TRAVELER

california

TRAVELER

california

by Greg Critser
photography by Gilles Mingasson

National Geographic
Washington, D.C.

PARKING

CONTENTS

Pages 2–3: The Pacific coast at sunset
Opposite: San Francisco's California cable car line, connecting the Financial District and Nob Hill

TRAVELING WITH EYES OPEN

Alert travelers go with a purpose and leave with a benefit. If you travel responsibly, you can help support wildlife conservation, historic preservation, and cultural enrichment in the places you visit. You can enrich your own travel experience as well.

To be a geo-savvy traveler:

- Recognize that your presence has an impact on the places you visit.
- Spend your time and money in ways that sustain local character. (Besides, it's more interesting that way.)
- Value the destination's natural and cultural heritage.
- Respect the local customs and traditions.
- Express appreciation to local people about things you find interesting and unique to the place: its nature and scenery, music and food, historic villages and buildings.
- Vote with your wallet: Support the people who support the place, patronizing businesses that make an effort to celebrate and protect what's special there. Seek out shops, local restaurants, inns, and tour operators who love their home—who love taking care of it and showing it off. Avoid businesses that detract from the character of the place.
- Enrich yourself, taking home memories and stories to tell, knowing that you have contributed to the preservation and enhancement of the destination.

That is the type of travel now called geotourism, defined as "tourism that sustains or enhances the geographical character of a place—its environment, culture, aesthetics, heritage, and the well-being of its residents." To learn more, visit National Geographic's Center for Sustainable Destinations at *www.nationalgeographic.com/travel/sustainable.*

TRAVELER

california

ABOUT THE AUTHORS & THE PHOTOGRAPHER

Greg Critser was born in Steubenville, Ohio, and raised in Whittier, California. He received his B.A. in history at Occidental College in Los Angeles and his M.A. from UCLA. His biographical research about the California author and social activist Carey McWilliams has appeared in the American Historical Association's *Pacific Historical Review* and the *UCLA Historical Journal.* Critser has worked as a senior editor at four magazines: *California Business, California* (formerly *New West*), *Buzz,* where he edited an award-winning stable of young Los Angeles writers, and *Worth,* where he was responsible for the magazine's first National Magazine Award nomination in public interest journalism. His own work has appeared in *Harper's,* the *Washington Post Magazine,* the *Wall Street Journal,* the *Los Angeles Times,* the *Washington Monthly,* the *New Yorker,* and *Worth.* Critser's acclaimed study of obesity, *Fat Land: How Americans Became the Fattest People in the World,* was published in 2003.

Gilles Mingasson grew up in Grenoble, France, and moved to Paris to pursue photojournalism. After arriving in the United States on an assignment, he traveled through Latin America before making Los Angeles his home base. In 2005, his work on Latinos in the United States won him an American Photography Award. His photography can be seen in the National Geographic *Traveler* guidebooks on Panama, the Dominican Republic, and France. Mingasson's website is *www.mingasson.com.*

California-based **Joe Yogerst** wrote the updates and sidebars for this edition. He is the co-author of *Traveler's Companion Peru* and has contributed to a number of National Geographic books about South America, including *Long Road South: A Journey Along the Pan American Highway, Enduring Treasures: National Parks of the World,* and *Sacred Places of a Lifetime.*

Charting Your Trip

Stretching nearly 800 miles (1,290 km) from north to south, California covers a massive expanse. Superimposed on the East Coast, it would extend from Philadelphia to Jacksonville, Florida—across *nine* states—with far more variety in climate and terrain than you find along the eastern seaboard. So think of your California trip as a journey not so much to a single state, but to a diverse collection of geographical areas with their own unique attributes and personalities.

Opportunities Abound

While it's certainly possible to hit the highlights in a single week, travelers with specific interests might want to focus on a particular area or theme. In Southern California, you could hit a brand new beach every day for a month and still not sample half the strands, let alone set aside time for the bounty of museums, theme parks, and historical attractions. Likewise, the state boasts enough ski and snowboard areas to keep you busy for an entire winter. California offers two types of desert—the sand dune-laden Colorado and the Joshua tree-studded Mojave—and experiences that range from Palm Springs posh to Death Valley solitude. The Sierra offer three of the country's oldest and largest national parks (Yosemite, Kings Canyon, and Sequoia), while the north coast throws up the planet's tallest trees and little-visited volcanic landscapes. With so much to see and do, California easily lends itself to multiple visits.

Getting Around

California created modern car culture—freeways, drive-in movies, and drive-time DJs—and cars are still the best means of exploring the state, especially given the scarcity of public transportation in many areas. Modern interstate freeways connect the big cities, but the most rewarding drives are off the beaten path—Calif. 1 along the Big Sur coast, Tioga Road over the crest of the Sierra, and the Redwood Highway—U.S. 101—through the big trees.

Still, the distances can be daunting. The fastest route between Los Angeles and San Francisco (Interstate 5) is still 380 miles (612 km) or roughly 6.5 hours of driving. Travelers who dislike long drives might want to consider flying between major destinations. Southwest Airlines (*www.southwest.com*) is a

Find film stars of every era on the Hollywood Walk of Fame.

popular option. Prices can be high on popular commuter routes (San Diego–Los Angeles, San Francisco–Sacramento), but you can often find bargains on flights into smaller airports like San Jose, Oakland, Burbank, and Long Beach.

Amtrak California (see Travelwise p. 347; *tel 800/872-7245, www.amtrakcalifornia.com*) stops at more than 175 California towns and cities on three services: the Pacific Surfliner, which runs between San Diego and San Luis Obispo (via Orange County, Los Angeles, and Santa Barbara); the San Joaquin, which connects the Bay Area and Los Angeles (via the Central Valley, with connections to Yosemite); and the Capital Corridor, running between the Bay Area and Sacramento.

Once you reach your destination, you might want to hold onto your rental car (see Travelwise p. 347). You can do without it in Yosemite Valley and San Francisco. But it's tough to get around much of California without your own wheels. Los Angeles is gradually expanding its bus, light rail, and subway network (see Travelwise p. 347; *www.metro.net*). Likewise, San Diego's red trolleys trundle along an ever-increasing track network *(www.sdmts.com)*. But enough holes exist in both systems to make private vehicles the preferred choice, especially for those short on time.

NOT TO BE MISSED:

Visitor Information

The state tourism commission has created Visit California *(www.visitcalifornia.com)*, a comprehensive and easy-to-use website with information on destinations, attractions, transportation, and places to stay.

California Welcome Centers are dotted throughout the state, some of them strategically placed along transportation corridors like Interstate 80 from northern Nevada (Truckee), U.S. 101 from the Oregon coast (Arcata), Interstate 5 from inland Oregon (Anderson), Interstate 15 from Las Vegas (Barstow), Interstate 10 from Arizona (Yucca Valley), and Interstate 8 from Arizona (Alpine).

If You Only Have a Week

If this is your first visit to California or if you've only got one week, it's possible to hit the highlights in seven days—but only if you are willing to rise early, hit the sack late, and cover plenty of ground each day. Our one-week travel plan requires your own vehicle. It can be done northbound or southbound, but our itinerary starts in San Francisco and ends in Los Angeles.

On **Day 1**, rent a car at San Francisco International Airport (see Travelwise p. 347) and drive 13 miles (21 km) into the city on the Bayshore Freeway (U.S. 101). Leave the car at the hotel because the rest of the day can be done on public transport. Hop a cable car up and over the hills to Fisherman's Wharf, where you can board a harbor cruise or ferry to Alcatraz Island. If time permits,

When to Visit

A state for all seasons, the best time to visit California depends on what you like to do and where you are likely to spend the bulk of your time. Owing to coastal overcast and fog in the spring and early summer, the best beach weather is generally July to early October. Triple-digit temperatures dominate the desert regions in summer, but desert winters are the stuff of snowbird dreams—clear skies and comfortably warm temperatures. The snow season stretches between Thanksgiving and Easter, but the best powder usually comes toward the end of that period.

peruse the tall ships at the San Francisco Maritime National Historic Park. Grab a quick seafood lunch along the wharf and head back downtown. Browse the chic boutiques around Union Square and the kitschy shops of Chinatown before tucking into an Asian dinner along Grant Avenue.

Begin **Day 2** with a short drive west to Haight-Ashbury and its lingering 1960s vibe. Then discover the treasures of nearby Golden Gate Park: the artistic de Young Museum, cutting-edge California Academy of Sciences, and Japanese Tea Garden. Plan for a picnic lunch in the park. Due north is the equally leafy Presidio, the historic former Army base with the best views of the Golden Gate Bridge. Then head to the South of Market area, with a stop at the San Francisco Museum of Modern Art.

Rise early on **Day 3,** and drive across the Golden Gate Bridge, 7 miles (11 km) from downtown. Stop for a quick breakfast along the Sausalito waterfront and continue north into Wine Country. Spend the rest of the day sipping vintages at Sonoma or Napa wineries, 54 miles (87 km) north of San Francisco. Spend the night in Wine Country. Drive south on **Day 4,** making your way around the eastern side of San Francisco Bay via Interstates 80 and 880. If you've got time, detour into Berkeley or Oakland for a dose of counterculture. Continue south to Monterey, 151 miles (243 km) south of Napa Valley, stopping in Salinas for lunch and a visit to the National Steinbeck Center. In the afternoon, cruise Cannery Row and visit Monterey Bay Aquarium. Take the 17-Mile Drive around the peninsula and have dinner in charming Carmel-by-the-Sea.

On **Day 5,** make your way south on Calif. 1 down the Big Sur coast. Along the way, stroll a secluded surf-swept beach and visit hilltop Hearst Castle. Continue the southward drive along U.S. 101 to Santa Barbara, 240 miles (386 km) south of Carmel, leaving time to visit the city's mission and waterfront. Dine along trendy State Street.

On **Day 6,** drive south into Los Angeles via Calif. 1 through Malibu, a total of 115 miles (185 km) from Santa Barbara. Cruise Sunset Boulevard through Brentwood to

Gas Prices & Gas Station Locations

Given the amount of driving you are likely to do in California, it's a good idea to keep track of fluctuating fuel costs on websites like Gas Buddy *(www.californiagasprices.com)*, which offers a dedicated California page. Covering the entire state, the site offers the lowest gas prices at thousands of gas pumps over the last 36 hours, as well as maps showing you where those stations are located.

The U.S. Department of Energy *(www.fueleconomy.gov)* offers access to several alternative gas price websites, including Automotive.com and MapQuest, through its online energy efficiency portal.

Guests enjoy lunch aboard a historic car on the popular Napa Valley Wine Train.

the Getty Center. Have lunch in Westwood next to the UCLA campus, and then continue along Sunset through Beverly Hills. In Hollywood, compare your hand and feet sizes to famous celebs' outside the Chinese Theater, take a studio tour, and view the city from the Griffith Park Observatory. After dark, see a show at the Hollywood Bowl.

End your trip on **Day 7** with a full-day visit to Disneyland and Disney California Adventure, 27 miles (43 km) south of L.A., using a dual-entry "Park Hopper" ticket.

If You Have More Time

If you have more time, you can venture beyond California's two urban meccas. Head to **San Diego,** 120 miles (193 km) south of L.A., and visit Balboa Park and the much ballyhooed zoo. Then go east into the desert, traveling north through **Anza-Borrego State Park** to **Palm Springs,** 123 miles (198 km) from San Diego. Continue across the desert to **Joshua Tree** and **Death Valley,** a further 287 miles (461 km) north. With time you could cruise up the **Owens Valley** and take Tioga Road across the top of **Yosemite National Park,** 244 miles (392 km) from Death Valley. Then head for **Gold Country** in the foothills between Yosemite and Sacramento. Spend a day and a night at **Lake Tahoe,** 134 miles (215 km) northeast of Yosemite, and end your trip with a riverside picnic in **Sacramento,** 114 miles (183 km) farther west. ■

Hotel & Campsite Reservations

To make hotel reservations, consult **Visit California** *(www.reservations.visitcalifornia.com)*. If you want to make a reservation at one of the campsites in California's state parks and state beaches, contact the **California Department of Parks and Recreation** *(tel 800/444-7275, www.parks.ca.gov)*. Campsite reservations for California's national parks, national forests, and other federal lands should be made through the federal government's outdoor recreation portal *(tel 877/444-6777, www.recreation.gov)*.

CHANDELIER
TREE

History & Culture

Padre Junípero Serra rises above the church of Mission Dolores.
Opposite: The Chandelier Tree, north of Eureka, a giant redwood that was carved in the 1930s to let cars drive through its trunk

California Today

The third largest state (after Alaska and Texas) in the United States, but by far the most populous, California comprises a dizzying potpourri of superlative landscapes. This, and a famously carefree lifestyle, have attracted an outdoorsy, entrepreneurial, forever upbeat, multicultural people inspired by California's open and inviting horizons. It's all part of the enviable California mystique.

Purely from a standpoint of numbers, Californians are remarkable: There are now more than 37 million of them, representing one in every eight U.S. residents. So great is California's allure to migrants that the state's population is expected to top 50 million well before the year 2050 (see sidebar p. 17).

The Hotel del Coronado, near San Diego, a distinctive late Victorian beach resort

Ethnically, Californians comprise the nation's most diverse population. While blacks represent less than 7 percent of the population—only half that of the U.S. average—and 40 percent are Caucasians of northern European descent, today more than one-third of the state's population identify themselves as Hispanic, a reflection of the state's geographic and historic intimacy with its neighbors to the south. More than one in ten Californians is Asian, ranging from Hmong villagers to Hindu software programmers to Chinese financiers. Fewer than half of Californians were born in the state, and fully one-quarter were born outside the U.S.

So great is California's allure to migrants that the state's population is expected to top 50 million well before the year 2050.

The result of this compressed ethnic migration, according to California novelist and social observer Donald Waldie, is a *mestizaje*, "the promiscuous amalgamation of Hispanic, African, Asian, and Native American peoples." It is really little wonder, then, that one California university recently renamed its old 1960s-inspired ethnic studies program as, simply, American studies.

Geographically, Californians are still largely a coastal people—more than one out of four reside in the five major metropolitan areas of Los Angeles, San Diego, San Francisco, San Jose, and Long Beach—all close to the sea. Many newer arrivals, together with a large number of second- and third-generation Californians, have been moving eastward to thriving inland suburban and new-town destinations with names like Rancho Bernardo and Santa Clarita. Meanwhile, new arrivals from abroad continue to coalesce where their native peers are established, resulting in high concentrations of specific ethnicities. Thus, for example, Vietnamese Americans constitute an astounding 40 and 29 percent, respectively, of the populations of Westminster and Garden Grove.

Californians are as diverse in lifestyle as in heritage and skin tone. The rusticity-seeking dwellers of the forested far north have more in common with the cowboys of Idaho than with California's urban sophisticates. And few commentators would argue with the observation that San Franciscans differ markedly from Angelenos. The state's multifaceted nature is epitomized by the differences (and rivalries) between the two urban centers. Progressive, heavily gay San Francisco (birthplace of anti–Vietnam War hippiedom) has always been open minded, even nonconformist, despite being the West Coast's bespoke-suited "Wall Street." Laid-back L.A. is more self-possessed and money oriented, as befits the world capital of Hollywood fame and glamour.

Money and boundless optimism wed to an entrepreneurial spirit and individuality drive Californians ever forward.

The annual Electronic Entertainment Expo in Los Angeles draws thousands of video game industry professionals, investor analysts, retailers, and journalists from more than a hundred countries.

In the past two decades they have reinvented their state's economy—the seventh largest in the world—weaning it from its onetime dependence on defense spending and redirecting it toward high technology and finance. Silicon Valley, centered around San Jose, is the birthplace and epicenter of the computing industry—Apple, Google, Hewlett Packard, and IBM are among the behemoths headquartered here—and the spawning ground not only of the technological future but also of overnight fortunes. L.A.'s economy and culture remain heavily dependent on the movie industry, and the fascination with youthful looks has spawned its own industry—cosmetic surgery. Meanwhile, California is the world's fifth largest producer of agricultural produce, although agriculture accounts for only 2 percent of the state's economy. Indeed, the vast San Joaquin/Sacramento Valley, colloquially known as the Central Valley, is the most productive and profitable agricultural center in the world, thanks to incredibly fertile soils and a constant stream of migrant labor.

While the very name "California" is synonymous with Hollywood, the cultural milieu runs broader and deeper than movies and TV sitcoms. Highbrow art looks back with pride to the plein air art movement, birthed here, while radiant works by British-born L.A. adoptee David Hockney have helped secure California's artistic place in the sun. In music, too, there's something to sing about. Los Angeles and San Francisco are bastions of classical music, as well as the spawning grounds for contemporary sounds, from the Beach Boys and Grateful Dead to the Black Eyed Peas and Green Day.

There is, of course, a cost to all of this growth and creativity, much of it borne by the environment. While it is true that much of the state remains pristine and unimaginably beautiful, it's also true that air and water quality in many urban areas has worsened. Even the Central Valley is now mired in smog as foul as anywhere else in the nation. But California, always at the forefront of national trends, is a trendsetter in efforts to legislate on behalf of a cleaner environment—a process accelerated under the tenure of governors Arnold Schwarzenegger and Jerry Brown. The state has spent much of its time in recent years responding to natural disasters. Fires, floods, and earthquakes have always been part of the bargain of being Californian, but they seem to grow ever more calamitous each year as the cities grow bigger and more crowded.

Yet Californians cannot be bowed down. Like the common concept of California's Mediterranean climate, their vision is always sunny. It is hard not to be so, one assumes, when blessed with such an abundance of sunshine and natural beauty. The ability of southern Californians to ski in the morning and sunbathe the same afternoon is the envy of anyone who doesn't actually live there. As East Coasters shiver through midwinter blizzards, Palm Springs residents sunnily sip iced martinis poolside in finger-snapping Sinatra style. True, chilling fogs smother much of the Pacific shoreline: Famously, San Francisco's coldest months are actually August and September, much to the surprise of many ill-equipped tourists. Anyone believing that even California's winter clime is always sunny should read up on the fate of the Donner party (forced to resort to cannibalism to survive when trapped by snowstorms in 1846 while attempting to cross the Sierra Nevada). And only mad dogs and Englishmen venture into Death Valley in the killer heat of midsummer.

But therein lies a deeper beauty. The physical diversity of both climate and terrain is astounding. North America's iconic low point, Death Valley (282 feet/86 m below sea level), is within a few hours' drive of the Sierra Nevada, where 15 peaks soar more than 14,000 feet (4,265 m). California's scale is big enough to guarantee amazing variety yet small enough to permit visitors to switch in a single day between mountain, coastline, desert, and forest. No wonder Californians are passionate about outdoor recreation. Mountain biking first evolved in the 1970s on the steep, winding trails of Mount Tamalpais. Whitewater rafting was birthed on the sparkling rivers that spill from the Sierra like effervescent champagne. And weekends are given to the health-conscious hedonism of sailing, snowboarding, surfing, or sundry other activities.

All this and more awaits visitors keen to sample the individual elements that combine to define the uniquely Californian quality of life. ■

By the Numbers

Population: 37,679,000
Area: 158,706 sq miles (411,046 sq km)
Coastline: 1,100 miles (1,770 km)
GDP: $1.95 trillion in 2011
Capital: Sacramento
State animal: Grizzly bear
State motto: "Eureka!"
Average number of earthquakes per year: 37,283
California is home to the highest and lowest elevations in the lower 48 states—Mount Whitney, 14,495 feet (4,418 m) high, and Death Valley, 282 feet (86 m) below sea level. It also has the world's tallest (coastal redwood), largest (giant sequoia), and oldest (bristlecone pine) trees.

The Land

Not everyone who comes to California reacts to its climate the way traveler Charles Dudley Warner did when he exclaimed, "Here is our Mediterranean!" (*Our Italy,* 1891). But few who have driven the state's byways and taken in the smells of orange blossom, sage, and sea remain impartial to its natural charms. If there ever were an American Mediterranean, California would be it.

The climate, in part, proceeds from the land, and the land—158,706 square miles (411,046 sq km) of it—proceeded from a series of giant tectonic collisions that began some 250 million years ago, when the offshore Farallon plate began to slip underneath the North American continent. In the process it formed a

With oceanic clouds blocked by mountains, Death Valley is one of the Earth's driest places.

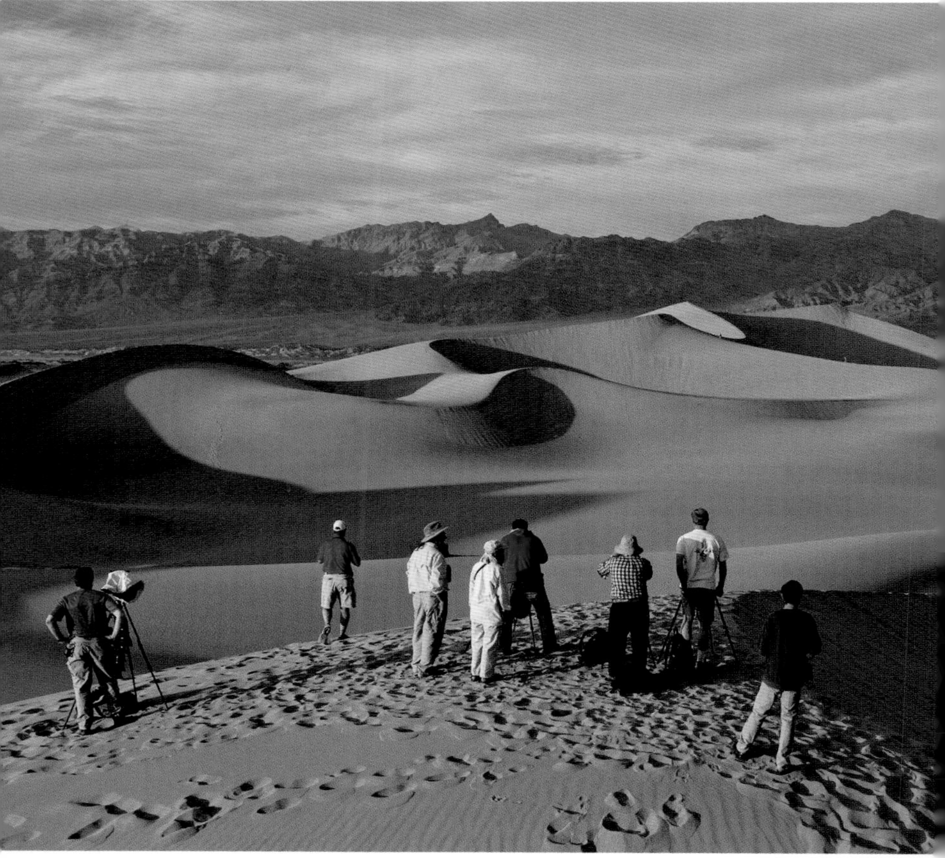

mountain range. Then: more collision, more mountains. And so, very gradually, the basic basin-and-range geography of the state was formed.

About 130 million years ago, these collisions heated up the underlying mantle of the Earth, liquefied it as lava, and, eventually, formed the Sierra Nevada. Once the North American plate overtook the Farallon, it bumped (this time laterally) into the Pacific plate. This formed what is known as a transform fault, the San Andreas, a network of terrestrial stresses and cracks that stretches northwest from the Gulf of California to Point Arena, above San Francisco Bay. The Pacific plate and the North American plate slide past each other along this fault, sometimes imperceptibly, at other times explosively in an earthquake.

Rim of Fire: Volcanism in California

California ia probably best known for its earthquakes. This tectonic shiftiness relates to the state's location within the Pacific Rim of Fire, as part of a section called the Cascade Volcanic Arc that also includes Washington, Oregon, and southern British Columbia. Sheer size and splendor make Mount Shasta (see pp. 284–287) the state's most famous volcano, although the snowcapped giant has been silent since 1786. Lassen Peak (see p. 288), another stratovolcano, last erupted in 1917 but remains a threat. The region's third rumbler is Medicine Lake, a massive shield volcano that last exploded about a thousand years ago.

The result of this upheaval is a land of extremes. At 14,495 feet (4,418 m), Mount Whitney, in Sequoia National Park, is the highest point in the coterminous United States. Badwater, in Death Valley, at 282 feet (86 m) below sea level, is the lowest. The consequential extremes in temperature and precipitation are aided and abetted by two major oceanic currents along the state's 1,100-mile (1,770 km) coastline. The deep, cool California Current sweeps south bringing frigid Arctic waters and is thus responsible for San Francisco's long, cool summers and legendary fogs. A secondary current, shallower and fragmented, flows along the eastward-veering southern California Bight, thereby accounting for the south of the region's remarkably balmy weather.

Not much fails to thrive here. Botanists estimate that, due to the abundance of singular habitats, more than one-third of California's 5,000 native flora may be unique to the state. In the foothills you can find the live oak, *Quercus agrifolia,* its tiny, hollylike leaves ingeniously suited to the high temperatures and low humidity of the region. *Sequoia sempervirens,* the coast redwood, thrives in the moist conditions near the coast. *Sequoia gigantea,* the giant sequoia, grows higher up in the Sierra Nevada. The pickleweed, *Salicornia,* has adapted so successfully to the harsh, salty waterline of inland estuaries that, from afar, it appears as swaths of russet-colored snow. And there are the imports—date, orange, and madrone. California has made them all its own.

Weather changes with the land, flora and fauna adapt to weather—and Californians to all three. Witness, if you travel here at the right time, the quintessential California rite of nature worship: the grunion

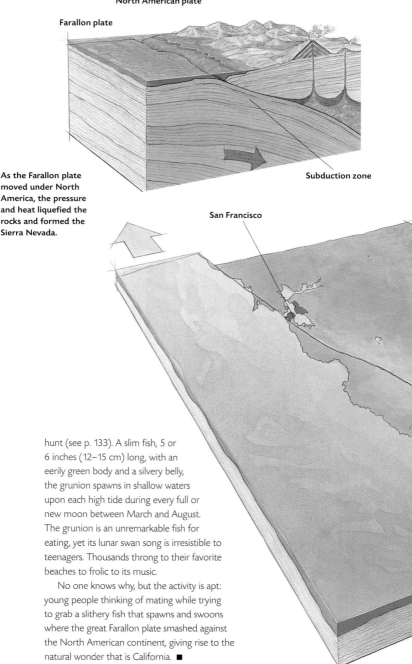

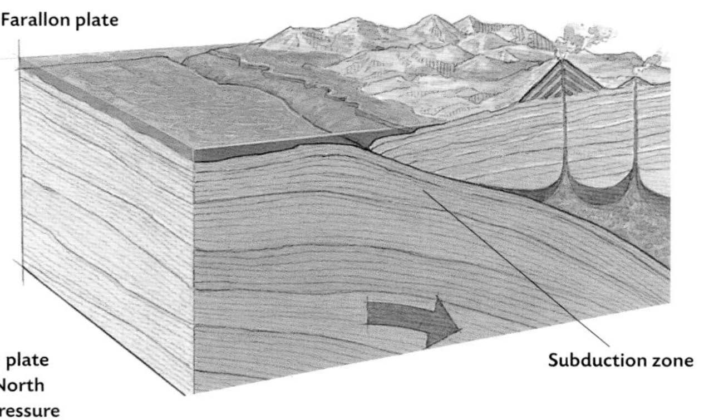

As the Farallon plate moved under North America, the pressure and heat liquefied the rocks and formed the Sierra Nevada.

San Francisco

hunt (see p. 133). A slim fish, 5 or 6 inches (12–15 cm) long, with an eerily green body and a silvery belly, the grunion spawns in shallow waters upon each high tide during every full or new moon between March and August. The grunion is an unremarkable fish for eating, yet its lunar swan song is irresistible to teenagers. Thousands throng to their favorite beaches to frolic to its music.

No one knows why, but the activity is apt: young people thinking of mating while trying to grab a slithery fish that spawns and swoons where the great Farallon plate smashed against the North American continent, giving rise to the natural wonder that is California. ■

Pacific plate

The North American plate and the Pacific plate slide past each other along the San Andreas Fault. Arising deep in the Earth's crust, earthquakes send primary waves (P-waves) pulsing through nearby rock; these set up slower, secondary waves whose shearing action can buckle the surface rocks and open up cracks and fissures along the fault line.

San Andreas Fault

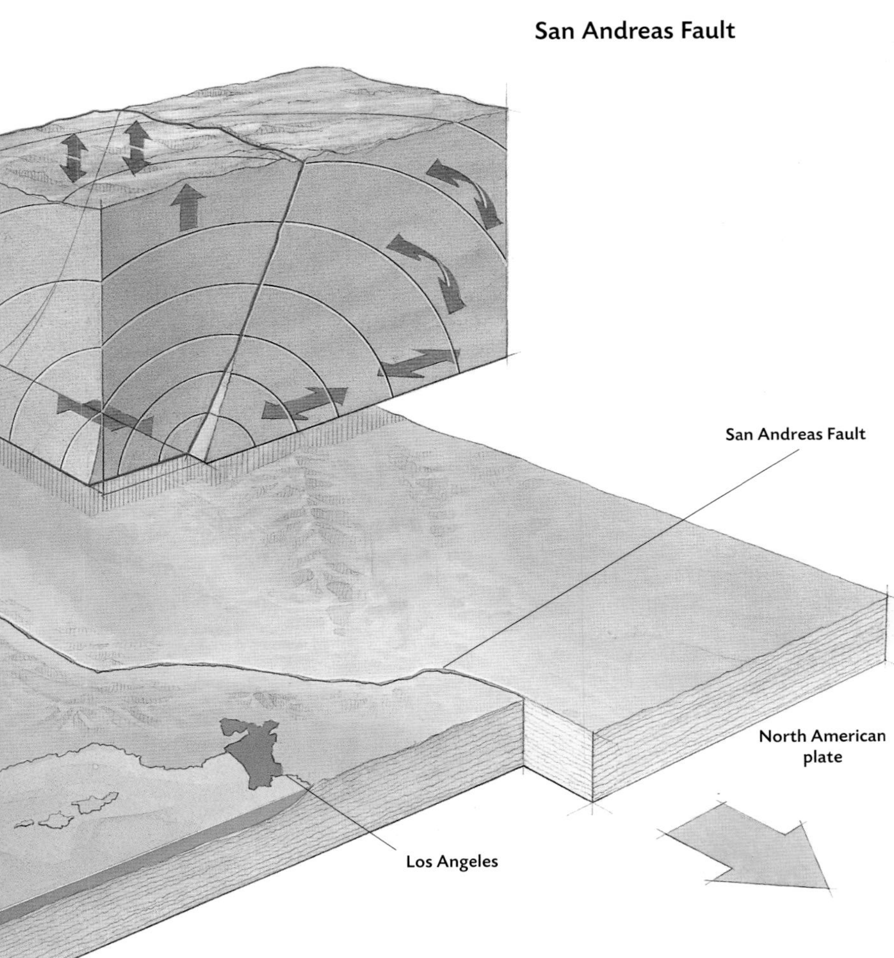

Food & Wine

For the past two decades, California has led the way in today's increasingly eclectic culinary world. The Golden State is the ultimate foodie mecca, offering gourmands a host of different cuisines. This diversity makes California cuisine hard to classify.

Sushi chef Tadashi Murakami prepares food at Hollywood's small, trendy Murakami.

Themes of California Cuisine

California cuisine embraces various **ethnic traditions.** The earliest sustained effort to create a California cuisine was made by *Sunset*, the "Magazine for Western Living." The publication was launched in 1898 by the Southern Pacific Railroad, whose aim was to exhort Easterners to "colonize the west and . . . travel in style to a new life of year-round sunshine and agricultural bounty." Almost immediately *Sunset*'s founders embraced the state's Mexican culinary past, launching an endless campaign to educate Golden Staters on everything about Mexican cuisine. Here was a way for a new Anglo migrant to invent a culinary history, a cuisine partly of memory and partly of psychological need.

Another theme—also one of *Sunset*'s editorial missions—was the notion that even middle-class Californians should have their own **kitchen gardens.** No issue of the magazine was (or, for that matter, is) complete without a gardening column and articles on topics like kiwi fruits or how to grow an Asian spice garden. Eating your own freshly grown food was not only pragmatic and thrifty; it could increase vigor, the key to fully appreciating all that California had to offer.

The third theme could be called the **"search for pure flavor,"** an activity born of the vast agricultural abundance and the belief among California chefs that theirs is a quest for absolute essence—whether it be of basil or orange or tomato or plum.

California Food Innovators

The first great modern synthesizer of these themes was Alice Waters, founder, in 1971, of the Berkeley restaurant **Chez Panisse** (see pp. 240–241). Having just returned from a trip to France, Waters applied the principles of Provençal cooking to California ingredients. As she later wrote, "My one unbreakable rule has always been to use only the freshest and finest ingredients; [my] quest led to Amador County for suckling pigs and peppery watercress; to Napa for Zinfandel made especially for our restaurant; to Gilroy for garlic; to Sonoma for locally made goat cheeses; to the ocean daily for oysters."

Inspired by Waters's injunction to "eat fresh from the garden," chefs from around the state literally reinvented all the classic cuisines—and a few nonclassic ones as well. In 1979 a young San Francisco Zen Buddhist named Annie Somerville, determined to make vegetarian cooking more, well, vegetarian, opened a new restaurant called, simply, **Greens** *(www.greensrestaurant.com)*. It was a refreshing contrast to the gloppy mess of overcooked grains and soy cheese that through the years had come to symbolize the genre.

In Los Angeles the innovators looked southward. The young chefs Susan Feniger and Mary Sue Milliken took up the old *Sunset* injunction about the importance of Mexico and started the **Border Grill** *(www.bordergrill.com)*, where intense poblano chilies met the mesquite-grilled flavors of modern Santa Fe. In 1984, cooks Viana La Place and Evan Kleiman opened **Angeli Caffe** *(www.angelicaffe.com)*, which reinvigorated traditionally heavy Italian-American restaurant food by treating the tastes of the southern Italian kitchen "in a light, modern manner." Rather than following the convention of serving foods either hot or chilled, they served theirs at warm-to-room temperature because "we know that the true flavors of food can be best appreciated at these temperatures." And, of course, there was Wolfgang Puck's celebrated **Spago** *(www.wolfgangpuck.com)* in Los Angeles, where

---

EXPERIENCE: Bay Area Breweries

The global repute of California wine has long overshadowed the fact that some of America's best beer is also made in the Golden State. San Francisco's Anchor Steam and Chico-based Sierra Nevada are the best known, but the state's microbreweries are where beer snobs quaff their amber nectar. In fact, a recent ranking of the nation's top beermakers was dominated by small California breweries, including three of the top ten.

Beer aficionados visiting San Francisco should consider the six-hour Nor Cal Brew Tour *($$–$$$$$)* offered by Brewery Adventures *(tel 800/230-BEER, www.breweryadventures.com)*. The tour includes round-trip transportation by bus to two breweries, beer samples, a brewery tour and gourmet lunch, and expert tour guides. Or stay in the city for the SF City Beer Tour *($$)*. Customized itineraries are also available.

Bay Area Brewery Tours *(tel 415/999-4989, www.bayareabrewerytours.com, $$$$$)* visits three area breweries Fridays to Sundays. The price includes round-trip transportation, tastings, and a souvenir glass. Book online; tours begin in the morning and leave from the Caltrain Station *(700 4th St., San Francisco)*.

California's entire ethnic archipelago fell onto a delicate pizza pie. No one would ever think of Beijing duck and goat cheese in the same way.

If the 1970s and '80s were about freshness and ethnic fusion, the 1990s were about the primacy of flavor, often in more traditional fare. At Napa Valley's **French Laundry** *(www.frenchlaundry.com)*, considered the "best restaurant in the United States" by Ruth Reichl of the *New York Times,* chef Thomas Keller draws from the surrounding countryside–and beyond from France and Italy–to create such startling dishes

Tex-Mex cuisine combines Mexican recipes with ingredients found in the southwestern U.S.

as white truffle custard, lobster in vanilla-saffron sabayon sauce, and pomegranate sorbet with champagne gelée. In San Francisco, Laurie Thomas's **Rose Pistola** *(www.rosepistolasf.com)* in North Beach captures the essence of rustic Genoese cooking in its chickpea-flour breads and whole roast snappers.

In Oakland's thriving farmers' market (see pp. 234–235) Hmong immigrants hawk fresh lemongrass and fiery Thai chilis, while African Americans offer bean pies and barbecue sauce. Nearby **Caffe 817** *(www.caffe817.com)* has pared its menu to the purest and freshest of what makes Italy Italy and California California. Over tiny Napa lettuce is drizzled only the freshest of local olive oils; over that, the most intense cured Italian ham the founders of *Sunset* could ever have imagined. A sliver of Parmesan. A sprig of lemon basil. *Perfetto!*

Wine

With more than 1,200 wineries across the state, perhaps the only thing more surprising than the variety of California wines is their overall quality. As John Doerper writes in *Wine Country,* his influential book on the subject, "The quality of the *average* wines produced in Napa and Sonoma is now so high that the gap between them and premium wines has narrowed . . . Winemakers now feel they have to widen that gap–to keep distinctive wines truly distinct–by raising the quality of premium wines ever higher." For the aficionado of wines, whether experienced or amateur, the situation spells bonanza. Today more than ever, California is a wine-lover's heaven, unparalleled anywhere in the world except for the ancient stands of France and Italy.

Today more than ever, California is a wine-lover's heaven, unparalleled anywhere in the world except for the ancient stands of France and Italy.

Modern California winemaking dates from as recently as 1966, when the Robert Mondavi Winery *(www.robertmondavi.com)* was founded in Oakville, near Napa, by Robert Mondavi and his elder son, Michael. Obsessed with elevating Napa Valley wines to world-class status, the Mondavis began experimenting with one of the mainstays of local viticulture, wines known as California sauternes. Soon they were applying contemporary European techniques learned during fact-finding expeditions across the Atlantic. The most important of their innovations involved sauvignon blanc grapes;

Established in 1973, the Domaine Chandon winery in Napa Valley offers private wine samplings.

like their friends in France, the Mondavis began to leave the skins on the grapes after the crush, and then ferment them in a stainless steel tank and transfer them to French oak barrels for aging. The result was one of the state's first blockbuster premiums—a new twist on an old favorite dubbed fumé blanc.

What followed was an explosion of vintners adapting similar classic techniques to California grape growing. Within ten years Mondavi's dream came true. At the Paris Wine Tasting of 1976, two California wines edged out French reds and whites. *Sacré bleu!*

The story since then has at times bordered on the tragicomic: So many nouveau winemakers have set up shop in the Napa and Sonoma Valleys that, during the summer tourist peak, there may be more traffic jams there than in the cities. And there has been, predictably, a small but notable Disney effect, with some large wineries becoming so adept at marketing and branding that one might wonder which comes first, the wine or the label.

Such cynicism evaporates when one returns to first principles—making world-class wines. Perhaps the most important trend in recent years is the increasing value placed on a wine's appellation, the special geographic and climatic area from which it comes. These regions—some vast, some only a few hundred acres—are capable of producing wines of extra-high quality that have special taste characteristics.

A particularly popular appellation at present is the Carneros region of southern Napa, which runs westward into Sonoma County. Here, the cool breezes and fogs from nearby San Pablo Bay help produce some of the state's most spectacular pinot noirs, as well as several outstanding chardonnays. Farther north and west, the Benziger family has used the various shade and sun combinations at its Sonoma Mountain vineyard to make a deep cabernet sauvignon. Still farther west, the nearly continuous cool weather of the Anderson Valley in Mendocino County has helped produce world-class gewürztraminers and rieslings.

History of California

"In contrast to history, the story of man in California would have different proportions, would take a longer view and recognize the Indians as the largest minority for a generation after 1849, heavily in the majority through the preceding 80 years, and the only residents for centuries and millennia prior to 1769."—John W. Caughey, California

Early Californians

If California's eccentric geography wrought a unique botany, its impact on human settlement was even stronger. Consider the archaeological record. Mainstream scholarship has long held that the first Californians probably arrived around 6,000 to

Ancestors of the Modoc painted the caves in Lava Beds National Monument.

7,000 years ago (a small but important group places the date as far back as 10,000 years). By the time Europeans arrived in the 16th century, however, Native Americans numbering about 300,000 had fragmented into some 105 linguistic groups dispersed widely throughout the state.

These groups fell loosely into one of three linguistic families. The Penutian family resided largely in the north and included the Miwok and the Wintun, who may have been among those greeting the Spaniards in the late 18th century. Among the Hokan speakers, occupying the central coast, were the Chumash, perhaps the most technically sophisticated of the southern tribes. The Uto-Aztecan group in the south were distant descendants of Mexico's Aztec and the American Comanche; their numbers included the so-called Gabrieleños, one of the first fully Christianized, or missionized, Indians.

If California's eccentric geography wrought a unique botany, its impact on human settlement was even stronger.

Details of daily life in pre-Columbian California remain scarce, but relatively new data suggest some compelling conjectures. Radiocarbon dating of inscribed animal bones found in the La Brea Tar Pits in Los Angeles, for example, indicates that the carvings were done on "green," or fresh, bones of now extinct animals, suggesting that early L.A. man led a life intricately tied to packs of wildly aggressive wolflike creatures. Reconstruction of the only complete human remains on the same site—those of a young woman—indicate that violence was not uncommon: Her skull had been bashed in with a blunt object. Close examination of the boats used by the Santa Barbara Chumash indicate that the tar pits were part of an important trade route. Modern-day Wilshire Boulevard in Los Angeles lies directly over the path they took to gather tar to waterproof their craft.

Still, the original Californians lagged significantly behind the Aztec, their brethren to the south, in several key areas. They had no organized system of agriculture, kept no domesticated animals (except for dogs), and were neither builders of roads nor creators of metallurgy. Their priesthood was relatively informal. Not surprisingly, these traits led the first European colonists to brand California's natives as rustics who lacked the self-sufficient backbone that Europeans considered a hallmark of civilization.

Yet there was little evidence that hunger was a problem for these people—at least until the Europeans came. This has led modern scholars to reconsider what, exactly, constitutes a "civilized" material culture. One item under their microscope is deer hunting as practiced by the Rumsen people of southern Monterey Bay. Far from being a simple, unplanned activity, Rumsen deer hunting not only involved high levels of skill, training, and knowledge but also demanded such religious and social preparations as praying, sexual abstinence, dietary restrictions, and even various mind-sharpening techniques. As scholar Malcolm Margolin points out, the hunter would usually give away part or all of his catch to elders and neighbors so that "hunting, in short, did not render a man 'self-sufficient,' but like other aspects of Indian life served to bind the hunter closer to others in a strand of reciprocity."

A fair question, then: Why did the Native Americans gravitate toward the mission system so easily and so freely (as was usually the case, despite assumptions to the contrary)? The answer must be found in what the Spaniards—with their legions of armored soldiers, exotic foods, elegant white horses, and sonorous-voiced padres—brought to the meeting when the two groups first encountered each other on a lonely beach in San Diego in 1769.

Spaniards & Mexicans

With few exceptions (among them the discovery of Point Reyes in 1579 by the English freebooter Sir Francis Drake), the pioneering of California was largely a Spanish undertaking. As such, its context was both medieval and colonial: medieval because it immediately followed the Spanish Inquisition and the expulsion of the Moors; colonial because it grew directly out of Cortés's 1521 conquest of the Aztec in Mexico.

Padre Junípero Serra founded 21 missions in California for Spain.

The new Pacific outpost derived its name from a 16th-century popular fantasy of chivalry, *The Exploits of Esplandian* (1510), by Garci Rodríguez de Montalvo. In it, the Christians of Constantinople must confront a great unknown: a force of Amazons led by a certain Queen Califia from the island of California, where everything was made of gold. Frustrated in his search for the fabled Seven Cities of Gold, Spanish explorer Francisco de Bolaños first applied the name to Baja in 1541—an allusion to a paradise, yet unfound.

Bolaños was followed by the better known Juan Rodriguez Cabrillo, who discovered San Diego Bay in 1542. Then came 125 years of benign neglect as Spain concentrated its resources on the silver and gold strikes in Mexico and the development of the Manila–Mexico spice trade. Only when incursions of British and Russian explorers threatened Spanish hegemony did Charles III of Spain finally make California a priority again: In 1768 he dispatched Gaspar de Portolà to secure the coast for Spain.

To do so, Portolà implemented the three most powerful elements of Spanish colonialism: the pueblo, the presidio, and the mission. The pueblo represented civil authority and was based on the medieval notion of a secure clustering of towns. The presidio, a fort, represented the military elite. The mission was the vehicle for the religious authorities charged with converting the Indians to Christianity.

Spain's most influential imperial cleric was the Franciscan Padre Junípero Serra, who founded the first mission, in San Diego, in 1769. A native of Majorca, Serra entered

Must-Read Books on California

Numerous novels and nonfiction books dealing with aspects of California history have been published since the 1840s. The following, listed in chronological order according to when their stories are set, rank among the best:

• ***Mark Twain's San Francisco*** This stirring anthology includes articles, essays, poems, and other scribbles drawn from the bard's 1860s sojourn in California.
• ***Ramona*** A runaway best seller when first published in 1884, this novel by Helen Hunt Jackson exposed the mistreatment of Native Americans in late 19th-century California.
• ***The Octopus: A Story of California*** Frank Norton's classic 1901 novel doubles as a scorching social commentary on the greed of the railroad robber barons and the Gilded Age.
• ***Ishi in Two Worlds*** Theodora Kroeber's popular nonfiction book tells the story of Ishi, who walked out of the northern California woods in 1911 as the last surviving member of the Yahi tribe.
• ***Oil!*** Published in 1927, Upton Sinclair's epic novel about the early scramble for oil in southern California was made into the 2007 film *There Will Be Blood.*
• ***The Grapes of Wrath*** John Steinbeck's 1939 classic tells the tale of the dirt-poor Joad family migrating to California during the Great Depression.
• ***L.A. Confidential*** James Ellroy exposes the gritty underbelly of 1950s L.A. in this "nouvelle noir" crime thriller.
• ***Tales of the City*** This first of eight novels in a series by Armistead Maupin brings to life the rainbow coalition that made 1970s and '80s San Francisco such a vibrant place to live.

the priesthood at 16, developed a reputation as an outstanding preacher, and was dispatched to the Americas in 1749. A stubborn, spirited, and often combative man, he was also a classic medievalist, believing, among other things, that pain and discomfort purified the soul. (Once he deliberately exposed himself to a swarm of insects, which caused an infection that left him permanently lame in one leg.) Serra's passion led him and his successors to establish 21 missions in California by 1821.

While few scholars doubt Serra's sincere religious motives, few also doubt that it was the mission system that led to the dramatic decline in the Indian population. This was tragedy laced with irony: The padres believed that they could only protect their neophytes from outsiders and often brutal Spanish soldiers by concentrating their wards together in large numbers. Yet by doing so, the padres also introduced the Indians to new European diseases. By the advent of the gold rush in 1848, Indian numbers had dropped from a pre-Columbian high of 300,000 to fewer than 35,000, and to fewer than 20,000 a decade later.

To this day, the destruction of the Indians in California is regarded as the original sin of the Golden State. Serra was eventually beatified by Pope John Paul II, but only after a 30-year, multimillion-dollar public relations campaign by some of California's richest and most influential Roman Catholics.

After Mexico won independence from Spain in 1821, California drifted under a succession of weak Mexican governors, who increasingly viewed the faraway colony as a drain on internal resources. To reward settlers and placate the ambitious, Mexico began granting large tracts of land to locals, or Californios. The result was the growth of an affluent rancho culture, with grizzly bear hunts and fiestas and rodeos. Eventually, these local land barons—the *gente de razón*—grew hostile to interference from Mexican authorities. In 1836, the Californio Juan Bautista Alvarado led a revolt against Mexican authorities and proclaimed California a free and sovereign state. Mexico soon regained sovereignty, but the stage was now set for independence—and eventual U.S. statehood.

Statehood of Gold

By 1846, two more potent elements had entered the amalgam of forces setting California on the path to independence and, eventually, statehood. Both of them resided among the 800 Anglo-Americans then living in Mexican California.

The first was mountain men, fur trappers, and reckless fortune seekers of mixed degrees of gentility, who resented Mexico's control. The second was Yankee settlers and entrepreneurs looking for opportunity. Among them were William B. Ide, who led a party of a hundred over the Sierra to the Sacramento area; James Wilson Marshall, the eventual discoverer of California gold; Sam Brannan, a Mormon pioneer and real estate entrepreneur; and John Sutter, a Swiss American who founded a colony named New Helvetia that later became the state capital. These Americans, of various stripes of religiosity, were united in their schemes to remake Mexican Catholic California into a more American Protestant version of paradise—Yankee paradise.

Into this cauldron of ambition and prejudice rode a young Army commander, John C. Frémont, the leader of a secret 1845 government investigation into California's political affairs. President James K. Polk had provoked the Mexicans on the Texas border and needed to know how the Californios would react to a declaration of war. Under the guise of a scientific expedition (although he could not explain the presence of a howitzer in its midst), Frémont and his small band were staying in the then capital, Monterey. José Castro, the *gobernador* in Monterey, grew suspicious and threw out the protesting Frémont, who retreated to Hawk's Peak overlooking the town and hoisted an American flag before going on to Oregon.

How Much Gold?

Given the random nature of gold prospecting and recordkeeping in the 19th century, it's almost impossible for historians to ascertain now the exact amount of gold that was discovered during the California gold rush of the late 1840s and early 1850s. The U.S. Geological Survey estimates that 12 million ounces was taken from Sierra foothill mines and streams during the first five years of the rush—an amount that is worth nearly $19 billion in today's dollars. By the turn of the 20th century, more than 40 million ounces of gold had been extracted, equivalent to about a third of the amount of gold that is currently stored at Fort Knox.

Frémont's camp soon became a magnet for disaffected mountain men and entrepreneurs, many of whom had heard of the Hawk's Peak incident and feared eviction by Mexico. On June 14 a band of these men descended on the Sonoma quarters of Mariano Vallejo, the *commandante* of Alta California, to demand his surrender. Vallejo, a longtime supporter of independence, entertained the men generously with alcohol; he had been expecting them. Arriving later to find his comrades drunk, Ide, the leader of the insurgents, negotiated Vallejo's surrender and then raised a quickly improvised flag featuring a grizzly bear and blazoning the words "California Republic."

A few weeks later, Frémont rode in and declared the republic a "permanent territorial possession" of the U.S., under military rule. Commander John Sloat sailed into Monterey Bay and, without firing a shot, took formal possession from Castro. A year and a half later, upon victory in Mexico proper, the Treaty of Guadalupe Hidalgo formalized Frémont's coup, and California was part of the U.S.

Before clear heads could begin to reckon how to organize this new U.S. possession, California exploded in gold fever. The discovery by Marshall at Sutter Creek on January 24, 1848, represented the ultimate slap in the face to the Old World, which had begun its exploration for the Seven Cities of Gold more than 300 years before. In the first months of excavation at Yuba alone, five California argonauts took out more than $75,000 worth of ore every month. At Placerville, the average daily yield per man often topped five pounds (2.2 kg), while a group of seven men from Monterey, using 50 Indian laborers, took out 273 pounds (124 kg) of gold in just seven weeks.

In 1849, a group of 48 men drew up a draft state constitution; one-quarter of them had come with the gold rush.

When the world beyond California heard of the strike, the young state's population began to soar. In San Francisco alone, more than 40,000 migrants arrived during the last weeks of 1848. The greatest and most lasting wealth was made by the businesspeople who rose to service this new population—from Levi Strauss, the inventor who (with a partner) patented the process for putting rivets into denim and so created an enduringly popular form of clothing, to hoteliers, bankers, and lawyers. Nonwhites played a substantial role in the gold rush. The number of black miners tripled to 2,000 during the first three years of the strike—literally a golden opportunity for men still not recognized as full U.S. citizens. Many so-called Free Negroes, for example, used their gold to buy freedom for other members of their families. And while racism was rampant throughout Gold Country, it was often tempered by the intimacy of side-by-side labor with whites, something quite new to many Free Negroes. As one freeman wrote to his wife from Cosumne Diggins mine, "This is the best place for black folk all over the globe. All a man has to do is work and he will make money."

The gold rush also ushered in official statehood. In 1849, a group of 48 men drew up a draft state constitution; one-quarter of them had come with the gold rush. Perhaps just as important was their youth: Only four of them were over 50, 30 were under 40, and nine were still in their 20s. The 31st state, admitted in 1850, would be run by some of the youngest old-timers in the country.

Boom Years

The 70-year period following California's admission into the Union witnessed a series of economic, demographic, and technological booms unparalleled in the nation's history. These booms were to shape the character and the image of the new state, which was perceived as a land of daring individualism and serendipitous success. California was where the young nation was able to act out its most youthful fantasies.

The story of the Central Pacific Railroad and the men who profited so mightily from it is a case in point. The line was originally the passionate vision of Theodore Judah, a young civil engineer who had successfully presided over the construction of the state's earliest line, the Sacramento Valley Railroad. As the gold rush towns rose around him, Judah was the first to connect California's economic dreams with the prevailing East Coast dream of a transcontinental railroad. Judah's idea (eventually fulfilled) was the so-called Dutch Flat route over the Sierra. Rebuffed by San Francisco politicians and private investors alike, he finally called a meeting of investors inside a Sacramento hardware store owned by Mark Hopkins and Collis P. Huntington. With Leland Stanford, a wholesale grocer, and Charles Crocker, a dry goods merchant, these men eventually convinced the increasingly desperate Judah to sell them one-hundredth of Central Pacific's outstanding stock and make them president, vice president, secretary, and treasurer of the new company. In 1863, as Judah traveled back east through Panama to stake his claim to the California leg of the transcontinental, he contracted yellow fever and died. Control passed to the men who would later be known as the Big Four.

All these new ways of doing things seemed to congeal in the explosive growth of the early 20th century's ultimate boomtown: Los Angeles.

Between 1880 and the onset of World War I, the number of miles of railroad in California increased from 2,195 (3,532 km) to more than 8,000 (12,875 km), creating new markets and fueling new industries. The boom in California agriculture—until then a small, regional affair—was led by the wheat growers, who planted such vast acreages that reapers would often have to camp at the end of a field, having completed but one pass during the day. Newly accessible markets led to all kinds of innovation. By the end of the 1880s, orange growers had figured out how to cool a railroad car sufficiently well to ship their goods to the East Coast; by 1892 they had succeeded in shipping their fruit to England.

The constant influx of immigrants from the rest of the U.S. and abroad also brought new ways of doing things. Where old-timers near Sacramento saw swampland, for example, the Japanese pioneer George Shima saw a veritable Eden for growing the potatoes he so loved in his homeland. Such was the road to success for the "Potato King." The expatriate Hungarian Count Agoston Haraszthy became the "father of California wine" when in 1857, reveling in the pleasant climate and rich soils of Sonoma Valley, he created the state's first winery, spurring on the labors of Charles Krug, Jacob Schram, and Paul Masson, who would make California wines world famous. Luther Burbank set up his horticultural laboratory in Santa Rosa, devoted to grafting and seed selection. The aggressive lending and collateral strategies of the Italian-American banker A. P. Giannini made his Bank of America the financial undergirding for generations of the state's farmers.

All these new ways of doing things seemed to congeal in the explosive growth of the early 20th century's ultimate boomtown: Los Angeles. The semidesert city used the latest engineering techniques to secure water from a faraway place called the Owens

Valley (which was left an environmental wreck). Advertising and the new motion picture industry lured residents to newly irrigated suburbs.

But how long would it look like that? Such growth might nurture the collective and the private pocket, but its price was the scarring of the landscape by mining and dumping and construction, the damming of great rivers, and the felling of great forests. A partial antidote was found in the activities of the Sierra Club and its rugged-mystic founder John Muir.

Muir, a Scot by birth, came to California in 1868. As a boy he had gone blind and, having regained his sight, had vowed to dedicate his life to the witnessing of nature. For decades he trekked the Yosemite Valley and other natural wonders, writing about them for various national newspapers and magazines. In 1892 he helped found the Sierra Club, was made its first president, and promptly went to war with the government over a plan to permit mining, lumbering, and grazing near Yosemite. Muir convinced the state to deed Yosemite to the federal government for use as a national park. It remains to this day an international symbol of a paradise rescued.

"The Road to California" (1871) depicts the Central Pacific's line into the Sierra Nevada.

Postwar Suburban Paradise

One would hardly have expected the good life to grow out of California's experiences in the Great Depression and World War II, yet that is precisely what happened. The Depression proved to Americans that California's much celebrated economic resilience was no fiction. The million new migrants who arrived during the 1930s experienced it for themselves. And what the Depression served to bolster, the war years cast in figurative and literal steel. Fueled by War Department contracts, California's total annual income almost tripled during the war. The Cold War kept the defense economy buoyant in the 1950s, and by 1960 California had a population of 15.8 million.

This growth and affluence, in proximity to the style-creating movie industry, helped give birth to the nation's first lifestyle culture. Here one could break with the past and, through personal consumer choices, become the person one wanted to be. A hypothetical composite of "California man" in 1960 might have read something like this: He works as a machinist or junior engineer at Douglas Aircraft, producing equipment for the U.S. Air Force or TWA. He holds a mortgage on a modern tract house in Lakewood, an "instant community" built from blueprint to landscape in two years. On weekends, dressed in a Hawaiian shirt and flip-flops, he attends a pool party in Palos Verdes. There, over barbecued steak and taco salad, he discusses contemporary politics—not conventional party politics, but specific ballot issues: a new tax to build the state university system into a world-class institution or maybe a measure to control handguns.

In the late 1960s and all through the 1970s, personal lifestyle culture broke new frontiers. California universities pioneered ethnic studies centers—one way for their students to regain the sense of personal history lost in the original race to become American. On the same campuses, the farmworker-rights leader Cesar Chavez found some of his most dedicated organizers—youths who truly believed in the justice of *la causa,* but who could also use the involvement to rethink traditional laissez-faire notions about economics and poverty. San Francisco became the world's first gay metropolis, with gay power parades and the country's first openly gay political figure, Supervisor Harvey Milk.

The conventional middle class also asserted the primacy of individual rights, first with the passage of Proposition 13, which severely limited the growth of property taxes, then in their overwhelming support of antitax political conservatives, from President Ronald Reagan to Gov. George Deukmejian. Bold new ventures by and for the spiritually aware ranged from outdoor churches in drive-in theaters (one formed by the Rev. Robert Schuller later became the Crystal Cathedral) to Zen Buddhist centers. Outdoor enthusiasts demanded and got several new state and national parks.

Coast Road

One of the most ambitious road projects in American history, California's State Route 1 (Calif. 1) along the Big Sur coast was the route that many people thought would never be built. The geography was just too severe: deep ravines and cliffs rising to 1,200 feet (365 m). But the need became too acute. Construction of the highway began in 1919, with much of the labor provided by prisoners from San Quentin. Civilians also joined the cause, including a young would-be writer by the name of John Steinbeck (see p. 44), who hailed from nearby Salinas. The highway was finished in 1934, when two crews working from opposite ends of the route finally came face-to-face.

Yet the most important contribution of the 1970s and '80s lay not in social or political developments, but in business. Heavy investment in education, combined with the stop-and-go nature of post-Vietnam defense spending, created a growing class of techno-whiz kids, concentrated around San Jose and the rest of the Bay Area. They included Steve Wozniak and Steve Jobs, who founded Apple; William Millard, an IBM dropout who started ComputerLand, the world's first computer retail chain; and Andrew Grove, a Hungarian immigrant who helped build Intel into the world's largest maker of microchips. Presiding over them all as father figure and mentor was David Packard, the founder of Hewlett-Packard.

Steve Jobs (*left*) and Steve Wozniak (*right*) helped found Apple in 1976.

To the south, the boom in L.A. and San Diego was due not so much to a substantial technological base but to an unstructured, fluid business establishment. With traditional banking concentrated in San Francisco, L.A. attracted financial experimenters. Michael Milken, the brilliant (if felonious) inventor of the junk bond, underwrote hundreds of successful but undercapitalized firms that later created thousands of new jobs.

By the late 1980s, however, several new challenges confronted Californians. Although the state had already begun to wean itself from defense contracts, it was unprepared for the enormous cuts that followed the end of the Cold War. Nor was it primed for the social costs of unchecked immigration, regardless of the net gain these new Latin and Asian immigrants brought to the economic table. The population was still increasing, and constrained state spending (largely the legacy of the antitaxers) exacerbated old inequities by beggaring poor school districts, libraries, and social welfare programs.

When the biggest race riot in the nation's history broke out in L.A. in April 1992, many Americans felt that Californians were finally getting their comeuppance. Referring to the faltering Golden State, social critic Michael Kinsley summed up the prevailing sentiment. "Ha ha!" he wrote in his nationally syndicated newspaper column. "Ha ha ha ha ha!"

Permanent Frontier

From 1989 through the first half of the 1990s, its economy adrift, California suffered a series of punishing environmental and social disasters. In October 1989 the Bay Area was struck by the most severe earthquake since 1906. A section of the Bay Bridge fell, and the Cypress Freeway collapsed, sandwiching traffic, while the Marina District crumbled, then burned. In October 1991 a wildfire hit the Oakland hills, destroying 3,000 homes.

Things were no better in Los Angeles. In 1991 a series of wildfires paralyzed the region from Malibu to Laguna. The 1992 riot erupted after an all-white jury acquitted four police officers accused of brutally beating Rodney King, an African American. The beating, captured on videotape and broadcast to a world audience, assumed epic proportions. When the acquittal was announced, the racially mixed south-central part of the city erupted. There followed four days of looting, burning, and shooting, leaving 58 dead and nearly 2,000 wounded. The National Guard was brought in to restore order. Measures taken to deal with race issues included changes in the police services and plans to build better schools in the inner city. In January 1994, the city was hit by a magnitude 6.7 earthquake originating in the San Fernando Valley. Some sections of freeway collapsed; neighborhoods of older tract housing crumbled. More National Guard troops and billions in federal aid were required.

The California Dream took on new meaning as tech-savvy youngsters became millionaires in the blink of an eye.

And yet, by 1995 new migrants were again arriving in droves. The most important reason was the state's economy, which was beginning to sing again. Dwindling trade barriers and a soaring global economy had created huge new markets for California's products: wine, rice, computer chips, electronic games. Another critical component was Hollywood. While the 1930s and '40s are traditionally thought of as the film industry's Golden Age, the 1990s became its Platinum Age. Pushed by worldwide demand for "entertainment product" and the flourishing of cable and pay-per-view TV, new jobs created in the entertainment industry had, by 1997, replaced nearly all the jobs lost in the defense cutbacks.

California—and specifically San Francisco—was the hub of the Internet boom of the late 1990s, when the Bay Area grew giddy on the most spectacular growth since the 1849 gold rush. The California Dream took on new meaning as tech-savvy youngsters became millionaires in the blink of an eye. The multiplying economy fostered a massive new wave of migration from out of state, adding fuel to a concomitant real estate boom. Californians had good reason to celebrate the new millennium. By 2002, however, they were suffering an almighty headache following the collapse of the Internet and stock-market bubbles. Employee stock-option fortunes

Jerry Brown served two terms as governor between 1975 and 1983, before starting a third in 2011.

evaporated overnight, along with jobs. With housing prices continuing to skyrocket, California witnessed a net exodus as residents headed out for greener pastures. In 2003, those that remained ousted the incumbent governor and voted in the Hollywood action-movie star Arnold Schwarzenegger on a "no new taxes" promise to resolve the state's overwhelming budget problems.

Schwarzenegger proved a popular governor at first due to his environmentally friendly agenda and his hands-on management of several devastating wildfires. However, his later years in office were plagued by a sexual scandal that led to separation from his wife, Maria Shriver, and by statewide economic malaise. Term limits prevented the "Governator" from running again.

The 2010 election to choose his successor pitted former governor Jerry Brown against eBay president Meg Whitman. Brown won in a landslide and has attempted to tackle the state's budget crises with austerity measures that have thus far proved unpopular with both sides of the political spectrum.

Demographically, the early 21st century continued trends evident since the 1970s, with Latinos increasingly dominating the traditional core cities and a multiethnic middle class moving to the older suburbs. Newer so-called exurbs, still farther from the core, continue to attract the upper middle class.

One new phenomenon is the popularity of "urban core boutique cities"—places like downtown San Francisco, which increasingly relies on San Jose for its main economic sustenance while marketing itself as the fashionable place to live. ■

The Arts

When asked why so many of his fellow painters were drawn to California, 19th-century artist John Gutzen Borghum answered that "such pure and living color is found in but few parts of the world, and such variety of strange and 'paintable' matter does not exist elsewhere." Today, California's vibrant art scene continues to draw sustenance from the state's diverse landscape.

Painting

That nature should preoccupy generations of California artists is hardly surprising. The state covers more than 158,000 square miles (409,218 sq km), much of it still undisturbed. Yet scale and remoteness alone do not quite explain the appeal. California as a phenomenon does. The state was born in a critical period for the U.S., a time when conventional frontiers were perceived as settled and when new lands were deemed necessary for the reinvigoration of the Democratic Experiment. It was the impact of Americans on the land, and vice versa, that bolstered the self-confidence of the young nation. The name for this was manifest destiny.

The first art to trickle out of the gold rush consisted largely of genre paintings of everyday life, a preoccupation among American artists all over the country. Yet these early works veered from the period's aesthetic norms by consistently portraying everyday scenes from heroic daily life. "Miners in the Sierras," the 1851 work by Charles Nahl and Frederick Wenderoth, shows four miners shoveling dirt into a sluice box. The work is hard, the earth yielding only to mighty swings of the pickax. But the real point of the painting is what lies ahead of the miners—an enormous rocky valley, unsettled but for one ramshackle cabin in the distance. Only a hero could work on, undaunted.

That nature should preoccupy generations of California artists is hardly surprising.

As the first impressions of California circulated—some of them accurate, many surely "stretchers," as Mark Twain would have it—more and more artists set out for the West. Although many of these first landscape painters were amateurs, not a few were professionals skilled in techniques of detail and illumination. Albert Bierstadt (1830–1902), a New Englander famed for his paintings of Yosemite Valley, was overwhelmed by his subject. "We are now here in the Garden of Eden," he wrote to one friend, "the most beautiful place I was ever in."

A sense of the mystic infuses Bierstadt's paintings. Trees

seem ready to burst with colorful sap; the folds of great mountain faces appear still pliable, the Creator not yet finished with them. The High Sierra, explains scholar Ilene Susan Fort in the book *Paintings of California*, "epitomized the idea of divine immanence that had become central to the American concept of nature."

Younger artists soon transformed the genre. Impressionism's preoccupation with light combined with a growing sense of regional uniqueness. The underrated William Keith (1839–1911), for example, began his career using Bierstadtian detail in his 1869 "San Anselmo Valley Near San Rafael"; by 1880 his style had mutated into a more van Gogh–like evocation in the "Sand Dunes and Fog, San Francisco." In the former, giant eucalyptus trees loom over plucky explorers. In the latter, the solitude of nature triumphs, the competing ecologies of sea grass, shrubs, and ocean quietly resolved.

Albert Bierstadt's "Half Dome, Yosemite" (1868) celebrates California's wild beauty.

Urban versions of this trend were rendered by William Hahn (1829–1887) in "Market Scene, Sansome Street, San Francisco," and by Theodore Wores (1859–1939) in "New Year's Day in San Francisco Chinatown."

These two impulses—localism and impressionism—made up a variety of movements spanning the period from the late 1890s through the late 1930s. The first recognizable group, the tonalists, focused on the Monterey Peninsula. Inspired by George Inness's "California" (1894), these artists looked to somehow evoke the essence of a scene via the use of tone, or, as Fort writes, "a narrow range of muted colors that emphasized spareness of land, solitary nature."

Yet localism did not imply timidity; Inness's gold-toned scene of a small rural settlement dominated by two gnarled trees is, after all, titled simply "California," as if it were somehow the final word on the subject. A similar sense of authority resounds in "The Summer" (1932), by Gottardo Piazzoni, who once answered the question "What is your religion?" with the reply "I think it is California." By 1933, San Francisco painter Arthur F. Mathews had pushed the tonalist form to a point of precision. His "Monterey Cypress #3" has the authority of a five-color woodblock print—brown, gray, green, blue, and an unforgettable butter gold.

The well-documented works of the Bay Area's Society of Six show how profoundly European trends inspired California painters.

The well-documented works of the Bay Area's Society of Six show how profoundly European trends inspired California painters. The group's "simple" use of brilliant hues and glowing palettes conspired to one end: to evoke the modern experience of nature. Yet, even in the works of one artist, the tactics of the typical Society of Six painter could be remarkably diverse. Was Selden Connor Gile (1877–1947), in his "Boat and Yellow Hills," a Post-impressionist? Or was he, as is suggested in his almost hallucinatory "The Soil" (1927), a modernist? How about a tonalist-modernist? The exercise in labeling may be silly, but it is irresistible, given the grandness of the works.

If the "modern experience of nature" was what enthralled the Society of Six, it was nature's pure "sensation" that preoccupied the southern California plein air scene. Painters such as Joseph Kleitsch and William Wendt seemed to proceed from the premise that the invariably perfect weather of southern California made for a perfectly invisible backdrop, allowing the subject of any painting there to vibrate with feeling. There is a wistful surrender to the everyday in Kleitsch's "Old Laguna" (1924), a surrender we would not trade for the world. In Wendt's "Where Nature's God Hath Wrought" (1925), a "typical" southern California hillock embodies the unknowable, the jagged geometry of purple rock rising forcefully from rolling green sage knolls—God's fist, raised in silent remembrance.

The onset of the Great Depression shook this Homeric idyll to its roots. The social and economic tumult of the nation was being played out on California's landscape, particularly upon its farms and orchards. Even before Steinbeck's groundbreaking *Grapes of Wrath* appeared in 1939, however, modern social realism flowed. Frances Brooks's "The Picnic" (circa 1930–1940) depicted the simple joys of the toiling class dancing in the evening shade after a long day in the fields. Painter Maynard Dixon's "Oakie Camp" and "No Place to Go" (both 1934) bear the indelible influence of his photojournalist wife, Dorothea Lange, known for her haunting photographs of the Depression dispossessed.

Watercolorist Millard Sheets (1907–1989) did some of his most memorable work in collaboration with Lange and fellow photographer Horace Bristol. Sheets's spare but charmingly forlorn "Miggs (Migrants), 1938" was used, in tandem with Lange and Bristol's works, by *Fortune* magazine in 1939 to illustrate the plight of migrant workers.

As in the rest of the country, the postwar period witnessed the rise of several modernist genres, from abstract expressionism to conceptual art. The content has been increasingly figurative, from the smudged impressionism of Elmer Bishoff (1916–1991) and Richard Diebenkorn (1922–1993). Landscape—the public landscape—has subsided.

Yet landscape—the private, personal landscape—remains at the core of the works of David Hockney (1937–), the preeminent figure of postwar California art. Using a self-described "playful" style of bold color and strong line, Hockney has consistently portrayed his, and by extension everyone's, private California. Intimate California. These are places that could only "feel" private in a state blessed with so much space and wealth: swimming pools ("A Bigger Splash," 1967), backyards ("A Lawn Being Sprinkled," 1967), even roads through deserts ("Pear Blossom Highway," 1986) and roads to Hollywood studios ("Mulholland Drive," 1980).

This last reveals how an artist's personal growth is often tied to the region itself. As Hockney tells it in his 1996 autobiography *That's the Way I See It*, "I'd moved to Los Angeles and was working on a painting of the view outside my studio on Santa Monica Boulevard. And it wasn't working. It was still stuffy, still asphyxiated by that sense of supposedly 'real' perspective. I gave up. I moved up to the Hollywood Hills and I began painting the drive down to the studio. The moment I moved up here into the hills, wiggly lines began appearing in my paintings. The only wiggly lines I'd had on my paintings before were those that were on water. I was painting ['Mulholland'] from memory—the memory of the drive down—[and it] was beginning to work. You see, it was all about movement and shifting views—although at the time I didn't yet fully understand the implications of such a moving focus."

EXPERIENCE: Listen to *la Música*

When it comes to live music festivals, California is perhaps best known for the alt- and modern-rock Coachella Festival *(www.coachella.com)* or the Stagecoach Festival *(www.stagecoachfestival.com)*, the state's biggest country-and-western bash. Fewer people, however, know about VivaFest *(www.vivafest.org)*, the world's largest mariachi music event.

Hosted in San Jose for more than 20 years, VivaFest lasts for about two weeks in September. And you don't have to spend a dime to enjoy its daylong outdoor concert, Feria del Mariachi. You might not recognize many performers' names, but they're internationally seasoned and acclaimed in Latin music.

Be sure to bring fare for the authentic Mexican food and art on offer. You can even take a workshop such as "Mariachi 101" or *folklórica* dance. You can also learn about Mexican heritage at film screenings, often alongside the directors and writers. Plan ahead for early-bird specials and to avoid sellouts, as interest in Latino culture continues to grow in this region.

Literature

About 20 minutes north of Angels Camp in Gold Country, in a quiet stretch of live oak and chaparral, sits a forlorn wooden shack. Here, in 1865, the young Mark Twain (1835–1910) wrote his most famous short story, "The Celebrated Jumping Frog of Calaveras County." The story concerns Jim Smiley, a betting man who is "always ready and laying for a chance," particularly when it comes to animal races. One day Smiley decides to catch a frog and train it to jump for competition. After three months of dedicated training, the frog, Dan'l, becomes Smiley's prize, "whomping" all comers.

One day a stranger in camp, hearing Smiley bragging about his frog, says: "Well, I'm only a stranger here, and I ain't got no frog; but if I had a frog, I'd bet you." No problem, says Smiley, spying an easy mark. He hands Dan'l to the stranger and asks him to hold him while he fetches another frog. Smiley returns, and the race begins. "The new

Kerouac, Ginsberg, and other Beatniks used to meet at San Francisco's famed City Lights bookstore.

frog hopped off lively, but Dan'l give a heave, and hysted up his shoulders—so—like a Frenchman, but it warn't no use—he couldn't budge: he was planted solid as a church." Smiley pays the man then discovers that the "stranger" had filled Dan'l with shotgun pellets.

In fewer than three pages, Twain had sketched the elements of what would fascinate him and so many others writing about the Western experience: Here was a place where men made themselves up as they went; freed from the conventions of the East, they could reinvent themselves—and their language—as conditions changed. Environment trumped heredity. Indeed, environment made the man: Bret Harte (1836–1902; see sidebar p. 43), one of Twain's contemporaries, would even speak of a place called Roaring Camp, where "the strongest man had but three fingers on his right hand; the best shot had but one eye."

To Harte and Twain, these were minor men—characters—yet somehow universal men as well, creating new lives and new rules in a land they perceived as a blank slate. What could be more American? No wonder the author-raconteur Ambrose Bierce (1842–1914) is best known not for his poignantly beautiful short stories ("An Occurrence at Owl Creek Bridge") but for his bitter truths about life in San Francisco. As in: "A morning newspaper says three unclaimed gold watches are in the hands of the police, and that it is not definitely known who stole them. It is definitely known who *will* steal them."

If the first literary explorers of California were wits who discovered what California was doing to the forty-niners, the next generation rendered precise regional portraits of the new state, seeking the truth in life's detail. One of these, Scottish author Robert Louis Stevenson (1850–1894), arrived in Napa for a nine-week honeymoon during the summer of 1880. Having been ill, he was quickly revived by the mild weather of the countryside and soon took to long walks and carriage rides, meeting a host of idiosyncratic fellows who were, by turns, making wine, playing at silver mining, squatting for land, and, like Stevenson, recovering from various ailments. Stevenson had discovered a land of tonics. Standing in Jacob Schram's vineyard one day, he looked over the valley and mused, "In this wild spot, I did not feel the sacredness of ancient cultivation. It was still raw, it was no Marathon, and no Johannesburg; yet the stirring sunlight, and the growing vines, and the vats and bottles in the cavern, made a pleasant music for the mind."

Another self-described literary explorer, Helen Hunt Jackson (1830–1885), was also at work during this period. A writer, traveler, and activist for the much-abused California mission Indians, Jackson published her most influential work, the romantic novel *Ramona*, in 1883. By setting her story of a doomed love affair between Señorita Ramona and a mission Indian, Alessandro, against the deplorable conditions of the tribes, Jackson hoped to draw attention to the plight of Native Americans.

Instead, *Ramona* was extolled as a glowing evocation of the region's Spanish Catholic past, glorifying the treatment of the Indians under the Spanish and Mexican dons and padres and laying almost all of the blame for Indian woes upon the later Anglo immigrants. To this day, the popularity of the book, along with the pageants, tour guides, and

California's Journalistic Giants

From John Steinbeck to William Saroyan, California boasts a wealth of famous fiction authors. But the state has also produced many celebrated journalists and newspaper icons. Having failed as a gold miner, **Mark Twain** (1835–1910) earned his first kudos as a writer in the 1860s working as a San Francisco–based journalist. Around the same time in the same city, **Bret Harte** (1836–1902) was honing a style that would make him one of the great correspondents of the Wild West and an early champion of Native Americans. Following the Civil War, a young Union Army officer named **Ambrose Bierce** (1842–1913) was posted to San Francisco, where he discovered a passion for the written word. He would shine as a columnist and critic. Although not a writer, **William Randolph Hearst** (1863–1951) had an indelible effect on American journalism as the longtime publisher of the *San Francisco Examiner* and other newspapers.

plays that it inspired, account for much of southern California's sweet-and-sour sense of itself—sweet for what once was (but really wasn't), sour for what is (but which may be better, if uglier).

By 1900, adventure writer Jack London (1876–1916), a former sailor, tramp, and gold miner, had settled down to write in the San Francisco Bay area. The hard-drinking London cut a wide swath. A self-educated socialist, he ran for mayor of Oakland and lost. He co-authored a book on sexual politics, then one about the underclass of London. Orating frequently on such subjects, he soon became America's best known socialist. Yet London seemed most at home on the Oakland waterfront. His short stories had a diverse cast of local characters: Mexican boxers, Portuguese wharf rats, Irish thieves, Chinese shrimp-catchers. Here were oyster-bed thieves with names like Porpoise, Centipede, and Barchi, who said things like, "You better slide outa this here or we'll fill you so full of holes you wouldn't float in molasses." So strong was London's writing—and so ambitious—that many critics believed he would become the West's first truly big author. By the eve of World War I, he had crafted some of the most compelling stories of his day. But a California Émile Zola he was not to be. In 1916, Jack London died of alcoholism. He was 40 years old.

Robert Louis Stevenson wrote of Napa Valley as "a pleasant music for the mind."

Writers of the next generation tended—not always successfully—to seek a national stage for their California experience. Poet Robinson Jeffers (1887–1962) evoked such strong admiration for his passionate, violent etchings of mankind's follies that his self-built Tor House, in Carmel, became a place of pilgrimage for writers and critics from around the world. Short-story writer and playwright William Saroyan (1908–1981), from farm country in Fresno, won similar fame for *The Human Comedy* and *My Name Is Aram.* The characters in the works of John Fante, writing in L.A., were luminous enough to garner the praise of even H. L. Mencken.

Yet in John Steinbeck (1902–1968) there would be a California Zola, or at least a California William Faulkner. A native of the little farm town of Salinas, Steinbeck wrote about the ways of "the small man, the small woman." His characters were mainly ordinary people trying to make their way in an American Eden where all was not well. Some of his subjects were cannery workers *(Cannery Row),* others tramps *(Of Mice and Men),* and still others the wandering *paisanos* who harvested the state's agricultural bounty *(Tortilla Flat).* Their world was that of the Great Depression. Steinbeck was clearly taken with their plight, making it the basis, even in his most overwrought scenes, of something that was irreducibly brilliant, unforgettable.

If Steinbeck was California's Faulkner, then Dashiell Hammett and Raymond Chandler would be its double-headed Balzac, peopling its landscape with cynical detectives, long-legged dames, and corrupt cops. Hammett's alter ego, Sam Spade, was the more hard-boiled of the two, although Humphrey Bogart's portrayal of him in *The Maltese Falcon* (1941) would forever leave Americans with the notion that he was somehow a good fellow beneath it all; apparently Hollywood did not believe the public could handle such amorality. The character of Philip Marlowe in Chandler's *The Big Sleep* (1939), however, *was* supposed to be a decent fellow, which the studios gladly accentuated. Yet the point of both characters is similar: What other reaction could an individual have to California? As critic Edmund Wilson later noted, bleak hard minimalism was the only logical reaction to a place where the only constant thing in life was the flat endless line in the sunset called the Pacific Ocean.

A native of the little farm town of Salinas, Steinbeck wrote about the ways of "the small man, the small woman."

Much of California's postwar literature continued in this vein, often embracing the decadent, as with Charles Bukowski's Meat School of inebriate poetry. From the 1970s (although arguably traceable as far back as Christopher Isherwood's *A Single Man*, about gay life, in 1963), new and more optimistic themes began to reassert themselves, principally through ethnic writers. Authors such as Amy Tan, for example, began exploring their interior immigrant worlds, fusing Old Country inheritances with New World domestic drama.

But it is through nonfiction that the newest minorities have made their most noticeable mark. Mexican American Richard Rodriguez, often seen on public TV's *NewsHour*, specializes in the post-postmodern paradox: How does California transform the Old World, and how does the Old World change California and, in turn, the whole nation?

Style & Design

While California's literary impact on the world has been relatively minor, its influence in the world of style and design has been sizable. One reason is one of today's principal makers of "culture"—Hollywood, which is in the business of digesting large amounts of information about audiences and then feeding it back to them in just recognizable forms. This is why you might hear one of today's smart college kids describe a postmodern building in downtown Los Angeles or San Francisco as having "a *Blade Runner* look."

But California's impact on the look of our world does not begin and end with cinema. Henry and Charles Greene, architects of the late 19th-century Arts and Crafts movement, are a case in point. The movement, which called for a return to simplicity and honesty in the arts, already had American proponents (such as the prairie school of architecture under Frank Lloyd Wright). However, it fell to the Greene brothers to find a distinctively California version of the style, more suited than the prairie style to the arid desert environs of much of the state.

Working in Pasadena from the early 1890s through 1915, the Greenes created a series of homes they dubbed "ultimate bungalows." The Gamble House (see pp. 112–113), designed for one of the country's biggest industrialists, may be the best of these efforts. Hallmarks of the style include Japanese-influenced overhanging eaves, the mission-influenced use of tile and stone, and a penchant for simple, handmade natural wooden furniture. The style was so resonant (and so widely imitated) that, to this day, the words "Arts and Crafts" and "Greene and Greene" are often used interchangeably.

The style is resurgent, reflected in Disney's Grand Californian Hotel, advertised as being in the "Greene and Greene craftsman style," as are hundreds of new tract homes now being built around the state.

In the U.S., architecture has often carried the extra burden of providing its own historical context; if a place has no past, the architect must evoke one. In California, this need for a past was exacerbated by the state's late entry into the Union and by its geographic remoteness. Thus architect Bernard Maybeck (1862–1957) imposed an imperial beaux arts style on his design for the 1915 Panama-Pacific Exposition, the better to signal to the world the grand ambitions of post–1906 earthquake San Francisco. Architect Bertram Grosvenor Goodhue (1869–1924) improvised a Spanish colonial revival style, replete with churriguresque ornamentation and tile domes, for San Diego's 1915 California Pacific Exposition. More recently, architect John Jerde has raised the profile of the genre, using larger-than-life signs and icons to create such faux landmarks as San Diego's Horton Plaza and the Universal Citywalk in Los Angeles.

Nevertheless, it may well have been the state's paucity of visual history that allowed internationalist Richard Neutra to create some of the world's best examples of modern architecture, particularly in the realm of private houses. An immigrant from Austria, Neutra had been trained in the modernist school of Bauhaus architecture, which advocated pragmatism, spare clean lines, and functionality. His 1933 V.D.L. House (see p. 108), in the Silverlake district of Los Angeles, represents the epitome of the style. The boxy, angular house is perhaps most distinctive for its use of large windows to blur the division between inside and outside. Copied by generations of architects, it is the DNA for much of what passes for contemporary architecture in the United States today.

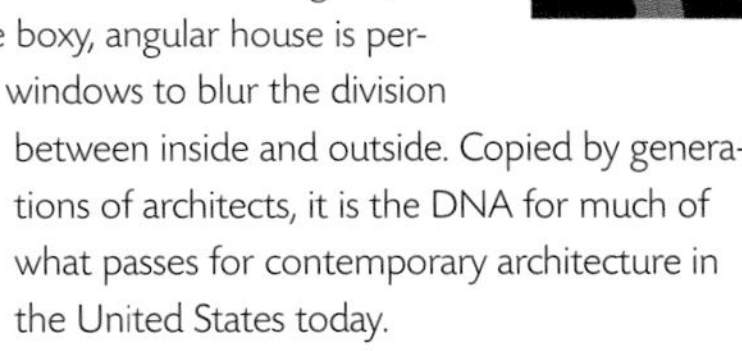

California, by virtue of history and climate, permitted the ultimate experiments in the functional. Where else, after all, could one dress in what came to be called "leisure wear"? In the postwar period, the state produced such fashion and design innovators as Cole of California, known for loose-fitting yet elegant beachwear, which was often worn far from the shore. The popularity of the singing group the Beach Boys, and the growth of surfing, helped launch such firms as Ocean Pacific, which now sells surfwear and Hawaiian shirts from Topeka to Tokyo.

The focus on comfort and "the essentials" was also a driving force behind the Venice Beach–based designers Charles and Ray Eames, who in the 1950s produced the stripped-down

California's Greatest Living Architect

Born in Canada, Frank Gehry (1929–) ran away to California as a teenager and worked his way from driving trucks to being the state's preeminent architect. Along with Zaha Hadid and Rem Koolhaas, Gehry has emerged as a leading light of an edgy postmodern movement that emphasizes both form and function, sometimes to startling effect. Although the Guggenheim Museum Bilbao (Spain) is probably his most celebrated work, he has plenty of masterpieces in California, most notably the Walt Disney Concert Hall (see p. 103) in downtown Los Angeles and the Gehry House in Santa Monica.

Pools and fountains cool the Museum Courtyard at the hilltop Getty Center.

"Potato Chip Chair," still much in evidence in offices around the world. And the need for easy mobility to cover routinely long distances in California soon elevated the automobile to icon status. No wonder that Detroit's most far-reaching innovations come from students at the Art Center College of Design in Pasadena.

Three recent buildings point to California's role in determining the look of tomorrow. With its defiantly bold lines and chock-a-block appearance, Frank Gehry's (see sidebar opposite) Air & Space Building for the California Science Center (see pp. 105–107) shows how functionality and the need for historic reference can be married without the misleading romanticism of earlier practitioners. Conversely, Richard Meier's Getty Center (see pp. 60–66) in Los Angeles, with its endless (and blinding) travertine plazas, may establish a new (and possibly troubling) coda for postmodernism.

And what of Spanish architect Raphael Moneo's Cathedral of Our Lady of the Angels (see p. 103) in Los Angeles? It may well represent what, at least for California, is the ultimate aesthetic achievement: a monument that is more Mexico City than Madrid, and more Golden State than United States.

Cinema

Although Hollywood, and by extension California, has long been synonymous with the film industry, conventional wisdom now holds that physical location plays only a secondary role in determining what regions will profit most mightily from this economic powerhouse. Citing the rise of computer animation, special effects technology, and soundstages in places as far flung as Austin, Texas, and Raleigh, North Carolina, some pundits have even proclaimed that the old Hollywood—the place where dreams are made—has ceased to exist. Yet time and time again, after flights of fancy to other ports, the film industry has reinvested in California, betting its existence on the combination of talent, technique, and location that the state possesses in such abundance.

Although the first full-length film made in L.A. was produced in 1907, it was not until 1910 that one filmmaker would fully exploit southern California's climatic, geographic, and historic attributes. That man was David Wark Griffith (1880–1948). A Kentucky-born actor who desperately wanted to be a playwright, the tall and lanky Griffith had by 1910 become a dominant director of one-reelers in the budding New York film industry. Taking his acting troupe west on seasonal filming forays, Griffith found that he could save money and time by using the region's abundance of sunlight. In the first four months of 1910, Griffith produced 21 films with southern California locations as background. Location soon began to dictate content, as the historic missions prompted Griffith to make a version of Helen Hunt Jackson's *Ramona* (see pp. 43–44), among other California-themed films.

In the process of manipulating all that sunlight to dramatic effect, Griffith discovered film's fundamental storytelling techniques: the angle shot, the flashback, and the close-up. All of these he used to stunning effect in his 1915 *The Clansman* (later retitled *Birth of a Nation*), a racist saga of Civil War reconstruction that President Woodrow Wilson called "history written with lightning." The film was so popular that it established Hollywood as the center of moviedom. By the late 1920s, Hollywood accounted for approximately 90 percent of all films made around the world each year.

By the late 1920s, Hollywood accounted for approximately 90 percent of all films made around the world each year.

Certainly no one needed to convince Louis B. Mayer—a Russian-born Jew and junk dealer turned Boston theater owner—that there was money to be made in Tinseltown. By the time Mayer moved to L.A. in 1918, he had already profited handsomely from movies. Among other wise moves, he had bought regional rights to such films as *Birth of a Nation.* More than money drew Mayer and a generation of Jewish emigré moguls to the West Coast: California, where everything was new and fluid, imposed none of the social constraints that Jews met in the East. Here, Mayer and his rivals Jack, Harry, Albert, and Sam Warner produced films that were more American than America. Optimistic and solidly midwestern, the Andy Hardy series, for example, starred Mickey Rooney as a rosy-cheeked teenager who loved sports, his wise "pop," and his nurturing "ma." At a time when the U.S. faced one of its greatest crises—its entry into World War II—Andy was unwavering in his belief that American values would always win out.

Mayer was also the creator of the studio system of film production, signing up young talent for years at a time and then driving them to make dozens of films, a kind of plantation system with champagne and silk scarves. His paternalism, combined with his studio's ownership of theaters, gave him formidable power over an actor's life. Writer

February 12, 1958: Director Stanley Donen holds up the final clapperboard as stars Cary Grant and Ingrid Bergman celebrate the completion of their film *Indiscreet*.

Billy Wilder recalls an afternoon spent writing a script at MGM in the early 1940s and seeing Mayer deal with the troublesome Rooney. "We looked out the window because there was screaming going on, and Louis B. Mayer held Mickey Rooney by the lapel. He says, 'You're Andy Hardy! You're the United States. You're the Stars and Stripes. Behave yourself! You're a symbol!'"

Although elements of this restrictive studio system remained in place until the early 1960s, its decline began as early as 1939, when the Department of Justice began investigating fair-trade violations involving studio control of theaters. By the late 1950s, the moguls had been forced to divest themselves of most holdings, stripping them of a lucrative source of capital with which to support their burgeoning stables of winsome stars, cranky directors, and megalomaniac producers. The story of Hollywood since has largely been the story of brilliant individuals—from Robert Towne (*Chinatown,* 1974) to Francis Ford Coppola (*The Godfather,* 1972)—trying, and usually failing, to refashion certain elements of the old system.

Of all these attempts, DreamWorks, the latest and most ambitious, may well be the one to succeed. At the core of DreamWorks, the first new studio in 50 years, are three men: mogul David Geffen (see sidebar p. 99), former Disney mastermind Jeffrey Katzenberg, and producer-director Steven Spielberg. The latter is the linchpin. An accomplished TV producer by his early 20s, Spielberg is the most commercially successful director in film history. Technology, in the form of special effects, has played a large role in making his work shimmer, as in *Jaws* (1975), *Raiders of the Lost Ark* (1981), *E.T.* (1982), *Jurassic Park* (1993), and *Shrek* (2003).

Spielberg has an extraordinary ability to zero in on tales with mythic resonance: *E.T.* as a coming-of-age in America story; *Jaws* as a modern *Moby Dick*, replete with Ahab-like shark hunter and an ending (costar Richard Dreyfuss paddling away on a piece of flotsam) evocative of Melville's hero clutching his dead friend's coffin.

Like Mayer, Spielberg and his partners also cultivate the special "people skills" (described by historian Garry Wills as "omnidirectional fawning") needed to secure the best stars, directors, and technicians. This is particularly apparent in the early success and quality of the trio's releases, including the *Shrek* films. However, Spielberg's approach to managing talent is very different from Mayer's. According to the *Wall Street Journal*, he ends every business call with the three little words every player in Tinseltown can't get enough of: "I love you."

TV in Hollywood

With so many early shows broadcast live on the East Coast, New York City dominated television production until the 1950s, when Hollywood entered the new medium. Among the first shows shot in Los Angeles were the iconic comedy *I Love Lucy* (1951–1957) and cop drama *Dragnet* (1951–1959). *Gunsmoke* (1955–1975) and *The Life and Legend of Wyatt Earp* (1955–1961) proved that TV could move outdoors. By the end of the decade, Hollywood was finally making more shows than New York. Many of them—like *Leave It to Beaver* (1957–1963) and *The Twilight Zone* (1959–1964)—remain small-screen classics.

Theater

The theater is one of the few enterprises in California to suffer from the presence of the film industry. The reasons are obvious, given some people's preference for wealth and fame. World-class playwrights such as Bertolt Brecht may sometimes take up residence but seldom stay under the palms for long enough to create the consistent audience demand that is required to sustain a distinct stage community.

Over the past few years, however, progress has been made. Director-provocateur Luis Valdez has pushed his Teatro Campesino to acclaimed performances of his Latino-themed plays, and San Diego's Old Globe theater (see p. 156) has won an international following for its presentations of modern and classical works. The brassy San Francisco Mime Troupe has refined the art of socially relevant drama. Another star of the California theater scene is the La Jolla Playhouse (see p. 146). Based on the campus of UC San Diego, the troupe was created in 1947 by Gregory Peck and other Hollywood actors craving a serious stage outlet closer to home. Starting in the 1980s, artistic director Des McAnuff crafted the playhouse into a national powerhouse of original plays, stunning revivals, and world premieres. Among its Tony Award–winning repertoire are *Jersey Boys, Memphis,* and *I Am My Own Wife.*

Under founding artistic director Gordon Davidson, L.A.'s Mark Taper Forum has also launched several Tony Award–winning plays. In 1993 the Forum took a gamble by throwing its weight behind the gay-themed *Angels in America* by Tony Kushner. The result was wide acclaim and the biggest compliment a California director can receive: a subsequent run on Broadway. ■

The nation's second biggest city, filled with art museums, beaches, and food and music scenes that have garnered vast acclaim

Los Angeles

The Chinese Theatre, host to many movie premieres

Los Angeles

It is, first and foremost, a flatland—a great desert plain. But it is a desert plain like no other. Irrigated with imported water, surrounded by glistening beaches and verdant foothills, and peopled by 18 million dreamers from the ends of the Earth, greater Los Angeles, North America's second largest metropolitan region, may well hold more surprises and delights than any other single destination in the world.

Certainly its short but action-packed history suggests so. Founded in 1781 by a group of Spaniards, Indians, and mestizos, the city was originally claimed for the king of Spain as el Pueblo de la Nuestra Señora la Reina de los Angeles—the City of Our Lady Queen of Angels. It quickly changed hands to Mexico in 1822, and then, reluctantly, to the United States in 1846. (The U.S. troops were initially so unpopular here that local *mujeres*—women—sent one stiff-necked U.S. Army lieutenant packing, along with a poignant sign of their regard: ripe peaches wrapped in cactus needles.)

After a brief period of lawlessness, the region underwent a still continuing pattern of real estate boom and bust. L.A.'s resultant sprawl (now of 80 contiguous towns) would thus reflect the values of the city's predominantly midwestern founders, men and women who sought to re-create the village society they had left behind in places like Iowa and

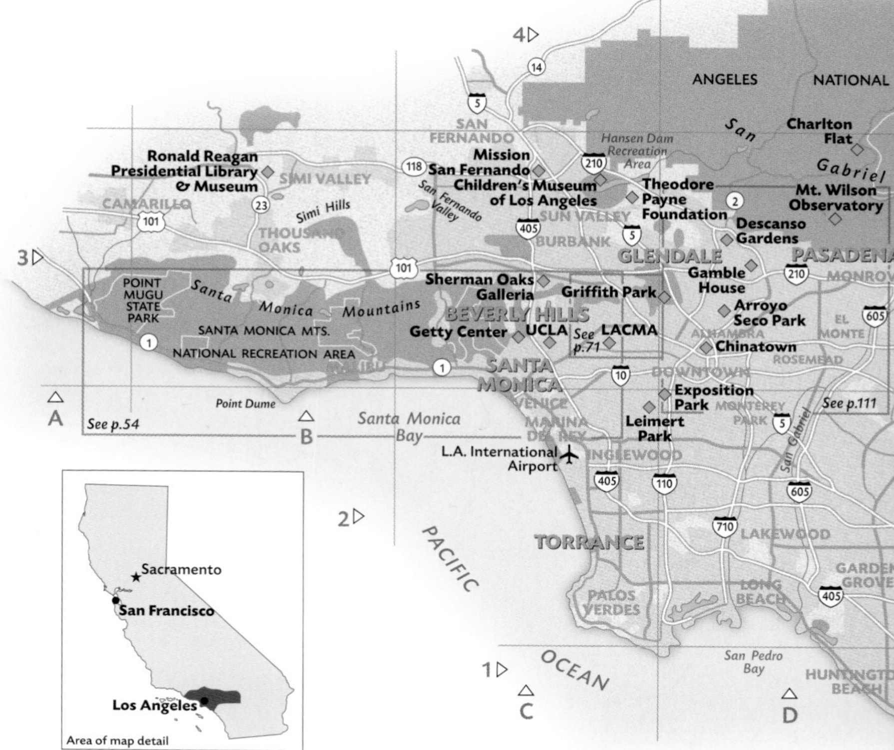

Indiana rather than become part of some looming cosmopolitan cluster.

Today these urban villages persist as identifiable, if constantly changing, regional cultures. The onetime beach resort town of Santa Monica is now a sophisticated, affluent city of achievers with one of the nation's most inclusive city governments, strong environmental laws, and a culture zone stretching from its historic pier to adjacent places like the Getty Center, which one critic has called the Athens of the West.

The Beverly Hills area offers world-class shopping (on Rodeo Drive), art (at the Los Angeles County Museum of Art), and people-watching (at the bustling Farmers Market). And, of course, Hollywood itself.

The late 19th-century "millionaires' retreat" of Pasadena, now a diverse community of Anglos, Asians, and Latinos, similarly thrives with art (the Huntington Library), food (nearby Monterey Park, the first suburban Chinatown), and architecture (as the capital of Craftsman-style homebuilding).

The traveler who settles into any one of these areas, all within 30 minutes' drive of each other, will be richly rewarded. ■

NOT TO BE MISSED:

A stroll along the Santa Monica–Venice Beach boardwalk **54–56**

Exploring 4,000 years of art at the Getty Center **60–66**

Shopping on Rodeo Drive **72–74**

Tinseltown's landmarks along Hollywood Boulevard **83–84**

An evening performance at the Hollywood Bowl **84**

Hiking in Griffith Park **86**

Enjoying the ethnic neighborhoods of Little Tokyo, Chinatown, and Olvera Street **92–95, 99**

The plush gardens and museums in and around Pasadena **110–117**

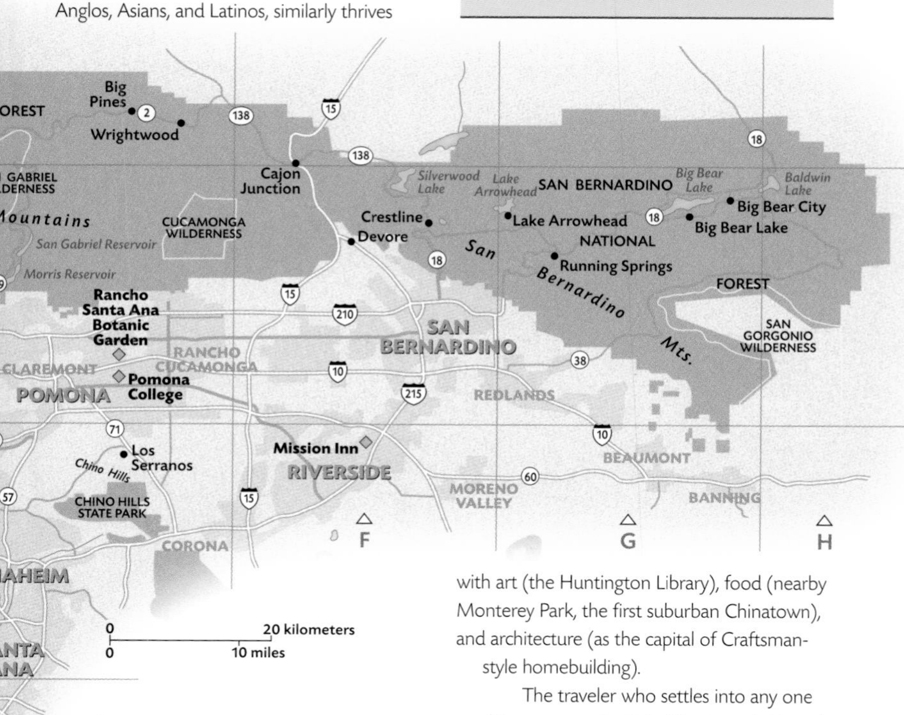

From the Beach

With more than 30 miles (48 km) of sparkling beaches, Los Angeles is a sun lover's dream. Continentals flock to Santa Monica for upscale shopping, while water sports fans go north to surf at Malibu or windsurf at Will Rogers. Dog lovers can take their pooches to Leo Carrillo still farther north. Young lovers seek out quiet Marina del Rey to the south, while bohemians, oddballs, artists, and anyone in need of a laugh and a decent hot dog in-line skate over to Venice.

Venice

52 C2 & 55 G1

Visitor Information

Marina del Rey Visitors Center, 4701 Admiralty Way, Marina del Rey

310/305-9545

www.visitthemarina.com

Just inland, pursuits turn to culture. The Getty Center has everything from van Gogh to Rembrandt in painting and outstanding decorative arts, as well as one of the most controversial public gardens in the country. UCLA, one of the state's most striking campuses, has more gardens (one of sculpture, one Japanese-style), as well as a stupendous museum devoted to cultural history.

Venice

Founded in 1904 as "the Venice of America" by enlightened tobacco tycoon Abbot Kinney, this part-bohemian, part-affluent jumble of wooden beach cottages, neo-Renaissance architecture, and idyllic canals is part of Marina del Rey.

Venice harkens back to L.A.'s original golden era, when beachgoers rode the Red Car line to Kinney's version of St. Mark's before jumping into a (now razed) saltwater plunge. "Old" Venice architecture can still be seen at **Windward Circle,** and enough remains to make the 3-mile (4.8 km) **boardwalk** one of the most frequented destinations for locals and tourists alike. At the southern end, near Venice

This lively skate park swirls alongside the Venice boardwalk, one of the best boardwalks in the U.S.

Boulevard, strollers will see the caged-in outdoor gym known worldwide as **Venice Weight Pen.** Muscle-bound exhibitionists, street artists, palm readers, musicians, religious preachers, and bikini-clad roller skaters add to the modern-day circus that defines Venice Beach. It was here that Arnold Schwarzenegger and a legion of Mr. Americas learned to pump iron.

The area around the last of the Venice canals *(near Dell Ave.)* is a placid, picturesque home to many of L.A.'s cultural elite, including Matt Groening, creator of *The Simpsons.* At the northern end stands the 30-foot-tall (9 m) public art piece **"Ballerina Clown"** *(corner of Main St. & Rose Ave.)* by Jonathan Borofsky.

Keep with the spirit of Venice by driving east to the **Museum**

Museum of Jurassic Technology

- 55 G2
- 9341 Venice Blvd., Culver City
- 310/836-6131
- Closed a.m. & Mon.–Wed.
- Donation

www.mjt.org

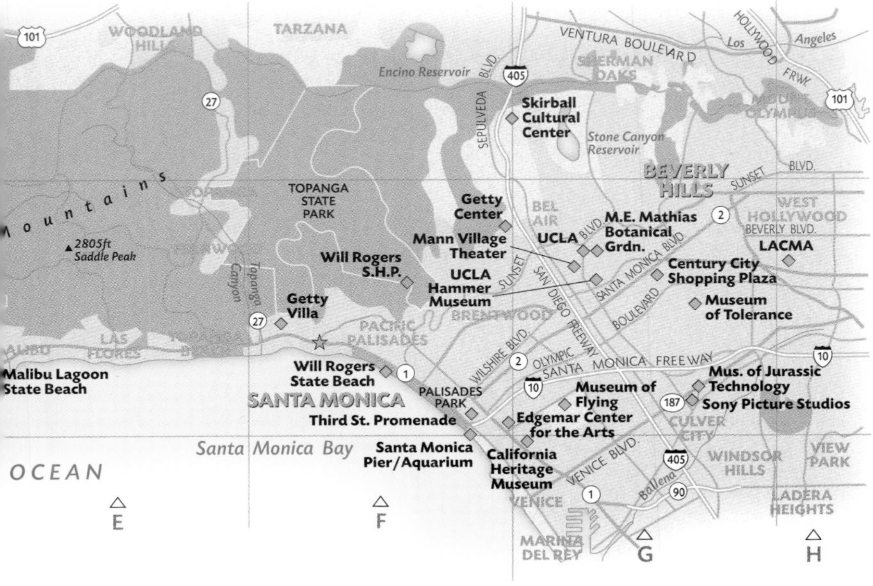

The Palm Tree

Decades of "creative landscaping" have resulted in L.A.'s towering palm trees. Many strains came from Chile and the Canary Islands; only the fan palm *(Washingtonia filifera)* is native to the Southwest. At more than 50 feet (15 m), with fronds up to 5 feet (1.5 m) long, this transplant from the Southwest desert serves as unofficial icon to the region.

Sony Pictures Studios
- 55 G2
- 10202 W. Washington Blvd., Culver City
- 310/244-8687
- Tours Mon.–Fri.
- $$$$$

www.sonypictures studios.com

Santa Monica
- 52 C3 & 55 F2

Visitor Information
- Convention & Visitors Bureau, 1920 Main St., Ste. B
- 310/393-7593, 800/544-5319

www.santamonica .com

Palisades Park
- 55 F2
- Ocean Ave., Santa Monica
- 310/458-8644

Santa Monica Pier
- 55 F1

www.santamonica pier.org

of Jurassic Technology, which boasts an eclectic collection of strange phenomena (such as the deprong mori, or "piercing devil" bat) and weird human accomplishments (micro-sculptures of Snow White and the Seven Dwarfs built inside the eye of a needle). The museum's avant-garde program of evening speakers is one of L.A.'s best kept secrets.

A tour of **Sony Pictures Studios** leads you through sets where Spiderman swung from buildings and agents from *Men in Black* (1997) battled aliens. You can even sit in on a filming of *Jeopardy!* or *Wheel of Fortune.*

Santa Monica

Santa Monica is no longer the sleepy beachside town so aptly evoked as "Bay City" by the detective novelist Raymond Chandler. With a population of more than 88,000 and some of the best eating and shopping in L.A., Santa Monica now sports more of a European ambience—the Nice of California. The various musicians who perform at the four-times-weekly farmers markets are an indication of another facet of Santa Monica: its prime position on the world music scene.

Fortunately for the seeker of old Santa Monica, there are still all the eternal beachside delights: salty air, tawny beaches, and magical sunsets. Perhaps the best place to take in the city's character is **Palisades Park.** Deeded to the city in 1875 by John Percival (J. P.) Jones, a city founder, this 26-acre (10.5 ha) strip of green lawn and Washington palm trees sits above Santa Monica Bay. The views sometimes include a glimpse of Catalina Island, some 22 miles (35 km) away.

A morning walk through Palisades Park could include several notable stops: The 110-year-old **Camera Obscura** *(1450 Ocean Ave.)* projects images through its rooftop lenses and prisms—a reminder of what passed for wonder before the age of Disney; the **statue of St. Monica** *(Ocean Ave. & Wilshire Blvd.)* by Eugene H. Monrahan is remarkable for its streamlined modern lines, as is the old **Shangri-La Hotel** *(1301 Ocean Ave., tel 310/394-2791, www .shangrila-hotel.com)* just across the street.

While the historic **Santa Monica Pier** now houses the reasonably priced **Pacific Park** *(tel 310/260-8744, www.pacpark .com)* amusement park, many come just to see the 1909 **Looff Hippodrome** and its refurbished carousel of hand-carved ponies.

On the south side of the pier is the original **Muscle Beach,** where the muscle-bound show off to the public. Underneath the pier is the **Santa Monica Pier Aquarium,** where three aquariums educate the public on marine science. Just north of the pier is the **Marion Davies Guest House** *(415 Hwy. 1)*, built for the star in 1929 by noted architect Julia Morgan.

On Main Street, the **California Heritage Museum** is well worth a visit. Housed in the 1894 former home of city founder J. P. Jones, the museum offers a number of exhibits in displays that change regularly. Some of its past shows have featured the work of 1920s California tableware makers, the origins of the Hawaiian shirt, and artifacts of early surfing culture.

The **Edgemar Center for the Arts** was originally designed as the Santa Monica Museum of Modern Art by architect Frank Gehry (see sidebar p. 46), whose work has included the American Center in Paris and the Guggenheim Museum in Bilbao, Spain. Architectural pilgrims can also see (from the outside only) Gehry's home at 1002 22nd Street.

Although closed at the time of writing, the **Museum of Flying** *(map p. 55 G2, 3100 Airport Ave., tel 310/398-2500, www.museumofflying.com)* is scheduled to reopen in 2013 on a new site on the north side of the Santa Monica airport. The airport is on the old site of the Douglas Aircraft Company which, for more than 60 years, dominated the construction of both commercial and military aircraft. The new museum will feature functioning World War II planes along with dozens of more recent aircraft.

People-watching and shopping at the **Third Street Promenade** *(map p. 55 F2, betw. Broadway & Wilshire Blvd., www.thirdstreetpromenade.org)* can be a full-time pursuit. The best time is on Wednesday, when the famous **Santa Monica Farmers Market** convenes at Third Street

(continued on p. 60)

Santa Monica Pier Aquarium
- Map: 55 F1
- 100 Ocean Front Walk, Santa Monica Pier, Santa Monica
- Tel: 310/393-6149
- Closed Mon. & a.m.
- $, children free

www.healthebay.org

California Heritage Museum
- Map: 55 G1
- 2612 Main St., Santa Monica
- Tel: 310/392-8537
- Closed Mon.–Tues.
- $

www.californiaheritagemuseum.org

Edgemar Center for the Arts
- Map: 55 F2
- 2437 Main St., Santa Monica
- Tel: 310/399-3666

www.edgemar.com

EXPERIENCE: Malibu Creek Horseback Riding

A visit to Los Angeles doesn't have to be confined to the city. Nearly 30 years of environmental activism has resulted in cleaner beaches, better water, and new state parks dedicated to preserving the ecologies of western Los Angeles County.

The most scenic of these parks is Malibu Creek State Park *(map p. 54 D2, 1925 Las Virgenes Rd., Calabasas, tel 818/880-0367, www.malibucreekstatepark.org)*, with reaches of rolling grasslands, sharp gorges, creeks, and towering old trees. One of the best ways to take in this backcountry is on horseback. Malibu Riders *(tel 818/510-2245, www.maliburiders.com)* offers daily one-hour, 3-mile (4.8-km) round-trip loop rides *($)* from Paramount Ranch into Malibu Creek. You will ride through the former Ronald Reagan Ranch and beautiful forests to a breathtaking view of Malibu Lake. An optional one-hour, 3-mile (4.8-km) extension *($$)* takes you deeper into the Santa Monica Mountains to Century Lake and back. Riders must be 8 years or older. Price includes horse rental and a guide.

Drive: Along Sunset Boulevard

Intrepid drivers can test their skills with a spin up scenic, winding Sunset Boulevard, memorably featured in one of moviedom's most stupidly terrifying chase scenes (*Against All Odds,* 1984). The sane motorist, however, begins the jaunt with a brunch at Gladstone's *(17300 W. Hwy. 1, Pacific Palisades, tel 310/454-3474, www.sbe.com/gladstones),* where French toast and coffee put you in the mood for an L.A. drive.

Heading east on Sunset Boulevard, the first stop is the **Self-Realization Fellowship Lake Shrine** ❶ *(17190 Sunset Blvd., tel 310/454-4114, www.yogananda-srf.org, closed Mon. & a.m. Sun.).* Founded in 1950 by the Paramahansa Yogananda, who preached that "there must be world brotherhood if we are to be able to practice the true art of living," the shrine underscores the highly ecumenical nature of Hinduism in Los Angeles. With its gardens of miniature roses and hydrangeas the size of basketballs, the shrine is a perfect place for an after-lunch nap. The gift store sells Indian curios, incense, and a range of self-improvement literature.

Still on Sunset, a left turn at Bienveneda Avenue will take you to the **Topanga Trailhead** ❷, the start of hikes into the mesquite-and-sage landscape of the Santa Monica Mountains. A nearby sign points to the easily negotiated **Phil Leacock Memorial Trail,** from which the view takes in Pacific Palisades as well as the ocean.

Continue up Sunset and past the famous **Gelson's Market** ❸ *(15424 Sunset Blvd. & Via de la Paz, tel 310/459-4483, www.gelsons.com),* where you can stock up on picnic items. Beyond it, look out for the turnoff for **Will Rogers State Historic Park** ❹ *(14253 Sunset Blvd., tel 310/454-8212, www.parks.ca.gov).* The beloved humorist deeded his estate to California, which has maintained his home and polo field; a free audio tour of Rogers's living room and living quarters, with its charming cowboys-and-Indians decor, is a must. A hike up **Inspiration Trail** will put a flush of sun and wind on your face.

NOT TO BE MISSED:

Self-Realization Fellowship Lake Shrine • Will Rogers State Historic Park • Bel Air Estates

On Sunset again, you pass infamous **Rockingham Avenue** ❺ (where noted non-killer O. J. Simpson's house has been razed). Stop for an espresso at Brentwood Village *(Barrington Ave., www.brentwoodvillage.org)* before passing

The 1.5-mile (2.4 km) portion of Sunset Boulevard known as the Sunset Strip is legendary for its nightlife.

I-405, the San Diego Freeway, and coming to **Bel Air Estates 6,** home of the rich and famous. Either of two ornate "gates" on the north side of Sunset admit the curious to a maze of small streets lined with some of L.A.'s priciest (if sometimes aesthetically troubling) estates. Note that the "star maps" hawked here are likely to be worthless. Content yourself with occasionally exclaiming, "That's gotta be Greta Garbo's house!" or "Isn't that where Don Johnson and Melanie Griffith got married?"

You can either end the drive here or continue to **UCLA** (see pp. 66–69) or to **Beverly Hills** (see pp. 70–89). Alternatively, turn right on Beverly Glen Boulevard to Santa Monica Boulevard and the **Century City shopping plaza** *(map p. 55 G2, 10250 Santa Monica Blvd., www.westfield.com/centurycity).*

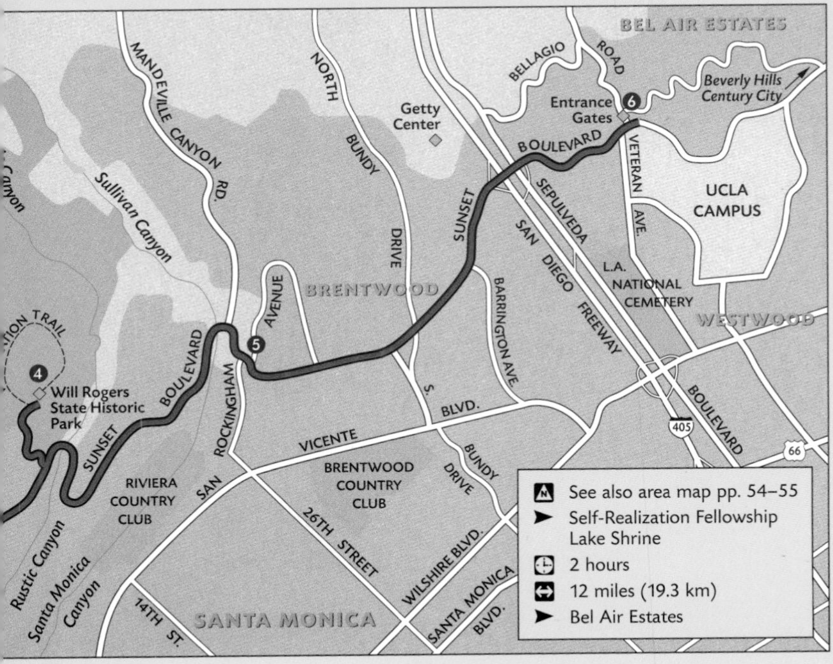

See also area map pp. 54–55
Self-Realization Fellowship Lake Shrine
2 hours
12 miles (19.3 km)
Bel Air Estates

Getty Villa
- 55 F2
- 17985 Hwy. 1, Pacific Palisades
- 310/440-7300, 310/440-7305 (hearing impaired)
- Closed Tues.
- $ (parking)

www.getty.edu

and Arizona Avenue. This is a "foodie" magnet, and a keen eye might spot celebrities and famous chefs scouting out the best organic mushrooms and brussels sprouts.

Getty Villa

The first home of oil billionaire J. Paul Getty's growing collection of antiquities and decorative arts was the recently restored Romanesque Getty Villa that Getty built in 1953 above Topanga Beach. The villa still houses his superb collection of more than 50,000 Greek and Roman antiquities. It also serves as an educational research center on ancient art and cultures.

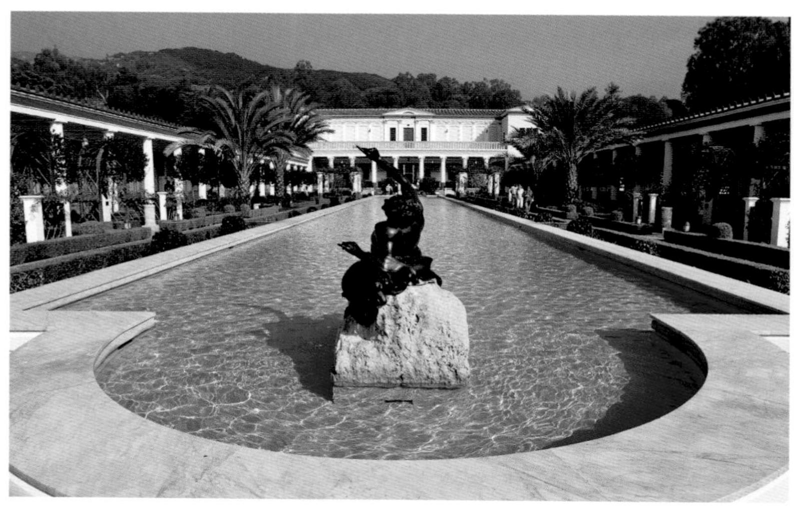

Plants favored by the ancients surround the Getty Villa's 220-foot-long (67 m) reflecting pool.

Getty Center
- 52 C3 & 55 F2
- 1200 Getty Center Dr., Getty Center exit from San Diego Freeway (I-405)
- 310/440-7300, 310/440-7305 for hearing impaired
- Closed Mon.
- $ (parking)

www.getty.edu

Getty Center

An eccentric with a reputation for being a skinflint, Getty surprised critics by leaving a $700 million trust. Astute financial management increased the trust to $4 billion, enabling its trustees to commit $1 billion to the building of a new museum.

Their choice of architect was Pritzker Prize–winner Richard Meier. The key design issue was how to make a modernist structure that inspired a classical sense of permanence. Meier's answer was to use travertine, a form of limestone quarried in Italy. The result is a hulking complex of shifting hues of white, ranging from a retina-scarring *blanc majeur* in the morning to a pleasant, late-afternoon-in-Rome gold by dusk.

Perched on its 110-acre (44.5 ha) campus high above the drone of I-405, the Getty Center, which was completed in 1997, inspires conflicting emotions. The dazzling complex bespeaks all the ambitions of a great art institution.

Yet the modernist campus also seems to be at once removed, reinforcing the old notion that in L.A. art has no organic connection with the community.

Yet since its opening, the Getty's actions have belied such concerns, and, through an outreach program, the center connects to the cultural life of the entire city. Key features are ongoing programs with local schools (guided and self-guided tours are offered, but must be reserved in advance) and educational programs covering photography, sculpture, and painting.

In addition, the Getty Center offers an eclectic range of events, from artist-at-work demonstrations and poetry readings to an annual Renaissance Family Festival, plus free "Friday Nights at the Getty" concerts featuring Afro-Latino, Cajun, folk, and blues music.

How to Visit: An electric tram shuttles visitors from the front entrance and parking to the museum **Arrival Plaza,** dominated by Martin Puryear's 45-foot (13.7 m) sculpture "That Profile." An orientation film is shown.

The Getty Center's five main buildings are arranged chronologically. All of them are connected, by either hallway or overpass, on both floors; at ground level, visitors can easily pass from 16th- to 18th-century works, then back to 17th-century, and so on. Mobile audio guides are programmed to respond to inquiries about individual paintings.

INSIDER TIP:

Regular films shown in the Getty auditorium include *Art Works: Behind the Scenes at the Getty* (30 mins.) and *Concert of Wills: Making the Getty Center* (90 mins.).

—GREG CRITSER
National Geographic author

North Pavilion: Paintings in the North Pavilion, which highlights art from before 1600, include the evocative "Mythological Scene," painted circa 1524 by the Italian Dosso Dossi *(room N205)*. The work perfectly illustrates the Venetian penchant for dreamscape and allegory, but also gives the museum the opportunity to fulfill its aim of educating the public about the history of paintings. Fra Bartolommeo's "Flight Into Egypt" is a good example of the luminous quality of this early 16th-century Italian's work. A 1330 panel by Bernardo Daddi depicting the Virgin, St. Paul, and St. Thomas Aquinas has been particularly well preserved. According to author Letitia Burns O'Conner, "the conservator who examined it prior to its purchase in 1993 declared he had never seen a *trecento* picture so well preserved, its glazes still intact to modulate the bright colors of the drapery, its punched gold background glowing softly."

(continued on p. 64)

Getty Center

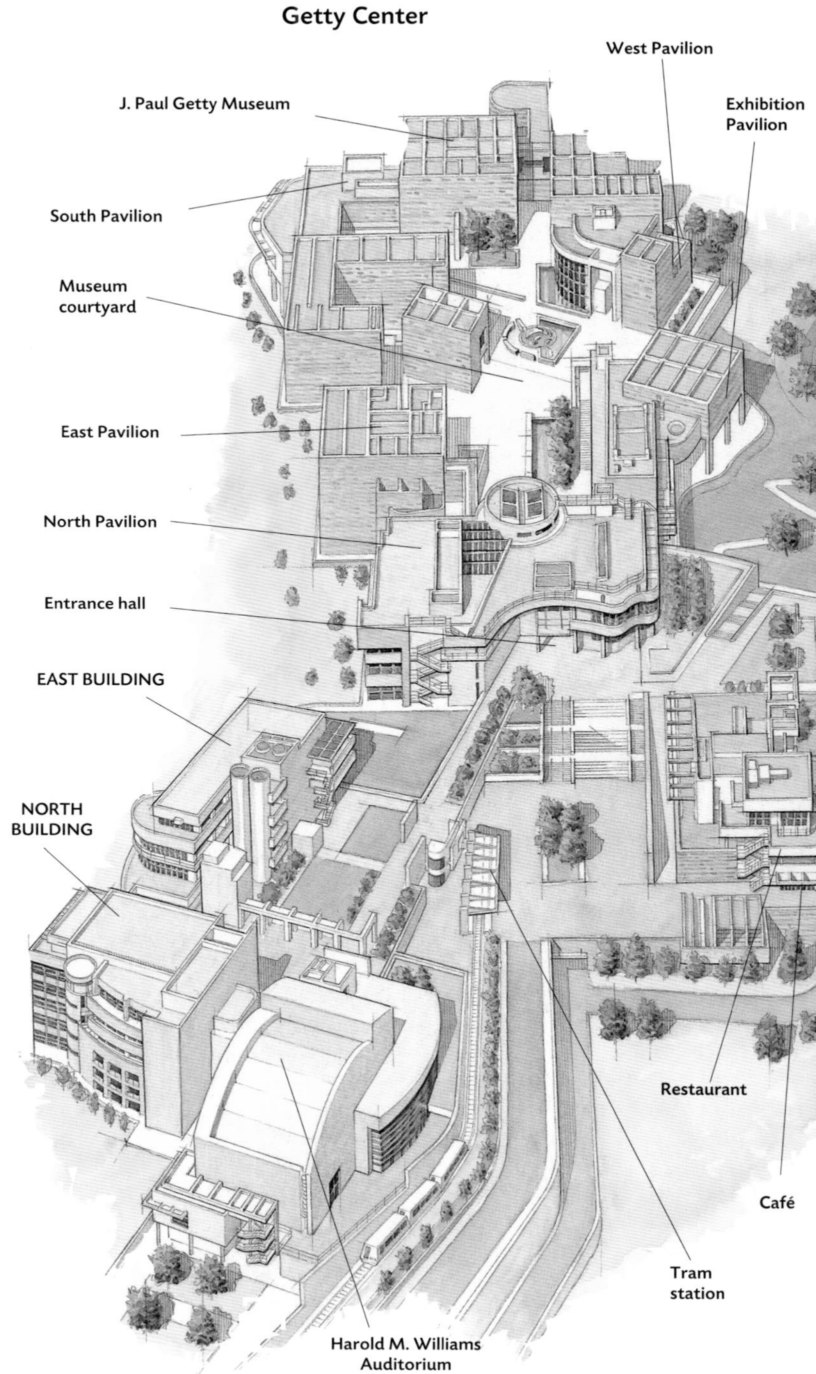
West Pavilion
J. Paul Getty Museum
Exhibition Pavilion
South Pavilion
Museum courtyard
East Pavilion
North Pavilion
Entrance hall
EAST BUILDING
NORTH BUILDING
Restaurant
Café
Tram station
Harold M. Williams Auditorium

Central garden
Getty Research Institute for the History of Art and the Humanities
Paintings
Changing exhibits
Education
Sculpture
Decorative arts
Manuscripts
Drawings
Photographs

In 2003, the Getty acquired Titian's "Portrait of Alfonso d'Avalos, Marchese del Vasto," painted in 1533. Considered the Getty Center's most important portrait, this masterpiece—of an illustrious noble in his suit of armor—by the leading exponent of Venetian Renaissance painting, set the standard for court portraiture and the evolution of Western art.

East Pavilion: The East Pavilion covers art from the period between 1600 and 1800. While the emphasis here is largely on Dutch and Flemish works, two small 17th-century paintings, Italian and French respectively, show the collection's range: Domenichino's "The Way to Calvary" is done on copper; Valentin de Boulogne's "Christ and the Adultress" *(both in room E201)* is noted in a museum caption by the neoconceptualist L.A. artist John Baldessari as "a kind of film noir."

What follows is a blur of giants, including Rubens ("The Entombment," "The Murder of St. Francis," both in room E202) and Rembrandt ("The Abduction of Europa" in room E205). A memorable piece by a lesser known 17th-century Dutch artist is Hendrick Ter Brugghen's "Bacchante With an Ape" *(room E204)*. Downstairs, the rotating collection of drawings in Gallery 103 is worth searching out for its spotlighted new acquisitions.

South Pavilion: The South Pavilion expands the scope by introducing decorative arts from

The Getty Center stands on a hill above Los Angeles with beautiful city views.

Jewish History in a Boutique Setting

Set on a hilltop just north of the Getty Center, the Skirball Cultural Center represents one of the best developments to come out of the growing trend toward boutique museums. This is because the Skirball has refined its mission—"to present Jewish culture and experience as part of the living fabric of American life as a whole"—and presents only the best and most comprehensive shows on the subject. There is a depth and singularity of experience here, matched by few such museums in the country.

At the core of the 125,000-square-foot (11,612 sq m) center is the exhibition entitled "Visions and Values: Jewish Life From Antiquity to America." Divided into 12 galleries, this rich display of artifacts, art, photos, texts, and objects from daily life takes visitors from the destruction of the Second Temple in A.D. 70 to modern-day America. Some of the displays are monumental, like the reproduction of the (later destroyed) New Synagogue of Berlin. Yet often it is the small, odd fragment that is most illuminating: a hand-painted handkerchief from China, the "Portrait of Mrs. Sarah Lyons" from Great Britain, and an ertrog container for citron used in the Sukkoth (harvest) ceremony.

The center has a program of arts and cultural events, including plays, music (including blues legend John Hammond), and readings.

1600 to 1800, the core of J. Paul Getty's personal collection. To do it justice, the museum brought in New York designer Thierry Despont to craft several period rooms, constituting a "museum within a museum." The effect is priceless, though some find it overwhelming. Despont's pale blue French-paneled room is a perfect medium for the ornate chairs, clocks, and furnishings. The enormous "Cabinet on Stand" (1675–1680) by André-Charles Boulle, in room S103, shows a craftsmanship unmatched by his contemporaries.

West Pavilion: Some visitors may prefer, with some justification, to make a separate trip to the Getty Center to see "Art after 1800," the exhibition in the West Pavilion. However, to do this would be to miss the effect of the dramatic buildup that the other pavilions provide. While many have cynically criticized this collection as "Europe's greatest hits," it is hard to underplay the delight provoked by the works of Monet, Renoir, Cézanne, Manet, and van Gogh that are hung here. "Irises" by van Gogh remains the biggest attraction. See it first thing in the morning before the crowds arrive. Lesser known paintings worth seeing here include Belgian painter James Ensor's huge 1888 work "Christ's Entry Into Brussels, 1889" *(room W204)*.

Juxtapositions of "smaller" works—a specialty of the Getty Center—make this gallery sing. Put Cézanne's "The Eternal Feminine" next to his "Still Life With Apples," and see if you ever think of fruit in the same way again. The brilliantly arranged photo gallery on the first floor makes a fitting coda.

Skirball Cultural Center

- 55 G3
- 2701 N. Sepulveda Blvd.
- 310/440-4500
- Closed Mon. & a.m. Tues.–Fri.
- $$

www.skirball.org

Gorgeous Gardens

UCLA has three outstanding gardens, all open to the public. The Mildred E. Mathias Botanic Garden *(map p. 55 G2, 100 Stein Plaza Driveway)* is a perfect place to read, write, or just sit and contemplate nature's wonder. The habitat diversity covers the spectrum from bamboo groves to streambeds and tropicals—some 4,000 plant species in all. The Franklin D. Murphy Sculpture Garden, behind the University Research Library, is a testimony to the former chancellor's breadth of interests. The 5-acre (2 ha) sculpture garden is the largest on the West Coast. Some 70 pieces of sculpture stand in the shade of the jacaranda trees. Among the artists are Auguste Rodin, Isamu Noguchi, and Alexander Calder.

Exhibitions Pavilion: No visit to the Getty Center would be complete without exploring the Exhibitions Pavilion, although its most famous and controversial piece, the Getty Kouros is no longer here. It was one of several antiquities returned to Greece and Italy after they were proved to have been stolen or excavated illegally.

Sculpture Garden: In 2007, the Fran and Ray Stark Sculpture Garden opened beside the tram station to display the bulk of 28 contemporary outdoor sculptures that Hollywood producer Ray Stark and his wife donated to the museum.

Central Garden: While there are many places at the Getty to pause and ponder or relax, nothing conjures the sense of discovery quite like the 134,000-square-foot (12,449 sq m) Central Garden. Created by artist Robert Irwin, the garden is an example of "site-generated art." Irwin's notion is that a person's intimate experience of nature can be heightened by accentuating the configuration of foliage, sunlight, and shade.

The focal point of the garden is a maze of floating azaleas, surrounded by a terraced round ravine marked by geometrically arranged cacti. Irwin interrupts the sense of botanical order with a series of "specialty gardens"—a meadow, a stream garden, terraces of hydrangeas and nasturtiums and irises. Just how well the scheme furthers the museum's aesthetic ideals is up to the individual stroller, but a better place to rest and soak up the sun is nowhere in sight.

UCLA
- 52 C3 & 55 G2
- 405 Hilgard Ave.
- 310/825-4321

www.ucla.edu

UCLA

Founded in 1919 as part of the University of California, the University of California at Los Angeles (UCLA) long languished in the shadow of its older sister, Berkeley (see pp. 238–239). Eventually, following a period of huge growth, the 400-acre (162 ha) campus began establishing a profile of its own (the turning point of which is said to have been former chancellor Franklin Murphy's command to answer the administration phones by saying "UCLA!" rather than "University of California"). Today UCLA ranks among the top ten research universities in the U.S., producing several recent Nobel Prize winners, and is fondly known as the "University of Caucasians, Latinos, and Asians," because of the diversity of its 25,000 undergraduates. South of Bel Air and north of Westwood Village, UCLA is at the heart of L.A.

Central Quad: Sitting on a low hilltop and overlooking surrounding valleys and mountain ranges, UCLA's Central Quad of four Romanesque-Renaissance-style buildings was built in 1929. Lush grounds and swaying old eucalyptus trees make it a perfect place for weekend strolls.

The university's **Powell Library** *(Quad, southwest corner)* is an architectural gem. Named for California bibliophile and longtime UCLA librarian Lawrence Clark Powell, the building has been restored to its 1929 grandeur. Soothing tile staircases lead to a reading room crowned by an ornate ceiling. The temporary structure used to house books during the remodeling, nicknamed "Towell," has won several architectural citations for its innovative use of materials.

Also restored is **Royce Hall** *(Quad, northwest corner),* another jewel. Named for California philosopher Josiah Royce, the Italianate auditorium is said to have been modeled on the Church of St. Ambrose in Milan.

The Museums: UCLA's main museum, the **UCLA Hammer Museum,** was founded by the late oil magnate Armand Hammer to house his then thin collection of old masters and Impressionist paintings. Since then, the institution has matured. Among the works in the collection are "Summertime" by artist Mary Cassatt (1844–1926), whose work was exhibited with that of the Impressionists in Paris in the 1880s. Other highlights include Rembrandt's "Juno" (1662–65), van Gogh's "Hospital at Saint-Remy" (1889), and Gauguin's "Bonjour Monsieur Gauguin" (1889). There are also a number of works by prominent American artists, including George Bellows, John Singer Sargent, Gilbert Stuart, and Andrew Wyeth.

INSIDER TIP:

Don't miss Richard Serra's "T.E.U.C.L.A." (Torqued Ellipse UCLA) in the sculpture garden: You can even walk through this beguiling plate of curved steel.

—KENNY LING

National Geographic contributor

Several other collections warrant attention. One is the largest U.S. collection of satirical drawings and watercolors by 19th-century French caricaturist Honoré Daumier. The other star, now also at the Hammer, is the **UCLA Grunwald Center for the Graphic Arts** *(tel 310/443-7078),* which features a wide range of paper works, from Dürer and Cruikshank to Picasso and Matisse. Because the Hammer is fond of

UCLA Hammer Museum

- 55 G2
- 10899 Wilshire Blvd., Westwood Village
- 310/443-7000
- Closed Mon.
- $$, free Thurs.

www.hammer.ucla.edu

Fowler Museum at UCLA

Fowler Hall, UCLA North Campus

310/825-4361

Closed a.m. & Mon.–Tues.

www.fowler.ucla.edu

traveling exhibitions—sometimes at the expense of its permanent collection—it is best to call before visiting for current information.

The Hammer's new initiative to amass a collection of contemporary works created since the 1960s focuses on drawing and photographs, with an emphasis on pieces since the millennium, while its **Billy Wilder Theater,** opened in December 2006, hosts provocative public programs and provides a cinematheque for the UCLA Film & Television Archive's vast documentary and movie collection.

The **Fowler Museum at UCLA** is a recent addition to the L.A. museum scene, but it has been making waves nonetheless. With its focus on non-European art and its emphasis on anthropology, the Fowler has staged acclaimed shows on subjects ranging from voodoo to the little-known Mochas people of pre-Columbian Peru.

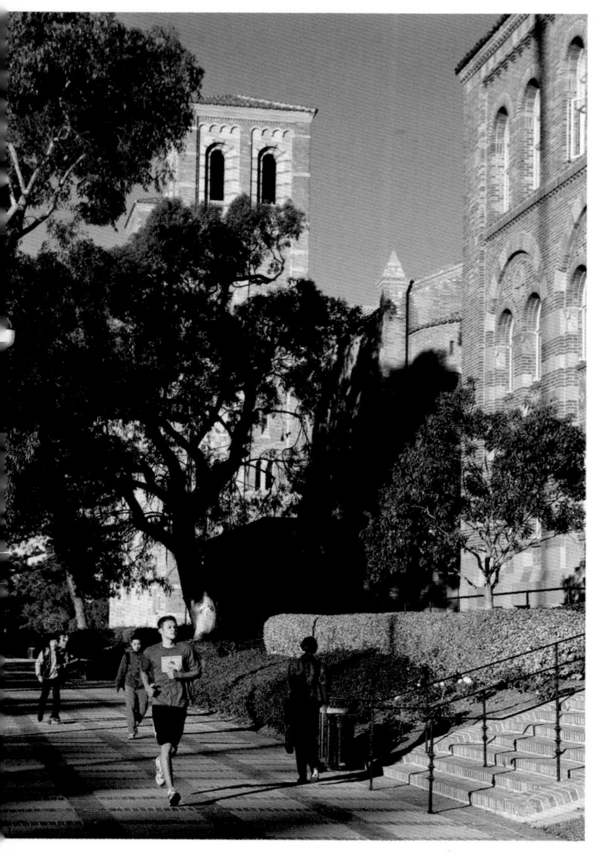

UCLA's Royce Hall: a study in Romanesque-Renaissance majesty

Athletics: Sports fans should check out the **UCLA Athletics Hall of Fame** in the J. D. Morgan Center. With more than a hundred NCAA championships under their belt, the Bruins have won more college championships than any other school. Among its athletic alums are basketball players Kareem Abdul-Jabbar and Bill Walton, baseball legend Jackie Robinson, Super Bowl quarterback Troy Aikman, and Olympic track star Jackie Joyner-Kersee.

Performing Arts: The **Center for the Art of Performance at UCLA** *(B100 Royce Hall, tel 310/825-4401, www.cap.ucla.edu)* is one of the city's premier cultural institutions, presenting world-class, cutting-edge works in dance, music, spoken word, and experimental theater. Inaugurated in 2001 by pop music icon Elvis Costello, the center spans the globe with its wildly eclectic and often experimental performances offered year-round. The center's programs are hosted at venues around UCLA's campus and beyond, including the Freud Playhouse, with its large proscenium stage, and Royce Hall (see p. 67), known for its state-of-the-art acoustics.

An infusion of funds from mogul-philanthropist David Geffen (see sidebar p. 99) and topflight Hollywood talent has made the **Geffen Playhouse,** in Westwood Village, a major L.A. theater venue.

Westwood Village: Just south of the main campus, Westwood Village serves as the proverbial (but pricey) "college town." Breakfast at Stan's Corner Donut Shop *(10948 Weyburn Ave., tel 310/208-8660)* is de rigueur, if only to experience the chocolate chip–peanut butter crullers. Bel Air Camera *(10925 Kinross Ave., tel 310/208-5150)* is in a building that looks like a camera (stock up here on photographic supplies).

Around UCLA: The restaurant scene around UCLA is constantly churning; one constant, just south of Wilshire Boulevard, is La Bruschetta *(1621 Westwood Blvd., tel 310/477-1052),* which serves up consistently good pasta dishes. Farther down Westwood is Junior's *(2379 Westwood Blvd., tel 310/475-5771),* the "Cadillac of Delis." Almost any of the Iranian restaurants on the east side of the street (known as Little Persia) serve up a decent lamb or chicken dish. To the west is Zen Bakery *(10988 Pico Blvd., tel 310/475-6727);* the breads and muffins are outstanding. At Westwood looms the neon-and-concrete Westside Pavilion Mall *(10800 W. Pico Blvd., tel 310/470-8752),* where West L.A.'s deeper pockets find just the right casual wear.

Driving east for ten minutes on Olympic Boulevard will take you to the **Museum of Tolerance,** a "teaching museum" dedicated to educating the public about racism and ethnic genocide. The focus is the Nazi Holocaust. The 90-minute guided tour of its interactive displays is unforgettable—and emotionally devastating. A recent addition, "Finding Our Families, Finding Ourselves," showcases the diversity and achievements of noted Americans. The museum's Tolerancenter includes a high-tech "time machine," which details human rights abuses around the world in different ages, and a re-created 1950s diner that "serves" a menu of controversial topics on video jukeboxes. ■

Cemetery to the Stars

The unofficial cemetery to the stars, Westwood Village Memorial Park *(1218 Glendon Ave., Los Angeles)* is the last resting place of Marilyn Monroe and numerous other luminaries of the big and small screens. Baseball legend Joe DiMaggio chose the tiny graveyard for his ex-wife after her controversial 1962 death because her mother was already buried there. Monroe's simple tomb lies in the wall near the northeast corner. Among the many others buried at Westwood are actors Natalie Wood, Jack Lemmon, George C. Scott, Walter Matthau, and Burt Lancaster, musicians Roy Orbison and Dean Martin, comedians Rodney Dangerfield and Don Knotts, writer Truman Capote, and director Billy Wilder. Visiting hours are daily 8 a.m. to dusk.

Geffen Playhouse

- 10886 Le Conte Ave., Los Angeles
- 310/208-5454

www.geffenplayhouse.com

Museum of Tolerance

- 55 G2 & 71 A1
- 9786 W. Pico Blvd., Los Angeles
- 310/553-8403
- Closed Sat. & public and Jewish holidays
- $$$

www.museumoftolerance.com

From Beverly Hills

The great urbanist Reyner Banham once referred to L.A.'s flat basin topography as "the plains of id." Here, life was so calm that anyone who lived in it for long would soon confront—or embrace—all their long-banished desires. If there is a "plain of id" in downtown and another at the beach, certainly there is a distinct one operating in and around the greater Beverly Hills area. This is the plain of money, both refined and crude—of money made and money spent.

The recently renovated Beverly Hills Hotel remains a classic celebrity hangout.

Beverly Hills
52 C3 & 71 A1
Visitor Information
Conference & Visitors Bureau, 239 S. Beverly Dr.
800/345-2210
www.lovebeverlyhills.com

It has always been that way in Beverly Hills. Founded in 1906 by real estate developer Burton Green, the city grew slowly until the 1920s. In 1920, movie star Douglas Fairbanks purchased a prominent hilltop in the area for $35,000. There he built the legendary Pickfair mansion for "America's sweetheart," actress Mary Pickford. Pickfair attracted all who aspired to be a Fairbanks or a Pickford, and the real estate market boomed.

Be warned: You will probably spend more on accommodations, food, and shopping in Beverly Hills than in other parts of the city. But this is a perfect place from which to explore several adjacent areas.

Just south, the Wilshire Corridor leads eastward to the Los Angeles County Museum of Art, perhaps the West Coast's best single art destination. Along the northern boundary of Beverly Hills runs Sunset Boulevard (see pp. 58–59), which also leads eastward, first to West Hollywood, a strip of famous restaurants and gay life, then on to old Hollywood, where so much of the money to sustain Beverly Hills was made in the first place.

INSIDER TIP:

To see *Homo holly-woodis* in action, have lunch at the legendary Polo Lounge in the Beverly Hills Hotel. Order the tortilla soup and fresh crab plate, and then sit back and watch the scene.

—GREG CRITSER
National Geographic author

From there the old Hollywood Freeway (U.S. 101) leads over to the San Fernando Valley, land of the quintessential shopping mall, offering yet more opportunities to part with your money.

Beverly Hills Hotel

There was a time when many people believed that the Beverly Hills Hotel—the old "Pink Palace"—had permanently lost its glow, its lovely yet outdated accommodations overshadowed by the gleaming new Peninsula Hotel down the way. No more. Ever since its purchase by the Sultan of Brunei in 1989, the hotel has mounted a strong comeback, investing heavily in a complete makeover. The result is a glamorous retreat, with all the modern conveniences, that evokes the best of Hollywood's Golden Age.

Have lunch under the old pepper tree in the **Polo Lounge,** then wander down to the **Fountain Coffee Room,** where you will

Beverly Hills Hotel

71 A2

9641 Sunset Blvd.

310/276-2251, 800/650-1842

www.beverlyhillshotel.com

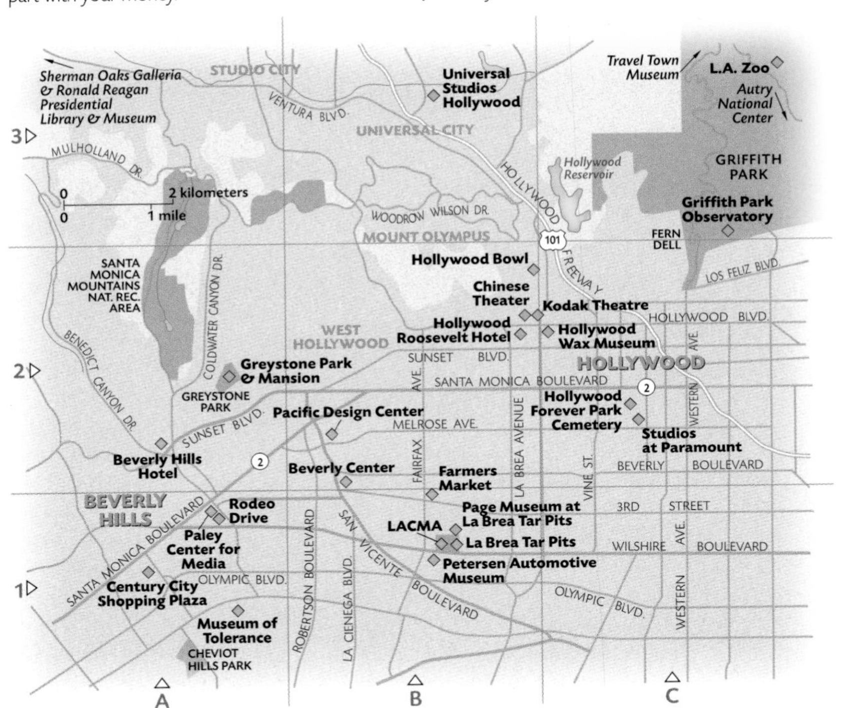

Cruise Through Hollywood's Past

For a trip into Hollywood history, drive **Mulholland Drive** along the crest of the Santa Monica Mountains. One of the most storied streets in the City of the Angels, Mulholland meanders 14.4 miles (23.1 km) from east to west, starting in the Cahuenga Pass above the Hollywood Bowl and twisting all the way to San Vincente Mountain Park, with its historic Nike missile launch pad. West of San Vincente Park, Mulholland continues as an unpaved hiking trail.

In addition to offering jaw-dropping views of Los Angeles and the San Fernando Valley, Mulholland Drive has also been home to myriad celebrities, including Jack Nicholson, Wilt Chamberlain, Britney Spears, Warren Beatty, John Lennon, Madonna, Marlon Brando, and Faye Dunaway.

Rodeo Drive
71 A1

often see younger stars preening, eating fatty no-no's, or irritably dealing with their equally irritated agents. Next, stroll the grounds and take in the architecture. If the mission-style exterior looks familiar, it may be because it was designed in 1912 by Elmer Grey, who with his partner Myron Hunt also did the Huntington Library (see p. 119–121). Paul Revere Williams was the architect for the newer Crescent Wing, built in 1949.

As the afternoon wears on and the heat rises, the hotel pool will look appealing. At poolside, cocktails are served 9 a.m. to 6 p.m.—or just jump in. After all, Katharine Hepburn did once—and she had all her clothes on. At night, celebs cluster at **Bar Nineteen 12,** the hotel's hip watering hole.

Rodeo Drive

The three blocks of Rodeo Drive north of Wilshire Boulevard rank among the most famous (and most expensive) shopping districts in the world, comparable to the Champs-Élysées in Paris or Florence's Ponte Vecchio. The one big difference is style; along Europe's great boulevards, one would never think of wearing a sweatshirt and jeans to go shopping for a $1,000 silk blouse. In Beverly Hills, a man in a tracksuit may well drop $15,000 in one afternoon, shopping at, say, House of Bijan. This does not mean you should not dress well to shop here—but if you choose to go casual, whip up a good dose of attitude to go with it.

Begin at Saks Fifth Avenue (just southwest of Rodeo), one of four large department stores on Wilshire. With its valet parking and attentive staff, Saks may well be the least snooty of the bunch.

North on Rodeo, the first area to your right is known as **Two Rodeo** *(www.2rodeo.com)*, a retail "alley" created in 1990 to house new outlets for Tiffany's and Ferre, along with several tasteful shops specializing in home decor. This was the first new street to be carved out of the city since it became independent from L.A. in 1914. Two Rodeo Drive was started in the 1980s by real estate developer Douglas Stitzel, who spared no expense with the imported Italian cobblestones. Several economic downturns later, shoppers still visit the Jimmy Choo, Lanvin, Buccellati, Lalique, or Versace boutiques.

People-watching reaches its peak in the block just north of Two Rodeo, where the palm-shaded sidewalks are flanked by posh fashion boutiques like Dolce & Gabbana, Yves Saint Laurent, and Christian Dior. North of that is Cartier, where diamonds are the prevailing art form, and Gucci, the Italian purveyor of handbags and accessories. The **Rodeo Collection,** just to the north, features five stories of cafés and stores, including such classy menswear outlets as Stefano Ricci. Guess tops the stroll northward. Watch for Anderton Court, on the east just north of Dayton. It was designed by Frank Lloyd Wright in 1952. You can take a narrated trolley tour of Beverly Hills architecture by meeting the bus at Rodeo Drive and Dayton Way *(tel 310/285-2442, Sat.–Sun., hourly 11 a.m.–4 p.m., $).*

Once relieved of your excess cash, it might be relaxing to drive over to the **Greystone Park & Mansion.** The 46,000-square-foot English Gothic Revival mansion was built in 1928 by oil baron Edward Doheny and then vacated after his son was found dead there in an apparent love suicide. Today a registered historic landmark, it is owned by the city of Beverly Hills, and the public enjoys its 18 acres (7.2 ha) of terraced gardens for picnics. Rangers lead guided tours of the mansion and grounds on Saturdays.

The **Paley Center for Media** is a delightful diversion for anyone interested in television and radio. Visitors can view news,

Rodeo Collection

- 268 N. Rodeo Dr.
- 310/276-9600

Greystone Park & Mansion

- 71 A2
- 905 Loma Vista Dr.
- 310/285-6830, 310/285-6850 (tours)
- Tour: $$$

www.greystonemansion.org

Paley Center for Media

- 71 A1
- 465 N. Beverly Dr.
- 310/786-1000
- Closed Mon.–Tues.
- Donation

www.paleycenter.org

Home to the toniest boutiques in Beverly Hills, Rodeo Drive beckons shoppers of all kinds.

Los Angeles County Museum of Art (LACMA)

52 C3, 55 H2, & 71 B1

5905 Wilshire Blvd.

323/857-6000

Closed Wed.

$$$ (Free 2nd Tues. of month)

www.lacma.org

entertainment, and sports footage preserved in the collection of 140,000 television and radio programs. Check out the *Steve Allen Show* (1956–1960) for an example of early audience participation.

Los Angeles County Museum of Art

"Oh! I just can't believe it. There is so much great art at that place, I mean great, that sometimes it's overwhelming for the rest of us. You're so lucky to be from a city with that much great art." This telling recommendation comes not from the public relations crew at the Los Angeles County Museum of Art (LACMA), but from a public relations person at one of San Francisco's leading art institutions. Anyone familiar with the intense rivalry between the two cities knows that such remarks are rare.

But rare is perhaps the best word to describe LACMA. In the three decades of its existence, the museum has gathered together the greatest collection of art in the western United States: 100,000 works, most of them of singular taste and quality. One reason for this is curatorial continuity. The American, modern, and Southeast Asian collections were each largely built under the regime of former curator Pratapaditya Pal; this makes for a cohesiveness rare in most large mainstream museums.

Initiated in 2004, a new master plan for the LACMA campus has entrusted world-renowned architect Renzo Piano to redesign the museum and transform it both in and out to create more dynamic, light-filled spaces while allowing visitors to navigate easily through galleries featuring work from ancient times to the present. New galleries, public spaces, gardens,

LACMA holds more than 100,000 works spanning the history of art from ancient times to the present.

and a new building devoted to exhibiting a collection of recently purchased contemporary works are woven together along a central concourse. LACMA's latest addition is a rotating exhibition area called the **Lynda and Stewart Resnick Pavilion,** the world's largest purpose-built, naturally lit, open-plan museum space.

Visitors enter the boldly imagined campus through the **BP Grand Entrance,** an open-air pavilion featuring landscaped piazzas, with the new **Broad Contemporary Art Museum** to the west. The latter's 60,000 square feet (5,574 sq m) of exhibition space includes "Band," one of two monumental Richard Serra sculptures of contoured weathered steel. In keeping with the eclectic nature of modern art, the new collection runs a broad gamut from the whimsical "Michael Jackson and Bubbles" and "Balloon Dog (Blue)" by Jeff Koons to iconic Roy Lichtenstein posters, Jean-Michel Basquiat graffiti art, and Cindy Sherman's offbeat portrait photography. Part of the fun is scaling the lipstick-red external staircase to the building's third floor.

Beyond the Broad, **LACMA West,** in a 1938 art deco building that once housed the May Company department store, is being renovated into a movie museum in a joint venture with the Academy of Motion Picture Arts and Sciences.

Ahmanson Building: The gateway to LACMA East is the historic Ahmanson Building, transformed into a soaring space connected to the plaza concourse by a Spanish-style staircase. Its four levels exhibit an extraordinary wealth of Far Eastern, European, African, and American art, but it is the collection of South and Southeast Asian art (on the third level) that is the most delightful and sensual example of LACMA's curatorial brilliance. Countries represented include Cambodia, Indonesia, and Nepal, but it is Indian art that is most exuberantly celebrated.

The world-renowned Madina Collection of Islamic Art spanning works from the 7th through 19th centuries is one of the world's preeminent Islamic holdings. The collection, also on the third level, focuses on decorative arts and calligraphy and includes a number of rare masterpieces. The ancient

How to Visit LACMA

The best time to visit LACMA is on a Friday evening, when the museum is open late and a free jazz concert thrums. The museum also hosts Latin Sounds on Saturday evenings and a classical concert series on Sunday evenings. During blockbuster exhibitions, the museum can become quite congested; if you want to see one of these shows, be sure to make a reservation.

The bulk of the collection is housed in six main buildings, with a seventh, the **Bing Center,** providing an auditorium with an ambitious calendar. Its weekend film series *(tel 323/857-6010)* is the place for film buffs—a legacy of author Christopher Isherwood's regular attendance in his later years. There is also a cafeteria, research center, and library *(by appt. only).*

world is also well represented, including an outstanding pre-Columbian collection boasting a rich cross section of objects from ancient Mexico.

To appreciate just how far artists have journeyed from their aesthetic forebears, take a look at the third level's majestic collection of European painting and sculpture. Stop at Rosso Fiorentino's "Allegory of Salvation" (1521). Rosso's portrayal of the young St. John, who has fallen faint at his mother's side after learning of her terrible prophecy of what will befall the Christ Child, is a clear comment on Michelangelo's "Pietà."

INSIDER TIP:

Visiting LACMA with kids? Head to the Boone Children's Gallery in the Hammer Building on a Monday or Friday at 2 p.m. for storytelling.

—MARY STEPHANOS
National Geographic contributor

An ever still spot in these galleries is in front of Rembrandt's stunning "Raising of Lazarus" (1630). So much is captured in the moment the picture portrays, and the artist has rendered it so skillfully, that gazing in silence seems the only appropriate reaction to such mastery. The main spot of light falls on the women at the graveside expressing their unfolding awe. Yet perhaps more arresting is the way the light falls on Christ. Even the Savior of All Mankind looks somewhat surprised at what he has done.

Hammer Building: The Ahmanson links east to the Hammer Building and its remarkable collection of Korean art, said to be the best in the world outside of Korea itself. The hundreds of objects on display in the second floor are primarily gleaned from the Three Kingdoms, Goryeo, and Joseon periods, including painting, ceramics, lacquer pieces, and sculpture.

The third floor is a trove of ancient Near Eastern art, a geographical arc that runs all the way from the eastern Mediterranean through Mesopotamia and Persia to the Indus Valley. Among its treasures are silver vessels, large Assyrian stone reliefs, and prehistoric Iranian pottery.

Elsewhere in the Hammer Building is the Boone Children's Gallery. Families can learn more about Korean and Chinese painting and actually practice the techniques at art workshops.

Pavilion for Japanese Art: Leaving the Hammer, walk eastward to reach the Pavilion for Japanese Art, an eccentric but perfect building for, among other things, the Shinenkan Collection of Edo-period screen art. Donated by philanthropists Joe and Etsuko Price, these scenes of nature—cranes flying, tigers prowling, roosters and hens foraging—have such a strong emotional impact that one leading Japanese art scholar confessed to having wept when he first saw them. That LACMA and the Prices agreed to build a pavilion with only natural lighting is a testimony to their good taste and sense of adventure. Particularly worth seeking out is Suzuki Kiitsu's "Seashells and Plums," painted, like almost all Edo art, without any preliminary sketching. As Price once explained, "He simply had to have the whole painting in his head before he executed one stroke."

Art of the Americas Building: To the south of the Hammer Building, the Art of the Americas Building exhibits art created since 1900. Although the building received unfavorable reviews, its layout permits natural light to reach every gallery, an accomplishment that not only complements the art but also makes for a pleasant atmosphere, an important attribute given the rather discomfiting nature of most modern art. The importance of some of the work here is open to question: Exhibits range from Alison Saar's indulgent "Sledge Hammer Mamma" to moments of brilliance, such as Ed Kienholz's "Back Seat Dodge '38" (deemed lurid in the 1960s, when museum trustees voted to ban it, today it seems, well, *quaintly* lurid). The pantheon of contemporary notables

LACMA's Cantor Sculpture Plaza & Garden features works by Rodin and Bourdelles.

Diners savor the relaxed mood of the original Farmers Market at Third Street and Fairfax Avenue.

represented includes Picasso and David Hockney, whose works here include "Mulholland Drive." LACMA's ongoing effort to collect and display the Mexican modernists is also proving fruitful, with fine examples of the works of Rivera, Orozco, and Siquieros (see sidebar p. 93). Look for Rufino Tamayo's "Study for America" (1955) or Rivera's "Women Washing" (1925).

A full range of American art comes together on the plaza level. Arranged chronologically, this collection highlights the great themes of American art. Key works include Winslow Homer's "The Cotton Pickers," painted in 1876, just before the artist retired to New England. Homer's experience as a correspondent-illustrator during the Civil War for *Harper's Weekly* propelled his rendering of rural America beyond the romantic pictures that were so preponderant at the time.

A joyful American send-up of Michelangelo and Rubens is all over Paul Cadmus's "Coney Island" (1934). The work succeeds because it is fleshy, resolutely hoi polloi, and yet humane about it all. Also displayed on the plaza are Arts and Crafts furniture and examples of work by Tiffany and others in the American decorative arts sections.

Cantor Sculpture Plaza & Garden: After the Americas, go left, down the steps to the sculpture garden, where the late Bernard Cantor's collection of Rodins cavorts silently in the grass. A number of large-scale contemporary works were recently added, including Christopher Burden's "Urban Light," incorporating more than 200 antique cast-iron lampposts.

Photography: LACMA's photography department puts on exhibitions drawn from its permanent collection of approximately 6,000 works, from the medium's invention in 1839 to the present, with works from the greats—Henri Cartier-Bresson, Walker Evans, Ansel Adams—to emerging artists. It also administers the Ralph M. Parsons Lectures on Photography series.

Around Museum Row

Mid-Wilshire has a number of other places to visit around LACMA. Among these attractions are the **La Brea Tar Pits.** Visitors can stroll the park grounds and watch excavations in process at a number of pits.

The adjoining **Page Museum at La Brea Tar Pits** displays some of the million fossils recovered from the pits. These Pleistocene remains are between 10,000 and 40,000 years old. The displays chronicle the animal life of L.A. in the Ice Age. There are skeletons of the saber-toothed tiger, an imperial mammoth with 12-foot (3.6 m) tusks, and a Harlan's giant ground sloth, which once stood more than 6 feet tall (1.8 m) and weighed about 3,500 pounds (1,587 kg). Don't miss La Brea Woman, more than 9,000 years old. The Paleontology Lab is a must for parents who help on their children's science projects, and don't miss the eerily bubbling tar lake in front of the museum.

Your ticket to the Page Museum is also valid for the **Petersen Automotive Museum**—150 cars from the collection of founder Robert Petersen, the auto magazine tycoon. Covering four floors, the museum traces the entire history of the automobile. For car buffs this is a must, but even car cynics have come away extolling these wonders. Among them are James Dean's 1950 Mercury, the 1948 Tucker, Mel Torme's 1937 Jaguar, and a 1981 DeLorean. A recent exhibition celebrating the 50th anniversary of rock 'n' roll featured 75 classic and custom guitars of the stars,

Page Museum at La Brea Tar Pits

- 71 B1
- 5801 Wilshire Blvd.
- 323/934-7243
- $$ (free 1st Tues. of month)

www.tarpits.org

Reliving Hollywood's Earliest Days

Grab a bag of popcorn and sink into Hollywood history at the **Silent Movie Theatre** *(611 N. Fairfax Ave., tel 323/655-2510, www.cinefamily.org).* The only local cinema that screens pre-sound films on a regular basis, the theater is located in the Fairfax District not far from CBS Studios and the Farmers Market (see p. 80). Some of the movies are presented with a recorded soundtrack, others with live organ music. Most of the films have been restored in recent years with help from the Academy of Motion Picture Arts & Sciences, and many are rarely screened for public viewing. **American Cinematheque at the Egyptian Theatre** *(6712 Hollywood Blvd., tel 323/466-FILM, www.americancinematheque.com)* also screens silent films on occasion.

Petersen Automotive Museum

- 71 B1
- 6060 Wilshire Blvd.
- 323/930-2277
- Closed Mon.
- $$

www.petersen.org

Farmers Market
71 B1
6333 W. 3rd St.
323/933-9211
www.farmersmarketla.com

Melrose Avenue
71 B2
Visitor Information
Convention & Visitors Bureau, 8687 Melrose Ave., Ste. M-38
310/289-2525, 800/368-6020
www.visitwesthollywood.com

along with Eric Clapton's 1940 Ford Coupe and Janis Joplin's 1965 Porsche. Other special exhibitions have ranged from "Speed: The World's Fastest Cars" to "Hollywood Star Cars" and "Alternative Power: Lessons From the Past, Inspiration for the Future."

Farmers Market

About 15 blocks away from Museum Row (a pleasant walk when the weather is cool) is a place just brimming with the simple pleasures of life. Here, at the junction of Third Street and Fairfax Avenue, is a celebration of the pure sensual enjoyment of eating old-fashioned meals in a festive environment. The original Farmers Market is a complex of more than a hundred shops catering to your every gustatory whim. A 1930s counterpart to downtown's Olvera Street (see p. 93), it is themed, but in a charming way.

Originated by oil tycoon E. B. Gilmore in the 1930s, the market serves as a kind of village green. The phrase "Meet me at Third and Fairfax" is still synonymous with meals of ham and eggs, gumbo, fried chicken, fresh fish and oysters, Belgian waffles, gallons of "Joe," tacos and beans, giant peanut butter cookies, submarine sandwiches, Armenian grilled meats, pots of pasta in red sauce—you get the picture. "The Farmers Market is what they call a 'great good place,'" remarks longtime L.A. chronicler Catherine Seipp. "It's that increasingly rare but vital locale where you can go to be alone with other people." Some of those others may well be from the film industry. Director Tim Burton *(Beetlejuice, Batman)* is sometimes seen near the waffle bar, Clint Eastwood at Phil's Deli, and a group of regulars led by director Paul Mazursky near Bob's Coffee and Donuts, near the east end. Stop by and give them a copy of your script. Bob's, by the way, makes about a thousand donuts a day.

The Ultimate Schmooze

If you are still hungry after the Farmers Market, a similar scene is repeated, around the clock, just across the street at Canter's Deli *(419 N. Fairfax Ave., tel 323/651-2030, www.cantersdeli.com).*

Located in the middle of Los Angeles' thriving Fairfax District, a hub of the Jewish community, Canter's serves up quintessential deli fare: bagels loaded with red onion, smoked salmon, and cream cheese; potato latkes; cheese blintzes; calf brains and eggs; *matzo brei* (a matzo-meal and egg pancake); brisket of beef; corned beef on rye; giant sour pickles; cream soda; and matzo-ball soup. The bakery counter sells outstanding fresh breads and pastries, but most clients prefer to dine in and be entertained by the waitresses' banter—a long-standing Canter's tradition.

Melrose Avenue

North of the Fairfax District, running east–west between La Brea Avenue and Robertson Boulevard, is a strip of ultimate urban grooviness. Melrose Avenue is responsible, among other things, for the resuscitation of Heather Locklear's career (via the hit TV show *Melrose Place*), for the popularity of

Melrose Avenue offers an eclectic mix of restaurants, tattoo parlors, and funky boutiques.

Harley-Davidson motorcycles among film stars (via its Johnny Rockets burger hangout), and for the $500 ripped T-shirt (via Comme des Garçons, a Japanese clothier with a penchant for bald-headed models who swear). It's just so swell—where should one start?

One of the gourmet treats at the avenue's eastern end is **Blu Jam** *(7371 Melrose Ave., tel 323/951-9191)*, which transforms from a casual café by day into a swanky bistro at night. For those getting a late start, breakfast is served until 5 p.m., and Sunday brunch is the way to refuel between bouts of shopping. The eclectic dinner menu is built around medium-size California cuisine dishes meant to share.

Farther west are clothing boutiques, specialty stores, and folk-art shops that sell affordable and interesting Mexican Day of the Dead works and painted tin *retabla* art. Despite its somewhat morbid name, **Necromance** *(7222 Melrose Ave., tel 323/934-8684)* is actually a curiosity shop filled with natural and historical curios, including skulls and skeletons, old cameras, beetles and butterflies, beads, and vintage medical instruments. At the other end of the Melrose shopping spectrum, **Kiki De Montparnasse** *(8280 Melrose Ave., tel 323/951-9545)* specializes in lingerie, leatherware, masks, and "instruments of pleasure."

Nearby is the **Pacific Design Center,** a collection of 130 showrooms offering furnishings by some of the best known designers in the world. The behemoth also houses a branch of the Museum of Contemporary Art (see p. 102–103). Back on Melrose, walk toward Robertson Boulevard for some outstanding tile, lighting, and furniture outlets.

Pacific Design Center

71 B2

7222 Melrose Ave.

310/657-0800

www.pacificdesigncenter.com

Beverly Center
71 B2
3rd St. & La Cienega Blvd.
310/854-0070
www.beverlycenter.com

From here, choose where to go next: north to West Hollywood, deemed the "Castro District of L.A."; south to the **Beverly Center,** the sine qua non of all galleria shopping experiences; or on to Hollywood itself.

Hollywood

For a city that is rightly considered the veritable engine of the world entertainment industry, Los Angeles is something of a letdown in this regard for most tourists. The reason is that the studios are no longer concentrated in old Hollywood, but spread about—some in the Valley, some in Burbank, others in Culver City and other unsexy destinations. Hollywood itself, that stretch of boulevard so often photographed, has for years looked quite down at heel, the remnants of its glamour dulled by the reality of a gritty street culture. Although there have been, and continue to be, several worthwhile redevelopment projects designed to "bring Hollywood back to Hollywood," the results are often disappointing, thinly veiled attempts to unload second-class tourist souvenirs.

So, these pages offer a selective iconic tour of Hollywood, covering few of the oft-cited theme museums and restaurants but, instead, a few choice destinations, real places that function now as they did in the old days. Those seeking the quintessential "studio tour" with plenty of fanfare and special effects will be more than satisfied by a day at Universal Studios (see p. 89).

To get a good sense of "working on the lot," as studio life is called, the best place to begin is the **Studios at Paramount** (see sidebar this page). From Melrose, you can pause for a photo of the famous Bronson Gates entrance, with its palm trees nodding in the wind and fountains gurgling in the background; these are the portals through which the limousine drove in *Sunset Boulevard* (1950). This is also where Fred Astaire and

Hollywood
71 C2
Visitor Information
Canvention & Visitors Bureau, 6801 Hollywood Blvd.
323/467-6412
www.hollywoodchamber.net

EXPERIENCE: Life on Screen

Paramount, the longest continuously running film studio in Hollywood, still holds some of the old magic. Two-hour guided tours of the Studios at Paramount *(map p. 71 C2, 5555 Melrose Ave., tel 323/956-1777, www.paramountstudiotour.com, $$$)* **grant an exciting behind-the-scenes look at the movie business. You can also make reservations to watch the taping of a sitcom episode, but the studio grounds are now off-limits.**

CBS Television City *(7800 Beverly Blvd., Los Angeles, CA, 90036, tel 323/575-2458, www.cbstelevisioncity.com)* **and Audiences Unlimited** *(tel 818/260-0041, www.tvtickets.com)* **offer free tickets for a number of sitcoms, game shows, and talk shows. Tickets for some popular shows are available only from the show's website. To see** ***Jimmy Kimmel Live, The Late Late Show with Craig Ferguson,*** **or** ***The Voice,*** **consult 1iota** *(www.1iota.com).*

Ginger Rogers danced and where Lucille Ball and Desi Arnaz literally invented the modern television production company.

For a relaxing, elegant lunch, drive north on Vine Street to the **Musso & Frank Grill** *(6667 Hollywood Blvd., tel 323/467-7788, www.mussoandfrankgrill.com, closed Sun.–Mon.)*, a Hollywood landmark where hip Angelenos take their out-of-town relatives who want to eat "flannel cakes" à la Philip Marlowe detective movies.

Sated, make your way along Hollywood Boulevard to the **Kodak Theatre,** home to the annual Academy Awards ceremony and permanent venue for a new Cirque du Soleil production called *Iris.* Next door is the new **Hollywood & Highland Center** *(www.hollywoodandhighland.com)*, a glitzy eating and shopping complex with architecture that must have been inspired by Cecil B. DeMille's epic films.

Just down the block is a much older Hollywood landmark, the **Chinese Theatre.** Built in 1927 by Sid Grauman, this may well be the most famous movie theater in the world. While many of the old landmarks are gone, the theater's extensive patio will certainly take you back a few years, containing as it does the hand- and footprints of many legendary movie stars. Even Roy Rogers's horse, Trigger, is honored here.

More commercial, or themed, enterprises abound in this area. Tacky or tantalizing, there is no denying the appeal of **Frederick's of Hollywood,** the legendary lingerie shop and museum that

Kodak Theatre

- Map: 71 C2
- Address: 6801 Hollywood Blvd.
- Phone: 323/308-6300
- Price: $$$ (tours daily)

www.kodaktheatre.com

Chinese Theatre

- Map: 71 B2
- Address: 6925 Hollywood Blvd.
- Phone: 323/464-8111

www.chinesetheatres.com

Frederick's of Hollywood

- Address: 6751 Hollywood Blvd.
- Phone: 323/957-5953

www.fredericks.com

Costumed characters interact with tourists for tips near the Hollywood & Highland Center.

Hollywood Wax Museum
71 C2
6767 Hollywood Blvd.
323/462-8860
$$$
www.hollywoodwax museum.com

Hollywood Museum
1660 N. Highland Ave.
323/464-7776
Closed Mon.–Tues.
www.thehollywood museum.com

Hollywood Forever Park Cemetery
71 C2
6000 Santa Monica Blvd.
323/469-1181
Map available at office
www.hollywood forever.com

Hollywood Bowl
71 B2
2301 N. Highland Ave.
323/850-2000, 323/850-2058 (museum)
Museum closed Mon.
www.hollywood bowl.com

sells all manner of saucy ladies' undergarments and, inevitably, boasts the Frederick's Celebrity Lingerie Hall of Fame. The **Hollywood Wax Museum** lets you feel part of a red carpet event with its exhibits of movie stars like Halle Berry and Angelina Jolie shown arriving for the Academy Awards. It also has a horror exhibit, plus re-creations of scenes from movies like *Men in Black* (1997), *The Matrix* (1999), and *Star Wars* (1977).

No visit to Hollywood is truly complete without stepping on the sidewalk of stars known as the **Hollywood Walk of Fame** *(www.walkoffame.com).* Orange signs mark the looped route, which features almost 2,000 bronze stars. The Hollywood visitor information center provides a map.

More fulfilling is the **Hollywood Museum,** in the Max Factor Building, which has been restored to its original 1935 splendor. The museum is chock-full of mementos regaling fascinating lore of the Hollywood region and movie industry. The world-famous **Mel's Drive-In** *(tel 323/465-3111, www.melsdrive-in.com)* all-American diner is next door.

Late afternoon might suggest a few quintessentially Hollywood outings. One is a visit to **Hollywood Forever Park Cemetery,** where Rudolph Valentino, Cecil B. DeMille, and other big names in movie history are buried.

When evening approaches, head to the **Hollywood Roosevelt Hotel** *(map p. 71 B2, 7000 Hollywood Blvd., tel 323/466-7000, www.hollywoodroosevelt.com),* where the first Academy Awards were held, a location chosen perhaps because its investors were Charlie Chaplin, Mary Pickford, and Douglas Fairbanks. The Roosevelt has been revived in recent years, and its Cinegrill is a nice place for a martini and live music.

The perfect end to a day in Hollywood would be a concert at the **Hollywood Bowl.** Founded in 1922, the Bowl is the summer home of the L.A. Philharmonic, which offers an affordable evening concert series ranging from the classics to show tunes to star vocalist combinations. The season is also peppered with several world-class special events, such as the International Mariachi Competition and the Playboy Jazz Festival.

INSIDER TIP:

Don't miss the swimming pool at the Hollywood Roosevelt Hotel. It was painted by David Hockney in the mid-1980s.

—MARY STEPHANOS
National Geographic contributor

Just as important—some would say more so—is the scene at the Bowl. On July 4, for example, long-time box seat holders turn out for the "1812 Overture" and a fireworks display. Among them will be dozens of movie and TV stars and, often, the very cream of old L.A. society, men in white pants and bow ties, ladies in pastel linens and cashmere wraps, for the cool night air.

Visitors take in the view of the sprawling city from the balcony of the Griffith Park Observatory.

Bring a picnic dinner, or you will end up quite ravenous. Arrive at least an hour early to see the **Hollywood Bowl Museum,** where you can watch famous Bowl performances on film, from the Beatles to Judy Garland.

Griffith Park

The best kept secret in Los Angeles, far from being small or tucked away, is right under everyone's nose. Griffith Park, whose more than 4,000 acres (1,618 ha) make it the largest urban park in the United States, is five times the size of New York's Central Park. That the park remains undiscovered by many would hardly surprise its founder, Col. Griffith J. Griffith. For years, he attempted to persuade the city fathers to turn his 1896 bequest of land, once part of Rancho los Feliz, into the hub of a city-wide park system. (Of course, Griffith's circumstances at the time may not have helped his cause: The hard-drinking Welshman had just returned from a two-year term in San Quentin prison for trying to kill his wife.)

While previous Angelenos periodically embraced the park, only recently has it become a preferred spot for weekend outings. The park is now a preferred spot for an estimated 10 million visitors each year. There are children's museums, a zoo, a museum for adults, a merry-go-round, and a place from which to gaze at the stars above and the city below.

Griffith Park

52 D3, 71 C3, & 111 A2

Visitor Information

Visitor's Center, 4730 Crystal Springs Dr.

323/913-4688

www.laparks.org

Griffith Park Observatory
71 C3
2800 E. Observatory Rd.
213/473-0800
Closed Mon., Tues., & a.m. Wed.–Fri. Laserium shows: call for times
$ for Laserium
www.griffithobs.org

Autry National Center
71 C3
4700 Western Heritage Way
323/667-2000
Closed Mon.
$$
www.theautry.org

Griffith Park Observatory: The renowned Griffith Park Observatory, is located at the top of Observatory Road. As recounted by local historian Letitia Burns O'Conner, the colonel had been so stunned by looking through the Mount Wilson telescope that he proclaimed, "If all men could look through that telescope, it would revolutionize the world!" Griffith was long gone before his dream finally came true here, in 1935. Since then, the observatory and its grounds have attained iconic status. Its exterior and the bronze statues of Galileo and company formed the backdrop to the famous switchblade fight in the James Dean movie *Rebel Without a Cause* (1955).

The classic 1935 building reopened in 2007 after a five-year restoration and now boasts 60 exhibits plus a state-of-the-art theater and a Wolfgang Puck café. The museum on two levels is burgeoning with sensational exhibits on astronomic sciences and includes an enormous rotating globe in the main rotunda. The east dome holds the **Hall of the Eye Exhibits,** displaying a camera obscura; the **Hall of the Sky Exhibits,** in the west dome, focuses on the sun and moon and holds solar telescopes. The central dome forms the **Samuel Oschin Planetarium,** known for outstanding laser-light and music shows, as well as more standard planetary projections. The lower levels feature exhibits relating to deep space, and the new **Leonard Nimoy Event Horizon** theater, with hourly shows.

Later, as the sun dips into the Pacific, the denizens of the City of Angels stroll onto the observatory's terrace to watch the horizon boil with pinks and reds and purples before it finally falls dark, winking with a million lights below and billions above.

EXPERIENCE: Hiking Griffith Park

The best way to discover Griffith Park is by hiking all or part of its 53-mile (85 km) trail network. The 1-mile (1.6 km) **West Observatory Trail,** between Fern Dell and the iconic observatory, is popular. There is lots of shade along the way, and the elevation gain is gentle. Those with stouter legs and lungs should try the **Charlie Turner Trail** to the top of Mount Hollywood. The 3-mile (4.8 km) hike entails 650 feet (198 m) of elevation gain, but the view from the summit is worth it. More spectacular views await at the top of the **Mt. Lee Trail,** which begins at the upper end of Beachwood Drive on the western side of the park. The 1.6-mile (2.5 km) path peaks right above the Hollywood sign. Hikers should watch out for coyotes and rattlesnakes, among other wildlife. Information on trail closures and restrictions are available at the Ranger Station *(323/913-4688).*

Autry National Center: The great surprise of Griffith Park's more recent additions is the Autry National Center, formed in 2003 by the merger of the Southwest Museum, the Women of the West Museum, and the Museum of the American West. The center today comprises a first-class educational institution plus two outstanding museums featuring permanent collections and special exhibitions dedicated to exploring the life and times of American cowboys and Native Americans. Don't miss it.

The **Southwest Museum of the American Indian,** with 250,000 pieces, is closed to the public while a new state-of-the-art facility is under construction. The sibling **Museum of the American West,** founded in 1989 with a $54 million gift from late cowboy film star Gene Autry, is arranged thematically. Starting on the ground floor, the **Romance Gallery** relies on the special quality of its objects rather than gallery themes. Paintings include John Gast's 1872 work "American Progress," Charles Deas's 1847 "Indian Warrior," Albert Bierstadt's "Sunset Over the Plains," and several Frederic Remington oils, as well as statues and animal figures by Charles Russell. In the same section you will also find Buffalo Bill's own saddle, later used in Robert Altman's film *Buffalo Bill* (1976).

Hollywood informs the **Imagination Gallery.** There are breakaway chairs, ricochet guns, bottles that shatter but don't cut, even Tom Mix's personal pistol. A collection of western movie posters begins with *Cimarron* (1931) and ends with *Thelma and Louise* (1991). It is a testament to Gene Autry's restraint that the display of his own film legacy is both strong in quality and modest in size.

The top floor is arranged thematically, beginning with the **Opportunity Gallery,** which strikes a particularly brave note in its presentation on pre-cowboy-era Native Americans. "With little thought for native peoples," one display states, " [Anglo migrants] aggressively began to populate and exploit the West." The impeccable collections of Native American weaponry make for imaginative conjecture about the practice of battlefield medicine at the time.

The **Conquest Gallery** shows meticulously preserved Gatling guns juxtaposed with displays on Plains bison culture. Also on view is Bierstadt's memorable "Herd of Buffalo and Indian" (1859).

INSIDER TIP:

If you visit the observatory early in the day, turn left on Los Feliz to Western, where a right turn brings you to a shady, brook-riven part of the park, perfect for a cool afternoon stroll.

—MARY STEPHANOS
National Geographic contributor

The **Community Gallery** looks at how emerging Anglo immigrant culture shaped already-existing Indian and Mexican culture. There is an original of the Cherokee Nation Constitution (in Cherokee) and a series of early photographs, while the **Greg Martin Colt Firearms Collection** includes firearms from tiny Derringers and early Smith & Wessons to Winchester rifles.

Animals From Around the Globe

The **Los Angeles Zoo** *(5333 Zoo Drive, Los Angeles, tel 323/644-4200)*, at the northeast corner of Griffith Park, has been busily bringing its facilities up to international par in recent years. Its collection of more than 1,100 mammals, birds, amphibians, and reptiles now attracts increasing numbers of tourists. The zoo has experimented with evolving novel habitats. Chimpanzees of Mahale Mountains presents chimpanzees frolicking on an acre (.4 ha) of grass and streams. Sea Life Cliffs, a saltwater habitat with underwater viewing of harbor seals, the new Elephants of Asia enclosure, and Campo Gorilla Reserve are other popular attractions.

The zoo also specializes in rare and unusual animals like the Komodo dragon, golden lion tamarin, South American maned wolf, okapi, and indigenous Channel Island fox, although its hottest stars are three Sumatran tiger cubs born here in August 2011.

Los Angeles Zoo
71 C3 & 111 A2
5333 Zoo Dr.
323/644-4200
$$$$
www.lazoo.org

Travel Town Museum
71 A2
5200 Zoo Dr.
323/662-5874
www.laparks.org

Live Steamers Railroad Museum
5202 Zoo Dr.
323/661-8958
www.lals.org

San Fernando Valley
52 C3–C4

The **Cowboy Gallery** thoroughly examines the relationship between horse and rider. There is a large exhibit of saddles, from the vaquero-style ones used by Mexican cowboys to today's highly technical saddles. Art in this gallery includes N. C. Wyeth's 1903 *Saturday Evening Post* cover "Bucking Bronco"; the masterful but largely underappreciated 1945 watercolor "California Vaquero," by former Hollywood stuntman Joe DeYong; and work by the well-known Maynard Dixon.

The **Family Discovery Gallery** honors the contribution of the Chinese and includes hands-on exhibits for children. The museum offers several special tours, and there is a restaurant-café.

Travel Town Museum: For railroad buffs small and large, the park's Travel Town Museum is a must-see. Travel Town is home to 14 steam locomotives, a number of specialty cars (as in the Union Pacific's luxurious "Little Nugget"), and two operating diesel locomotives. A miniature train takes visitors around the grounds, and in addition to the museum's own historical exhibits and fire engines, there is a huge N-gauge model train track maintained by a local group of rail enthusiasts. It is up and running on weekends.

A different free train ride can be had by going to the nearby **Live Steamers Railroad Museum,** whose enthusiasts operate an elevated 2-mile (3.2 km) line on which 7-inch-gauge model trains run on Sundays.

San Fernando Valley

Earthquakes such as the 1994 one centered in Northridge have brought a certain notoriety to the San Fernando Valley, between Hollywood and San Fernando. This, the essential valley, is home to almost one-third of L.A.'s population and to one of the city's most popular attractions, Universal Studios.

The huge success of the themed **Universal CityWalk** *(www.citywalkhollywood.com)* has been something of a shock to

L.A.'s self-proclaimed arbiters of cool. After all, the two-block-long congeries of neon and pop architecture is the kind of urban confection that most deep thinkers love to hate. CityWalk has become one of the leading destinations in the area precisely because it entertains people so well. The entertainment lies in three activities: eating, shopping, and people-watching. There are also street performers, including fire-jugglers, musicians, puppet masters, and all manner of eccentrics. CityWalk is eclectically hip enough to hold the attention of child, parent, and even the most jaded of eyeball-rolling teens.

Next door, Hollywood meets Disneyland at **Universal Studios Hollywood,** whose movie-themed rides and attractions are visitor favorites. The Backlot Tram tour is the way to see the huge site and its dozens of movie and TV locations. A visit to Universal is an all-day affair, and you can stay on in the valley into the evenings, perhaps taking in a concert at the **Gibson Amphitheatre** *(tel 818/622-4440, www.gibson-amphitheatre.net).*

Mulholland Drive (see sidebar p. 72), which cuts between the valley and L.A. proper, is accessible from several of the north–south thoroughfares including I-405 and Sepulveda Boulevard. It gives breathtaking views of mansions, mountains, and the ocean. Back down on Ventura Boulevard, a 2-mile (3.2 km) strip of stores and restaurants culminates in Jerry's Famous Deli *(12655 Ventura Blvd., tel 818/980-4245, www.jerrysfamous deli.com),* frequented by celebrities.

Burbank is home to a number of movie and television studios, including Walt Disney and DreamWorks. One of the oldest and largest in Hollywood is **Warner Bros. Studio** *(3400 W. Riverside Dr., Burbank, tel 877/492-8687, www.vipstudiotour.warnerbros.com, closed Sun., $$$$$),* where *Casablanca* (1942), *The Maltese Falcon* (1941), *My Fair Lady* (1964), *Ghostbusters* (1984), and *Jurassic Park* (1993) were filmed. Behind-the-scenes VIP tours take visitors through the studio's backlot streets, sound stages, film sets, and craft shops. ■

Universal Studios Hollywood

- 71 B3
- Universal City Dr. (off U.S. 101)
- 800/864-8377
- $$$$$

www.universalstudioshollywood.com

A rare summer storm produces a double rainbow over the San Fernando Valley.

From Downtown

Almost every pundit worth his or her salt has cadged a cheap laugh over downtown Los Angeles. "An enormous village" is how author Louis Adamic saw it in the 1920s. A "harlot city," said author Carey McWilliams, viewing its "mob mad" yokelry intoxicated on cheap religion and bad movies. "It is as if one tilted the nation on its side and let all the loose nuts roll down into one corner," proclaimed Frank Lloyd Wright.

Painted red and white by commuters, U.S. 101 snakes through downtown L.A. to Hollywood.

Much of this hostility derives from the fact that Los Angeles has little of a traditional downtown social scene. Yet even early on, L.A. did have an identifiable core, still present today, bounded by the Old Pueblo district to the north, the Santa Monica Freeway to the south, Central Avenue to the east, and the Pasadena Freeway to the west. So why all the jokes?

One answer may be that downtown L.A., either then or now, cannot be considered an American city at all, but rather a city of the desert. Moreover, this desert city was, and is, a Latin American phenomenon. None has caught its essence as well as Mexican Nobel Laureate Octavio Paz.

"When I first arrived in the United States I lived for a while in Los Angeles, a city inhabited by over one million persons of Mexican origin," Paz wrote in his 1961 masterpiece, *The Labyrinth of*

Solitude. "At first sight, the visitor is surprised not only by the purity of the sky and the ugliness of the dispersed and ostentatious buildings, but also by the city's vaguely Mexican atmosphere, which cannot be captured in words or concepts. This Mexicanism—delight in decorations, carelessness and pomp, negligence, passion and reserve—floats in the air. I say 'floats' because it never mixes or unites with the other world, the North American world based on precision and efficiency. It floats, without offering any opposition; it hovers, blown here and there by the wind."

Union Station

One might start a tour of Paz's floating world in the north by parking in the blacktop lot surrounding Union Station *(map below, Alameda St. at Cesar Chavez Ave.)*. Erected in 1939 (by some accounts on the site of an ancient Indian village), this was the last great train station to be built in the United States. A walk about its interior reveals many elements unchanged since then, from the massive wooden waiting benches to the muted earth tones of the designs modeled on Native American patterns.

Visitors might recognize the glistening travertine and marble interior from scenes in such movies as *Pearl Harbor* (2001), *Star Trek: First Contact* (1996), and *Blade Runner* (1982). From the station's rear, equally spiffy and super-efficient subway cars offer an air-cooled ride to Long Beach (see pp. 132–133) or MacArthur Park. Intended to

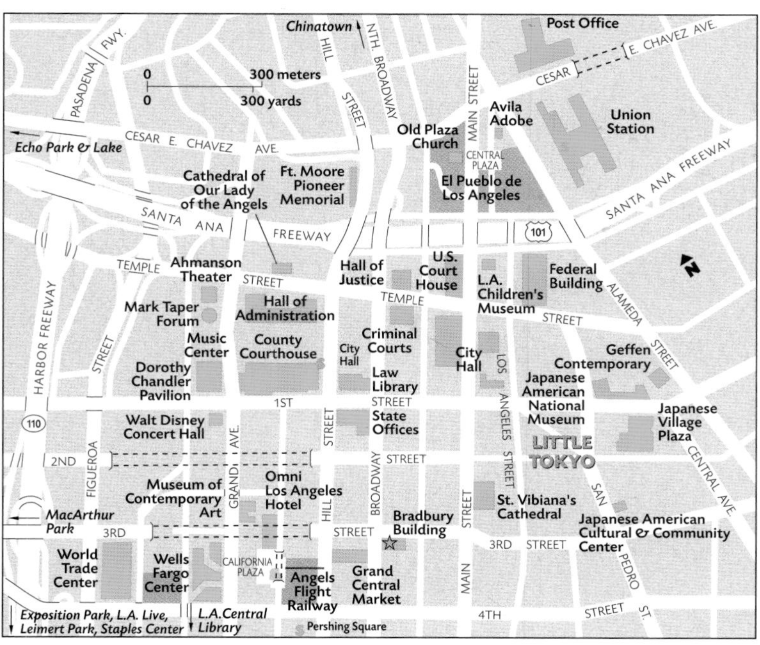

El Pueblo de Los Angeles
91
Visitor Information
Visitors' Center, 622 N. Main St.
213/628-1274
Closed Sun.
www.elpueblo.lacity.org

revolutionize travel in the city, the new Metrorail system is estimated to have cost L.A. taxpayers a billion dollars a mile. Make use of it!

Outside the station, take a moment to look at the cityscape, the palms waving in the breeze, the old pueblo church beckoning, the cars zooming by on Alameda. This was the scene that millions of new Angelenos laid eyes on when they first arrived. To get a better idea of what they saw, take a historical tour offered by the Los Angeles Conservancy *(523 6th St., Ste. 826, tel 213/430-4219, www.laconservancy.org, $).*

El Pueblo de Los Angeles

This 44-acre (18 ha) historic monument contains what might best be thought of as the sociological DNA of Los Angeles. In it are not only the remains of the historic pueblo but also several sites documenting the early presence of Italians, Chinese, Spaniards, and, of course, Native Americans. For these reasons, it hangs heavy with symbolism for so many in L.A., yet El Pueblo is nevertheless a place increasingly concerned with the present and the future. Its historic Roman Catholic church welcomes a new generation of Angelenos, learning the language and ways of a strange but promising land. Pretty high school girls practice folk dances on the Plaza Pavilion, calling home to mama on their cell phones. Toddlers squeal with delight under the blooming jacarandas, tearing apart giant pink clouds of sticky cotton candy proffered by street vendors.

After crossing Alameda Street from Union Station, you reach **Placita Dolores,** site of many festivals and celebrations, then

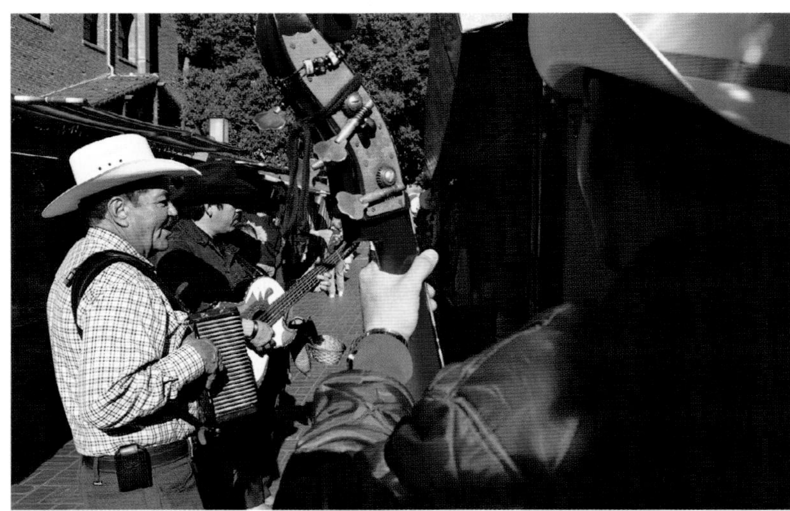

Enjoy lunch on Olvera Street and you just might be serenaded by a mariachi band.

"American Tropical"

Between the Hammel Building on Olvera Street and the Italian Hall in El Pueblo, you will find a remarkable mural painting by Mexican artist David Alfaro Siqueiros (1896–1974). Entitled "American Tropical," the work was almost immediately covered up after Siqueiros, an ardent trade unionist and onetime revolutionary (he fought to overthrow Porfirio Días in 1910–1911), was expelled from the U.S. in 1932.

Siqueiros went on to found the Center for Realist Art in Mexico City, eventually becoming one of the leading artists of 20th-century Mexico. "American Tropical" has in recent years been uncovered and "stabilized" by the progressive Getty Conservation Institute.

A guide to both old and new public art around downtown can be found by searching the Public Art in Los Angeles website *(www.publicartinla.com).*

go past the **Indian Garden** before arriving at the **Central Plaza,** built in 1825–1830. The statue in front of you is of Felipe de Neve, the stoic *gobernador* who led the original settlers to the site in 1781; the one behind you is of his employer, King Juan Carlos III of Spain. To the east is the **Biscailuz Building,** which now houses a Spanish-language library and bookstore. Follow the sign to the **Mexican Cultural Institute,** which often stages exhibitions by contemporary Mexican artists.

Don't miss the outdoor shops along **Olvera Street** *(www.olvera-street.com),* named for Agustin Olvera, who fought against Frémont during the war of American conquest (see pp. 30–31). Closed to through traffic since 1930, Olvera Street today is a kind of pre-Disney ethnic theme park, complete with roving mariachi bands and guys who sell shaved-ice confections from rickety carts. What makes it so jolly today is its lack of slickness; it is a genuine anachronism. The food at the restaurants tends to be pretty average, but the range of Mexican folk art (see sidebar above) and leather *huarache* sandals on sale here are hard to beat. Buy some before visiting the **Avila Adobe** *(10 E Olvera St.),* built in 1818 by one of the first ruling families of Los Angeles, the Avilas. (Francesco Avila was an early Mexican *alcalde,* or mayor.) Many of its beams are said to have been made from cottonwood trees that once grew along the Los Angeles River.

Across from the Avila Adobe is **Sepulveda House,** where the visitor center on the first floor shows a free, short film on early L.A. history. The house, built by Señora Eloisa Martinez de Sepulveda in 1887, is in the Eastlake Victorian style—an early sign of the region's troubling aesthetic malleability. The center offers free morning tours, Tuesday through Saturday.

Leaving Sepulveda House on Main Street and walking westward, one can visit the **Old Plaza Church** *(map p. 91),* taking care to respect worship hours. Built in 1818 and restored and rebuilt several times since, it is worth walking

Mexican Cultural Institute

✉ 125 Paseo de la Paz, #100

☎ 213/624-3660

http://mexicanculturalinstitute-la.org

Chinese American Museum
425 N. Los Angeles St.
213/485-8567
Closed Mon.
$
www.camla.org

through simply to witness how the church continues to be the principal portal into the existing society for new Americans.

On the south side of the park, the restored 19th-century Garnier Building (said to be the last surviving structure from the city's original Chinatown) today houses the **Chinese American Museum,** which opened in late 2003 and is dedicated to fostering an understanding of Chinese-American heritage. The twin-level museum displays artifacts, photographs, period clothing, jewelry boxes, decorations, musical instruments, and ornamentation from years past to the present day.

Shifting perspectives: Los Angeles's new Chinatown was originally the site of the city's Little Italy.

Chinatown
52 D3 & 91
Visitor Information
727 N. Broadway, Ste. 208
213/680-0243
www.chinatownla.com

Chinatown

Because the epicenter of Asian cuisine in L.A. has shifted farther east, to the San Gabriel Valley, many have taken to asking why they should even bother with the "old" Chinatown, sandwiched between Hill and Broadway just south of Chavez Ravine. The answer is simple: If you haven't eaten dim sum at Empress Pavilion, you haven't eaten it at all.

Located on the second floor of Bamboo Plaza, **Empress Pavilion** *(988 N. Hill St., tel 213/617-9898, www.empresspavilion.com)* is the epitome of a classic Hong Kong restaurant, cavernous, cooled almost to the point of hypothermia, and filled with little rolling steam carts stuffed with delectables ranging from *shiu mai* (shrimp dumpling) to pork *bao,* a baseball-size bun filled with sweet pork and golden nuts. In between, watch the guy outside spin little sugar candies out of thin air.

Just down Hill Street is **Chinatown Central Plaza,** marked by the wildly gay **Gate of Filial Piety.** Both were built in the late 1930s. Inside is a statue, erected in 1966, of Sun Yat-Sen, the father of independent China, whose daughters later invested heavily in California banking and real estate.

On the Broadway side of the plaza is the **Phoenix Bakery** *(969 N. Broadway, tel 213/628-4642, www.phoenixbakeryinc.com),* packed at night with families from all over town buying almond cookies, gooey Rice Krispy bars, and, of course, fortune cookies. A mark of L.A.'s diversity is Superior Poultry, a store on the east side of Broadway with a 6-foot (1.8 m) plaster rooster on top. It signs are also in Spanish *(¡Pollo Vivo!)* and Chinese.

If the north end of Chinatown still evokes the era of Suzy Wong and *Flower Drum Song* (1961), the south end feels more like something out of a John Woo film, with plenty of modern multistory mini shopping malls and ginseng parlors on every corner.

Little Tokyo

If L.A.'s Chinatown feels a bit like an empty stage, Little Tokyo, the heart of the nation's largest Japanese-American community, feels like the third act in a Busby Berkeley musical. Once threatened by the tragic aftereffects of World War II internment of Japanese Americans, it now hums with a revived community spirit, not to mention millions in real estate investments.

The eastern anchors of Little Tokyo consist of two thriving arts complexes, the Geffen Contemporary at MOCA (see pp. 101–102) and the **Japanese American National Museum.** This thoughtfully curated institution occupies two spaces, one inside a 1920s Buddhist temple, the other in a modern center on the corner of First Street and Central Avenue. Particularly moving is the permanent exhibition of old home movies on the ground floor of the old church.

Two blocks south and one block west, the **Japanese American Cultural & Community Center** has exhibits on aspects of Japanese culture such as bonsai and ikebana and is considered one of the best such centers in the United States. A must, if time permits, is one of the performances sponsored by the center, which often include world-class

(continued on p. 99)

Little Tokyo

Map p. 91

Japanese American National Museum

91

369 E. 1st St.

213/625-0414, 800/461-5266

Closed Mon.

$$

www.janm.org

Japanese American Cultural & Community Center

91

244 S. San Pedro St.

213/628-2725

www.jaccc.org

EXPERIENCE: Japanese Rituals

Get in touch with your inner Zen via Asian-style treatments and rituals in and around Little Tokyo. Combine shiatsu and reike treatments at Spa Relaken at the Miyako Hotel *(328 E. First St., tel 213/617-0004, www.miyakoinn.com, $$$$$)* with Japanese meals at the hotel's Tamon restaurant and sushi bar. Yoga Circle Downtown *(400 S. Main St., tel 213/620-1040, www.yogacircledowntown.com, $$–$$$,),* on the western edge of Little Tokyo, offers a variety of daily yoga, alignment, and pilates classes. Visitors are welcome at the weekly Sunday morning services at the Higashi Honganji Buddhist Temple *(505 E. 3rd St., tel 213/626-4200, www.hhbt-la.org).*

Broadway Walk

Nowhere is the floating world of Octavio Paz's Los Angeles better illustrated than in the greater Broadway area. You can best appreciate this part of the city by taking a walk through its heart. In the 1930s, this was the closest thing the city had to a "traditional" American city center, complete with big law firms, expensive restaurants, and opulent movie theaters.

The Grand Central Market offers fresh food and small eateries in an informal, authentic setting.

NOT TO BE MISSED:

Bradbury Building • Grand Central Market • Angels Flight Railway • Museum of Contemporary Art

Today, Broadway is the undisputed capital of Latin L.A., an exuberant Les Halles in the making. There are Bible-thumpers on every corner, and thrumming, bopping music emanates from a dozen discount audio stores, where you can buy classic rumba and mambo at one-third of the usual prices.

Having parked at Third Street and Broadway, start at the **Bradbury Building** ❶ *(304 S. Broadway, www.bradburybuilding.info)*, the extraordinary 1893 structure now best known for its appearance in the movie *Blade Runner* (1982). With its five stories of glorious glazed brick, ornamental iron, and filigreed windows, the Bradbury's design was inspired by its architect's eerie session with a Ouija board ("Take the Bradbury!" it allegedly commanded), and by the 1887 science fiction novel *Looking Backward,* by Edward Bellamy. The book posited the typical commercial building as a "vast hall full of light, received not alone from the windows on all sides, but from the dome, the point of which was a hundred feet above." After walking about the lobby, jog across the street and visit the **Farmacia y Botánica Million Dollar** *(301 S. Broadway)*. Here you will find one of the biggest and most colorful collections of traditional Santeria folk medicines in the country, with more than 60 different types of "spiritual baths" alone. If not too busy, the presiding pharmacist will gladly explain items and their uses.

Farther on, the **Million Dollar Theater** ❷ *(307 S. Broadway, tel 213-617-3600, www.milliondollartheater.com)* was built by Sid Grauman in 1918 with a Hollywood baroque fantasy terra-cotta facade. It now screens a wide range of classic and popular films.

Walk south on Broadway to reach the back entrance to the **Grand Central Market** ❸ *(317 S. Broadway, www.grandcentralsquare.com)*, where all manner of foodstuffs, both raw and cooked, are for sale. Try the tasty El Salvadoran *pupusas* (stuffed tortillas) at Sarita's Pupuseria, or stand in line at the old-fashioned China Café, where you can get a plate of traditional fried rice. On the second floor, past the bargain spices at Del Rey Productos Latinos, is the Tropical Zone, where you can buy any of a hundred different combinations of fresh juices. Sitting in the Grand Central Market watching everybody eat reaffirms what writer Carey McWilliams observed about Los Angeles in 1932: The city

See also area map p. 91
➤ Bradbury Building
1 hour
1 mile (1.6 km)
➤ L.A. Central Library

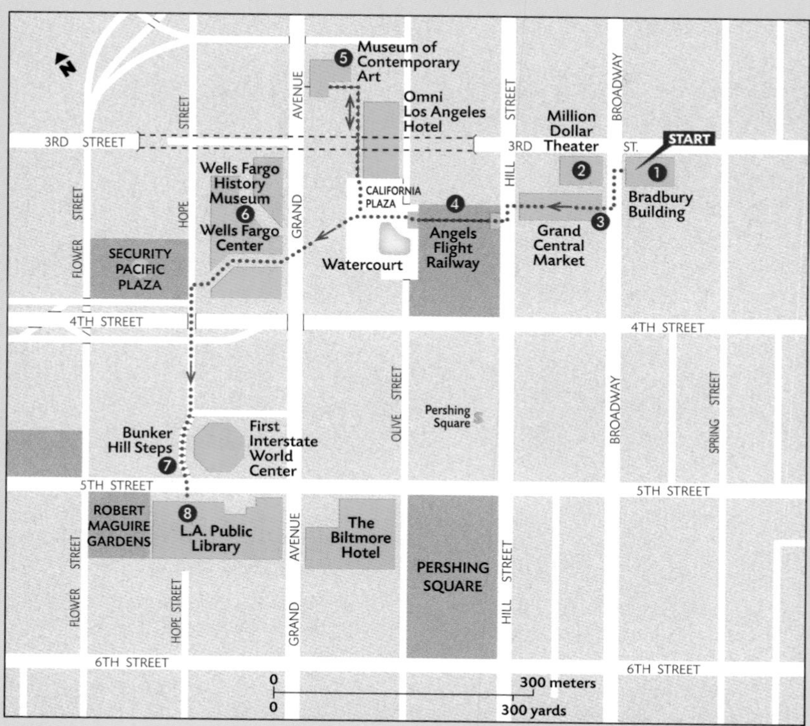

Angels Flight Railway, which has two cars, began operation on a different site in 1901.

"is a nation of munchers. In L.A., no one misses a meal."

Cross Hill Street from the market to the **Angels Flight Railway** ❹ *(www.angelsflight.com),* a beautifully restored 1901 funicular, which will whisk you up historic **Bunker Hill** to **California Plaza** on Grand Avenue. To the north, next to the **Omni Los Angeles** hotel, is the **Museum of Contemporary Art** ❺ (see pp. 99–101), and in the distance is the Music Center (see p. 103), home to the renowned L.A. Philharmonic and the L.A. Opera.

Circular steps lead to the sun-filled **Watercourt at California Plaza,** a lunch spot with entertainment provided by syncopated water spouts and fountains. Across Grand is the **Wells Fargo Center** ❻, where several large pieces of public art include works by Louise Nevelson, Robert Graham, and Jean Dubuffet. The **Wells Fargo History Museum** *(333 S. Grand Ave., tel 213/253-7166, closed Sat.–Sun.)* houses a perfectly preserved 19th-century stagecoach.

Go down the escalator to Hope Street, past the Calder sculpture, and onto the Hope Street overpass to the **Bunker Hill Steps** ❼, L.A.'s version of the Spanish Steps in Rome. At the top is the highly symbolic sculpture by Robert Graham entitled "Source Figure" (1992). Down the steps and through the lush landscaping is the pride of modern downtowners, the restored **L.A. Public Library** ❽ *(630 W. 5th St., tel 213/228-7000, www.lapl.org).* Designed by Bertram Goodhue, who also worked on Caltech and Balboa Park, the building displays many elements that might be called neo-Byzantine, neo-Spanish, or neo-Egyptian. Inside the second-floor rotunda is a chandelier representing the solar system, and a 1933 mural by Dean Cornwell depicting the romance of L.A.'s past.

Outside, the art deco sculptures of Homer, St. John, Shakespeare, and others are by Lee Lawrie, best known for his sculpted main entrance to the RCA building in New York's Rockefeller Center. The **Robert Maguire Gardens** to the west have been restored to Goodhue's basic design, embellished by modern elements, including the Grotto Fountain.

The L.A. Conservancy *(523 W. 6th St., tel 213/430-4219, www.laconservancy.org)* offers many great and reasonably priced tours.

acts such as the Grand Kabuki of Japan.

Return to First Street to find **Fugetsu-do** *(315 E. 1st St., tel 213/625-8595, www.fugetsu-do .com),* a traditional Japanese candy store that still uses antique wooden forms to press sweets into delicate patterns. In **Japanese Village Plaza** *(map p. 91, www.japanesevil-lageplaza.net),* near the intersection of First Street and Central Avenue, you can experience several Japanese culinary pleasures. Joy Mart Restaurant specializes in Izaakaya-style cuisine—small, tapas-like dishes that go well with sake and beer. After dinner, pop into the nearby Mikawaya café for traditional Japanese ice cream and *wagashi* pastries.

Museum of Contemporary Art

It has often been observed that when young artists want to make a name for themselves, they go to Manhattan. When they want to make art, however, they go to L.A., where the lack of a clear arts hierarchy and a less corporate culture has always made dreaming a respected art form in itself. But it was not until 1984, when MOCA opened, that L.A. had the clout, the will, and the money from younger patrons that are all necessary to make a modern art museum successful. Fueled by generous contributions from Hollywood's younger moguls, MOCA has quickly established itself as an institution with which to be reckoned, amassing in just a few years the most prestigious collection of postwar art in the western United States.

The works are displayed in the MOCA Gallery at the Pacific Design Center (see p. 102–103), the Geffen Contemporary at MOCA (see pp. 101–102), and the main MOCA campus itself, two red sandstone pavilions on Grand Avenue, north of California Plaza. While it pays to phone for an exhibition schedule, the cavernous Geffen ensures that some of the museum's permanent collection remains on display for at least part of the year.

Museum of Contemporary Art (MOCA)

- Map: 91
- Address: MOCA Grand Avenue, 250 S. Grand Ave.
- Phone: 213/626-6222
- Hours: Closed Tues. & Wed.
- Price: $$ (ticket valid for all venues). Free Thurs. 5 p.m.–8 p.m.

www.moca.org

Arts Sponsor

Movie mogul, record producer, and stage impresario, David Geffen (1943–) is one of the most powerful people in show business and one of the greatest art collectors in the world (see pp. 101–102). Along with Steven Spielberg and Jeffrey Katzenberg, Geffen formed DreamWorks in 1994. But he was already famous as the money behind *Cats, Dreamgirls, Little Shop of Horrors,* and many other Broadway hits, as well as the producer of such music icons as Bob Dylan, Janis Joplin, the Eagles, and John Lennon. He has channeled much of his billion-dollar-plus fortune into modern American art, a private collection that runs the gamut from Jackson Pollack and Jasper Johns to Willem de Kooning and Robert Rauschenberg.

The best strategy for seeing the two main facilities (one ticket admits you to both) is to start in Little Tokyo at the Geffen, where you can buy your ticket and enjoy the capacious, light-filled building before eating lunch at one of the affordable restaurants over on

First Street. Then walk or drive over to MOCA *(parking available in the garage under California Plaza).* If you are more interested in the MOCA building, designed by Japanese architect Arata Isozaki, reverse the order. But you may then regret that you spent too much time in MOCA's ill-lit exhibition space when you could have lingered at the Geffen.

Neon!

Gas and glass come together at the Museum of Neon Art ***(tel 213/489-9918, www.neonmona.org),*** **in the midst of moving from downtown L.A. to Glendale's Culture Arts District (2014). MONA offers popular workshops and nighttime neon cruises of Hollywood and downtown in an old double-decker London bus, as well as the Lumens Project to restore and relight historic neon signs across the metropolis.**

MOCA's core collection was procured by the museum trustees in 1984 from Giuseppe and Giovanna Panza; by most critical measures, the acquisition is considered a coup. Among the 80 pieces in the Panza collection are works by Robert Rauschenberg, Mark Rothko, Roy Lichtenstein, and Claes Oldenberg. The latter's installation piece "The Store" (1961–62) grounds the collection in the 1960s, in this case underscoring the era's emergent genres of pop art and "happening" art. Lichtenstein's "Man With Folded Arms" (1962) shows the fullness of the Panzas' taste, opting for a subdued, almost woodblock-print illustration rather than one of the artist's more over-the-top, comic-book-style works.

The museum has aggressively entered the fray over photographic art, scooping up 2,000 prints in 1995 alone. This makes for one of its best standing displays—the works of Larry Clark, known most recently for his disturbing film *Kids* (1995). In a series of 50 black-and-white photos taken in 1980, Clark, in pieces such as "Tulsa," documented the world of young white Texas outcasts: among them drug addicts, boozers, and gun freaks. The pictures are spooky, not just for their content but also for the way they seem to prefigure the age of video.

In 1989, MOCA received perhaps its single most discerning collection, 18 works of sculpture, painting, and drawing from Rita and Taft Schreiber. Two bronze figures by Alberto Giacometti, "Tall Figure II" and "Tall Figure III" (1960), are at its heart; redolent of the Etruscan-era *Uomo sull'Ambras* found in Italy's oldest towns, the delicate forms cast one of mankind's oldest fears—that of evaporating in sunlight—and render it permanent. Some of the other pieces from the Schreibers are by Alexander Calder, Arshile Gorky, Joan Miró, Piet Mondrian, and Jackson Pollock.

The **Scott D. F. Spiegel Collection** is more problematic, perhaps reflecting the fact that some members of this group of "emerging artists" are still alive. The works

INSIDER TIP:

Use the Advanced Parking System lot on First Street and Central Avenue, which is cheap and open 24/7. But remember, the Geffen is closed on Tuesdays and Wednesdays.

—DANIELLE FISHER
National Geographic contributor

by Jean-Michel Basquiat, with their icons of urban tribalism, are still vexing: Were they the work of a genius whose life was cut tragically short, or was it simply Basquiat's mentor Andy Warhol's longest-running joke? Robert Longo's series of falling men surely provokes ("It makes me want to choke him," was one recent comment), as does Susan Rothenberg's "The Hulk."

To its credit, MOCA has made a strong commitment to site-specific artworks, something requiring an enormous effort in audience education. This has created a platform for the works of Robert Irwin. Irwin is principally concerned with the manipulation of light and space, as his seminal garden at the Getty illustrates (see p. 66).

Geffen Contemporary at MOCA: Unlike its brother on the hill, the Geffen Contemporary is free from the obligations of being an institutional showplace. Named for its mogul-contributor David Geffen (see sidebar p. 99), this is a more flexible venue, its size and light allowing for the accommodation of large-scale works. Initially dubbed the "Temporary Contemporary," the giant old warehouse, just up the street from the Japanese American National

Geffen Contemporary at MOCA

- 91
- 152 N. Central Ave.
- 213/626-6222

MOCA is L.A.'s only museum devoted entirely to modern art.

MOCA Pacific Design Center
✉ 8687 Melrose Ave.
☎ 310/289-5223

Museum, has taken on a life of its own in recent years, often outperforming MOCA itself.

One major exhibition featured the works of sculptor Richard Serra. A Californian who worked in Paris and Florence before settling in New York, Serra works primarily with sheet steel, which he uses to produce large-scale minimalist works—giant cubes of steel plates leaning against each other and acres of sheet metal winding around city blocks. Usually encountered outdoors as public art, Serra's works take on a strangely fragile quality at the Geffen.

Similarly, L.A. performance artist Chris Burden, known for shooting himself and hammering nails through his hands—and recording the whole affair—has a rare permanent exhibit here, a whimsical piece entitled "Exposing the Foundations of the Museum," which he did with pick and shovel.

The Geffen has also expanded MOCA's ability to present architectural subjects, as in its successful "Blueprints for Modern Living: The History and Legacy of the Case Study Houses," which highlighted an important theoretical architectural movement with L.A. roots.

MOCA Pacific Design Center: In 2001, MOCA opened a gallery at the Pacific Design Center (see p. 81), with an emphasis on architecture and design. Housed in the "Blue Whale" building, designed by Cesar Pelli, its inaugural exhibition surveyed a tendency in Japanese art, animation, fashion, and graphic design toward two-dimensionality. The museum has staged a number of large-scale exhibits documenting some of the century's most visionary architects, from MOCA designer Arata Isozaki and Geffen designer Frank Gehry (see sidebar p. 46) to Louis Kahn.

The First Electronic Evangelist

Sitting in the northwest corner of Echo Park, just beyond the quacking ducks, is the historic **Angelus Temple** *(1100 Glendale Blvd., www.angelus temple.org)* founded in 1923 by the Foursquare Gospel preacher Aimee Semple McPherson. One part actress, one part evangelist, and one part entrepreneur, "Sister Aimee" attracted thousands to her church by using highly theatrical techniques to engage their imaginations.

The Works Progress Administration guide to California gives this description of the temple in its heyday: "The ceiling of the huge unsupported dome is sky-blue behind fleecy clouds, and light enters through tall stained glass windows. The temple has four robed choirs, several orchestras, bands, and smaller musical organizations, an expensive costume wardrobe, a vast amount of stage scenery, and a 5,300-glass communion set. Also in the structure are the technical room and studio of Radio Station KFSG—the 'Glory Station of the Pacific Coast'—the Choir Studio and the Prayer Tower, where alternating shifts of men and women have prayed in continuous session night and day since the Temple opened in 1923. A display of X-ray photographs and discarded crutches is offered as testimony to the 'healing power of prayer.'"

The Music Center

The Music Center is the West's preeminent performing arts venue, offering a critically acclaimed, year-round program of music and theater. The center itself is worth visiting during a trip downtown; its public art includes sculptures by Robert Graham and Jacques Lipchitz, the latter perched inside an inviting water sculpture.

The 7-acre (2.8 ha) complex has four separate halls. The **Dorothy Chandler Pavilion** is home to the L.A. Opera and the L.A. Master Chorale. The **Ahmanson Theater** presents large-scale theatrical blockbusters, and the **Mark Taper Forum** is a more intimate house for innovative drama. The jewel in the crown is the **Walt Disney Concert Hall** *(111 S. Grand Ave., tel 323/850-2000, tours: 213/972-4399, www.laphil.com)*, designed by Frank Gehry (see sidebar p. 46) and home of the L.A. Philharmonic. Recalling the Guggenheim in Bilbao, this bold statement in stainless steel is one of the most acoustically sophisticated concert halls in the world. Completing the complex is the new, cubist-inspired **Cathedral of Our Lady of the Angels** *(map p. 91, 555 W. Temple St., tel 213/680-5200, www.olacathedral.org)*, by architect José Rafael Moneo. Replacing the old cathedral damaged beyond repair by a 1994 earthquake, it has an adjoining plaza and gardens with a **Native American Memorial.**

Echo Park & Lake

A drive west along Sunset Boulevard to Echo Park Avenue will take the adventurous to a delightful, if often overlooked, section of old Los Angeles: Echo Park and Lake. Here it is possible to get an idea of what early Angeleno civic planners hoped would be the heart of the city, a kind of West Coast Central Park under the palms. Today the park is a center of the thriving Central American community. Strollers can buy colorful shaved ices, roasted corn, and mango sticks sprinkled with chili powder and lime juice. Pedal boats can be rented for an invigorating turn about the lake.

The 21-acre (8.5 ha) park hosts

The Walt Disney Concert Hall boasts some of the world's best acoustics.

The Music Center

- Map: 91
- Address: 135 N. Grand Ave.
- Tel: 213/972-7211, 213/972-4399 (tours)

www.musiccenter.org

Echo Park & Lake

- Map: 91 & 111 A1
- Tel: 323/860-8874
- $: Donation for walking tours

www.historicechopark.org

Exposition Park
52 D2 & 111 A1
www.expositionpark.org

Natural History Museum of Los Angeles County
900 Exposition Blvd.
213/763-3466
$$
www.nhm.org

two yearly events, the Cuban Music Festival in May and the Lotus Festival in July.

Just to the park's east is **Carroll Avenue,** one of the city's earliest Victorian neighborhoods. You can arrange a tour of the area through the L.A. Conservancy *(523 W. 6th St., tel 213/430-4219, www.laconservancy.org).*

A bit farther to the west, down Sunset Boulevard, are numerous *panaderias*, Latino bakeries.

Exposition Park

Just west of I-110 and south of the University of Southern California (see p. 107) stands a cluster of buildings and greens known as Exposition Park. Founded in 1872 as a place for agricultural fairs, it became a public park at the turn of the 20th century. At its center is the 15-acre (6 ha) sunken **Rose Garden,** planted in 1913. The park's two main attractions can be found on its northern edge.

Natural History Museum of Los Angeles County:

With more than 35 million specimens, the Natural History Museum of Los Angeles County is the second largest museum of its kind in the United States, outranked only by the Smithsonian. Faced with the prospect of seeing such a huge collection, you would be well advised to do some advance planning. The museum's website is extremely useful, outlining upcoming exhibitions and talks and detailing much of the permanent collection. The museum has a wealth of child-centered exhibits, as well as reading areas.

Of all the museum's permanent exhibits, none brings visitors back as often as its hallmark "Dueling Dinosaurs," in the foyer behind the main entrance, the complete, full-scale skeletons of a *Tyrannosaurus rex* and a triceratops posed in deadly battle. This memorable exhibit had its roots in a decision by museum trustees more than 30 years ago to fund a series of expeditions to Hell Creek in Montana. By 1969 the venture had reaped a treasure trove of dinosaur remains, including an enormous tyrannosaur skull that, after five years of reassembly, proved to be the largest ever found (a distinction later conceded to a new find in South Dakota's Black Hills).

INSIDER TIP:

During the week, visit the Natural History Museum in the afternoon, when field trips and school groups taper off and the galleries are quiet.

—CHRIS MAES
National Geographic Television production manager

Unveiled in 2011, the cutting-edge **Dinosaur Hall** revolves around a young adult *rex* nicknamed "Thomas" (one of the world's best preserved *T. rex* skeletons), a massive mamenchisaurus, bigger than a bus, and an armored triceratops created from bones discovered at four different digs. Thomas is part of the world's only *T. rex* growth series, a unique exhibit that also includes baby and juvenile skeletons. The hall is fitted with interactive screens and touch stations where visitors can handle genuine dinosaur bones. Innovative displays and mounting techniques bring paleontology to life, revealing never-before-seen details like skin textures, internal organs, and even stomach contents.

Another major component of the museum's aggressive expansion campaign is the new **"Becoming Los Angeles,"** a 14,000-square-foot (1,300 sq m) exhibit that traces the city's human history from ancient Native American times through the Spanish mission era, the Mexican hacienda period, the early American decades, and L.A.'s emergence into a global city in the 20th century. Opened in 2012, the exhibit embraces an eclectic array of original artifacts, from Spanish colonial religious objects and weapons to Walt Disney's first animation workshop, built in his uncle's garage in 1923.

The museum's **Gem and Mineral Hall** displays more than 2,000 precious stones and nuggets, including one of the world's largest gold exhibits. The **Schreiber Hall of Birds** has avian specimens from around the world, including more than 400 species found in southern California.

Fresh from a recent remake, the museum now features the **Ancient Latin America Hall,** with superb exhibits of ancient South American and Meso-American cultures, while the **Lando Hall of California History** traces events and culture since the 1500s.

Finally, the recently renovated **Parsons Discovery Center** takes the current fad for interactive museum displays to a wonderful and unusual extreme. The 6,000-square-foot (557 sq m) pavilion not only lets visitors touch dinosaur bones, mammal fur, and fish scales but also has a live insect zoo stocked with tarantulas, scorpions, Madagascan hissing cockroaches, and dung beetles.

L.A. LIVE

Downtown Los Angeles is expanding southward on the coattails of massive projects like the $2.5 billion L.A. Live *(map p. 91, 800 W. Olympic Blvd., tel 213/763-5483 or 866/548-3452, www.lalive.com)* entertainment complex, near the L.A. Convention Center. Set around an outdoor plaza that hosts the annual X Games and pro wrestling events, the complex includes the 7,100-seat Nokia Theatre *(www.nokiatheatrelalive.com)*, where the *American Idol* finals and other live music events take place, as well as the ESPN broadcast studio. Its other anchor is the new Grammy Museum *(tel 213/765-6800, www.grammymuseum.org, $$)*, an interactive multimedia collection dedicated to the artists who have captured America's top music award since it was established in 1959. Across the street from L.A. Live is the Staples Center *(map p. 91, 1111 S. Figueroa St., tel 213/742-7326, www.staplescenter.com)*, an arena that seats up to 21,000 for various sporting events.

California Science Center: In the northeast section of Exposition Park is the California

California Science Center

- 700 Exposition Park Dr.
- 323/724-3623, 213/744-7400 (IMAX)
- $$ (IMAX)

www.californiasciencecenter.org

The California Science Center is one of southern California's most popular museums.

Science Center (CSC), which teaches scientific and technological literacy in interactive ways. Encompassing almost 500,000 square feet (46,450 sq m), its many marvelous exhibits include the **Air and Space Gallery,** dedicated to explaining the principles of air, space, and flight and how humans design aircraft and spacecraft. Housed in a 1984 Frank Gehry structure with an F-104 Starfighter bolted to its facade, the gallery displays stunning exhibits, including a full-scale model of the 1894 Lilienthal glider that inspired the Wright brothers' flight, the Bell X-1 (the world's first supersonic aircraft), a Gemini capsule, and a full-scale model of Sputnik. CSC has been chosen as one of only four museums nationwide that will receive a NASA Space Shuttle Orbiter for permanent display, in this case the *Endeavour.* In an **Air and Space Discovery Room,** kids can learn about the moon, explore the planets, and pretend to be pilots on a plane or space shuttle. The **Science Court** has hands-on demonstrations ranging from molecular science to an exciting high-wire bicycle.

One central exhibit, **World of Life** (in Edgerton Court), draws rave reviews. Divided into several mini pavilions, this is a high-touch, high-tech exploration of how living things function and survive. The emphasis is on the human cell, highlighted in a huge multimedia Cell Lab and Cell Theater, where audiences are surrounded by enormous projections of cell functions. Five life-process galleries dramatize how organisms defend themselves, reproduce, make energy, and control interaction with their environments. In the gallery showing how organisms are supplied with food, visitors can compare the effort needed to transport blood from the heart to the brain of a boy with that needed to do the same for a giraffe.

Another state-of-the-art exhibit, **Creative World,** looks at the ways in which human endeavor has shaped—and will shape—the world around us. In its three galleries, visitors can help to build structures which then undergo environmental tests to test their endurance and strength in natural disasters. There are interactive displays about "smart highways," robotics, computer technology (through a "virtual volleyball" exhibit), long-distance communications, and a child-size TV studio.

In the **IMAX Theater,** a variety of science films are projected both three-dimensionally and at several times their normal size.

California African American Museum: Set at the eastern edge of Culver City, home to much of Los Angeles's African-American community, Exposition Park is also home to the California African American Museum, with changing exhibitions honoring the contribution of blacks to American settlement and culture.

University of Southern California

Just to the north of Exposition Park is the campus of the University of Southern California, where the architecturally inclined can enjoy an educational—and free—90-minute walking tour past several graceful Gothic- and Renaissance-style buildings. ■

California African American Museum

- 600 State Dr.
- 213/744-7432
- Closed Mon.
- $$ (parking)

www.caam.ca.gov

University of Southern California

- Exposition Blvd. & Pardee Way
- 213/740-2311 (walking tours)

www.usc.edu

EXPERIENCE: African-American Culture

About 2 miles (3.2 km) west of Exposition Park (see pp. 104–107), you'll find a trove of African-American culture at Leimert (la-MERT) Park. One of Los Angeles's first planned communities, Leimert takes its 1920s design from the two sons of architect Frederick Law Olmsted, who designed New York's Central Park. Although its property deeds originally prohibited minorities from moving in, a mid-20th-century black migration and a Supreme Court strike-down of the restrictive deeds flip-flopped the racial ratio. Today Leimert is a Galápagos of African-American culture, with an evolved diversity of jazz, poetry, gallery art, shopping, and political activism.

Try Southern-style collard greens and macaroni at **Babe's & Ricky's Inn** *(4339 Leimert Blvd., tel 323/295-9112, www.bluesbar.com)* as jazz musicians serenade you from the same stage Duke Ellington, B. B. King, Cab Calloway, Eric Clapton, and countless others have played. In summer, catch celebrity author readings, book signings, and music at the free **Book Fair** *(www.leimertparkbookfair.com)*. If you visit in winter, the **Kwanzaa Heritage Festival** *(www.kwanzaaheritage.org)* kicks off New Year's Eve with candles, drums, international food, and a petting zoo. The celebration takes place in the parking lot of the historic 1931 Vision Theatre.

To check for festivals during your trip, visit *www.leimertparkbeat.com.* If nothing is scheduled, a single-digit donation will buy you—novice or pro—a spot in a weekly jazz workshop at the **World Stage** *(4344 Degnan Blvd., tel 323/293-2451, www.theworldstage.org)*. Or visit the park plaza, where you might stumble upon a jam session.

Architecture Drive

Between 1920 and 1950, perhaps no single region in the United States produced as much first-rate modern architecture as did the Los Feliz–Silver Lake area of Los Angeles. Why this is so is still the subject of debate. Whatever the reason, few areas of the world seemed to grasp with such intensity the words of the leading Bauhaus architect Walter Gropius, who in 1926 declaimed: "Modern man, who no longer dresses in historical garments but wears modern clothes, also needs a modern home."

This drive takes in a selection of these buildings, still architecturally stunning, though it is perhaps harder now to grasp just how innovative they were when first built. (Remember that they are private residences, so look at them from your car or from the sidewalk.)

NOT TO BE MISSED:

Schrage House • V.D.L. House • Daniels House • Alexander House • Hollyhock House

Travel north from downtown on I-110 to the Los Feliz Boulevard exit, then head west to Commonwealth Avenue. Turn right to find Raphael Soriano's **Schrage House** ❶ *(2648 N. Commonwealth Ave.),* built in 1951. Mentored by Richard Neutra, Soriano was a modernist known for his experimentation with steel and aluminum framing.

Return to eastbound Los Feliz. Make a quick right on Rowena Avenue and a quick left on Lowry Road to see two houses by Frank Lloyd Wright, Jr., the son of Frank Lloyd Wright: the **Carr House** ❷ at Lowry and Rowena, and the **Farrell House** ❸ at 3209 Lowry. While Wright's son was building these fine small private houses in 1925–26, his father had just finished four of his enormously weighty "cast-block" houses.

Continue south on Rowena, past Hyperion Avenue, to Glendale Boulevard and turn left, then right on Waverly to Nos. 2717–2721. Here, R. M. Schindler's **McAlmon House** ❹ of 1935 reflects the architect's search for a style that could be judged "not by the eyes, but by living."

Return to Glendale and proceed south to Silver Lake Boulevard. Here, turn right, follow the boulevard to the left to a cluster of houses by Richard Neutra, who began developing the area into a modernist housing colony in the late 1940s. (Nos. 2250, 2242, 2238, and 2232 East Silver Lake Boulevard are just four of the houses he built between 1948 and 1961.) The architect's own home, the **V.D.L. House** ❺ at 2300 Silver Lake, was originally built in 1933 with funds from a client named Van der Leeuw. Tours can be arranged by appointment *(tel 323/953-0224, www.neutra.org/tours.html).* The house has an interesting history; after a fire, it was completely rebuilt by Neutra's son, Dion, who added some questionable elements such as the reflecting pools while trying to outdo his father.

The easiest route (albeit longer) to the next stop is simply to proceed south on East Silver Lake to Sunset Boulevard, turning right to Micheltorena Street, where you will see two outstanding examples of houses designed in 1939 by Gregory Ain: the **Daniels House** ❻ *(1856 Micheltorena St.)* and the **Tierman House** *(2323 Micheltorena St.).* Ain used space, particularly small spaces, in a particularly masterful way, "framing" a home's volume to accentuate capacities, both functional and emotional.

Also on Micheltorena are two houses designed by John Launer, a Wright apprentice

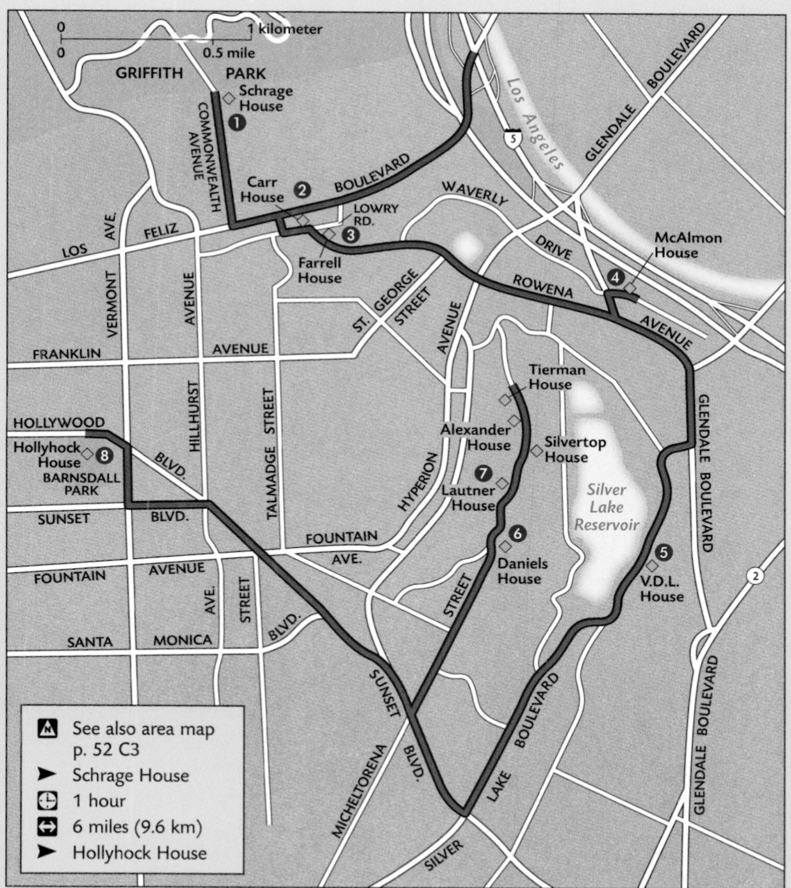

who attempted to create highly individualized modern houses. He often integrated water features and a garden into the plan, as with the **Lautner House** ❼ *(2007 Micheltorena St.)*, built in 1939, and the **Silvertop House** *(2138 Micheltorena St.)*, built in 1957. At 2265 Micheltorena is the **Alexander House.** Built in 1940 by Harwell Harris, it reflects Harris's unique blending of Craftsman concern for natural materials with the modular configurations of Neutra, who was his mentor in the early 1930s.

Return to Sunset and follow it westward past Santa Monica Boulevard and Hillhurst onto Hollywood Boulevard. Go past Vermont Avenue and on the left you will see the sign for Barnsdall Park. Here is the last and most famous stop, Frank Lloyd Wright's **Hollyhock House** ❽ *(4800 Hollywood Blvd., tel 323/644-6269, www.hollyhockhouse.net, tour: $$)*, a spectacular concrete block residence built for an oil heiress in 1917–1920. The wonderfully light and airy interior is still complete with its original Wright furniture. Tours of the house are offered daily.

For more information about these and other L.A. architects, try the online Great Buildings Collection *(www.greatbuildings.com)*.

From the Foothills

Along the foothills of the San Gabriel Mountains lies a swath of forests, unique architecture, and a lively cultural life. No wonder that famous people from all walks of life—from Albert Einstein to Jon Bon Jovi—have chosen to call it home.

Dotted with sage and live oak, the foothills of the San Gabriel Mountains form one of the primordial historic landscapes of California, redolent of old Spanish dons on horseback, padres nodding in siesta after Mass, señoritas with the local Matalija poppy behind one ear. With that as a backdrop, today's foothill culture, located mostly on the borders of the Angeles National Forest, can be thought of as a hybrid: part Midwestern migrant, part Latin, and part Asian. Where else could one find a stucco office building with a sign on it saying "Chinese Rotary Club of San Gabriel"?

The west entrance of Pasadena's City Hall, completed in 1927, culminates in a grand dome.

Pasadena

At the center of the region is Pasadena, "Crown of the Valley." Founded in the late 19th century by high-minded folk from Indiana who wanted "to get where life is easier," Pasadena evolved as one of southern California's wealthiest communities, complete with a Millionaires' Row (south on Orange Grove from Colorado), a Valley Hunt Club (still private), and more debutantes than there are flowers on a Rose Parade float.

Although conservative, the city of Pasadena could be politically tolerant, putting up with radicals such as writer Upton Sinclair in the 1930s. World War II made Pasadena a more representative town, open to light industry and affordable housing.

Inaugurated in 2003, the Gold Line *(tel 626/471-9050 or 800/266-6883, www.metrogoldline.org)*, a light-rail system, now links Old Pasadena with Union Station (see pp. 91–92) in downtown Los Angeles and with Azusa.

The city has experienced a renaissance in recent years as a hub of commerce, education, and the arts. Much of the impetus has come from neighborhood groups and architectural preservationists known as "bungalow huggers" for their defense of the small Craftsman houses that, at one time, were only considered fit for the bulldozer. As a result, the city's **Old Town** *(Fair Oaks Ave. & Colorado Blvd.)* is one of the best examples of downtown renewal in the state.

To the east, you'll find the new **Plaza Las Fuentes** *(N. Los Robles Ave. & N. Euclid St.)*, which consists of a hotel and restaurants. The plaza successfully merges with the historic revivalist architecture of Pasadena's **City Hall** *(100 N. Garfield Ave., www.ci.pasadena.ca.us)*, designed by Bakewell & Brown, and the **Pasadena Public Library** *(285 E. Walnut Ave., www.ci.pasadena.ca.us)*, by Myron Hunt.

The ornate tile-and-plaster **Pasadena Playhouse** *(39 S. El Molino Ave., tel 626/356-7529, www.pasadenaplayhouse.org)* is one of the top stages in the area.

Pasadena

111 B2 & 52 D3

Visitor Information

Convention Center, 300 E. Green St.

626/795-9311, 800/307-7977

www.pasadenacal.com

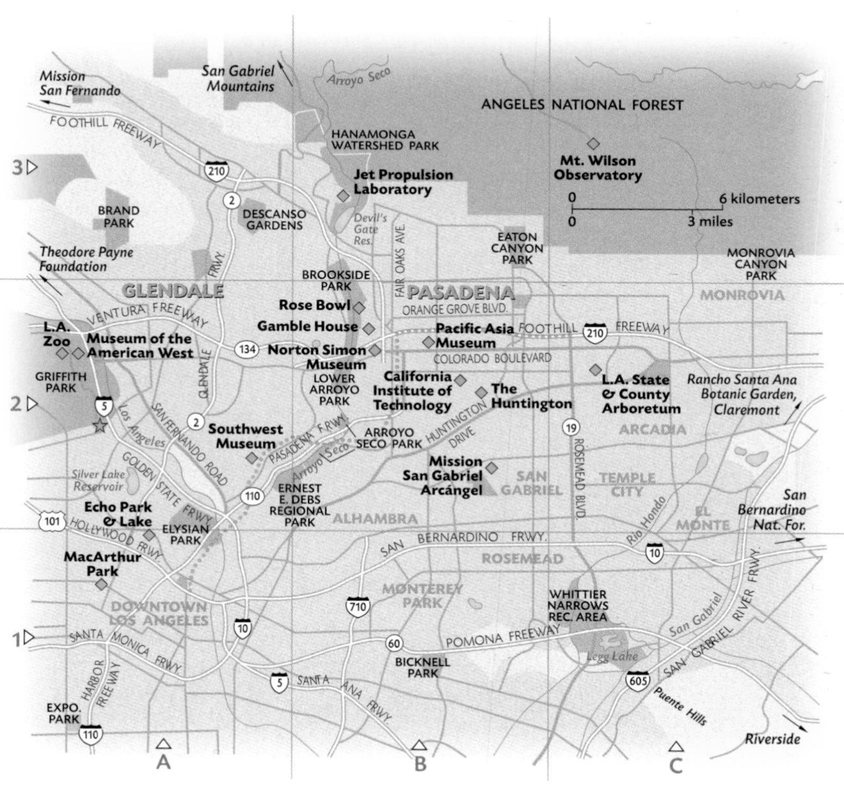

UCLA Bruins quarterback Kevin Prince scans for a receiver in a game at Pasadena's Rose Bowl.

Gamble House
111 B2
4 Westmoreland Pl. (off Orange Grove Blvd.), Pasadena
626/793-3334
Closed a.m. & Mon.–Wed. Soft-sole shoes required (coverings provided otherwise)
$$
www.gamblehouse.org

Gamble House: Built in 1908 by the architect brothers Charles Sumner Greene and Henry Mather Greene for wealthy industrialist David Gamble, the Gamble House represents the epitome of the American Arts and Crafts movement. One can imagine the satisfaction the Greenes might now experience were they to rematerialize some sunny weekend afternoon and surreptitiously take one of the meticulous and informative afternoon guided tours of their "ultimate bungalow."

With all the hype surrounding the Craftsman aesthetic (fueled in no small part by singer and actress Barbra Streisand's $250,000 purchase of a Stickley side cabinet), it is easy to forget that the original impulse of the bungalow movement was rather mundane. It was, above all, an attempt to create an affordable, regionally appropriate architecture. In southern California, this means three things: a patio, a covered porch, and large rooms with no dark hallways. It is a form that peppers the landscape in countless stucco houses in and around Pasadena.

In the Gamble House, however, the architects were given the resources to explore the outer limits of naturalism, emphasizing simplicity of construction, honesty of materials, and a deference to the designs of Mother Nature. "In a sense," California historian Kevin Starr has eloquently written, "the craftsman bungalows were themselves planted on the landscape as arboreal forms."

With its Japanese-inspired overhanging eaves and wooden shingles, the exterior of the Gamble House certainly suggests a radical departure from the fussy Victorianism that prevailed in late 19th-century Pasadena homebuilding. Gone are the tiny, lace-puddled windows, the faux English gardens, the gingerbread crenellations above lintel and column. In their place are wide windows, spare lighting fixtures, and Japanese koi ponds amid river stones and creeping mint. One can almost hear John Ruskin and William Morris cheering in the background.

The Gamble's interior, however, may be the greater masterpiece. One highlight is the **Tiffany doorway and entry room.** The rear of the hall is the best place from which to admire the cumulative effects of sunlight beamed through stained glass onto an endless variety of wood and glass surfaces. The interlocking wood casements and panels become structure and decoration, harmonizing organically with the light fixtures that were inspired by Japanese lanterns.

The spare **master bedroom** on the second floor carries the Japanese nature theme forward. Finished in rare Port Orford cedar, the room gets indirect lighting via wooden light fixtures dangling on leather straps and embedded with abalone shells. The fireplace is done in an earthy brown—a stone cedar, in effect. The furniture is linked together by a repeating oval shape inspired by the handguard on a Japanese sword known as a *tsuba*. A door leads to three open-air sleeping porches.

The **butler's pantry** and its tile wall and wooden cabinets represent the pinnacle of careful hand craftsmanship, everything fitting as if it had grown together.

No tour of the Gamble is complete without a brief tour of its **grounds.** The old garage now serves as a gift store, well stocked with books on California homebuilding and reproduction Arts and Crafts tiles, lamps, clocks, and bric-a-brac. You can also buy a map of the surrounding neighborhood that shows the location of dozens of Greene brothers houses within walking distance of the Gamble and identifies several ultimate bungalows in other parts

(continued on p. 115)

The Rose Bowl

One of the world's most celebrated stadiums, the Rose Bowl *(Arroyo Seco Park, Pasadena, tel 626/577-3101, www.rosebowlstadium.com)* was built in 1922 to host the annual showdown between the best college football teams from the Midwest and Pacific coast. The 90-year-old behemoth is now a national historic monument and host to a number of special events each year. The Rose Bowl game between the winners of the Pac-12 and Big-10 conferences takes place the first week in January, but the stadium is also the home field of UCLA Bruins football, scene of a grand Independence Day fireworks spectacular, and venue for a huge monthly flea market (the largest in California), with more than 2,500 vendors.

Arroyo Culture

Stand in the middle of the sweeping Arroyo Seco Bridge and, instead of looking toward the mountains, look southward. There flows the old arroyo, down a cement flood-control culvert and on into the ocean some 20 miles (32.1 km) away. It was this landscape, wilder than it is now and certainly without the cement, that inspired L.A.'s unique turn-of-the-20th-century culture, the arroyo movement.

Like their upscale brethren up on Millionaires' Row, the rustic bohemians who lived along the arroyo were transplants from the East, men and women who had come here, first tentatively, then with enthusiasm. But if the Valley Hunt Club types on Orange Grove sought to replicate eastern institutions, the rustics of the arroyo sought roots in the region's past, with its innocent natives and Spanish dons, its life lived close to the wild.

The acme of the "Arroyo type" was Charles Fletcher Lummis, an itinerant newsman who, in 1885, walked to L.A. from Ohio, sending missives along the way to the *Los Angeles Times*, where he was later to become city editor. Lummis used boulders taken from the arroyo (see sidebar right) to build his home, **El Alisal** *(200 East Ave., tel 323/222-0546, www.socalhistory.org, closed a.m. & Mon.–Thurs.)*, now home of the Historical Society of Southern California. The floor plan was one of rustic simplicity, with a patio and every manner of native basket and blanket. By 1907, he had founded the **Southwest Museum** *(234 Museum Dr., Avenue 43 exit off I-110, tel 323/221-2164, www.museumsofthearroyo.com, closed Mon.)* for the preservation and study of Indian folk art.

His friends were of like mind. Bookseller John Vroman, whose Vroman's Bookstore *(695 E. Colorado Blvd., tel 626/449-5320, www.vromans bookstore.com)* is still central to Pasadena literary life, photographed local Native Americans. The period's leading plein air painters took up residence just upriver from Lummis, rendering the canyon rock and sumac in faded yellow and pale sage. Painter Maynard Dixon designed Lummis's enormous hand-carved doors. His friend, university dean William Lees Judson, whose stained-glass studios became a center of the local Arts and Crafts movement, even emulated Lummis's homebuilding techniques.

By the 1920s, however, Lummis's star had fallen. Los Angeles had entered the 20th century with a great surge of urbanity; the simple precepts of Arroyo culture could certainly no longer contain it. Increasingly ill, Lummis lived out his final years at El Alisal, dying in 1928.

Yet everywhere in southern California are remnants of Lummis's rustic bohemianism. It is found in the patio outside even the tiniest apartment or condominium, in the inexpensive Tijuana serape hanging on a restaurant wall, and in the "mission" roof tiles atop the cheesiest strip mall in the San Fernando Valley or Chinatown.

EXPERIENCE: Reclaiming the Arroyo

The most recent resurgence of California's early 20th-century arroyo movement is found in Arroyo Seco Park *(map p. 111 B2)*, where, through the efforts of city government and business, the old riverside habitats are being revived. Exotic plants have been weeded out and replaced with native coffeeberry, elderberry, and willows, and parts of the concrete arroyo have been redirected to natural streams and ponds. Hawks, killdeers, and mallards have returned. Contact the Arroyo Seco Foundation *(tel 323/405-7326, www.arroyoseco.org)* for volunteer opportunities that include planting trees, ridding streams of trash, and clearing trails for horses and hikers.

of Pasadena—well worth the drive. Please remember that they are private houses, to be viewed only from the sidewalk.

One nearby house, behind a shrub-lined fence at 645 Prospect Crescent, is **La Miniatura,** Frank Lloyd Wright's first adobe-block house. The famous architect once described it as a "genuine expression of California in terms of modern industry and American life." Unfortunately it is not open to the public.

Also in the area, on Grand Avenue, is the restored **Arroyo Hotel** *(125 S. Grand Ave.),* in its heyday a gathering place for wintering millionaires. Converted, it now hosts the U.S. Ninth Circuit Court of Appeals. Nearby is the **Colorado Street Bridge,** which sweeps over the Arroyo Seco riverbed and park. Once known as "suicide bridge" for the convenient height it afforded despairing financiers of the 1930s, the bridge is a focal point for preservationists.

Norton Simon Museum:

Though Pasadena had long nurtured its own art museum, it was not until 1974, when the brilliant industrialist Norton Simon entered the picture, that the city's museum scene finally came to the fore. It was Simon who agreed to acquire the foundering Pasadena Art Museum and infuse it with talent, funds, and, most importantly, his own collection of art.

Called "picture for picture, the greatest painting collection in town—indeed the Western United States" by the discerning *L.A. Times*

Norton Simon Museum

- 111 B2
- 411 W. Colorado Blvd., Pasadena
- 626/449-6840
- Closed a.m. & Tues.
- $$

www.nortonsimon.org

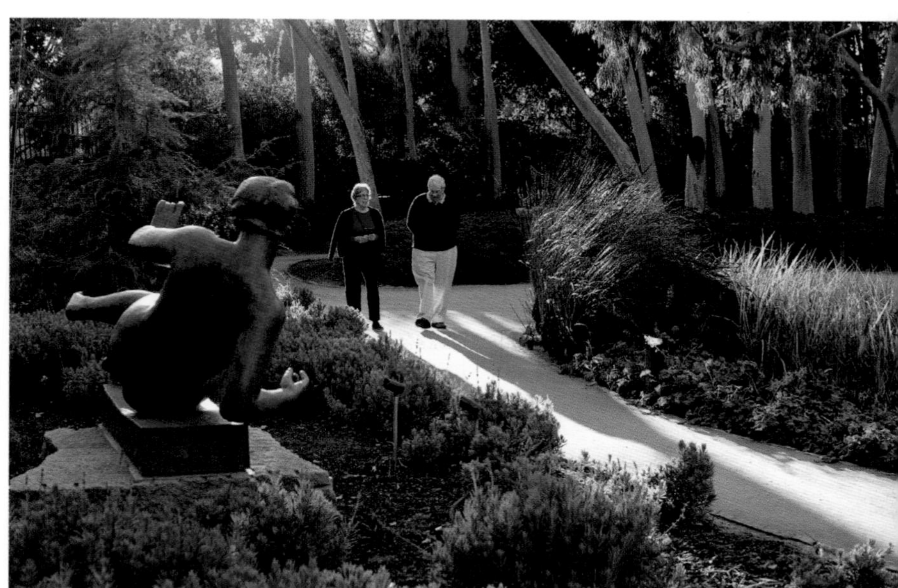

The expansive sculpture garden at the Norton Simon Museum impresses in every season.

critic Christopher Knight, the selections demonstrate Simon's affinity for what might be called the "primary example." That aesthetic informs the entire museum, from its stunning choice of old masters to the bronze gods and goddesses in the South Asian section. Simon's dedication has been carried forward by his widow, actress Jennifer Jones, who presided over the museum's recent three-million-dollar redesign.

Asian Art, New & Old

Housed in a 1924 building that was built in Chinese imperial style, the Pacific Asia Museum *(map p. 111 B2, 46 N. Los Robles Ave., Pasadena, tel 626/449-2742, www.pacificasiamuseum.org, closed Mon.–Tues., $$)*, **a long-standing Pasadena institution, takes a rare pan-Asian approach to its exhibitions. Its displays have included Burmese, Nepalese, Chinese, Thai, and Japanese art complemented by nontraditional showings of art from New Guinea and "Oriental" woodblock prints by Western artists such as Paul Jacoulet and Lillian Miller.**

Visit the serene Chinese garden in the inner courtyard and the bookstore, and take a look at the small permanent collection, all well worth the time. Walk up the street to Plaza Los Flores for lunch or a drink afterward.

The fine art collection commences with works from the 14th century. The choice of "Saints Benedict and Apollonia" by Filippino Lippi (1483) is indicative of Simon's eye for color, texture, hue, and tone. Robes enfold all but the essentials—only the strong hands and purposeful gaze of the saints are revealed. The museum likes to mix media, standing four gold panels by Giovanni di Paolo and Pietro Lorenzetti near the oil paintings of Raphael, Bassano, Cranach, and Memling. The depth and breadth of the collection is greatest in the baroque period, with works from Spain, Italy, France, Holland, and Belgium. Francisco de Zurbarán's "Still Life With Lemons, Oranges and a Rose" (1633) is an outstanding example of the period, its sensuous rendering of oversize fruits approaching realism. The rococo is represented by 18th-century French and Venetian works by Fragonard, Chardin, and Canaletto. One can nearly smell the baby powder in Giovanni Battista Tiepolo's glorious "Triumph of Virtue and Nobility Over Ignorance" (1740–1750).

The museum's holdings from the modern period remain the envy of the American curatorial world. Paul Cézanne's "Tulips in a Vase" (circa 1890–92) is a wistful, light-filled evocation of a humble glazed vase and imperfect flowers, the biomorphic agitation of the leaves a reminder of the obviously hasty arrangement of the flowers, the *ma'mselle* perhaps rushing off to scold an errant child. Monet, Renoir, and van Gogh follow.

The 20th-century exhibit also holds all the touchstones—Picasso, Klee, Braque, Kandinsky. The bohemian woman in Matisse's "Odalisque With Tambourine (Harmony in Blue)" (1926) is at once bawdy and delicate. Picasso's "Woman With a Hairnet" documents the artist's fascination with the female form.

Later in his life, Simon took an interest in Southeast and South Asian art. Fortunately, he was living in L.A. where the great curator Pratapaditya Pal was monomaniacally amassing the Los Angeles County Museum of Art's (see pp. 74–79) collection from that part of the world. In an age when so many Asian antiquities were flooding into American institutions, Pal was brave enough to play the role of dour editor, throwing out showier, second-rate items and investing in high-quality essentials. That attitude simply reinforced Simon's own picky tendencies. The result is a splendid group of sculptures, primarily from Nepal, Thailand, Cambodia, and India. The 14th-century Nepalese bronze gilt "Tara" is a favorite.

The **Garden Café** in the sculpture garden (closed during rains), part of a 79,000-square-foot (7,339 sq m) garden planted in 1870, is a delightful place of repose. The museum also offers a film series and lectures *(tel 626/449-6840 ext. 6906)*.

Descanso Gardens

Founded in 1939 by Los Angeles publisher Manchester Boddy, the 160-acre (65 ha) Descanso Gardens sit in a natural bowl at the foot of the San Rafael Hills, once prime food-gathering territory for the Gabrieleño Indians, who used the nut of the live oak as a dietary staple. Its unique location in a cool spot amidst hot foothills has afforded Descanso

Descanso Gardens is an urban retreat of year-round natural beauty.

Descanso Gardens

111 A3

1418 Descanso Dr., La Cañada-Flintridge

818/949-4200, 818/949-4290

$$

www.descansogardens.org

Gardens a remarkable range of plantings, from its internationally recognized camellia garden to its native plant garden. This results in a succession of year-round colors.

Begin your tour in the **Camellia Forest,** the pride of Descanso. Situated under the canopy of a 25-acre (10 ha) live oak forest (some of the trees are more than 300 years old), the camellia collection is the largest in North America, with more than 700 varieties. Filtered light and fertile soil collaborate to produce some truly remarkable specimens. Several varieties of the red Chinese camellia are the result of founder Boddy's tenacious negotiations with the Chinese for propagation rights.

The **Japanese Garden,** next, contains authentic Japanese structures and its own Japanese teahouse, garden bridge, and ponds. Not far away is the **Lilac Garden,** featuring some 400 of the fragrant shrubs, among them Sierra Blue and Mountain Haze, developed for the mild southern California climate. From the Lilac Garden, walk to the 5-acre (2 ha) **International Rosarium,** where much of the work of the famous hybridizer Walter E. Lammert remains in such classic cultivars as Sunny June, High Noon, and Chrysler Imperial. The **Iris Garden** is a seasonal delight, as is the **Spring Show,** with acres of tulips and other spring bulb plantings.

The 8 acres (3.2 ha) of **California Native Plants,** developed with naturalist Theodore Payne, are well worth the walk. In the **Lake and Bird Sanctuary,** grebes and mallards are commonly spotted from a bird observation station.

The gardens provide a number of guided tours, both on foot and by tram, as well as plant sales and lectures. A delightful children's railroad takes families to the home of founder Boddy, now a display area for the work of local artists.

INSIDER TIP:

In the zen calm of the Descanso's Japanese Garden, take time for contemplation and a cool drink at the Full Moon Tea House.

—LARRY PORGES
National Geographic Travel Books editor

Other Botanical Wonders

The **Los Angeles County Arboretum & Botanical Garden** *(301 N. Baldwin Rd., Arcadia, tel 626/821-3222, www.arboretum.org)* has impressive stretches of Australian and African plants, tropical greenhouses, and herb gardens.

Farther out of the city, off I-210, you will find a sizable display of desert flowers at **Rancho Santa Ana Botanic Garden** *(1500 N. College Ave., Claremont, tel 909/625-8767, www.rsabg.org)*, with 86 acres dedicated solely to plants native to California.

Closer to Pasadena are the Huntington Botanical Gardens (see p. 122) and **Burkard's Nursery** *(690 N. Orange Grove Blvd. & Lincoln Ave., Pasadena, tel 626/796-4355, www.burkardnurseries.com)*.

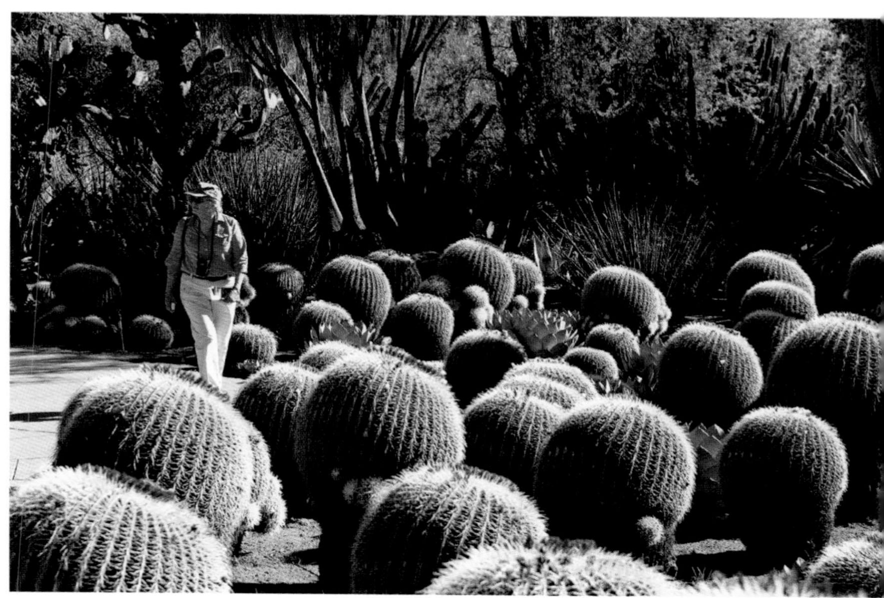

The Huntington's stunning Cactus Garden is one of the largest and oldest of its kind in the world.

The Huntington

Like its modern equivalent the Getty Center (see pp. 60–66), the Huntington represents nothing if not huge ambitions. And, like the Getty, these ambitions—research library, art collection, and garden—are realized with elegance, taste, and, for the most part, depth.

What makes the Huntington something the Getty Center should strive for can be described in one word: consistency. For more than 80 years, this brainchild of Henry E. Huntington, nephew of railroad baron Collis P. Huntington, has single-mindedly pursued excellence of the caliber found only in some of Europe's best-edited collections (the Musée d'Orsay in Paris comes to mind as one).

Huntington was a great booster of early 20th-century L.A.; his mark, in fact, is everywhere discernible in the routes of the modern freeway system, which still often follow the tracks of his Red Car line, a once popular trolley car system. (Urban legend—revived in the 1988 movie *Who Framed Roger Rabbit?*—has long blamed its demise on an evil oil company–car company lobby, but scrutiny reveals that, ultimately, Angelenos simply preferred cars to rail trams.) The Huntington was one of Henry's later passions, coming after his divorce from his first wife and his marriage to Annabelle Huntington, his aunt, in 1914.

The Huntington complex is set on 207 acres (83 ha) of breathtaking gardens. Its three art galleries and library preserve

The Huntington

- Map: 111 B2
- 1151 Oxford Rd., San Marino
- 626/405-2100
- Closed a.m. Mon.–Fri. & all day Tues.
- $$$

www.huntington.org

and show such masterpieces as a Gutenberg Bible, Rogier van der Weyden's "Madonna and Child," Gainsborough's "Blue Boy," Mary Cassatt's "Breakfast in Bed," and Edward Hopper's "The Long Leg." The botanical gardens range from an extensive collection of old roses to tropical plants and desert landscapes (look for the creeping devil cacti in the Baja California desert bed).

Each individual attraction is covered by an outstanding free brochure. Smart travelers will allocate an entire leisurely day to take in all the Huntington's sights, lunching at the restaurant near the Shakespeare Garden and having late afternoon tea as a relaxing finale. Bring a hat or umbrella in the summer—even with all that greenery, the Huntington can be hot, hot, hot.

The Bard's Blooms

The Huntington makes it possible for visitors to escape the noise and confusion of Los Angeles and commune with the Bard. Its Shakespeare Garden—which is located between the Art Gallery and the Scott Gallery—creates the illusion of a traditional English garden surrounded by forest. Poppies, marigolds, carnations, irises, pansies, and other beautiful blooms blanket a boggy dell that is at once pastoral retreat and literary lesson. This English-style perennial garden pays tribute to the Library's collection of rare editions of Shakespeare. Originally designed in 1959, the Shakespeare Garden aims to show the relationship between plants and the playwright's works. Watch out for the less obvious Shakespearean flora in the garden including woodbine, myrtle, lemon balm, and crab apple.

INSIDER TIP:

Take the primrose path in the Huntington's Shakespeare Garden and watch for plants and flowers mentioned in his plays. Small plaques quote the relevant lines.

—JUSTIN KAVANAGH
National Geographic International Editions editor

Passing through the **Entrance Pavilion** on Allen Avenue, bear right past the Palm Garden and into the **Library Exhibition Hall.** The high ceilings and large galleries in this building are a perfect place to cool off while taking in the remarkable Ellesmere manuscript, from 1410, of the *Canterbury Tales.* These pages, with their colorful border ornaments and renderings of the Wife of Bath, remind how far away is the world that first moved Geoffrey Chaucer to pen the great mythical yarns. Their foreignness is a reminder that the stories may well have origins not in Western civilization at all, but in the great Hindu tales of the *Pancatantra*, written about A.D. 200. Rarely does mere type prove so moving.

After looking at the Gutenberg Bible and admiring Audubon's exquisite illustrations in *Birds of America*, move on to the beaux arts **Huntington Gallery,** the onetime residence designed, with nods to the Mediterranean, by Elmer Grey and Myron Hunt. By

2006, the mansion, completed in 1911, had deteriorated markedly. Hence, the Huntington Gallery closed in 2006 and reopened in May 2008 after extensive restoration. This huge gallery contains the country's largest collections of British and French painting from the 18th and 19th centuries. But don't spend too long in front of Gainsborough's "Blue Boy" or Lawrence's "Pinkie." The gallery has so many treasures, and with a few inquiries to the hovering guards, you might see some of William Blake's watercolors, which the museum owns in quantity.

The **Shakespeare Garden** (see sidebar p. 122) leads to the **Scott Gallery,** which traces the history of American art over three centuries. Here you may recognize Gilbert Stuart's "George Washington" (1797), the stern visage forever emblazoned on the memory of American schoolchildren everywhere.

Adjoining the Scott Gallery, the **Erburu Gallery** opened in 2005 as a showcase for the institution's growing collection of American art, while nearby, Henry Huntington's garage has been transformed into the **Boone Gallery,** a world-class art venue for changing exhibitions.

Visitors admire Thomas Gainsborough's "Blue Boy" and other paintings in the Huntington Library.

On the way out, pass through the rose and herb gardens and linger for a while in the **Japanese Garden.** It has four main features: a formal garden, a Zen rock garden, a 19th-century Japanese teahouse, and an ikebana pavilion. Don't miss the view from the

Getting in Touch With Nature

California the way it used to be is the theme of **Eaton Canyon Park** *(map p. 111 B3)* in northeastern Pasadena, an oasis of wildlife and natural vegetation on the outer edge of the vast metropolis. Cutting through the foothills of the San Gabriel Mountains, the canyon falls under the purview of both the L.A. County Department of Parks & Recreation and the U.S. Forest Service. So great was its repute in pioneer times that John Muir came to have a look at both the canyon and its eponymous **waterfall,** which the great naturalist described as "a charming little thing, with a low, sweet voice, singing like a bird." The park's other landmark is the old **Mount Wilson Toll Road,** constructed in the 1890s and now a strenuous hiking route that leads deep into the mountains. The fulcrum of the modern park is the **Eaton Canyon Nature Center** *(1750 N. Altadena Dr., tel 626/398-5420, www.ecnca.org),* which showcases the native flora and fauna of the San Gabriel Valley. Rangers and docents lead a variety of guided hikes.

California Institute of Technology

111 B2

1200 E. California Blvd., Pasadena

626/395-6811

www.caltech.edu

Zen garden to the house, where the zigzag bridge affords a rare Western insight into the spare, asymmetrical aesthetic of Japan.

Another must, particularly in spring when it is in flower, is the peach tree and stone pagoda in the canyon of the Japanese Garden proper. Intrepid strollers will also delight in the **Australian and Desert Gardens,** as well as the **Chinese Garden,** opened in February 2008 with 12 acres (4.8 ha)–the largest such garden outside of China–and a lake.

Caltech

Long synonymous with technological prowess, the California Institute of Technology produced some of the 20th century's biggest scientific breakthroughs. This was where, in the 1930s (while a fuzzy-haired fellow named Einstein rode around the campus on an old bicycle), Theodore Von Karmen pioneered the mathematical principles of aeronautics and where the Richter system for measuring earthquakes was developed. More recently, the subatomic particle dubbed the quark was discovered here. That the grounds should be such a marvelous repository of architectural finds makes them all the more worth a visit, perhaps on a Saturday afternoon between visits to the Gamble House and Pasadena's Old Town (see pp. 111–113).

Caltech originated as a vocational school in the late 19th century. It evolved along a master plan by the great architect Bertram Grosvenor Goodhue, who went on to do such memorable projects as the L.A. Public Library (see p. 98) and San Diego's Balboa Park (see pp. 152–156). Goodhue envisioned a dual-axis campus with portals, cypresses, and a central pool–something of the effect of the one leading to the Taj Mahal in India. Certainly Goodhue was into Spanish Renaissance, as indicated by his floral volutes and sculptured shells around the entry to the **Parsons-Gates Hall of**

Administration. Two remaining structures by Goodhue are the **Bridge Laboratory of Physics** and the High Voltage Research Laboratory (now called the **Sloan Laboratory**). Both of these structures have been modified, but close inspection reveals many of the signature Goodhue touches: vaulted ceilings, water fountains, large expanses of plain exterior wall punctuated by regular patterns of windows. In fact, architectural detail plays a huge role in maintaining the campus's muted religious bearing, as in the old Alexander Calder sculptures preserved in the current facade of the **Beckman Laboratory of Chemical Synthesis.**

Campus social life centers on the **Athenaeum,** built in 1930 by British architect Gordon Kaufman. Again, a kind of eclectic Mediterranean style reigns. The **Beckman Institute** maintains the **Caltech Science Museum** *(tel 626/395-6520, open by appt. only)* devoted to Caltech alumnus Arnold O. Beckman, a pioneer of scientific instrumentation, including a re-creation of the chemistry lab when he was a student. The college offers talks by visiting scholars, plus regular musical and cultural events *(tel 626/395-4652).*

Mission San Gabriel Arcángel

Founded by Spanish Franciscans in 1771 as the fourth in a chain of 21 California missions, Mission San Gabriel Arcángel has a rich heritage. It was from here that Gobernador Felipe

(continued on p. 126)

Mission San Gabriel Arcángel

- 111 B2
- 428 S. Mission Dr., San Gabriel
- 626/457-3048

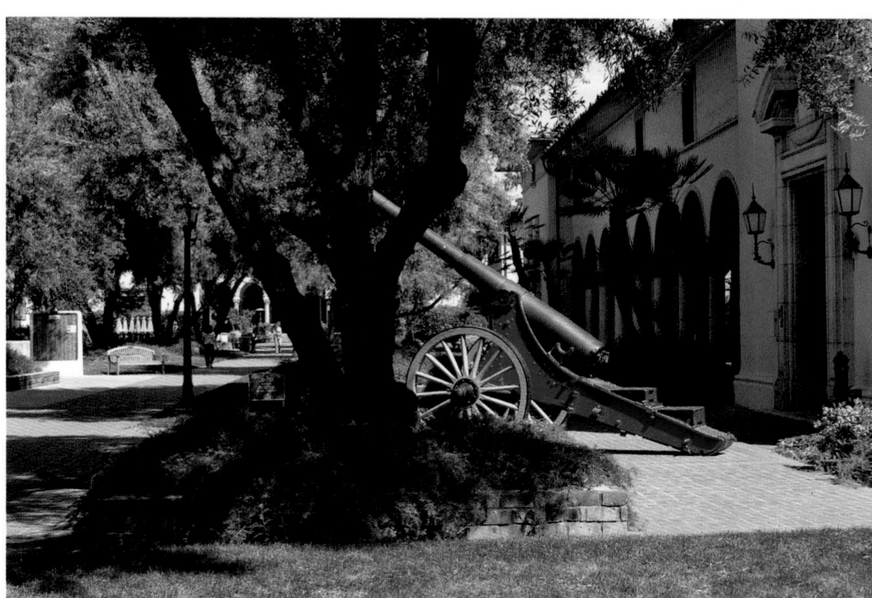

Following World War II, Caltech's expanding campus became a microcosm of architectural styles.

Monterey Park

For travelers who consider food a destination in itself, the four-city area of Monterey Park, Alhambra, San Gabriel, and Rosemead may well be heaven. This part of the San Gabriel Valley, known as Monterey Park, is home to L.A.'s burgeoning Asian populations, many of whom come from Taiwan, Hong Kong, mainland China, and Vietnam. The result, as the august *Atlantic Monthly* pronounced, is that the "best Chinese food in the world is now being served in Los Angeles's new Sino-suburbs."

Chinese Americans celebrate the new year at one of Monterey Park's must-dine restaurants.

It was not always thus. Until the mid-1970s, Monterey Park was just another of southern California's largely Anglo middle-class suburbs, where adventurous eating began and ended at the local taco house. Beginning in the early 1970s, however, a few Chinese immigrants began promoting the area's real estate in overseas Chinese newspapers. Loosened immigration laws made sales easier, and Hong Kong's imminent return to the People's Republic of China increased the heat on the middle class to move. By the mid-1980s, Monterey Park was 60 percent Asian, a booming Chinese-American suburbia with its own supermarkets, banks, and restaurants.

Travelers take note: This is not the Chinese food of your youth. While elements of the old "sweet-and-sour pork" menu remain, by and large this is the cooking of modern China, highly regional and very fresh. This means you must remain open-minded and willing to ask questions. While their employees may occasionally struggle with the vexing English language, most shops will have someone fluent enough to answer basic questions. But the watchword is *experiment*, rather than ordering as though you were taking a legal deposition.

Unless you are into bird's-nest soup and platypus beaks, the food here is inexpensive, so try several different dishes.

Ready? To get the full range of the experience, start at **San Gabriel Square,** once a drive-in theater and now lined with restaurants and dubbed the Great Mall of China. A good introduction to Taiwanese cuisine can be found here at **Happy Family** *(140 W. Valley Blvd., tel 626/282-8986),* where L.A. food guru Jonathan Gold recommends the pan-fried string beans and the home-style tofu. The less adventurous can try any of the fish and seafood entrées, and the spicy eggplant is memorable.

Farther down Valley Boulevard, directly across from the Red Rose nightclub, is one of many smaller plazas; in it is **Mei Long Village** *(301 W. Valley Blvd., San Gabriel, tel 626/284-4769).* Presided over by its businesslike but congenial owner, the restaurant is usually packed with Chinese families and the occasional Caucasian foodie. Order the crab dim sum for starters. Now order another—they're that good. The stir-fried pea greens are a must, as is the pièce de résistance, a huge piece of the most delicious pork, rather uncharmingly named Pork Pump.

Now try something different—perhaps at **Jazz Cat Café** *(1281 E. Valley Blvd., San Gabriel, tel 626/288-5200),* a hip Asian fusion eatery that specializes in a range of souplike dishes, including Japanese shabu-shabu, Chinese hot pots, and herbal broths.

Duck across the street to the **Hawaii Supermarket,** where the exotic stock runs a broad gamut from seaweed and sake to bok choy, pork feet, mung beans, and dried udon noodles. Five blocks east, stop in at the **Saigon Sandwich & Bakery** *(718 E. Valley Blvd., San Gabriel, tel 636/288-6475),* one of colonial France's few contributions to the culinary world. This is the place to buy perfect, fresh-baked baguettes (crunchy exteriors and cloud-soft innards) and Vietnamese *bahn mi* sandwiches with fresh veggies and jalapeños, and the flan is delicious. Buy three sandwiches and get a free baguette.

The ultimate, and slightly more pricey, seafood meal can be had at **Empress Harbor Seafood** *(111 N. Atlantic Blvd., tel 626/300-8833).* Here the food is so fresh that it prompted the following passage from food critic Gold: "We had an almost perfect Chinese meal here. First there were giant prawns, fished out of the tank one by one with a net, tossed thrashing into a bucket. Then, a few seconds later, shrimp, steamed, the flesh of the banana-sized creatures sweet and firm. Next, a live lobster, which splashed everyone at the table when it was scooped from the tank." You get the idea. Now get going!

EXPERIENCE: Chinatown Summer Nights

Visit L.A.'s Chinatown in July and August when the area bursts into life during Chinatown Summer Nights ***(Central & West Plazas, 943–951 N. Broadway, Los Angeles, tel 213/680-0243, www.chinatownsummernights.com).*** **You'll experience three lively evenings of food, live music, and art. This free outdoor celebration lets you enjoy cooking competitions, live music performed by local bands, art displays, and video projections. Kids will enjoy the colorful Chinese cultural activities on offer. Kick up your heels on the large outdoor dance floor to music spun by local DJs, or relax in the craft beer garden. Just be sure to bring a good appetite; local food trucks and Chinatown's excellent restaurants provide an exotic array of choices.**

Events take place from 5 p.m. to midnight. If you're taking the Los Angeles Metro, take the Gold Line and exit at the Chinatown station. Check the website for dates and a map.

Angeles National Forest

111 B3–C3 &52 D4–53 E4

Visitor Information

Big Pines Information Center, Angeles Crest Hwy. (Hwy. 2), Wrightwood

626/574-1613

Closed Tues.–Thurs.

www.fs.usda.gov/angeles

de Neve led a party of soldiers and settlers in 1781 to establish El Pueblo de Nuestra Señora la Reina de los Angeles. It was from this mission (once dubbed San Gabriel de los Tremblores for the area's earthquakes) that the padres ruled more than 1.5 million acres (607,000 ha) of farmland, making them a formidable economic power.

Like all the other missions, secularization in 1833, and subsequent Americanization, led to San Gabriel's decline. For the past century, it has been subject to restoration efforts, the latest in 1996.

EXPERIENCE: Mountain High Thrills

Perched at 6,000 feet in the San Gabriel Mountains, Wrightwood *(map p. 53 E4)* is the most popular ski and snowboard resort in southern California. Located just west of town, Mountain High Resort *(tel 888/754-7878, www.mthigh.com)* comprises three distinct snow zones, with beginner, intermediate, and advanced pistes and terrain served by 14 lifts. The snow season generally runs early November to late April, with night skiing five times a week. Mountain High also offers ski and snowboard classes for children, adults, and seniors. During summer, hiking, mountain biking, and adventure zip lines take over the Wrightwood slopes.

What remains of the original church has been carefully restored. The main chamber consists of a simple rectangular vault with an **altar** of Spanish design. The colorful **sculptures** of various saints, one donated by Queen Maria in 1773, are in remarkably good condition. The **capped buttresses** of the belfry underscore a decidedly Moorish subtext to San Gabriel. Scholars have noted its resemblance to the cathedral of Córdoba, birthplace of Padre Antonio Cruzado, who is credited with building the mission.

As with many of the missions, the surrounding grounds and cemetery provide ample opportunity to ponder the mixed legacy of Spanish colonization. Underneath are said to be the remains of some 5,000 Gabrieleño Indians.

Around the Foothills

Looming above the foothills and stretching from the San Fernando Valley east to San Bernardino is **Angeles National Forest.** This 650,000-acre (263,045 ha) area features hiking trails, picnic sites, and ski areas. Devastating fires often blaze through the forests, as in 2009.

At the old **Mount Wilson Observatory** *(map p. 111 C3, tel 310/476-4413, www.mtwilson.edu, open April–Nov.)*, you can see the telescope used by generations of Caltech scientists to probe the mysteries of space or watch the hang gliders jump off the cliff and sail home to Altadena below. The **Charlton Flat** picnic area, farther up, is a prime spot for bird-watching. Still farther on, at **Jarvi Memorial Vista,** watch for bighorn sheep.

Back down the mountain, a worthwhile side trip to the west is to **Mission San Fernando** *(map p. 52 C3, 15151 San Fernando*

Mission Blvd., Mission Hills, tel 818/361-0186). Founded by Padre Fermín Lasuén in 1797, this mission served early L.A. in much the same way as its counterpart in San Gabriel, by providing the new pueblo with food, clothing, and fuel. Lasuén was a masterful inculcator of the faith, and by 1819 San Fernando had a neophyte population of more than a thousand.

The fully restored chapel is worth viewing for its Indian and Spanish colors and ornamentation. The wide, tiled walkways under the mission loggia are a pleasure to stroll, particularly on a hot, dry summer day when the stillness encourages contemplation.

On the way back from the mission, everyone interested in the flora of the Southwest should visit the **Theodore Payne Foundation,** a shrine to native California botany that is a must for those wishing to buy Californian plants. In spring, the 23 acres (9.3 ha) are ablaze with wildflowers.

Driving back into Pasadena on I-210, you will pass the exit for the **Jet Propulsion Laboratory** *(map p. 111 B3, 4800 Oak Grove Dr., tel 818/354-4321 or 818/354-9314, www.jpl.nasa.gov).* You need to make reservations at least a month in advance in order to visit this wonderland of real space pioneering. It was from here that NASA explored the solar system with missions ranging from the first *Explorer* to the latest *Sojourner*.

The road farther eastward (I-210) is dotted with small, down-home towns full of yesteryear

Theodore Payne Foundation

- Map: 52 C3
- Address: 10459 Tuxford St., Sun Valley
- Tel: 818/768-1802
- Hours: Closed Sun.–Mon. mid-Oct.–June & Sun.–Wed. July–mid-Oct.

www.theodore payne.org

Mount Wilson Observatory's 60-inch (1.5 m) telescope is among the world's largest.

The sun rises over Big Bear Lake, 25 miles (40 km) northeast of San Bernardino.

charm. A stop in the town of **Monrovia** (Myrtle exit; *www.ci.monrovia.ca.us*) finds clusters of inexpensive antique stores. The quaint college town of **Claremont** *(map p. 53 E3, www.ci.claremont.ca.us)*, a 20-minute drive farther east, has a New England feel and several artistic and architectural places of pilgrimage, from Myron Hunt's Bridges Hall of Music at **Pomona College** *(map p. 53 E3, N. College Way, tel 909/621-8000, www.pomona.edu)* to the first mural painted in the U.S. by José Orozco, at the school's Frary Hall.

It is an hour-long drive to the city of **Riverside** *(map p. 53 F2, www.riversideca.gov)*, where the restored **Mission Inn** *(3649 Mission Inn Ave., tel 951/784-0300, www.missioninn.com)* is a prime example of blended Mexican and Spanish architectural styles, with ornate loggias and fountains.

The **San Bernardino National Forest** *(map p. 53 G3, tel 909/382-2600, www.fs.usda.gov/sbnf)* is an everlastingly popular vacation destination. In the 1920s, such stars as Charlie Chaplin made **Lake Arrowhead** the resort destination of preference. Now it is home to numerous mountain water-sports outfits in the summer and skiing in the winter.

The particularly scenic **Bluff Meadow,** at the end of **Champion Lodgepole Pine Trail,** can be found south of neighboring **Big Bear Lake** *(tel 800/424-4232, www.bigbearinfo.com)*, where you can see bald eagles during the winter months.

Good for biking and hiking in summer, Big Bear wears a snowy shawl for much of winter, drawing skiers and snowboarders to **Big Bear Mountain Resorts** *(tel 909/866-5766, www.bigbearmountainresorts.com)*, offering southern California's premier ski runs. ■

Balmy evening breezes and azure blue skies, plus San Diego's Balboa Park and the fine architecture and good food of Santa Barbara

Southern California

Palm trees in Heisler Park, Laguna Beach

Southern California

Despite occasional efforts to repackage its name into something more memorable (or marketable), "Southern California" remains the moniker of choice for the vast region unfolding south from the Tehachapi Mountains to the Mexican border.

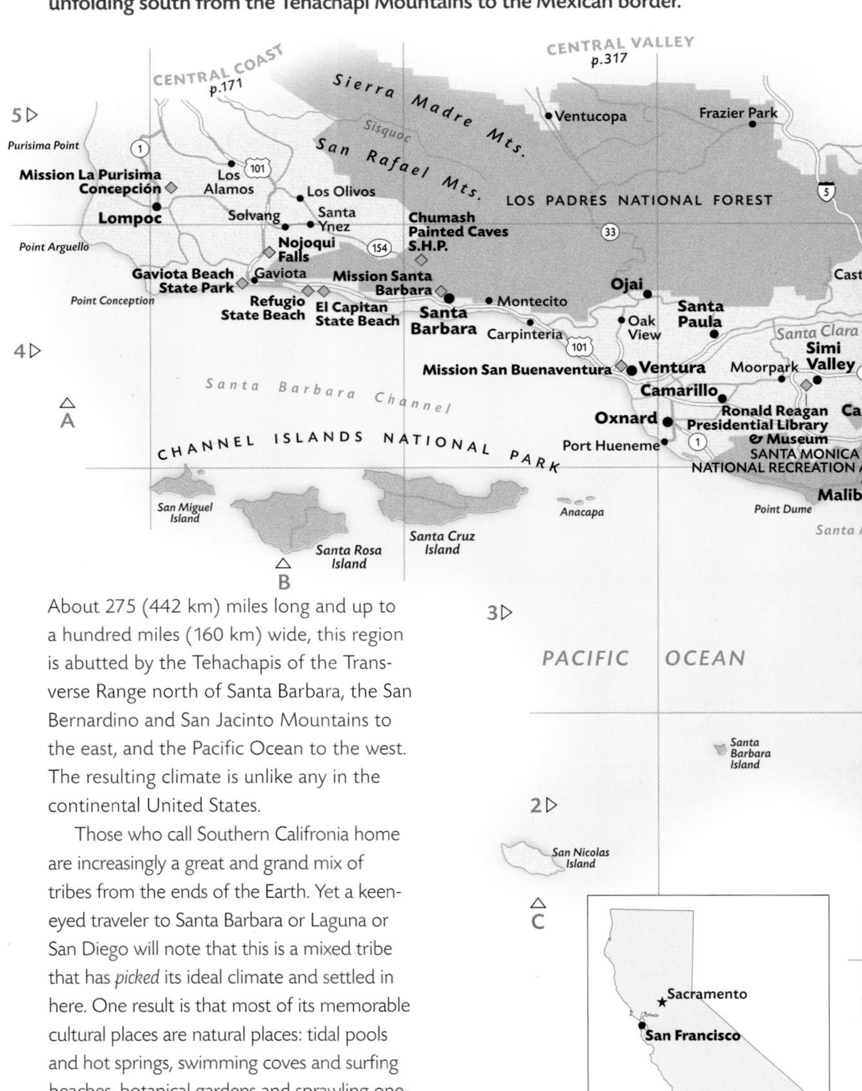

About 275 (442 km) miles long and up to a hundred miles (160 km) wide, this region is abutted by the Tehachapis of the Transverse Range north of Santa Barbara, the San Bernardino and San Jacinto Mountains to the east, and the Pacific Ocean to the west. The resulting climate is unlike any in the continental United States.

Those who call Southern Califronia home are increasingly a great and grand mix of tribes from the ends of the Earth. Yet a keen-eyed traveler to Santa Barbara or Laguna or San Diego will note that this is a mixed tribe that has *picked* its ideal climate and settled in here. One result is that most of its memorable cultural places are natural places: tidal pools and hot springs, swimming coves and surfing beaches, botanical gardens and sprawling one-time ranchos. Is beach spelled with a capital "B" anywhere but in southern California?

The beaches to the south, from Long Beach to San Diego, are nirvana to sun worshippers the world over; inland are theme parks galore (Disneyland, Knott's Berry Farm), a new wine country (Temecula), and several great art and culture palaces. The beaches to the north, from Santa Barbara on, are cooler, more urbane places to stroll and explore. If you can tear yourself away from these beaches, inland you will discover still another new wine country, lots of horses, and a bucolic little gem of a place called Ojai, where the intrepid might find the roots of the region's vaunted new spirituality. ■

NOT TO BE MISSED:

The original Magic Kingdom and the revamped Disney California Adventure **134–138**

Posh seaside living in Laguna and Newport Beaches **140–143**

Balboa Park's eclectic museums and world-famous zoo **152–158**

San Diego's historic waterfront and Cabrillo National Monument **158–160**

Shamu, sharks, and sea lions at SeaWorld **160–161**

Santa Barbara's Spanish mission and charming city center **163–166**

The wide open spaces of Channel Islands National Park **170**

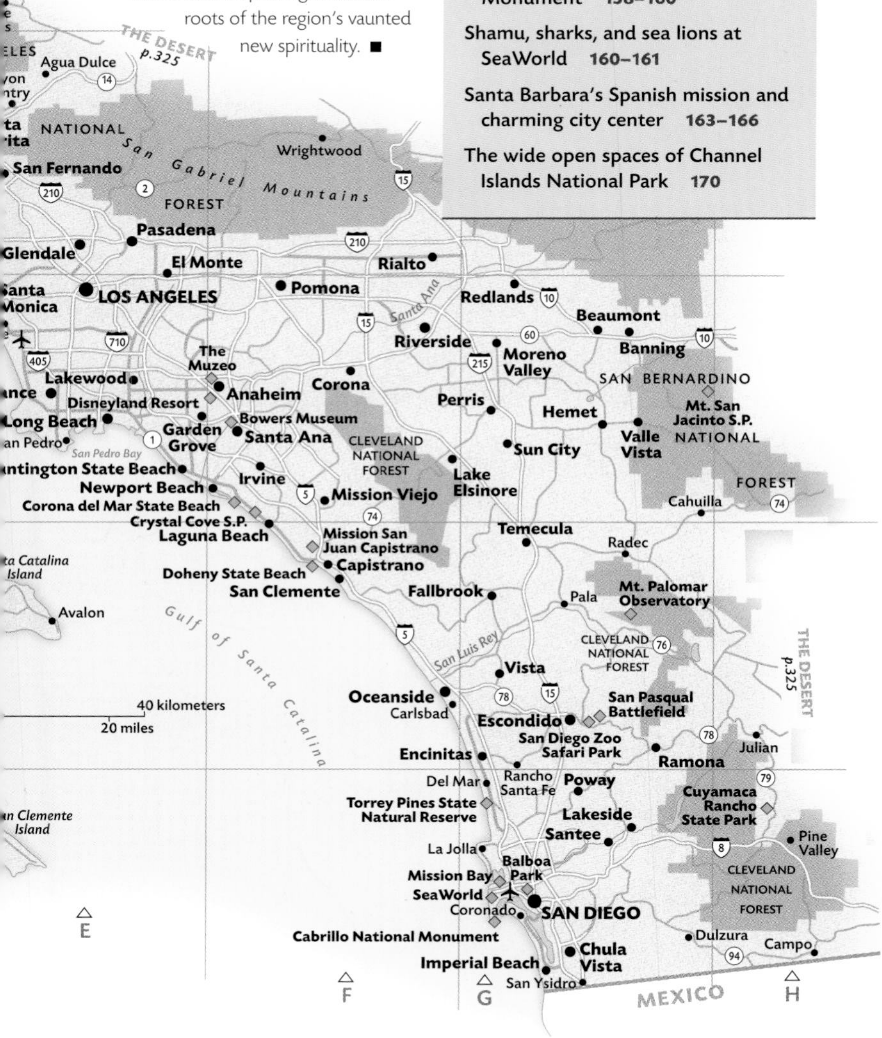

Long Beach & Around

Situated on the 8-mile (13 km) coastline of San Pedro Bay, Long Beach has always been in the shadow of Los Angeles, its more glamorous sister to the north. In recent years, however, Long Beach has resuscitated itself. It now claims one of the best ports in the world, a high quality of life, and several worthwhile attractions for visitors. At its hub is the multibillion-dollar Pike at Rainbow Harbor project, the largest seaside development in California history.

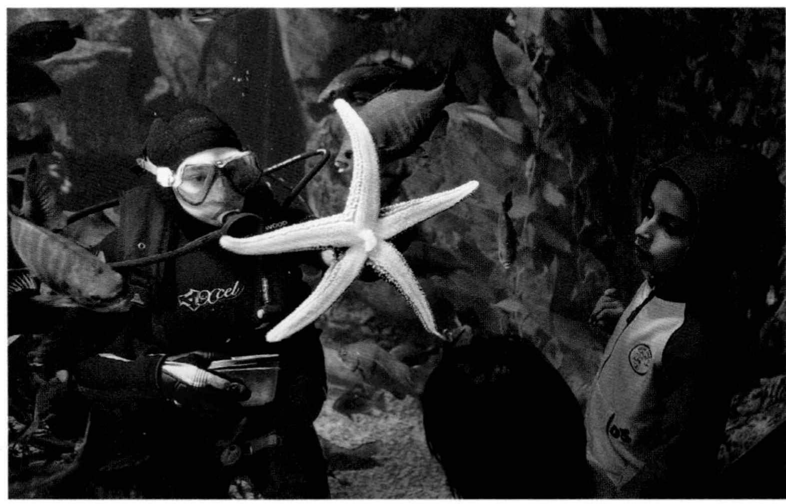

Feeding time at the Aquarium of the Pacific

Long Beach
131 E3

Visitor Information

Long Beach Convention & Entertainment Center, 300 E. Ocean Blvd., #1900, Long Beach

562/436-3645, 800/452-7829

www.visitlongbeach.com

The outstanding **Aquarium of the Pacific** *(100 Aquarium Way, tel 562/590-3100, www.aquariumofpacific.org, $$$$$)*, one of the country's largest, displays 11,000 marine creatures in 19 major habitats. The vast **Shark Lagoon** is worth the visit alone. Opened in 2011, the **Arctic & Antarctic exhibit** unveils how climate change is threatening those fragile ecosystems. Among the wildlife on display are polar fish, red crabs, and arctic foxes as well as a sea jelly touch tank. Also new is the **Ocean Science Center,** which uses high-tech "Science on a Sphere" technology to explore the planet and spin stories about ocean phenomena and their impact.

From the aquarium entrance, catch the AquaBus to Long Beach's other big attraction, the ***Queen Mary*** *(1126 Queens Hwy., tel 877/342-0738, www.queenmary.com, $$$$)*. This imperious ocean liner, launched in 1936, has been restored to its art deco glory. Admission includes a shipwalk tour and access to such special exhibits as "Russian Cold War Submarine *Scorpion*."

For shopping or dining, return downtown to **Pine Avenue,** where Melrose meets the Pacific. Or visit the **Long Beach Museum of Art** *(2300 E. Ocean Blvd., tel 562/439-2119, www.lbma.org, closed Mon.–Wed., $$, free Thurs. p.m. & Fri.).* This little jewel, located in a historic house overlooking the ocean, presents exquisitely curated shows on Western artists.

Also in Long Beach is the **Museum of Latin American Art** *(628 Alamitos Ave., tel 562/437-1689, www.molaa.com, closed Mon.–Tues., $$),* which focuses on local Latino artists. Many of them draw inspiration from David Siquieros (see sidebar p. 93), who painted in the Los Angeles area in the 1930s, and José Orozco.

San Pedro

Once the hub of maritime culture in the Los Angeles area, San Pedro is now filled with quaint shops and seafood cafés. Worth a visit is the **Cabrillo Marine Aquarium,** focusing on local marine life. During nighttime high tides between March and August, the museum leads guided viewings of the grunion runs, when millions of small fish land on local beaches, burrow into the sand to mate, and then retreat to die in local waters.

Catalina Island

Situated 22 miles (35 km) offshore, and once favored by famous figures like gum magnate William Wrigley, this rugged island is lapped by pristine waters abounding in marine life. Ashore, explore the 42,000-acre (16,996 ha) **Catalina Island Conservancy** *(tel 310/510-1445, www.catalinaconservancy.org),* home to fox, buffalo, and bald eagles, as well as a botanical garden. The art deco Casino Building houses the **Catalina Island Museum** *(tel 310/510-2414, www.catalinamuseum.org),* which has an outstanding archaeological collection. ■

San Pedro

131 E3

Visitor Information

- San Pedro Convention & Visitor Bureau, 510 W. 7th St., San Pedro
- 310/729-9828

www.spcvb.com

Cabrillo Marine Aquarium

- 3720 Stephen White Dr., San Pedro
- 310/548-7562
- Closed Mon. & Tues.–Fri. a.m.
- $$ ($ suggested donation)

www.cabrilloaq.org

Catalina Island

131 E2

Visitor Information

- Visitors Bureau, #1 Green Pleasure Pier, Avalon
- 310/510-1520

www.catalina.com

EXPERIENCE: The Crossing to Catalina

Getting to Catalina Island from the mainland is usually half the fun, especially on one of those crystal-clear southern California days when you have the snowcapped mountains on one side and the endless Pacific on the other. Dolphins are frequent companions, and it's not uncommon for travelers to spot gray, humpback, or finback whales during the hour-plus crossing.

Ferries depart from five different ports along the Los Angeles/Orange County coast. **Catalina Express** *(tel 800/481-3470, www.catalinaexpress.com, $$$$$,)* runs boats from downtown Long Beach, San Pedro, and Dana Point to Avalon town and Two Harbors village at the north end of Catalina. The most convenient service from L.A.'s west side is **Catalina Ferries** *(tel 310/305-7250, www.catalinaferries.com, $$$$$),* which uses high-speed catamarans. The only service from Newport Beach is the **Catalina Flyer** *(tel 800/830-7744, www.catalinainfo.com, $$$$$).* Short on time? Opt for a helicopter crossing between Long Beach and Avalon with **Island Express** *(tel 800/228-2566, www.islandexpress.com, $$$$$).*

Disneyland Resort

For many travelers the principal destination in southern California, Disneyland has been the subject of so many interpretive essays in recent years that one might think that the Happiest Place on Earth, founded in 1955, had lost its happy sense of innocence and wonder. Nothing could be further from the truth. People keep coming in record numbers, spending tons of cash, and feeling happy, happy, happy!

Walk through the gate of Sleeping Beauty Castle, the oldest Disney castle, and step into a fairy tale.

Disneyland Resort

- Map: 131 F3
- Address: 1313 Harbor Blvd., Anaheim
- Phone: 714/781-4565, 714/781-4400 (tickets only)
- Price: $$$$$ (children under 3 free)

www.disneyland.com

Disneyland Resort is a 500-acre (202 ha) park comprising Disneyland Park and Disney California Adventure.

Disneyland Park

Disneyland Park is organized into eight themed "lands."

Main Street, U.S.A.: This section of the park is organized as a typical American burg of around 1890. Favorite attractions here are the various coin-operated games and **Great Moments with Mr. Lincoln,** in which an Audio-Animatronic Abe delivers his greatest oratory. The experience proves moving, even to Nintendo-jaded teens. While you are on Main Street, be certain to take in one of the park's many elaborate

The Battle Plan

There are ways to maximize your enjoyment and minimize your discomfort during a visit to Disneyland Resort. First, the night before you go, get an idea of what your family absolutely must see in the park. The company's website is quite helpful, with maps, hotel and food information, and a list of rides scheduled to "go dark" for service and cleaning.

Then think about what you want to eat—you can't bring food in with you, so consider a hearty breakfast at one of Anaheim's local eateries before entering the park, preferably as early as possible. Food in Disneyland is not bad, but not great either. You may want to make sure you will have a decent dinner by employing one park fanatic's plan: "Whenever we go, we make an immediate beeline for the Blue Bayou Restaurant in New Orleans Square and make a reservation for later that day," she says. "It is the most comfortable, appetizing, sit-down eating place in the park, and you can't beat it after eight hours on your feet."

Another strategy is to take in the park's live attractions, shopping, and dining during the day, saving the more popular—and more crowded—rides for the cooler nights, when they are generally less crowded.

Lastly, there are now a number of specialized guidebooks to the park for families with small children.

parades; at night, they end with a memorable fireworks show.

Adventureland: This was once considered one of the park's quieter sections, dominated by such low-tech attractions as the **Enchanted Tiki Room** and the **Jungle Cruise.** But Adventureland's character was revved up with the addition of the ultrafast **Indiana Jones Adventure,** which has some of the most consistently long lines in the park. Late evening may be the best time for this popular attraction.

Fantasyland: This section of the park enchants with **Sleeping Beauty Castle, Peter Pan's Flights,** and **Snow White's Scary Adventures,** while **Mr. Toad's Wild Ride** is well attended by teenagers and even young adults. For children, two must-rides are **It's a Small World,** the theme song of which you will memorize, and **Dumbo the Flying Elephant.** More ambitious is the fast and wet **Matterhorn Bobsleds**. A word of warning: Don't ride too soon after eating.

Tomorrowland: Walt Disney's idea of the future, Tomorrowland puts the emphasis on action, though there are still some attempts at education. **Innoventions,** for example, has guests board a slowly rotating "loading pod," where they are introduced to the exhibits in five thematic areas: transportation, health and sports, home, work and school, and entertainment. Guests are then free to play with hundreds of hands-on displays of new products and technologies.

The **Autopia**—where a second generation of supercharged cars hits the street—is best seen as a mechanized rendition of Disney cartoon characters.

The **Finding Nemo Submarine Voyage** is an underwater adventure. Hop aboard the submarine to experience a sub-shaking volcanic eruption and explore coral reefs while Nemo and his fishy friends go along for the ride thanks to a futuristic projection technology.

Critter Country: One of the newer sections of Disneyland, Critter Country has a slower pace and gentler entertainments that make it perfect for tots and burned-out parents. The **Many Adventures of Winnie the Pooh** fun ride for honey is one highlight here. Another is the more action-oriented **Splash Mountain,** a highly recommended ride in the form of a superslick log flume. You can get wet on this ride.

Frontierland: Frontierland is one of the more traditional sections of the park, with attractions like the **Mark Twain Riverboat,** the **Pirate's Lair on Tom Sawyer Island,** and the **Frontierland Shootin' Exposition** show.

A classic park showcase for special effects as well as new and old Disney characters, **Fantasmic!** takes the viewer on a trip "through Mickey's imagination" along the many rivers of America. If you become bored by such fare, wake yourself up with a ride on the **Big Thunder Mountain Railroad.**

New Orleans Square: Perhaps the most memorable ride in the park is **Pirates of the Caribbean,** found in lively New Orleans Square. "Pirate"

Downtown Disney District

Between the entrances to Disneyland Park and Disney California Adventure lies the Downtown Disney District, a lively promenade lined with shops, restaurants, and open-air cafés. In addition to a megaplex theater, entertainment possibilities include live gospel and other music performances at the **House of Blues,** jazz shows at **Ralph Brennan's Jazz Kitchen,** and the **ESPN Zone Sports Arena,** which offers dining plus games for kids of all ages. Professional musicians help stoke the party atmosphere outside with live performancces of everything from classical to blues.

The district charges no entry fee and is within walking distance of both theme parks. You can also take the Disneyland Monorail (see sidebar p. 138) or drive. Parking is free for the first three hours, or up to five hours with validation. The parking lot is located on Disneyland Drive, between the Mickey & Friends Parking Structure and the Disneyland Hotel.

And if you need a place to rest your head after all this excitement, consider the **Grand Californian Hotel & Spa,** a 751-room deluxe hotel built in the Arts and Crafts style.

Board the Indiana Jones Adventure for a trip inside the mysterious Temple of the Forbidden Eye.

guests ride on a "floating" boat that, after two hair-raising plunges, lands them in a pirate- and damsel-filled land of Audio-Animatronic boozers, wenches, and assorted ne'er-do-wells. The line moves quickly, but waits of an hour are not uncommon. The square is a good place to hop aboard one of four steam-powered locomotives that tour the park.

Mickey's Toontown: A three-dimensional cartoon world, Mickey's Toontown benefits from new technologies and a younger, more aesthetically sophisticated group of designers and architects. **Roger Rabbit's Car Toon Spin** is an old-fashioned pod ride in the tradition of Mr. Toad; guests can spin their vehicles as they career through various cartoon worlds. Other attractions here include **Goofy's Play House, Donald Duck's Boat,** the **Chip 'n' Dale Treehouse,** and **Gadget's Go Coaster.**

INSIDER TIP:

If you plan to visit both Disney parks, purchase a Park Hopper ticket, which will save you money on the cost of admission.

—JOE YOGERST
National Geographic author

Disney California Advenure Park

Visitors to Disneyland Resort can also choose Disney

California Adventure Park. According to Barry Braverman, its producer, the idea behind this attraction is to "immerse guests in compelling stories, evocative places, and fantastic adventures that will bring the California dream to life." This it does through a series of elaborately themed California districts—from beach to deserts to mountains—that capture northern, central, and southern California on 55 acres (22 ha).

One ride, **Soarin' Over California,** allows guests to virtually "soar" on hang gliders over a re-creation of Yosemite National Park. Another attraction conjures up the "Hollywood of the imagination." **The Twilight Zone Tower of Terror,** will make your hair stand up. The setting is the once-glamorous Hollywood Tower Hotel, now vacant and full of "ghastly ghostly guests." Adrenalin junkies experience a fright night as lightning strikes and you are plunged 13 stories down an abandoned elevator shaft into the "most thrilling recesses of the Twilight Zone."

California Adventure got an extreme makeover in 2012 that included a new entrance plaza called **Buena Vista Street** (based on 1920s Los Angeles) and several new attractions. Foremost among these is **Cars Land,** with rides like **Radiator Springs Racers** and **Mater's Junkyard Jamboree** based on the animated movie series.

Also new is an after-dark multimedia spectacular called **World of Color** and **The Little Mermaid–Ariel's Undersea Adventure,** where giant clamshells take visitors on a journey beneath the sea that features animatronics, immersive special effects, and the movie's well-known songs. ■

EXPERIENCE: Photograph Disneyland by Monorail

To capture the feel of the "old" park, take your camera with you on the Disneyland Monorail. The first of its kind in the U.S. when it opened in 1959, the environmentally friendly train runs on electricity and does not emit exhaust or other pollutants. Riding the monorail is free, but Disneyland admission is required. Board the train at the Tomorrowland station or in the Downtown Disney District (see sidebar p. 136). The ride circles the park in about 15 minutes, passing over the main entrance and affording wonderful aerial views of Fantasyland (see p. 135) and Tomorrowland (see pp. 135–136). Set your camera to pan focus or landscape mode, and be sure to get your hand stamped for reentry.

INSIDER TIP:

If visiting Disneyland around the holidays, check out the candy cane making at Candy Palace. It's very popular—be sure to get tickets ahead of time.

—MARCELLA PLEGGE
National Geographic contributor

Around Orange County

If you haven't run out of energy and money by the time you have finished with the Magic Kingdom, you may want to explore some of Orange County's other attractions.

With a mission to preserve, study, and exhibit the fine arts of the Americas, Africa, and the Pacific Rim, the **Bowers Museum** *(2002 N. Main St., Santa Ana, tel 714/567-3600, www.bowers.org, closed Mon., $$, free 1st Sun. of month)* turns a fine curatorial eye on everything from late 18th-century Mexican copper brandy stills to funerary ritual objects from New Guinea.

If you need some non-Disney inspiration, head to the remarkable **Crystal Cathedral** *(12141 Lewis St., Garden Grove, tel 714/971-4013, www.crystalcathedral.org, closed Sun. except services)*, built for Rev. Robert Schuller, who started here 30 years ago. If you need a dose of reality, however, the fascinating **Richard Nixon Presidential Library & Birthplace** *(18001 Yorba Linda Blvd., Yorba Linda, tel 714/993-5075, www.nixonlibrary.org, $$)* has galleries on Nixon's life, world leaders, and the Berlin Wall, as well as Pat Nixon's rose garden with the tiny house where the President was born.

In downtown Anaheim, **The Muzeo** *(241 S. Anaheim Blvd., tel 714/956-8936, www.muzeo.org, $$$)* cultural center, art gallery, and museum for world-class traveling exhibitions opened in 2007 with a lavish exposition on Imperial Rome.

Angel Stadium in Anaheim is home field to the Los Angeles Angels, one of the top Major League Baseball teams in recent years. Across the freeway is the **Honda Center** *(www.hondacenter.com)*, which hosts major concerts and the Anaheim Ducks of the National Hockey League. ■

The Crystal Cathedral gleams with 10,000 panes of glass.

Knott's Berry Farm

Disneyland (see pp. 134–138) may get most of the publicity, but Orange County's first theme park was **Knott's Berry Farm** *(8039 Beach Blvd., Buena Park, tel 714/220-5200, www.knotts.com, $$$$$)*. The kernel for today's modern park took root in the 1920s when Walter and Cornelia Knott began adding onto their berry farm, starting with a fried chicken restaurant and Wild West ghost town with stagecoach rides and gunslinger shows. These original attractions remain, but Knotts is better known today for its thrill rides, plus a **Soak City** *(www.soakcityoc.com)* water park that's open only in summer.

Laguna Beach

Homesteaded by Mormons in the 1870s and developed as an artists' retreat and resort town in the early 1900s, Laguna Beach has long proven irresistible to both visitors and natives seeking respite from inland heat and noise. All crisp sea air and primal canyonland, its geography holds a clue to why.

The town of Laguna Beach is fronted by a series of stunning coves with waters sometimes shimmering a light blue and sometimes brooding, nearly purple. Rising from the coves are a series of sculpted cliffs, which give way to a small basin flat enough for what many have called "a permanent village." Looming behind that are the *cañons de los lagunas*, or canyons of the lakes.

Laguna Beach offers Orange County residents a thriving beach and arts culture.

Water, sand, canyon. Such are the features that attracted California's plein air painters, many of whom set up here in the early 1900s. Although the Hollywood crowd soon followed, Laguna Beach has always retained a strong identification with the arts, as represented by its **Pageant of the Masters** *(tel 949/494-1145 or 800/487-3378, www.foapom.com)*, a live staging of masterpieces from Tiepolo to Toulouse-Lautrec.

The modern visitor might begin an exploration of the coves at any number of Laguna's beaches. **Main Beach,** situated at the foot of Laguna Canyon Road, is the epicenter of the city's beach culture, with a thriving volleyball and skateboarding scene. Its waters are often calm enough for a pleasant swim. Main Beach is also within walking distance of downtown Laguna Beach, fine for strolling and shopping in the summer months.

A more tranquil beach experience can be had by driving about a mile (1.6 km) north of Main Beach to **Crescent Bay.** This aptly named stretch of sand is known for its great body-surfing waves and ample sunning areas. The tidal pools to its north are easily explored (take some old tennis shoes), and on a good day visitors may see the rare red sea anemone, sometimes bigger than a baseball glove. The more aquatically skilled can rent snorkeling or scuba equipment and swim out to **Seal Rock,** a protected sanctuary for the honking, boisterous California sea lion. The beds of giant sea kelp around the rock are particularly mesmerizing when viewed through a diving mask.

INSIDER TIP:

The annual Sawdust Art & Craft Festival *(www.sawdustfestival.org)*, where you can see and buy the work of more than 200 Laguna Beach artists, is a summer must.

—MARY STEPHANOS
National Geographic contributor

The unique ecology of Laguna's cliffs is the focus of the relatively new **Crystal Cove State Park,** to the north off the Pacific Coast Highway. Situated on onetime cattle-grazing land, with 3.2 miles (5.1 km) of beach, the park has undergone extensive vegetation with native plants. An extended boardwalk takes guests through the park and onto the beach below, and it serves as an educational nature trail. You may spot red-tailed hawks and northern harriers swirling above; below, roadrunners career about. Down on the beach, explore **Reef Point** for more tide-pooling adventures.

One benefit of a disastrous 1992 fire that ravaged Laguna's canyons was the creation of the 7,000-acre (2,832 ha) **Laguna Coast Wilderness Park.** Two walks justify taking the trouble to make a reservation. The first is the 3.5-mile (5.6 km) **Laurel Canyon Nature Trail,** its air perfumed with wild sage and sycamore, its undulating rockscape as dramatic today as it was in the early 20th century, when such painters as Guy Rose and Norman St. Clair depicted the area in their plein air canvases.

Farther up Laguna Canyon Road, past groves of old eucalyptus trees, is the **James Dilley Greenbelt Preserve.** Visitors follow a trail around a landscape of bulrushes, prickly pear, hemlock, and sycamores. Egrets and ospreys are common in the main lake to the north (known as Lake Number One).

Just north of the Inn at Laguna Beach (the preferred vacation residence) is **Gallery Row,** on North Coast Highway. The work of many local painters, some doing a form of neo-plein air painting, is worth a look; prices are reasonable for good living room art. Some of the originals that inspired this work can be seen at the **Laguna Art Museum.** The delight of seeing William Wendt's original of "Spring in the Canyon" is just one thing that makes a visit here worthwhile. ■

Laguna Beach
Map: 131 F2
Visitor Information
Address: Laguna Beach Visitors Center, 252 Broadway St., Laguna Beach
Phone: 949/497-9229
www.lagunabeachinfo.com

Crystal Cove State Park
Map: 131 F3
Address: N. of Laguna Beach off Pacific Coast Hwy. (Calif. 1)
Phone: 949/494-3539, 949/497-7647 (interpretive walks)
Price: $$$
www.crystalcovestatepark.com

Laguna Coast Wilderness Park
Address: 18751 Laguna Canyon Rd. (near El Toro Rd.)
Phone: 949/923-2235, 949/923-3702
Price: $
www.ocparks.com/lagunacoast

Laguna Art Museum
Address: 307 Cliff Dr.
Phone: 949/494-8971
Price: $$$
www.lagunaartmuseum.org

Beach Cities

North and south of Laguna Beach, a string of beach cities edges the coast and offers the casual visitor an extreme close-up of the southern California surfing scene. On virtually any morning, the earlier the better, you can watch the practice sessions of some of the world's most skilled wave riders. Later in the day, check out the surfwear shops, health food cafés, and seafood restaurants.

Surfers are rewarded with great waves near the pier, Huntington Beach.

Huntington State Beach

131 E3

Visitor Information

Headquarters, 17851 Pacific Coast Hwy., Huntington Beach

714/377-2481

www.parks.ca.gov

North of Laguna Beach

Huntington State Beach: South of central L.A., the wide, clean stretches of Huntington State Beach beckon sunseekers. Those interested in marine life can drive the few miles to **Bolsa Chica Ecological Reserve** *(3842 Warner Ave., tel 714/846-1114, www.bolsachica.org).* Here a 1.5-mile (2.4 km) trail leads around a tidal lagoon, where stingrays and least terns are among the wildlife. Overlooks provide vistas of the restored wetlands.

Newport Beach: Farther south is fast-paced, glamorous Newport Beach. The principal social activity here is boating, which takes place in the "largest small craft harbor in the world." Even for those who can't afford the $200 deck shoes (let alone the boat), **Newport Harbor** provides ample sun-filled entertainments, from the historic **Balboa Pavilion** to **ExplorOcean** *(600 E. Bay Ave., Newport Beach, tel 949/675-8915, www.nhnm .org, $),* which examines the past, present, and future of local and global maritime exploration.

For shopping, **Fashion Island** *(Jamboree Rd., off E. Pacific Coast Hwy.)* offers ultra-exclusive shops that rival those of Rodeo Drive (see pp. 72–73). For art, the permanent collection of postwar California art at the **Orange County Museum of Art** *(850 San Clemente Dr., Newport Beach, tel 949/759-1122, www.ocma.net, closed Mon.–Tues., $$$, free 2nd Sun. of month)*, known for some rather remarkable exhibitions, is worth a trip.

Farther inland, head for the **Upper Newport Bay Nature Preserve** *(2301 University Dr., Newport Beach, tel 949/923-2290, www.ocparks.com)*, a lush 750-acre (303 ha) salt marsh that is home to approximately 70 percent of the remaining population of the light-footed clapper rail.

EXPERIENCE: The Ocean Institute

If you're maritime minded, don't miss the experience of diving into marine lab activities, watching octopus and jellyfish feedings, piloting a remotely operated underwater vehicle, and cruising offshore on the *Sea Explorer* research vessel or the *Spirit of Dana Point* schooner. Tucked down at the southern end of Orange County, the Ocean Institute at Dana Point *(24200 Dana Point Harbor Dr., tel 949/496-2274, www.ocean-institute.org)* is a nonprofit, educational facility specializing in marine and environmental science and maritime history. Weekday programs are reserved for schools and members, but on weekends the institute's exhibits and aquariums are open to all. During spring and summer, the historic brig *Pilgrim* is the venue for maritime-themed dramas and musicals.

Other Beaches: Back south on the Pacific Coast Highway (Calif. 1), you'll find two remarkable beaches. **The Wedge** is known mainly for its huge, bone-crunching waves. **Corona del Mar State Beach** *(tel 949/644-3151)* is the epitome of the southern California bathing beach: swimmable waters, pristine sands, and a backdrop of palms, seagulls, and even the occasional pelican.

South of Laguna Beach

The picturesque coves and rugged cliffs of Laguna continue southward well beyond the city's limits. There is public access to all of these beaches, and they are well worth the effort to escape the summer crowds. The pier and marina are the main attractions at **Dana Point** *(Pacific Coast Hwy. & Street of the Golden Lantern)*, and a walk to the lookout yields memorable views.

Inland, off I-5, is **Mission San Juan Capistrano**, perhaps the most picture-perfect California mission. The Moorish-style architecture and burnished bells and arcades lend a romantic hue, while the gardens make a pleasant stroll. Migratory swallows return here every spring and are welcomed with a festival on March 19.

Returning to the Pacific Coast Highway, three contiguous beaches give you a choice for a fun-filled day of sunning and swimming: **Doheny State Beach, Capistrano Beach,** and **San Clemente Beach.** ■

Newport Beach

131 F3

Visitor Information

1600 Newport Center Dr., Suite 120, Newport Beach

949/644-3035, 800-94-COAST

www.visitnewportbeach.com

Corona del Mar State Beach

131 F3

Mission San Juan Capistrano

131 F2

26801 Ortega Hwy., San Juan Capistrano

949/234-1300

www.missionsjc.com

North Coastal San Diego

North of San Diego (see pp. 150–161) stretches an expansive coastal region noted for its exquisite beaches, protected wild places, and miles of open space. From Carlsbad south to La Jolla, just north of San Diego, you'll find a landscape dotted with picturesque small towns and unbeatable oceanside vistas. Whether you are after art and antiques or sunning and swimming, the area north of San Diego is bound to delight.

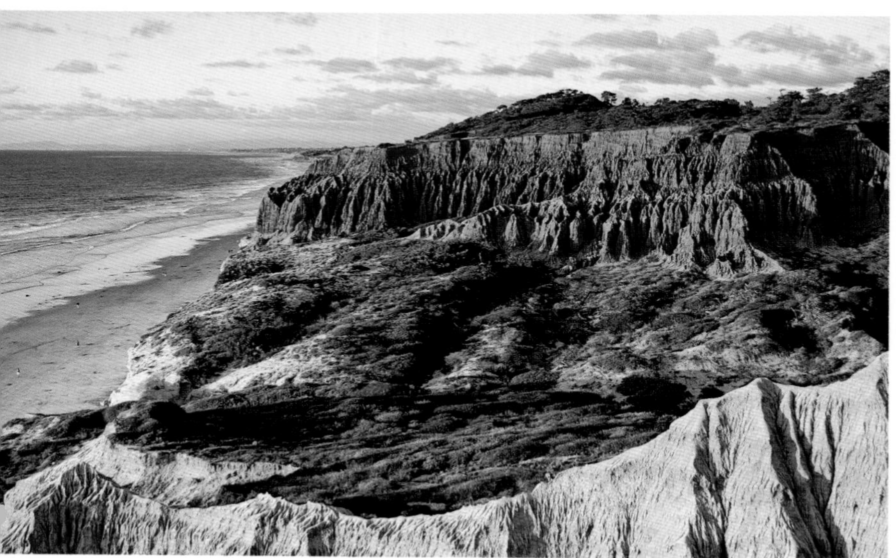

The rugged coastline north of San Diego has attractive small towns and a laid-back atmosphere.

Carlsbad
131 F2

Visitor Information

Visitor Center, 400 Carlsbad Village Dr., Carlsbad

760/434-6093

www.carlsbadca.gov

Carlsbad

Located south of Laguna Beach (see pp. 140–141), Carlsbad is known for its flower farms and the interactive **Museum of Making Music** *(5790 Armada Dr., tel 760/438-5996, www.museumofmakingmusic.org, closed Mon., $$)*. Its biggest attraction, however, is **Legoland California Resort** *(1 Legoland Dr., tel 760/918-5346, http://california.legoland.com, $$$$$)*, a high-tech American version of the celebrated Danish theme park.

The 128-acre (51 ha) park offers innovative rides, shows, and attractions, including the popular Pharaoh's Revenge laser game and Pirates Cove water-based rides. At the heart of the park are diminutive versions of Manhattan, Washington, D.C., Las Vegas, and others rendered in Lego bricks. One of the newest attractions is the interactive Sea Life aquarium, specially designed to introduce children to the wonders of the sea. The Legoland Water Park opens during warmer months.

INSIDER TIP:

Rates are reasonable at the Torrey Pines Golf Course *(www.torreypinesgolfcourse.com)*, considered one of the world's most scenic places to tee off.

–GREG CRITSER
National Geographic author

From Carlsbad, I-5 continues into **Encinitas,** hub of southern California surfer culture., followed by Solana Beach and Del Mar (see sidebar below).

Torrey Pines State Natural Reserve

Of all southern California's parks, the 1,750-acre (708 ha) Torrey Pines State Natural Reserve, an area of seaside cliffs and lagoons south of Del Mar, may well be the most sensuous. The scents of wild fennel, sage, and pine combine with sand, sun, and spray to make a heady mixture. Alas, only 9,000 of the drought-tolerant trees that give the reserve its name, *Pinus torreyana,* remain in all America.

Start with a short hike (about two-thirds of a mile/1 km) around the **Guy Fleming Trail** *(leaflets from the visitor center).* The eerily eroded cliffs and twisted pines are a joy, particularly from February through May when native California flowers blossom in hues of red, orange, purple, and green. Omnipresent is the "sticky" monkey flower, with its tiny orange trumpets; here also are the yellow mariposa lily, the lemonade berry, and the purple coast cholla.

Near the bottom of the **Broken Hill Trail** is the overlook for **Flat Rock,** dramatic in its simplicity. From January through March, you may spot a California gray whale on its annual migration. Seals, cormorants, and gulls add to the spectacle. Red-throated loons and great blue herons are found year-round.

On the park's north edge is **Los Peñasquitos Marsh,** once a Native American encampment and now an extensive mudflat, home to fiddler crabs and jackknife clams. Access is controlled; check with the ranger station for tours.

Torrey Pines State Natural Reserve

- Map: 131 G1
- Visitor Center, 12500 N. Torrey Pines Rd. (exit off I-5)
- 858/755-2063

www.torreypine.org

Del Mar & Solana Beach

The seaside resort of Del Mar *(see map p. 131 G1; visitor information, City Hall, 1050 Camino del Mar, tel 858/755-9313 or 858/755-2794, www.delmar.ca.us, closed Sat.–Sun.)* lies at the mouth of the Dieguito River north of Torrey Pines. The city has long been famous for its horse-racing track, run by the Del Mar Thoroughbred Club *(tel 858/755-1141, www.dmtc.com).* Balmy summer evenings are pleasant here even when Lady Luck isn't going your way.

North of Del Mar is the laidback city of Solana Beach, with its Cedros Avenue Design District *(www.cedrosavenue.com),* two and a half vibrant blocks of interior design shops, funky bistros and cafés, art galleries, hip fashion boutiques, and bustling young architecture firms. A farmers market operates Sunday afternoons.

La Jolla
131 G1

Visitor Information

Visitor Information Center, 7966 Herschel Ave.
619/236-1212
Closed Wed. in winter

www.lajollabythesea.com

Museum of Contemporary Art San Diego at La Jolla

700 Prospect St., La Jolla
858/454-3541
Closed Wed.
$$$

www.mcasd.org

Birch Aquarium at Scripps

2300 Expedition Way, La Jolla
858/534-3474
$$

www.aquarium.ucsd.edu

La Jolla Playhouse

2910 La Jolla Village Dr., La Jolla
858/550-1010

www.lajollaplayhouse.org

La Jolla

Founded in the early 20th century, the exclusive suburb of La Jolla shimmers with the essence of the Good Life. Its shopping arcades along sunny Prospect Street are vaguely European, and its homes, a fusion of modernism and recherché mission style, seem perfectly matched to the always changing ocean sky.

Many travelers head for the famed **La Jolla Caves** and **La Jolla Cove** (along Coast Walk). The former is a group of seven natural sea caves ripe for exploration; the latter is one of the most picturesque, albeit tiny, beaches on the coast, its deep blue waters attracting many snorkelers.

Back up on Prospect, the **Museum of Contemporary Art San Diego at La Jolla** offers a constantly changing palette of postwar art and design. Many visit this museum just to bear witness to the architecture of Irving Gill, who designed the sleek but site-sensitive building. The musem's extensive collection includes Ellsworth Kelly, Niki de Saint Phalle, and Robert Irwin. Don't miss the Nancy Rubins kayak-canoe-surfboard sculpture "Pleasure Point" (2006) in the garden.

Those with a certain literary inclination should take time to walk over to **Windansea Beach** *(Neptune Pl. & Bonair St.)*, immortalized in journalist Tom Wolfe's essay "The Pump House Gang."

"Spectacular" sums up the **Birch Aquarium at Scripps** *(N on Torrey Pines Rd. to Expedition Way)*, the interpretive center for the Scripps Institute of Oceanography. In the **Hall of Fishes,** state-of-the-art tanks display Pacific marine life. Of hypnotic interest here is the giant kelp forest, located inside a sunlit 55,000-gallon (208,197 L) tank equipped with a wavemaking machine.

INSIDER TIP:

Before taking in a play at the La Jolla Playhouse, enjoy cocktails at La Valencia *(1132 Prospect St., tel 858/454-0771, www.lavalencia.com).*

—GREG CRITSER
National Geographic author

One of the aquarium's most popular exhibits, **There's Something About Seahorses** features more than a dozen seahorse species. The **Tropical Seas Gallery** has especially lively exhibits on coral reefs, while **Feeling the Heat: The Climate Challenge** addresses issues of global warming. Launched in 2012, the interactive exhibit called **Boundless Energy** explores various ways that natural forces like wind and water can be used to power everyday life.

The aquarium's activities schedule includes snorkeling with sharks and "Tidepooling for Tots." A visit to the **Tide Pool Plaza,** with its panoramic view of the La Jolla shoreline, is a stunning coda to the visit and perfect preparation for tide pool explorations (see pp. 148–149). ■

Going on Safari

Sprawling across 1,800 acres (728 ha) of landscaped gardens and native chaparral terrain, the San Diego Zoo Safari Park offers visitors the chance to see more than 3,500 animals from around 400 species, many of them rare or endangered.

Located about 35 miles (56 km) north of San Diego (see pp. 150–161), the **San Diego Zoo Safari Park** *(15500 San Pasqual Valley Rd., Escondido, tel 760/747-8702, www.sdzsafaripark.org, $$$)* is country cousin to the San Diego Zoo (see pp. 156–158) and a major center for the captive breeding of rare and endangered species.

Much of the park's space is taken up by huge, open-air exhibits of African and Asian wildlife. It is home to the world's largest veterinary hospital and also boasts the **Institute for Conservation Research (ICR),** which contains a "frozen zoo" with the embryos of hundreds of endangered animals from around the globe. The efforts of the ICR have helped save several species from extinction, including the California condor, white rhino, and Arabian oryx.

Centered around a lake with flamingos and other waterfowl, the **Nairobi Village** area contains restaurants, shops, and exhibits for smaller animals, as well as the main gorilla habitat and an amphitheater where a popular bird show takes the stage several times each day.

You can explore everything by following the trails that meander through the park, but the best way to explore the park is by "going on safari."

No reservations are needed for the **Africa Tram Safari** *($$$, included in park admission),* a 25-minute open-air expedition on one of the park's colorful vehicles. Sit back and relax as your expert guide explains the behaviors and personalities of the African animals in the park. You'll see everything from giraffes and rhinos to ostriches and cranes—and maybe even a lion or two. Children 11 and younger must be accompanied by an adult.

For something that's a little closer to an actual African motor safari experience, try the **Caravan Safari** *($$$$$)*. You have four options to choose from. All of them offer the opportunity to ride in the back of an open-top truck and to feed giraffes and rhinos. The "Kids' Caravan Adventure" and "Adventure" options last 2 hours each and visit two or three field exhibits, respectively. The "Deluxe Adventure" lasts 3.5 hours, visits five field exhibits, and includes a snack stop. Check the park's website for the "Night Moves" option, a 2.5-hour, after-dinner excursion offered on select dates. Dessert and drinks are available.

The popular **Roar & Snore** adventure *($$$$$)* includes overnight accommodation in a private safari tent, dinner and breakfast on a bluff overlooking the African grasslands, campfire programs, kid's crafts, guided walks, and an after-hours glimpse of the wildlife.

See giraffes up close in the San Diego Zoo Safari Park.

In the Tide Pools

The typical southern California tide pool consists of five zones, each with its own ecology. The topmost is the spray zone; then come, in descending order, the high, medium, and low intertidal zones, where most of the action is. The last is the subtidal, where many of these creatures live when not looking for food in the intertidal.

With its warm waters and accessible cliffside pools, La Jolla (see p. 146) provides some excellent opportunities for tide pooling. Linda E. Tway, author of *Tidepools of Southern California*, is a local expert. Her advice is to prepare by checking the local tide tables (in the newspaper daily). Remember that removing any marine life from the pools is against the law.

Although there are several outstanding tidepooling sites in La Jolla, the location known as **Big Rock** *(enter from Camino de la Costa between Cortez Place & Via del Norte)* offers the opportunity of seeing some rare and colorful species. Come at low tide—but watch for strong surf surges.

The most continually exposed of the zones, the spray zone, is a treasure trove of thriving marine life. Outstanding examples of creatures that are numerous at Big Rock include the periwinkle, a snail-like mollusk about five-eighths of an inch (1.7 cm) long and spherical in shape, and the striped shore crab, a crustacean normally two inches (5 cm) long with green stripes.

Inhabitants of the **high intertidal zone** must be able to tolerate a good deal of sun and air; one response is for them to close up or seal themselves within a shell, preventing dehydration. The masters of this, found in abundance at Big Rock, are the California mussel and the leaf barnacle. The mussel grows to six inches (15 cm) in length and is brown to purple-black. It attaches itself to a rock with a single foot. The barnacle, up to five inches (12.7 cm) long, white, and more or less leaf-shaped, clings with grayish brown stalks in large numbers, often one on top of another. Also watch for the giant keyhole limpet, a shell-covered conical oval, gray to brown, clamped to the rock with a single yellow-orange foot.

As exposure to air decreases in the **medium intertidal zone,** coralline algae transform the gray-green sandstone into a wonderland of pinks and purples. Into this surface burrows the troglodyte chiton, brown and one-and-a-half inches (3.8 cm) long. These remnants from dinosaur days spend their 20-year lives scraping into the sandstone. The result is the pockmarked surface of Big Rock.

Because the **low intertidal zone** is mostly submerged, more permanent "homes" are built. One of the most remarkable is that of the sandcastle worm. Two inches (5 cm) long, cream colored with a black tip and lavender tentacles, *Phragmatopoma californica* builds honeycomb-like clusters of delicate sand tubes (watch your step). Another star of this zone is the giant green anemone. A member of the same class of invertebrates as corals, anemones use their tentacles to catch passing prey. The green anemone can grow as large as seven inches (17.7 cm) wide. Also look for the giant acorn barnacle, which resembles a tiny volcanic crater.

The **subtidal zone** is where you will see fishes and the larger seaweeds of the area.

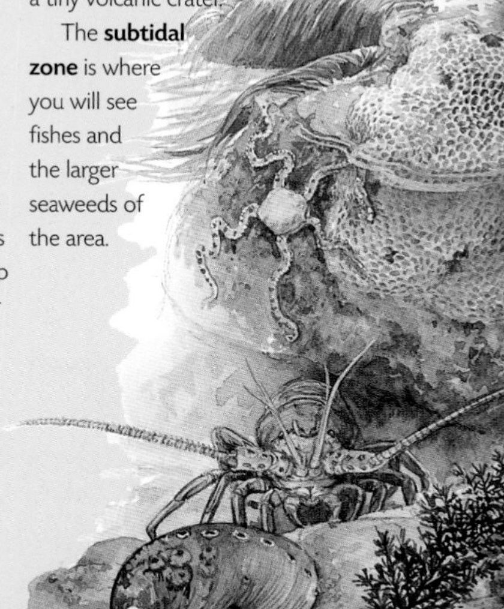

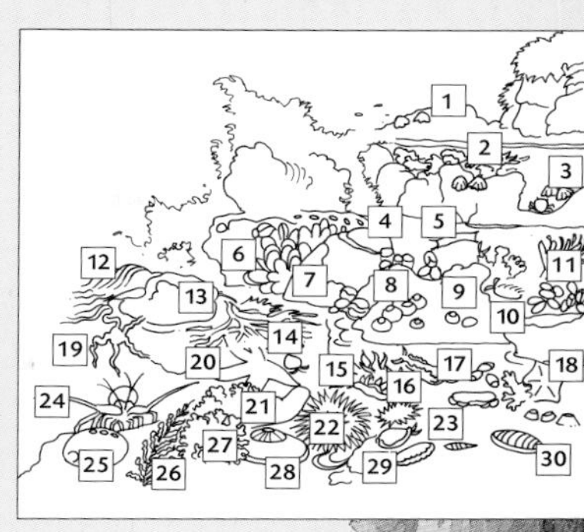

KEY TO DIAGRAM

1 rough limpet
2 sea lettuce
3 striped shore crab
4 giant owl limpet
5 striped sea slug
6 California mussels
7 pink encrusting coralline algae
8 volcano barnacles
9 velvety red sponge
10 Spanish shawl nudibranch
11 leaf barnacles
12 common surfgrass
13 sandcastle worms
14 rockweed
15 giant green anemone
16 Hopkins' rose
17 California sea hare
18 bat star
19 Panama brittle star
20 ochre star
21 warty sea cucumber
22 sea urchin
23 rock crab
24 spiny lobster
25 black abalone
26 sargasso weed
27 coralline red algae
28 giant keyhole limpet
29 chestnut cowry
30 chitons

San Diego

If its neighbor to the north, La Jolla (see p. 146), represents the ultimate California Good Life, then San Diego conjures the ultimate California Outdoor Life. With its huge range of water-sports facilities, its giant municipal culture parks, and the largest zoo in the United States, it is a giant adult playground. The fact that it is surrounded by frontierland—desert to the east, the Mexican border to the south, and the Pacific to the west—only underscores the city's relatively late development. Though it sprawls, it has yet to break out into megasprawl.

San Diego, America's eighth largest city, is surrounded by 70 miles (112 km) of beaches.

San Diego
131 G1
Visitor Information
San Diego Convention & Visitors Bureau, 750 B St., Ste. 1500, San Diego
619/232-3101
www.sandiego.org

From its birth in 1769 as the first Spanish settlement in Alta (Upper) California, San Diego has followed much the same pattern of development as other great Californian cities. The initial spurt of missionizing was so aggressive that, in 1775, the neophytes at Mission San Diego openly revolted and slew Padre Luis Jayme, making him the first martyr of Alta California. A period of Mexican neglect and wildcat Anglo fur trading was followed by a spate of Yankee entrepreneurialism, much of it focused on the area's climate and natural harbor.

The Yankees stuck. In 1870, Alonzo Horton, considered the founder of modern San Diego, began touting the city as a mecca of tourism and health; eventually he built one of the most celebrated hotels of his time (see sidebar p. 158). Nowadays Horton is honored in the popular Horton Plaza outdoor mall.

By 1915 the city of San Diego was confident enough to enter the "world exposition" game, hiring gifted architect Bertram Grosvenor Goodhue, who was responsible for Caltech (see pp. 122–123) and L.A.'s Public Library (see p. 98), to design Balboa Park (see pp. 152–156), where the city fathers promoted the 1915 Panama-California International Exposition.

John D. and Adolph B. Spreckels, sons of a sugar magnate, caught the alfresco bug as well, building in 1915 the world's largest outdoor organ. To this day, on any warm Sunday afternoon, numerous San Diegans and visitors can be found in Balboa Park's open-air Spreckels Organ Pavilion (see p. 155), the music and sun washing over them as they sit like seals on a sandy beach.

During the mid-20th century, San Diego boomed. A heavy dose of federal government largesse, largely coming through the burgeoning naval complex, allowed the city to avoid some of the planning mistakes made by its northern neighbors, cities that often sabotaged their own zoning laws in order to attract new corporate residents. In San Diego, debate over growth has traditionally been framed by the phrase "Smokestacks versus Geraniums." Even the conservative former governor of California Pete Wilson, who was the mayor of San Diego in the late 1970s, is remembered as a proponent of restrained growth in the city.

More recently, huge population gains and economic shifts (the naval presence has been replaced in part by high-tech

EXPERIENCE: Wine Tasting in the Wild West

Fewer than 60 miles (96 km) north of San Diego along I-15 you'll discover Temecula *(map p. 131 G2; visitor information, Convention and Visitors Bureau, 28690 Mercedes St., Ste. A, tel 888/363-2852, www.temeculacvb.com)*, an old Wild West town that has boomed again on a bounty of wine. Here more than 30 wineries produce a variety of reds, whites, and grape-based drinks.

If you're a sparkling wine aficionado, then **Wilson Creek** *(35960 Rancho California Rd., tel 951/699-9463, www.wilsoncreekwinery.com)* is your first stop. Try the almond-flavored champagne and peach bellini. Next head to breezy, hilltop **Falkner Winery** *(40620 Calle Contento, tel 951/676-8231, www.falknerwinery.com)*, where you can picnic on the lawn and sip the exquisite syrah. For a killer white port and pinot gris, try **Wiens Family Cellars** *(35055 Via del Ponte, tel 951/694-9892, www.wienscellars.com)*. Mechanically-minded wine lovers should stop at the Argentine-owned **Doffo Winery** *(36083 Summitville Rd., tel 951/676-6989, www.doffowines.com)* where an exotic motorbike museum can be enjoyed with a fine malbec.

The **Temecula Valley Winegrowers Association** *(34567 Rancho California Rd., tel 951/699-3626 or 800/801-9463, www.temeculawines.org)* offers maps and itineraries. Be sure to check out the association's various events like the annual **World of Wine** gourmet food, the wine weekend in March, and the **Harvest Celebration** in November.

Balboa Park
131 G1
Visitor Information
Visitors Center, 1549 El Prado, San Diego
619/239-0512
www.balboapark.com

industries) have made planned growth more difficult. San Diego is now the eighth largest city in the United States. Urban sprawl, as in the area around Qualcomm Stadium near the old mission, is becoming more common.

Yet any discerning visitor would be hard pressed to come away from San Diego unhappy. The old California Tower in Balboa Park shines in the sun *and* in evening spotlights. Old San Diego is joined with new Tijuana in Mexico via an efficient, low-cost trolley car system and new Bridge of the Americas. There are plays and concerts under the stars every night. Out on Mission Bay (see pp. 160–161), water-skiers skip over lacy wave crests like dolphins leaping. Don't forget the suntan lotion.

Balboa Park

Of the two major "exposition cities" built in 1915 to commemorate the opening of the Panama Canal (San Francisco and San Diego), San Diego is home to unquestionably the best preserved and most culturally vibrant relic of that era:

The Casa del Prado is a reconstruction of a Panama-California Exposition building.

1,100-acre (445 ha) Balboa Park (see sidebar p. 153). In the park are 17 distinct museums and art institutes, three theaters, 19 formal and informal gardens, the nation's largest zoo, and more Spanish colonial architecture than anywhere else in the state.

The park is arranged in a series of plazas along the main road, El Prado, with the landmark tower at the east end. It was designed with two purposes, one pragmatic, one aesthetic. By building a giant

Pacific "Dream City," the park's founders hoped to establish San Diego as the preferred port of call for ships arriving through the new Panama Canal. By bringing in architect Bertram Grosvenor Goodhue, known for his flashy Mediterranean style, the city fathers also sought to communicate San Diego's vision of itself as a merging of garden and city.

If Balboa Park's official purpose was, as its founders said in one 1930s pamphlet, "to illustrate the progress and possibility of the human race," the unofficial one was not unlike that of today's sophisticated relocation ads used to lure new companies to new cities. This effort was redoubled in 1935, when the city held another world exposition, adding Moorish and Italianate elements to the original Mediterranean aspects. As state librarian Kevin Starr notes, this was architecture as "romantic text." Yet it was the continuing enlistment of the city's mercantile elite that saved Balboa Park and preserved it for what it is today: one of the best kept secrets in American tourism.

The Look of Balboa

Balboa Park as we know it today is largely the result of two world's fairs: the 1915 Panama-California Exposition and the 1935 California Pacific International Exposition. Inspired by the recent opening of the Panama Canal, the 1915 event produced many of the park's Spanish Renaissance Revival landmarks, including the California Tower, Cabrillo Bridge, and Organ Pavilion, as well as the San Diego Zoo (see pp. 156–158). Aimed at boosting the local economy during the Great Depression, the 1935 fair brought a far different style to Balboa—the distinctive art deco buildings that now house the aerospace, automotive, and sports museums, but also the beloved Old Globe theater.

How to Visit: To take full advantage of all that Balboa Park has to offer, set aside at least two days. The Passport to Balboa Park *(hwww.balboapark.org/parkpass)*, on sale at any of the park's museums, affords onetime access to each venue and is good for one week.

Park near the zoo and walk in, take the tram, or stroll across **Cabrillo Bridge,** which links the Prado area with the historic Banker's Hill district in the west. Ask your hotel concierge to make reservations at one of the evening theater performances in the park.

The San Diego Museum of Art

Although all of them are worth a visit, three Balboa Park museums warrant particular note. The largest of the city's museums, the **San Diego Museum of Art** has a significant collection of Renaissance and post-Renaissance works by Spanish artists. The best known work is "Quince, Cabbage, Melon, and Cucumber," painted in 1602 by Juan Sánchez Cotán. One wonders how a man could produce such a realistic depiction of fertility and then the following year, as Cotán did, renounce the world and become a monk. An outstanding work is Diego Rivera's "The Hands of Dr.

San Diego Museum of Art

- ✉ 1450 El Prado, Balboa Park
- ☎ 619/232-7931
- 🕒 Closed Sun a.m. & Mon.
- $ $$$

www.sdmart.org

Timken Museum of Art–Putnam Collection
1500 El Prado, Balboa Park
619/239-5548
Closed Sun. a.m. & Mon.
www.timkenmuseum.org

Moore" (1940), with an anthropomorphic tree that represents both the natural world and the female anatomy. Although born in Greece, El Greco did his best work in Toledo, Spain, and belongs here among the Spaniards. "The Penitent St. Peter," painted in 1600, startles with its use of light, reminiscent of Rembrandt's "Raising of Lazarus."

EXPERIENCE: Balboa in December

Although Balboa Park is great at any time of year, nothing beats December Nights *(www.balboapark.org/decembernights)* during the yuletide season. Normally held on the first weekend in December, the event draws as many as 300,000 people to the park for holiday foods, drinks, crafts, and entertainment. All of the park's museums are open for free from 5 p.m. to 9 p.m., and a number of local arts groups stage free dance, drama, and music performances. Other highlights include international holiday foods at the House of Pacific Relations cottages, the Santa Lucia Procession, the Spanish Village arts fair, and carnival rides in the Pan American Plaza.

Mingei International Museum
1439 El Prado, Balboa Park
619/239-0003
Closed Mon.
www.mingei.org

The museum also has a notable grouping of American painters, chief among them Thomas Eakins. His "Elizabeth Crowell With a Dog," painted in 1871, will strike a chord with any animal lover.

Timken Museum of Art —Putnam Collection

Just east, the **Timken Museum of Art–Putnam Collection** is housed in the only nonrevivalist building in Balboa Park, a cool modern temple of marble and glass. This eccentric grouping of European and American masterworks is marked by its even more eccentric juxtaposition with a world-class collection of Russian iconography. From late 16th-century Russia, the wood panel "St. Basil the Great and Scenes From His Life" is full of quiet power; religious icons were, after all, conceived as a medium for meditation upon God's kingdom. From 1838 comes a painting by Jean-Baptiste-Camille Corot. Entitled "View of Volterra," the work is a masterful evocation of the long approach from Siena to the old Etruscan town of Volterra, which Corot first sketched on a summer visit to Italy in 1834. The sensuous realism of late 19th-century American painters is found in "The Magnolia Flower," painted in 1888 by Martin Johnson Heade.

Mingei International Museum

Scholars and folk art buffs flock to see the most dynamic of the park's museums, the **Mingei International Museum,** which is dedicated to world folk art, both contemporary and historical. Titles of past exhibitions hint at the diversity: "American Expressions of Liberty"; "India: Village, Tribal, Ritual Arts"; "Folk Toys of the World"; and "¡Viva los Artisanos!" If you are lucky, you may catch one of Niki de Saint Phalle's exhibitions. French born, New York City raised, and part-time La Jolla resident until her death in 2002, Saint Phalle is known for her colorful and fantastic images, some as big as a small house.

INSIDER TIP:

Unlike L.A., San Diego is wonderfully walkable. Just pull out a street map and discover all the city has to offer on foot.

—LARRY PORGES
National Geographic Books editor

Other Museums

Other museums in the park include the **Museum of Photographic Arts,** which offers an extensive collection of the 20th century's leading practitioners. The **San Diego History Center** charts several hundred years of local history through temporary displays and a new permanent exhibit called "Place of Promise."

The Space Theater at the **Reuben H. Fleet Science Center** contains a planetarium and IMAX theater, while the **San Diego Air & Space Museum** has a superb collection of historic aircraft and exhibits on space exploration.

The collection at the **San Diego Automotive Museum** includes late 19th-century horseless carriages, muscle cars, and cars of the space age. The **Model Railroad Museum** *(Casa de Balboa, tel 619/696-0199, www.sdmrm.com, closed Mon.)* specializes in train scenes of San Diego and southern California.

Learn about the city's contributions to more than 40 sports at the **San Diego Hall of Champions** *(2131 Pan American Plaza, tel 619/234-2544, www.sdhoc.com).*

The **Museum of Man** *(1350 El Prado, tel 619/239-2001, www.museumofman.org)* looks at humankind's evolution from cultural and physical perspectives. Lastly, the **San Diego Natural History Museum** *(1780 El Prado, tel 619/232-3821, www.sdnhm.org)* specializes in exhibits explaining broad habitats and in the geology of gems and minerals.

Gardens & Organ Pavilion:

The **Spreckels Organ Pavilion** *(just S of the Plaza de Panama on El Prado)* also harks back to a simpler time, when, in 1915, civic leaders John D. and Adolph B. Spreckels spent the then huge sum of $100,000 on building the world's largest outdoor organ. On Sunday afternoons, young musicians try out this old classic. Free **Twilight in the Park** concerts are held on midweek evenings in summer.

East of the organ pavilion, the **Japanese Friendship Garden** is one of the more recent additions to the park. Its 11-acre (4.4 ha) site features winding paths, stone lanterns, and Zen rock gardens.

Built with more than 12 miles (19 km) of redwood lath, the **Botanical Building & Lily Pond** *(between Casa del Prado & museum of art)* houses a wide variety of exotic plants.

The enormous lily pond has proven highly adaptable over the years. During World War II, when many park buildings were used as troop hospitals, it served as a rehabilitation pool. In the blistering summer of 1945, the pond became a swimming pool for 22,000 local children.

Museum of Photographic Arts

✉ 1649 El Prado, Balboa Park
☎ 619/238-7559
🕒 Closed Mon.
www.mopa.org

San Diego History Center

✉ 1649 El Prado, Balboa Park
☎ 619/232-6203
🕒 Closed Mon.
$ $
www.sandiegohistory.org

Reuben H. Fleet Science Center

✉ 1875 El Prado, Balboa Park
☎ 619/238-1233
$ $$
www.rhfleet.org

San Diego Air & Space Museum

✉ 2001 Pan American Plaza, Balboa Park
☎ 619/234-8291
$ $$$
www.sandiegoairandspace.org

San Diego Automotive Museum

✉ 2080 Pan American Plaza, Balboa Park
☎ 619/231-2886
$ $$
www.sdautomuseum.org

EXPERIENCE: Behind the Scenes at the Zoo

As well as regular admission, the San Diego Zoo offers visitors special behind-the-scenes experiences for an additional price.

The zoo's popular **Backstage Pass** *($$$$$)*, for example, affords visitors a rare opportunity to interact with the zoo's wild animals. You'll have your photo taken with a cheetah, brush or feed a rhino, and perhaps even help train a kangaroo or other animal. You'll also hear stories about the animals you visit and learn about the zoo's ongoing conservation efforts. Offered daily, the Backstage Pass is suitable for everyone 5 years old and older. Children 15 and younger must be accompanied by an adult.

Designed especially for children age, 3 to 6, the **Junior Inside Look Tour** *($)* is a 2-hour family-friendly adventure that will introduce you to the methods that the zoo uses to care for its animals. You'll travel by cart in small groups to off-exhibit areas and pay a visit to the Discovery Outpost (see p. 158) for an up-close animal encounter.

Interested in something a little less "wild"? Then try the **Horticulture Tour** *($)*, which focuses on the park's lush gardens and many exotic plant species. Tours last 1.5 or 2 hours and can be customized. Plant lovers can choose a general overview of the zoo's flora, or focus on a specific garden area such as Fern Canyon.

The Old Globe

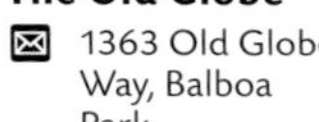

1363 Old Globe Way, Balboa Park

619/231-1941

www.oldglobe.org

San Diego Zoo

2920 Zoo Dr., Balboa Park

619/894-8425

$$$$$

www.sandiegozoo.org

Theaters: Some of the best theater on the West Coast takes place at Balboa Park's three-venue complex. Built for the 1935 California Pacific International Exposition, the **Old Globe** theater was dedicated to abbreviated performances of Shakespeare. After a series of fires, the Old Globe was incorporated into today's triplex to make this San Diego's largest arts institution. In 1984, it received a Tony award for Outstanding Regional Theater, and since then the complex has launched several new works.

Two other theaters operate alongside the Old Globe. They are the **Sheryl and Harvey White Theatre** and the **Lowell Davies Festival Theater,** each with its own unusual seating configuration—the former in the round, the latter open air.

San Diego Zoo

Founded in 1916 by the enterprising Dr. Harry Wegeforth, the San Diego Zoo has grown far beyond even its founder's grandest dreams. Resting on a hundred acres (40 ha) of northern Balboa Park, this state-of-the-art animal park now displays and cares for 3,700 animals representing more than 650 species. Its botanical credentials (more than 6,500 plant species) startle as well; with only a little imagination, one can, within one park, experience jungle, tundra, and rain forest. Many come to San Diego to see this attraction alone. Only excessive marketing detracts from the experience.

The zoo is divided into nine animal zones representing different continents or geographical areas. Right behind the flamingos at the entrance is the **Lost Forest,** a lush tropical habitat with streams, waterfalls, and meandering paths. Hidden among the trees is the **gorilla exhibit**—one of the zoo's top attractions—2.5 acres (1 ha) of simulated African rain forest within an 8,000-square-foot (745 sq m) enclosure that is home to a troop of western lowland gorillas. Inside the same zone is the **Scripps Aviary,** with more than 130 African birds in free flight.

In the canyon west of the great apes is the stunning **Tiger River,** where visitors walk down a misty forest path before coming to ten enclosures housing more than a hundred animals (including Burmese pythons, narrow-snouted crocodiles, and Malaysian tapirs). The tigers prowl about on a grassy hillside, their appearance made all the more dramatic by the rain forest environs.

At the bottom of the canyon is **Hippo Beach,** where you can view these 4,000-pounders (180 kg) both aboveground and underwater, through a two-inch-thick (5 cm) window of laminated glass.

If the weather is hot, the **Polar Rim,** located at the park's outer boundary, provides a soothing scene. Conjuring two acres (.8 ha) of Arctic tundra, complete with Siberian reindeer and arctic foxes, the plunge features a group of playful polar bears busily cavorting in a 130,000-gallon (492,103 L) tank. Their underwater antics are visible through a large acrylic window. Many swim right up to the glass, curious about the odd creatures on the other side.

If you backtrack, the **Giant Panda Research Station** is next. The zoo keeps adding to its population of these endangered creatures: Bai Yun, who arrived

The gorilla exhibit is always a crowd-pleaser. A visit to the zoo late in the day is most rewarding, as the crowds have thinned and animals become more active.

Julian

131 H2

Visitor Information

Chamber of Commerce, 2129 Main St., Julian

760/765-1857

www.julianca.com

from China in 1996, has since given birth to several cubs, most recently in August 2009. The exhibit area includes an interactive **Giant Panda Discovery Center.**

The zoo's newest zone, the highly creative **Elephant Odyssey** on the east mesa, revolves around extinct animals that lived in southern California 12,000 years ago and their living relatives. The Pleistocene creatures come alive in full-scale models and a replica tar pit filled with fossils. The living animals—lions and jaguars, tapirs and capybaras, elephants and pronghorn antelope—roam large habitats in between.

Between these major stops are dozens of specialized habitats, each designed for the particular needs of its inhabitants. There are the requisite kangaroos and koalas and rhinos and giraffes.

To your left upon entering is the outstanding **Discovery Outpost,** complete with reptile house and a display of increasingly rare Galápagos tortoises. A **Nighttime Zoo** is open in summer.

INSIDER TIP:

In October, head north and east of San Diego to the old gold-mining town of Julian, known nowadays for its art galleries and annual Apple Festival.

—JOE YOGERST
National Geographic author

Historic San Diego

As the oldest Spanish settlement in California, San Diego and its environs are full of historic places, some major, some minor. The City of San Diego has made visiting several nearby sites both easy and comfortable. A trolley system offers an outstanding

California's Iconic Hotel

The centerpiece of the 4,100-acre (1,659 ha) Silver Strand Peninsula that separates San Diego's harbor from the Pacific Ocean is the fanciful Victorian **Hotel del Coronado** *(1500 Orange Ave., tel 619/468-3533 or 800/468-3533, www.hoteldel.com).* Built in 1888 by Elisha Babcock, Jr., and H. L. Story, the hotel has been an enduring attraction ever since.

A favorite getaway of blue bloods and Hollywood doyens, the gleaming white structure oozes dated opulence and has hosted the likes of the Duke and Duchess of Windsor, Henry James, and L. Frank Baum, who wrote the *Wizard of Oz* (1900) here and supposedly modeled his Emerald City on the view from his room. Most famously, Marilyn Monroe paraded the hallways in *Some Like It Hot* (1959).

While the hotel is still a fanciful place to visit, with historical tours available, the wise traveler will limit outings here to the off-season or midweek, when the tour buses dwindle in number.

Today's "Hotel Del," often busy and crowded, is a place to see but not one to linger in, even for a meal. Instead, enjoy a drink in the woodsy old lobby bar, then jump back on the San Diego-Coronado ferry *(tel 619/234-4111, www.sdhe.com)* and return across the water to see a play in Balboa Park (see pp. 152).

two-hour narrated tour, with the advantage that you can debark and reboard the trolley all day.

Among the attractions are the revived **Gaslamp Quarter** *(Broadway & 4th–6th Aves.)*, where Wyatt Earp ran such a bawdy operation that he caused his more uptight neighbors to move north. Since the 1980s, the quarter has become the place to shop and eat in historic San Diego.

Old Town State Park, protected as the site of the early settlement, also offers the splendid **Junípero Serra Museum,** which holds relics and pieces of art from the original mission. Nearby you can view the restored **Victoriana of Heritage Park** *(2460 Heritage Park Row, www.heritageparksd.com)*, while kids can romp amid interactive displays at the **New Children's Museum.**

Besides taking you to **Balboa Park** (see pp. 152–156) and the **Coronado Peninsula** (see sidebar p. 158), the trolley also travels along San Diego's seafront. There, maritime buffs can explore the **Maritime Museum,** where the spectacular "San Diego's Navy" exhibit opened in 2007, depicting the history of the U.S. Navy in San Diego; the 1860s *Star of India* is another highlight. Nearby is the **USS *Midway* Aircraft Carrier Museum** *(Navy Pier, tel 916/544-9600, www.midway.org)*, showcasing the flattop that berthed here permanently in 2004 after a 47-year career and today rewards visitors with a virtual-reality flight experience, plus military aircraft spanning five decades.

An ongoing redevelopment of downtown San Diego is transforming the long-dormant area into a vibrant neighborhood anchored by the new 42,000-seat **PETCO Park** *(www.sandiegopadres.mlb.com)* baseball stadium and the award-winning **Horton Plaza Shopping Center,** replicating a European market with more than 140 shops and cafés. Also in the downtown area is the **Museum of Contemporary Art** *(1100 Kettner Blvd., tel 858/454-3541, www.mcasd.org, closed Wed., $$$)*, a counterpart to the one in La Jolla.

San Diego's historic Gaslamp Quarter fills more than 16 blocks.

Farther Afield

From San Diego, take Calif. 209 to **Cabrillo National Monument** *(map p. 131 G1; 1800 Cabrillo Memorial Dr., tel 619/557-5450, www.nps.gov/cabr)*, at the tip of the Point Loma Peninsula. As the name suggests, this is where Juan Rodriguez Cabrillo, the great Portuguese explorer—in service to Spain—became the first European to set foot in California. More appealing than

Junípero Serra Museum

✉ 2727 Presidio Dr., San Diego

☎ 619/297-3258

$ $

www.sandiegohistory.org/serra_museum.html

New Children's Museum

✉ 200 W. Island Ave., San Diego

☎ 619/233-8792

$ $$

www.thinkplaycreate.org

Maritime Museum

✉ 1492 N. Harbor Dr., San Diego

☎ 619/234-9153

$ $$$

www.sdmaritime.org

Ocean Beach

Visitor Information

- MainStreet Association, 1868 Bacon St., #A, San Diego
- 619/224-4906

www.oceanbeachsandiego.com

Belmont Park

- 3146 Mission Blvd., San Diego
- 858/488-1549

www.belmontpark.com

Mission Bay

- 131 G1

Visitor Information

- Visitors Information Center, 2688 Mission Bay Dr., San Diego
- 619/276-8200

the monument and the **Cabrillo Museum** is the surrounding parkland, 144 acres (58 ha) offering spectacular views of city and bay, as well as extensive hiking trails. You may also visit the lower rooms of the 1855 **Old Point Loma Lighthouse,** a short walk from the monument.

On the northwestern edge of Point Loma is the funky seaside neighborhood of **Ocean Beach,** where antiques shops, coffeehouses, and counterculture outlets line Newport Avenue. At the end of the avenue are the Ocean Beach pier and a broad, white-sand strand with a special area where dogs can frolic in the surf.

On the north side of the San Diego River estuary is **Mission Beach,** a tightly packed neighborhood that hugs a narrow isthmus between Mission Bay and the ocean. Walking and biking paths run along both shores.

But the area's main attraction is **Belmont Park,** an old-fashioned seaside amusement park founded in 1925. Among its iconic features are the Giant Dipper roller coaster (listed on the National Register of Historic Places) and a huge indoor swimming pool called the Plunge.

On the north side of the bay is **Pacific Beach,** where the historic Crystal Pier Hotel *(tel 800/748-5894, www.crystalpier.com)* offers the only over-water accommodation along the California coast.

Mission Bay & SeaWorld

Jubilant **Mission Bay** is a 4,600-acre (1,861 ha) aquatic park that is dedicated to just about every water-based activity imaginable (see sidebar p. 161). It's also where San Diegans go to stay healthy and let rip.

Every April, the bay hosts

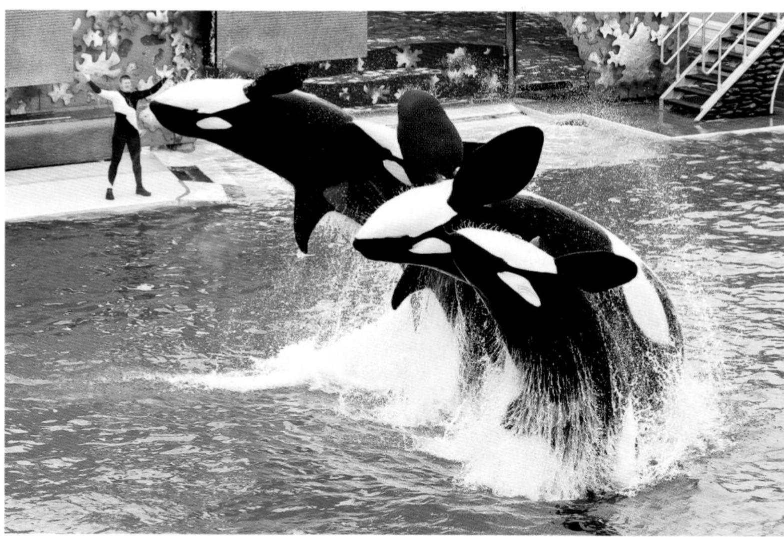

SeaWorld San Diego's killer whales are housed in 7-million-gallon (26,497,880 L) habitats.

EXPERIENCE: Ocean Life, Southern California Style

Mission Bay has 17 miles (27 km) of beaches, with eight swim-only areas. You'll find sandy beaches open to the public at **Leisure Lagoon** and **De Anza Cove,** along the eastern shore, and **Ventura Cove,** on the west side. **Sail Bay,** in the northwest part of the park, is reserved for sailing and paddle craft. **Fiesta Bay,** in the northeast, is the domain of powerboats and those who like to water-ski, wakeboard, or tube.

Mission Bay Sportscenter *(1010 Santa Clara Pl., tel 858/488-1004, www.missionbaysportcenter.com)* rents a wide variety of watercraft, including sailboats, powerboats, pontoon boats, kayaks, paddleboards, and surfboards. It also offers guided sunset cruises, Jet Ski tours, and summer evening rentals to watch the SeaWorld fireworks.

The nearby **Mission Bay Aquatic Center** *(1001 Santa Clara Pl., tel 858/488-1000, www.mbaquaticcenter.com)* offers year-round instruction in a variety of water sports, including wakeboarding, stand-up paddling, and windsurfing.

The bay is flanked by 14 miles (22.5 km) of bike paths. The most popular of these are the fishhook-shape route between the Bahia Resort and the tip of Crown Point, and the meandering path between De Anza Cover and the big Tecolote Shores playground. **Cheap Rentals** *(3689 Mission Blvd., tel 858/488-9070, www.cheaprentals.com)* rents bikes, rollerblades, and other sports equipment.

the boisterous **San Diego Crew Classic** *(www.crewclassic.org)*, which attracts collegiate teams from around the U.S. and Canada. In September comes **Bayfair** *(www.sandiegobayfair.org)*, the World Series of powerboat racing.

Located on the bay's southern shore, **SeaWorld San Diego** has long been at the leading edge of animal marine entertainment, education, rescue, and research. The park's emblematic attraction is Shamu, the star of killer whale shows in an outdoor stadium with underwater viewing windows and giant LCD screens. Other popular shows include the **Blue Horizons dolphin theater,** the **Clyde and Seamore sea lion cabaret,** and **Pets Rule.**

Animal habitats include those for sea otters and sea turtles, and the popular **Shark Encounter,** with an underwater tunnel that lets you get within inches of the prehistoric predators.

The chilly **Penguin Encounter** features 300 of the cute, aquatic birds. Next door, **Wild Arctic** presents a unique combination of live animals (polar bears, walruses, and white beluga whales) and thrill ride—a flight simulator that takes you on a virtual journey through frozen Arctic landscapes.

Three other thrill rides round out the SeaWorld experience. You are almost guaranteed to get soaked running the **Shipwreck Rapids** in giant inner tubes. An imaginary voyage to the mythical lost city is the theme of **Journey to Atlantis,** which starts with a 60-foot (18 m) plunge into a lagoon. New in 2012 is the biggest of them all—the **Manta** roller coaster, which soars sideways and upside down through the midde of the park. ■

SeaWorld San Diego

131 G1

500 Sea World Dr., San Diego

619/226-2901, 800/257-4268

$$$$$

www.seaworldparks.com

Mexican Folk Art

The Mexican city of Tijuana is a 15-minute trolley car ride south from San Diego (see pp. 158–159). These days, many come to this once rough border town not for the illicit delights of drink, dames, and gambling—although those still abound—but for Mexican tribal art. However, U.S. visitors to this city, a battleground in Mexico's drug wars, should exercise caution and follow State Dept. advisories *(www.travel.state.gov/travel)*.

Figurines made to celebrate one of Mexico's most important holidays, the Day of the Dead

The origins of the Mexican folk art industry lie in 18th-century Mexico, when village priests and lay artisans began crafting ornamentation for new churches. These pieces often combine colorful pre-Columbian nature worship and traditional Old World religious iconography. The result is rustic, hallucinatory, festive, and even provocative.

To get to Tijuana by car, take I-5 or Calif. 805 south past San Ysidro to the International Border Crossing. Park, cross the bridge on foot, and pick up a cab on the other side. (Ask the driver how much he charges for the trip downtown.) If you choose to drive across the border, one-day insurance is available at several sites. A better way to see "TJ" is by trolley, available at a number of sites around the city. For the closest, call **San Diego Trolley** *(tel 619/233-3004, www.sdmts.com)*. The inexpensive journey takes just 45 minutes. U.S. citizens should carry proof of citizenship for reentry.

While folk art of varying quality, new and old, can be found throughout Tijuana, one of the better shops is **Tolán** *(between Calles 7 & 8 on Ave. Revolución, tel 011 52 66/88-3637)*. Go there first to get an idea of top price and top quality, *then* explore alternatives along the various *calles* to make comparisons. The key is to have fun. Bargain, but don't take it seriously.

What to Buy

Among the most popular items are ***retablos,*** painted tin-and-wood plaques used as votives in tiny household shrines across Mexico. They often bear the likeness of the Virgin of Guadalupe. Some of the best come from the state of Oaxaca. Look, too, for ***ceramicas festas,*** brightly colored ceramics used to commemorate the Day of the Dead. These range in size from the tiny clay skulls made in Oaxaca to the fantastic candelabra and Nativity scenes made in Puebla. Renderings of various **mythical beasts** are usually made in Metepec, outside Mexico City. You will also find ***santos*** and ***bultos*** (saints and "figures") in tin, clay, wood, and ceramic, and ***milagros,*** tin representations of body parts, often pinned to statues of saints in hope of a healing miracle.

Woven goods, both everyday and precious, include the ***sarapes*** of northern Mexico, ***rebozos,*** and ***huipils,*** tunics made popular by the Mixtec peoples, who dye them with colors from insects and sea snails. The Zapoteca people are known for their copying abilities. Huipils and ***quechquemitls,*** or capes, made during the 1920s and '30s, often display such European influences as Escher and Miró.

Santa Barbara

North from Los Angeles, Santa Barbara benefits from a near-perfect climate of sunny skies, refreshing sea breezes, and pleasantly warm temperatures. Outdoor enthusiasts come here for horseback riding, surfing, camping, and bicycling. There are also botanical gardens to explore and interesting wine country. Downtown, the street scene thrives with a diverse crowd of students, couples on holiday, and old-timers who stay for the late afternoon breeze.

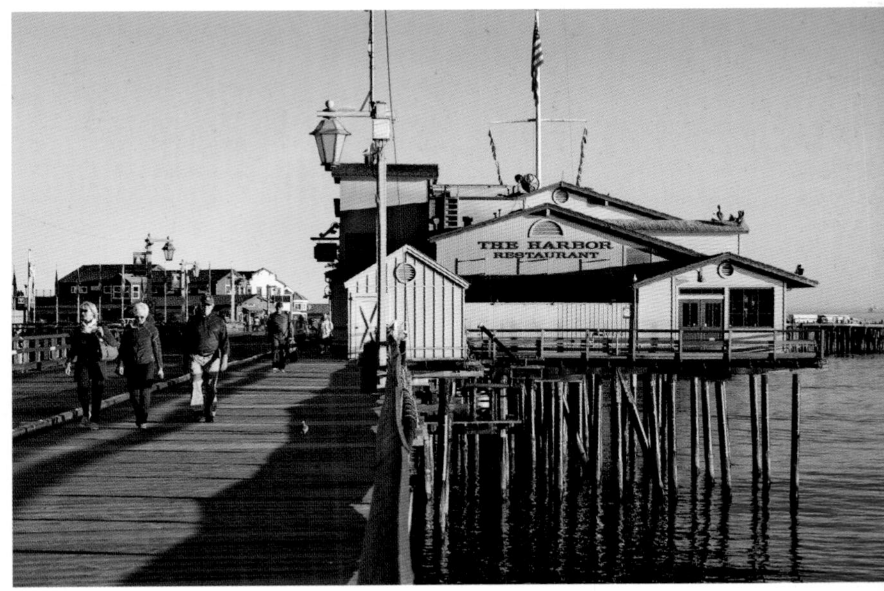

Stroll along Stearns Wharf for boutique shops, fishing opportunities, and on-the-water dining.

Santa Barbara, which has nurtured its Hispanic roots, revels in red-tiled roofs and mission revival architecture. But the atmosphere is not kitsch. The Chumash word *anacapa* ("pleasant illusion") seems to sum it all up.

Mission Santa Barbara

Founded in 1786 but not completed until 1820, Mission Santa Barbara *(2201 Laguna St. via Alameda Padre Serra, tel 805/682-4713, www.sbmission.org, $)* is one of California's most architecturally distinguished missions, its Ionic columns and Roman facade taking their cues from the drawings of Vetruvius Pollio, dating from 27 B.C. The Roman connection derives from St. Barbara, the mission's namesake, an early Christian martyr. Some of the leading hidalgos and Americanos of the era were educated in its mid-19th-century boys' school. A big attraction

Santa Barbara

130 C4

Visitor Information

Santa Barbara Conference & Visitors Bureau and Film Commission, 1601 Anacapa St.

805/966-9222

www.santabarbaraca.com

Arlington Theatre

✉ 1317 State St.

☎ 805/963-4408

www.thearlingtontheatre.com

Casa de la Guerra Historic House Museum

✉ 15 E. de la Guerra St.

☎ Tours: 805/965-0093

🕒 Closed a.m. & Mon.–Fri.

$ $

www.sbthp.org/casa.htm

is the mission's interior colors, which still glow. Be sure to see the **baptismal font.**

The grounds bear extensive Native American influence. The mission fathers still minister to the area's remaining Chumash, and the commemorative seal to "Juana Maria," a Chumash woman, is the only such plaque dedicated to a Native American in the entire mission system.

The City

The focal point of Santa Barbara's street scene is **State Street,** with its shops, restaurants, and mission revival landmarks like the 1931 **Arlington Theatre,** where concerts, lectures, and movies are part of an ever-changing entertainment menu.

Another relic of the same style and era is the nearby **El Paseo** *(812 State St.),* a shop-filled pedestrian zone created in the early 1920s. The shopping precinct incorporates a much older structure, the **Casa de la Guerra Historic House Museum,** built in 1819 by the Spanish commandante, José de la

Mission Santa Barbara

A missionary bedroom circa 1800

Guerra. It was de la Guerra who, after Mexico won California from Spain, became the small pueblo's commercial leader. His wife was the daughter of Don Raimundo Carrillo, a veteran of the Sacred Expedition of 1869 that had founded the city. A look at the highbrow European furnishings so lovingly acquired by the Carrillo family brings to life the early days of the community here.

The immediate area is filled with other well-preserved remnants of Spanish days, including the **Hill-Carrillo Adobe** (1825–26) at 11–15 E. Carrillo Street, the **Lugo Adobe** (1830) at 114 E. de la Guerra Street, and the **Rochin Adobe** (1856) at 820 Santa Barbara Street. Five blocks east is the **Presidio Chapel** (1788), which contains the original fort's 18th-century decor. It offers a short slide show and a scale model of the Old Presidio.

To the north, the outstanding **Santa Barbara Museum of Art** has important holdings of works by O'Keeffe, Remington, and

Santa Barbara Museum of Art
✉ 1130 State St.
☎ 805/963-4364
🕒 Closed Mon.
$ $$
www.sbmuseart.org

Santa Barbara County Courthouse

- 1100 Anacapa St.
- Tours: 805/962-6464
- Guided tours 2 p.m. Mon.–Sat. & 10:30 a.m. Mon.–Tues. & Fri.

www.sbcourts.org

Santa Barbara Botanical Gardens

- 1212 Mission Canyon
- 805/682-4726
- $

www.sbbg.org

Santa Barbara Zoo

- 500 Ninos Dr. (off Cabrillo)
- 805/962-6310
- $$

www.sb2000.org

Hopper. Two blocks east is the pièce de résistance of Spanish colonial revival, the **Santa Barbara County Courthouse** (1929), considered one of the most beautiful municipal gems in the U.S. Designed by architect William Moser, the courthouse offers daily guided tours. Don't miss it.

North of the mission district, the **Santa Barbara Botanical Gardens** are the most remarkable of Santa Barbara's public gardens. More than 5 miles (8 km) of trails wander through 78 acres (31.5 ha) of California native plants.

Directly east of the mission is 18-acre **Franceschi Park** *(1501 Mission Ridge Rd.)*, named for Emmanuele Franceschi, who lived in Santa Barbara between 1893 and 1912. The panoramic views and old stone pathways through aloe gardens make this an intriguing botanical getaway.

Southeast, nearer the beach, are the **Santa Barbara Zoo,** a small zoo in a garden of an old estate, and, farther up Cabrillo, the 32-acre (13 ha) **Andree Clark Bird Refuge** *(Los Patos Way, Cabrillo exit from U.S. 101)*, where you can bicycle through lush gardens squawking with waterbirds.

Many of the area's most scenic beaches are north of the city, but for plain seaside fun try **Leadbetter Beach** or **West Beach,** adjacent to historic **Stearns Wharf.** The wharf itself is a major attraction, with several good seafood restaurants, a vintner's shop, and **Ty Warner Sea Center** *(211 Stearns Wharf, tel 805/962-2526, www.sbnature.org/seacenter, $)*. You could rent a bicycle and take in **Chase Palm Park,** also adjacent to Stearns.

EXPERIENCE: Riding Horses in Wine Country

Long before the advent of boutique wineries, the Santa Ynez Valley was known for its horse ranches. Spreads like **Magali Farms** *(3951 Baseline Ave., Santa Ynez, tel 805/693-1777, www.magalifarms.com)* have produced a steady stream of thoroughbred champions over the years. Often seen riding the range, President Ronald Reagan transformed the Rancho del Cielo into the Western White House. Michael Jackson morphed another ranch into his Neverland nirvana.

Today, you can find equine adventures throughout the valley. In addition to scenic trail rides, **Little Big Riding School** *(Rancho Olivos, 2390 Refugio Rd., Santa Ynez, tel 805/886-2215, www.santaynezvalleyhorsebackriding.com)* hosts lessons and camps *($$$$–$$$$$)* for adults and children. As the name suggests, **Vino Vaqueros** *(tel 805/944-0493, www.vinovaqueros.com, $$$$$)* outside of Los Olivos combines horseback riding through scenic vineyards with a tasting at a local winery. **Alisal Guest Ranch** *(1054 Alisal Rd., Solvang, tel 805/688-6411, www.alisal.com)* offers rides to its overnight guests along 50 miles (80 km) of trails, as well as private lessons and a rodeo every Wednesday during the summer.

One of the valley's most unique establishments is **Return to Freedom** *(tel 805/737-9246, www.returntofreedom.org)*, a wild horse sanctuary that provides a haven for more than 400 mustangs from around the West. Although not open to the public on a daily basis, the ranch hosts educational tours and hikes.

At sunrise and sunset, the glowing waves around Santa Barbara lure visitors to stunning Pacific vistas.

North of Santa Barbara

To get a sense of Santa Barbara's historic grandeur, drive northwest on U.S. 101, past three remarkable state beaches: **El Capitan, Refugio,** and **Gaviota.** The rangers can tell you where the old **hot springs** are located, just to the north off Vandenburg Road.

From here, the highway veers inland through some of the most beautiful oak and chaparral in the state. Stop at **Nojoqui Falls** *(off Alisal Rd.)* for a short hike up to the area's only major waterfall. Continuing north, take Calif. 246 to **Solvang** *(see map p. 130 B4; visitor information, Solvang Conference & Visitors Bureau, 1639 Copenhagen Dr., tel 800/468-6765, www.solvangusa.com),* a Danish village that is also home to **Mission Santa Inés.**

Drive through the Santa Ynez Valley before joining scenic Calif. 154. In tiny **Los Olivos** *(see map p. 130 B5; visitor information, www.losolivosca.com),* you can browse for antiques and California art. Look for prints by California artist Joe DeYong—a kind of cowboy-meets-Zen landscape and figure painter.

Return to Santa Barbara via Calif. 154, which parallels the old stagecoach route. Stop at **Chumash Painted Caves State Historical Park** to see the Native American cave art.

South of Santa Barbara

Go southwest on U.S. 101 to the exclusive enclave of Montecito where, by appointment, you can visit **Casa del Herrero,** a private, 11-acre (4.4 ha) estate known for its outstanding Spanish-Moorish-style garden. Then explore the antique shops in nearby **Carpinteria,** at the end of Calle Ocho Road and a grand lookout point.

Farther south on U.S. 101 is the harbor town of **Ventura,** known for its bargain antiques and the recently opened **Murphy Auto Museum** *(2230 Statham Blvd., tel 805/487-4333, www.murphyautomuseum.com, closed Mon.–Fri.),* displaying autos spanning the last hundred years. Little **Mission San Buenaventura** *(see map p. 130 C4, 211 E. Main St., Ventura, tel 805/643-4318, www.sanbuenaventuramission.org)* was rebuilt in 1809 after being destroyed by fire. ■

Mission Santa Inés

✉ 1760 Mission Dr., Solvang

☎ 805/688-4815

www.missionsantaines.org

Chumash Painted Caves State Historical Park

Map: 130 C4

✉ Painted Cave Rd.

☎ 805/733-3713

www.parks.ca.gov for directions

Casa del Herrero

✉ 1387 E. Valley Rd., Montecito

☎ 805/565-5653

Hours: Tours twice daily Wed. & Sat. Closed mid-Nov. to mid-Feb.

$ $$$$

www.casadelherrero.com

Ventura

Map: 130 C4

Visitor Information

✉ 101 S. California St., Ventura

☎ 800/333-2989

www.ventura-usa.com

Mission La Purisima Concepción

There may be more beautiful missions than La Purisima Concepción, a humble grouping of adobe buildings, but no other mission better captures the essence of mission life in the early 19th century. Completely restored by the Civilian Conservation Corps in the 1930s, La Purisima—"the most pure"—is a perfect place to spend a meditative morning away from the crowds, wandering among the old mission buildings and delighting in the outstanding garden of herbs and native plants.

Mission La Purisima Concepción

 130 B5

2295 Purisima Rd., Lompoc (off Calif. 246, 3 miles NE of central Lompoc)

805/733-3713

$

www.lapurisimamission.org

Completed in 1822 after its original structure was destroyed by the great earthquake of 1812, La Purisima is a repository of colonial history. And while much of its story underscores the tragedy wrought on the Chumash by newcomers to their lands, much also serves to dispel the stereotype of the Indian as a passive rustic.

Beyond the **visitor center,** which provides an introductory overview, is the **cemetery,** starting point for the mission's one-hour guided tours. Here you come face to face with the blunt fact that, between 1804 and 1807, more than 500 Chumash died at La Purisima from exposure to European smallpox and measles.

Next to the cemetery, the long, narrow **church** once accommodated up to a thousand worshippers for Sunday Mass. Its uneven floors and austere ornamentation reflect the rawness of mission life. The "river of life" pattern on the main doors suggests that the Chumash imbued their churches with their own art.

The nearby **soldiers' quarters, carpenter's shop,** and **weavery** tell of the entrepreneurial nature of the mission system. Each unit was expected to grow and prosper through its own labors. Grain was milled and tallow processed for soap on the back patio. Nearby stands the **dormitory** for unmarried women.

In 1824, the tension between the Chumash and soldiers grew so great at La Purisima that neophytes here joined a rebellion that had begun at nearby Mission Santa Inés (see p. 167). Surrounding La Purisima, a group of Chumash seized two cannon, built a wooden wall around the mission, and held their Spanish captives for a month before backup troops arrived to quash the action.

The last major building consists of the **padres' quarters,** a **convent,** and a small **chapel**. From here, Padre Mariano Payeras designed the mission's irrigation system and managed a shop that sold candles, wool, and goods made of leather.

The **herb and flower garden** outside the compound has been completely restored to its original glory. In what might these days be called "Mission Ayurvedic," Chumash and padres created the first bicultural apothecary. ■

Ojai

Among the rites of passage for young Angelenos, a trip to Ojai to explore variants of Hinduism and other non-Western religions stands as the only proper antidote to that other L.A. rite—the drunken coming-of-age bar crawl in Tijuana.

The venerable **Krotona Institute of Theosophy** *(46 Krotona Hill, tel 805/646-1139, closed Mon., www.theosophical.org)* was founded by American followers of Annie Besant, a 19th-century proponent of Theosophy, a universalistic amalgam of Hindu and Christian thought. Regardless of one's religious orientation, a visit to Krotona will help explain the more complex spiritual landscape behind this region's flighty reputation.

The other culture in Ojai—that of rest and civilized sport—can best be found at the **Ojai Valley Inn & Spa** *(905 Country Club Rd., tel 805/646-1111, www.ojairesort.com)*. The renovated hotel, in the mission revival style, sits in spectacular country, which you can explore on a rented bicycle. For pure bliss afterward, try a soak at **The Oaks** *(122 E. Ojai Ave., tel 800/753-6257, www.oaksspa.com)*, an outstanding full-service spa.

For real food in classic Ojai fashion, go to the **Ranch House** *(S. Lomita Ave. & Besant Rd., tel 805/646-2360, reservations recommended)*, where the roasted pork and pâté are out of this world.

Farther east, you can visit the **Ronald Reagan Presidential Library & Museum.** The Gallery of Presidents honors 200 years of the Presidency. The museum also hosts rotating exhibitions, and you can tour Air Force One. ■

Ojai

- Map: 130 C4

Visitor Information

- Address: Visitors Bureau, 206 N. Signal St., Ojai
- Phone: 888/652-4669

www.ojaivisitors.com

Ronald Reagan Presidential Library & Museum

- Map: 130 D4
- Address: 40 Presidential Dr., Simi Valley
- Phone: 805/577-4000, 805/522-2977
- Price: $$$

www.reaganfoundation.org

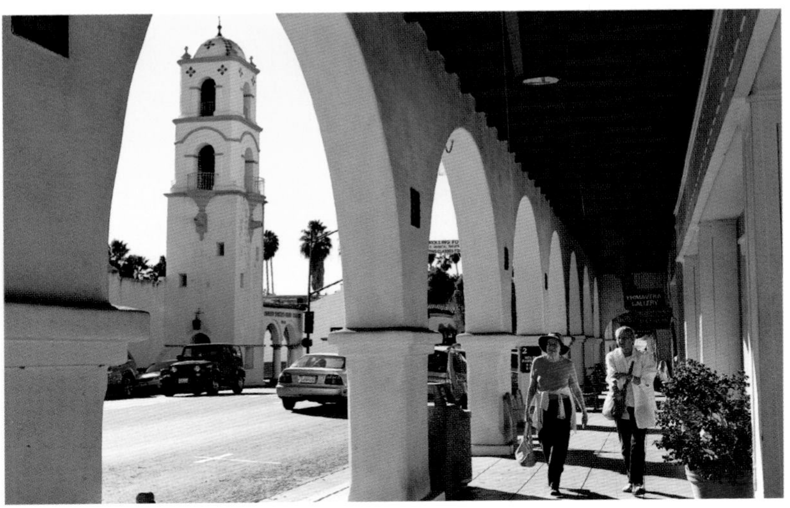

Spanish arches frame the colonial-revival-style post office in Ojai.

Channel Islands National Park

Surrounded by giant beds of gleaming green kelp, punctuated by deep blue coves and the mysterious remains of ships sunk long ago, the Channel Islands became a national park in 1980. From January through March, nature adds a further attraction: the gray whale migration. Visitors can spot the 40-foot (12 m) beasts swimming in schools, often with calves, their spouts shooting high in the air. Bald eagles soar overhead after recently being reintroduced.

Channel Islands National Park

 130 B3–D2

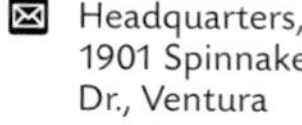
Headquarters, 1901 Spinnaker Dr., Ventura

805/658-5730

www.nps.gov/chis

HOW TO VISIT

To get a closer look, or simply to take in the adventures and scenery offered by these five islands, make a reservation with **Island Packers** *(tel 805/642-1393, www.islandpackers.com),* the official day boat concessionaire.

On **Anacapa,** itself composed of three islets, watch for whales, bottlenose dolphins, California sea lions, and northern elephant seals. Explore the tide pools at **Frenchys Cove,** and then go on to Anacapa, where, just offshore, you can see the remains of the *Winfield Scott*, which sank here in 1853.

Santa Cruz Island is the largest in the chain. The Chumash were its principal inhabitants for nearly 6,000 years, fishing and plying the waves in their sophisticated canoes. The island is an ecological miracle, home to 600 plant species, nine of which occur only here.

Santa Rosa Island is home to almost 200 bird species. Keep an eye out for dinosaur fossils; in 1994, explorers discovered the skeleton of a dwarf mammoth.

On **San Miguel Island,** explore the beaches and hike 3.5 miles (5.6 km) to the caliche forest to see mineral casts of old tree trunks and 10-foot-tall (3 m) specimens of the flowering plant *Coreopsis*.

Some 50 miles (80 km) to the southeast is **Santa Barbara Island.** Because it had no source of fresh water, the region's Native Americans did not reside on this island. Park authorities aim to restore the island's native flora, once overrun by foreign grasses. ■

EXPERIENCE: Kayaking the Channel Islands

Channel Islands National Park offers ample attractions for experienced paddlers, from gliding alongside migrating gray whales to exploring cathedral-size sea caves. Cart your own kayak on the ferries from Santa Barbara and Oxnard, or join a guided excursion.

Aquasports *(111 Verona Ave., Goleta, tel 800/773-2309, www.islandkayaking.com, $$$$$)* offers adventurous one-day trips to Santa Cruz, Anacapa, and Santa Barbara Islands, as well as three-day trips to Santa Cruz with overnight camping at Prisoner's Harbor and Scorpion Landing.

Those with limited or no paddling experience should consider a trip with **Blue Ocean Kayaking** *(3001 S. Victoria Ave., Oxnard, tel 805/204-0977, www.blueoceankayaking.com)* around skinny Anacapa Island. Based at Channel Islands Harbor in Oxnard, Blue Ocean keeps the mother boat close at hand, ready to retrieve paddlers at any point during the trip.

Before setting out, you should always check with park authorities for the latest information on weather, currents, and sensitive habitats that are off-limits.

The pull of the Pacific revealed in Hearst's fabulous castle, Steinbeck's novels, cozy Carmel, rugged Salinas, and beyond

Central Coast

The beautiful Pacific Coast Highway (Calif. 1), lined with wildflowers, along the Central Coast

Central Coast

A single image conveys the essence of California's Central Coast. A Monterey cypress, alone and defiant, is cast against the bruised blue sky of the Pacific. Fog rolls by in great puffs and swells over Cypress Point in Pebble Beach. First photographed by Carleton Watkins in 1885, the Monterey cypress has become a kind of visual haiku, denoting a primal Eden by the sea. Certainly John Steinbeck, who hailed from here, thought so.

Bixby Creek Bridge in Big Sur, opened in 1932

The drama of the Central Coast grows directly from its geography, particularly its relationship with the sea. Between Santa Cruz and Morro Bay is the nation's largest marine sanctuary. Under the waves, Monterey Canyon–the size of the Grand Canyon–wells with the cold, nutrient-rich waters that start the food chain that reaches up to the sea otter, the elephant seal, and the blue whale. It also has one of the world's largest kelp beds.

Land and sea create drama where the Santa Lucia Range tumbles into the Pacific at Big Sur, or on Point Lobos, where oak-and-cypress-dotted cliffs finally relent to the turbulence below. It's little wonder that photographers Ansel Adams and Edward Weston created some of their most memorable images here.

Travelers in search of drama will be rewarded by many historic sites. Spanish troops and padres settled here in 1770, and five years later the king made Monterey the capital of Spanish California. Here, too, the "original sin" of California history was committed. In 1775, Padre Junípero Serra ordered the recapture of a band of Native American converts who had fled Mission Carmel. The forced return of indigenous peoples to a culture that eventually wiped them out has haunted Serra's march toward sainthood ever since. The historical drama climaxed in Monterey in 1845–46, when Thomas Larkin, consul to Mexican California, began a series of intrigues that led to the state becoming a U.S. territory.

The Central Coast offers outdoor delights galore. Golfers can play at outstanding courses such as Pebble Beach. The offshore canyons of Monterey Bay yield spectacular scuba diving, while hikers can spend days exploring the trails of the Santa Lucia Range. Bird-watchers find their mecca north of Monterey on the Elkhorn

NOT TO BE MISSED:

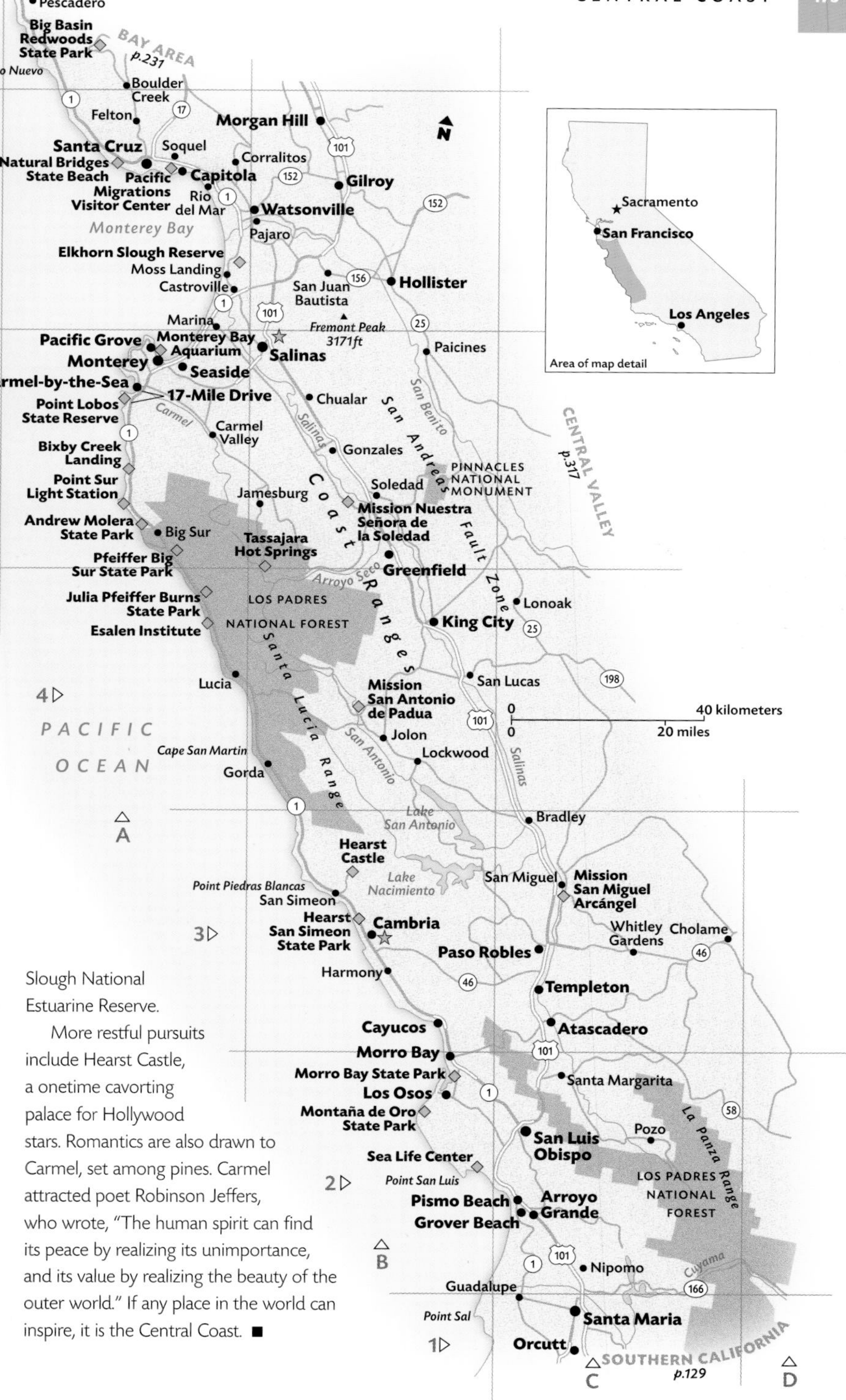

Slough National Estuarine Reserve.

More restful pursuits include Hearst Castle, a onetime cavorting palace for Hollywood stars. Romantics are also drawn to Carmel, set among pines. Carmel attracted poet Robinson Jeffers, who wrote, "The human spirit can find its peace by realizing its unimportance, and its value by realizing the beauty of the outer world." If any place in the world can inspire, it is the Central Coast. ■

Hearst Castle

As a boy traveling in Europe, publisher-tycoon William Randolph Hearst had told his mother that he would one day occupy Windsor Castle and buy the Louvre. Hearst kept his grand aspirations, and in 1919 commissioned his own *castello grande.* "Would it not be better," he wrote to his architect Julia Morgan, "to do something a little different than other people are doing in California as long as we do not do anything incongruous?" The result was an eclectic fusion of Mediterraneanism, tempered by California botany and topography.

Neptune Pool at Hearst Castle, built at 1,600 feet (487 m), holds 345,000 gallons (1,305,967 L) of water.

Hearst Castle
- 173 B3
- 750 Hearst Castle Rd., San Simeon
- 805/927-2020, 800/444-4445 (ticket information; reservations recommended)
- $$$$$

www.hearstcastle.com

The Hearst-Morgan collaboration (as he saw it) produced **La Casa Grande,** the estate's centerpiece. Choosing acquired elements of European decoration, such as the Spanish and Italian choir stalls used as wainscoting, Morgan fashioned a stunning new aesthetic, a mix of traditional European creations and modern techniques.

La Casa Grande was Hearst's salon, where he and Marion Davies entertained celebrities. As one account has it, guests were free to do as they liked as long as they followed four rules: congregate nightly in the ornate **Assembly Room** around the 16th-century French fireplace, take dinner in the adjoining **Refectory,** view the evening's motion picture in the **Theater,** and, most important, never utter the word "death" in the presence of their host.

The three guesthouses—**Casa del Mar** (often used by the Hearsts during construction of the main house), **Casa del Monte,** and **Casa del Sol**—were built in the Mediterranean style and are all mansions in their own right.

Around Hearst Castle

An easy side trip from Hearst Castle is to take Calif. 1 south to Hearst **San Simeon State Park,** where gorgeous scenery unfolds beneath rocky promontories and jagged cliffs. The park incorporates **Pa-Nu Cultural Preserve,** a significant archaeological site dating back almost 6,000 years. In winter, northern elephant seals gather at the state park beach up the coast from San Simeon Cove.

Farther south, at **Morro Bay State Park,** you may spot peregrine falcons and great blue herons.

At **Montaña de Oro State Park,** the Bluff Trail leads to interesting rock formations and tide pools. Inland is **San Luis Obispo** *(map p. 173 C2; Visitor Center, 1039 Chorro St., tel 805/781-2777, www.visitslo.com),* a good base for exploring two exciting new wine regions, **Paso Robles** *(map p. 173 C3; Visitor Center, 1225 Park St., tel 805/238-0506, www.pasoroblesschamber.com)* and **Arroyo Grande** *(map p. 173 C2; www.arroyogrande.org).*

Pismo Beach *(map p. 173 C2; Visitor Information Center, Hinds Ave. & Dolliver (tel 800/443-7778, www.classiccalifornia.com)* becomes the clam capital of the West Coast in October. Nearby, the **Sea Life Center** *(map p. 173 B2; 50 San Juan St., Avila Beach, tel 805/595-7280, www.sealifecenter.org)* has hands-on marine science exhibits.

Most people's best memory of Hearst Castle is the 104-foot-long (31 m) **Neptune Pool.** Tiled in deep blue and set in front of a Greco-Roman temple facade, it overlooks one of the estate's most spectacular vistas. The smaller indoor **Roman Pool** is lined with Venetian and gold-leaf tiles.

Hearst ordered that the estate be kept in year-round color. To do so, he built five **greenhouses** and hired a huge gardening staff to raise more than 500,000 annuals for rotational planting. Into these **gardens** he carefully positioned several gigantic coastal live oaks and California bay trees and built a 1.25-mile (2 km) pergola.

Like many gilded-age millionaires, Hearst acquired a collection of **European art** to decorate his home: antique ceilings, Greek vases, tapestries, and wall panels. Adriaen Ysenbrandt's 16th-century "Madonna and Child" adorns one wall in the main house. In the Gothic Suite sits "La Virgen de la Leche," a tiny statue carved in Spain some 500 years ago. Outside are four colossal stone lion-face goddesses carved in Egypt during the 13th century B.C.

How to Visit

Road access to the castle is restricted, so visitors must take a scheduled tour. One tour includes the ground floor of La Casa Grande, one of the guesthouses, both pools, and part of the gardens. Another tour visits the upper rooms of the main house. Three new daytime tour options include self-guided access to the grounds after the guided portion indoors. Evening tours in spring and fall are guided by docents in period costume. Special evening dinner events include an annual Christmas Holiday Feast. ■

Hearst San Simeon State Park

Map: 173 B3

Visitor Information

Address: Park Office, Van Gordon Creek Rd. at San Simeon Creek Rd., Cambria

Tel: 805/927-2020

www.parks.ca.gov

Morro Bay State Park

Map: 173 B2

Address: Morro Bay State Park Rd., Morro Bay

Tel: 805/772-2560

www.parks.ca.gov

Montaña de Oro State Park

Map: 173 B2

Visitor Information

Address: Park Office, Pecho Rd.

Tel: 805/528-0513

www.parks.ca.gov

Drive: Cambria to Carmel

With its dramatically twisting roads and stunning scenic promontories, Calif. 1 between Cambria and Carmel is to many Californians a kind of modern pilgrimage, the object of reverence being the Big Sur River (crossed by the awe-inspiring Big Sur Bridge) and its beautiful forested hinterlands.

Begin a trip north on Calif. 1 by first getting gas and a meal in **Cambria** ❶ *(visitor information, Chamber of Commerce, 767 Main St., tel 805/927-3624, www.cambriachamber.org)*; the distances between the few towns are long, and the road is a workout in itself at times.

Beyond the small town of **Lucia** (the southernmost limit of the redwood tree) lie the three state parks of central Big Sur. First is **Julia Pfeiffer Burns State Park** ❷ *(tel 831/667-2315, www.parks.ca.gov)*. A trail leads to Saddle Rock, location of the only waterfall on the Pacific Coast that falls directly into the ocean. Behind it looms **Anderson Peak,** at 4,099 feet (1,249 m) the highest point of the Santa Lucia Range. A few miles farther north is the **Henry Miller Memorial Library** ❸ *(48603 Calif. 1, Big Sur, tel 831/667-2574, closed Tues., www.henrymiller.org)*, in the place where the writer spent the postwar years with a coterie of fellow artists.

The star of the Big Sur coast is **Pfeiffer Big Sur State Park** ❹ *(tel 831/667-2315, www.parks.ca.gov)*, the largest of the three state parks, with a substantial stand of redwoods. A good swim in the Big Sur River before making a campsite is an old California tradition.

About 6 miles (9.6 km) north again is **Andrew Molera State Park** ❺ *(tel 831/667-2315, www.parks.ca.gov)*, where the scenic Big Sur River ends in a fine habitat for birds and wildlife. Look for mule deer, gray foxes, and raccoons. Much in the way of classic drama surrounds the location of **Point Sur Light Station** *(tel 831/625-4419, www.pointsur.org, walking tours: $$)*, built in 1889 after two shipwrecks.

The Big Sur area has a series of interesting places to stay or eat. The cabins at **Deetjens Big Sur Inn** *(48865 Calif. 1, Castro Canyon, Big Sur, tel 831/667-2377, www.deetjens.com)*, which has a good Norwegian restaurant, are named for various literary figures. Not far away is the restaurant-bar **Nepenthe** *(48510 Calif. 1, Big Sur, tel 831/667-2345, www.nepenthebigsur.com)*, designed by a student of Frank Lloyd Wright. The deck overlooks the Pacific.

Long considered the ultimate in Big Sur lodging, the **Ventana Inn** *(48123 Calif. 1, Big Sur, tel 831/667-2331, www.ventanainn.com)* has spacious luxury cabins (with kitchens) built on a sun-flecked hillside. The massages and spa treatments are outstanding, and you can enjoy the Japanese baths, stroll among the trees in Ventana's white bathrobes, and enjoy the peace.

At the **Loma Vista Café & Gardens** *(tel 831/667-2818)*, you can enjoy a cup of coffee and great views of the Santa Lucia Range.

Approaching Carmel (see pp. 180–181), you reach **Point Lobos State Natural Reserve** ❻ *(tel 831/624-4909, www.pointlobos.org)*, whose coves are home to sea lions, sea otters, and pelicans. Literary experts believe this was the inspiration for Spyglass Hill in *Treasure Island* (1883), which Robert Louis Stevenson wrote after visiting in 1879. Follow the **Sea Lion Point Trail** past stands of wild red buckwheat to a lookout onto Sea Lion Rocks, or take the **Cypress Grove Trail** around a grove of ancient cypress hung with green-blue moss.

NOT TO BE MISSED:

Julia Pfeiffer Burns SP • Point Lobos SNR • Nacimiento Fergusson Road

---

The environs support delicate coastal orchids, which grow along the branches of fallen trees.

Return from Carmel by taking County Road G16 up the Carmel Valley. After 20 miles (32 km), Tassajara Road on the right takes you to **Tassajara Zen Mountain Center** ❼ *(39171 Tassajara Rd., Carmel Valley, tel 831/659-2229, www.sfzc.org/tassajara)*, with natural hot springs. Overnight stays are possible in summer.

Return to G16 and continue via Arroyo Seco Rd. to **Greenfield.** A few miles down U.S. 101, turn off on County Road G14 to the small town of **Jolon,** the setting for John Steinbeck's novel *To a God Unknown* (1933), about a pioneering California family. In a quiet valley to the north is the restored **Mission San Antonio de Padua** ❽ *(Mission Rd., tel 831/385-4478, www.missionsanantonio.net)*, founded in 1771.

Return to the coast road down **Nacimiento Fergusson Road** ❾. In the foothills of the Santa Lucia Range, wildflowers surround you, particularly in spring. The great variety of plant life here includes wild fennel, a non-native that is slowly dominating the coastal underbrush; white-plumed our lord's candle; bright green-yellow mustard (said to have been sown by the padres); and coastal agave, its tendril-like biomorph twisting and looking like a beached octopus.

Ecology of Light, Sea, & Stone

The artwork of Edward Weston, Ansel Adams, & Robinson Jeffers

Of the many reasons artists and writers came to the Central Coast, the most important are its physical elements—light, sea, and stone. The evanescence of the first, the promise of the second, the hard reality of the third—these the artists of Big Sur cannot avoid. Their combined hardness, as Ansel Adams once put it, forces the artist to focus on "really seeing."

Edward Weston

For photographer Edward Weston (1886–1958), the Central Coast represented both escape and maturation. He came here in 1923, after leaving his wife and taking up with an exotic Italian actress. He began an association with Mexican art "radicals" David Alfaro Siquieros (see sidebar p. 93) and Diego Rivera, and his style became increasingly direct, documentary, erotic. Nude portraits of his many lovers were conscientiously unretouched. In the early 1930s, he settled in Carmel and, with Ansel Adams, founded the f/64 Movement, which pronounced that photography must be severed from the confining strictures of formalistic art.

Weston's photo "The Fishing Fleet, Monterey" captures *his* Central Coast. It shows Monterey Marina in the late afternoon. There is a small rock in the foreground, gulls sunning; in the background bob the little workboats, waiting for their masters. This was an exotic, but contained, aesthetic moment.

Ansel Adams

Weston's friend Ansel Adams (1902–1984) was equally passionate about nature and photography: "I believe in stones and water, air and soil, people and their future, and their fate." This directness with his subjects bursts from all Adams's photographs, the most well known of which are of Half Dome in Yosemite (see pp. 304–309). Travel down to the shoreline of Point Lobos State Natural Reserve (see p. 176), as Adams did, to see *his* Central Coast. Here shadow and light seem to hold their own vast territories, a block of light here, of darkness there. There is a Zen quality to Adams's Big Sur photographs. They are momentary yet hard—a visual "belief" in stones and water.

Robinson Jeffers

It was poet Robinson Jeffers (1887–1962) who perhaps better than anyone fused Weston's personal coast with Adams's natural coast. Jeffers went even further than Adams's and Weston's stripped-down coastal images. For him, *only* nature mattered, mankind being but a passing presence. Only

EXPERIENCE: Enlightenment

To find *your* Central Coast, pay a visit to the Esalen Institute *(map p. 173 A4; 55000 Calif. 1, Big Sur, tel 888/837-2536, www.esalen.org)*, where Ansel Adams was once an instructor.

Founded in 1962 on a cliff top overlooking the ocean at Big Sur, the institute was a nexus for spiritual studies and alternative philosophies during the flower power era. Since then, it has evolved into a highly respected learning center that presents more than 500 seminars and workshops annually. Workshop topics range from yoga meditation to photography and creative writing. Typical workshops *($$$$$)* last one week. You can also sign up for a "personal retreat."

"Autumn Tree in Cathedral Rocks" is one of many photographs Ansel Adams took in Yosemite.

those who understood this, he believed, had any chance of finding some peace in an increasingly inhumane world.

The early local population in Big Sur, described in a 1939 guidebook as a folk given to "inbreeding, passion, moroseness, and suspicion," filled Jeffers's prose. Bixby Creek Landing, north of Point Sur, was the setting for his "Thurso's Landing," about a woman who takes up with her husband's only friend, a dynamiter for a roadbuilding crew. In one scene, the wife, Helen, says to her lover: "Do you ever think about death? I've seen you play with it. Strolling away while the fuse fizzled in the rock." "Hell no," the dynamiter replies, "that was all settled when they made the hills."

Carmel-by-the-Sea & Around

An artists' colony developed by two nimble real estate developers eager to exploit the post-1906-earthquake residential needs of the rich, Carmel has from its very beginnings epitomized what we have come to call the "lifestyle community." Its cachet lies in its "themed exclusivity" as an arts community. Residents have included poet George Sterling, regionalist Mary Austin, radical Lincoln Steffens, and increasingly conservative Robinson Jeffers (see pp. 178–179).

Carmel is known for its easy pace, quintessential English charm, and rich art history.

Carmel-by-the-Sea

173 A5

Visitor Information

Visitor Center, San Carlos, betw. 5th St. & 6th St., Carmel

831/624-2522, 800/550-4333

www.carmelcalifornia.com

In Carmel, business always took a back seat to aesthetics, something even Clint Eastwood had to admit after his failed attempt as mayor to bring the village into the entrepreneurial age. To this day, the recherché tumble of small boutiques on Ocean Avenue epitomizes the word "cute."

Not surprisingly, visitors come to Carmel for peace and quiet. That's good, as there is not a lot to do here except admire the scenery and the wildlife, hike, and wander through art galleries. Stock up on outstanding picnic supplies at the Mediterranean Market *(Ocean Ave. & Mission St.)* before heading off to **Carmel River State Beach** *(off Scenic Rd., S of Carmel Beach, tel 831/649-2836, www.parks.ca.gov).* Here, slopes flushed with pine and oak fall to a brilliant white beach, perfect for hiking and bird-watching.

When you tire of the beach, return to town for a little browsing along **Ocean Avenue,** where shops sell everything from proper nautical wear to handmade cardigans and shawls. For some hearty food in a family-style atmosphere, go to **Little Napoli** *(Dolores St.*

near 7th Ave., tel 831/626-7373, www.pepemag.com), where the food is straightforward and satisfying, the service friendly, and the atmosphere warm and jolly.

Since lounging and sitting by cozy fireplaces are two principal Carmel activities, three inns are worth noting (see also Travelwise p. 363). The first is **Quail Lodge** *(8000 Valley Greens Dr., tel 831/620-8866, www.quaillodge.com),* which sits in the Carmel Valley. For a more eco-New Age experience, try the **Highlands Inn** *(Calif. 1, S of Carmel, tel 831/620-1234, www.highlandsinn.hyatt.com).* With their balcony views, in-room hot tubs, spas, personal sound systems, and wood-burning fireplaces, the rooms here make for a memorable experience.

Nearer to the center of town, **The Normandy Inn** *(Ocean Ave. & Monte Verde St., tel 831/624-3825, www.normandyinncarmel.com)* is charming and located near the shops and the beach.

Tor House & Hawk Tower

Perhaps the most original feature in all Carmel is Tor House and its adjoining Hawk Tower, both built by poet Robinson Jeffers between 1914 and 1930 (with later additions). Jeffers and his wife, Una, were attracted to the dramatic site, a *tor* or craggy hill near the outflow of the Carmel River, and the structures reflect the couple's idiosyncrasies. Almost inseparable from the elements to which it is so exposed, the house is an unforgettable California monument to creativity, individualism, and strength.

Festivals & Art Venues

As might be expected, Carmel hosts several outstanding cultural events and venues. The **Carmel Bach Festival** *(tel 831/624-1521, www.bachfestival.org)* takes the spotlight in July and August, when concerts and classes on the composer take center stage. In October, the **Carmel Art and Film Festival** *(tel 831/625-3700, www.carmelartandfilm.com)* offers the works of leading modern artists. The **Pacific Repertory Theater** *(tel 831/622-0100, www.pacrep.org)* runs year-round.

EXPERIENCE: Artista Art Vacation

If the creative urge overtakes you before visiting Carmel—and you happen to be a woman—check out the wide range of residential "creative safaris" at Artista *(tel 831/625-5748, www.artistacreative.com, $$$$$).* Classes in abstract painting, encaustic (hot wax) painting, and artistic collage are combined with a two-night/three-day stay at a local boutique inn. The cost includes art supplies, daily yoga session, and two meals each day. Artista's instructors are accomplished artists in their fields.

It is worth checking out the works by locals at the **Carmel Art Association** *(Dolores St. between 5th & 6th Aves., tel 831/624-6176, www.carmelart.org).* Many visitors end up returning again and again, following and acquiring the works of one artist, year after year.

Tor House & Hawk Tower

26304 Ocean View Ave. (betw. Stewart Way & Bay View Ave.), Carmel

831/624-1813

Foundation open Mon.–Thurs. Hourly tours Fri.–Sat. No children under 12. Reservations required.

$$

www.torhouse.org

17-Mile Drive
173 A5
Scenic Tour
831/373-3304
$$
www.pebblebeach.com

17-Mile Drive

A toll road worth every cent, the legendary 17-mile (27 km), coast-hugging drive along the Carmel peninsula encompasses some of Monterey Bay's most spectacular coastal vistas and natural features. The private roadway (closed to motorcycles) snakes through the gated community of Pebble Beach, stippled with luxurious mansions and a mecca for golf enthusiasts. Even on foggy days, it's hard to get lost thanks to red dotted markings along the route.

EXPERIENCE: Coastal Golfing

Other than winning the Masters with a long 18th-hole putt, playing Pebble Beach Golf Links *(tel 800/654-9300, www.pebblebeach.com/golf)* is the most enduring dream of golfers nationwide. The famed seaside course was founded in 1919 and annually hosts the National Pro-Am tournament that pairs the world's best golfers with celebrity show-biz partners. Unlike many exclusive golf clubs, the Pebble Beach links are open to the general public. The cost of a round of 18 holes *($$$$$)* does not include cart fees.

Heading north from the Carmel Gate *(off Calif. 1 at N. San Antonio Rd.)*, the road loops up to **Huckleberry Hill,** smack in the middle of the Del Monte Forest.

The road meets the shore at **Spanish Bay,** where explorer Gaspar de Portola anchored in 1796, believing it to be Monterey Bay. Rising above the southern end of the beach, the rocky pinnacles of **Point Joe** lured many a mariner to their fate in the false belief that the point marked the entrance to Monterey. The colliding currents here stir up nutrients that feed fishes that in turn bring pelicans, cormorants, and other seabirds in vast numbers. **Bird Rock** is a favored roost; seals and sea lions often snooze at nearby **Seal Rock** and **Fanshell Beach.**

INSIDER TIP:

Be sure to pick up the brochure available at the start of the drive. It spells out all the details of the route.

—JOE YOGERST
National Geographic author

Nearby, various species of native cypress and pine are a highlight of **Crocker Grove**, a 13-acre (5.2 ha) nature reserve. The lone twisted tree at **Cypress Point** must be one of the world's most photographed living things.

To end, stop for a drink or meal at the **Lodge at Pebble Beach** *(tel 831/647-7500)*, a world-class resort renowned as the setting for **Pebble Beach Golf Links** (see sidebar), where crooner Bing Crosby launched the Pebble Beach National Pro-Am, which still draws the world's top golfers.

Auto aficionados flock in each August for the **Concours d'Elegance** *(tel 831/622-1700, www.pebblebeachconcours.net)*, a showcase of historic cars.

Mission Carmel

The second mission built in California by Padre Junípero Serra, **Mission San Carlos Borromeo del Rio Carmelo**—or Mission Carmel—is historical ground zero for almost all modern discussions of the mission system and its legacy. This was Serra's place of great toil, the center of his attempt to re-create Spanish civilization in a raw new world. Between 1770 and 1836, he and his successors confirmed more than 4,000 neophytes here.

Today the deep interconnectedness of Serra and California's self-identity can be seen in the statue located in the restored **Old Quadrangle.** Entitled the "Serra Cenotaph" and sculpted in 1924 by local artist Jo Mora, the work portrays a triumphant Serra, a California grizzly bear at his feet.

In the ornate **basilica** are the graves of the mission's founders, including Serra, whose living quarters, or **cell,** has also been restored, albeit with some creative revisionist spin: The leather scourges or whips that used to hang here have been removed, likely out of fear that visitors might "misinterpret" their use. (The padres used them on themselves and, occasionally, on their converts.) On a lighter note, the restored **kitchen** gives an idea of the simplicity of mission life. The **garden** possesses a fine collection of native plants and a range of dahlias, some of them as large as eight inches (20.3 cm) in diameter.

Built in 1770, the Carmel Mission is still an active place of worship today.

Other Missions

Two lesser known missions are within driving distance of the Carmel mission south on U.S. 101. Founded by Padre Lasuén in 1791, **Mission Nuestra Señora de la Soledad** was one of the most remote of the missions. As such, it offered a hiding place to padres and neophytes in 1818 when French pirate Hippolyte de Bouchard was ravaging the other missions. A fine icon is its statue of the Virgin, dressed in the black of a Spanish doña in mourning.

Farther south on U.S. 101 is **Mission San Miguel Arcángel** *(see map p. 173 C3; 775 Mission St., tel 805/467-3256, www.missionsanmiguel.org)*. Founded in 1797 as an agricultural outpost, this mission has kept some original interior art. Created by neophytes, it is an original fusion of Old World medievalism and New World fecundity of color. ■

Mission San Carlos Borromeo del Rio Carmelo (Carmel Mission)

✉ 3080 Rio Rd., Carmel

☎ 831/624-1271

www.carmelmission.org

Mission Nuestra Señora de la Soledad

Map 173 B5

✉ 36641 Ft. Romie Rd., off U.S. 101, 3 miles SW of Soledad

☎ 831/678-2586

www.missionscalifornia.com

Driving in Steinbeck Country

It would take too long to list all the many real-life touchstones found in the stories of John Steinbeck. It is enough to say that his writing is inextricably woven into the vast Salinas Valley and points just beyond. These two drives convey much of the atmosphere of Steinbeck country. The Steinbeck Center in Salinas has a brochure with other tours.

Drive One: Salinas & the "Long Valley"

Orient yourself to Steinbeck country in **Salinas** ❶ *(visitor information, 119 E. Alisal St., tel 831/424-7611)* at the **National Steinbeck Center** *(1 Main St., tel 831/796-3833, www.steinbeck.org),* a modern facility rising out of the author's cherished **Old Town.** The center has an extensive collection of Steinbeck memorabilia—including Rocinante, the pickup truck in *Travels With Charley* (1962)—and several interactive exhibits. There are also displays of Hollywood's various renditions of his work. The Rabobank Wing celebrates the valley's rich agriculture heritage.

Just down the street is the **Steinbeck House** *(132 Central Rd., tel 831/424-2735, www.steinbeckhouse.com),* where the author was born and raised, and where you can have lunch. Other attractions here include the **Roosevelt School** *(120 Capitol St.),* the West End School in the epic *East of Eden* (1952). The author attended grades 3–8 here. On Main Street in Old Town are several sites mentioned in the same book, among them the San Francisco Chop House *(No. 116),* Krough's Drug Store building *(No. 156),* and Elks Building *(No. 247).* The **Garden of Memories Cemetery** *(850 Abbott St.)* is where the author is buried, along with several of the real-life characters in *East of Eden,* including the Hamilton Family, William J. Nesbitt (Sheriff Quinn), and Mary Jane Reynolds (Jenny).

Leave Salinas on U.S. 101 south. The town of **Soledad** ❷ *(visitor information, Visitor Center, 248 Main St., tel 831/223-5000, www.ci.soledad.ca.us)* was the setting for *Of Mice and Men* (1937); the general store is still here. Continue on U.S. 101, then turn northeast on County Road. G13 to **King City** ❸ *(visitor information, Visitor Center, 200 Broadway, Ste. 40, tel 831/385-3817, www.kingcity.com, closed Sat.–Sun.),* where Steinbeck set scenes in *The Red Pony* (1937). Return to U.S. 101 and go west to the G14 turnoff. Take this road to **Jolon** ❹**,** where the action takes place in *To a God Unknown* (1933).

Return to Salinas on U.S. 101, and take Calif. 68 west to pass the scenic **Salinas River Basin** ❺**,** where Steinbeck swam and hunted rabbits. Farther along is the mountainscape known as **Corral de Tierra** and **Castle Rock.** The latter was an inspiration for Steinbeck's *The Acts of King Arthur and His Noble Knights* (1976).

Continue on Calif. 68 into **Monterey** ❻ (see pp. 186–187). The town's **Cannery Row** was the setting for the 1945 novel of the same name, as well as *Tortilla Flat* (1935) and *Sweet Thursday* (1954). The lab of the real-life Ed Ricketts, Steinbeck's raconteur-marine biologist protagonist, is at 800 Cannery Row; Wing Chong's Market (now simply the Old General Store) is at No. 835. La Ida's Café (now called Kaliso's) is at No. 851. At 399 Alvarado Street, you can see the second-floor room in which Steinbeck wrote *The Pearl* (1947). It was from **Fisherman's Wharf** that Steinbeck and Ricketts set out for the Gulf of California in 1940, the inspiration for *Sea of Cortez* (1951).

NOT TO BE MISSED:

National Steinbeck Center • Cannery Row • Fisherman's Wharf • Fremont Peak • Pinnacles National Monument

---

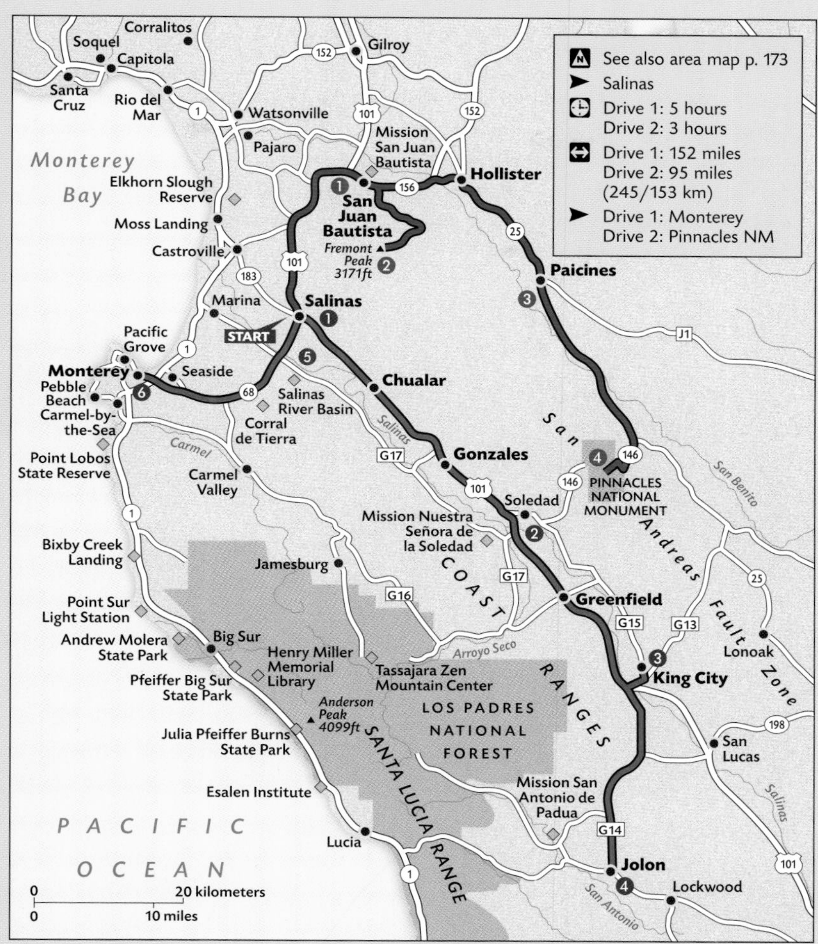

Drive Two: The Badlands

Heading north from Salinas on U.S. 101, go east on Calif. 156 to **San Juan Bautista** ❶ *(www.san-juan-bautista.ca.us).* The restored **Mission San Juan Bautista** *(N side of Plaza, tel 831/623-2127, www.oldmissionsjb.org)* has an altarpiece painted by Thomas Doak, the first American settler in Alta California. Steinbeck was fond of the mission and its stories.

From Calif. 156, exit on San Juan Canyon Road and head to **Fremont Peak State Park** ❷ *(tel 831/623-4255, www.parks.ca.gov).* It was on Fremont Peak that Steinbeck, in *Travels With Charley,* chose to go east, never to see his beloved valley again. To the west is the old Steinbeck ranch.

Down from the peak, continue east on Calif. 156, then go south on Calif. 25. In the tiny town of **Paicines** ❸ you can still buy a soda at the store where in 1873 the *bandito* Tiburcio Vásquez shot his last victim. **Pinnacles National Monument** ❹ *(tel 831/389-4486, www.nps.gov/pinn),* a mass of volcanic rock formations with hiking trails, looms to the south.

Historic Monterey

Claimed for Spain in 1770, Monterey remained the political, social, and economic core of California until the mid-1850s, when the Americanos decided to locate their new statehouse elsewhere. As an economic force, Monterey kept surging ahead, its fishing industry fueled by successive waves of immigrants. Today this bayside city teems with new enterprise, museums, art galleries, and an extensive restored historic district. Fisherman's Wharf is a favorite place to grab a bite to eat, shop, and stroll.

Popular with tourists, Cannery Row reminds visitors of the bayside city's long fishing history.

Monterey

173 A5

Visitor Information

Visitor Center, Franklin St. & Camino El Estero

877/666-8373

www.historicmonterey.com

Monterey State Historic Park

20 Customs House Plaza, Monterey

831/649-7118

www.parks.ca.gov

Monterey State Historic Park

With headquarters near the Customs House, the park links more than 30 historical places. Peppered with historical adobes, Monterey-style mansions, and public gardens, its "path of history" is well marked, beginning with the restored **Customs House,** the oldest government building in California. Here, in 1846, Commodore John Drake Sloat proclaimed California part of the United States. The **Larkin House,** a two-story adobe built during the Mexican period, was home to Thomas Oliver Larkin, the first and only U.S. consul to California under Mexican rule.

One of the more remarkable old-time adobes is the **Casa Soberanes Adobe,** also known as the House of the Blue Gate. Built in the 1840s, it has been beautifully restored, complete with original furnishings.

The **Pacific House,** originally used during the 1847 U.S. occupation of California, contains museums on early Monterey and Native American life. Perhaps the best single place to get a sense of early merchant life in Monterey is the **Cooper Molera Adobe,** named for trader John Rogers Cooper, who married into a prestigious Mexican family. The grounds include barns, farm animals, and vegetable and fruit gardens. **Colton Hall,** where the California constitution was signed, is another outstanding example of Monterey architecture. It now contains a museum about early state history.

The **Stevenson House** *(530 Houston St.)* is best known for Scottish writer Robert Louis Stevenson, who stayed here in 1879, recovering from an illness, before marrying and setting off for Napa Valley.

Away from the historic park, the **Presidio of Monterey** *(www.monterey.army.mil)* affords access to Sebastián Vizcaíno's 1602 landing site and the location of Padre Junípero Serra's first Mass in 1770. More recent military history is explored at the **Presidio of Monterey Museum** *(Corporal Ewing Rd., Bldg. 113, tel 831/646-3456, closed Sun. a.m., Mon. p.m., & Tues.–Wed.)*, which houses materials on local military history from the Spanish period through WWII.

The **Old Whaling Station** on Pacific Street was built in 1847 and later served as headquarters of the Old Monterey Whaling Company. The adobe's front walkway is paved with whale vertebrae. Nearby is the **Museum of Monterey,** which has broadly expanded its mission in recent years to encompass local art, history, innovation, and maritime activities. Housed in the waterfront Stanton Center, the collection ranges from early California decorative arts and clothing to model ships amassed by former ship captain and Carmel mayor Allen Knight.

Since its early days, Monterey has attracted more than its share of ambitious young artists. The **Monterey Museum of Art** *(www.montereyart.org)* holds an outstanding collection of their work and that of other Californians in its two locations (on Via Mirada and at the Civic Center).

Museum of Monterey

- 5 Customs House Plaza, Monterey
- 831/372-2608
- Closed Sun. a.m. & Mon.
- $$ (free 1st Tues. p.m. of month)

www.montereyhistory.org

Monterey Museum of Art

- 720 Via Mirada & 559 Pacific St., Monterey
- 831/372-3689 (Via Mirada), 831/372-5477 (Civic Center)
- Closed Mon.–Tues.
- $$

www.montereyart.org

EXPERIENCE: Hollywood's Wildlife

Perched on a hilltop overlooking the Salinas Valley and just a 30-minute drive from historic Monterey, Vision Quest Ranch *(400 River Rd., Salinas, tel 800/228-7382, www.visionquestranch.com)* offers a true California experience: Guests can stay overnight at a "safari style" bed & breakfast: canvas-walled cabins set on wooden platforms around the edge of an elephant sanctuary. The ranch is the home of many of the creatures that appear in Hollywood television and movie productions. From tarantulas and Bengal tigers to bears, birds, and baboons, animals of all types relax on the ranch between gigs. The ranch includes a compound for exotic animals and an equestrian center. Tours *($–$$$)* range from one-hour guided walks to daylong "full contact" experiences and customized photo safaris. Vision Quest also arranges summer camps and sleepovers for kids, as well as animal training courses and scuba diving in Monterey Bay.

Monterey Bay Aquarium
173 A5
886 Cannery Row, Monterey
831/648-4800
$$$$$
www.montereybay aquarium.org

Monterey Bay Aquarium

One of the world's preeminent education/research establishments of its kind, the excellent Monterey Bay Aquarium is dedicated to the vast realm of Monterey Bay, the nation's largest marine sanctuary, located just outside its door. Allow about three hours for your visit. If you intend to see one of the various regular specialty shows such as the feeding of the sea otters, check for scheduled times at the front information desk as you enter.

The aquarium's Open Sea exhibit includes not only sharks but also sea turtles and schools of fish.

The aquarium provides a tour of the world's oceans and Monterey Bay's four principal habitats. The central attraction of the first section is the **Kelp Forest.** This huge tank perfectly simulates a kelp environment, complete with surging waters and a variety of ichthyological inhabitants, including tightly knit schools of anchovies streaming between the long amber fronds. Try to see the twice-daily feeding show, in which scuba divers descend into the tank to hand-feed the creatures. On the second floor, the expanded and interactive **Splash Zone** grants a more detailed look at kelp forest, rocky shore, and coral reef habitats.

Among the new exhibits in the **Ocean Gallery** is a habitat for the giant Pacific octopus, a striking velvet-red creature that is rarely seen in the wild. Surprisingly intelligent, the octopuses recognize individual aquarium workers and have enough brain power to find extra food in plastic mazes.

The **Sand Shore Aviary** harbors birds found along the shoreline of Monterey Bay and adjacent wetlands like Elkhorn Slough (see sidebar opposite),

Elkhorn Slough

Located on a tidal channel teeming with wildlife and fish, Elkhorn Slough National Estuarine Research Reserve encompasses 1,400 acres (566 ha) of marshland and tidal flats and is home to more than 400 species of invertebrates, 80 species of fish, and 200 species of birds. Leopard sharks and bat rays cruise these shallow waters, and this is one of the last known reaches of the clapper rail.

After a morning at Elkhorn, stop at Moss Landing, where several stores deal in reasonably priced antique California and Arts and Crafts–era pottery. The cafés offer outstanding oyster dishes. The used bookstore is a reader's dream. If you come in early spring, stop at one of the roadside stands and try a fresh artichoke—or have some shipped back home; nearby Castroville is the artichoke capital of the world.

including the western sandpiper, red phalarope, long-billed curlew, and ruddy turnstone.

In the **Rocky Shores** tank, visitors can watch the tiny creatures that thrive at the water's edge. Eels slither about between bizarre-looking nudibranches and their whirls of newly hatched eggs. The focal point is a walk-through acrylic tunnel that lets you experience the power of waves that crash overhead.

The **Tide Pool Life** exhibit uses man-made waves to enliven several tidal habitats, including that of the hermit crab, sculpin, sea stars, and various forms of anemone. New to this area are the African blackfooted penguins, which thrive in the cold-water currents of the South Atlantic.

The aquarium's **outdoor decks** provide a perfect spot from which to watch for the various marine mammals that routinely make their way through the bay: harbor seals, harbor porpoises, white-sided dolphins, orca whales, and elephant seals. The 50,000-gallon (189,270 L) **Sea Otter** tank gives visitors a close-up look at these playful creatures, which the aquarium obtained as rescued orphans. Nearby are some of the aquarium's newest residents: North Atlantic puffins, juvenile sea turtles, and sea horses.

Mission to the Deep combines high-definition video footage with interactive computer animations of underwater robots and other high-tech tools used in underwater research.

Be sure to leave time for the last section, the **Open Sea,** which contains two of the aquarium's most memorable displays. Focusing on the submerged world starting 200 miles (322 km) offshore, the exhibit explores a world of light, temperature, and salinity. Perhaps the most spectacular of these seafarers are the ocean travelers, everything from plankton to crab larvae to predatory jellyfish. In dramatically lit tanks, rare jellyfish glow like diamonds against a vast black velvet robe. The purple-striped jelly can reach up to 30 inches (76 cm) in diameter. The million-gallon (3,785,410 L) Open Sea tank holds giant ocean sunfish, schools of tuna and bonito, sharks, and sea turtles. ■

Elkhorn Slough National Estuarine Research Reserve

Map: 173 A6

Address: 1700 Elkhorn Rd., Elkhorn

Phone: 831/728-2822

Hours: Closed Mon.–Tues.

Price: $

www.elkhornslough.org

Moss Landing

Map: 173 A6

Visitor Information

www.mosslandingchamber.com

Castroville

Map: 173 A6

Santa Cruz & Around

For those with a slightly more bohemian approach to travel, the beach town of Santa Cruz is an outstanding destination. The city and its surrounding areas, now fully recovered from the devastating 1989 Loma Prieta earthquake, offer reasonably priced lodging, excellent seafood, and stunning scenery.

Santa Cruz
173 A6

Visitor Information
303 Water St. #100, Santa Cruz
831/425-1234, 800/833-3494
www.santacruz.org

Frans Lanting Gallery
207 McPherson St., Santa Cruz
831/429-1331
www.lanting.com

Natural Bridges State Beach
173 A6
2531 W. Cliff Dr., Santa Cruz
831/423-4609
www.parks.ca.gov

Big Basin Redwoods State Park
173 A7
21600 Big Basin Way, Boulder Creek
831/338-8860
www.bigbasin.org

Soquel
173 A6

The main attraction in town is the **Santa Cruz Beach Boardwalk** *(400 Beach St., tel 831/423-5590, www.beachboardwalk.com)*, an historic amusement park. Nearby is the **Frans Lanting Gallery,** displaying the works of great nature photographers.

A favorite activity is to rent a bicycle and ride the bike path on the bluffs above. The exhilarating 5-mile (8 km) round-trip to the stunning rock formations at **Natural Bridges State Beach** is unforgettable. On the way back, stop by the **Santa Cruz Surfing Museum** *(1305 E. Cliff Dr., www.santacruzsurfingmuseum.org)* for its vintage surfboards and shark attack photos.

Mission Santa Cruz, *(126 High St., tel 831/426-5686, www.holycrosssantacruz.com)* is a 1931 reproduction of the original. Nearby, at **Roaring Camp Railroads** *(tel 831/335-4484, www.roaringcamp.com)*, steam trains puff to the Bear Mountain summit.

The Santa Cruz Mountains are rich in early pioneer history, with sites such as the 1892 **Felton Covered Bridge** *(Calif. 9, 5 miles/8 km N of Santa Cruz, www.scparks.com/felton.html)* in the San Lorenzo Valley. Farther north, off Calif. 9, is **Big Basin Redwoods State Park,** where you can rent tent cabins *(tel 800/444-7275)* set beneath towering coast redwood trees. The park has more than 80 miles (128 km) of trails. To the east, **Soquel** is now part of a wine-growing region with more than 70 wineries *(tel 831/685-8463, www.scmwa.com)*. Try **Bargetto Winery** *(3535 N. Main St., tel 831/475-2258, www.bargetto.com)*.

INSIDER TIP:

With its creekside setting, Shadowbrook restaurant in Capitola *(www.shadowbrook-capitola.com)* promises an evening to long remember.

—BARBARA A. NOE
National Geographic Travel Books senior editor

South of Soquel, the city of **Capitola** *(see map p. 173 A6, www.ci.capitola.ca.us)* is now a romantic's redoubt, complete with quaint beach cafés and several inns with beautiful views of northern Monterey Bay. The **Pacific Migrations Visitor Center** *(see map p. 173 A6, tel 831/464-5620, closed in winter)*, at New Brighton Beach in Capitola, explores the interactions of human and animal migratory patterns in California. ■

Art museums flush with new acquisitions, Victorian architecture on bold display, and cuisine supremely gourmet, in the city by the Bay

San Francisco

An iconic cable car climbs Hyde Street with Alcatraz Island visible across the bay.

San Francisco

Affluent yet bohemian, cosmopolitan yet provincial, gay yet buttoned-down, old-worldly yet youthful—San Francisco has something for every contemporary urban traveler. Part Florence (for its artisanal culture) and part Boston (for its endless ethnic politics), the city is compact, electric, romantic, exotic.

During the gold rush, the population of San Francisco rose from a sleepy 500 in 1847 to a raucous 20,000 in 1849. Then came the Yankee merchants, intent on making the city, as Richard Henry Dana had observed decades before, "the emporium of a new world." They would succeed beyond their wildest dreams.

Devastation came with the great earthquake and consequent fire of 1906. But the success of the Panama-Pacific Exposition in 1915 declared that the city was back. While the Depression certainly burnished the city's liberal democratic reputation, it was the AIDS crisis of the

1980s and beyond that once again invigorated San Francisco's eclectic character.

Travelers in San Francisco today confront a feast of cultural and culinary delights. Fueled in large part by Silicon Valley money, the city has become the site of America's most venturesome high cuisine. Money from "the valley" is also remaking venerable cultural institutions, such as the new Civic Center location of the Asian Art Museum. The city's fine-art museums have also benefited from public commitment. And the Golden Gate National Recreation Area, a vast expanse of meadows, windswept beaches, gnarled madrone trees, and misty forest trails, beckons.

NOT TO BE MISSED:

Espresso and homemade pasta in North Beach **198–199**

The view from Nob Hill **202–205**

Fresh seafood and historic ships at Fisherman's Wharf **206–207**

Soaking up the creepy criminal ambience of Alcatraz Island **208**

Driving, biking, or walking across the Golden Gate Bridge **212**

Perusing world-class art at the de Young Museum **217–218**

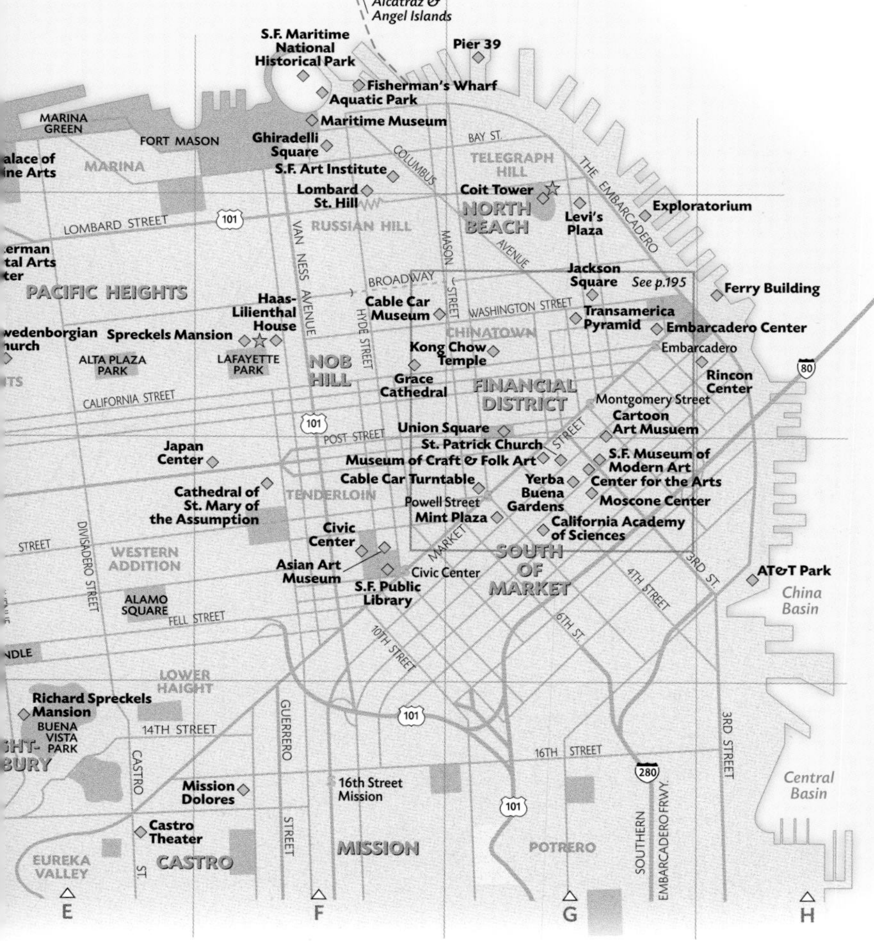

Financial District

The Financial District (between Pine, Washington, Montgomery, and Drumm Streets) features several interesting buildings. With its foundations in the era of the gold rush, San Francisco's banking industry has long maintained a high profile. Since the late 1960s, its buildings—literally—have, too.

The Transamerica Pyramid covers an entire city block.

Financial District
193 G3 & 195

The first of the city's skyscrapers were the 1969 Bank of America Building *(555 California St.)*, at 52 stories, now called **555 California Street,** followed by the distinctive 853-foot (260 m) **Transamerica Pyramid** *(Clay & Montgomery Sts., www.transamericapyramidcenter.com)* in 1972. Older buildings worthy of a look include the **Pacific Exchange** *(301 Pine St.)*, remodeled in 1930, and the 1903 **Merchant's Exchange** *(465 California St.)*.

The 1875 **Palace Hotel** *(2 New Montgomery St., tours tel 415/512-1111, www.sfpalace.com)*, rebuilt in 1909 and now lavishly refurbished, is known as the place where President Warren Harding drew his last breath in 1923. The **Garden Court** astounds with its incredible architecture, dome stained-glass ceiling, and Austrian crystal chandeliers and in its early 20th-century heyday was the setting for some of the nation's most prestigious events. Today it's a perfect setting for afternoon tea.

At the modern end of the scale are the **Schwab Building** *(101 Montgomery St.)*, headquarters for Charles Schwab & Co., and the shopping arcade-cum-plaza known as the **Embarcadero Center** *(Clay St. betw. Drumm & Battery Sts., tel 415/772-0700, www.embarcaderocenter.com)*.

Montgomery Street

Access to many Financial District buildings is restricted, but looking from the outside is free, as is the lively **Montgomery Street** scene—watch the brokers either looking depressed or ordering caviar for breakfast. A swell place from which to view it all is the Starbuck's café *(tel 415/788-1363)* at Kearny & Bush.

Jackson Square, up the street, offers perhaps the single best congregation of buildings from the gold rush era. Take a look at the 1852 **Golden Era Building** *(730–752 Montgomery St.)* and the gorgeous Italianate facade of the **Hotaling Building** *(451 Jackson St.)*. The shop called W. Graham Arader III *(435 Jackson St.)* has a huge selection of antique prints and rare maps.

Back down Montgomery Street, stop at the **Wells Fargo History Museum** to learn how the West was financed—largely through the efforts of this prestigious bank. The jewels here are the well preserved, mid-19th century stagecoaches. San Francisco's "other" downtown centers around **Union Square** *(Geary St. at Stockton St., www.unionsquareshop.com)*, the historic center of the downtown retail trade. Nearby, at Powell and Market Streets, is the Powell Street **Cable Car Turntable,** from where you can begin a scenic journey to Nob Hill (see pp. 202–205), Fisherman's Wharf (see pp. 206–207), or Chinatown (see pp. 196–197). ■

Wells Fargo History Museum

- Map p. 195
- 420 Montgomery St.,
- 415/396-2619
- Closed Sat.–Sun.
- Cable car: California St.; Bus: 1, 12, 15, 42

www.wellsfargohistory.com

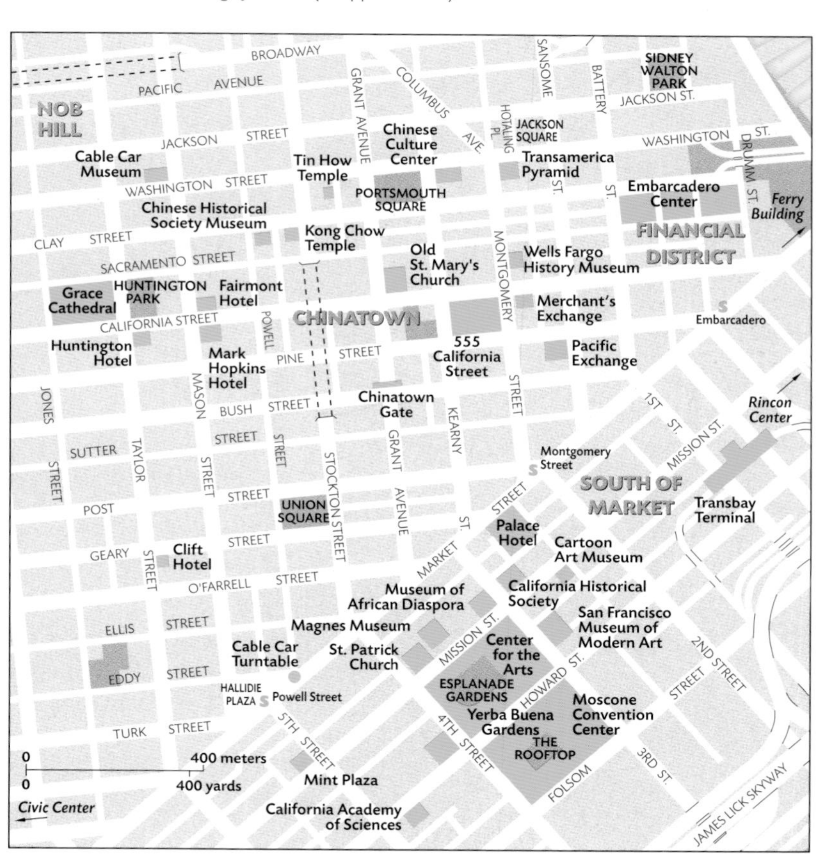

Chinatown

Founded in the mid-19th century, San Francisco's Chinatown has long served as a historical touchstone for the city's now highly assimilated but ethnically proud Chinese-American community. It is, to be sure, somewhat faded by age, and many of its older Chinese families have moved elsewhere. Yet this noisy quarter (bounded by Broadway, Powell, Kearny, & Bush Sts.) remains a vibrant and richly evocative travel destination.

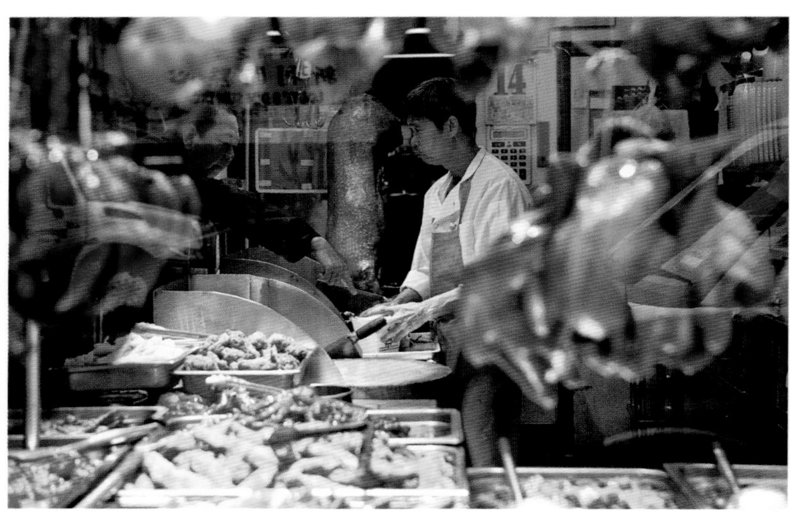

After roast duck? Head to Stockton Street, the center of commerce—and food—in Chinatown.

Chinatown

193 G3 & 195

 Cable car: California St., Powell-Hyde, Powell-Mason; Bus: 1, 9X, 15, 41, 45, 83

www.sanfranciscochinatown.com

Shopping looms large in Chinatown, from cheap Asian curios and timeless San Francisco souvenirs to jade pieces and gold jewelry. The ornate, green-tiled **Chinatown Gate** *(map p. 195, Bush & Grant Sts.)* marks the start of the quarter. Those with a bent for shopping can visit the many shops along historic **Grant Avenue.**

Specialty shops include Golden Gate Fortune Cookies *(56 Ross Alley, tel 415/781-3956)* and Chinatown Kite Store *(717 Grant Ave., tel 415/989-5182)*, where the stock ranges from traditional Chinese dragon and goldfish kites to modern power foils and sports kites. Foodies should take to **Stockton Street,** where produce sellers hawk their wares next to outstanding Chinese herbal medicine stores.

One of Chinatown's best views is from the rooftop restaurant Empress of China *(838 Grant Ave., tel 415/434-1345, www.empressofchinasf.com)*, with its over-the-top Hong Kong decor, delicious Cantonese cuisine, and panoramic views of North Beach (see pp. 198–199) and Coit Tower (see p. 200). Afterward pop into the Li Po Lounge *(916 Grant Ave., 415/982-0072)*, where the signature drink is the Chinese Mai Tai.

The **Chinese Culture Center** exhibits local art, as well as musical instruments and other cultural items. Its real specialty, however, is its historical walking tours, well worth the cost.

Among the traditional historical stops is **Old St. Mary's Cathedral** *(map p. 195, Grant Ave. & California St., www.oldsaintmarys.org)*, the West Coast's first Roman Catholic cathedral and one of the few buildings here to survive the 1906 earthquake and fire. In the park across the street, you'll find mah-jongg players and a rendering of Sun Yat-Sen by local artist Benjamin Bufano.

The relatively new (1977) redbrick **Kong Chow Temple** contains one of the oldest Taoist shrines in America; on its ruby-red walls is a 19th-century statue, from Canton, of the patron deity Kuan Ti. The statue was rescued from the ashes of the original temple on Pine Street after the 1906 earthquake.

Colorful Waverly Place has restaurants and both churches and temples, including the **Tin How Temple** *(map p. 195, 125 Waverly Pl.)*. Established in 1852 by Day Ju, one of the city's first Chinese immigrants, the temple is dedicated to the "Queen of the heavens and goddess of the Seven Seas." The remarkable "Life of Confucius" altar has been a spiritual and social core ever since.

The **Chinese Historical Society Museum**—occupying architect Julia Morgan's 1932 Chinatown YWCA, with its towers and painted ceiling panels, focuses on early Chinatown. Other sites offering a sense of the early neighborhood include the **Old Chinese Telephone Exchange** *(743 Washington St.)* and **Chinese Six Companies** *(843 Stockton St.)*—which once informally "ran" the enclave. ■

Chinese Culture Center

Map p. 195
Hilton Hotel, 3rd Floor, 750 Kearny St.
415/986-1822
Closed Sun.–Mon. Call for tours.
Tour: $$$$$

www.c-c-c.org

Kong Chow Temple

193 G3 & 195
855 Stockton St., 4th floor
415/788-1339

Chinese Historical Society Museum

Map p. 195
965 Clay St.
415/391-1188
Closed Sun. & Mon.

www.chsa.org

EXPERIENCE: Sampling Chinatown

For some guidance on Chinatown food, it is worth turning to a local expert. **Wok Wiz** *(250 King St., Ste. 268, tel 650/355-9657, www.wokwiz.com)* offers two outstanding culinary tours that also include a good dose of local history.

The **Wok Wiz Daily Tour** *($$–$$$)* will introduce you to the history and architecture of Chinatown, with visits to an herbalist, tea shop, and local farmers market. The tour begins at 10 a.m. at the Hilton Financial District *(750 Kearny St.)*. For an extra fee, you can finish with an excellent dim sum lunch at one of Chinatown's oldest restaurants.

The three-hour **I Can't Believe I Ate My Way Through Chinatown! Tour** *($$$$$)* begins with a traditional Chinese breakfast—congee and dumplings. You'll then sample tea at a local tea shop and visit some of the neighborhood's best food markets. The tour, which is led by food-loving chef Shirley Fong-Torres, ends with a fabulous lunch. Space is limited, so book early.

If you prefer to plan your own food tour, two reliably delicious restaurants are the **House of Nanking** *(919 Kearny St., tel 415/421-1429)* and **Lucky Creation** *(854 Washington St., tel 415/989-0818)*.

North Beach

From its mid-19th-century days as a point of disembarkation for Italian and French immigrants to its 1950s flourishing as a Beat literary center, North Beach has long been the city's entertaining and unself-conscious theater of street life. With its bounty of hearty food, camp (if now somewhat tacky) sex shows, historic literary cafés, and outstanding boutique shopping, it has travelers returning to it again and again.

Much of life in North Beach—alive with cafés and restaurants—revolves around eating and drinking.

North Beach
193 G3

The Beat Museum
Map p. 201
540 Broadway
800/537-6822
$
www.kerouac.com

Bounded by Broadway to the south, Montgomery Street to the east, Lombard Street to the north, and Mason Street to the west, North Beach was defined by the Italians who settled here late in the 19th century and claimed it for their own after the 1906 earthquake and fire. Today the Italian presence is unmistakable in such establishments as Tosca, Caffè Trieste, and Rose Pistola (see Travelwise p. 370).

The Italian community's place of worship is the 1922 Romanesque **Sts. Peter and Paul Church** *(map p. 201, 666 Filbert St., tel 415/421-0809, www.stspeterpaul.san-francisco.ca.us)*. Here, in 1957, baseball hero Joe DiMaggio and his bride, Marilyn Monroe, had their wedding photos taken. The twin spires of the church overlook **Washington Square,** whose daily parade of Chinese tai chi practitioners and old-style *paisanos* evokes a unique American ambience.

For a bigger draft of the past, visit the **Beat Museum,** where an extensive photo collection

INSIDER TIP:

Picnic in Washington Square Park near Sts. Peter and Paul Church for a vibrant slice of North Beach.

—ERIN STONE
National Geographic contributor

documents the district's bohemian history. Recent work by local artists is found at the beautiful **San Francisco Art Institute** (see p. 201), which also houses the **Diego Rivera Gallery.**

A pilgrimage point for bookish types is **City Lights.** Still owned by Beat generation poet Lawrence Ferlinghetti (the city's former poet laureate), the bookstore stocks a wide selection of literary fiction and politically charged nonfiction. There is, of course, a deep shelf of Ferlinghetti's fellow poet Allen Ginsberg and the official martyr of the Beat movement, Jack Kerouac, whose *On the Road* (1957) fueled the wanderlust of 1960s youth. Just across **Jack Kerouac Alley** is **Vesuvio** *(map p. 201, 255 Columbus Ave., tel 415/362-3370, www.vesuvio.com)* another Beat-era touchstone.

Clubs and bars line **Broadway;** a walk along the strip is essential, if only to see the **Condor Club** *(map p. 201, 560 Broadway, tel 415/781-8222, www.condorsf.com),* where, in 1964, Carol Doda stunned America by dancing topless. In **Club Fugazi,** the musical spoof *Beach Blanket Babylon* will tickle you with its mad satire and over-the-top hats.

The antique shops of North Beach are worth checking out for their Italo-Americana. Or wander a few blocks up to **Grant Avenue,** where you will discover some highly individualistic shops. Number 1529B was the **workshop of Peter Macchiarini,** a former Works Progress Administration artist whose sculptures and jewelry still evoke the best of that period's folk modernism. Across the street, the items at **Aria** *(1522 Grant Ave., tel 415/433-0219)* range from architectural remnants and figures of saints to antique games. ■

San Francisco Art Institute

- Map: 193 F4 & 201
- Address: 800 Chestnut St.
- Tel: 415/771-7020
- Transit: Cable car: Powell-Hyde, Powell-Mason; Bus: 30

www.sfai.edu

City Lights

- Map: Map p. 201
- Address: 261 Columbus Ave.
- Tel: 415/362-8193
- Transit: Bus: 8X, 30, 41, 45

www.citylights.com

Club Fugazi

- Map: Map p. 201
- Address: 678 Green St.
- Tel: 415/421-4222
- Transit: Cable Car: Powell-Mason; Bus: 9X, 20, 30, 45

www.beachblanketbabylon.com

Riding Through History

The Cable Car Museum *(map pp. 193 F3 & 195, Mason St. & Washington St., tel 415/474-1887, www.cablecarmuseum.org)* has a small but exquisite collection of cable car artifacts and history. The city's machine-age (but still digital-era-functioning) cable cars were originally constructed to solve a transportation problem: how to get people up a hill too steep for horses. San Francisco industrialist Andrew Hallidie came up with the idea of using cable traction to power public transport; the system was inaugurated on August 2, 1873—and hasn't stopped since.

Some of the old cable cars here date from as far back as the 1870s. It is worth going downstairs to see the "brains" of the system. The massive wheels carrying the cable that moves the cars along are beautiful in their early industrial-age simplicity.

Present-day cable cars start at Powell and Market and at Powell and Van Ness and run from 6:30 a.m. to 1 a.m. daily *(tel 311 or 415/701-3000, www.sfmta.com).*

Telegraph & Russian Hills Walk

Notable for stunning views of both the bay and the city, Telegraph Hill and Russian Hill hold a number of delights (particularly the singularly crooked Lombard Street) within reasonable walking distance.

The iconic curves of Lombard Street were added in 1922 so cars could safely descend.

Walk One: Coit Tower to Russian Hill Park

Chief among the sights on this walk is **Coit Tower** ❶ *(1 Telegraph Hill Blvd., tel 415/362-0808, www.sfrecpark.org/CoitTower.aspx)*, a 284-foot (86.5 m) fluted tower designed by architect Arthur Page Brown—architect of City Hall and the Swedenborgian Church (see p. 209), among other buildings—and set at the top of Telegraph Hill. It was built with funds left to the city after the death of eccentric philanthropist Lillian Coit in 1929. The tower is her memorial to the city's firefighters: An obsessive devotion to them was one aspect of Coit's eccentricity. She wore a diamond-studded fireman's badge everywhere she went, even to elegant balls.

The **elevator ride** *($)* to the top of Coit Tower promises superb views of the city and the bay. The building's other highlights are its **murals,** which line the inside walls. Painted in the early 1930s by a group of artists employed by the Public Works of Art Project (a precursor to the Works Progress Administration, or WPA), the paintings were controversial in their time. Today they are icons of the city's vaunted tolerance for the politically charged. Particularly arresting is the mural titled "Banking and Law," created in 1933–34 by artist George Harris.

A multimillion-dollar renovation has brought new life to the already splendid

---

NOT TO BE MISSED:

Coit Tower • Lombard Street • San Francisco Art Institute • Filbert Steps

---

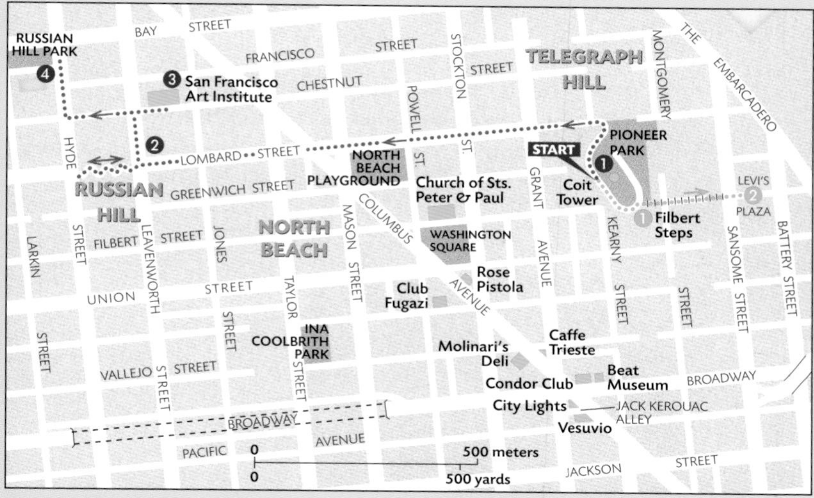

See also area map p. 193 G3
➤ Coit Tower
2 hours
1.1 miles (1.7 km) to Russian Hill Park
➤ Russian Hill Park or Levi's Plaza

Pioneer Park, surrounding the tower, with a series of new terraces and lookout points, making this an even more perfect place for a picnic. Buy the makings for one at **Molinari's Deli** *(373 Columbus Ave., tel 415/421-2337, www.molinarisalame.com).*

From Telegraph Hill, you have two main paths of discovery. The first is more traditional. Stroll down **Lombard Street 2.** Then cross Columbus Avenue and head uphill, still on Lombard, to Leavenworth Street. From here, Lombard Street—called the "world's crookedest street"—twists and turns its way uphill.

A right turn on Leavenworth and again on Chestnut takes you to the **San Francisco Art Institute 3** (see p. 199). The prize here is Diego Rivera's "Making of a Fresco" (1931), but the 1926 Spanish Colonial building and all its contents are worth a stop. From here, walk along Chestnut to Hyde Street and turn right to **Russian Hill Park 4,** a wonderful place to rest, recoup, and gaze out on the bay.

Walk Two: Telegraph Hill Toward the Waterfront

An alternative walk from Coit Tower, and a splendid end to an afternoon on Telegraph Hill—or perhaps a good prelude to a day on the waterfront (see pp. 206–207)—is to go down the **Filbert Steps 1,** just to the east of the tower. Beginning by a notable art moderne apartment building, the steps descend amid a series of terraced gardens, all of them flush with basketball-size hydrangeas, lush ivies, loquat trees, and magnolias.

The Filbert Steps end at **Levi's Plaza 2** *(map p. 193 G3; 1155 Battery St., tel 415/391-7305, www.levistrauss.com),* near the waterfront. Here you will find the headquarters of the legendary jeans manufacturer whose fame stretches from the gold rush to the global era.

"The Irish they live on th' top av it,
And th' Dagoes they live on th' base av it,
And th' goats and th' chicks and th' brickbats and shticks
Is joombled all over th' face av it."

—Wallace Irwin, from *Telygraft Hill*

Nob Hill

As the highest point in the city (338 feet—103 m—above sea level), it is hardly surprising that Nob Hill *(California & Taylor Sts.)* has long been San Francisco's most visible indicator of wealth and status. A good way to take in the hill's main attractions is to visit its grand early 20th-century hotels. For an understanding of how the modern city communes with the traditional, older era, visit Nob Hill's architectural gem: Grace Cathedral.

California Street on Nob Hill offers a view of the Bay Bridge.

The Hotels

Nob Hill's three principal hotels—the Mark Hopkins, the Fairmont, and the Huntington—are well worth a visit. The Mark Hopkins and the Huntington, in particular, warrant consideration by the traveler in search of a memorable San Francisco experience. Given the prices at the deluxe chain hotels, these gracious old piles offer sumptuous spas, unbeatable dining, and often good value.

Mark Hopkins: At the Mark Hopkins *(map p. 195, 1 Nob Hill, tel 415/392-3434, www.intercontinentalmarkhopkins.com)*, built in 1926, take the elevator up to the art deco-ish **Top of the Mark** *(tel 415/616-6916, www.topofthemark.com)*, the hotel's grande dame of a watering spot. It is without peer as a place from which to view the entire cityscape and has an outstanding wine and mixed drinks list. Sunset is the time to be here.

Fairmont: Across California Street is the Fairmont *(map p. 195, 950 Mason St., tel 415/772-5000, www.fairmont.com/sanfrancisco)*, saved from the earthquake wreckage by architect Stanford White in

King of the Hills

Its name cribbed from the Hindi *nabob,* roughly meaning "big shot," Nob Hill was the residence of choice for such late 19th-century figures as business and railroad barons Leland Stanford, Charles Crocker, and Mark Hopkins. Men like these led lives of such ostentation as to provoke Irish labor leader Denis Kearny to lead an angry mob of workers up the hill in protest in 1878.

Only the earthquake and fire of 1906 put a (temporary) stop to the bacchanal. The great mansions were replaced—by luxury hotels, city clubs, churches for the wealthy, and parks for the few hoi polloi who made it up the hill for the views. Today the views are still free and still stunning. Most wealthy residences are now in other parts of the city, but Nob Hill stands as glorious as ever.

1907. Take in the ornate lobby, the oldest in the three hotels. An extensive renovation has restored its Florentine mirrors and gold leaf. Its Laurel Court, Venetian Room, and facade have also been restored. The Fairmont sits on the foundations of the mansion built by the daughter of James G. "Bonanza Jim" Fair, an also-ran in the "robber baron" coterie alongside the Big Four: Crocker, Stanford, Hopkins, and Collis P. Huntington (see sidebar above).

INSIDER TIP:

Pop into the Venetian Room at the Fairmont Hotel to see where Tony Bennett first performed "I Left My Heart in San Francisco."

—JUSTIN KAVANAGH
National Geographic International Editions editor

Huntington: To cap a perfectly opulent day in this perfectly opulent terrain, the restaurant at the Huntington *(map p. 195, 1075 California St. at Taylor St., tel 415/474-5400, www.huntingtonhotel.com)* is hard to beat. Named the Big Four in reference to city plutocrats of old, it successfully conjures the best of the old days. Its crab cakes and rack of lamb, not to mention rabbit, quail, and champagne, are exactly what the Big Four would be eating today.

Clift Hotel: The recently renovated Clift Hotel *(map p. 195, 495 Geary St., tel 415/775-4700, www.clifthotel.com)* boasts the **Redwood Room,** a moderne-style 1934 cocktail lounge wrought from the wood of a single redwood tree and overhauled with a mirrored bar, "digital art," and dim lighting—at once romantic and decadent.

Grace Cathedral

The nation's third largest Episcopal cathedral measures 329 feet (100 m) long, with a spire rising 247 feet (75 m). It is modeled on Paris's Notre Dame, but unlike a European cathedral,

Nob Hill
193 F3 & 195

Grace Cathedral
193 F3 & 195
1100 California St. at Taylor St.
415/749-6300
Cable car: all lines; Bus: 1

www.gracecathedral.org

it was built not of stone but of reinforced concrete—a material perhaps incongruous for a sacred space. (It was used for earthquake safety.) Here, where old-line Episcopalianism meets the globally minded ways of the urban affluent, you will find the focal point of a unique and modern religious culture.

Officially established in 1853, Grace Cathedral had as its first bishop William Ingraham Kip, a Yale-trained historian. Although orthodox and East Coast urbane, Kip quickly saw a unique opportunity for Episcopalianism in the West. (He was not without a few initial doubts; the bawdy excesses of the gold rush period, he wrote, were "enough to convince one of the doctrine of total depravity.") Kip quickly took to his role as an evangelizing "frontier bishop," delighting in California's Roman Catholic past and Mediterranean climate. By embracing the state's past, aesthetically, oratorically, and socially, Kip believed that Episcopalianism could plant its rich apostolic traditions in an unfolding new world. His would be a Californian Episcopalianism, orthodox but open, its eye on the past yet, as scholar Kevin Starr has noted, "redeemed in futurity . . . and the aesthetic elaboration of the present." That this doctrine might produce the wide-open, progressive spirit now abundantly in evidence at Grace would likely startle Kip were he alive today. But he would likely come to embrace it. Everywhere here, the modern and the ancient combine in a spirit of mystical openness.

Some highlights of the church bear this out. The classic French Gothic architecture is fronted by bronze **entrance doors,** duplicates cast from the originals of Lorenzo Ghiberti's "Doors of Paradise" in the baptistry of the cathedral in Florence. Just inside the doors, to the right, is the **AIDS Interfaith Chapel,** with its altarpiece by the late graphic artist Keith Haring. There is also an AIDS quilt panel, the most universal memorial to victims.

A joyful noise rises in Grace Cathedral when the bells ring.

Inside the cathedral proper, directly behind the **Meditation Labyrinth** (modeled on that of Chartres), is a beautifully wrought statue of St. Francis by San Francisco artist Benjamin Bufano. An interesting way of linking the 1930s part of the building with the 1960s section can be seen by standing here and looking up and back, toward the entrance. Here you will see the **East Rose Window,** a copy of the "Canticle of the Sun," by Gabriel Loire of Chartres in France. The canticle was inspired by St. Francis's celebratory poem in praise of the Creator and Creation. Looking down at the floor of the nave, you will discover another iteration of that theme, this time in the form of the Chi Rho, a Greek monogram for Christ.

INSIDER TIP:

Attend yoga classes with 60 or 80 locals every Tuesday night at Grace Cathedral near Union Square.

—KAY RABIN
City guide, San Francisco Public Library

Perhaps the best expression of the uniquely Californian and progressive religious aesthetic can be found in the sanctuary. The **altar** is made of granite from the High Sierra and a piece of 2,000-year-old coastal redwood. The altar rail cushions are stitched with wildflowers of various Californian Episcopal dioceses.

The many outstanding original works of Renaissance art include the "Madonna and Child" plaque by Antonio Rossellino, just to the right of the choir stall.

The most memorable and moving works are probably the more recent ones in the **Chapel of Grace Baptistry,** to the left of the choir stall. Two icons done in 1990 by painter Robert Lenz seem an appropriate coda to the Grace experience. The first, to your left, is of John Donne, the 17th-century mystic poet and preacher, dean of St. Paul's Cathedral in London. The other is of Mary Magdalene holding in her hand an egg, the instrument by which she is said to have taught Emperor Tiberius the story of the resurrection. This icon was dedicated in 1990 to Bishop Barbara Harris, the first woman bishop in the Episcopal Church.

A brochure map is on sale in the lobby and gift shop, and afternoon tours are available. ■

The Other Cathedral

To the south, between Nob Hill and Pacific Heights (see pp. 209–211), is the Cathedral of St. Mary of the Assumption ***(map pp. 193 F2 & 211, 1111 Gough St., tel 415/567-2020, www.stmarycathedralsf.org).*** **Completed in 1970, the cathedral is one of the most dramatic buildings in California. Covering two city blocks, it has a sweeping modern ceiling and outstanding interior sculptures by Mario Rudelli and Enrico Manfridi. The building's remarkable postmodernist shape—a cruciform cone on a square base—evokes the optimistic era of post–Vatican II American Catholicism.**

The Waterfront

Second only to Chinatown in popularity with tourists, Fisherman's Wharf anchors the waterfront, a triptych extending for five miles (8 km) from the foot of Market Street westward to Crissy Field and the Golden Gate Bridge. There was a time when the urban shoreline was synonymous with a stroll-and-spend on the highly themed Pier 39. No more. Today, the city's shore can fill an entire day and fit a wide range of interests.

The huge sign in Ghiradelli Square went up in 1915.

Ferry Building
- 193 H3
- Embarcadero at Market St.
- 415/983-8030

www.ferrybuilding marketplace.com

Exploratorium
- 193 G3
- Piers 15 & 17
- 415/561-0360
- Closed Mon. except some holidays
- $$$. Free 1st Wed. of month
- Bus: 22, 28, 30, 41, 43, 45

www.exploratorium .edu

A good starting point for exploring is the historic **Ferry Building.** Opened in 1898 to serve the ferries connecting San Francisco to the East Bay, it entered a long period of disuse after the opening of the Bay Bridge in 1937. Recently restored, it is now a magnificent marketplace, and the 240-foot-tall (73 m) clock tower again serves as a welcoming beacon.

Joggers and historic trams run the length of the **Embarcadero** *(map p. 193 G4–H3)*, lined with piers used by cruise ships.

Founded by physicist Frank Oppenheimer in 1969, the popular **Exploratorium** utilizes every piece of technological wizardry imaginable to engage young minds in the sciences. Its 800 interactive exhibits, displays, and original artworks include a computer-simulated flight over the city, a distorting room that makes children look bigger than their parents, and even an antigravity mirror. A giant prism teaches the principles of light refraction, while visitors can learn about water dynamics by creating their own vortex in a 7-foot (2 m) Plexiglas beaker. The Exploratorium has become something of a media darling in recent years. But be warned: This place is *loud.*

Farther west, **Pier 39** *(map p. 193 G4, Beach St., www.pier39.com)* delights tourists with its shops, restaurants, and amusements, including a carousel. Sea lions often laze on the boat docks. At **Aquarium of the Bay** *(Embarcadero at Beach St., tel 415/623-5300, www.aquariumofthebay.org, $)*, a moving walkway goes through a see-through tunnel, while sharks and other sea creatures swim about you. Ferries run from here to Sausalito (see p. 245), Tiburon (see p. 244 and opposite), and Alcatraz and Angel Islands (see p. 208).

Farther west, **Fisherman's Wharf** *(map p. 193 F4, www.fishermanswharf.org)* is named for the brightly painted fishing fleet that has berthed here since the late 19th century. The area is now mostly a jumble of kitschy boutiques and tourist traps, but with some splendid restaurants and streetside stalls where you can buy the city's famous Dungeness crab. Attractions include **Ripley's Believe It or Not! Museum** *(175 Jefferson St., tel 415/202-9850, www.ripleysf.com, $$$$)* and the **Cannery** *(2801 Leavenworth St., tel 415/771-3112, www.delmontesquare.com)*, a former peach cannery now housing shops and eateries.

The **USS *Pampanito*** *(Pier 45, tel 415/775-1943, $$)*, a World War II submarine open to the public, is part of the **San Francisco Maritime National Historical Park.** Located in a streamlined art deco building, the park's mainstay, the **Maritime Museum,** exhibits model ships and nautical miscellany that document San Francisco's maritime grandeur. The park's historic vessels include the 1886 *Balclutha* (of Cape Horner style); the 1895 *C. A. Thayer* (a lumber schooner); and the last of the city's paddle-wheel steam-powered ferryboats, the 1890 *Eureka*.

The Maritime Museum abuts **Fort Mason,** a former Army barracks and now a lively cultural center with three outstanding theaters and several small museums.

To the south, **Ghiradelli Square** *(map p. 193 F4, 900 N. Point St., tel 415/775-5500, www.ghirardellisq.com)*, a brick-terraced 19th-century chocolate factory, today comprises shops and fine restaurants.

The **Marina Green** *(map p. 193 E3–E4)* is a fun place to stroll, roller-skate, or fly a kite. The esplanade leads to the **Palace of Fine Arts,** a lone but grand reminder of the 1915 Panama-Pacific Exposition. It is well worth a visit, if only to get an idea of how early 20th-century San Franciscans viewed the city's future in the wake of the 1906 earthquake and fire. ■

San Francisco Maritime National Historical Park

- 193 F4
- Jefferson & Hyde Sts.
- 415/447-5000
- $ to board historic ships
- Cable car: Powell-Hyde, Powell-Mason; Bus: 30, 41, 45; Streetcar: F-line

www.maritime.org

Fort Mason

- 193 E4–F4
- Marina Blvd. & Buchanan St.
- 415/345-7500

www.fortmason.org

Palace of Fine Arts

- 193 E4
- 3301 Lyon St.
- 415/563-6504

www.palaceoffinearts.org

EXPERIENCE: Out on the Bay

Those who crave their own sail on the bay have a number of choices. Start by consulting **Sailing San Francisco** *(www.sfsailing.com)*, which lists yacht charters, sailing schools, and races. Or try one of the cruises offered by the **Blue & Gold Fleet** *(tel 415/705-8200, www.blueandgoldfleet.com, reservations recommended, $$$$)*. Boats depart several times a day from Pier 41 on Fisherman's Wharf and Pier 39. One option is a trip to **Tiburon** (see p. 244), a quaint, small former railroad town across the bay, good for food and with an excellent bike path *(rent a bike when you depart from Pier 41)*. Or take a cruise along the waterfront, passing such landmarks as the Palace of Fine Arts and the Golden Gate Bridge (see p. 214).

Captain Kirk's Sailing Adventures *(tel 650/492-0681, www.sfbaysail.com, $$$$$)* offers lessons and several beneath-the-canvas adventures, including a 4-hour sail around the bay, Angel Island barbecue, open ocean sail beyond the Golden Gate, and harbor porpoise excursion. **Adventure Cat Sailing Charters** *(tel 800/498-4228, www.adventurecat.com, $–$$$$$)* organizes similar sailing trips on two huge catamarans.

Alcatraz & Angel Islands

A trip to Alcatraz Island has become an essential part of any first-time visit to San Francisco. The thrill in walking in the steps of Al Capone and "Machine Gun" Kelly is tempered by the melancholic nature of the world's most famous prison, but visitors agree that it is a uniquely memorable experience. Nearby Angel Island—the "Jewel of the Bay"—provides the freedom that Alcatraz once denied.

Alcatraz Island
- Map: 233 B3
- Tel: 415/561-4900; Ferry bookings: 415/981-7625
- $: $$$$$

www.nps.gov/alcatraz

Angel Island
- Map: 233 B4
- Tel: 415/435-5390; Ferry bookings: 415/435-2131

www.parks.ca.gov

Alcatraz Island

On Alcatraz, guides tell of escape attempts (all convicts who tried were either shot, recaptured, or presumed drowned) and the various criminal personalities. Among these are Robert Stroud, the original "birdman of Alcatraz"; Al Capone, whose five-year stint in isolation left him mentally deranged; and the Anglin brothers, who escaped by chipping through the walls of their cells but most likely drowned. The prison also held the Native American rebel Kaetena (a friend of Geronimo), who in 1887 had led a mutiny against the government in Arizona.

INSIDER TIP:

Be sure to get tickets for an Alcatraz cruise and tour early as they often sell out. Tickets are available up to 90 days in advance.

—CHARLES KOGOD
National Geographic contributor

Try to leave time during your visit to Alcatraz for a walk along the **Agave Trail.** The quarter-mile (.4 km) trail leads through the island's bird sanctuary. Pelicans, for which Alcatraz was named, dominate, but different seasons bring dozens of other species.

Alcatraz Cruises *(tel 415/981-7625, www.alcatrazcruises.com)* offers various themed interpretive tours of the island, including a night trip.

Angel Island

Unlike Alcatraz, Angel Island remains a relatively untouristy destination. The largest island in the bay, at 1 square mile (2.5 sq km), it is known for the old **Immigration Station at China Cove,** where hundreds of thousands of Asian and Russian immigrants were "processed" around the turn of the 20th century. During World War II, it served as a prisoner of war camp and, later, a missile base.

Angel Island also offers miles of outstanding hiking trails as well as an interesting Civil War camp and fort. A perimeter trail winds about the entire island; a trail near the marina in Ayala Cove takes you to the highest peak, 771 feet (235 m), for sweeping views.

The Angel Island Company *(tel 415/435-3544, www.angelisland.com)* offers tram and Segway tours, plus bike rentals. ■

Around Pacific Heights

If one end of the San Francisco architectural aesthetic is historicism—the attempt, whether through Victorian homes or a beaux arts civic center, to create a selective European past—the other end is naturalism or Bay Area regionalism.

The prime example of naturalism is the **Swedenborgian Church.** This little structure was built in 1894 for followers of Emmanuel Swedenborg, an 18th-century Swede who preached "reverence for the divine in nature." Although a tiny commission by the day's gilded-age standards, the project nonetheless attracted the leading craftsmen of the period, including A. C. Schweinfurth and Arthur Page Brown, artists Bruce Porter and William Keith, and architect Joseph Worcester, who also happened to be pastor of the new church. Another strong influence was Bernard Maybeck, architect of the Palace of Fine Arts (see p. 207).

The Swedenborgian Church has been called the "church of the simple life."

A stroll through the church and its grounds reveals a central theme: "The interpenetration of the spirit and nature, of the seen and unseen," as historian Kevin Starr explains. The madrone tree ceiling supports, which were Maybeck's idea, heighten the rustic-Zen quality of the church, making a visit here a prized moment for those interested in American architecture. Two circular stained-glass windows by Porter lend a calm glow to the Shaker-simple seating below. Outside, the garden is planted with olive trees, cedar of Lebanon, elm, pine, plum, and crabapple.

If you walk north from the Swedenborgian, there's a fine photo opportunity of the bay from the **Lyon Street Steps.** For those interested in Victoriana, it is worth visiting the classic 1866 **Haas-Lilienthal House,** a beautifully restored and furnished Queen Anne structure.

To the south, the **Japan Center** *(map pp. 193 F2 & 211, 1730 Geary Blvd., www.sfjapantown.org)* is the historic heart of the area's Japanese-American community. Enjoy Japanese food, art, and, most refreshing after a long day, a dunk in the old-style Japanese baths at the **Kabuki Springs & Spa** *(1750 Geary Blvd., tel 415/922-6000, www.kabukisprings.com)*. A shiatsu massage and scrub are available by appointment. ■

Swedenborgian Church

- 193 E3
- 2107 Lyon St.
- 415/346-6466
- Bus: 3, 12, 22, 24

www.sfswedenborgian.org

Haas-Lilienthal House

- 193 F3 & 211
- 2007 Franklin St.
- 415/441-3000
- Tours Wed., Sat., & Sun.
- $$
- Bus: 1, 12, 19, 27, 47, 49

www.sfheritage.org

Pacific Heights Walk

During the years following the 1906 earthquake and fire, the epicenter of wealth and power in San Francisco shifted westward to the hills now known as Pacific Heights. Here, as one WPA writer put it, the rich "could dwell surrounded by gardens overlooking the Golden Gate." In grand style, modern San Franciscans carry on that tradition, everywhere evident during a pleasant morning's walk.

The remarkable Spreckels Mansion covers an entire block and has 26 bathrooms.

There are some wonderful surprises on this walk and many highlights. (Please remember that nearly all the buildings are privately owned and not open to the public, so view them only from the sidewalk.)

The French baroque **Spreckels Mansion ❶**, just west of Gough Street at 2080 Washington Street, is a good starting point. The architect of the Palace of the Legion of Honor, George Applegarth, built the house in 1912 for sugar magnate Adolph Spreckels. From here Spreckels's wife, Alma, the doyenne of early 20th-century San Francisco, ruled the social scene. Writer Danielle Steel now lives in the "Sugar Castle."

Walk west up Washington, passing the **Phelan House** (four houses up on the right), where Sen. James D. Phelan entertained when the city was run by an oligopoly in the late 19th century. Turn south through **Lafayette Park ❷**, at the top of which are some of the best views in town. On the southern side, pass the

NOT TO BE MISSED:

Spreckels Mansion • Century Club • Row house Victorians

Atherton House, at Octavia and California. It is perhaps the most eclectic hodgepodge of Victorian styles anywhere.

Proceeding east on California Street past Gough, you will see two outstanding examples of Victoriana. The **Wormser House ❸**, at 1834 California Street, was built in 1877 by San Francisco merchant Isaac Wormser. It is interesting for its mix of styles: Queen Anne on the left side and the vertically exaggerated Stick style on the right. At 1818 California sits the **Sloss Home.** Built in 1876 by a fur trade millionaire, it is also in the Stick style, with Italianate lines on the side and cornice.

At 1701 Franklin (at California) is the **Edward Coleman House ❹**, built in the Queen Anne style in 1895. If you walk south down Franklin, you can see the remarkable stained-glass enclosed stairway in the rear. A true historic gem is the former **Century Club,** located at Franklin and Sutter. Its architect was the renowned Julia Morgan, who also designed Hearst Castle (see pp. 174–175). The Spanish consulate now occupies the building.

Go west on Sutter to Gough Street and the **Hotel Majestic ❺** *(1500 Sutter St., tel 415/441-1100, www.thehotelmajestic.com).* In the 1960s, this 1905 Victorian gem was run as the notorious Brothel, a hotel for gay men. Closed by Mayor Dianne Feinstein (along with the bathhouses) during the early AIDS epidemic, it is now an excellent bed-and-breakfast hotel, known for its elegant Butterfly Lounge.

Walk north on Gough Street and turn west on Bush Street. More examples of the area's architectural heritage warrant note on Bush. Houses called **row house Victorians** ❻ can be seen here–middle-class houses of mixed styles, ranging (often in one house) from Queen Anne to Stick. The house at 1803 Bush is Italianate; next door is an example of a "smothered" Victorian, a description that refers to mid-20th-century "improving" of 19th-century houses with stucco and brick.

An architectural oddity is the **Ohabai Shalome Temple** ❼ ("Loves of Peace") synagogue near Bush and Laguna. Modeled on the Doge's Palace in Venice, it is redwood right down to its "stone carved" exterior.

Continue west on Bush Street and turn north on Pierce. You can enjoy another aspect of Pacific Heights as you walk northward on Pierce through **Alta Plaza Park** ❽**,** with its stunning views, and on north to the junction with Broadway, into the wealthier section of town. Several houses on Broadway have famous associations. The **Mary Martin House** at Pierce and Broadway once belonged to the actress. The real pièce de résistance of the neighborhood is the **Casebolt House** ❾ *(2727 Pierce St.)*, built by a hardware magnate in 1915. Appearing to be a kind of inflated Brooklyn brownstone, it is made completely of carved redwood. Its owners came from New York and wanted to feel at home.

Return to Broadway. The Victorian at No. 2311 is where the hit TV show *Party of Five* was filmed, while the house at Broadway and Steiner Street was the location of the 1993 movie *Mrs. Doubtfire*. Go east, and then turn south on Gough Street to your starting point.

See also area map p. 193
Spreckels Mansion
2 hours
3.2 miles (5.1 km)
Spreckels Mansion

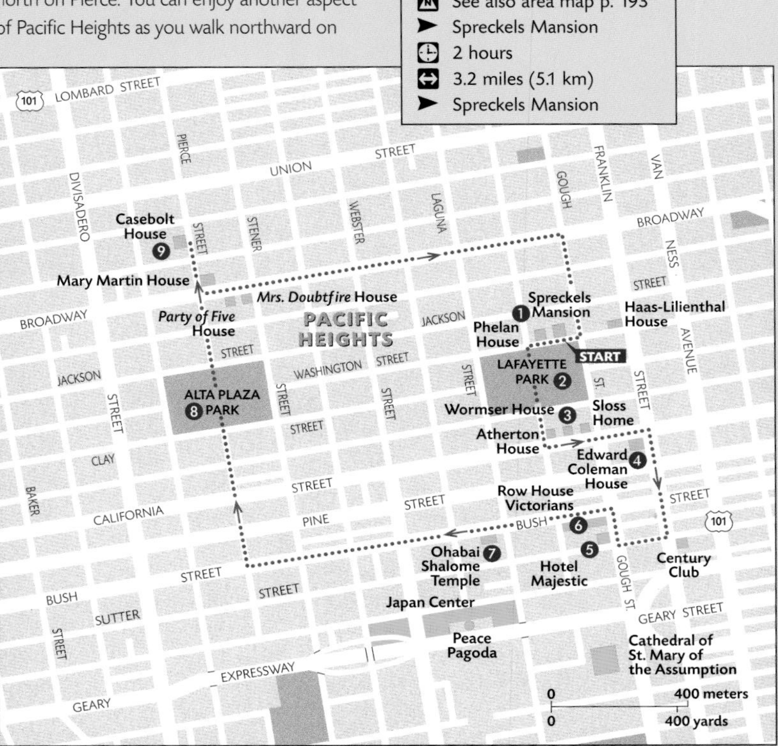

Golden Gate Bridge & Around

In San Francisco's northeast corner lies a 1,491-acre (603 ha) haven of forests, grasslands, and sea cliffs—a miracle considering how much the rest of the city is built up. You'll find hiking trails, beaches, and some of the most magnificent views in the United States. Tour some of the 19th-century structures (there are 477 of them) and then head for Golden Gate National Recreation Area, which links the Golden Gate Bridge with the California Palace of the Legion of Honor.

Want some postcard shots? Baker Beach offers superb views of the Golden Gate Bridge.

Golden Gate Bridge
192 C4

Golden Gate Bridge

A remarkable piece of art, the Golden Gate Bridge—an elegant 8,900 feet (2,712 m) of concrete and steel supported by just two deftly designed piers—symbolizes San Francisco for locals and people the world over. As a feat of engineering, it represents a pure force of will and is a testimony to the engineering skills of Joseph Strauss, the architectural brilliance of Charles Ellis and Leon Moisseiff, and the financial acumen of A. G. Giannini, whose Bank of America floated the bond issue that paid for it. When the bridge was dedicated in 1937, it was the largest single structure in the world.

Today it would be hard to imagine a better place from which to begin a romantic trip to San Francisco. Mornings, misty and cool, are the perfect time for a bracing walk across the bridge to gain an overview of the city and its setting.

Almost 2 miles (3.2 km) long, the bridge is open to walkers (east walkway only) from April through October, and from 6 a.m. to 6 p.m. the rest of the year *(access from Lincoln Blvd.)*. Wear a jacket as winds are often strong. To the northwest, a silvery stream might light up the Marin Headlands (see p. 244); behind them stands mysterious Mount Tamalpais (Mount Tam to the locals). To the northeast are the lonely shapes of Alcatraz and Angel Islands (see p. 208), flocks of gulls and pelicans floating on the air as if hanging from invisible rope. Across the bay are Berkeley and Oakland. To the southeast is the skyline of the city itself, perhaps the most memorable in all America.

Below you, on the south shore, sits **Fort Point National Historic Site.** This redbrick fortress was built during the Civil War to protect San Francisco from Confederate attack. Cannon-loading demonstrations are held here, and Civil War reenactments bring the fort to life.

The bridge is a jewel in the crown of the **Golden Gate National Recreation Area.** This stretch of beach, forest, and grasslands runs from **Fort Funston** *(map p. 192 A1, tel 415/561-4700, www.parksconservancy.org)* in the south, eastward to **Fort Mason** (see p. 207), and north as far as **Tomales Bay** (see p. 246). The best place to take photographs of the city skyline is from the aptly named **Vista Point,** on the Marin side of the bridge.

Presidio

First established by the Spanish in 1776, the Presidio served as an army post commanding the Golden Gate straits. In 1994, the U.S. Army pulled out and the vast green swath was incorporated into the Golden Gate National Recreation Area.

Fort Point National Historic Site

Map: 192 C4

Tel: 415/556-1693

www.nps.gov/fopo

Golden Gate National Recreation Area

Map: 192 B3–D4

Visitor Information

Fort Mason, Bldg. 201

Tel: 415/561-4700

www.nps.gov/goga

Presidio

Map: 192 C3–D4

Visitor Information

Visitor Center, 50 Moraga Ave.

Tel: 415/561-4323

www.nps.gov/prsf

Getting Around San Francisco

Although San Francisco is a fine city to visit on foot, there comes a time when you'll want to avoid climbing yet another hill. Luckily, the city is well supplied with user-friendly and affordable public transportation (see inside the back cover for more information).

The **Bay Area Rapid Transit** (BART; *tel 415/989-2278, www.bart.gov*) is a sleek, well-groomed, 104-mile (167-km) rail system that links San Francisco and the peninsula with cities in the East Bay (via a 3.8-mile-long–6.1-km–transbay tube), making outings to Oakland (see pp. 234–237) and Berkeley (see pp. 238–242) an easy day trip; an extension feeds the San Francisco International Airport. The trains run from dawn to midnight. You can purchase multi-excursion passes at any of five BART stops along Market Street—Van Ness, Civic Center, Powell, Montgomery, and Embarcadero.

For information on the **Muni bus system** and advice on which bus to take, call the Muni information line *(tel 311 within San Francisco or 415/701-3000, or go to www.sfmta.com)*.

The historic **cable cars** (see p. 199), start at Powell and Market and Powell and Van Ness and run all day. Passes, which are also accepted on the city's Muni bus system, can be purchased at Muni kiosks.

California Palace of the Legion of Honor
- 192 B2
- 100 34th Ave.
- 415/750-3600
- Closed Mon.
- $$ (free 1st Tues. of month)
- Bus: 1, 18, 38

www.famsf.org/legion

Thanks to the restoration of several historic gems and an intelligent conversion of former military installations, the park features well-preserved military buildings, a museum, mile upon mile of looping roads, and great stands of eucalyptus trees, plus hiking trails and picnic areas with stupendous views of the Golden Gate Bridge.

The Spanish originally built the Presidio to discourage the Russians; as usual, this was a sad tale for the Ohlone, who had lived here for about 5,000 years. In 1822, the site fell under Mexican rule until the U.S. Army took control in 1846. During the next 148 years, the Army transformed the mostly empty windswept dunes and scrub into a verdant jewel-in-the-crown of military posts. The U.S. Army Corps of Engineers planted thousands of cypress and eucalyptus trees. The result is a splendid urban forest enclosing sweeping lawns where military history topples over itself.

Start at the **Presidio Visitor Center** *(map p. 192 D3)*, in the former barracks, facing onto the original Spanish parade ground. This Spanish mission-style building was erected around the original Spanish adobe fort, which can be seen. Nearby, the U.S. Army's oldest general hospital today houses the **Letterman Digital Arts Center,** a division of LucasFilms. Visit the *Star Wars* exhibit in Building B, which is open to the public.

On the bay shorefront, windsurfers launch from beach-lined **Crissy Field** *(map p. 192 D4, Mason St.)*. Here, the **Farallones Marine Sanctuary Visitor Center** *(map p. 192 D4, tel 415/561-6622, www.farallones.org, closed Mon.–Tues.)* features hands-on exhibits about local marine life. On the park's south side, the public **Presidio Golf Course** *(map p. 192 D3, 300 Finley Rd., tel 415/561-4661, www.presidiogolf.com)* enfolds **Mountain Lake,** popular with waterfowl and picnickers.

INSIDER TIP:

Head to Baker Beach in the morning, when crowds are light and fog hovers around the Golden Gate Bridge.

—ERIN STONE
National Geographic contributor

Lincoln Boulevard *(map p. 192 C3)* leads past a series of batteries pointing their cannons toward the Pacific and across the Golden Gate. **Baker Beach** *(map p. 192 C3)* is a popular spot for strolling the sands.

Before leaving, pay your respects at the **World War II Memorial** *(map p. 192 C3, Lincoln Blvd. & Kobbe Ave.)* and **San Francisco National Cemetery** *(map p. 192 D3, Lincoln Blvd. & Crissy Field Ave.)*, burial place of more than 26,000 American soldiers killed in battle.

California Palace of the Legion of Honor

The westernmost part of San Francisco, known as **Lands End,** lies within the Golden Gate National Recreation Area.

Rodin's "The Thinker" graces the entrance of the California Palace of the Legion of Honor.

Enshrined in **Lincoln Park** *(map p. 192 B2–B3)*, this craggy region boasts one of the city's premier art galleries in the neoclassical California Palace of the Legion of Honor—the 1924 gift of social doyenne Alma Spreckels.

The stupendous museum exhibits an extensive collection of old masters, including Rembrandt, Rubens, and Watteau; Impressionist paintings by Monet and Cézanne; works by Picasso and Matisse; and a vast collection of works by Auguste Rodin, not least an original cast for "The Thinker."

One particularly spectacular piece is the circa 1500 "Last Judgment Triptych," by an unknown artist. The exquisite collection of antiquities includes Egyptian, Grecian, and Roman pottery, sculpture, and metalwork. Other highlights include an entire 15th-century Spanish ceiling, plus a superb grouping of furniture and decorative items with a vast hoard of English and French 18th-century porcelain. The more eclectic offerings include the Reva and David Logan Collection of Illustrated Books.

The museum also hosts temporary exhibitions, as well as a Sunday brunch with live music in the Legion Café.

Cliff House

To the southwest, at **Point Lobos,** the renovated Cliff House, now a restaurant, overlooks the ocean, and you can watch the sea lions and pelicans offshore on **Seal Rocks** *(map p. 192 A2)*. On Sundays, this restaurant hosts excellent champagne buffets. Eastward, the coastal trail takes you to **China Beach** *(map p. 192 C3)*, ideal for picnicking. ■

Cliff House

- Map: 192 A2
- Address: 1090 Pt. Lobos Ave.
- Phone: 415/386-3330
- Bus: 18, 38

www.cliffhouse.com

Golden Gate Park

Established in 1870 on a thousand acres (404 ha) of sand and windswept dunes, Golden Gate Park remains the single best daytime destination in San Francisco. Among its attractions are several world-class art and science museums, gardens representing flora and fauna from near and far, and a wide variety of picnic and hiking areas.

The beautiful blooms on show at the Conservatory of Flowers are a floral inspiration.

Golden Gate Park

192 B2–D2

Visitor Information

Visitor Center (inside Beach Chalet), 501 Stanyan St.

415/750-5105

www.golden-gate-park.com

The park's varied landscapes—hillocks, glens, lakes, knolls, and meadows—are largely the work of a Scotsman, John McLaren, who nurtured it from 1887 to 1943. McLaren succeeded William Hammond Hall, the park's first superintendent, after many in the San Francisco establishment ridiculed the notion of creating a park from wasteland.

Experimenting with various native grasses and trees, McLaren eventually prevailed over the park's apparently self-destructive tendencies. (As well as bureaucratic ones: He once faced down his own Public Works board by directing his staff to remove a parking lot and replant it with oaks.) So popular was "Uncle John" that an attempt to force him into retirement resulted in a minor uprising, causing the city to adopt a special exemption for him.

How to Visit

Walking (or cycling) is the best way of getting around inside the park. Wear comfortable shoes—the park is three miles (5 km) long! Many roads within the park are closed on weekends to enhance the safety of pedestrians and cyclists. Trams serve seniors and disabled travelers.

The Museums

Often bypassed in the rush to take in the entire park in one day, the museums located here are superb, whether it is art that draws you or the excitement of science.

De Young Museum: The de Young is one of those quiet old California institutions that only slowly yields its treasures—at least at first. In fact, it holds one of the most comprehensive collections of art on the West Coast. Anyone who spends more than an hour here will end up spending a day. Don't miss it.

Erected in 1895, the original Egyptian Revival–style buildings of San Francisco's oldest public museum were irreparably damaged by the 1989 earthquake. The museum is now in a brand-new state-of-the-art structure.

Among the treasures of the museum's vast **American collection,** look for "Dinner With Threshers" (1934) by Grant Wood, the pop art classic "Three Machines" (1963) by Wayne Theibaud, and "Rainy Season in the Tropics" (1866) by landscape maestro Frederic Edwin Church.

The collection presents a veritable pantheon of other 19th- and early 20th-century Americans, including Bill Copley, Paul Revere (silverware), Frederic Remington, Winslow Homer, John Singer Sargent, and Mary Cassatt. Many works expand on Western themes, such as Charles Nahl's troubling 1867 "Sacramento Indian with Dogs" and Thomas Cole's 1847 "Prometheus, Bound." Along these lines, it is well worth seeking out George Caleb Bingham's "Boatmen on the Missouri" (1846). "Susanna and the Elders" (1938) by Thomas Hart Benton is a Depression-era retelling of the classic Biblical tale about moral depravity and a prime example of the artist's proclivity for testing America's moral hang-ups.

Many of these works were donated by California's most aggressive late 19th-century capitalists and were supplemented in 1979 by acquisition of the Rockefeller Collection of American Art.

The permanent collection also includes sculpture by Joan Miró, Louise Nevelson, Isamu Noguchi, and Claes Oldenburg in the **Barbro Osher Sculpture Garden.**

De Young Museum

- 192 D2
- 50 Hagiwara Tea Garden Dr.
- 415/750-3600
- $$

www.deyoung.famsf.org

Recreation in Golden Gate Park

The park offers all kinds of outdoor pursuits, from soccer and jogging to fishing and archery. Some popular activities are:

Biking/In-line Skating: Bikes can be rented in the park, as can in-line skates *(tel 415/668-1117).*

Boating: Pedalboats and rowboats are available for rent on Stow Lake *(tel 415/752-0347).*

Golf: The park has an eccentric nine-hole course *(47th Ave., tel 415/751-8987).*

Tennis: There are 21 courts *(John F. Kennedy Dr., opposite Conservatory, tel 415/753-7131).*

Lawn Bowling: Free lessons are given on Wednesdays *(near Sharon Meadow and the Carousel, tel 415/487-8787).*

For a comprehensive listing of park facilities, consult the maps available at all major sites throughout the park.

California Academy of Sciences
192 D1
55 Music Concourse Dr.
415/379-8000
$$$$$
www.calacademy.org

Another mission of the de Young is expressed in the **Arts of Africa, Oceania, and the Americas** collection. Far from the catchall that its title might imply, this collection maintains a fine emphasis on the most primary of pieces, from the Central Asian door rugs in the Wiedersperg Collection to the terra-cotta vessels from seventh-century Teotihuacan in Mexico. The textile collection alone includes more than 13,000 items, from European tapestries and oriental silks to fashionable 18th-century dress and fine African costumes.

The **photography collection** includes early daguerreotype portraits, pre-1906-earthquake snaps of San Francisco, and the groundbreaking locomotion photography of Eadweard Muybridge.

California Academy of Sciences: Across the concourse from the de Young is the California Academy of Sciences, established in 1853. After complete rebuilding, the academy reopened in 2008 with an advanced **aquarium** and spectacular **natural history museum.** Highlights include a **rain forest dome,** where visitors can take a vertical journey; a **replication of a U.S. swamp,** complete with alligators; and the **Tusher African Center,** with zoological dioramas. The new facility, designed by Pritzker Prize–winning architect Renzo Piano, has a shape that suggests hills with a **living roof,** where native plants thrive.

The lower level features exhibits from the academy's former Steinhart Aquarium in a new environment. Visitors walk through a glass tube inside the **Amazon Flooded Forest.** Jellyfish, giant octopuses, and sharks teem inside the 100,000-gallon (378,541 L) **Northern California Coast** exhibit. A 212,000-gallon (802,507 L) **Philippines coral**

The 2.5-acre (1 ha) Living Roof at the California Academy of Sciences bursts with 1.7 million native plants.

EXPERIENCE: National AIDS Memorial Grove

Take a quiet walk in this grove, which defines itself as "a dedicated space in the national landscape where millions of Americans touched directly or indirectly by AIDS can gather to heal, hope, and remember." Or you can pitch in as a volunteer to maintain the grove by weeding, mulching, and planting.

Begun in 1991, the project rehabilitated the overgrown de Laveaga Dell at the east end of Golden Gate Park. It brought together professional landscape architects and designers with volunteer workers, who have donated more than 60,000 hours in clearing overgrowth and planting new trees and shrubs, as well as creating six gathering spots.

Free 20-minute tours of the grove are offered from March through October on the third Saturday of the month. On the same days, visitors can take part in volunteer workdays *(tel 415/765-0497, www.aidsmemorial.org).*

Donors of $1,000 or more can engrave a name in the **Circle of Friends** to honor someone they love and/or miss.

INSIDER TIP:

The botanical garden in Golden Gate Park is a treat anytime, but visit at twilight and walk quietly, and you may see families of quail out for a stroll.

—FORREST MCGILL
Chief curator, Asian Art Museum

reef habitat is the world's deepest such interior ecosystem. And the multimedia **Water Planet** brings to life an array of ocean and freshwater environments. The three-story state-of-the-art **planetarium** has a real-time NASA data link.

The Gardens

One of McLaren's legacies is the patchwork of special garden-meadows throughout the park. Although not as intensively curated as other attractions, they are pleasant places for picnics and walks. They include the **National AIDS Memorial Grove** (see sidebar above), **Shakespeare Garden, Rose Garden,** and McLaren's own **Rhododendron Dell.** The park service visitor center provides a map of the gardens.

San Francisco Botanical Garden at Strybing Arboretum: Of the three formal botanical sites, the San Francisco Botanical Garden at Strybing Arboretum is the most spectacular. The arboretum was founded in 1937 with a gift from Helen Strybing, widow of a wealthy San Francisco merchant. Strybing was particularly interested in indigenous botany and plants with medicinal purposes.

Many of the early collections focused on plants from Mediterranean climates: coastal California, South Africa, western Australia, the central coast of Chile, and the Mediterranean itself.

One of the most striking of these collections is the **Cape Province Garden,** which displays a

San Francisco Botanical Garden at Strybing Arboretum

- 192 D1
- 9th Ave. & Lincoln Way
- 415/661-1316
- Call for tours
- $
- Bus: 5, 21 26, 42, 47

www.sfbotanicalgarden.org

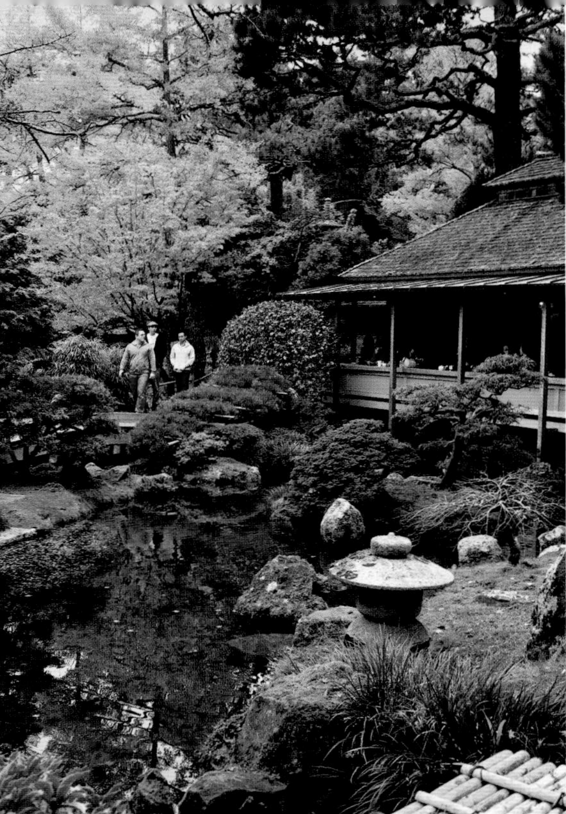

Koi ponds add to the serenity of the Japanese Tea Garden.

Japanese Tea Garden
192 D1
75 Hagiwara Tea Garden Dr.
415/752-1171 (tour information)
$

www.japanesetea gardensf.com

Conservatory of Flowers
192 D2
100 John F. Kennedy Dr.
415/666-7001
Closed Mon.
$
Bus: 5, 7, 21, 33, 44, 71; Streetcar: N

www.conservatory offlowers.org

number of amazingly well adapted plants from this unique botanical region on the southern tip of Africa. The various heaths, for example, can bloom year-round because their small needle-like leaves diffuse heat so well. The Cape Province Garden also showcases several varieties of aloe, kniphofia, and ice plant (the last are showier than their freeway-strip cousins might suggest).

One of the more recent additions to the Strybing is the **Meso-American Cloud Forest,** which is a testing ground for tropical plants, many of which are endangered in their native habitats. The garden is using the Bay Area's natural fogginess to approximate conditions in tropical cloud forests such as those in Chiapas, Mexico. Check out the giant lobelias, salvias, and daisies as large as small trees.

Japanese Tea Garden: Built for the 1894 Midwinter Exposition, the Japanese Tea Garden, at the north entrance to the Strybing, is the oldest Japanese-style garden in the United States. Take in the perfectly manicured grounds, and then relax in the open-air pavilion with tea and cookies. Do not miss Nagao Sakurai's 1953 **Zen Garden,** with its astonishing bonsai cypress. In spring, cherry and azalea blossoms explode in a riot of color.

Conservatory of Flowers: The Conservatory of Flowers, which attracts more visitors than any other place in Golden Gate Park, is a huge Victorian greenhouse filled with a riotous profusion of tropical plants. The Western Hemisphere's oldest existing conservatory, it was erected from a "kit" acquired from the estate of business magnate James Lick, who had planned to assemble it on his property in the Santa Clara Valley. Erected in 1879, the greenhouse was badly damaged in the 1990s in a windstorm. After eight years and $25 million worth of restoration, it reopened in 2003. Today, plants from more than four dozen countries—some 1,500 species—are displayed under one vast roof of glass.

Enter the **Lowland Tropics** section and you step into a realm of palm canopies and immense leaves (look for the 100-year-old imperial philodendron). There are "economic plants"—coffee, chocolate, vanilla—that have had worldwide commercial importance for centuries, as well as cycads, a species that dates back before the age of dinosaurs.

Orchids star in the **Highland Tropics** gallery, growing among ferns and creepers. The conservatory boasts the world's best public collection of Dracula orchids.

The **Aquatic Plants** gallery showcases huge lilies (one variety has leaves of up to six feet/two meters in diameter) and flowers that float. Another wing holds seasonal displays and special exhibits.

Historic Buildings

Fittingly, park headquarters is in the **McLaren Lodge.** Uncle John lived in this Moorish-cum-Gothic confection at the eastern end of the park until his death in 1943.

Opposite the Japanese Tea Garden is the ornate Spreckels Temple of Music, now known as the **Bandshell** *(map p. 192 D1)*. Built in 1899, it is home to the oldest continuously operating municipal band in the U.S.

Near Stow Lake is the **Pioneer Log Cabin,** a restored 1911 structure made from Humboldt redwoods. For an example of 1930s Works Progress Administration architecture, see the **Angler's Lodge,** opposite the historic **Buffalo Paddock** *(map p. 192 B1)*, with its herd of shaggy beasts.

If you are heading east, take a walk through the neighborhood of **Haight-Ashbury** (see sidebar below). If you are going west, see the **Beach Chalet.** The café, with its Depression-era frescoes, is a great place to eat. ■

McLaren Lodge
- Map: 192 D2
- Address: 501 Stanyan St.
- Tel: 415/831-2700
- Hours: Closed Sat.–Sun.

Beach Chalet
- Map: 192 A1
- Address: 1000 Great Hwy.
- Tel: 415/386-8439

www.beachchalet.com

San Francisco's Sixties Heritage

Just to the east of Golden Gate Park lies the venerable old neighborhood of Haight-Ashbury ***(map p. 193 E1)*****, which began life as a Victorian escape from the city center. Growth boomed after the 1906 fire, which left the area untouched. In the 1930s it declined, the Victorian houses split into flats. Drawn by low rents, Beats and African Americans arrived in the 1950s, followed by hippies and the flower-power generation.**

In the 1960s, Haight-Ashbury had its 15 minutes of fame, becoming the locus of just about everything that characterized the decade, from peace signs and tie-dyed clothing to black-light posters and head shops. By night, the area's musical denizens took the stage at Fillmore West, the legendary concert hall that lives on as the modern Fillmore ***(1805 Geary Blvd., tel 415/346-6000, www.thefillmore.com)*****.**

By the 1970s, however, Haight-Ashbury was a trash-littered ghetto with boarded-up shops. Remarkably, it made a comeback. Young professionals and gays moved into restored Victorian houses, and interesting shops opened (look for vintage clothes and records).

Stroll past the Victorians on Masonic Avenue or by the Queen Anne Richard Spreckels Mansion ***(map p. 193 E1, 737 Buena Vista Ave. W., not open to the public)*****. Continue up Buena Vista (daytime only) to Buena Vista Park** ***(map p. 193 E1)*** **and take in the views. South Haight has a fine community of retailers and specialty shops.**

Victorians on the Bay

Although many American cities flirted with Victorianism, few reveled in it in quite the same way as 19th-century San Francisco. Victorian architecture was, after all, a perfect synthesis of everything the booming city's new rich craved: status (the style had rich European antecedents), conformity, domesticity, and order (each room had a special purpose, unlike the boardinghouses that were the principal domiciles of the gold rush).

Quintessential Victorian row houses—the famed "Painted Ladies"—line Alamo Square.

And yet no city confounded, or continues to confound, Victorian stereotypes as much. Consider, for example, the story of the building now known as the **Queen Anne Hotel** at 1590 Sutter Street. With its domed turret, peaked gables, and gingerbread details, it certainly embodies Victorianism externally. But what happened inside its doors? It was built in 1889 for Sen. James G. Fair, one of the Comstock Lode silver kings and the force behind the Nob Hill landmark now known as the Fairmont Hotel (see pp. 202–203). At the time, the senator had already been sued by his first wife on grounds of "habitual adultery," according to an account by San Francisco historian Bob Bills.

This was apparently not a happy house. Although the senator kept custody of his two sons, both of them went on to blaze decidedly non-Victorian trails in the annals of family dysfunction. His son James, following a long battle with alcoholism, killed himself in 1892 at the young age of 27. The very next year, the other son, Charles, publicly married one of the era's most prominent prostitutes. In 1890, the building was sold to the Miss Mary Lakes School for Girls, which trained young women in more proper pursuits. It later went through iterations as a men's club and as an Episcopal girls' lodge before being boarded up in the late 1950s.

The most pronounced element of the Victorian style was **ornamentation**—ways to call attention to one's own individual taste while remaining safely inside the framework of Victorian architecture. To do this, the typical San Franciscan could employ several forms of artifice, some interesting, others frilly, and some outlandishly garish. There were the wall textures known as fishscaling and gingerbread, or the window decoration known as puddling, in which one layer of curtain was piled upon another to lend a regal effect. An Italian style could be added to a house by adding a simple eyebrow dormer.

Center of 1960s counterculture, Haight-Ashbury managed to retain its Victorian grandeur.

INSIDER TIP:

For an inside look at a true-blue San Francisco Victorian, don't miss the Hass-Lilienthal House *(www.sfheritage.org/haas-lilienthal-house)*, the only private home open to the public.

—BARBARA A. NOE
National Geographic Travel Books senior editor

Color, too, functioned as a social barometer. Although the average late 19th-century home might not have been as bright as some of today's candy-colored versions, color was often used to set off various exterior elements.

From the 1930s through the postwar years, as these neighborhoods declined, many of the Victorians became run-down housing stock, rented out on a month-to-month basis and seldom appreciated by their owners. The dominant color was battleship gray. Tour guide Jay Gifford *(tel 415/252-9485, www.victorianhome.com)* credits the hippie movement with saving the Victorian row houses. "Painting those drab buildings with bright colors saved them because it renewed interest in all those lost and faded details that no one had noticed for so long."

But what also transformed "those drab buildings" was the combination of two social trends: the remaking of downtown San Francisco as a financial center, and the growing population of gay professionals who worked there and needed housing. Author Richard Rodriguez has noted the irony that "it was thus a coincidence of the market that gay men found themselves living within the architectural metaphor for family."

The late 1990s wrought new changes in San Francisco's Victorian houses. Outrageous colors went out of fashion, but an indicator of the boomtime stock market was the use of gold leafing as ornamentation.

Castro District

Although well past its prime as "gay capital of the world," the Castro, with its many cafés, clubs, and bars, still offers fast-paced entertainment and busy street life.

The pink neon of the Castro Theatre *(reflected in car window)* acts as a beacon in San Francisco's gay center.

Castro District
193 E1–F1

It was here during the 1970s that gay men first began the often difficult process of leading openly gay lives. Their patron saint was Harvey Milk (see sidebar), a flamboyant and politically astute man who became the city's first openly gay supervisor before being shot, along with San Francisco mayor George Moscone, in 1978.

Two longtime Castro hangouts are the **Midnight Sun** *(4067 18th St., betw. Castro & Hartford Sts., tel 415/861-4186, www.midnightsunsf.com)* and **Badlands** *(4121 18th St., tel 415/626-9320, www.sfbadlands.com).*

For film buffs, the ornate **Castro Theatre** *(429 Castro St., tel 415/621-6120, www.castrotheatre.com),* a 1922 film palace, features a Wurlitzer organ that rises from the floor and plays before the featured film. ■

Leader of Gay Community

Elected to the San Francisco County Board of Supervisors in 1977, Harvey Milk was the first openly gay person to hold elected office in the U.S. Born on Long Island, Milk moved to San Francisco in 1972 and opened a camera shop in the Castro District, quickly becoming an activist for both his neighborhood and the gay movement. "If a gay man can win," declared Milk on the night of his election victory, "it proves there is hope for all minorities." Little more than a year later, Milk and Mayor George Moscone were assassinated by fellow supervisor Dan White inside City Hall.

Mission District

San Francisco's Mission District, which is situated east of the Castro (see p. 224), has made great progress toward revitalization in recent years. The Hispanic murals that have brought life to the streets remain, but new immigrants to the area are the key to more recent changes. Their flower stands and produce marts, and the great variety of Salvadoran, Indian, Chinese, and Vietnamese eateries that have popped up, astound even the locals. And the neighborhood continues to evolve.

The main attraction of this district is in fact a mission nicknamed **Mission Dolores,** after a now dried-up creek called Arroyo de Nuestra Señora de los Dolores; *dolores* meaning "sorrow." Its real name is San Francisco de Asís, for its founder's patron saint. Founded five days before the signing of the Declaration of Independence, Mission Dolores is rather plain and spare by the standards of its own era. It is, however, remarkable for its seamless blending of Old World and New World aesthetics, from its colorful **roof beams** (originally painted by Ohlone Indians) to the **statue of the Archangel Michael,** dressed as an Indian vanquisher. The **reredos,** or decorative altar, was made in San Blas, Mexico, in 1796.

The **cemetery** is also worth visiting. In its center is a statue of Junípero Serra by California artist Arthur Putnam. The surrounding **garden** contains many native plants, from huge Mexican sages to Matilija poppies. Here lie the remains of some of early San Francisco's most important figures, including Don Luis Antonio Arguello, the first governor of Alta California under Mexican rule. ■

INSIDER TIP:

At Mission Dolores cemetery, fans of Alfred Hitchcock's film *Vertigo* can look for the grave of the fictional Carlotta Valdes.

—KENNY LING
National Geographic contributor

Mission District
Map: 193 F1

Mission Dolores
Map: 193 F1
Address: 3321 16th St.
Phone: 415/621-8203
Transit: Muni: J car, Van Ness Station

www.missiondolores.org

More than 200 murals adorn walls and garage doors in the Mission.

Civic Center

The hub of San Francisco's government, the Civic Center is an impressive urban landscape dominated by the classical columns and gleaming dome of the 1915 City Hall. But this is also a neighborhood of serious culture, boasting a symphony hall, the War Memorial Opera House, and most recently the Asian Art Museum, with its treasures of many lands and materials.

The Asian Art Museum displays more than 2,000 objects, including this Chinese seated Buddha.

Civic Center
193 F2

City Hall
Polk St. betw. Grove & McAllister Sts. For tours, go to Van Ness Ave. entrance
415/554-6139
Tours Mon.–Fri. 10 a.m., 12 p.m., & 2 p.m.
Bus: 5, 19, 21, 47, 49; BART: Civic Center

www.sfgov.org/cityhall

After the 1906 earthquake and the devastating fire that followed it, San Franciscans vigorously debated how they wanted their rebuilt city to look. Their loftiest hopes for a "City Beautiful," contained in the Burnham Plan, were largely abandoned for more practical ideas, with the lone exception of the splendid Civic Center.

Located between Market, McAllister, and Gough, the Civic Center is still one of the nation's most complete collections of beaux arts buildings set in a formal plan. Broad red plazas and buildings with gold domes, Doric columns, and masses of California granite, convey the city's regal sense of itself after the earthquake. After some years of decline, the Civic Center has been revitalized, centering on **City Hall,** whose recent $300 million refurbishing brought back to life an urban temple of granite, marble, and gilded ironwork.

The 1995 **San Francisco Public Library** *(map p. 193 F2, 100 Larkin St., tel 415/557-4400, www.sfpl.org, closed Fri. & a.m. Sun.)* attracts people of all ages conducting research at computers and in specialized study centers whose scope ranges from Native American and African-American materials to the nation's first library center for gay and lesbian studies.

Asian Art Museum

Asian culture and art come to life in a stunning setting: the Italian Renaissance–style old public library designed by Brown and Bakewell and in 2003 given a new interior by contemporary architect Gae Aulenta, known for the Musée d'Orsay in Paris. The museum—the nation's largest devoted entirely to Asian art—displays works from (in the order they are encountered) India, the Persian world/West Asia, Southeast Asia, the Himalaya/Tibet, China, Korea, and Japan. Exhibits explore three major themes: Buddhism, trade and cultural exchange, and local beliefs.

India, Southeast Asia, & the Himalaya/Tibet: Religious statuary illuminates India's diverse religions, and an exhibit explains Hindu temples as symbolizing the holy mountains where gods dwell. From Thailand and Southeast Asian islands come ornate daggers (krises), while Cambodian sculptures show the refined temple decorations created by the Khmer people of the Angkor kingdom. Tibetan arts are represented by monastery scrolls, 15th-century ritual objects of gilded metal, and lacquered wood figures. Works from Nepal include mystical diagrams, or mandalas, that aid meditation.

China: Neolithic oracle bones show China's first written language. Other objects include the first Chinese Buddha (A.D. 338), ceramics, fan paintings, Ming calligraphy, and a large collection of jade objects, ranging from a rare symbolic disk (2500 B.C.) to openwork carvings and 1930s tourist trade items. Also in the collection: textiles, cloisonné, ivory, bamboo, and glass.

Asian Art Museum

- 193 F2
- 200 Larkin St.
- 415/581-3500
- Closed Mon.
- $$ (free 1st Sun. of month)
- Bus: 5, 19, 21, 26, 47; BART: Civic Center

www.asianart.org

Embracing the Seedy Side

Wedged between the Civic Center and Union Square is one of San Francisco's most colorful areas, 50 square blocks that comprise the once seedy Tenderloin neighborhood *(map p. 193 F2)*. As the city's favorite "underbelly," the Tenderloin hosted gambling dens, burlesque shows, speakeasies, and brothels as far back as the 1890s. The area was also home to many down-and-out artists, including budding jazz greats and a young Dashiell Hammett, who set *The Maltese Falcon* (1930) and several other books in the district. Although vice has faded in recent years, the dramatic arts continue to thrive in dozens of local theaters.

Korea & Japan: The finest collection of Korean objects outside Korea includes Bronze Age slate daggers, earthenware vessels, gilded Buddha figures, and paintings on silk. A broad survey of Japanese art takes in painted screens, notably an 18th-century example depicting a scene from the tenth-century poetic narrative *The Tales of Ise,* dry lacquer figures, glazed stoneware and porcelain, bronze bells, carved netsuke, and hanging scrolls. ■

SoMa & Yerba Buena

SoMa is the universally recognized abbreviation for the area of San Francisco that lies south of Market Street. Yerba Buena, named for the landing cove on its seaward side, was the city's business epicenter well into the 20th century. In recent decades, both areas have been reborn. With museums, playhouses, galleries, and the San Francisco Giants' AT&T Stadium, SoMa and Yerba Buena easily compete with Golden Gate Park and the waterfront as lively destinations.

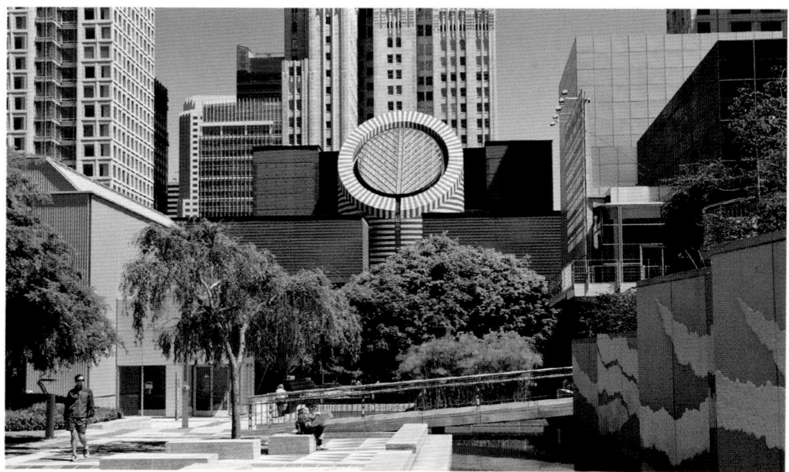

The San Francisco Museum of Modern Art features an outstanding contemporary building.

SoMa & Yerba Buena
193 G2 & 195
Visitor Information
www.visityerbabuena.com

San Francisco Museum of Modern Art
193 G2 & 195
151 3rd St.
415/357-4000
Closed Wed.
$$$ (free 1st Tues. of month)
Bus: 5, 9, 12, 14, 15, 30, 38, 45
www.sfmoma.org

San Francisco Museum of Modern Art

The main draw in the area is the San Francisco Museum of Modern Art (SFMOMA), partly housed in a red-orange structure designed by Swiss architect Mario Botta and opened in 1995. With its wide, open galleries and airy interior, it is the perfect place to view this outstanding collection of modern and contemporary art. Its **Caffè Museo** downstairs is one of the few museum eateries worth its salt and pepper. Spend the bulk of your time here on the atrium-lit **second floor** viewing a permanent installation of 250 works pulled from the museum's 27,000 holdings.

Given its location in the city that helped invent the 1960s counterculture, it comes as no surprise that SFMOMA boasts works by iconic pop art figures like Andy Warhol. "National Velvet" (1963) is far more typical of Warhol's distinctive style than his chromatic self-portrait in the same gallery. One of the more compelling abstract works is Jackson Pollack's cryptic "Guardians of the Secret" (1943), a painting you can ponder for hours without reaching a definitive conclusion about what the mystery might be. Pablo Picasso is amply represented by "Women of Algiers" (1955), one of a series by the Spanish master inspired by a 19th-century Delacroix painting of North African concubines. Cranking back the clock to cubism, the collection includes a quintessential George Braque entitled "Violin and Candlestick" (1910). Another SFMOMA favorite is Henri Matisse, whose range of paintings here show his artistic progression from "Woman With a Hat" (1905) to "The Conversation" (1938).

INSIDER TIP:

A favorite brewery is 21st Amendment *(563 2nd St.)*. Try the Hell or High Watermelon Wheat beer.

—RYAN GADDUANG
Supervisor, Sir Francis Drake Hotel

The museum has a fine representation of Mexican modernists. A triumph is Diego Rivera's 1935 "The Flower Carrier," which fuses the abstract concern for primal shape with the realist's attraction to biomorphism (how the body works). Though one can almost count the number of elements in the painting, any geometric staleness is flushed with the blood of Rivera's masterful palette work.

The collection has Hockneys, Lichtensteins, and Diebenkorns, as well as single works by the lesser known. SFMOMA has made significant acquisitions in recent years, including works by Francis Bacon, Jasper Johns, Willem de Kooning, and Robert Rauschenberg. The biggest coup came in 2009, when Gap founders Doris and Donald Fisher inked an agreement with the museum to show pieces from their private collection—more than 1,100 works by 185 artists, including Alexander Calder, Roy Lichtenstein, Agnes Martin, Richard Serra, and Andy Warhol. All of these new works will be displayed in a $555 million extension slated for completion in 2016.

Other Attractions

The newest addition to Yerba Buena's burgeoning culture is across the street at the **Rooftop** at **Yerba Buena Gardens**. Ten acres of child-size gardens, labyrinths, play spaces, and a glass-enclosed antique carousel are atop the **Moscone Center,** offering some of the liveliest daytime entertainments in town. Also on the Rooftop is the interactive **Zeum (Children's Creativity Museum),** which explores the visual and performing arts. Young people can learn to produce their own animated shorts and do 3-D modeling and audio mixing. The Rooftop also runs the **Yerba Buena Ice Skating & Bowling Center.**

Nearby is the **Yerba Buena Center for the Arts,** which features changing exhibitions of local art and includes the **YBCA Theater,** whose works reflect the cultural diversity of San Francisco. Relax in the adjoining **Esplanade Gardens** *(map p. 195)*, and see the **Martin Luther King Memorial** while you are here.

Yerba Buena Gardens

Map: 193 G2 & 195
Address: Betw. 3rd., 4th, Mission, & Howard Sts.
Phone: 415/820-3550

www.yerbabuenagardens.com

Zeum (Children's Creativity Museum)

Address: 221 4th St.
Phone: 415/820-3320
Price: $

www.creativity.org

Yerba Buena Ice Skating & Bowling Center

Address: 750 Folsom St.
Phone: 415/820-3541
Price: $

www.skatebowl.com

Yerba Buena Center for the Arts

Map: 193 G2 & 195
Address: 701 Mission St.
Phone: 415/978-2787
Price: $$ for galleries (free 1st Tues. of the month)
Bus: 9, 12, 14, 15, 30, 45, 76

www.ybca.org

EXPERIENCE: Baseball by the Bay

The Giants of Major League Baseball moved from New York to San Francisco in 1958. But the biggest move the franchise has made in recent years was the long-awaited migration in 2000 from windy Candlestick Park to a new stadium, AT&T Park *(map p. 193 H2, http://sanfrancisco.giants.mlb.com)*. Set in the revitalized South Beach neighborhood, the 41,000-seat stadium—named America's Sports Facility of the Year in 2008—is considered one of the nation's best places to watch baseball. Tickets are available online for a season that runs April to October. For a unique San Francisco experience, join a guided tour with City Kayak *(South Beach Harbor, tel 415/357-1010, www.citykayak.com, $$–$$$)* to McCovey Cove, where floating fans await home-run balls smacked over the right field wall.

Cartoon Art Museum

- 193 G3 & 195
- 655 Mission St.
- 415/227-8666
- Closed Mon.
- $$

www.cartoonart.org

California Historical Society

- Map p. 195
- 678 Mission St.
- 415/357-1848
- Closed Sun.–Tues.
- $

www.calhist.org

Across the street, **St. Patrick Church** *(map pp. 193 G2 & 195, 756 Mission St., tel 415/421-3730, www.stpatricksf.org)* presents Latin Mass at 10:30 a.m. on Sundays. Behind the church, the **Museum of Craft & Folk Art** *(map p. 193 G2, 51 Yerba Buena Ln., tel 415/227-4888, www.mocfa.org, closed Mon. & holidays, $)* features exhibits from around the world.

Pedestrian-only **Mint Plaza** *(map pp. 193 G2 & 195, www.mintplazasf.org)* hums with cafés, public art, cultural programs, street fairs, and a farmers' market.

The **Cartoon Art Museum** showcases selections from its collection of 6,000 pieces of original art—ranging from *Li'l Abner* and *Peanuts* drawings to cels from Walt Disney cartoon features. Highlights include animation drawing from *Gertie the Dinosaur* (1914) by the "father of the animated cartoon," Winsor McCay; underground comix (R. Crumb, *Zippy the Pinhead*); and an early character sheet from Disney's *Snow White and the Seven Dwarfs* (1937) showing some dwarfs who didn't make it to the film, among them Jumpy and Baldy.

The **Contemporary Jewish Museum** *(736 Mission St., tel 415/655-7800, www.thecjm.org, closed Wed., $)* stands on the site of the former power station. The **California Historical Society** puts on some of the best historical shows anywhere. It has 500 works by such artists as Albert Bierstadt and Thomas Hill, not to mention photos by Carleton Watkins, Eadweard Muybridge, and Arnold Genthe.

The Museum of the African Diaspora *(map p. 195, 685 Mission St., tel 415/358-7200, www.moadsf.org, closed Mon.–Tues. & a.m. Sun., $$$)* looks at the journeys and achievements of Africa-descended people around the world. Permanent exhibitions include the highly moving "Slavery Passages."

While you are in the SoMa area, stroll up Market Street to the **Rincon Center** *(map p. 193 H3, 121 Spear St.)*. This complex of stores and offices incorporates the 1930s **Rincon Annex Post Office.** The draw here is the post office's murals, painted in 1941–1948 by Russian artist Anton Refregier. The works were so critical of the city establishment that the artist had to make 92 changes to placate various interest groups. The murals also withstood a McCarthy-era attempt to destroy them for being "communistic" in tone. ■

Offering Muir Woods in Marin, the coast at Point Reyes, Berkeley's funky street scene, a great museum in Oakland, and Silicon Valley

Bay Area

The San Jose Museum of Art, Silicon Valley's leading art institution

Bay Area

If the charms of San Francisco seem to radiate outward, its surrounding territories (though substantial in size and at some distance from it) at times seem wholly directed toward the city, as if it were the very reason for their being. That is far from true, but each area's principal attributes do figure heavily in the city's character.

From the east comes much of the region's political, artistic, and literary history. Oakland gave the world Jack London (whose Yukon cabin stands on the bayfront mall) as well as many of the great plein air painters (whose works hang in the Oakland Museum of California). The much lampooned neighboring city of Berkeley (columnist Herb Caen dubbed it "Berserkeley") still exports the revolutionary impulse, but today it is more likely to be culinary, as at Alice Waters's Chez Panisse restaurant, than political. Still, the university named for the 18th-century Irish philosopher Bishop Berkeley ("Westward lies the course of empire . . .") remains a great excursion in tolerance, learning, and intellectual inquiry.

NOT TO BE MISSED:

From the rugged north—the Muir Woods and the Marin Headlands—comes much of the region's avid environmental ethos. There, between the mystical sea fogs and mists, visible from many points in the city, is nature preserved for all . . . and harvested for all. Travelers here find some of the best produce in the country: the famed oysters of Tomales Bay, found in luxury restaurants around the nation; the cheeses of Point Reyes Station; and the produce of the Marin Farmers' Market. Today's visitors to this whole remarkable area also find an outstanding travel infrastructure, and many small inns and bed-and-breakfasts featuring world-class cuisine, historical ambience, and comforts galore.

And the south? The land south of the city—best seen on the way to the Central Coast (see pp. 171–190) or on a day trip—is still very much the great experiment. San Jose and its environs are the land of technology entrepreneurs, their fortunes, like their mini-mansions, quickly made. Here technology is king. San Jose's most recent sight is the Technology Museum of Innovation, and its most popular tours include that of the giant Intel Corporation, world leader in the production of semiconductors.

By contrast, nearby Palo Alto has one of the world's greatest private colleges, Stanford University. Built with a 19th-century railroad fortune, its little university area is a more genteel version of Berkeley. ■

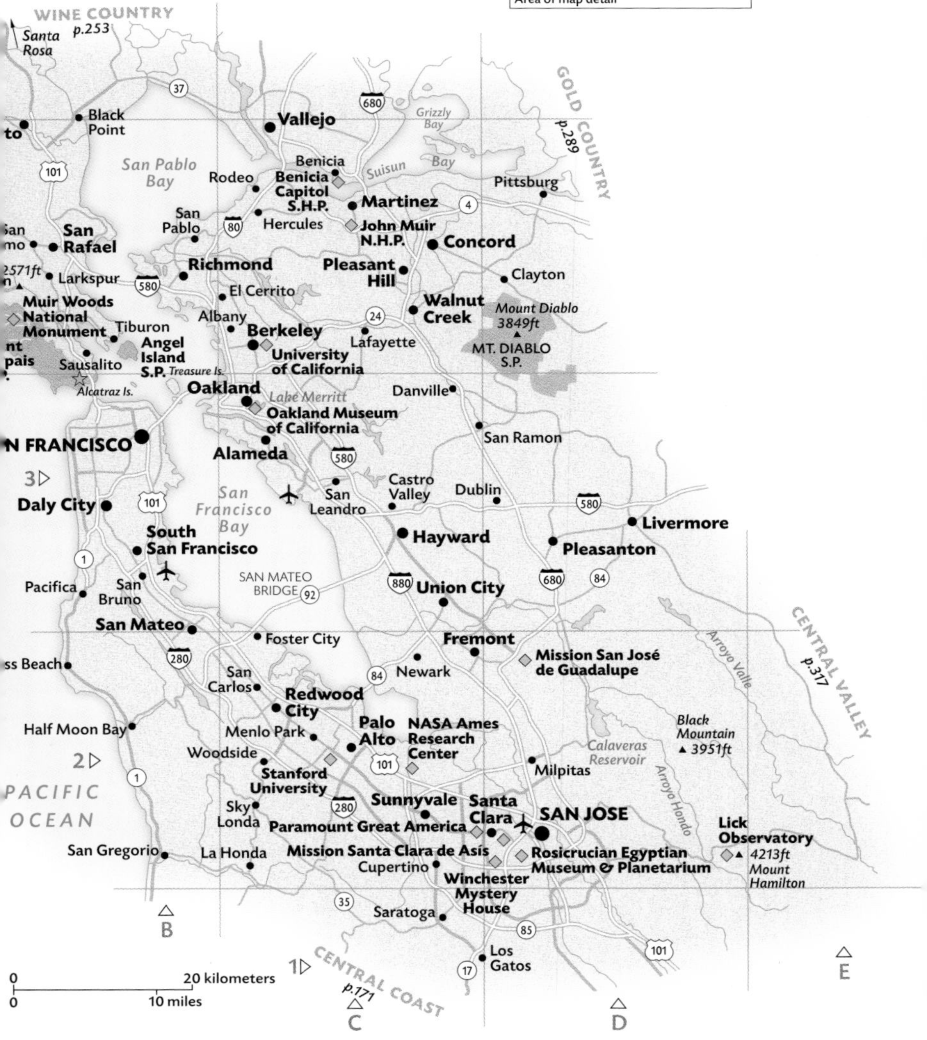

Oakland

Oakland has long labored under Gertrude Stein's memorable, if misquoted, comment—that "there is no *there* there." However, it possesses more than its share of classic American qualities. Oakland's character derives from its history: In 1869, the city fathers accepted an offer from the Central Pacific to become the railroad's western terminus—something its snootier neighbor to the west had fought against with all the money and political might it could muster.

Shedding its long-held reputation as a gritty port city, Oakland now attracts young professionals.

Oakland

233 C3

Visitor Information

Oakland Convention and Visitors Bureau, 463 11th St., Oakland

510/839-9000

www.visitoakland.org

In one sense, Oakland's genius was to turn San Francisco's throwaways into one of the West Coast's most dynamic industrial cities, a distinction it held until well after World War II. If a steel mill, a chemical plant, or a new shipyard was too dirty for the swells across the bay, Oakland would have it. Even today, the city's broad harbors and numerous light industrial areas thrum with commerce, though much has been lost to Seattle and Los Angeles in recent years. Under recent mayor—former and current California governor—Edmund G. "Jerry" Brown, Oakland began to surge forward again.

A good notion of the new Oakland can be found inside the old one, particularly on Friday mornings at the **Old Oakland Farmers Market** *(9th St. betw. Broadway & Clay, tel 510/745-7100, 8 a.m.–2 p.m.)*. This is an electric scene, vibrant with entrepreneurship of Latinos, Asians, and African Americans. A typical lineup might include an Armenian olive-oil maker from Modesto, a seller of sweet-potato pies and other African-American pastries, a Hmong tribeswoman in bright red selling fresh ginger and lemongrass, and a Vietnamese youngster hawking slippery shrimps and gleaming snapper.

A more historical slice of Oakland can be seen at **Jack London Square** *(tel 510/645-9292, www.jacklondonsquare.com)*, located on the waterfront Embarcadero south of Broadway. Few modern literary figures have been quite so intertwined with a city as was London (see p. 44 & sidebar p. 237). Born in 1876 and raised in Oakland, he found fame as a working-class adventure novelist *(The Call of the Wild* and *White Fang)*. London's **Yukon cabin,** from his days in the Klondike gold rush, has been relocated to the square. You can also visit the **Heinhold's First and Last Chance Saloon** *(48 Webster St., tel 510/839-6761, www.firstandlastchance.com)*, still a bar, with its unnervingly slanted floor. The square hosts free concerts, and a weekend farmers' market. Nearby, the **U.S.S. *Potomac*,** President Franklin D. Roosevelt's "floating White House," welcomes visitors at **FDR Pier.**

INSIDER TIP:

Gertrude Stein's oft-misquoted "There's no *there* there!" referred to her demolished childhood home in Oakland. To discover the city's charming *there*, walk the Rockridge district.

—CHRISTOPHER BAKER
National Geographic author

EXPERIENCE: Black Panthers

Hotbed of the civil rights and free speech movements during the turbulent 1960s, Oakland keeps its revolutionary heritage alive with "The Spirit of '66" from Black Panther Tours *(tel 505/884-4860, www.blackpanthertours.com, $)*. You will see Bobby Seale's home, the first Black Panther party office, and the place where Huey P. Newton was murdered. Tours begin at the West Oakland Branch Library *(1801 Adeline St.)*.

Lake Merritt, in the city's heart, is a relaxed weekend destination. Its pathways frame **Lakeside Park,** on its north shore, where a wildlife sanctuary draws wild geese and other waterfowl. You can rent boats, or Gondola Servizio *(tel 510/663-6603, www.gondolaservizio.com)* will punt you around the lake. The thickly forested Oakland Hills are studded with giant redwoods, including those within the 500-acre (202 ha) **Joaquin Miller Park.** Here you'll find hiking trails, equestrian areas, and an amphitheater hosting summertime musicals.

Oakland Museum of California

In 1969, the citizens of Oakland combined the collections of three older institutions to form

U.S.S. *Potomac*

FDR Pier, 540 Water St.
510/627-1215
$$
www.usspotomac.org

Lakeside Park

1520 Lakeside Dr.
510/238-7275

Joaquin Miller Park

3450 Joaquin Miller Rd.
510/238-7275
www.oakland.net/joaquinmillerpark

Oakland Museum of California

233 C3
1000 Oak St.
510/318-8400
Closed Mon.–Tues.
$$. Free 1st Sun. of month
www.museumca.org

the Oakland Museum of California, one of the finest regional museums in the country. Lodged in a sprawling but spare modern complex, dotted with verdant gardens and placid ponds, the museum brilliantly grounds its patrons in the ecology, history, and art of the state. Its atmosphere is relaxed, and the staff is helpful and knowledgeable.

After undergoing extensive renovation, the museum reopened

An exhibit at the Oakland Museum of California retraces the journey of settlers during the Dust Bowl.

in 2010. The remake features more interactive and multimedia experiences and an offbeat blend of history, art, and science.

Gallery of Art: Perched on the third floor, the new Gallery of Art features selected works from the museum's 70,000-strong collection, including painting, sculpture, photography, decorative arts, and new media, as well as documentary materials like sketchbooks and artists' tools. The space is divided into separate areas for works that represent California land, people, and creativity.

The collection hints at the scale and achievement of California's artistic community, which in a little more than 200 years has confronted colonialism, industrialization, the enclosure of the wild, and the emergence of the world's first "permanent" frontier.

Many of these themes are readily identifiable in such works as Thomas Hill's "El Capitan," an 1866 piece with strong leanings toward the impressionist style of later years; the brilliant early tonalism of George Inness's "California, 1894"; and the early plein air works of J. H. E. Partington and his 1890 "Lake Temescal."

One particularly memorable section is dedicated to the Society of Six (see p. 40), a 1920s group of Oakland-based painters who used a style of bold, simple brushstrokes. Aiming to communicate a "joy of vision" via the arrangement of abstract elements, such artists as William H. Clapp ("Bird-Nesting") and Maurice Logan ("Point Richmond") reveled in the state's sky and soil colors. The great Millard Sheets explored the more human dimensions of this aesthetic in paintings such as "California Dock Scene" (1929).

One of the museum's great joys is its inclusion of less celebrated artists from the state's past, many of whom are only now growing in stature. One of these is Rinaldo Cuneo, whose transfixing "Earth Patterns" (1932) will forever change the way you look at the furrowed landscape of California agriculture. Other delights lie in the museum's collection of decorative and ceramic arts.

Of particular interest to photography enthusiasts is the museum's extensive holding of photos by Dorothea Lange; her 1936 "Migrant Mother" holds a special fascination for those interested in the artistic response to the Great Depression.

The gallery is topped off with a significant collection of California moderns, from Richard Diebenkorn and Joan Brown to some lesser known work of David Park and M. Louise Stanley.

Gallery of California History: Down one level, this gallery uses an abundance of artifacts to present a detailed chronology of the state, including actual covered wagons, gold-mining equipment, and some of the earliest correspondence between pioneers and their "folks back home." Some of the daguerreotypes are particularly entertaining, as in Gabriel Harrison's 1848 "California News," depicting the enthusiastic response of Eastern newspaper readers to the discovery of gold at Sutter's Creek. Early examples of mythmaking shine in the museum's collection of souvenir lettersheets used by illiterate miners to send home the "good news"—even when it was bad.

Gallery of California Natural Sciences: Down one more level is an extensive (38,000 square feet/3,530 sq m) display of elemental California, from flora and fauna to lava beds and the Great Basin. The gallery simulates a walk across the state's many habitats.

Try to make time to visit the **California Library of Natural Sounds**—a unique "sound walk" across California that includes audio recordings of the state's indigenous animals as well as ambient soundscapes. ■

Jack London: Call of the Wild

Not only did Jack London master the adventure novel—his style carried over into other genres, too. His later reporting of sporting events is also characterized by his trademark inclinations toward the working class, as demonstrated in this excerpt from *The Night Born* (1913):

"To his ears came a great roar, as of the sea, and he saw Danny Ward, leading his retinue of trainers and seconds, coming down the center aisle. Everybody proclaimed him. Everybody was for him. Even Rivera's own seconds warmed to something akin to cheerfulness when Danny ducked jauntily through the ropes and entered the ring. His face continually spread to an unending succession of smiles, and when Danny smiled he smiled in every feature, even to the laughter wrinkles of the corner of the eyes and into the depths of the eyes themselves. Never was there so genial a fighter. His face was a running advertisement of good feeling, of good fellowship. He joked, and laughed, and greeted his friends through the ropes. Those farther away cried 'Oh, you Danny!' It was a joyous ovation of affection that lasted a full five minutes."

Berkeley

Although it traces its roots to the breakup of one of California's most powerful 19th-century ranchos, the town of Berkeley did not emerge from the shadow of San Francisco until the early 20th century, when the 1906 earthquake sent many San Francisco folk in search of new homes and Phoebe Apperson Hearst, mother of William Randolph Hearst, transformed the small Christian college of Berkeley into one of the nation's preeminent educational institutions.

University of California at Berkeley

Hearst money also made the University of California at Berkeley such a fine architectural gem, with such masters as John Galen Howard, Julia Morgan, and Bernard Maybeck brought in to design its key buildings.

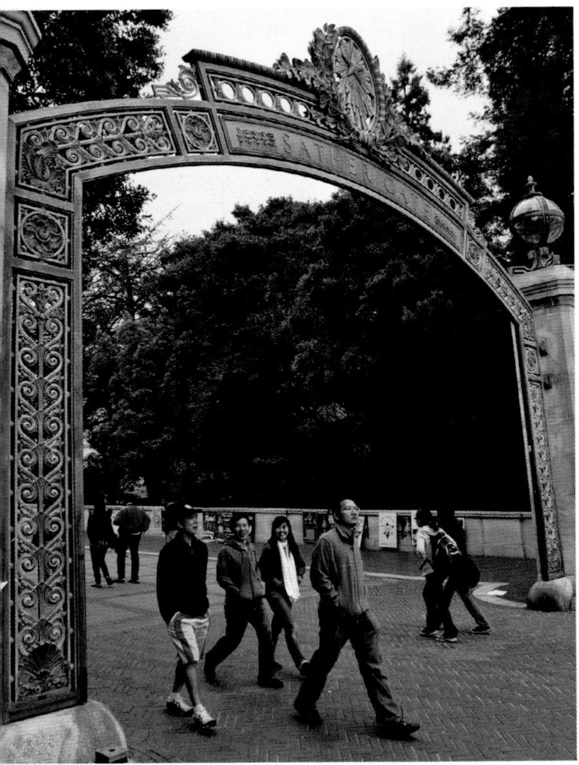

The restored Sather Gate

A walk through the campus, starting perhaps at the Telegraph Avenue entrance, takes one past **Sproul Hall** and the **Sather Gate,** site of many 1960s free-speech demonstrations. To the north is the principal landmark, **Sather Tower,** also known as the **Campanile.** Built by Howard in 1914, it is said to have been modeled on the tower of the Piazza San Marco in Venice. Farther north sits the regal **Hearst Mining Building,** built by Howard in 1907. To the east of it is the **Hearst Greek Theater** where, in 1903, Theodore Roosevelt delivered the commencement address. To the west is the **Life Sciences Building,** a huge concrete edifice with lovely external ornamentation in the shape of fishes, reptiles, and mammals. For a relaxing coda, stroll to the **Faculty Glade,** between **Stephen's Union** and the **Men's Faculty Club;** the glade is full of oaks, cedars, and restful green spaces.

The **Berkeley Art Museum and Pacific Film Archive** *(2625 Durant Ave. #2250, tel 501/642-0808, www.bampfa.berkeley.edu, closed Mon.–Tues., $$)* was established in 1963 by abstract expressionist painter Hans Hofmann and later housed in this engaging, playful fan-shaped building. There are the requisite Cézannes and

Monets expected of any modern museum, but the Berkeley's unique strength lies in the core collection of Hofmann's own works. See them in Gallery A.

The **University Botanical Garden** showcases another of the university's areas of expertise, with more than 13,000 botanical specimens. The 34-acre site

INSIDER TIP:

Berkeley's "gourmet ghetto" is a gourmand's paradise. Chez Panisse (see pp. 240-241)—the birthplace of California nouvelle cuisine—is at the ghetto's crux, at Shattuck Ave. and Cedar St.

—CHRISTOPHER BAKER
National Geographic author

contains a huge variety of exotic species, acquired since the university first began collecting them in 1890. If you plan to visit the Mendocino Coast later, be sure to see the **pygmy forest** to get a scholarly view of the phenomenon so prevalent at Van Damme State Park (see pp. 272–273).

For a shot of astronomy, visit the **Lawrence Hall of Science** *(1 Centennial Dr., off Stadium Rimway, tel 510/642-5132, www.lawrencehallofscience.org, $$$)*, where the brains behind some of today's top research put together planetarium shows. The museum and its workshops make science accessible and fun. Its hilltop perch offers spectacular vistas across the bay.

The **Hearst Museum of Anthropology** holds the keys to one of the great anthropological puzzles of modern times: How did a lone man named Ishi, the last known representative of the Stone Age Yahi people, come to be discovered in the Central Valley town of Oroville in 1911? A permanent exhibition of his work with UC scholars is on view, along with artifacts from ancient Egypt and Peru. Do not miss this gem.

For those not inclined to meander among the bookstores and cafés of Telegraph Avenue, **Tilden Regional Park** *(N of the university, tel 510/544-2747)* is a tonic. The park's gardens emphasize California's native plants. Romantics (and their kids) will love the old carousel and steam trains *(Closed Mon.–Fri. in winter)*.

Around Berkeley

Not surprisingly, the hills and glens of Berkeley hold several one-of-a-kind architectural gems. This is partly due to the freethinking, creative atmosphere that has long characterized the town's academic community. Another factor is money: This was a wealthy community with the resources to commission some of the top architects of the day.

For example, when Phoebe Apperson Hearst underwrote Berkeley's early 20th-century expansion, she also made Berkeley into a stage for the era's leading architects. Competition, ego, and

(continued on p. 242)

Berkeley

233 C4

Visitor Information

Convention & Visitors Bureau, 2030 Addison St. #102, Berkeley

510/549-7040, 800/847-4823

Closed Sat.–Sun.

www.berkeleycvb.com

University of California at Berkeley

233 C4

Visitor Information

Visitor Center, 101 Sproul Hall, Bancroft Way & Telegraph Ave.

http://visitors.berkeley.edu

University Botanical Garden

200 Centennial Dr., off Stadium Rimway

510/643-2755

$$

http://botanicalgarden.berkeley.edu

Hearst Museum of Anthropology

103 Kroeber Hall, Bancroft Way & College Ave.

510/642-3682

Closed Mon.–Tues. Tours by appt.

Bus 7, 40, 51, 52, 64

http://hearstmuseum.berkeley.edu

California Cuisine

"All I cared about was a place to sit down with my friends and enjoy good food while discussing the politics of the day. And I believed that in order to experience food as good as I'd had in France, I had to cook it myself." So explains Alice Waters, founder of Berkeley's famed Chez Panisse restaurant, of the inspiration that launched her now famous culinary career.

Founded in 1971, Berkeley's Chez Panisse features a different menu every night.

Anyone who follows food knows that Waters has far exceeded her own modest goals. More than 40 years after the creation of Chez Panisse, she is widely credited for the popularity of California cuisine.

The hallmarks of Waters's cuisine are classic French technique (albeit with a lighter hand with fats) combined with the freshest local, seasonal ingredients obtainable. A sample spring menu might include wild mushrooms on croutons, thin pasta with spring vegetables, charcoal-grilled salmon with grilled red onions, and buckwheat crêpes with tangerines, glacé fruit butter, and eau-de-vie. A summer menu could offer yellow squash and blossom soup, grilled whole filet of beef with deep-fried onion rings, and honey ice cream with lavender. Fall brings smoked trout mousse with chervil butter and champagne sauerkraut. Winter? Try oysters on the half shell with champagne sausages and mignonette sauce.

Waters has also deeply influenced the way we think about food, particularly restaurant food. To this day, she has kept the European

EXPERIENCE: Marin County Cooking Classes

If you are among the many foodies who flock to California panning for culinary gold in a state with a long tradition of top-notch cuisine, you'll discover a wide choice of cooking classes in Marin County.

Pine Point Cooking School *(tel 415/332-4352, www.pinepointcooking.com, $)* in Sausalito offers year-round adult culinary workshops as well as summer camps and holiday season classes for kids. You'll find an emphasis on fresh Mediterranean cuisine made with organic produce, dairy, poultry, and sustainable seafood. Your training will include blind tastings to differentiate between organic and industrial fruit and vegetables.

The posh **Cavallo Point Lodge** *(tel 888/651-2003, www.cavallopoint.com, $$$)*, at the southern tip of Marin, organizes monthly cooking classes and tastings with its own chefs and visiting experts. Themes run a broad gamut from artisan cheesemaking and Malaysian cuisine to winter comfort food and soufflés.

At Tiburon-based **Gourmet Gatherings** *(tel 415/717-1649, www.gourmetgatherings.com, $–$$)* you can enjoy interactive cooking classes and culinary parties for groups of ten or more. Guests are divided into culinary teams to prepare dishes you'll later feast upon. Epicures who don't live or work in the Bay Area can plan their session in the kitchen of top restaurants in San Francisco, Napa, and elsewhere. Just over the Marin county line, the **Ramekins Culinary School** *(tel 707/933-0450, www.ramekins.com, $–$$$)* in Sonoma offers a selection of classes in two kitchens. The mouthwatering courses include Tuscan cuisine, Asian noodles, Basque tapas, custards, curry workshops, and French Quarter cuisine.

tradition of a single, five-course, prix-fixe menu (a preference shared now by many California chefs, including Thomas Keller at Napa's French Laundry). "When people come to the restaurant, I want to insist that they eat in a certain way, try new things, and take time with the food," she writes. "For me food is a totally painless way of awakening people and sharpening their senses. I opened a restaurant so that everybody could come and eat."

You will need to make a reservation if you want to eat at **Chez Panisse.** Choose between the restaurant *(1517 Shattuck Ave., Berkeley, tel 510/548-5525, www.chezpanisse.com)* and the less pricey café *(tel 510/548-5049)* upstairs.

Other Berkeley Restaurants

Two other brilliant eateries in Berkeley are worth the time and the often inevitable wait. **Café Rouge** *(1782 4th St., tel 510/525-1440, www.caferouge.net)* offers some of the best bistro meals in the area. Try the steak, the salmon, or even the hamburger. At **Bette's Oceanview Diner** *(1807 4th St., tel 510/644-3230, www.bettesdiner.com, closed dinner)* locals line up for outstanding down-home breakfasts.

Afterward, stroll the outstanding Fourth Street Shopping District for some of the city's best gardening, cooking, and design boutiques.

INSIDER TIP:

The Ferry Building in San Francisco is one of the great "foodie" destinations in the world. Amid culinary-related stores, you'll find the Slanted Door, considered the best Vietnamese restaurant in the U.S.

—STEPHEN C. FERNALD
Culinary arts program director, Lake Tahoe Community College

inspiration fueled their architectural brilliance.

Two examples can be found at the corner of Dwight and Bowditch Ways. If some modern-day architects regard San Francisco's Swedenborgian Church (see p. 209) as the primal altar of the native Arts and Crafts movement, many others revere Berkeley's **First Church of Christ, Scientist** *(2619 Dwight Way, www.1stchurchberkeley.org).* Designed by Bernard Maybeck, who also had a hand in the Swedenborgian, this 1910 structure shows the style in full experimental swing. With its great gilded cruciform truss and Romanesque columns of exposed concrete, the church illustrates two of Maybeck's aesthetic concerns, according to historian Jefferey W. Limerick: the "love of grandeur, mood and atmosphere" and the "concern for craftsmanship and the rustic."

Opposite is the **American Baptist Seminary of the West** *(2606 Dwight Way, www.absw.edu),* formerly the Berkeley Baptist Divinity School, designed in 1918–19 by Julia Morgan of Hearst Castle (see pp. 174–175) fame. With its slate roof, bay, and turret, the school represents one of the earliest American attempts at an English institutional style.

Another example of Morgan's work can be found at the **Berkeley City Club** *(2315 Durant Ave.),* originally the Berkeley Women's City Club. Built in 1929 in what she called the "late medieval style," the club included a 25-by-75-foot (7.6 by 22.8 m) pool. As historian Sara Holmes Boutelle writes, "Every aspect of pool life was considered and planned for: changing, swimming, watching, sunning. Morgan's dressing rooms shine in comparison with most of the mildewed dungeons set aside for this purpose."

Of lesser caliber, but still monumental, is the **Claremont Resort Hotel** *(Ashby & Domingo Aves., tel 510/843-3000, www.claremontresort.com).* A white castle set against verdant hills, the hotel offers bay views, a spa, and tennis courts. Its restaurant, Meritage, is a fine eatery, and its Paragon martini bar combines contemporary chic with live jazz. ■

John Muir National Historic Site

Although John Muir, grandfather of the environmental movement, is most often linked with Yosemite and the Sierra Nevada, he kept his permanent address in Martinez, a laid-back town in Contra Costa County. His rambling Victorian home is now part of the John Muir National Historic Site *(4202 Alhambra Ave., Martinez, tel 925/228-8860, www.nps.gov/jomu).* The site's visitor center offers exhibits on Muir and a 20-minute film about his life. Guided tours of his 17-room mansion are offered daily. Much of the ranch is also open for exploration, including the orchards and Mount Wanda, where Muir often took his daughters for nature walks. An exhibit housed in the Martinez Adobe on the ranch grounds traces the route of Spanish explorer Juan Bautista de Anza from Mexico to the Bay Area in 1775–76.

Benicia

Situated northeast of San Francisco, east of the entry to the scenic Carquinez Strait, is Benicia—calm, with crisp sea air, a significant history, and abundant small-town delights.

Benicia is home to the **Benicia Capitol State Historic Park,** a perfectly preserved piece of California history. Originally built to be City Hall, it housed the state legislature from February 1853 through February 1854, when Sacramento took over. The first Women's Suffrage Act, permitting women to own property under their own names, was passed here. One of the legislators was Mariano Vallejo, who had originally sold the land to the town founders on the condition that it be named for his wife, Francesca; the city fathers later settled on her middle name, Benicia, to avoid conflicts with their growing neighbor, San Francisco.

For military buffs, the **Benicia Historical Museum** *(2060 Camel Rd., tel 707/745-5435, www.beniciahistoricalmuseum.org, closed a.m. & Mon.–Tues., $, free 1st Wed. of month)* displays artifacts from the history of Benicia and the U.S. Army arsenal. The road name derives from the camels originally brought west to transport troops over desert terrain.

Others will enjoy the **First Street Antiques District** *(C St. to F St.)*, whose shops offer a wide variety of Americana.

Visitors seeking something a bit more romantic should head to **St. Dominic's Cemetery.** There you'll find a gravestone to Sister Mary Dominica Arguello. Born Maria Concepción Arguello, the daughter of the military commandante in San Francisco, she had fallen in love with a visiting Russian, Count Nicolai de Rezanov. Her father opposed the union, but Maria won a compromise: If the count went to Rome and received the permission of the Holy Father, then they could wed. The count hurried off, but died while crossing Siberia. For ten years, Maria pined, unsure of Rezanov's fate. Finally, in 1816, his death was confirmed. Maria became a nun and died in 1857, "the first native daughter," as her headstone reads, "to receive the Dominican habit in California." ■

Of California's early capitol buildings, Benicia's is the only one still surviving.

Benicia
233 C4

Visitor Information
250 E. L St., Benicia
707/746-4202
www.visitbenicia.org

Benicia Capitol State Historic Park
233 C4
115 W. G St.
707/745-3385
www.parks.ca.gov

St. Dominic's Cemetery
585 Hillcrest Ave.
www.stdominicsbenicia.org

Drive: Marin Headlands to Mount Tamalpais

Mysterious fogs, lush redwood forests, and dramatic rocky shorelines make the Marin Headlands a popular yet unspoiled destination. That rare combination—the result of a century of environmental activism by Bay Area citizens—yields a seemingly endless parade of spectacular and accessible treats.

Arriving on the Marin Headlands via the Golden Gate Bridge on U.S. 101, go west on Bunker Road to the **Marin Headlands Visitor Center** ❶ *(Fort Barry Chapel, Field Rd. & Bunker Rd., 415/331-1540, closed Thanksgiving & Christmas)*. Nearby are the starting points for hikes along the **Miwok Trail.** Access other trails by driving north on U.S. 101 to Tennessee Valley Road, which leads to the **horse stables** *(tel 415/383-8048)*.

Consider a detour to sleepy **Tiburon** *(visitor information, Chamber of Commerce, 96B Main St., tel 415/435-5633, www.ci.tiburon.ca.us)*, an attractive little town noted for houseboats pulled onto land and used as shops and restaurants. The **Richardson Bay Audubon Center & Sanctuary** *(376 Greenwood Beach Rd., Tiburon, tel 415/388-2524, www.tiburonaudubon.org)* has self-guided trails and wetlands full of waterfowl.

Head north on U.S. 101. Take Calif. 1, the dramatic **Shoreline Highway,** west past **Green Gulch Farm Zen Center** *(1601 Shoreline Hwy., tel 415/383-3134, www.sfzc.org/ggf)*, which offers courses, lectures, retreats, and overnight stays.

Farther along Calif. 1, at the **Muir Beach Overlook** ❷ *(tel 415/388-2596)*, get your first view of the shore and, in late January to March, possibly of migrating California gray whales. Then drive north to **Stinson Beach** ❸ *(tel 415/868-0734, www.stinsonbeachonline.com)*, popular with surfers and swimmers.

Bird-watchers should visit the **Audubon Canyon Ranch** *(4900 Calif. 1, Stinson Beach, tel 415/868-1699, www.egret.org)*, a breeding site for Great Egrets and Great Blue Herons, and the **Point Reyes Bird Observatory** ❹ *(Mesa Rd., Bolinas, tel 415/868-0655, www.prbo.org)*.

NOT TO BE MISSED:

Muir Beach Overlook • Mount Tamalpais • Muir Woods NM

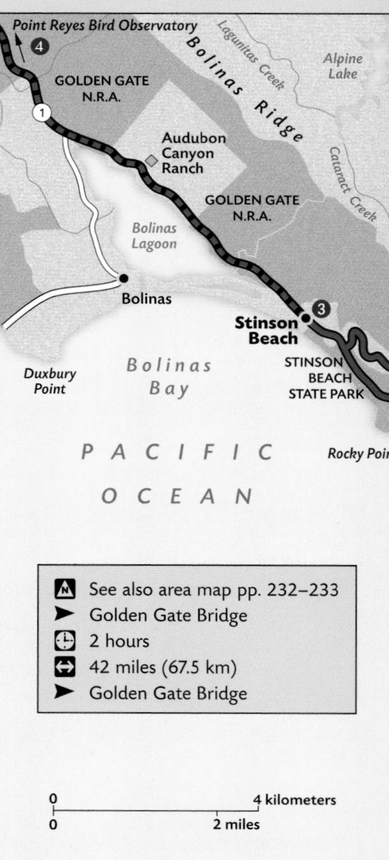

Inland from Stinson Beach stretches **Mount Tamalpais State Park** ❺ *(801 Panoramic Hwy., tel 415/388-2070, www.parks.ca.gov)*. You can drive to the 2,571-foot (783 m) East Peak of Mount Tam's double peak via the Panoramic Highway, which goes east from Calif. 1 a mile (1.6 km) south of Stinson Beach and Ridgecrest Boulevard. The 2-mile (3.2 km) **Pantoll Easy Grade Trail** is perfect for an afternoon hike. Or take to the trails on a mountain bike.

Farther south on the Panoramic Highway is **Muir Woods National Monument** ❻ *(Muir Woods Rd., Mill Valley, tel 415/388-2595, www.nps.gov/muwo)*, where a nature trail takes you through every element of the redwood forest—from salmon and steelhead trout of the Redwood Creek to the ferns, huckleberries, and violets of the forest floor.

Take the Panoramic Highway to U.S. 101 and back toward San Francisco. Stop in the quaint waterside town of **Sausalito** ❼ *(Visitor information, Visitor Center, 780 Bridgeway Ave., tel 415/332-0505, www.sausalito.org)*. A unique attraction here is the **Bay Model Visitor Center** *(2100 Bridgeway Ave., Sausalito, tel 415/332-3871, www.spn.usace.army.mil/bmvc)*, a detailed 1.5-acre (.6 ha) hydraulic model of San Francisco Bay complete with tides and currents.

Point Reyes

Point Reyes, at the core of the 75,000-acre (30,350 ha) Point Reyes National Seashore, lies on the eastern edge of the Pacific plate, which creeps northwestward past the North American plate at about two inches (5 cm) a year. At the Bear Valley Visitor Center, you can stand on the spot where, during the 1906 San Francisco earthquake, the peninsula leaped 20 feet (6 m) to the northwest. It is perhaps the most dramatic place in California to view the San Andreas Fault.

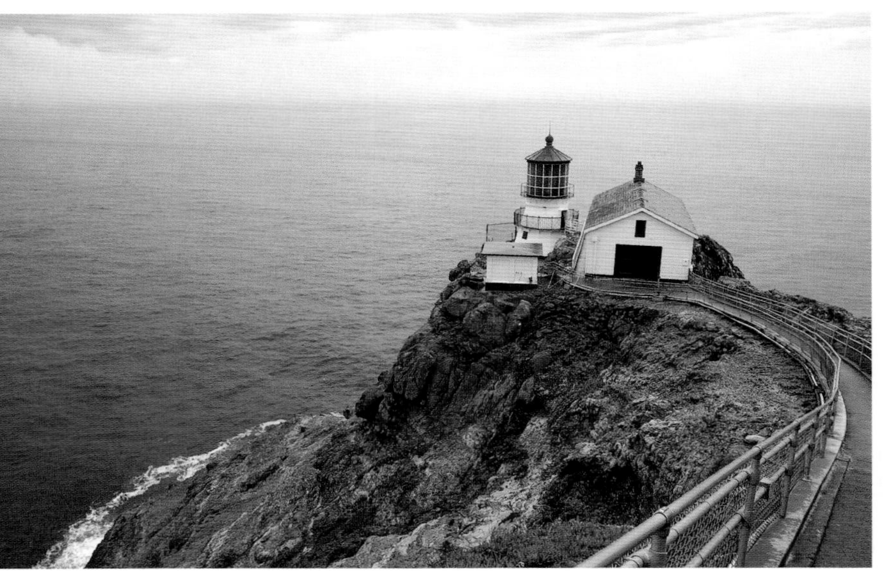

The Point Reyes Lighthouse guided ships through dangerous wind and fog for more than a century.

Point Reyes National Seashore

232 A4–A5

Visitor Information

Bear Valley Visitor Center, 1 Bear Valley Rd. (off Calif. 1 at Olema)

415/464-5100

www.nps.gov/pore

Ruler-straight Tomales Bay runs along the fault line; **Tomales Bay State Park** *(1208 Pierce Point Rd., Inverness, tel 415/669-1140, www.parks.ca.gov)* protects wetlands and surf-free beaches good for picnics. Full of natural and historic wonders, the point was discovered in 1579 by English explorer Sir Francis Drake. It was later claimed for the English crown, unbeknown to the Miwok Indians who had helped Drake resupply his ship, the *Golden Hind.*

At the northern end of Point Reyes is the historic **Pierce Point Ranch.** Founded in 1858, it is perhaps the oldest dairy farm in California; the state now manages the original structures and maintains a self-guided trail. Not far away is the **Tule Elk Preserve,** where, after a century of near-extinction, this magnificent mammal is staging a comeback. To the south lies **Abbotts Lagoon,** where bird-watchers may paddle canoes to see the annual water-fowl migration.

INSIDER TIP:

Point Reyes Lighthouse is often shrouded in cold, dense fog in summer. Arrive in a T-shirt and shorts, and you'll be in for a chilly surprise!

—CHRISTOPHER BAKER
National Geographic author

To catch the grand sweep of Drakes Bay itself, make the pilgrimage to the **Point Reyes Lighthouse** *(Sir Francis Drake Blvd., tel 415/669-1534, closed Tues.–Wed.)*. The original tower, with a 3-ton lens ground in France, was constructed in 1870 to prevent ships from running aground in the area's notorious fogs. Despite its 24-mile (38-km) visibility, the lighthouse has not prevented several crashes, including at least one involving an airplane. The estuary called **Drakes Estero,** where the explorer is said to have repaired his ship, is woven with hiking trails; some pass by oyster beds. Bring binoculars in the winter months to scan the horizon for migrating gray whales.

The town of **Point Reyes Station** on the eastern edge of the park has emerged as a hub for both adventure sports and the "farm-fresh food" movement. **Blue Waters Kayaking** *(60 4th St., tel 415/669-2600, www.bwkayak.com)* offers guided trips and canoe/kayak rentals for exploring the peninsula and its many inlets on your own. In 1994, **Tomales Bay Foods** *(80 4th St., tel 415/663-9335)* started to market locally produced vegetables and cheeses. A key to its success is access to one of the state's oldest organic dairies, the **Strauss Family Creamery** *(www.straussfamilycreamery.com)*. At **Bovine Bakery** *(tel 415/663-9420)*, you can buy great desserts and breads. Ask local retailers for the best places to buy the noted Hog Island oysters. ■

Point Reyes Station

232 A4

Visitor Information

415/663-9232

www.pointreyes.org

POINT REYES PICNICS

Michael Bauer, food editor of the *San Francisco Chronicle,* has recommended four picnic spots less than 30 minutes' drive from Point Reyes Station: **Chimney Rock,** on the road to Point Reyes Lighthouse; **Heart's Desire Beach,** located in Tomales Bay State Park; **Drakes Beach,** southwest of Inverness along Sir Francis Drake Boulevard; and **Samuel P. Taylor State Park,** near Olema, with picnic tables under a redwood canopy.

EXPERIENCE: Mountain Biking in Point Reyes

The Bay Area boasts some of the nation's best mountain biking trails, routes that are both scenic and technically demanding. Although mountain biking is prohibited in much of Point Reyes National Seashore *(www.nps.gov)*, the park has several challenging trails. Perfect for summer, the shady **Bear Valley Trail** follows the valley for a relatively easy 4 miles (6.4 km) to the coast. The trail starts at the visitor center parking lot in Olema. After a stiff climb, the 5.2-mile (8.3-km) **Olema Valley Trail**—which begins at the Five Brooks Trailhead in Olema—follows the eastern edge of Inverness Ridge in a gradual descent to the sea. Despite its bumpy climbs and descents, the 4.4-mile (7-km) **Estero Trail** rewards the brave with views across the coastal grasslands. You can pick up the trail along the western shore of Tomales Bay. Consult the park website for more mountain biking trails. Top trails are also found at **Annadel State Park** *(www.parks.ca.gov)* in Santa Rosa, **Henry W. Coe State Park** *(www.parks.ca.gov)* in the mountains south of San Jose, and at **Skeggs Point** on the peninsula.

Urban Marin County & Around

The hippie-turned-yuppie townsfolk of Marin have, over the past few decades, earned for themselves a reputation for being trendy, health conscious, self-involved, and politically correct. The resulting farmers' markets, boutiques, New Age galleries, and healing centers all make for pleasant and stimulating outings (whether or not you share the philosophy behind them). Many of the region's towns have outstanding historical and architectural sites, too.

Mountain biking was born in Marin County in the 1970s and has grown in popularity ever since.

San Rafael
233 B4
Visitor Information
Chamber of Commerce, 817 Mission Ave., San Rafael
415/454-4163
www.sanrafaelchamber.com

San Rafael

Mission San Rafael Arcángel *(5th & A Sts., tel 415/454-8141, www.saintraphael.com)*, the 20th mission established in California, was founded in 1817, when Lt. Gabriel Moraga convinced the padres at Mission San Francisco to allow their more sickly neophytes to move to San Rafael's warmer and drier climate. The neophytes recuperated, and San Franciscans have ever since sought relief from their winters (and summers) in this gem of a town.

The pristine, small-town atmosphere was not lost on local resident George Lucas, who used it as a backdrop to his classic movie *American Graffiti* (1973). The surrounding geology also fueled one of the last great projects of architect Frank Lloyd Wright, who called it "one of the most beautiful landscapes I have ever seen." Wright's **Marin County Civic Center** *(3501 Civic Center Dr., tel 415/473-6800, www.co.marin.ca.us/mc)*, finished after his death, was conceived as a "bridge between hills," illustrating the harmony Wright sought to bring between his medium and, as he would have

Modern Cuisine in a 19th-Century Setting

Founded in the late 19th century, the town of Larkspur *(Convention and Visitors Bureau, 1013 Larkspur Landing Circle, tel 415/499-5000, www.visitmarin.org)* has a pleasant mix of architecture, ranging from Victorian to log cabin to mission, and brick-lined **Magnolia Avenue,** a colorful shopping district, is listed on the National Register of Historic Places.

However, most folk come here for another reason: the **Tavern at Lark Creek** *(234 Magnolia Ave., tel 415/924-7766, www.larkcreek.com),* a world-renowned restaurant helmed by chef Bradley Ogden. After one of his brilliant New American meals of, say, pot roast and homemade ravioli, take a stroll to the north end of town to see the remains of the historic **Escalle Winery.** Notice the wildflowers, for which the town is said to have been misnamed (they are actually lupins!).

Located just 3 miles (4.8 km) south of the city of San Rafael near Mount Tamalpais, Larkspur has a busy ferry terminal, conveniently connecting the town with San Francisco.

put it, "Nature with a capital *N*."

The **Marin Veterans' Memorial Auditorium** at the Civic Center hosts a wide range of world-class performing arts, including music, dance, comedy, and the prestigious Marin Speaker Series.

The Thursday **farmers market** *(tel 415/492-8007, www.sanrafaelmarket.org)* along Fourth Street in downtown San Rafael mixes fresh food with local wines, live music, vintage clothing, handcrafted jewelry, and other local fortes. The civic center also hosts two weekly farmers' markets *(415/472-6100),* on Sundays and Thursdays.

San Anselmo

Founded in 1875 as the result of a legendary feud between the wives of two railroad men, San Anselmo is now known as the capital of the antiques trade in northern California. Buyers be warned: Prices are high. The town also has its share of cafés and restaurants, with an especially lively and rather upscale Sunday brunch scene.

Novato

The north Marin competitor of San Rafael, Novato offers many of the lures of its southern sister, from an **Old Town** district to a summer Tuesday evening **farmers market.**

Above all, it is the town's deep identification with the area's Native American days that distinguishes it for the traveler. An **adobe wall** just outside the Old Town, a former part of Rancho Burdell, once belonged to the home of Camillo Ynitia, last chief of the Olompali. Ynitia is believed to have been killed by his brother for not sharing the proceeds of the sale of the land to a pioneer family.

The **Marin Museum of the American Indian** *(Miwok Park, 2200 Novato Blvd., tel 415/897-4064, www.marinindian.com, closed Mon.)* is a must for anyone interested in the region's history before the arrival of Europeans. ■

San Anselmo

233 B4

Visitor Information

415/454-2510

www.sananselmochamber.org

Novato

233 B4

Visitor Information

Chamber of Commerce, 807 DeLong Ave., Novato

415/897-1164

www.visitnovato.com

San Jose & Around

Although its history dates back to 1777, when the Spanish attempted to found a mission and agricultural outpost at the southern end of San Francisco Bay, San Jose clearly takes its cues from a more modern moment. The Hewlett-Packard Company began in nearby Palo Alto in 1939, fueling the growth of the premier technopolis in the U.S. Apple, Google, IBM, and Intel are all headquartered here, in a one-time piece of farmland now known as Silicon Valley.

San Jose's Tech Museum of Innovation appeals to the "inner techno geek" in every visitor.

San Jose
233 D2
Visitor Information
Convention & Visitors Bureau, 408 Almaden Blvd., San Jose
408/295-9600
www.sanjose.org

The Tech Museum of Innovation
201 S. Market St., San Jose
408/294-8324
$$$
www.thetech.org

For a long time, much of the new wealth tended to travel to San Francisco and other cities. That pattern has changed in recent years with the formation of several new museums and cultural institutions in San Jose. The most glamorous of these is the **Tech Museum of Innovation,** with more than 250 exhibits and interactive displays, an interactive media lab, and an IMAX theater. Eight permanent galleries demonstrate every techie aspect of modern life.

Three other museums are worth your time. By far the best is the **San Jose Museum of Art** *(110 S. Market St., tel 408/271-6840, www.sjmusart.org, closed Mon., $$).* The museum focuses on works by West Coast artists since 1980. Particularly engaging are the many artists who fuse the area's rich agricultural history with its present fixation on technology.

The **Rosicrucian Egyptian Museum & Planetarium** *(1600 Park Ave., tel 408/947-3635, www.egyptianmuseum.org, closed Mon.–Tues., $$)* houses the largest collection of Egyptian artifacts in the western U.S. It includes a large collection of human and animal mummies, a full-scale reconstruction of an Egyptian noble's tomb, walls of hieroglyphs, a collection of Coptic textiles, extensive gardens, and free hieroglyphic workshops on weekends.

The **San Jose Museum of Quilts & Textiles** *(520 S. First St., tel 408/971-0323, www.sjquilt museum.org, closed Mon.)* prides itself on an international mix, with changing exhibitions.

San Jose is perhaps best known for the **Winchester Mystery House,** a Victorian mansion famous for its weirdness: 160 rooms (many too tiny to be useful) and staircases, corridors, and doorways that lead nowhere. The owner, rifle heiress Sarah Winchester, was convinced that she would die if the building was completed, so work continued for nearly 40 years. Special flashlight tours are given periodically.

Santa Clara

In Santa Clara, just 4 miles (6.4 km) west of San Jose, thrill-seekers are drawn to **California's Great America** *(tel 408/988-1776, www.cagreat america.com),* a 100-acre theme park. Or visit the **Intel Museum** to see chips being made in one of the industry's "clean rooms."

While in the Santa Clara area, visit the **Mission Santa Clara de Asís,** on the campus of Santa Clara University. Nothing remains of the 1777 mission, but later buildings can be seen, as well as a beautiful facsimile of the original church; many of the old garden's roses—including an 1822 Castilian rose bush—are now classified as antiques by experts. **Mission San José de Guadalupe** *(map p.233 D2, 43300 Mission Blvd., Fremont, tel 510/657-1797, www.missionsan-jose.org)* lies northeast of the city.

Farther Afield

Aerospace buffs might like to visit the famed **Lick Observatory,** on 4,213-foot (1,284 m) Mount Hamilton, and the **NASA Ames Research Center** *(Moffett Field, tel 650/604-6274, www.arc.nasa .gov).* Here, the NASA Ames Exploration Center lets visitors experience NASA technology and missions firsthand and includes an IMAX theater. ■

Winchester Mystery House
- Map: 233 D2
- 520 S. First St., San Jose
- 408/247-2101

www.winchester mysteryhouse.com

Intel Museum
- 2200 Mission College Blvd., Santa Clara
- 408/765-0503
- Closed Sun.

www.intel.com/ museum

Mission Santa Clara de Asís
- Map: 233 D2
- 500 El Camino Real, Santa Clara
- 408/554-4000

www.scu.edu/ mission

Lick Observatory
- Map: 233 D2
- 408/274-5061

www.ucolick.org

San Jose's "Urban Village"

One of California's most creative urban renewal projects in recent years is the bold, brash Santana Row *(tel 408/551-4611, www.santanarow.com)* in San Jose. Packed into 42 acres (17 ha or roughly ten city blocks), the development opened in 2003 to rave reviews and several national design and engineering awards. A blend of residences, restaurants, and upscale shops, this "urban village" draws its architectural inspiration from several sources, including the Mediterranean and art deco. Extra-wide sidewalks, grassy plazas, benches, open-air cafés, and courtyards make Santana Row pedestrian friendly. Among the 90 shops and restaurants are Brooks Brothers, Gucci, Urban Outfitters, LB Steakhouse, and El Jardin Tequila Bar. Other tenants include the CinéArts 6 movie house and the boutique Hotel Valencia Santana Row *(tel 866/842-0100, www.hotelvalencia -santanarow.com).* Park Valencia hosts live music and a popular hot dog stand.

Stanford University

Stanford, one of the world's most prestigious academic institutions, was founded in 1887 in Palo Alto by railroad baron Leland Stanford and his wife to honor their son, who had died at age 16 from typhoid fever. From the beginning, it set high-minded goals. With the grand Romanesque architecture, red-tiled roofs, and wide brick plazas, form certainly followed ambition. The university visitor service offers free one-hour walking tours daily from Memorial Hall.

Stanford Memorial Church holds regular multifaith services.

Stanford University
233 C2
Visitor Information
Memorial Hall, 295 Galvez St., Stanford
650/723-2560
www.stanford.edu

Hoover Institution
434 Galvez Mall
650/723-1754
Closed Sat.–Sun.
www.hoover.org

Although there are many interesting historical sites to see, the **Stanford Memorial Church** *(Central Quad)* warrants special note. The church was the special project of Jane Stanford, who commissioned Maurizio Camerino, a great 19th-century Italian mosaicist, to render a reproduction of Cosimo Roselli's fresco of the Last Supper in the Vatican's Sistine Chapel. At the time of its completion in 1903, it was the largest mosaic in the United States. Like the church, it had to be rebuilt after the 1906 earthquake.

A more recent addition (1999) is the beautifully realized **Cantor Arts Center** *(Lomita Dr. at Museum Way, tel 650/732-4177, www.museum.stanford.edu, closed Mon.–Tues.),* which combines many of the university's older collections—including works by Goya, Piranesi, and Delacroix—with more recent acquisitions. The centerpiece is the Cantor collection of sculptures by Auguste Rodin, the largest in the world. There is also an extensive collection of Asian and American art.

INSIDER TIP:

When visiting Stanford University, don't miss nearby Filoli *(86 Cañada Rd., Woodside, tel 650/364-8300, www.filoli.org)*, a breathtaking English-style estate with spectacular gardens.

—GREG CRITSER
National Geographic author

The influential **Hoover Institution,** named for its founding alumnus President, was one of the first "think tanks" in the U.S. The library holds Herbert Hoover's 150,000-piece collection of manuscripts and documents on international relations. ■

Emerald green valleys, where wine is a way of life and simple outdoor pleasures reign

Wine Country

Sonoma Valley's Sebastiani Winery, one of the largest wineries in the U.S.

Wine Country

Although many have written about the grandeur of California's wine country, few have captured it as well as author Robert Louis Stevenson, who, in the summer of 1880, visited pioneer winemaker Jacob Schram. "In this wild spot, I did not feel the sacredness of ancient cultivation," Stevenson wrote. "Here . . . earth's cream was being skimmed and garnered, and customers can taste, such as it is, the tang of the earth in this green valley."

Today, as California wine country increasingly becomes an oenophile theme park, it is easy to forget the primal pleasures of the land itself. True, the crush of summer traffic, the jockeying for dinner reservations, and the collecting of the newest vintages make traveling in this region exciting. But the joy is in the land—seeing it, smelling it, feeling it connect in your belly with that first drop of a simple cabernet.

Some planning before you arrive is certainly worthwhile. First, when to come? California's wine country is at its best in late fall or early winter, when the crowds thin and the foliage puts on a spectacular show. Second, where to go? Consider staying away from the main action, perhaps in Calistoga, where the food is outstanding and the room rates more reasonable (albeit not cheap). Make reservations if you want to eat at any of the top restaurants. Lastly, bone up on your wine basics. It is hard even for the uninitiated to buy a bad bottle of wine here, but a little background knowledge always helps. ■

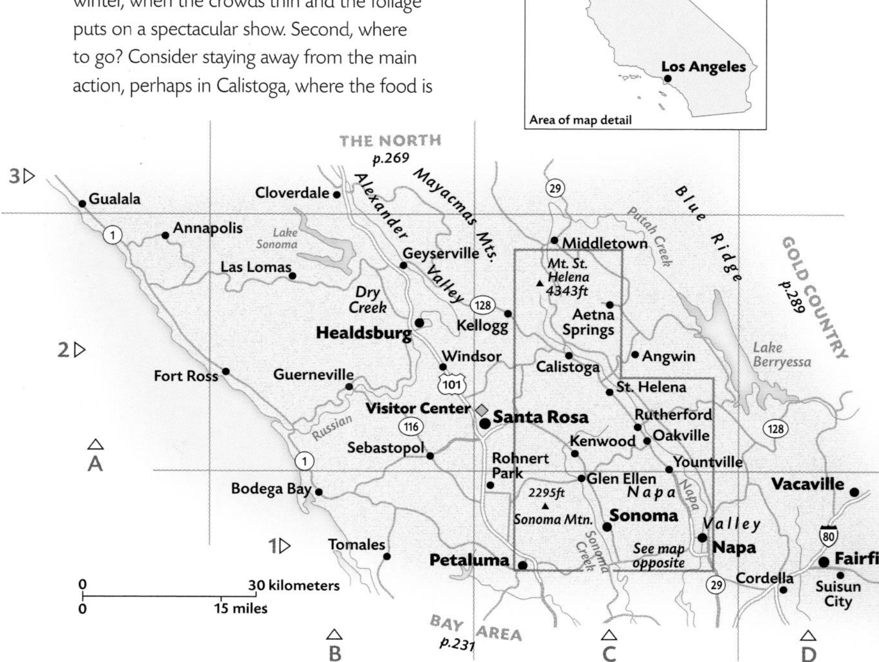

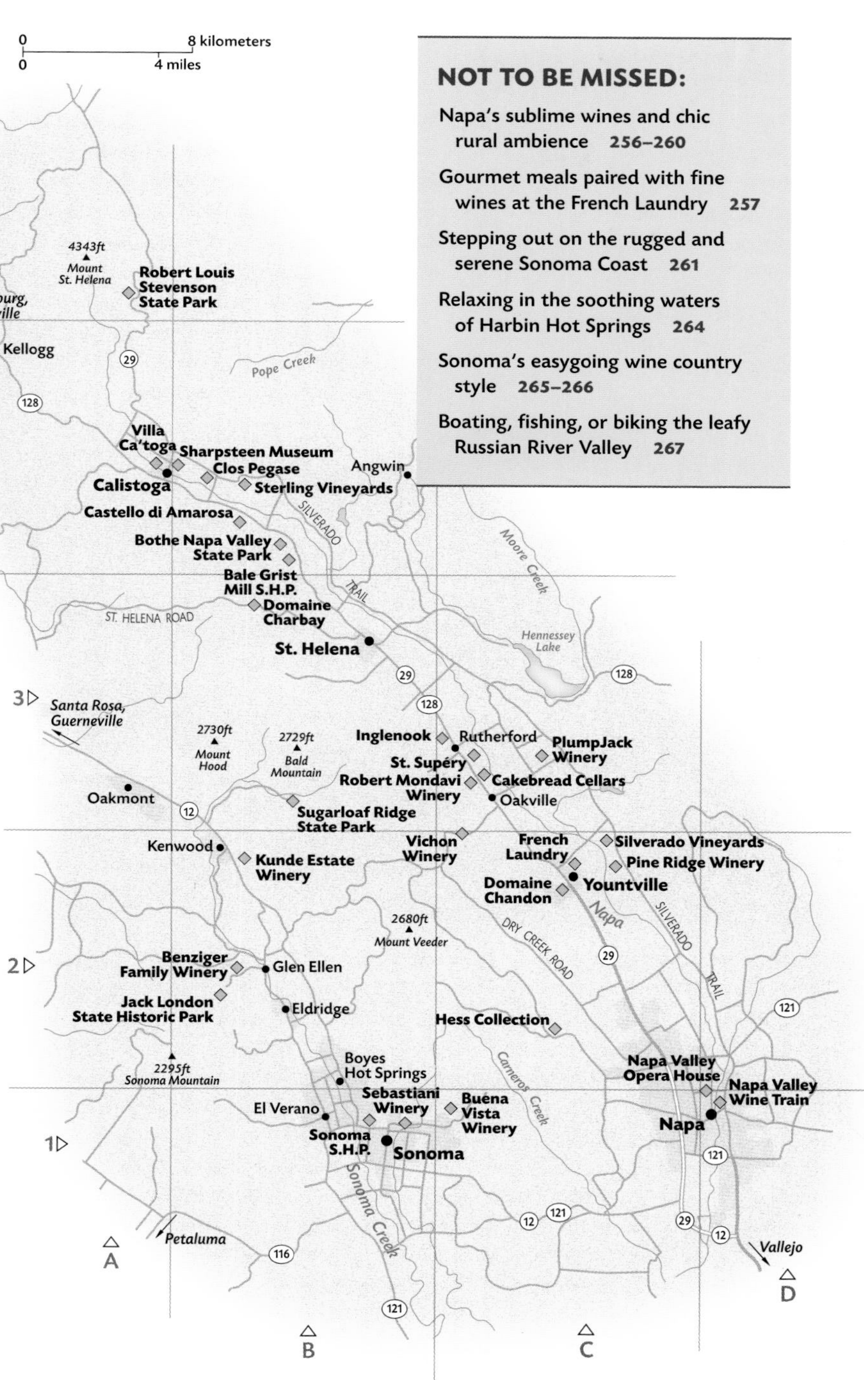

NOT TO BE MISSED:

Napa's sublime wines and chic rural ambience **256–260**

Gourmet meals paired with fine wines at the French Laundry **257**

Stepping out on the rugged and serene Sonoma Coast **261**

Relaxing in the soothing waters of Harbin Hot Springs **264**

Sonoma's easygoing wine country style **265–266**

Boating, fishing, or biking the leafy Russian River Valley **267**

Napa Valley

The heart of California's wine country begins at Napa, about an hour's drive north of San Francisco (see pp. 191–230). Volcanic soils and a favorable climate first attracted vintners to the region in the mid-19th century. Today, the valley stretching from Napa to the old spa of Calistoga, some 30 miles (48 km) northwest, has more than 200 wineries, some of them world famous and very much geared to visitors. They need to be. Annually, more than five million people make the pilgrimage up Calif. 29, the backbone of Napa Valley.

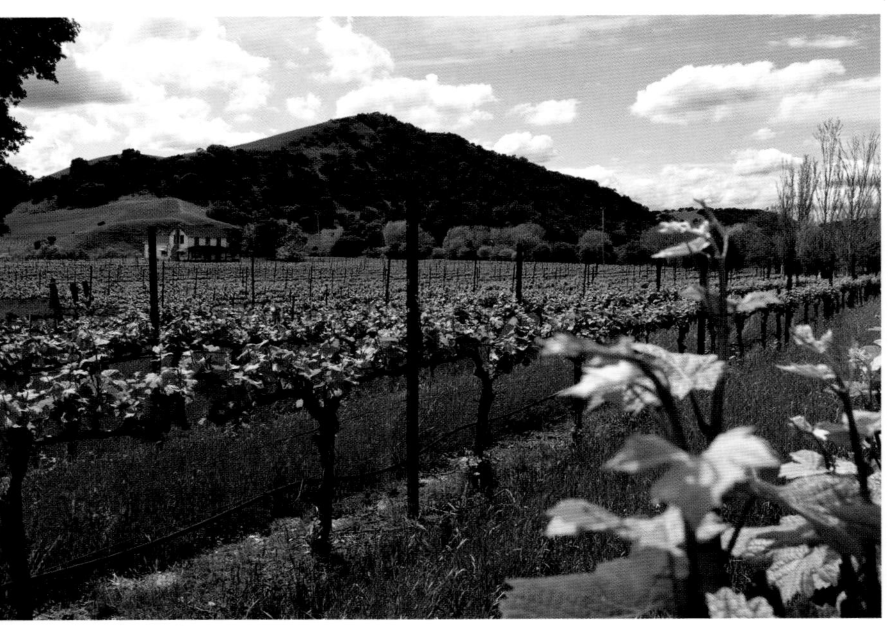

Nearly all of Napa Valley's agricultural land is given over to the cultivation of grapes for wine.

St. Helena
254 C2 & 255 B3
Visitor Information
Chamber of Commerce, 657 Main St., St. Helena
800/799-6456
www.sthelena.com

St. Helena

At the heart of the oasis, St. Helena is the perfect spot for the **Culinary Institute of America** *(2555 Main St., tel 800/333-9242, www.ciachef.edu).* With its fragrant herb gardens and food-is-all atmosphere, it would be engaging enough as a travel destination. The addition of a restaurant makes it a foodie theme park, where you can spend half a day eating. The seasonal menu is influenced by new Mediterranean cuisine, and the emphasis is on local foods and wines.

The good life continues at the luxury resort of **Meadowood** *(900 Meadowood Ln., tel 800/458-8080, www.meadowood.com),* where gabled hillside cabins are set in a 250-acre (101 ha) valley of oaks, pines, azaleas, and rhododendrons.

Best Meal in the U.S.

A food lover's dream, the **French Laundry** *(map p. 255 C2, 6640 Washington St., Yountville, tel 707/944-2380, www.frenchlaundry.com)* serves food that many believe is the nation's best. Some samples from a recent prix-fixe tasting menu: Sabayon of pearl tapioca with poached Malpeque oysters and Osetra caviar; new potatoes and French winter truffles; butter-poached Maine lobster with wilted arrowleaf spinach and saffron-vanilla sauce. These chef Thomas Keller serves in, as critic Ruth Reichl put it, "small, intense bites that add up to the valley's most incredible dining experience."

Although the courses are small, there are so many of them that, as one diner remarked, "It was like that movie *Groundhog Day.* Just when we thought we had finished, here came the waiter with another round!"

Reservations can be made between 10 a.m. and 7 p.m., two months to the day before you plan to dine. In other words, make this reservation before you buy your plane ticket. It is worth it.

INSIDER TIP:

Cycling is a great way to see wine country. Napa Valley Bike Tours *(www.napavalleybiketours.com)* also offers hot-air balloon rides.

—BOB HOLMES
Author, A Traveller's Wine Guide to California

Many come for the food, the golf course, and summer opera.

St. Helena also has associations with Robert Louis Stevenson, who spent his honeymoon near here in 1880. The **Silverado Museum** *(1490 Library Ln., tel 707/963-3757, www.silveradomuseum.org, closed Mon., donation)* recalls his stay.

Calistoga

Reposing, in Stevenson's words, "on a mere film above a boiling, subterranean lake," is the spa town of Calistoga. Founded by pioneer Sam Brannan as a health resort in 1859, Calistoga offers good bed-and-breakfasts, cafés, boutiques, and restaurants.

For the past 50 years, Calistoga has also provided balm to the weary by means of **Dr. Wilkinson's Hot Springs Resort** *(map p. 255 A4, 1507 Lincoln Ave., tel 707/942-4102, www.drwilkinson.com),* which offers reasonably priced spa services: massages, salt glow rubs, and "the mud," a complete immersion in warm volcanic ash and natural hot spring water.

The **Sharpsteen Museum** *(map p. 255 B4, 1311 Washington St., tel 707/942-5911, www.sharpsteen-museum.org, $ donation)* displays artifacts dating back 200 years. Nearby, the sumptuously decorated **Villa Ca'toga** re-creates the feel of ancient Rome.

Napa

At the valley's southern end, the **Napa Valley Opera House** *(map. p. 255 D1, 1030 Main St., tel 707/226-7372, www.nvoh.org)* hosts worthwhile dramatic performances by the American Conservatory Theater. ■

Calistoga

Map: 254 C2 & 255 A4

Visitor Information

Visitor Center, 1133 Washington St., Calistoga

707/942-6333, 866/306-5588

www.calistogavisitors.com

Villa Ca'toga

Map: 255 A4

3061 Myrtledale Rd., Calistoga

707/942-3900

Closed Nov.–April. Tours 11 a.m. Sat.

$$$$$

www.catoga.com

Napa

Map: 254 C1 & 255 D1

Visitor Information

Welcome Center, 600 Main St., Napa

707/251-5895

www.legendarynapavalley.com

Napa Valley Wineries

Sitting in one of Napa's glamorous but rustic tasting rooms or restaurants, it's hard to believe that just a few decades ago the idea that California wineries would ever be anything more than a footnote in the annals of wine would have been a joke. But now the footnote is a tome.

Extravagant Domaine Carneros sits atop a vine-lined knoll.

Inglenook

In 1975, director Francis Ford Coppola bought part of the Niebaum estate, which had been involved in winemaking since 1872. Three years later, he made his first vintage of Rubicon. Now Inglenook, formerly Niebaum-Coppola, is known as an outstanding producer of wines, from its trademark Rubicons (labeled by *Wine & Spirits* as "dense, rich, sumptuous—even when young") to its newer Rosso and Bianco line of family-style blends.

Robert Mondavi
- 255 C3
- 7801 St. Helena Hwy. (Calif. 29), Oakville
- 888/766-6328
- Tastings: $$$$

www.robertmondaviwinery.com

Inglenook
- 255 C3
- 1991 St. Helena Hwy., Rutherford
- 707/968-1100 (tours by appt. only)
- Tastings: $$$$$

www.rubiconestate.com

Robert Mondavi Winery

Set in a stylish country villa headquarters, this winery was the brainchild of Robert Mondavi, who departed the family's old Charles Krug Winery to experiment with realizing the world-class potential of Napa's rich soils and outstanding climate. He studied French winemaking techniques with the masters, bringing home new ideas, experimenting, adapting, failing, succeeding. In 1976, Napa entries in the Paris Wine Tasting won top honors, proving Mondavi right and launching Napa and California onto the world stage. Today, Mondavi's legacy winery offers some of the more (deservedly) popular tours in the valley.

INSIDER TIP:

Visit Napa Valley in February or March and you won't have to make restaurant reservations weeks in advance.

—BOB HOLMES
Author, A Traveller's Wine Guide to California

The winery's **Centennial Museum** blends artifacts from the early Inglenook winery, which originally stood here, with items from Coppola's films, right down to a vintage Tucker automobile and Don Corleone's desk.

St. Supéry

St. Supéry's Sauvignon Blanc and Chardonnay are considered outstanding among wines made to be drunk fresh. The tour includes a visit to the Victorian **Atkinson House,** built in 1881. Among the other delights here are a display vineyard, and, for the technophile, an exhibit dubbed "SmellaVision," a hands-on display to help one understand the language of aroma, appearance, and taste.

The Silverado Trail

Founded in the 1970s, **Silverado Vineyards** is situated along the scenic Silverado Trail, a 19th-century Napa Valley mining road that runs along the eastern side of the Napa River. Grown under the retreating cool air from San Pablo Bay, its merlots and cabernets are especially known for their "rounded" flavors and silky textures. A tour takes in the dining room, with original works by such California painters as Thomas Hill and William Keith. From the back terrace of the house, there is a stunning view of Mount St. Helena, to the northwest, and of the surrounding countryside.

Not far away on the Silverado Trail, the acclaimed daily tours of the **Pine Ridge Winery** *(5901 Silverado Trail, tel 707/737-1410 or 800/575-9777, www.pineridgewinery.com, tastings $$$$)* concentrate on various aspects of the growing process. A visit to the winery's hillside caves is followed by a tasting of Pine Ridge's fine cabernets, merlots, and chardonnays.

Calistoga (see p. 257) marks the northern end of the Silverado Trail. Here, **Clos Pegase** *(1060 Dunaweal Ln., tel 707/942-4981, www.clospegase.com),* founded by Jan and Mitsuko Shrem in 1987, manages to pull off a triple treat—art, wine, and architecture—with grace and aplomb. True, the award-winning headquarters at first shocked the valley's more traditionally minded vintners. But the Shrems have integrated much tradition at their winery, the most engaging being their aging caves, 20,000 square feet (1,858 sq m) of wooden barrels buried below a nearby rocky knoll. Sculptures by Henry Moore, Richard Serra, and Anthony Caro dot the property. The winery offers free "Grand Tours" every day, plus the Harvest Bacchanal and Grape Stomp in October.

Vintners & Gardeners

Several Napa Valley wineries take great pride in their gardens. Don't miss the innovative vegetable gardens at Cakebread Cellars ***(map p. 255 C3, 8300 St. Helena Hwy., Rutherford, tel 707/967-8620, www.cakebread.com);*** **the rustic landscaping at Sterling Vineyards** ***(map p. 255 B4, 1111 Dunaweal Ln., Calistoga, tel 800/726-6136, www.sterlingvineyards.com);*** **or the tomato extravaganza at the Robert Mondavi Winery (see p. 258). One of the valley's finest gardens flourishes at Peju Province Winery** ***(8466 St. Helena Hwy., Rutherford, tel 800/446-7358, http://peju.com).*** **As professional landscape gardeners and floral nursery owners, Tony and Herta Peju were well equipped to design and nourish a garden when they started the winery in 1983.**

St. Supéry
- Map: 255 C3
- Address: 8440 St. Helena Hwy., Rutherford
- Tel: 707/963-4507, 800/231-9116
- $: Tastings: $$$$$. Tours: $$$$$ (by appt. only)

www.stsupery.com

Silverado Vineyards
- Map: 255 C2
- Address: 6121 Silverado Trail, Napa
- Tel: 707/257-1770
- $: Tastings: $$$

www.silveradovineyards.com

Castello di Amorosa
- 255 B4
- 4045 N. St. Helena Hwy., Calistoga
- 707/967-6272
- Tastings: $$$

www.castellodiamorosa.com

Hess Collection
- 255 C2
- 4411 Redwood Rd., Napa
- 707/255-1144
- Tastings: $$

www.hesscollection.com

Domaine Charbay
- 255 B3
- 4001 Spring Mtn. Rd., St. Helena
- 707/963-9327
- $$$$. Visits by appt. only.

www.charbay.com

Castello di Amorosa

The most sensational newcomer is Castello di Amorosa. Thirteen years in the making, this 121,000-square-foot (11,240 sq m) Tuscan-style castle perched on a hill south of Calistoga features a frescoed great hall, secret passageways, and even a torture chamber. Other castle activities include horse-drawn carriage rides and hiking vineyard tours.

Hess Collection

The most outstanding art collection belongs to the Hess Collection, in the hills west of Napa. Established in 1896, the winery occupies a centenarian, three-story stone structure built into the side of Mount Veeder. The self-guided tour begins in the theater, where visitors are introduced to Hess's traditional Burgundian winemaking practice, resulting in quality wines of richly satisfying complexity. The second- and third-floor galleries meld a contemporary redesign into the historic sandstone shell, with 13,000 square feet (1,207 m) of art space displaying 115 contemporary pieces, including works by such masters as Francis Bacon and Franz Gertsch.

Domaine Charbay

In recent years, many wineries have begun producing grappa, port, and various trendy spirits. The family-run Domaine Charbay, a mountaintop aerie outside St. Helena, leads the spirited pack with its apple brandy, black walnut liqueur, and award-winning trademark fruit-flavored vodkas. It also produces the world's only dessert chardonnay, as well as California's first pastis, a California vermouth, and even a sunroot spirit—the first original, purely American spirit—made from sunflower tubers. ■

Meals on the Move

As you might expect, picnics in the Napa Valley are an art form. To get just the right cold chicken, salads, cheeses, and, of course, wine, try the **V. Sattui Winery** *(1111 White Ln., St. Helena, tel 707/963-7774, www.vsattui.com)*, which offers an extensive deli and a fine picnic area. Among prime picnic spots on the wine circuit for locals in the know are the **Vichon Winery** *(map p. 255 C2)*, which has its own bocce ball court, and the picnic tables at **PlumpJack Winery** *(map p. 255 C3)*.

As you also might expect, there is no shortage of places to buy picnic supplies. The famed **Oakville Grocery** *(7856 St. Helena Hwy., Oakville, 707/944-8802, www.oakvillegrocery.com)* offers outstanding specialties, from fig-olive tapenade to local fruits and salads. The more commercial (but delightful) **Dean & DeLuca** *(607 S. St. Helena Hwy., St. Helena, tel 707/967-9980)* has its own charcuterie. In Calistoga try the **Palisades Deli Cafe** *(1506 Lincoln Ave., tel 707/942-9549)*.

If you don't want to picnic but are tired of the restaurant scene, try a jaunt on the **Napa Valley Wine Train** *(1275 McKinstry St., Napa, tel 707/253-2111, www.winetrain.com)*. A restored 1917 Pullman dining car trundles you through wine country at a leisurely clip as you eat brunch, lunch, or a gourmet dinner.

Sonoma Valley

If Napa Valley is the Florence of American viticulture, full of talent, pomp, and wealth, then Sonoma Valley is its Siena, a place just as deeply committed to the art of wine but with a quieter air about it. In sheer number of wineries, Sonoma is outdone by its neighbor; in landscapes and ambition, it is its equal. And as the site of California's most northerly mission and the Bear Flag Revolt, the town of Sonoma has a historical importance that Napa can never match.

Sonoma's historic district is part of Sonoma State Historic Park, comprising six sites.

Sonoma

Bear Flag Monument in Sonoma's **Central Plaza** marks the place where, on June 14, 1846, a ragtag group of fur trappers and mountain men charged the quarters of Mexican commandante Mariano Vallejo, took him into custody, and raised a crude flag bearing a star, a grizzly bear, and the words "California Republic." The republicans were independent for less than a month. On July 9, U.S. Army captain John C. Frémont declared them part of the territorial United States.

The **Sonoma Barracks** *(20 E. Spain St., tel 707/939-9420)*, built for the Mexican army and later occupied by the Americans, is also in the plaza, as is **Lachryma Montis** *(Spain & 3rd Sts., tel 707/938-9560)*, the Gothic Revival mansion built in 1852 near a mineral water spring–hence the name, meaning "tears of the mountain."

Just off the plaza is **Mission Solano,** the last of California's missions to be built. Founded in 1819, it represented the ambitions of its founder, Padre José Altamira. He hoped to use it to usurp the leadership of Mission Dolores and Mission San Rafael to the

(continued on p. 264)

Sonoma

254 C1 & 255 B1

Visitor Information

Visitors Bureau, 453 1st St. E., Sonoma

707/996-1090, 866/966-1090

www.sonomavalley.com

Mission Solano

114 E. Spain St., Sonoma

707/938-1519

Anatomy of a Sparkling Wine

First associated with the kings of France, champagne—or sparkling wine as it is more properly called in general—came to be linked across Europe, in the 17th to 19th centuries, with power and royalty. Later, upwardly mobile middle classes adopted the drink for festivals and rites of passage, a potent symbol of the levels of luxury and wealth to which they aspired.

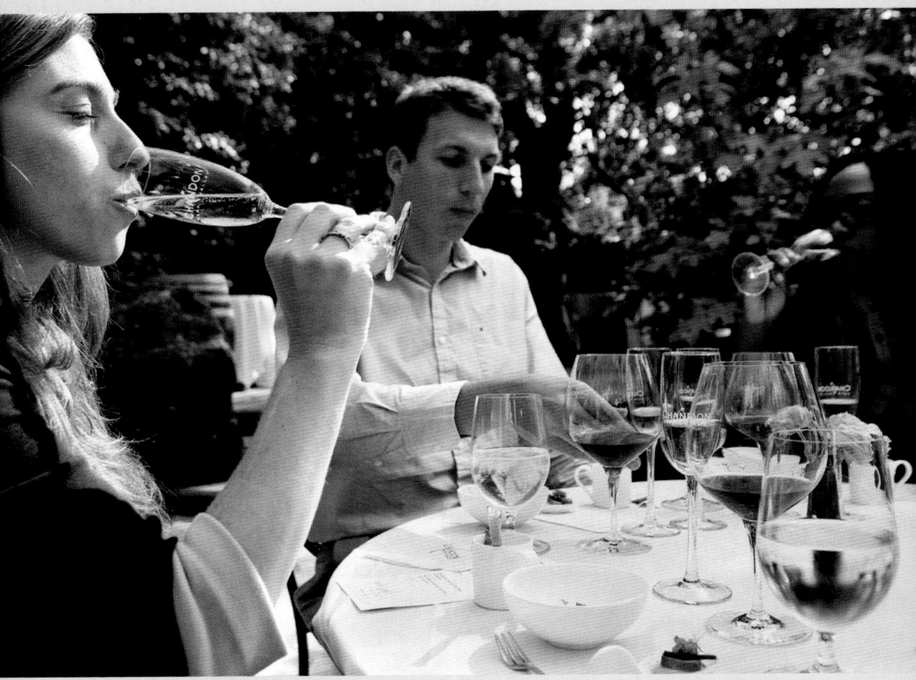

Established in 1973, Domaine Chandon was Napa's first French-owned sparkling wine producer.

Although it is fairly easy to learn about the making of wine in the U.S. these days, the same cannot be said of sparkling wine. Its production continues to be a European affair, even to the extent that, in recent years, there has been bitter controversy over the use of the name "champagne" to refer to wines produced anywhere except in the Champagne region of France.

In wine country, however, there are several places where you can get an idea of what goes into a bottle of the drink that, as Woody Allen said, "tingles the tongue as it mangles the brain." One such place is **Domaine Chandon** *(map p. 255 C2, 1 St. Helena Hwy., Yountville, tel 888/242-6366, www.chandon.com)*. Here they still use the ancient and revered *méthode champenoise,* as worked out by a 17th-century monk named Dom Pérignon, to create a sparkling wine.

The first step in the method is the crush—or, rather, **the press.** Sparkling wine requires a lighter hand than still wine in order to minimize the presence of tannin, a bitter chemical compound that comes from grape skins. The juice then goes into its first fermentation in giant stainless steel tanks.

Next comes the **blending** process, a careful addition and mixing of various grape juices that will produce the desired flavors. To this *cuvée* the winemaker adds a *liqueur de tirage,* a mixture of yeast and sugar that activates another round of **fermentation** as the liquid is poured into bottles and sealed. This causes the wine to produce more carbon dioxide, infusing itself with champagne's characteristic bubbles. Now the bottles are put in storage for two to five years, depending upon the cuvée.

During this period of **autolysis,** the wine takes on its unique characteristics–its smell, texture, and color. To collect the yeast sediment, the bottles are riddled, or turned, several times a day. At Domaine Chandon, the process is done by a machine called a gyropallette, or by hand. Winemakers have devised an ingenious method to disgorge the sediment by first freezing the neck of the bottle, then unplugging it and letting the built-up carbon dioxide jettison it. The bottle is then corked, wired shut, and labeled.

EXPERIENCE: Making Your Own Wine in Wine Country

Always wanted to try your hand at making wine? You're in luck because there are a few locals in wine country who will help you experience winemaking firsthand. One option is the Hope-Merrill Inn *(21253 Geyserville Ave., Geyserville, tel 707/857-3356, www.hope-inns.com, $$$$$)*, which offers a five-day pick-and-press winemaking event. Come in September for two and a half days of picking and hand-pressing grapes from the inn's own vineyard, and then return in May for another two and a half days that includes a tasting as well as two cases of wine to take home. The price includes four nights at the inn, plus breakfast and dinner. The interactive education center at the Napa Valley Museum *(55 Presidents Circle, at the California Veterans Home exit, Yountville, tel 707/944-0500, www.napavalleymuseum.org, closed Tues.)* teaches all of the winemaking processes.

Sparkling wine is stored in tanks at Domaine Chandon, which also produces still wines.

Glen Ellen
254 C1 & 255 B2

Jack London State Historic Park
255 B2
Visitor Information
2400 London Ranch Rd., Glen Ellen
707/938-5216
www.parks.ca.gov

Santa Rosa
254 C2
Visitor Information
Convention & Visitors Bureau, 9 4th St.
707/577-8674
www.visitsantarosa.com

Charles M. Schulz Museum
2301 Hardies Ln., Santa Rosa
707/579-4452
Closed Tues. Sept.–May
$$
www.schulzmuseum.org

south, but his plans were found out. Altamira nonetheless built a substantial plantation, though his abused Native American laborers rebelled in 1826 and sacked the mission. The chapel on display today was built in 1841.

The elegantly restored gold rush–era **El Dorado Hotel** *(405 1st St. W., tel 707/996-3220, www.eldoradosonoma.com)* features a good restaurant offering contemporary California cuisine. For a snack, visit the **Sonoma Cheese Factory** *(2 W. Spain St., tel 707/996-1931, www.sonomacheesefactory.com)*, where you can watch the making of the famed Sonoma Jack.

Glen Ellen

For an introduction to California's olive oil industry, drive up the valley to Glen Ellen. In the center of town is the **Olive Press** *(24724 Arnold Dr., tel 707/939-8900, www.theolivepress.com)*, featuring a tasting bar and pressing mill, in operation October to early February.

An outstanding place to stay is the **Fairmont Sonoma Mission Inn** (see Travelwise p. 376) at Boyes Hot Springs, a 19th-century bathhouse rejuvenated, tastefully, in modern mission style. The inn is within reach of **Jack London State Historic Park,** where the author is buried. His legacy to the valley was a nickname: the title of his book *Valley of the Moon*, by which this area is still known.

Santa Rosa

At the northern end of the Sonoma Valley, the historic town of **Santa Rosa** warrants a visit to see the **Charles M. Schulz Museum,** celebrating the life and art of the eponymous cartoonist who created *Peanuts*, and the **Luther Burbank Home & Gardens** *(204 Santa Rosa Ave., tel 707/524-5445, www.lutherburbank.org)*, where the famed horticulturist experimented with everything under the California sun. Some of Burbank's great triumphs are on display, including the Burbank russet potato and the Shasta daisy. ■

EXPERIENCE: Ancient Valley Retreat

Tucked into oak-strewn foothills about 50 miles (80 km) north of Sonoma Valley, you'll find the 1,600-acre (647 ha) **Harbin Hot Springs** *(18424 Harbin Springs Rd., Middletown, tel 707/987-2477 or 800/622-2477, www.harbin.org)*. Visit this nonprofit retreat and workshop center to explore its New Age benefits such as holistic healing and universal spirituality. Water is the main event here, with manmade pools of various temperatures fed by seven different springs. But you can also experience plenty of other activities, including yoga lessons, massage and meditation sessions, shamanic circles and Kirtan chanting, Native American sweat lodges, and Tantric sex workshops.

You'll sleep well, too: Harbin offers a wide range of crash pads, from dorms and motel rooms to cottages and geodesic domes. You can also visit the complex without reservations with a six-hour *($$)* or 24-hour *($$$)* pass. Camping is available nearby. No one under 18 is admitted.

Sonoma Valley Wineries

In recent years, Sonoma wineries have attracted increasing attention for their diversity of flavor and mood—probably due to the weather, influenced by the Mayacmas Mountains, and to the largely volcanic soils. People come to Sonoma when they just want to embrace nature and drink a good glass of California vino. Even Robert Mondavi bragged about his Sonoma holdings.

Visitors taste wine at Buena Vista Winery, said to be the oldest winery in the region.

Benziger Family Winery

A great place to start a Sonoma journey is at the **Benziger Family Winery,** near Jack London State Historic Park (see p. 264). To quote the prestigious *Wine Spectator* magazine, this is "one of the top ten winery visits in California." The winery was founded in 1980 by Mike Benziger, a native New Yorker. Later joined by his father and siblings, Benziger is focused on building a world-class *terroir,* or soil.

The tour, winding through unmatched wine country scenery complete with a redwood grove, brilliantly explicates the Benziger mission. Innovative trellising techniques, visible near the Viticulture Discovery Center, allow for maximum regulation of light, which in turn enables the vineyard to produce 25 different wines and 350 different flavors. Visitors also see how vines are grafted, trained, and maintained. There is a fine exhibit on cooperage—the art of barrelmaking—and a working bug farm, where natural methods of fighting pests are developed. Finally, there is the wine tasting room. The wine seems even better after a few hours spent wandering around in this blissful landscape of flavor.

Benziger Family Winery

- 255 B2
- 1883 London Ranch Rd., Glen Ellen
- 707/935-3000, 888/490-2739
- Tastings: $$. Tours: $$$$

www.benziger.com

EXPERIENCE: Fishing & Boating Clear Lake

The largest natural freshwater lake entirely in California, Clear Lake basks in the uplands 80 miles (129 km) north of Sonoma Valley. Its hundred miles (160 km) of shoreline support boating, fishing, waterskiing, and windsurfing. As the self-proclaimed "Bass Capital of the West," the lake hosts several national fishing competitions and is renowned for the immense size of its largemouth bass.

Travelers who have their own watercraft can launch from 11 free public ramps around the lakeshore. A number of outfitters rent boats and equipment, including **Disney's** *(401 S. Main St., Lockport, tel 707/263-0969, www.disneyswatersports.com)*. Alternatively, let someone else do the "driving" and sign up for a 1.5-hour cruise on the lake aboard the ***Lady of the Lake*** *(Seawall, Clear Lake, tel 641/357-2243, www.cruiseclearlake.com, $)*.

For a list of local fishing guides, log onto the Lake County tourism website *(www.lakecounty.com)*.

Buena Vista Winery
- 255 C1
- 18000 Old Winery Rd., Sonoma
- 707/938-1266, 800/926-1266
- Tastings: $$

www.buenavistawinery.com

Kunde Estate Winery
- 255 B2
- 9825 Sonoma Hwy, Kenwood
- 707/833-5501
- Tour & Tastings: $$$$$

www.kunde.com

Sebastiani Winery
- 255 B1
- 389 4th St. E., Sonoma
- 707/933-3230
- Tastings: $$

www.sebastiani.com

The Benziger family's **Imagery Estate Winery & Art Gallery** *(14335 Hwy. 12, Glen Ellen, tel 707/935-4515 or 877/550-4278, www.imagerywinery.com, tastings: $$)* produces rare wines. Its "Artists Collection," numbering almost 200 uncommon varietals, features labels specially commissioned from leading contemporary artists.

Buena Vista Winery

Historic Buena Vista Winery, in the Carneros region east of Sonoma, certainly lives up to the regal aspirations of its founder, Agostin Haraszthy. This Hungarian noble-turned-émigré-farmer came to Sonoma seeking a rustic empire. By 1860, after a tumultuous stint as an official at the U.S. Mint in San Francisco, Haraszthy had amassed some 6,000 acres of pristine valley floor. Not content with the local vines, he returned to Europe in 1861 and sent back more than 200,000 cuttings from 1,400 grape varieties. Among them were some of a pest-resistant strain that would save the nascent industry time and time again in subsequent decades. The result of his labors, much of it in evidence today, has earned him the uncontested title of father of California viticulture.

Kunde Estate Winery

Buena Vista may be Sonoma's most historic winery, but, with 800 acres (323 ha), the largest vineyard owner in the valley is the **Kunde Estate Winery.** The tour here includes a walk through hillside caves engineered by Russell Clough, who "dug the tunnel" for San Francisco's BART subway system (see sidebar p. 213). Try the viognier, a white wine from a French grape. If you're lucky, the winery may also have a store of zinfandel made from 1882 vines.

Sebastiani Winery

Just a few blocks from the plaza in Sonoma lies the **Sebastiani Winery.** Its tour has been highly praised by *Wine Spectator*. ■

Russian River

The area most favored by Bay Area weekenders for nearly a century, this lush and scenic river valley offers outdoor pursuits—canoeing, fishing, swimming, and bicycling, to name just a few—and is dotted with a number of outstanding wineries.

Guerneville, in the lower part of the valley, offers one of the most interesting wineries: **Korbel Champagne Cellars.** Founded about 130 years ago on the site of a lumber mill, the winery is like a tiny piece of history preserved in amber. An old blacksmith shop and general store remain for viewing. A rose garden, with more than 250 varieties of antique roses, is the subject of a half-hour tour.

Farther north, in Dry Creek Valley, is the Sonoma operation of wine giants E.&J. Gallo. In the grand tradition of California agriculture, the Gallos have rearranged the landscape, rebuilt historic bridges, and replanted groves of oaks. The **Gallo Family Vineyards** is entirely organic and worth driving by, even though there are no tours of this clannish family's estate. The Gallo family offers wine sampling at its new tasting room in charming **Healdsburg** *(map p. 254 B2, 320 Center St., tel 707/433-2458).*

For a good sandwich, stop at the Dry Creek General Store on Dry Creek Road just outside of Healdsburg. Then go on to the splendid **Ferrari-Carano Winery.** The wine is outstanding, but so are the 5-acre (2 ha) gardens, with 18,000 tulips in spring.

North of Santa Rosa is lush Alexander Valley. In summer, **Stryker Sonoma** offers food and wine events; as well as a series of evening concerts. The setting alone is worth the drive. **Trentadue Winery** *(19170 Geyserville Ave., Geyserville, tel 707/433-3104 or 888/332-3032, www.trentadue.com),* founded in 1969, is known for its outstanding sangiovese. ■

The heat of summer recedes with a float down the Russian River.

Guerneville

254 B2

Visitor Information

Visitor Center, 16209 1st St., Guerneville

707/869-9000

www.russianriver.com

Korbel Champagne Cellars

13250 River Rd., Guerneville

707/824-7000

www.korbel.com

Gallo Family Vineyards

3387 Dry Creek Rd., Healdsburg

877/425-5696

www.gallosonoma.com

Ferrari-Carano Winery

8761 Dry Creek Rd., Healdsburg

707/433-6700, 800/831-0381

www.ferrari-carano.com

Stryker Sonoma

5110 Calif. 128, Geyserville

707/433-1944, 800/433-1944

www.strykersonoma.com

The Sonoma Coast

Due west of wine country is the gorgeous Sonoma Coast, a 50-mile (80-km) stretch of seaside hamlets, tranquil farmland, and rugged seascapes that rivals Big Sur in terms of sheer beauty.

Dramatic golden cliffs surround Bodega Bay.

Bodega Bay

Start your exploration of the Sonoma coast at its southernmost point, **Bodega Bay** *(map p. 254 B1; visitor information, Chamber of Commerce, tel 707/347-9645, www.bodegabayca.org)*, named for Spanish mariner, Juan Francisco de la Bodega y Quadra, who charted this coast in 1775. This is also the place where Alfred Hitchcock filmed ***The Birds*** (1963), and visitors still flock to the town in search of movie locations like the old Potter Schoolhouse in inland Bodega village.

Get out on the water during a 3-hour voyage with **Bodega Bay Sailing Adventures** *(tel 707/318-2251, www.bodegabaysailing.org, $$$$)*, which also organizes 4-hour eco cruises *($$$$)* with local naturalist Katja Svendsen. Afterward, dine along the waterfront at **Spud Point Crab Company** *(1860 Westshore Rd., Bodega Bay, tel 707/875-9472, www.spudpointcrab.com)*, or buy your own picnic fixings at **Diekmann's Bay Store** *(1275 Calif. 1, Bodega Bay, tel 707/875-3517, www.diekmannsbaystore.com)*.

Sonoma Coast State Park *(tel 707/875-3483, www.parks.ca.gov)* begins on the northern outskirts of Bodega Bay, a sprawling reserve broken into several sections that embrace some of the most dramatic scenery along the Sonoma shore. Among its many natural landmarks are the **Bodega Dunes** and a rocky headland called **Bodega Head; Goat Rock,** near the mouth of the Russian River (see p. 267) and its resident harbor seals; and **Salmon Creek Beach,** with its tranquil lagoon, sandy spit, and turbulent surf. The circular drive around **Duncan's Landing** provides a great vista up and down the coast. The visitor center in Jenner is open only on weekends during the summer months.

Fort Ross

A dozen miles (19 km) north of Jenner is **Fort Ross** *(map p. 254 B2, tel 707/847-3286, www.fortrossstatepark.org)*, one of California's more remarkable historic sites. Established in 1812 as Russia's southernmost point in the New World, the fort was abandoned in 1841 when the Russians left California. The reconstructed stockade and its redwood buildings reflect what life must have been like in this far-flung outpost.

Just beyond Fort Ross, enjoy a gourmet meal at Alexander's at **Timber Cove Inn** *(21780 Calif. 1, Jenner, tel 707/847-3231 or 800/987-8719, www.timbercoveinn.com)*, on a cliff-top perch above the waves.

Gualala

The Gualala River marks the northernmost extent of the Sonoma coast. Wedged between the river and the ocean is **Sea Ranch,** a sprawling resort community that includes the **Sea Ranch Golf Links** *(42000 Calif. 1, tel 707/785-2468, www.searanchgolf.com)* and **Gualala Point Regional Park** *(42401 Calif. 1, tel 707/785-2377)*. ■

Cooler, greener, and full of natural wonders—home to coast redwoods and a paradise for outdoors folk

The North

One-room schoolhouse at Stone Lagoon, Orick, north of Eureka

The North

If much of California imagines itself as Mediterranean, its northern reaches identify with lands of higher latitudes. This is, after all, a land that Russian settlers tried (and failed) to claim in the early 19th century; it is a coast where Finns and Swedes dominated the fishing and shipping industries. Central to it is a storm system known as the Aleutian Low, which sends icy winds down from the Gulf of Alaska.

This is the California of great natural resources, its rugged terrain sprouting fine woods for the lumber industry, its waters giving bounty to generations of fishermen. Fortunately for travelers, much still remains. In and around Mendocino, great conifers still dominate the coastal rain forests. Farther north, coast redwoods tower over the junglelike vegetation of Redwood National Park. Here giant ferns and wild orchids create a dream world of filtered sun and foliage. Inland, at Mount Shasta, the manzanitas appear, their red stems hoisting aloft great low clouds of foliage.

In the Trinity Alps, you can drive all day through towering pines blanketed with fresh snowfall. Farther east, in remote Lassen Volcanic National Park, you can explore bubbling volcanic fumaroles, take a horseback ride

NOT TO BE MISSED:

Redwood wine country **274–275**

Victorian architecture in Eureka and other north coast towns **276–277**

The world's tallest trees in Redwood National Park **278–279**

The snowcapped majesty of Mount Shasta **284–287**

Wide open spaces in Modoc National Wildlife Refuge **287**

The geological oddities of Lassen Volcanic National Park **288**

Houseboating on Shasta, Trinity, or Whiskeytown Lakes **288**

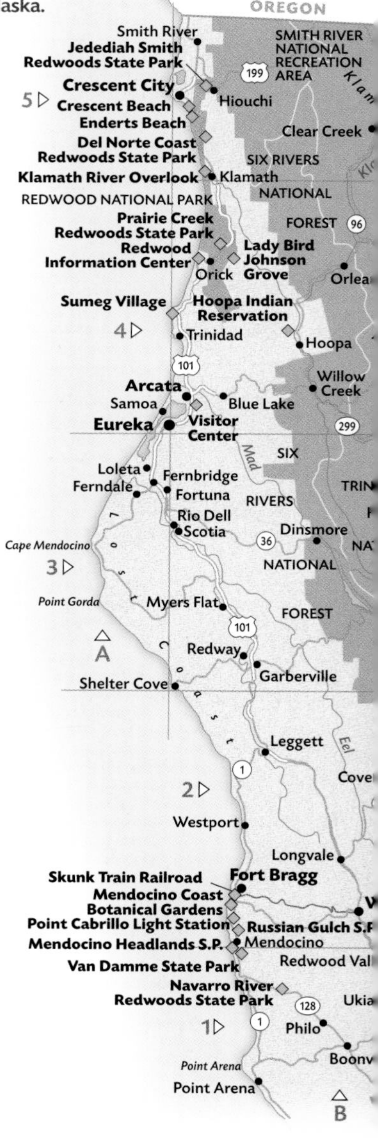

through wildflower meadows, and stay at an old-fashioned summer lodge where hot springs run through the outdoor swimming pool.

Close to the Oregon border is Lava Beds National Monument, where battles once raged between Native Americans and settlers. Today, amateur cavers can climb through the lava tubes that have been preserved here.

Alturas, in the northeastern corner of the state, is the capital of California bird-watching. Stay the night, and wake to the sounds of migrating wildfowl. ■

Van Damme State Park

Its floor carpeted with lush ferns and redwood sorrel, its paths dotted with little log benches, Van Damme State Park makes for a perfect stopover on the long, windy road between San Francisco and Mendocino. Here, in a small area beside Calif. 1, is a classic northern rain forest with streams containing coho salmon, masses of wild rhododendrons, and one of the world's greatest stands of pygmy pine trees.

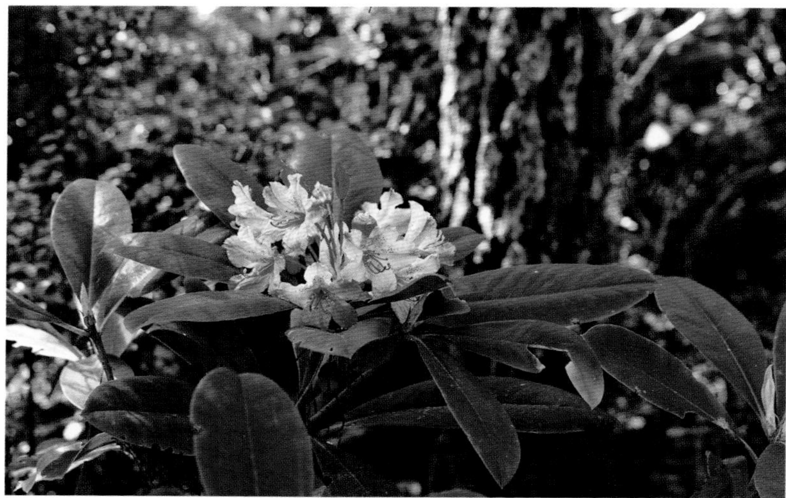

The cheery pink blooms of the Pacific rhododendron pepper the forest floor beneath tall redwoods.

Van Damme State Park

 270 B1

E side of Calif. 1, 2 miles (3.2 km) S of Mendocino

 707/937-5804

www.parks.ca.gov

For the best views of the park, follow the **Fern Canyon Trail** from the end of the entrance road. Flat and well-marked with a series of numbered salmon sculptures, the trail originated as a logging road in the late 1800s. In 1936, the Civilian Conservation Corps built nine stream crossings and a series of rock embankments along the side of the streams. An idea of the difficulties encountered by the workers comes across in a staff report from the era: "This project is without a doubt the most disagreeable project we are working on . . . the walls of the canyon are steep and heavily timbered and at this season, the sun seldom reaches that portion of the canyon where the men are working."

An opportunity to view the silvery coho salmon can be had nearby along the **Little River.** They were once so numerous that it was possible to catch them with bare hands, but the coho has in recent years suffered from increasing salinity and dwindling spawning habitats. A few moments spent by the stream will reveal the fish in one of three states. In winter, large adult fish begin to spawn, lodging themselves in pebbly basins and laying eggs before drifting down to the sea to die. In spring, the eggs hatch, producing dense schools of young. For the rest of the year, these young salmon feed, growing to a length of four to six inches (10–15 cm). By spring, they're ready for their journey to the sea; having memorized the scent of their home stream, they develop the silvery color required for survival in salt water. After two years in the ocean, they return to the Little River to repeat the cycle.

Visit during May and June and you'll witness another remarkable sight: the blooming of the Pacific rhododendron. Long studied for its adaptive abilities, this member of the heath family has leaves that roll under during the summer heat and pink, bell-shaped flowers in six-inch (15 cm) clusters.

The Pygmy Forest

The park's main attraction is the **pygmy forest**, reached by the old logging road. A self-guided trail leads through this wonderland of cypresses, Bolander pines, and bishop pines that stand only a couple of feet tall. The unique geology, heavy rainfall, and poor soil combine to produce the dwarf effect: Nutrients leached from the topsoil form a hard, impenetrable pan beneath the surface. With reduced nourishment, the trees' growth is stunted.

Various shrubs also grow here, particularly the (edible) huckleberry and the (inedible) manzanita. Walk the entire circumference for some outstanding photo opportunities. You can rent mountain bikes in Mendocino (see p. 274) and ride the trail, but bring a bike rack to avoid having to ride along the perilous Coast Highway. ■

Plant Life of the North

Just about everyone knows about northern California's coast redwoods (see pp. 278–283), but the plant life of the upper reaches of the state offers many other discoveries, too.

Closed-cone pines and cypresses: Four species of pine and ten of cypress dominate this group. All can thrive in infertile soils. Although they grow throughout the state, several species form concentrations in the north, from Van Damme State Park to Humboldt County. The most common are bishop pine, Douglas fir, Mendocino cypress, and Bolander pine. Their cones open only when exposed to intense sun or fire.

Manzanita *(Arctostaphylos):* A dramatic, low-growing brush with red trunk and lustrous leaves, the manzanita comes in several forms. Inland, at such places as McArthur-Burney Falls Memorial State Park (see p. 287), look for the stunning greenleaf manzanita, often found growing near magnificent incense cedars. On the coast, look for the low-growing Fort Bragg manzanita or the aptly named hairy manzanita.

Sagebrush *(Artemisia):* Although widely distributed throughout the state, sagebrush dominates much of the northeastern high desert. The plains are sometimes covered with shrubby sagebrush, while the big sagebrush grows on the eastern edge of the Sierra. Both are highly aromatic, the stuff of Native American and New Age apothecary alike.

Mendocino & Around

Inhabited by the valley-dwelling Pomo tribe from approximately 9500 B.C., the area was named by 16th-century Spanish settlers for Antonio de Mendoza, viceroy of New Spain. At the mouth of the Big River's outflow into the ocean, Mendocino's first Yankee pioneers quickly set up a lumber mill, and a town sprang to life. Its New England cast and stunning views attracted lumber barons as well as tourists and artists, who continue to revel in its many natural delights.

The Lost Coast offers secluded beachside camping.

Mendocino & Fort Bragg

270 B2

Visitor Information

Chamber of Commerce, 217 S. Main St., Fort Bragg

707/961-6300

www.mendocinocoast.com

Today, the buffed-up village of Mendocino offers several good bed-and-breakfasts and lovely restaurants located in restored Victorians. Galleries on and around Main Street offer local art, some of it by nationally known landscape painters. Artists here are known for their interesting use of natural materials such as wood and stone.

An excellent way to explore Mendocino's hinterland is by canoe, rentable at the Stanford Inn (see Travelwise p. 380). The canoes are fitted with special outrigger-style stabilizing devices, allowing even novices to explore the lush reaches of the **Big River.** Along the way to the **Mendocino Woodlands,** a wooded upland area, lies a series of breathtaking scenic canyons, salt marshes, and streambeds populated with great blue herons, ospreys, and even harbor seals.

If you are here in winter, go to **Mendocino Headlands State Park** *(map p. 270 B1, off Calif. 1 just S of town, tel 707/937-5804, www.parks.ca.gov)* for gray whale-watching. To the north, **Russian Gulch State Park** *(map p. 270 B2, tel 707/937-5804, www.parks.ca.gov)* offers 36 miles (58 km) of coastal trail and the unique Devil's Punch Bowl—a collapsed sea cave through which waves churn dramatically. Just up the coast, the restored 1909 **Point Cabrillo Light Station** *(map p. 270 B2, tel 707/937-6122, www.pointcabrillo.org)* is open for public tours.

In midsummer do not miss the **Mendocino Music Festival** *(tel 707/937-2044, www.mendocinomusic.com),* held on the bluffs above the sea!

Redwood Wine Country

Situated southeast of Mendocino along Calif. 128, the wine country of the redwood region is known for its diverse microclimates, producing leading labels of chardonnay, pinot noir, and sauvignon blanc. Many of the 300 vineyards center on the scenic Navarro River; in recent years, **Navarro Vineyards** *(5601 Calif. 128, Philo, tel 707/895-3686, www.navarrowine.com)* has received high praise for its pinot gris and the rarely made (in the U.S.) *verjus,* a tart, green grape juice perfect for the nondrinker and the kitchen, where the French have used it for centuries as a replacement for vinegars and lemon juice.

A nice intermezzo to a day of winery touring is a picnic at the nearby **Navarro River Redwoods State Park** *(map p. 270 B1, just off Calif. 128, 2 miles/3.2 km E of Calif. 1, tel 707/937-5804, www.parks.ca.gov),* an 11-mile-long (18 km) "redwood tunnel to the sea," as local literature puts it.

Fort Bragg

The working lumber town of Fort Bragg was founded in 1857 as a military outpost and named for Gen. Braxton Bragg, hero of the Mexican War. On the edge of a redwood forest, it sits between two bodies of running water, the Noyo River to the south and Pudding Creek to the north. A charming way to see much of the hinterland is via the old **Skunk Train Railroad.** Constructed by lumber barons in the 1880s, the 40-mile (64 km) line takes its passengers through dense stands of redwoods to **Willits,** where the notorious Black Bart robbed 27 coaches between 1875 and 1883, when he was "retired" to San Quentin prison in Marin County.

On the coast to the south are the **Mendocino Coast Botanical Gardens.** Founded in 1961, the gardens specialize in colorful rhododendrons, including hybrids, with collections of heathers, dahlias, camellias, and ivies. There are picnic areas, winding grass paths, and an ocean overlook. ■

Skunk Train Railroad
✉ Laurel St., Fort Bragg
☎ 707/964-6371, 866/457-5865
$ $$$$$
www.skunktrain.com

Willits
Map 270 B2
Visitor Information
✉ Chamber of Commerce, 299 Commercial St., Willits
☎ 707/459-7910
www.willits.org

Mendocino Coast Botanical Gardens
Map 270 B2
✉ 18220 N. Calif. 1, Fort Bragg
☎ 707/964-4352
$ $$$
www.gardenbythesea.org

EXPERIENCE: Hiking the Lost Coast

North of Fort Bragg, California's celebrated Pacific Coast Highway (Calif. 1) suddenly jogs inland around shoreline too wild and rugged for even the most ambitious road engineers. Beyond this point, the roughly 80-mile (128 km) stretch of redwoods and amber-colored sea cliffs, pristine beaches, and secluded hamlets, is known as the Lost Coast. Much of this region—the most remote stretch of coast between Canada and Mexico—is preserved within the **King Range National Conservation Area** *(U.S. 101 N to Garberville, follow signs, tel 707/825-2300, www.blm.gov/ca/arcata/kingrange)* and the **Sinkyone Wilderness State Park** *(1 hr. N of Fort Bragg, Calif. 1/mile 90.88, tel 707/986-7711, www.parks.ca.gov),* both of which offer top-notch coastal hiking.The easiest access to the Lost Coast is via Shelter Cove *(map p. 270 B3),* 23 miles (37 km) west of Redway off U.S. 101 along a country road. Shelter Cove offers the area's only noncamping accommodation. The 60-mile (96 km) **Lost Coast Trail** starts at the Sinkyone visitor center and ends in Mattole, where the campground *(tel 707/986-5400, $)* sits right on the beach at the north end of King Range. Rangers recommend about a week for the trip, which requires hikers to pack in all equipment and supplies.

Eureka & Around

The center of California's massive lumber industry since the late 1800s, Eureka is like many midsize towns in the state—sprawling, without a core, sometimes pretty and sometimes ugly. Yet Eureka (Greek for "I have found it") holds several delights, both within its city limits and just beyond. Anyone planning to trek through some of the number of memorable national and state parks in this part of northern California will likely end up staying—or at least dining—here.

The William Carson Mansion is made mainly of redwood.

Eureka
270 A4
Visitor Information
Convention & Visitors Bureau, 1034 2nd St., Eureka
707/443-5097, 800/346-3482
www.redwoodvisitor.org

Eureka

Eureka's **Old Town** includes three fully restored Victorians. The extraordinary **William Carson Mansion** *(143 M St., closed to the public)*, built in 1884 and now a private club, is a combination of Queen Anne, Italianate, and Stick-Eastlake styles. Also look for the 1889 **J. Milton Carson House** *(202 M St., closed to the public)* and the **Clarke Historical Museum** *(240 E St., tel 707/443-1947, www.clarkemuseum.org)*, built in 1888.

Before looking outside the city limits for travel destinations, try the 75-minute **Humboldt Bay Harbor Cruise** *(tel 707/445-1910, operates summer only, $$$)* on the old *Madaket*, a 1910 passenger ferry. The **Humboldt Bay Maritime Museum** *(foot of C St., next to Samoa Cookhouse, tel 707/445-1910, www.humboldtbaymaritimemuseum.com, closed Sun.–Mon. & Thurs.)* features a number of exhibits about local shipwrecks. At the **Blue Ox Millworks Historic Park** *(1 X St., tel 707/444-3437, www.blueoxmill.com, closed Sun., $$)* you can watch craftspeople use vintage machinery to make the gingerbread so evident in regional Victoriana. Finally, look in on the **Fort Humboldt Museum & State Historic Park** *(3431 Fort Ave., tel 707/445-6567, www.parks.ca.gov)* and find out about Ulysses S. Grant, who was stationed in Eureka in 1854.

South of Eureka

Several places of interest lie south of Eureka on or around U.S. 101. The first is **Fortuna,** where an 1893 railroad depot is home to the **Fortuna**

Depot Museum *(3 Park St., tel 707/725-7645, closed p.m. Mon.–Wed. Sept.–May)*, specializing in antique train, fishing, and logging memorabilia.

Off U.S. 101 to the west is the delightful town of **Ferndale,** where one can ride in a horse-drawn carriage through a largely untouched 1890s town. Farther south on U.S. 101, at the riverside town of **Scotia** *(map p. 270 B3)*, visitors can tour the **Scotia Museum** *(tel 707/764-5063, 122 Main St., open summer only)*, which spins the story of the local logging industry and the world's largest redwood mill.

South again, midway between Eureka and Fort Bragg, lies the little town of **Garberville** *(map p. 270 B3; visitor information, Chamber of Commerce, 784 Redwood Dr., tel 707/923-2613, www.garberville.org)*, blessed with turn-of-the-century architecture. One not to be missed is the Tudor-style **Benbow Inn** (see Travelwise p. 380), host to the stars in its heyday. Spencer Tracy, Clark Gable, and Joan Fontaine all stayed here.

Around Humboldt Bay

Across Humboldt Bay from Eureka is the historic **Samoa Cookhouse** *(79 Cookhouse Ln., Samoa, tel 707/442-1659, www.samoacookhouse.net)*, the last logging-camp cookhouse in the western U.S. Enjoy a very hearty meal here and see the intriguing logging museum adjacent.

On the north side of the bay is the town of **Arcata.** Here the **Arcata Railroad Museum** *(Jacoby's Storehouse, 791 8th St., tel 707/822-4500)* will please railroad buffs with its collection of historic maps and artifacts, and the **Arcata Marsh & Wildlife Sanctuary** *(569 S. G St., tel 707/826-2359)* is a perfect place for watching northern shorebirds. Just a bit farther north, the beach town of **Trinidad** *(map p. 270 B4)* stands on a dramatic seaside point.

Local Specialties

Regional specialties abound. Visit the Loleta Cheese Factory *(252 Loleta Dr., tel 707/733-5470, www.loletacheese.com)*, in nearby Loleta, where you can watch the company's award-winning cheese being made and try some free samples. Thin out your blood at Eureka's Lost Coast Brewery *(617 4th St., tel 707/445-4480, www.lostcoast.com)*, which makes no fewer than eight award-winning brews. The Nectar ales and "beer cuisine" are served in a brewpub full of football memorabilia.

Nearby is **Sumeg Village** *(map p. 270 B4, 4150 Patrick Point Dr., Patrick Point State Park, tel 707/677-3570, www.parks.ca.gov, $$)*. This 1990 re-creation of an ancient village has a working reconstruction of a traditional sweathouse. Today, the large Hoopa Indian reservation *(map p. 270 B4)*, about 60 miles (96 km) inland from Eureka, is home to some 2,000 of the tribe. The **Hoopa Tribal Museum** *(Hoopa Shopping Center, Calif. 96, tel 530/625-4110, www.hoopa-nsn.gov, closed Sun. & Sat. in winter)* includes examples of dugout canoes and ceremonial regalia and offers tours of local villages and ceremonial sites. ■

Fortuna
270 A3
Visitor Information
Chamber of Commerce, 735 14th St., Fortuna
707/725-3959, 800/426-8166
www.fortunachamber.com

Ferndale
270 A3
Visitor Information
Visitor Center, 5683 2nd Ave., Ferndale
360/384-3042
www.ferndale-chamber.com

Arcata
270 B4
Visitor Information
Chamber of Commerce, 1635 Heindon Rd.
707/822-3619
www.arcatachamber.com

Redwood National Park

A 1968 cartoon by the Pulitzer Prize–winning *L.A. Times* artist Paul Conrad shows a caravan of suitcase-laden cars driving into a tunnel bored through an enormous redwood tree. A sign tacked onto its trunk proclaims: "Redwood National Park." For years, Conrad's vision was not far from the truth. Many travelers rushing along the interstate barely got out of their cars to see the majestic trees; when they did, it was merely to snap a photo of the family standing in front of an enormous mass of furrowed bark—the tree, of course, being too big to get into the photo.

The parks' natural rain forest ecosystem incubates a diversity of plant life under the canopy.

Redwood National Park
270 B4
Visitor Information
Information Centers: 1111 2nd St., Crescent City; U.S. 199 at Hiouchi; & U.S. 101, S of Orick
707/464-7335
www.nps.gov/redw

Today, thanks to the renewed interest in the outdoors, California's redwoods are again the subject of human scrutiny. In fact, so many backpackers head into the wilderness that it has become necessary to control their numbers and activities more closely. Yet so far-reaching and awe-inspiring are these parks that, on a hike or even stopping for a picnic, it is still easy to feel you are the only person for miles around.

Four major redwoods parks in northern California lie close to the coast north of Orick, on coastal U.S. 101 north of Eureka, stretching almost to the state border with Oregon. Redwood National Park (1968) is by far the largest and the youngest. Together

Redwood Flora & Fauna

First, a few redwood facts: The coast redwood *(Sequoia sempervirens)* is the world's tallest tree, but not the thickest or the oldest. Those distinctions belong, respectively, to the giant sequoia *(Sequoiadendron giganteum)* or Wellingtonia of the Sierra and the bristlecone pine *(Pinus longaeva)*, also an inland species.

Although some specimens have been known to reach more than 2,000 years old, California's coast redwoods average between 500 and 700 years in age. Suffering from no known pestilence or fatal disease, the tree thrives on a vast system of ancillary roots that supports its main taproot. It can reproduce via sprouts as well as seeds, and new stems and roots can shoot from burned or cut-down trunks.

Redwoods are denizens of fog: The mild, moist climate of the dinosaurs was their birthright, a climate somewhat replicated today when warm inland air passes over the coastal lands bordering the Pacific here, which are cooled by the sea current flowing south from the Arctic Ocean.

With a natural rain forest ecosystem feeding it moisture and nutrients, the floor of redwood forests teems with many smaller but equally fascinating and rare plants. Look for deer and sword ferns, redwood sorrel, redwood violet, and western trillium. Chanterelle mushrooms and many other fungi also thrive in this habitat.

The most common animals include Roosevelt elk, chinook salmon, and the huge banana slug, which flourishes in the damp conditions. Among birds to look for in the redwood parks are small seabirds called murrelets, and Steller's jay, a dark blue woodland bird with a black crest.

with three redwood-filled state parks (see pp. 280–283), it forms the heart of both a World Heritage site and an International Biosphere Reserve.

At the **Kuchel Visitor Center** in Orick, you will find maps, books, displays, and helpful park rangers. (Requests for campground reservations should be made several months beforehand, particularly if you are planning a summer visit.)

To see the **Tall Trees Grove,** home of the world's second largest tree (360 feet/112 m); a 378-foot (115 m) tree, Hyperion, was discovered in 2007 but is inaccessible by trail), you must first obtain one of a limited number of permits that allow you to drive to the trailhead. To get a permit, arrive at the visitor center early. The round-trip takes about four hours.

INSIDER TIP:

If your time is limited, take in a 45-minute ranger-led forest walk at Stout Grove in Jedediah Smith Redwoods State Park (see p. 282).

—MICHAEL GLORE
Park ranger, Redwood National & State Parks

Lady Bird Johnson Grove can be reached by a self-guiding loop trail that goes through mature forest and, finally, into the majestic grove dedicated by the former first lady in 1968. A flatter trail to the north, just south of the Prairie Creek park, is **Lost Man Creek.** This fern and moss forest has some fine rain forest flora. ■

Redwoods State Parks

Together with Redwood National Park (see pp. 278–279), California's three redwoods state parks—Prairie Creek, the farthest south; Del Norte Coast; and Jedediah Smith, in the north—offer a diverse range of attractions for forest hikers of all ages and skill levels. The parks, and the redwood forests they protect, spread along the northern coast of California and are the high points of any tour to the north.

Once used by logging trucks, dirt roads in California's redwoods parks now carry bike riders.

Keep in mind that the entire coast redwood area is likely to be damp, misty, and often rainy—these are the climatic conditions in which redwoods flourish. But do not let the weather deter you from a thorough exploration of this area.

Prairie Creek Redwoods State Park

The 70 miles (112 km) of hiking trails in Prairie Creek Redwoods State Park range in difficulty from easy to very strenuous. There is also a scenic, 3-mile (4.8 km) drive, **Cal-Barrel Road,** to which any ranger can direct you, as well as the **Revelation Trail,** specially created for blind and partially sighted visitors.

At center stage of the Prairie Creek experience are the Roosevelt elk, which graze placidly on the **Elk Prairie** and on **Gold Bluffs Beach.** A member of the deer family, the elk or, as the Shawnee knew them, wapiti, have a tawny brown coat and a thatch of white on their rump. The animal, which is so fat it ought to be called the William Howard Taft elk, is native to the Pacific Northwest, with a population numbering approximately 2,000. Do not approach them. Rather, use the well-marked **Elk Prairie Trail,** a

INSIDER TIP:

The Klamath River Overlook is a must-see. On a clear day, you can often spot Pacific gray whales, sea lions, harbor seals, osprey, and bald eagles as the river empties into the Pacific Ocean.

—MICHAEL GLORE
Park ranger, Redwood National & State Parks

1.3-mile (2 km) loop skirting the eastern edge of the Elk Prairie.

From here begin a number of hiking trails *(maps from the visitor center at park entrance)*. If time is limited, try the **Five-Minute Trail,** which begins just behind the visitor center. Along this trail are several trees that have been hollowed out by fires; a close look may reveal traces—carved initials, gougings, seat-worn spots—of the families who lived here during the Great Depression.

The **Fern Canyon Loop,** about half a mile in length, takes in a spectacular natural feature where 50-foot (15 m) canyon walls tower above a mossy floor. Among the species of fern that grow luxuriantly in this sheltered, moist spot are the five-fingered, deer, lady, and sword varieties.

A favorite trail is the beautiful **South Fork–Rhododendron–Brown Creek Loop.** A walk of just over 3 miles (4.8 km), it takes in ghostly stands of moss-covered redwoods, ancient tree trunks covered with red, green, orange, and yellow mushrooms, and placid ponds, their surfaces mirrorlike in stillness. For mountain bikers, who are discouraged from most state and national parks, there is a designated 19-mile (30 km) **Bicycle Trail.** It begins where the Elk Prairie campground road links with the jogging trail.

Prairie Creek Redwoods State Park

270 B4

Turn off U.S. 101 at Newton B. Drury Scenic Parkway

707/465-7347

www.parks.ca.gov

Klamath River Overlook

270 B5

Turn off U.S. 101 at Requa Rd.

CAMPING: Prairie Creek Redwoods State Park, Elk Prairie Campground, 127011 Newton B. Drury Pkwy., tel 707/465-7354

The Indian Jerusalem

North of Prairie Creek, near Klamath at the **Klamath River Overlook**, you can visit a place that is the source of an enchanting Native American myth. Walk down the hillside path, past fragrant wild fennel. At the top of an old wooden stairway, as you gaze out onto the mouth of the Klamath River, contemplate the following story.

Once upon a time, according to Klamath oral tradition, the river's outlet was located 6 miles (9.6 km) to the north, retained in its path by two sharp parallel bluffs. Then came the Klamath version of Jesus Christ, a man named Po-Lick-O-Quare-Ick. The Wise One, as he was known, had a long and fruitful mission among his people and was greatly loved. When his mission ended, his subjects grieved as he paddled down the river, out to sea. Then, as the Wise One wound his way downriver, he issued a command, obeyed immediately by the twin bluffs, which separated, allowing the river to run a more natural course. Po-Lick-O-Quare-Ick then disappeared into the gold rays of the Pacific sun. Ever since, the Klamath has followed his course, and the Wise One's people have had something by which to remember him.

EXPERIENCE: Mountain Biking in the Redwoods

Encompassing more than 9,600 acres (3,884 ha), Jedediah Smith Redwoods State Park *(see below, and www.redwoodhikes.com)* is home to many of the world's oldest redwood trees. In the early 1900s, the park's **Howland Hill Road** was a thoroughfare for logging operations. Today, the hard-packed dirt road that ascends gently through these silent giants is great for mountain biking.

Begin the ride (5 miles/8 km each way) at the point where the park's paved road becomes gravel and dirt. As you begin pedaling, the hill slopes gently down on your right into Mill Creek. The old-growth trees are dense here, and the towering canopy filters most of the sunlight. The mostly shaded forest floor is smothered with all kinds of green understory, including ferns, redwood sorrel, and wild rhododendron. Continue past several hiking trails and through an intersection with a paved road to the left. When the path levels, park your bike and hike the **Stout Grove Trail** to see some of the park's oldest trees. The Howland Hill Road is an easy, nontechnical trail that is suitable for most riders, even children.

Del Norte Coast Redwoods State Park

- 270 B5
- U.S. 101, 13 miles (21 km) N of Klamath
- 707/465-2146

www.parks.ca.gov

Crescent City

- 270 B5

Visitor Information

- Chamber of Commerce, 1001 Front St.
- 800/343-8300

www.northerncalifornia.net

Jedediah Smith Redwoods State Park

- 270 B5
- U.S. 199 (off U.S. 101)
- 707/458-3018
- Closed Oct.–mid-May

www.parks.ca.gov

Del Norte Coast Redwoods State Park

This 6,400-acre (2,590 ha) park stretches along the Pacific shore for some 8 miles (12.8 km) south of **Crescent City,** the most northerly town on the California coast. Del Norte's shoreline is spectacularly wild, and much of it is fairly inaccessible—not to mention foggy. Almost half of Del Norte consists of old-growth trees, from coast redwood to tan oak, madrone, red alder, and bigleaf maple. The dense understory vegetation supports a wide range of wildlife, from bobcat and coyote to bear and deer. Maps and guides for Del Norte, and other parks in the area, are available either from the visitor center in Orick (see p. 278), to the south, or from the main information center for the redwoods state parks in Crescent City, to the north.

A tsunami triggered by an Alaskan earthquake swept through much of Crescent City in 1964, causing several fatalities and wiping out most traces of the town's history as a focus for the surrounding gold mines.

From Crescent City, you can reach the ocean by car, driving south for 2 miles (3.2 km) to **Crescent Beach** and **Enderts Beach** *(map p. 270 B5)*. A map of the coastal Damnation Trail is available at the visitor center. During the summer, guided tidepool walks take place at Enderts Beach, which is known for its teeming marine life.

Jedediah Smith Redwoods State Park

Named for the 19th-century pioneer-explorer who opened a trail to Oregon, Jedediah Smith Redwoods (east of Crescent City) is the northernmost of California's redwoods parks. Because of its situation a few miles inland, this park is sometimes sunny when the nearby coast is blanketed in the fog that is such a feature of the Pacific Northwest seaboard. However, the weather is often wet and cold. The **Hiouchi Information Center** *(tel 707/458-3294, closed mid-Nov–mid-May)* is situated on U.S. 199.

Jedediah Smith has a range of hiking trails. A popular short hike, just half a mile (.8 km), is the **Simpson-Reed Discovery Trail,** which passes through a stand of western hemlock, Douglas fir, and tan oak. Another begins at the trailhead and goes to the 44-acre (17.8 ha) **Stout Grove** (see sidebar opposite), where some coast redwoods are 1,500 to 2,000 years old.

You can also enjoy the park from the **Smith River** on a guided kayak tour. Fishing enthusiasts know the Smith for its runs of chinook and steelhead trout, but it is also popular for swimming and other water-based activities. Rent rafts, kayaks, and bicycles in little **Hiouchi** *(map p. 270 B5)*, where U.S. 199 crosses the Smith River in the far north of the state. ■

In Search of Sasquatch

Bigfoot legends have been around for centuries, but the hairy creature didn't become a household name until 1967, when Roger Patterson and Robert Gimlin filmed a creature walking casually along Bluff Creek in the Six Rivers National Forest of northern California. Although derided as a hoax by scientists, the film kicked off a bigfoot craze that endures to this day. Those interested in undertaking their own Sasquatch search can hike the Bluff Creek Trail, near the town of Orleans *(map p. 270 B4)*, off Calif. 96. The Willow Creek–China Flat Museum *(www.bigfootcountry.net)*, in nearby Willow Creek *(map p. 270 B4)*, boasts plaster cast footprints and other alleged proof of the creature's existence.

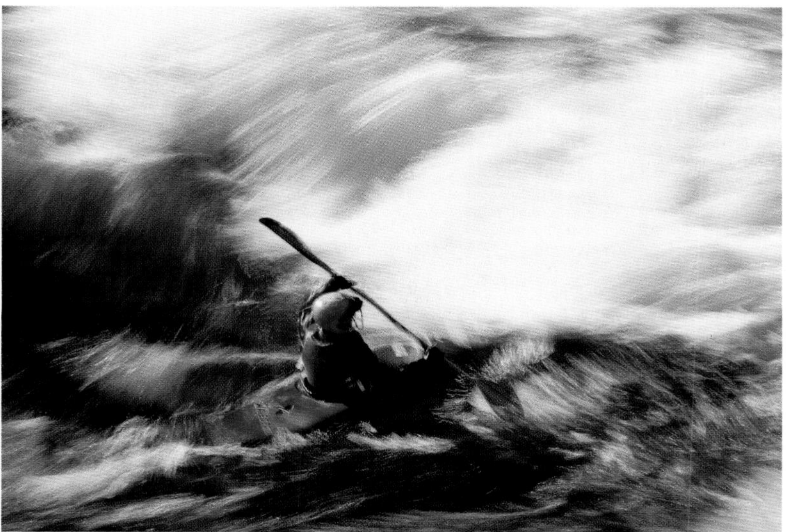

A whitewater kayaker runs a rapid in Oregon Hole Gorge on the Smith River.

Drive: Mount Shasta

This driving tour, lasting up to a leisurely week, will take you to the major attractions of the remote and beautiful north, which is blessed with some of the state's most stunning scenery and least crowded parks. Depending on your schedule, you can treat it as a series of separate drives or opt for a shorter circular route by omitting the section north of Mount Shasta. Each major stopping point has accommodations and places to eat.

Start in the small town of **Red Bluff** ❶ *(visitor information, Chamber of Commerce, 100 Main St., tel 530/527-6220, www.redbluffchamber.com)*, reached from the south on I-5 or from the west on Calif. 36, which cuts across the scenic South Fork Trinity River. (If you are coming from the coast, the latter entails a full day's drive. Be sure to check your brakes before departing.) Red Bluff, set on the Sacramento River at the junction of several routes, has a long tradition of hosting travelers.

Take I-5 north and make a brief stop, about a mile north of Red Bluff, at the **William B. Ide Adobe State Historic Park** *(21659 Adobe Rd., tel 530/529-8599, www.parks.ca.gov)*. Ide was an early settler, an entrepreneur, and a leader of the 1846 Bear Flag revolt in Sonoma (see p. 261). In early Red Bluff, he literally served as judge, clerk, prosecutor, and defense attorney in trials of horse thieves. After a jury found them guilty, he would invariably sentence them to be hanged. His home has been preserved here, along with some fascinating relics of mid-19th-century ranch culture.

Passing through the towns of Anderson *(visitor information, 1699 Hwy. 273, 530/365-7500, www.shastacascade.org)*, where the U.S. Fish and Wildlife Service runs the **Coleman National Fish Hatchery** *(24411 Coleman Fish Hatchery Rd., tel 530/365-8622, www.fws.gov/coleman)*, and Redding.

Turtle Bay Exploration Park *(840 Sundial Bridge Dr., tel 530/243-8850, www.turtlebay.org, closed Mon.–Tues.)* is worth a stop. This sprawling campus includes a 200-acre (81 ha) arboretum and garden, plus wildlife exhibits and educational activities tracing the relationship between humans and nature.

NOT TO BE MISSED:

Shasta Lake • Mount Shasta area • Lava Beds National Monument • Modoc National Wildlife Refuge • McArthur-Burney Falls Memorial State Park • Lassen Volcanic National Park

---

I-5 now cuts through increasingly interesting terrain, crossing an arm of scenic **Shasta Lake** ❷, California's largest reservoir (29,740 acres/12,035 ha). If you have time for a detour, visit **Lake Shasta Caverns** *(tel 530/238-2341, www.lakeshastacaverns.com, $$$$ including ferry from Lakeview Marina, E of O'Brien exit off I-5 on Shasta Caverns Rd.)*, on the lake's eastern shore. Here, you'll find an illuminated display of stalagmites and stalactites.

Farther north, as you approach Dunsmuir, **Castle Crags State Park** *(I-5, 6 miles/9.6 km S of Dunsmuir, tel 530/235-2684, www.parks.ca.gov)* looms dramatically. Its 6,000-foot (1,828 m) spires mark the site of a war in 1855 between settlers (and their Shasta allies) and the Modoc. The Modoc fled, their numbers greatly reduced.

At 14,162 feet (4,316 m), **Mount Shasta** ❸ is almost permanently snow covered. A volcanic peak that last erupted more than 200 years ago, it is still considered an active volcano. The mountain left John Muir with a less than pleasant memory—so bad was the frostbite he suffered there one winter that the great man walked with a limp for the rest of his life. Today, with some planning, the area is at least as

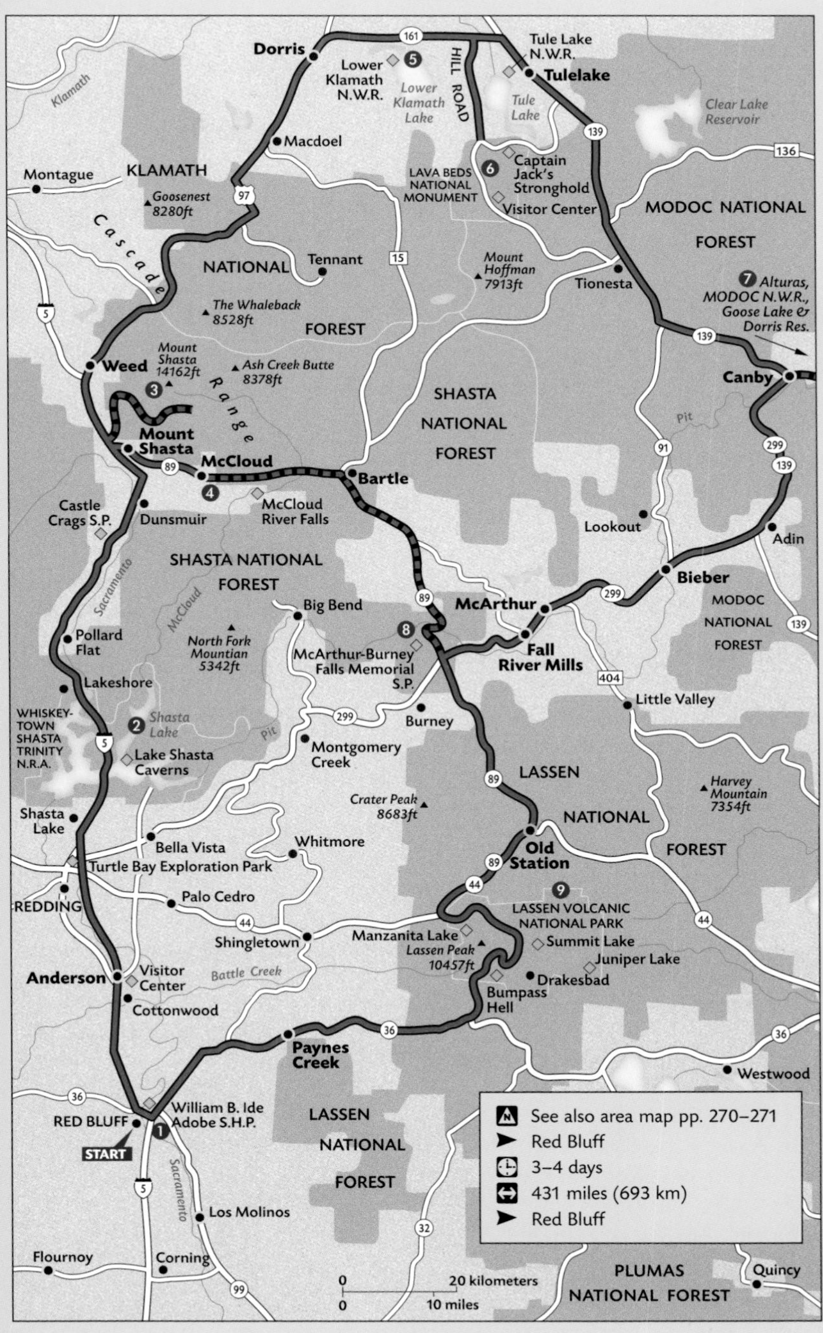
Dorris
Lower Klamath N.W.R.
Lower Klamath Lake
HILL ROAD
Tule Lake N.W.R.
Tulelake
Tule Lake
Clear Lake Reservoir
Klamath
Macdoel
Montague
KLAMATH
Goosenest 8280ft
Captain Jack's Stronghold
LAVA BEDS NATIONAL MONUMENT
Visitor Center
MODOC NATIONAL FOREST
Cascade
NATIONAL
Tennant
FOREST
Mount Hoffman 7913ft
Tionesta
Alturas, MODOC N.W.R., Goose Lake & Dorris Res.
The Whaleback 8528ft
Weed
Mount Shasta 14162ft
Ash Creek Butte 8378ft
Range
Canby
SHASTA NATIONAL FOREST
Pit
Mount Shasta
McCloud
Bartle
Castle Crags S.P.
Dunsmuir
McCloud River Falls
Lookout
Adin
SHASTA NATIONAL FOREST
Bieber
Sacramento
McCloud
Big Bend
McArthur
MODOC NATIONAL FOREST
Pollard Flat
North Fork Mountain 5342ft
McArthur-Burney Falls Memorial S.P.
Fall River Mills
Lakeshore
Little Valley
WHISKEY-TOWN SHASTA TRINITY N.R.A.
Shasta Lake
Pit
Burney
Lake Shasta Caverns
Montgomery Creek
LASSEN
Harvey Mountain 7354ft
Shasta Lake
Crater Peak 8683ft
NATIONAL
Bella Vista
Whitmore
Old Station
FOREST
Turtle Bay Exploration Park
REDDING
Palo Cedro
LASSEN VOLCANIC NATIONAL PARK
Shingletown
Manzanita Lake
Summit Lake
Lassen Peak 10457ft
Juniper Lake
Anderson
Visitor Center
Battle Creek
Drakesbad
Bumpass Hell
Cottonwood
Paynes Creek
Westwood
RED BLUFF
START
William B. Ide Adobe S.H.P.
LASSEN NATIONAL FOREST
Sacramento
Los Molinos
Flournoy
Corning
0 20 kilometers
0 10 miles
PLUMAS NATIONAL FOREST
Quincy
See also area map pp. 270–271
Red Bluff
3–4 days
431 miles (693 km)
Red Bluff

The snow-covered cone of volcanic Mount Shasta last erupted in 1786.

comfortable—and every bit as scenic—as other ski country. Mount Shasta may also be of interest for its mystical legends and spiritual vortices.

A good place to stay, particularly when you are traveling in the summer, is the old lumber town of **McCloud** ❹ *(visitor information, tel 530/964-3113, www.mccloudchamber.com)*, a few miles east of I-5 on Calif. 89. The restored McCloud Hotel (see Travelwise p. 380) offers fine bed-and-breakfast service with beautiful rooms. During the day, visit one of the three local natural waterfalls in the area, where you can swim, picnic, and hike along easy trails *(maps available at the hotel)*.

At this point, you can opt for an abbreviated version of this drive: Rather than heading into the northern section, proceed southeast from McCloud on Calif. 89 and rejoin the drive at McArthur-Burney Falls.

The main drive continues north on I-5 to the old lumber town of **Weed** *(visitor information, Chamber of Commerce, 34 Main St., tel 530/938-4624, www.weedchamber.com)*. Bear northeast on U.S. 97 to cross the **Cascade Range.** The Great Basin region is represented here by the **Modoc Plateau**—high, dry, and flat. The **Klamath Basin National Wildlife Refuges Complex** *(tel 530/667-2231, www.fws.gov/klamathbasinrefuges)*, encompassing six refuges, extends across the Oregon-California border and is home to spectacular bird populations.

Just before the state border, don't miss the turnoff on Calif. 161. Head east, cutting across California's northernmost reaches. A worthwhile first stop is at the **Lower Klamath National Wildlife Refuge** ❺. This refuge and the nearby **Tule Lake National Wildlife Refuge** are a dream come true. The vast basin of marshes and shallow lakes is a winter haven for bald eagles and for more than a million migrant ducks, geese, and swans. During the breeding season, it is common to see herons and egrets, double-crested cormorants, and cinnamon teal.

Just to the south of Tule Lake is **Lava Beds National Monument** ❻ *(turn off Calif. 161 on Hill Rd. S, tel 530/667-8113, www.nps.gov/labe)*. Be prepared here for extremes: of heat during the day, of cold in the evening. Clustered near the park's visitor center are the famous lava tubes. These 30,000-year-old signs of volcanic activity were formed when the exterior of long lava flows cooled and hardened before their centers. When the flow stopped and the remaining molten lava ran out of the other end, a tube resulted. Many of these tubes contain brightly colored lichens. Some are open for visitors to explore. To do so, you will need warm clothes, hard-soled shoes, a helmet, a flashlight (the visitor center provides these), and a lot of common sense—for example, do not go alone. Park rangers conduct regular walking tours. They can also direct you to a number of petroglyphs, ancient Native American rock carvings.

Before leaving the park on Calif. 139, take the rare opportunity to visit a battleground most Americans do not even know about—that of the Modoc War. **Captain Jack's Stronghold,** at its center, is named for the ingenious Modoc warrior who in 1872 startled the U.S. Army by beating them in a series of skirmishes over land policy. Two short walking trails take visitors around Captain Jack's fortifications.

A detour for wildlife enthusiasts is to take Calif. 299 east from Canby to the little town of

Alturas ❼ *(visitor information, Chamber of Commerce, 600 S. Main St., tel 530/233-4434, www.cityofalturas.org),* the focal point of an area that is outstanding for bird- and animal-watching. For a hearty meal, drive over to the Brass Rail (see Travelwise p. 379), which serves up giant portions of Basque-style cuisine in a family setting.

The big attraction in the Alturas area is the **Modoc National Wildlife Refuge** *(5364 Cty. Rd. 115, Alturas, tel 530/233-3572, www.fws.gov/modoc),* a 7,000-acre (2,832 ha) park dedicated to the management and protection of migratory waterfowl. Don't underestimate its popularity; it may be remote, but professional ornithologists flock here every year. The reason: The refuge is an important resting and feeding area for migratory birds on the Pacific flyway. A total of 246 bird species have been spotted on the refuge, including 40 accidentals. In spring and fall, Canada geese and teal, mallard and widgeon, are everywhere. In summer come wading birds such as willets and avocets, plus several species of gulls and herons. In winter, you might spot a bald eagle. On your way, you may see a herd of pronghorn gathered on the edge of a local wild-rice farm. The best birding is April to May and September to October, when the greatest diversity of species is present. **Dorris Reservoir** permits boating and fishing April to September.

Anyone interested in pioneer history should make a further side trip north from Alturas on U.S. 395 to **Goose Lake.** Here, close to the point where California, Oregon, and Nevada meet, two important migrant trails converged. One, the **Applegate Trail,** was made in 1846 by a party of 15 men following cartographic information developed by the Hudson's Bay Company's trappers in the 1820s. The second, the **Lassen Trail,** was first trekked in September 1848; after a winter of few supplies and rough weather, the party was rescued, 40 miles (64 km) north of Sacramento, by Peter Burnett, who later became the first governor of California. Staff of the Modoc National Wildlife Refuge information center will give you information on these trails. Continuing the drive from Canby, follow Calif. 299 southwest, then head north on Calif. 89 for the entrance to **McArthur-Burney Falls Memorial State Park** ❽ *(tel 530/335-2777, www.parks.ca.gov).* Its 129-foot (39 m) waterfall—Theodore Roosevelt proclaimed it the "eighth wonder of the world"—is reached by a well-maintained footpath. Teeming with wildlife (the rare black swift nests here) and stands of fantastic incense cedar and ponderosa pine, the park is yet another of this region's undervisited gems. Several campsites are available, as are cabins, and small motels and inns just outside the park offer a restful natural getaway.

On the road once more, drive south on Calif. 89 to reach **Lassen Volcanic National Park** ❾ (see p. 288). The spectacular drive across the park on Calif. 89 is closed to travelers in winter, and occasionally even in summer in bad weather. Check current conditions with the park. Continue on Calif. 89 to Calif. 36, and go west to return to Red Bluff. In winter, take Calif. 44 to Redding, and then drive down I-5.

Scaling & Skiing Mount Shasta

Towering more than 14,000 snowcapped feet (4,267 m), Mount Shasta is a magnet for year-round outdoor activities. The most popular climbing route is Avalanche Gulch, on the southwest flank, an 11-mile (17.7 km) round-trip with 7,200 feet (2,195 m) of vertical gain that experienced hikers can knock off in a single day. Even during the peak of summer, crampons, helmets, and ice axes are highly recommended. During winter, Avalanche Gulch morphs into a gnarly backcountry ski piste that sometimes lives up to its deadly name.

More sedate slopes can be found at nearby Mount Shasta Ski Park *(104 Siskiyou Ave., Mount Shasta, tel 530/926-8610, www.skipark.com),* where the terrain ranges from beginner to black diamond.

Lassen Volcanic National Park

One of the best kept secrets of the northwest is this 100,000-acre (40,468 ha) wilderness. Anyone wishing to impress friends with their summer vacation photos and have a great time in truly stunning scenery, away from the crowds of Yosemite, will find this place pure magic.

Lassen Volcanic National Park
271 D3 & 285
Visitor Information
Calif. 36 E., Mineral
530/595-4480
www.nps.gov/lavo

The park centers on 10,457-foot (3,187 m) **Lassen Peak,** a volcano that last erupted in 1915, producing an immense cloud of dust and covering the land around it with deep mud. The effects are still visible where Calif. 89, or Lassen Park Road, crosses the **Devastated Area** to the north of the peak.

The park's extraordinary volcanic landscape includes hot springs, bubbling mud pots, and gas seeping from holes called fumaroles at **Bumpass Hell** in the southwest. Elsewhere there are blue-green volcanic ponds, crystal-clear lakes, forests, and, in spring, wonderful verdant wildflower meadows.

Trails have been laid out by the National Park Service to enable visitors to explore the park's wonders. Keep to them—it goes without saying that hot springs, steam, and unstable ground can be hazardous and that care and common sense are necessary as you follow the trails.

The free "Lassen Park Guide" includes a list of accommodations. Choose from six campsites, most close to dramatic natural features, among them **Manzanita Lake** in the northwest, **Butte** in the east, and **Summit Lake** in the center. For a more comfortable stay, make reservations at Drakesbad Guest Ranch (see Travelwise p. 379). ■

California's Lake District

Perched in the Cascade Range just north of Redding are three large reservoirs—Shasta, Trinity, and Whiskeytown—that comprise the sprawling **Whiskeytown National Recreation Area** *(map p. 271 C3–C4; visitor information, Visitor Center, Calif. 299 & John F. Kennedy Dr., tel 530/246-1225, www.nps.gov/whis).* The watery wilderness lends itself to numerous outdoor pursuits, among them fishing, swimming, boating, waterskiing, and waterfront camping.

Jointly managed by the National Park Service and U.S. Forest Service, the three enormous lakes are best explored by houseboat over several days or even weeks. Larger than San Francisco Bay, Lake Shasta is the largest of the trio, with 370 miles (595 km) of shoreline and seven marinas. **Shasta Marina Resort** *(tel 800/959-3359, www.shastalake.net, $$$$$)* rents luxury houseboats with full kitchen, multiple bathrooms and satellite TV that sleep as many as 16 people. **Trinity Lake Resorts** *(tel 800/255-5561, www.trinitylakeresort.com, $$$$$)* operates two marinas with similar houseboat rentals on secluded Trinity Lake. Those wishing to boat Whiskeytown, smallest of the lake, must bring their own vessel. No overnight mooring is allowed on Whiskeytown Lake, but skippers can dock at **Oak Bottom Marina** *(tel 530/359-2269, www.whiskeytownmarinas.com).*

The historic—and dramatic—core of California, now mined for great wines and stunning scenery

Gold Country

Old-fashioned sign advertising gold prospecting for modern tourists

Gold Country

Based on a chain of picturesque towns along Calif. 49, from Mariposa to Nevada City, Gold Country is a traveler's delight. Drive through it in a day, or probe, ponder, and explore it for a week. Unlike the far north, Gold Country has a strong tourist infrastructure (perhaps the best visitor centers of any region), relatively short distances between major points, and (in season) a pleasant, warm climate. No wonder that its beautiful landscapes inspired the plein air painters of the early 20th century.

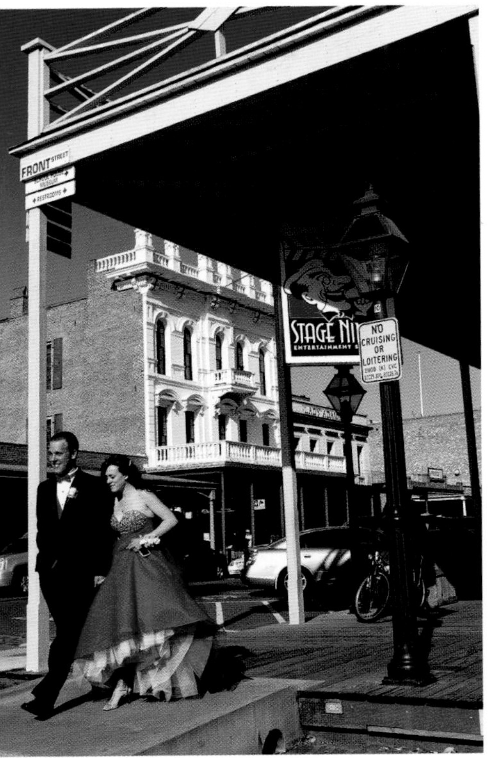

Old Sacramento, commercial hub of the gold rush

It is a region of grand, epic history. On January 24, 1848, a New Jersey émigré named James Marshall, working at a wood mill on the American River, spotted a lentil-size speck of yellow ore. He picked it up and then smashed it between stones. It was soft. It was gold. Word spread–to the bay, then back east, then around the world. California was transformed. By 1850, its population had soared from 15,000 to nearly 100,000. As historian J. S. Hallidie wrote, "The world had rushed in."

The refined version of the story adds nuance, tragedy, and color. The gold rush was a triumph for some, but a disaster for the Native Americans routinely stripped of land and made ill with white man's diseases. It was also, in a sense, the end of Latin Catholic California, bringing as it did many Anglo Protestants and Yankee reformers. It was also a multicultural world, where Chinese mixed with Peruvians and blacks and Swedes and mountain men.

NOT TO BE MISSED:

Sacramento's splendid State Capitol building **292**

Contrasting contemporary and Victorian architecture at the Crocker Art Museum **292**

Bustling Old Sacramento **292–293**

Historic trains at the California State Railroad Museum **292–293**

Panning for gold **295**

Sutter's Mill, where the story of the gold rush began **296**

Getting cold and muddy in the region's celebrated caverns **298**

Historic gold rush towns of Murphys and Jamestown **298–300**

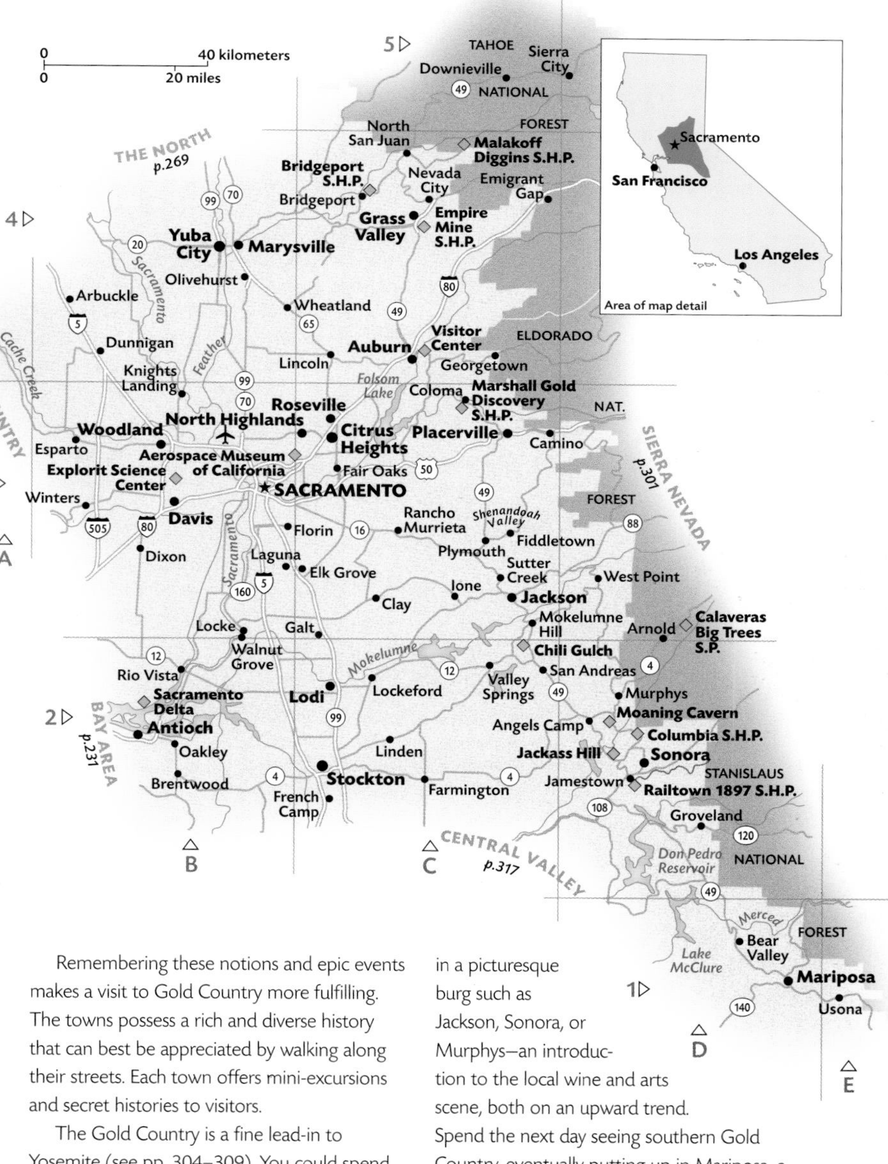

Remembering these notions and epic events makes a visit to Gold Country more fulfilling. The towns possess a rich and diverse history that can best be appreciated by walking along their streets. Each town offers mini-excursions and secret histories to visitors.

The Gold Country is a fine lead-in to Yosemite (see pp. 304–309). You could spend the first night in Grass Valley, with its fine restaurants and inns. Next day, explore the famous Empire Mine before heading south to Marshall Gold Discovery State Historic Park. Then stay in a picturesque burg such as Jackson, Sonora, or Murphys—an introduction to the local wine and arts scene, both on an upward trend. Spend the next day seeing southern Gold Country, eventually putting up in Mariposa, a morning's drive away from Yosemite.

As with all historical destinations, it is a good idea to bone up before departing (for some suggestions, see Travelwise p. 347). ■

Sacramento

Founded in 1839 by Swiss-born entrepreneur John Augustus Sutter, what is now the capital of California began its postcolonial life as one man's attempt to build his own feudal agricultural colony at the confluence of the American and Sacramento Rivers. When the gold rush came, the workers on Sutter's estate—a polyglot bunch from the ends of the Earth—abandoned him. The agricultural part fared little better. By the 1850s, Sutter was broke.

Find the center of California politics at the State Capitol in Sacramento.

Sacramento
291 B3
Visitor Information
Convention & Visitors Bureau, 1002 2nd St., Sacramento
916/442-7644
www.discovergold.org

Sutter's Fort State Historic Park
2701 L St.
916/445-4422
Closed Mon.
$
www.parks.ca.gov

You can view what remains of Sutter's Fort, including copper and blacksmith's shops, a bakery, and a prison, on a self-guided audio walking tour of **Sutter's Fort State Historic Park.**

Sacramento's most distinctive building is the elegant 19th-century neoclassic **State Capitol** *(10th St. & Capitol Mall, tel 916/324-0333, www.assembly.ca.gov/museum)*. Some of its rooms are open to the public.

Although politics dominates Sacramento's social landscape, the art scene thrives. Located in a 19th-century mansion and the futuristic new Teel Family Pavilion, the **Crocker Art Museum** *(216 O St., tel 916/808-7000 or 916/808-1184, www.crockerartmuseum.org, closed Mon., $$)* has works by many European painters, from Albrecht Dürer to Hendrick Goltzius, as well as contemporary works by California artists.

In revitalized **Old Sacramento,** a 28-acre (11.3 ha) site on the Sacramento River and onetime mercantile epicenter of the gold rush days, wooden sidewalks in front of historic buildings give the town a Wild West flavor. Don't miss the **California State**

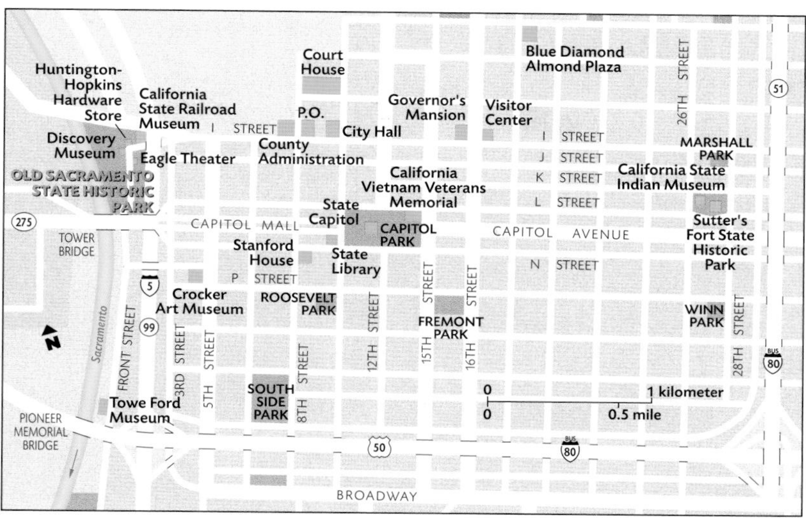

Railroad Museum *(125 I St., tel 916/445 6645, www.csrmf.org)*, the largest interpretive railroad museum in North America. From April to September, you can take a 40-minute train ride. The Big Four masterminded the transcontinental railroad (see pp. 31–32) at the adjoining **Huntington–Hopkins Hardware Store** *(125 I St., tel 916/323-7234, call ahead)*.

The interactive **Discovery Museum** *(3615 Auburn Blvd., tel 916/264-7057, www.thediscovery.org, closed Mon. & a.m. Tues.–Fri., $$)* examines topics like science, space, natural history, archaeology, and robotics. The **California State Indian Museum** *(2818 K St., tel 916/808-3942, www.parks.ca.gov, closed Mon.–Tues., $)* presents a different perspective on regional history. The **Explorit Science Center** *(3141 5th St., tel 530/756-0191, www.explorit.org)*, in the nearby university town of Davis, is a hands-on science museum, while the **Aerospace Museum of California,** on the former McClellan Air Force Base, showcases 34 aircraft from early prop planes to supersonic jets.

For a novel and relaxing view of Sacramento, hop aboard the ***Delta King*** stern-wheel riverboat *(1000 Front St., tel 916/444-5464, www.deltaking.com)*. ■

Aerospace Museum of California

- 291 B3
- 3200 Freedom Park Dr., McClellan
- 916/643-3192
- Closed Mon.
- $$

www.aerospacemuseumofcalifornia.org

Sacramento Delta

Many of the towns of the Sacramento Delta were founded by Asian immigrants. The "Potato King," George Shima, a 19th-century Japanese immigrant, created a potato empire on delta soil regarded as wasteland by his Anglo contemporaries.

The tiny town of Locke *(map p. 291 B3)*, on Calif. 160, was the first community in the U.S. built entirely by Chinese for Chinese. Once a rowdy Wild West town full of booze, prostitutes, and opium, it now stands, picturesque and weathered, as a piece of working history. A museum traces its past.

Northern Gold Country

The towns of California's northern Gold Country are characterized by a cooler climate than those to the south, a strong community spirit, and a local pride in historical continuity–a history that stretches back to the mid-19th century.

Old mining equipment and a prospector statue greet visitors in historic Auburn.

Downieville
291 C5

Nevada City
291 C4

Visitor Information

Chamber of Commerce, 132 Main St., Nevada City

530/265-2692

www.nevadacitychamber.com

Downieville

Established in 1851 by Maj. William Downie, Downieville, on Calif. 49, sat on so much gold that, as legend has it, a man boiling a locally caught fish found gold dust at the bottom of the pot. In the town center, on Main Street, is the 1855 **Sierra County Courthouse,** where several men were sentenced to swing from the gallows on Piety Hill, just behind. The **Downieville Museum** *(330 Main St., tel 530/289-3580, closed in winter)* displays a wide range of gold-rush artifacts. Amateur gold seekers can buy equipment at Sierra Hardware *(305 Main St., tel 530/289-3582).*

Nevada City

To the southwest on Calif. 49 is Nevada City, established in 1849 by miners seeking the rich gravel beds of the Lost Hill section, which yielded $8 million in gold dust in two years. The **National Hotel** *(211 Broad St., tel 530/265-4551, www.thenationalhotel.com)* here claims to be the "oldest continuously operating hostelry west of the Rockies."

Nevada City is still a welcoming tourist town with comfortable amenities. It is also a base for gold-panning tours (see sidebar p. 295) and for visiting **Malakoff Diggins State Historic Park,** to the northeast. The broken landscape there still demonstrates the rapacious nature of the early (and fortunately short-lived) practice of hydraulic gold mining.

For a change of scene, admire the beautiful wildflowers along the **Buttermilk Bend Trail** near the South Yuba River State Park visitor center. Nearby is the 1862 **Bridgeport Covered Bridge,** at 229 feet (69 m) thought to be the longest single-span wooden covered bridge in the world.

Grass Valley

Grass Valley is acknowledged as the richest of California's mining towns, with production of more than $400 million over the course of a century following its founding in 1849. It was the birthplace, in 1855, of Josiah Royce, a Harvard scholar noted for his idealism and emphasis on the importance of the individual. Royce's childhood home, now the site of the city library, is on Mill Street, close to the 1852 home of sultry dance-hall performer Lola Montez, known for her Spider Dance and the fact that she divorced her husband because he killed her pet bear when it attacked him.

The historic **Holbrooke Hotel** *(212 W. Main St., tel 530/273-1353, www.holbrooke.com)* was home away from home for Mark Twain, Bret Harte, and several U.S. presidents; the bustling hotel now offers fine cuisine in the restaurant, including local mushrooms and wild lettuce in the fall. Outside town is **Empire Mine State Historic Park,** the oldest, richest mine in California.

Malakoff Diggins State Historic Park

291 C4

23579 N. Bloomfield Rd., Nevada City

530/265-2740

$

www.parks.ca.gov

Grass Valley

291 C4

Visitor Information

248 Mill St., Grass Valley

530/273-4667, 800/655-4667

www.grassvalleychamber.com/visitor

EXPERIENCE: Panning for Gold

Although the Mother Lode is long gone, searching for gold remains a popular pastime and is generally allowed on public lands, including state and national parks. Many of the region's state parks also offer panning lessons. Among these are **Marshall Gold Discovery State Historic Park** (see p. 296) in Coloma and **South Yuba River State Park** *(tel 530/432-2546, www.parks.ca.gov)* near Nevada City (see pp. 294–295).

Check with local chambers of commerce about conditions and the best places to pan. Or join an expedition with **Gold Prospecting Adventures** *(18170 Main St., tel 209/984-4653, www.goldprospecting.com, $$$)*, in Jamestown, which offers panning experiences and multiday prospecting courses in placer mining and mineral claims. **Roaring Camp Mining Company** *(Calif. 88, Pine Grove, tel 209/296-4100, www.roaringcampgold.com, $$$$$)*, on the Mokelumne River, blends its gold-panning experience with a pioneer-style barbecue dinner on Saturdays.

Silicon Valley Gold Prospectors *(www.wix.com/kitfoxchumash/clubsite)*, in San Jose, organizes events that teach gold panning and introduce would-be miners to California's prospecting laws and regulations. SVGP also recommends other prospecting clubs that own their own mining claims and allow members and their families to camp and prospect for gold, which they are allowed to keep.

Buy pans, pickaxes, and sluice box kits at **Matelot Gulch Mine Supply Store** *(Washington & Main Sts., tel 209/532-9693)* in historic Columbia or **Big Valley Metal Detectors** *(8153 Juli Ct., Citrus Heights, tel 916/225-9150, www.bigvalleymetaldetectors.com)*, near Sacramento.

Empire Mine State Historic Park

Empire St., off Calif. 49 E of Grass Valley

530/273-8522

$$

www.empiremine.org

Auburn

291 C4

Visitor Information

Visitors Bureau, 13411 Lincoln Way, Auburn

530/887-2111

www.visitplacer.com

Coloma

291 C3

Visitor Information

www.coloma.com

Marshall Gold Discovery State Historic Park

291 C3

30 Back St., off Calif. 49, Coloma

530/622-3470

$

www.parks.ca.gov

Sutter Creek

291 C3

Visitor Information

Visitor Center, 71A Main St., Sutter Creek

209/267-1344

www.suttercreek.org

Sutter Ridge Winery

14110 Ridge Rd., Sutter Ridge

209/267-1316

www.sutterridgewine.com

Auburn

Established in 1848, the town of Auburn, at the junction of Calif. 49 and I-80, sits on a streamlet named Auburn Ravine, once the site of the richest placer gold mines in the state. The handsome 19th-century **Placer County Courthouse** *(101 Maple St.)* presides over the Old Town, and its museum *(tel 530/889-6500)* has several interesting historical exhibits.

Coloma

Coloma, farther south on Calif. 49, was the site of James Marshall's gold discovery. Spend an afternoon picnicking, hiking, and investigating the historical sites at the **Marshall Gold Discovery State Historic Park.** Trails lead from the visitor center to the Marshall Monument and Gravesite, to the Gold Discovery Site, and then along to the site of **Sutter's Mill,** and eventually to **Bekeart's Gun Shop.**

Shenandoah Valley

The rolling, oak-dotted hills around the **Shenandoah Valley** *(map p. 291 C3)* are well suited to farms and fruit orchards. This is also the center of Amador wine country, which is focused along Shenandoah and Fiddletown Roads. A beautiful back-roads drive can be made northward from Fiddletown to the Apple Hill farm collective, off U.S. 50 near the little town of **Camino** *(map p. 291 C3)*; a more direct route runs east from **Placerville** *(map p. 291 C3)* on U.S. 50. Back south, on Shenandoah School Road near the town of Plymouth *(map p. 291 C3)*, the **Amador Flower Farm** *(tel 209/245-6660, www.amadorflowerfarm.com)* specializes in daylilies. Nearby is the tasting room for Deaver Vineyards.

Sutter Creek

Sutter Creek played a key role in gold-rush history, attracting a number of investors to mine the Widman, Lincoln, and Central Eureka sites. The last, once almost abandoned by Leland Stanford, eventually produced the funds for him to invest in the Central Pacific Railroad. Sutter Creek is now the center of its own thriving mini wine country, typified by **Sutter Ridge Winery.**

INSIDER TIP:

In Coloma, stop into Bekeart's Gun Shop *(329 Calif. 49, tel 530-295-1850)*, where you can try your hand at panning for gold in a small demonstration tank.

—LARRY PORGES
National Geographic Travel Books editor

The town, formerly a key gold-foundry center, has a fine historic district. Many old mercantile buildings built by Italian immigrants can be toured with the help of a map from the visitor center. On weekends from March to October, you can also explore the productive **Kennedy Gold Mine** *(tel 209/223-9542, www.kennedygoldmine.com).* ■

Southern Gold Country

It was in southern Gold Country that, with the stakes so palpably high, the gold rush turned violent. Here the "Mexican Robin Hood," Joaquín Murieta, is said to have begun his bloody pillaging. Here the first Chinese Tong wars were fought, and here slaves were allegedly sold and race riots fought over mining rights. Today the quiet, picturesque streets of southern Gold Country—from "Moke Hill" (Mokelumne Hill) to Mariposa—betray none of that churning, fugitive, and violent history. Instead, there is a placid ambience of a wine country in the Sierra.

Costumed guides at Columbia State Historic Park show visitors how to pan for gold.

Jackson to Angels Camp

Once a prominent stop on the old Carson Emigrant Trail and now the crossroads of north–south Calif. 49 and east–west Calif. 88, **Jackson** came into its own as a town in 1850. Its early name, Bottileas, was a reference to the many broken whiskey bottles found on its hell-raising streets. The Argonaut Mine, still visible south of Calif. 88, sunk its shafts more than one mile below the surface. The town briefly became the seat of Calaveras County after ambitious Jacksonians literally pilfered government archives from nearby Double Springs, only to be out-politicked the next year by neighboring "Moke Hill," which then assumed the title. Today Jackson is a bustling town, full of cafés, Italian restaurants, and bookstores (see sidebar p. 300).

Established as a Mexican mining camp in 1849, **Mokelumne Hill,** farther south on Calif. 49, was once one of the most boisterous gold towns, where shootings were a weekly affair. A walking tour map can be obtained from the Hotel

Jackson

291 C3

Visitor Information

Visitor Center, 125 Peek St., Jackson

209/223-1646

www.ci.jackson.ca.us

Mokelumne Hill

291 C3

Calaveras County Museum & Visitor Center

30 N. Main St., San Andreas

209/754-4658

www.gocalaveras.com

Angels Camp

291 D2

Visitor Information

Visitor Center, 584 S. Main St., Angels Camp

209/736-2181

www.angelscamp.gov

Murphys

291 D2

Leger *(830 Main St., tel 209/286-1401, www.hotelleger.com)*, but it hardly does justice to the region's eventful past. For example, French Hill, just to the south, is where the so-called French War was fought in 1851, when American miners literally took up their picks to drive off overly aggressive French upstarts. South of there on Calif. 49 is **Chili Gulch** *(map p. 291 C2)*, site of the Chilean War of 1849. This time, the Americans were driven out by Chileans angered by attempts to expropriate their mining claims.

Another Mexican camp, established in 1848, **San Andreas** *(map p. 291 C2)* may be the site of the tavern portrayed in Mark Twain's story "The Celebrated Jumping Frog of Calaveras County" (see p. 42). Ask at the **Calaveras County Museum & Visitor Center** if you can see the reputedly genuine red sash of the local bandito Joaquín Murieta (see Murphys, below). The museum also has relics of the Miwok, who once dominated the region.

Then again, **Angels Camp,** say locals, is where Twain got the inspiration for the bar scene in "Jumping Frog." ("I found Simon Wheeler dozing comfortably by the barroom stove of the dilapidated tavern in the decayed mining camp of Angel's.") Today this is a rather unremarkable destination, with several boutiques, a few cafés, and a gold rush museum.

EXPERIENCE: Spelunking

Caves of all shapes and sizes riddle the ground beneath Gold Country. Moaning Cavern *(map p. 291 D2)*, south of Murphys, began attracting the curious during pioneer days. Cave & Mine Adventures *(9565 Cave City Rd., Mountain Ranch, tel 209/736-2708, www.caverntours.com)* offers several ways to see the cavern, from an easy, 45-minute walking tour *($)* to a three-hour "Adventure Trip," with or without rappeling *($–$$$)*. The same outfitters organize descents into Black Chasm Cavern, a designated national natural landmark near the town of Volcano in Amador County. The Yokut once used the Mercer Caverns *(1665 Sheep Ranch Rd., Murphys, 209/728-2101, www.mercercaverns.com)* in Calaveras County as a place to bury their dead, but nowadays the living limestone wonder is open to visitors.

Murphys & Around

Established in 1848, Murphys, off Calif. 49 on Calif. 4, is said to be where Joaquín Murieta got his ire. A three-card monte dealer in 1851, Joaquín had watched as his brother was hanged on a bogus charge of horse thievery. After Joaquín himself was flogged, he embarked on two years of his own brand of bloody thieving, in which, as Richard Rodriguez writes in his 1992 book of essays *Days of Obligation,* he "stole horses, beautiful horses. He was like the wind stealing clouds." Murieta was eventually killed near Fresno. The Yankees hated him so much they cut his head off and displayed it in a jar.

Today Murphys is one of the best preserved gold rush towns. **Murphys Historic Hotel** *(457 Main St., tel 209/728-3444, www.murphyshotel.com)* is worth a look—after all, Mark Twain and

For a taste of the Old West, take a walk down Main Street in Angels Camp.

President Ulysses S. Grant both slept there. The **Murphys Creek Theatre** *(tel 209/728-8422, www.murphyscreektheatre.org)* produces excellent year-round drama, ranging from Shakespeare and Moliére to Henry James and Stephen Sondheim.

To see giant sequoias close up, travel northeast from Murphys on Calif. 4 to **Calaveras Big Trees State Park,** near the little town of Arnold.

Murphys is a good place from which to explore Calaveras wine country, particularly the beautiful **Ironstone Vineyards** *(1894 Six Mile Rd., tel 209/728-1251, www.ironstonevineyards.com)*. The winery occupies a stunning building modeled on a 19th-century gold stamp mill. Pick up a picnic lunch in Ironstone's deli and drive south on Parrotts Ferry Road to **Columbia State Historic Park,** a preserved gold rush town with a difference: Here it is not only the buildings that recall the 1850s. A stagecoach, costumed guides, gold panning, live theater, and music in historic saloons all help Columbia to re-create the days when its importance made it a rival of Sacramento (see pp. 292–293) in the race to be state capital.

While there may be disputes over aspects of Twain's "Jumping Frog," no one contests its provenance—now a tiny, dilapidated wooden shack perched in a quiet grove of black and live oaks on **Jackass Hill** *(map p. 291 D2, turn left up Jackass Hill Rd. from Calif. 49, S of Carson Hill, N of Turtletown)*. Here Twain, puffing his pipe and worrying over his San Francisco debts, crafted his tale. Anyone with a literary soul should make this pilgrimage. Yet few do, making this a lonely and beautiful site.

Established in 1848 by Mexican miners, **Sonora** teemed with political intrigue during its early years. A riot almost occurred in 1850, when the new U.S. government imposed a $20 tax on foreign-born miners. Eventually the Mexicans fled, but not before a group of Anglo settlers had marched in a display of bellicosity. Today Sonora is an exciting little town, replete with cafés, restaurants, shops, and cultural events such as the blues

Calaveras Big Trees State Park

291 D3

1170 Calif. 4, Northeast of Murphys

209/795-3840

www.parks.ca.gov

Columbia State Historic Park

291 D2

11255 Jackson St., Columbia

209/588-9128

www.parks.ca.gov

Sonora

291 D2

Visitor Information

Visitors Bureau, 542 W. Stockton Rd., Sonora

209/533-4420, 800/446-1333

www.tcvb.com

Railtown 1897 State Historic Park

5th Ave., Jamestown

209/984-3953

Closed Tues.–Wed. No trains Nov.–March

$$$

www.railtown1897.org

Mariposa

291 D1

Visitor Information

Tourism Bureau, 5158 Calif. 140

209/966-7081

www.yosemiteexperience.com

and rock music festival held here in August *(tel 209/533-3473).* See gold rush memorabilia at the **Tuolumne County Museum & History Center** *(Bradford Ave., off Washington St., tel 209/532-1317, www.tchistory.org).*

Jamestown *(map p. 291 D2),* established in 1849 by Col. George James, is now a tiny burg with many cute shops. The main attraction here is the **Railtown 1897 State Historic Park,** an extension of the California State Railroad Museum in Sacramento (see pp. 292–293). A 40-minute, 6-mile (9.6 km) ride in an old steam-powered train is a fine way to end a day of exploring, and there is a collection of locomotives, carriages, and mementoes.

Mariposa

A gateway to Yosemite (see pp. 304–309), Mariposa has an interesting old courthouse and jail. Details of its days as a 19th-century mining and railroad center are preserved at the **Mariposa Museum & History Center** *(5119 Jessie St., tel 209/966-2924, www.mariposamuseum.com, $)* and the **California State Mining & Mineral Museum** *(off Calif. 49, S of Mariposa, tel 209/742-7625, www.parks.ca.gov, closed Mon.–Wed., $).* After his run for the Presidency failed in 1856, John C. Frémont lived in a house on Calif. 140 with his wife, whose *Mother Lode Narratives* gives insight into her remarkable life. ■

Gold Country Shopping

Although Gold Country shopping has its requisite share of cute, it also has a great variety of refreshingly down-to-earth establishments. **Antiques:** An outstanding antique collective is **Creekside Shops** *(22 Main St., Sutter Creek, tel 209/267-5520),* where you might pick up anything from a McCoy vase to a first edition of an 1896 Bret Harte biography. Two popular items are turn-of-the-20th-century stereographs and period postcards. **Antiques Etcetera** *(S. Washington St., Sonora, tel 209/532-9544)* specializes in early 20th-century dinnerware. **Art:** Gold Country is alive with talented artists, many of whom established their reputations in San Francisco before heading upriver. The **Holbrooke Hotel** in Grass Valley has prints by Peggy Swan, a brilliant printmaker. A sampling of the region's talent can be seen at the **Calaveras County Arts Council Gallery** *(22 Main St., tel 209/754-1774)* in San Andreas. A coterie of young painters has grown up in and around Sonora. **The Vault** *(42 S. Washington St., Sonora, tel 209/533 1384, www.vaultart.com)* represents many of them. Sonora native Jack Cassinetto's neo-tonalist plein air works echo the early Californian great Gottardo Piazonni. **Books:** Several outstanding secondhand book stores include **Hein & Company** *(204A N. Main St., Jackson, tel 209/223 9076),* where you might find a 1930s Maxfield Parrish album or a rare hardcover edition of Gertrude Atherton's *Rezanov.* **Produce:** Local produce and many things made from it are available through the **Apple Hill Growers Association** *(www.applehill.com)* in Camino, east of Placerville. In the fall, try **Mill View Ranch** *(2740 Cable Rd., tel 530/644-4408)* for homemade apple pies and jams; the **Marvin Larsen Ranch** *(2721 Mace Rd., tel 530/644-1396)* for cider, pears, and honey; or **Boa Vista Orchards** *(2952 Carson Rd., Placerville, tel 530/622-5522, www.boavista.com)* for fruit, wine, pies, and pastries.

Wildest California, from the wonders of Yosemite, Sequoia, and Kings Canyon National Parks to Lake Tahoe's ski slopes

Sierra Nevada

"Powder hounds" enjoy all the adventure the Sierra Nevada has to offer

Sierra Nevada

The Sierra Nevada mountain range runs from south of Mount Lassen to beyond Sequoia National Park. This 400-mile (644 km) chain is the result of massive volcanic activity some 130 million years ago. Today it is a paradise of deep forests, ice-blue lakes, glacier-carved valleys, and snowy mountain peaks.

Camping in the High Sierra, Kings Canyon

Travelers interested in the flora and fauna (not to mention weather) of this region will need to know the basics of Sierra topography before setting out. Ascending the range compares to a trip into Arctic tundra, with every 1,000 feet (305 m) of elevation equivalent to traveling 300 miles (482 km) northward.

The Sierra Nevada can be broken down into four ecological zones. The first, the mixed conifer zone (3,500–6,000 feet/1,065–1,830 m), is a zone of frequent precipitation and dense vegetation. Here giant sequoias, Jeffrey pines, and Douglas firs provide cover for deer, bears, and other forest mammals. The lodgepole pine–red fir zone (6,000–8,500 feet/1,830–2,590 m) is a region of deeply shaded forests, increasing snowfall, and wet mountain meadows—perfect for western and lodgepole pine and Sierra juniper. In the third zone, the subalpine (8,500–10,500 feet/2,590–3,200 m), the effects of wind and snow begin to contort the natural landscape; vegetation is low growing, often gnarled and twisted. The alpine zone (from 10,500 feet/3,200 m) marks the timberline; here precipitation falls off dramatically and vegetation grows sparsely.

One interesting adaptation by plants growing in the Sierra Nevada is their distinct lack of scent; fragrance uses up scarce water. But the nose's loss is the eye's gain: Many plants here compensate with large flowers to attract pollinators.

The centerpiece of the "Sierra experience" is Yosemite National Park. But in recent years, the area's two other national parks—Kings Canyon and Sequoia—have also become first-choice destinations. The great expanse of Lake Tahoe to the north has always been a draw, particularly for those seeking the added distractions found

NOT TO BE MISSED:

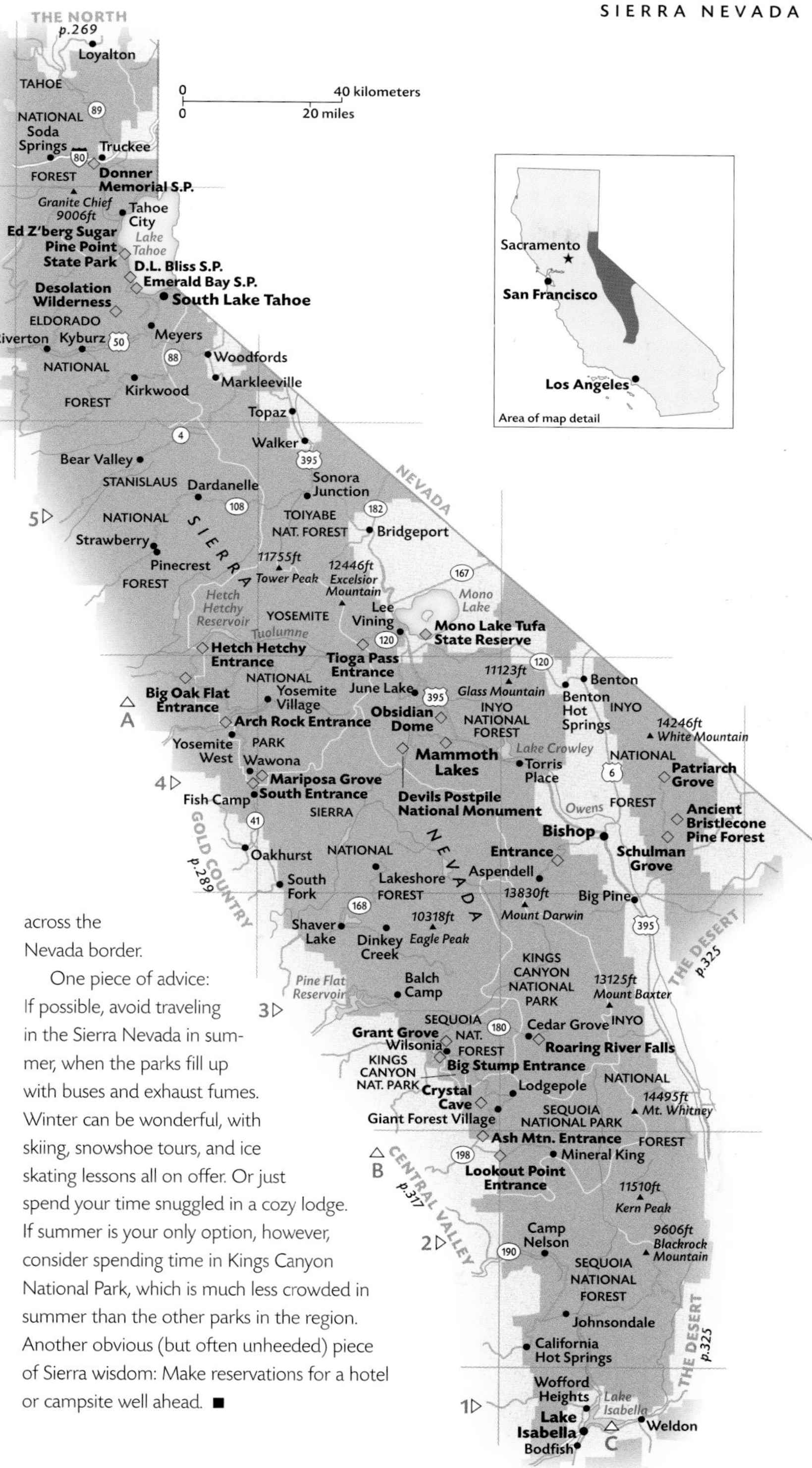

across the Nevada border.

One piece of advice: If possible, avoid traveling in the Sierra Nevada in summer, when the parks fill up with buses and exhaust fumes. Winter can be wonderful, with skiing, snowshoe tours, and ice skating lessons all on offer. Or just spend your time snuggled in a cozy lodge. If summer is your only option, however, consider spending time in Kings Canyon National Park, which is much less crowded in summer than the other parks in the region. Another obvious (but often unheeded) piece of Sierra wisdom: Make reservations for a hotel or campsite well ahead. ■

Yosemite National Park

For more than 9,000 years, Indian communities inhabited the Yosemite Valley. For the last thousand years, it was the home of the Miwok, a subgroup of the Ahwahneechee. *Ahwahnee* means "valley that looks like a gaping mouth," a vivid description of this glacier-carved slash across the Sierra.

El Capitan *(left)*, Bridalveil Fall *(right)*, and Half Dome in the distance distinguish Yosemite Valley.

Yosemite National Park

303 A4–B4, 305

209/372-0200 (24-hour updates on weather and trail conditions, plus campground info.); 877/444-6777 (campground reservations); 801/599-4884 (lodging reservations)

www.nps.gov/yose
www.yosemitepark.com

In 1851, the governor of California asked the Mariposa Brigade of the U.S. Army to put an end to the conflicts between Native Americans and miners. Following a group of Native Americans into the mountains, the troops came upon this magical valley, the first non-Native Americans to see it. The great naturalist John Muir (1838–1914) was seduced by Yosemite's spell and spent much of his life defending it. In 1890, the spell conjured a miracle—Congress created Yosemite National Park. Today, with more than four million visitors each year, Yosemite, a World Heritage site, is one of the world's most famous wilderness areas.

The valley at the heart of the park, formed by glaciers and further cut by the Merced River, is surrounded by awesome peaks: the 8,842-foot (2,695 m) **Half Dome,** its other half crushed by glaciers; the massive bulk of the 7,569-foot (2,307 m) **El Capitan** at the western end of the valley, the world's tallest exposed granite

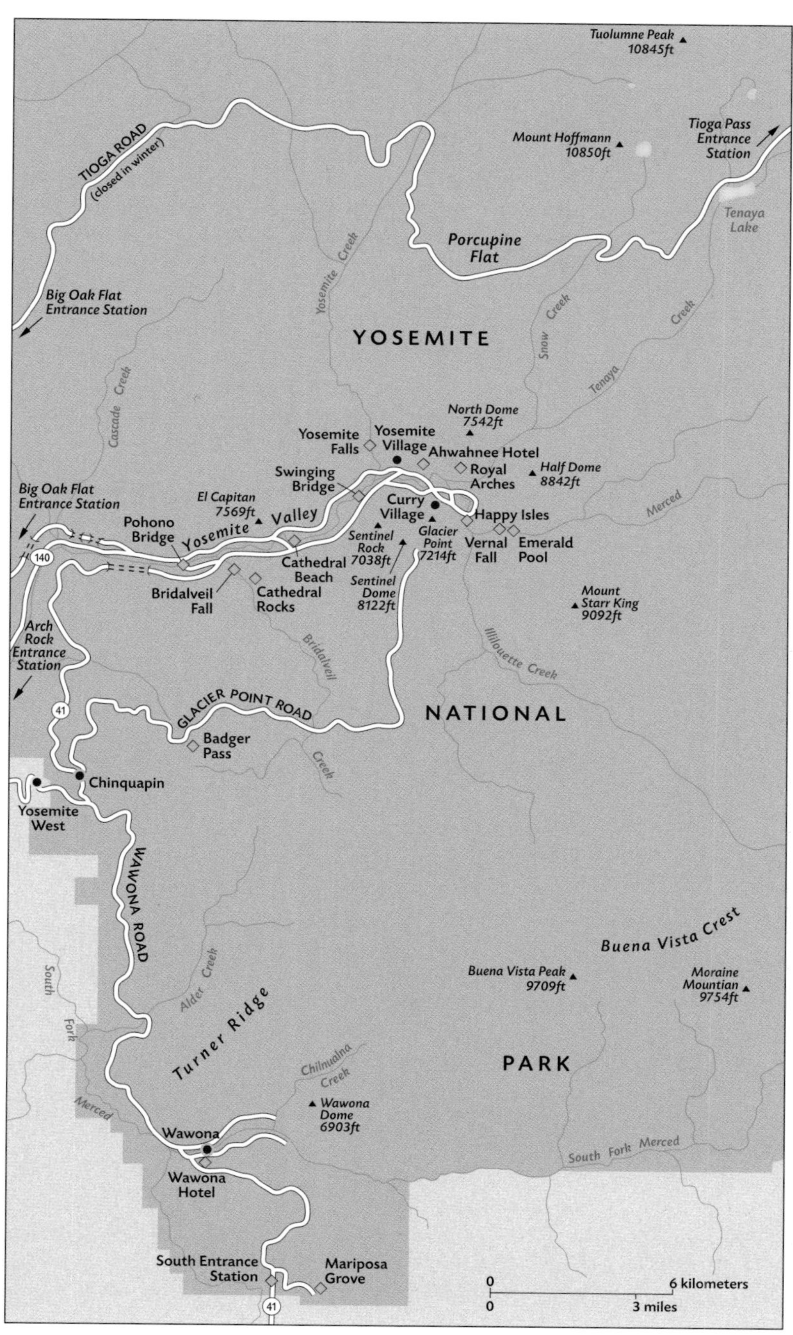
Tuolumne Peak 10845ft
Mount Hoffmann 10850ft
Tioga Pass Entrance Station
TIOGA ROAD (closed in winter)
Tenaya Lake
Porcupine Flat
Yosemite Creek
Big Oak Flat Entrance Station
YOSEMITE
Snow Creek
Tenaya Creek
Cascade Creek
North Dome 7542ft
Yosemite Falls
Yosemite Village
Ahwahnee Hotel
Royal Arches
Half Dome 8842ft
Swinging Bridge
Big Oak Flat Entrance Station
El Capitan 7569ft
Curry Village
Happy Isles
Merced
Pohono Bridge
Yosemite Valley
Sentinel Rock 7038ft
Glacier Point 7214ft
Vernal Fall
Emerald Pool
140
Cathedral Beach
Sentinel Dome 8122ft
Bridalveil Fall
Cathedral Rocks
Mount Starr King 9092ft
Arch Rock Entrance Station
Bridalveil
Illilouette Creek
41
GLACIER POINT ROAD
NATIONAL
Badger Pass
Creek
Chinquapin
Yosemite West
WAWONA ROAD
South Fork
Alder Creek
Turner Ridge
Buena Vista Crest
Buena Vista Peak 9709ft
Moraine Mountian 9754ft
PARK
Chilnualna Creek
Merced
Wawona Dome 6903ft
Wawona
South Fork Merced
Wawona Hotel
South Entrance Station
Mariposa Grove
41
0
6 kilometers
0
3 miles

EXPERIENCE: Rafting the Sierra Nevada

The Tuolumne is one tough river, an untamed torrent of melting snow and spring rain that starts high in the Sierra Nevada of Yosemite National Park and churns its way through deep Tuolumne Canyon on its long journey to the Central Valley and eventually the Pacific Ocean. Given its isolation and fluvial dangers, the only way to explore the watercourse is on a guided whitewater rafting trip.

Based in Angels Camp (see p. 298), **O.A.R.S.** *(tel 800/346-6277, www.oars.com)*—one of the oldest whitewater rafting outfits in the world—offers guided trips *($$$$–$$$$$)* on the Tuolumne lasting one, two, or three days. The trips begin and end in Groveland, just outside Yosemite. Along the way are abandoned mines and pioneer towns, relics of the day when even this remote corner of California was part of the gold rush, as well as sandy beaches, swimming holes, and small waterfalls that provide cool respite from the blazing summer sun. Camp beneath the stars, and fall asleep to the sound of the rushing river.

Other Sierra rivers ripe for adventurous rafting include the gnarly Kern River in Sequoia National Forest *(map p. 303 C2)*, the Stanislaus River near Calaveras Big Trees State Park (see p. 299), and the American River near Sacramento (see pp. 292–293). Farther south, **Kern River Tours** *(tel 800-573-7238, www.kernrivertours.com)* runs single and multiday trips on Lake Isabella *(map p. 303 C1)*.

monolith; **Glacier Point,** at the top of a 3,200-foot-high (975 m) rock wall. These are among the most photographed natural wonders of Yosemite. Visitors flock to the valley to see them, resulting in traffic jams, pollution, and all the accompanying problems. However, at 7 miles long by 1 mile wide (11 km x 1.6 km), the valley represents only a tiny fraction of the park's total area of more than 1,000 square miles (2,590 sq km). In much of the rest of Yosemite, the park's spell is unbroken—especially for those who can leave their cars and walk its trails.

Tioga Pass Road *(closed spring & winter)* crosses the park from Crane Flat, near the Big Oak Flat entrance. The road climbs to the high country of the Sierra and crosses **Tuolumne Meadows** to Tenaya Lake and on to the 9,945-foot (3,031 m) Tioga Pass and the eastern entrance of the park.

INSIDER TIP:

From Glacier Point, you can see Yosemite Valley, the Clark Range, Vernal and Nevada Falls, and a great profile of Half Dome.

—SCOTT GEDIMAN
Assistant superintendent, Yosemite National Park

This is serious hiking country, and the park offers some 800 miles (1,287 km) of marked trails, many of which are fine for inexperienced hikers. Discovering Yosemite's colors and smells can be as easy as the stroll to **Mirror Lake** or as taxing as the steep haul to the top of North America's highest waterfall, 2,425-foot

(739 m) **Yosemite Falls.**

The park is remarkably user friendly, with major information stations at Yosemite Village, Wawona, and Tuolumne Meadows. The park information service provides excellent trail maps and weather information.

Valley Floor Trek

This flat, 5-mile (8 km) trail loops through the most popular part of the park. Set out early and plan on spending most of a morning. Pick up a map at the Valley Visitor Center and take the free bus to the Yosemite Falls stop.

After walking the gentle slope up to the foot of the falls, go downhill to the lovely **Cooks Meadow.** From here, the entire pantheon of Yosemite icons looms upward like great granite sentries—as well as Half Dome and Glacier Point, look out for **Sentinel Rock** and the **Cathedral Rocks.**

Cast your eyes lower and the meadow's flora and fauna come into view. Spring is the best time for the wildflowers here. The meadow lands are often alive with red-wing blackbirds, robins, and Steller's jays; predators such as owls, peregrines and other falcons, and even golden eagles are sometimes spotted hunting over the valley.

Keeping the burbling Merced River to your left, you will come to **Leidig Meadow,** named for Charles Leidig, the first non-Native American male born in Yosemite. This is one of the largest remaining meadows in the valley. Follow the bike path to its edge and to the river, where you may see stunning reflections of **Sentinel Falls.** Follow the trail along the north side of the meadow to **Rocky Point,** easily recognizable by the rubble at its base, then continue to the river and a large wooded area. Now stick to the trail along the river to an area known as **Indian Swamp.** In spring, the meadow here floods, giving amazing reflections of Cathedral Rocks and Spires.

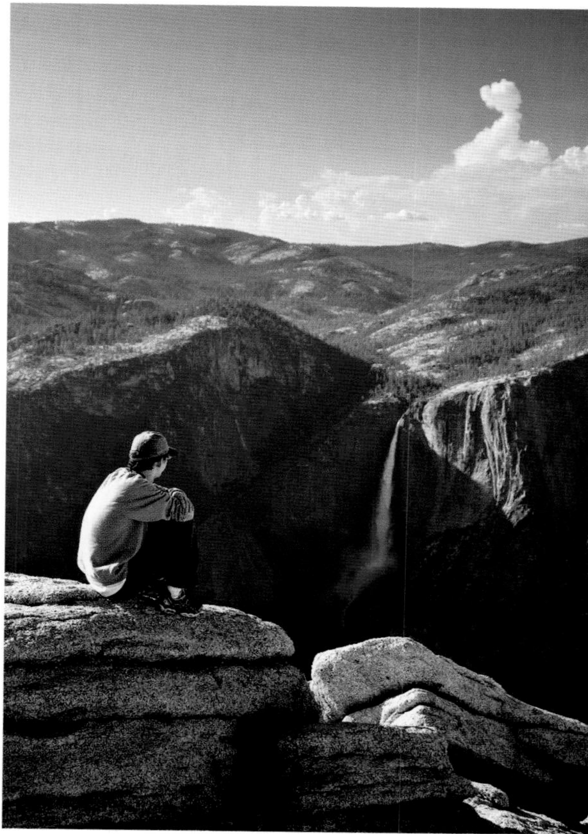

The view from the top of Sentinel Dome is spectacular.

Yosemite Essentials

There are several entrance stations to the park. The south entry *(Calif. 41)* is the most popular. During peak season, you will save time and frustration by using one of the three western gates: Arch Rock *(off Calif. 140)*, Big Oak Flat *(off Calif. 120)*, or Hetch Hetchy *(N of Mather on Hetch Hetchy Rd.)*. To the east is the Tioga Pass entrance *(off Calif. 120)*, closed winter through spring.

The main sources of information for the park are the entrance stations and the visitor centers, where one can obtain up-to-date weather and trail condition reports and the "Yosemite Guide."

Camping is allowed only in designated campgrounds. You may need to make a reservation up to three months in advance to be sure of your preferred site at popular times. There are also a number of first-come, first-served sites, for which you register at an entrance.

The three hotels within the park itself (see Travelwise pp. 382–383) are the Ahwahnee, beyond Yosemite Village; the Wawona, near the southern entrance; and Yosemite Lodge, near Yosemite Falls. All suggest advance booking; for the Ahwahnee, make reservations several months in advance.

The trail then takes you to **El Capitan Meadow,** where you can view the towering sheer slab of granite, the subject of so many Yosemite photos. Across the valley is **Bridalveil Fall,** a spectacular 620-foot (189 m) vertical torrent in spring. Continue along the riverside to **Gates of the Valley,** one of the best spots from which to view the entire valley.

At **Pohono Bridge,** cross the river to **Fern Spring.** From here, you can either follow the trail to the base of the fall or return along the Merced River going through a gate to **Cathedral Beach.** The view of the **Three Brothers** is outstanding. Continue to the **Swinging Bridge** for a final sweeping view.

Happy Isles to Vernal Fall

To begin this two-hour out-and-back trek, take the bus to Happy Isles, then go along the trail beneath Glacier Point to the popular **Mist Trail.** After about 50 minutes of steady climbing, a bridge appears. From here, you have your first clear view of 317-foot (96 m) **Vernal Fall.** Return to the Happy Isles bus or go farther up the trail to the brilliant view near **Emerald Pool.** Return on the **John Muir Trail** (see sidebar p. 312).

Mariposa Grove Trail

If you are going south out of Yosemite, this 5-mile (8 km) hike to see the giant sequoias is a perfect farewell. Take the trail just before Calif. 41 leaves Yosemite to the south. Walk through the lower grove until you reach the **Fallen Monarch.** At the 1-mile point, you will come upon the **Grizzly Giant,** thought to be more than 2,700 years old. The trail winds past the **Faithful Couple** and **Clothespin** trees. A loop at the top passes a log-cabin museum *(open in summer)*, then returns to the trail. ■

EXPERIENCE: Yosemite in Winter

Yosemite is a far different park in winter than the one that most people know or imagine. When the cold weather comes, the crowds vanish, making even normally crowded Yosemite Valley feel like it must have a hundred years ago when John Muir wandered the landscape. Storms bring a shroud of fresh snow to the granite domes, alpine meadows, and towering trees. And the park throws on its winter sports coat.

Outdoor Activities

Developed for Yosemite's bid to host the 1932 Winter Olympics (it lost out to Lake Placid), **Badger Pass Ski Area** *(tel 209/372-8430, www.yosemitepark.com/badgerpass.aspx)* is now considered one of the best places in California for kids to learn how to ski or snowboard. Lifts operate from 9 a.m. to 4 p.m. Equipment rentals and lift tickets are available from 8:30 a.m. to 4 p.m. *(tel 209/372-1000 for current snow conditions).*

Guided snowshoe tours, another way to explore the white wilderness, range from relatively easy, ranger-led, 2-hour jaunts around Badger Pass to a 6.5-hour "adventure hike" to Dewey Point run by the **Yosemite Mountaineering School** *(tel 209/372-8444. www.yosemitepark.com/rockclimbing.aspx)*. YMS also gives cross-country skiing lessons and leads guided trips along Old Glacier Point Road. One of the holy grails of American cross-country skiing, the 21-mile (33.7 km) round-trip normally includes an overnight at the Glacier Point Ski Hut overlooking Half Dome and Yosemite Valley.

Down in Yosemite Valley is another vestige of the '32 Olympics bid: the **Curry Village Ice Rink** *(tel 209/372-8341)*, with two to four skating sessions per day between November and early March. After dark, big band music fills the air and skaters can curl up around a fire pit blazing at one end.

Last but not least, the giant sequoias of the Tuolumne Grove are magical to trek or snowshoe with snow all around.

Indoor Activities

Among the park's indoor cold-weather activities is **Winter Theater Live!** at Yosemite Lodge. One recent production was *The Spirit of John Muir: Stories of Ice and Snow.*

Gourmet events in Yosemite during the winter months include the celebrated **Bracebridge Dinners** *(tel 801/559-5000, www.bracebridgedinners.com)* at the Ahwahnee Hotel in December and other special events like the **Vintners' Holidays** in November and December and **Chefs' Holidays** in January and February *(tel 801/559-4884 to book either culinary experience).*

Hiking and driving options may be limited in Yosemite in winter, but there is no shortage of natural beauty to be experienced.

Sequoia & Kings Canyon National Parks

Along the wet, western side of the Sierra Nevada crest east of Fresno lie two breathtakingly beautiful national parks, almost as dramatic as Yosemite (see pp. 304–309) to the northwest but not as well known. One reason is elevation. Much of Sequoia and Kings Canyon is perched above 11,000 feet (3,352 m)—about 4,000 feet (1,219 m) above the highest road. Fortunately, several roads wind through the park, with viewing points all along the way. But, as in Yosemite, the best way to see these 862,000 acres (348,840 ha) is to get out there and sweat a little.

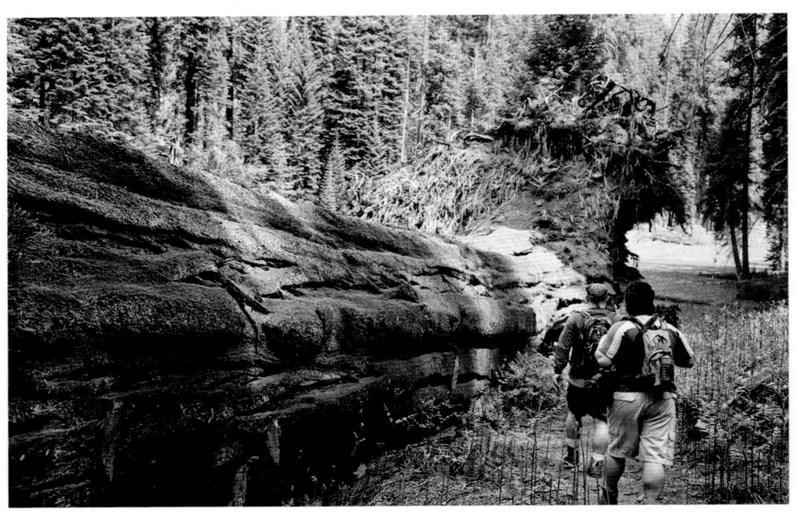

Giant sequoias here die not from disease but from toppling over—they simply grow too big.

Sequoia & Kings Canyon National Parks

303 C2–C3

Visitor Information

Visitor Center, 47050 Generals Hwy., Three Rivers

559/565-3341

www.nps.gov/seki

If Sequoia and Kings Canyon were a movie, its stars would be the giant sequoias. Of the 75 groves of these trees in the world, only eight grow north of the Kings River, and those are scattered over more than 200 miles (321 km); the rest are close together in a 60-mile-long (96.5 km) area south of the river. The ecology of Sequoia and Kings Canyon—their precipitation, elevation, and soil—is perfect for these trees.

Sequoia National Park

Sequoia National Park has been organized with a variety of fitness levels in mind. The campgrounds (first come, first served), many of which sit along cool, clear streams, are close to interesting hike destinations, and none are too far from ranger outposts. The popular **Lodgepole Campground** and **Dorst Campground** *(tel 877/444-6777)* require you to book in advance; each offers educational

INSIDER TIP:

Wake early and go for a sunrise hike. You're more likely to catch sight of a grazing mother deer and her fawn.

—ERIN STONE
National Geographic contributor

services and fireside entertainment in summer. Built of cedar and stone, the 102-room **Wuksachi Lodge** *(tel 888/252-5757, www.visitsequoia.com/lodging.aspx)* offers overnight and dining options in the Giant Forest area.

Entering Sequoia National Park on Calif. 198 (Generals Highway) from Three Rivers brings you to **Amphitheater Point;** stop for a stunning view of the San Joaquin Valley before driving on to see the astonishing sequoias of the **Giant Forest,** one of the great altars of the American environmental movement and an area explored and named by John Muir.

Starting at the **General Sherman Tree**—at 52,500 cubic feet (1,486 m^3) the world's largest living thing (though not the tallest)—visitors can take the 2-mile (3.2 km) **Congress Trail** past all of the major giant sequoias here, including the **House** and **Senate** groups, as well as the **President** and **McKinley** trees.

Giant Forest Village marks the start of a 3-mile (4.8 km) road that will take you, either on foot or by shuttle (in summer), to two outstanding sights. About 2 miles (3.2 km) down is the steep, quarter-mile staircase up to **Moro Rock.** From the top of this granite dome is a spectacular view, particularly at sunset. Below stretches the blue-green Kaweah River, while to the west one can see beyond the San Joaquin Valley and over into the Coast Range.

At the road's end is **Crescent Meadow,** perhaps the finest of all midaltitude meadows. It was here, in 1875, at the lodge of pioneer Hale Tharp, that Muir spent several nights, later crowning this meadow the "gem of the Sierras." If you get ambitious, you can start the **High Sierra Trail** here; it finishes at **Mount Whitney,** the highest point in the coterminus United States, 14,495 feet (4,418 m) tall and 71 miles (114 km) away.

Four-and-a-half miles (78.2

HOW TO GET THERE
If you are arriving from the south on Calif. 99, take Calif. 198 northeast to Sequoia; from Fresno, follow Calif. 180 east to Kings Canyon. As in almost all national parks, entrance stations provide maps and more detailed trail and climate information.

The Yokut

Reflect for a moment on the original inhabitants of the Kings Canyon area, the Yokut. Although at first these Native Americans welcomed their mid-19th-century pioneer acquaintances, by 1862 the same Anglo newcomers were already forcing the Yokut into the meager backcountry. Simultaneously the Yokut began to perish from the first infection by the white man's diseases—smallpox, measles, and scarlet fever. A particularly poignant moment came in 1864, when the chief of the remaining Yokut directly asked a leading pioneer, Hale Tharp, to leave. According to the contemporary accounts, when Tharp refused, "the chief and his brave sat down and cried." By the following year, all of the Yokut had retreated to the remote back canyons, where they would scratch out only a shell of their former existence.

Crystal Cave

 303 B3

12 miles W of Lodgepole Visitor Center

559/565-3759

Closed winter

$$$ (45-minute tour; tickets at Lodgepole or Foothills Visitor Centers)

km) north of the Giant Forest is Lodgepole Camp. The **Tokopah Falls Trail** starts here. The walk ascends steadily (but manageably), leading along the magnificent Marble Fork Kaweah River and on into a series of cliffs and the waterfall of Tokopah Canyon, 2 miles (3.2 km) from the start.

A short drive west of Lodgepole is **Crystal Cave,** a series of underground caverns with superb specimens of stalactites, stalagmites, and other geological formations. The tour is worthwhile. In summer, when temperatures can reach the 90s, the cave's cool interior is welcome.

Kings Canyon National Park

North and west, Generals Highway goes to Kings Canyon National Park and reaches **Grant Grove.** The giant sequoia called **General Grant** is the world's third largest living tree, at more than 42,000 cubic feet (1,189 m^3). It is also, in the words of the Park Service, a "designated national shrine" and "the only living memorial to those who gave their lives for freedom."

The 1.5-mile (2.4 km) **North Grove Loop** gives a closer look at the trees. The **Redwood Canyon Trail,** beginning at Redwood Saddle, is the start of two easy, 6-mile (9.6 km) loops through sequoia groves; the **Sugarloaf Trail,** at Sunset Meadow, is a moderate effort for 2 miles (3.2 km) along a spectacular glaciated canyon.

North and then east along Calif. 180 (this part is only open in summer) brings hikers into **Sequoia National Forest** and then on to a remote corner of Kings Canyon and **Cedar Grove.** The grove is pleasantly quiet, even during peak season. To get an idea of the glacial history of Kings Canyon, take the **Canyon View** turn a mile (1.6 km) past Cedar Grove Village. Another mile east is the entrance to **Roaring River Falls,** where a five-minute walk leads to a waterfall pulsing through a narrow ravine. A farther 1.5 miles (2.4 km) east is the scenic **Zumwalt Meadow.** ■

EXPERIENCE: Hiking from Yosemite to Sequoia

The shortest path between Yosemite National Park (see pp. 304–309) and Sequoia National Park is the 215-mile (346 km) **John Muir Trail** *(www.johnmuirtrail.org)*, but you'll have to walk it. The route follows the crest of the High Sierra between Yosemite Valley and Mount Whitney, threading a landscape mottled with alpine tarns and snow-capped peaks, rocky cirques, and sun-splashed meadows that only ardent hikers ever see. Thirty days is the recommended time for walking the entire trail, but shorter sections can be navigated in a week or even less. Hikers must pack in all of their supplies and pack out all of their garbage; bear canisters are a must. A backcountry permit is required from the national park or forest where you commence your hike.

Mono Lake & Mammoth Lakes

Although technically well north of the official California deserts, Mono Lake bears contemplation as a desertified ecology. Since 1941, water agencies in southern California, thirsty for the liquid gold necessary to grow new suburban communities, have diverted the freshwater streams that used to feed this ancient lake. This has caused the water level to drop by some 45 feet (13.7 m), concentrating already high salt levels. Mono is two-and-one-half times as salty as the ocean, wreaking havoc for many indigenous birds, fish, and flora.

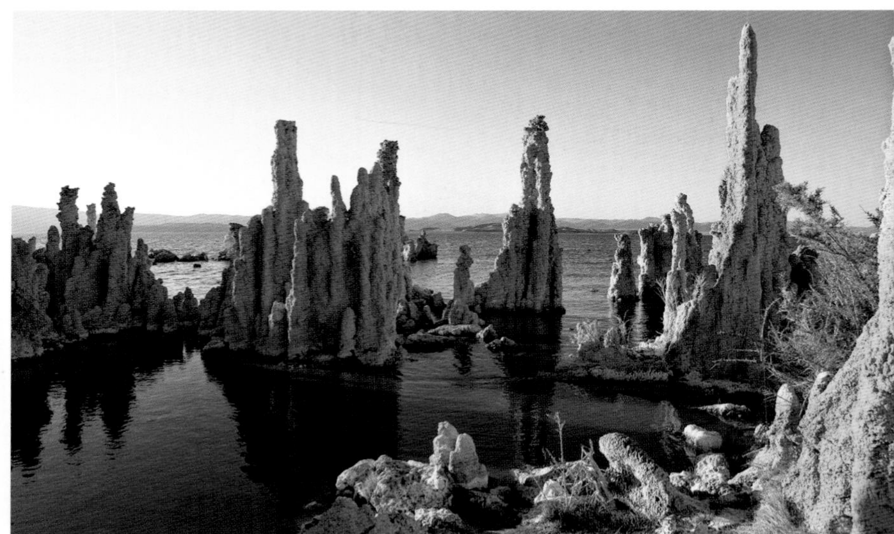

Dramatic towers rise at South Tufa in Mono Lake Tufa State Natural Reserve.

As Mono Lake's water level has dropped, spectacular geological formations called tufa towers have been exposed. Resembling stalagmites, these towers—formed when freshwater underground springs mix their calcium with the carbonate-rich lake water—conjure the effect of a city skyline against the background of snowy mountain peaks. They are one of the most peculiar and beautiful sights in the state. Some of the best are preserved at **Mono Lake Tufa State Natural Reserve.**

Some species of wader and waterfowl have successfully adapted to the unusual environment here, and it is a popular destination for bird-watchers. Between August and April, the lake is home to one of the largest populations of eared grebes in the Northern Hemisphere; the Audubon Society estimates their numbers at up to

Mono Lake Tufa State Natural Reserve

303 B5

Visitor Information

Park Office, 395 & 3rd St., Lee Vining

760/647-6331

www.parks.ca.gov

Ancient Bristlecone Pine Forest
303 C4
Visitor Information
Visitor Center, White Mtn. Rd. off Calif. 168, NE of Big Pine
760/647-6595
Closed winter

Inyo National Forest
303 B4–C4
Visitor Information
Visitor Center, 351 Pacu Ln., Bishop
760/873-2400
www.fs.fed.us

Mammoth Lakes
303 B4
Visitor Information
Visitor Center, 2520 Main St., Mammoth Lakes
760/934-2712, 888/466-2666
www.visitmammoth.com

Tamarack Cross-Country Ski Center
Tamarack Lodge, 163 Twin Lakes Rd., Mammoth Lakes
760/934-2442
www.tamaracklodge.com

Mammoth Ski Museum
Edison Hall, 100 College Pkwy., Mammoth Lakes
760/934-6592
www.mammothlakesfoundation.org

800,000. Snowy plovers, avocets, and phalaropes also overwinter here, while in spring and summer the lake hosts a large breeding population of California gulls.

Ancient Bristlecone Pine Forest

It is something of an effort to visit this remote forest, which lies deep inside **Inyo National Forest,** south of Mono Lake. But the inconvenience is outweighed by the thrill of seeing some of the world's oldest living trees.

There are two principal groves worth visiting. The first is the 4,000-year-old **Schulman Grove,** named for naturalist Julius Schulman, who was the first to announce the grove's antiquity in 1958. The Forest Service maintains a **Discovery Trail** off White Mountain Road that takes you past dozens of the trees. One of the grove's most stunning features is its brilliant palette of primary colors, heightened by the crystal-clear mountain air: cinnamon red trunks against deep blue skies, beige trunks with striking black grain, rich red-orange wood, and purple-black tips to the branches.

The second grove, of even older bristlecones, is the **Patriarch Grove.** It is a few miles farther along White Mountain Road and several hundred feet higher, just south of the White Mountain Natural Area. In it is the venerable **Methuselah,** a tree estimated to be more than 4,700 years old.

The bristlecone pine *(Pinus longaeva)* acquired its twisted, stunted form in response to its extremely cold and windy environment. Trunk bark grows in beleaguered thin strips, forcibly restraining growth and making for the dense cells and abundant resin that are a resilient and necessary life-support system.

INSIDER TIP:

Check out Mammoth Lakes' secret astronomical show: Pick a dark night, head up to Horseshoe Lake, lay out a blanket, and view a star display like you've never seen before.

—JUDY FARNETTI
Mammoth Lodging, www.MammothSierraOnline.com

Mammoth Lakes

One of North America's most volcanically active regions, Mammoth, 20 miles (32 km) south of Mono Lake, is named for the crystal-clear lakes filled with fish in summer. In winter, Mammoth favors skiing, snowmobiling, and dog-sled adventures. The **Tamarack Cross-Country Ski Center** offers 19 miles (30.5 km) of trails. The **Mammoth Ski Museum** tells the sport's tale in the High Sierra. Calif. 203 snakes west from US 395 past Mammoth Mountain to **Devils Postpile National Monument** *(map p. 303 B4)*, featuring huge columns of ancient basalt lava. North of Mammoth Lakes rises **Obsidian Dome** *(map p. 303 B4)*, a great dome of solid volcanic glass. ■

Lake Tahoe

German skiers have their own fond name for Lake Tahoe: *der Blaue*—the blue one. It is often also called one of the most beautiful lakes in the world. Even Mark Twain lost his characteristic bluster when first seeing "the mountains brilliantly photographed upon its surface . . . surely it must be the fairest picture the whole earth affords."

The lake's sublime color is due to weather, elevation, and depth.

Tahoe is 1,640 feet (500 m) deep, making it the world's tenth deepest inland body of water. Created when the Tahoe Basin sank between parallel faults two million years ago and lava blocked the water's outflow, the lake is now 22 miles (35.4 km) long and 12 miles (19 km) wide. Its environs are an undisputed delight. Golf, fishing, waterskiing, boating, biking, and swimming are among summer activities here; skiing, snowmobile riding, and snowboarding are the main winter pastimes. (For skiing information, see Travelwise, p. 390.) The lake's 72-mile (115 km) shoreline, straddling the California-Nevada border, is home to everything from quiet forests to glamorous casinos. There is something here for everyone. The summer peaks with 100,000 visitors, so if you're looking for peace and quiet, come in spring or fall.

The lakefront on Tahoe's California side includes a number of state parks, historic sites, and ski resorts. **South Lake Tahoe,** the biggest city in the region, is a good place for an overview. Here one can board the authentic ***Tahoe Queen* paddle wheeler** *(900 Ski Run Blvd., South Lake Tahoe, tel 775/589-4906 or 800/238-2463, www.laketahoecruises.com, $$$)* and sail to Emerald Bay and back, taking in the vast shore and the mountain skyline.

Many prefer to spend their first day here doing the 72-mile (115 km) **Shoreline Drive,** which takes you around the lake's entire circumference. A fun way to do this is to buy the two-hour audio tour "Drive Around Lake Tahoe," available from the South Lake Tahoe Chamber of Commerce. The commentary provides a series of colorful facts, tales, and legends about the area as you drive.

Another popular outing is to take the **Heavenly Valley Gondola** *(tel 775/586-7000)* at Heavenly Ski Resort *(3860 Saddle Rd., South Lake Tahoe, tel 530/541-4418, www.skiheavenly.com),* which

Lake Tahoe

303 A6

Visitor Information

Visitors Authority, 3066 Lake Tahoe Blvd., South Lake Tahoe

530/544-5050

www.visitinglaketahoe.com

www.tahoesouth.com

Emerald Bay State Park
303 A6
22 miles S of Tahoe City
530/541-3030
www.parks.ca.gov

D. L. Bliss State Park
303 A6
17 miles S of Tahoe City on Calif. 89
530/525-7277
www.parks.ca.gov

Ed Z'berg Sugar Pine Point State Park
303 A6
Follow signs from Sugar Pine Point
530/525-7982
www.parks.ca.gov

will whisk you up 3,000 feet (914 m) to the peak restaurant.

There are plenty of places to visit around the lake. **Tallac Historic Site** *(Calif. 89, tel 530/543-2600 or 530/543-0956, www.fs.usda.gov, closed Oct.–May)*, northwest of South Lake Tahoe, boasts a resort of late 19th-century houses built as vacation homes by rich San Franciscans.

On the lakeshore 10 miles (16 km) north of South Lake Tahoe is **Emerald Bay State Park,** where you can visit **Vikingsholm,** an eccentrically brilliant, perfect reproduction of a 10th-century Norse fortress. The site can be reached via a short hiking trail or by boat. Vikingsholm was the dream home of Lora J. Knight, a wealthy Chicago widow who, in 1928, asked Swedish architect Lennart Palme to build it "without moving a single tree." He did. Emerald Bay also offers hiking trails and picnic areas.

Farther along the shoreline are two other state parks. The first, 3 miles (4.8 km) north of Emerald Bay, is **D. L. Bliss State Park,** laced with scenic hiking trails, outlooks, and the outstanding **Lester Beach.** Farther north still is **Ed Z'berg Sugar Pine Point State Park,** with the 1903 **Hellman-Ehrman Mansion** *(closed Oct.–May, $$)*, a lighthouse, and a log cabin. A bike trail to Tahoe City starts here.

Desolation Wilderness *(map p. 303 A6)* consists of 63,000 acres (25,495 ha) of alpine and subalpine lakes, and can only be traversed by foot, bike, or horse *(tel 530/644-6048 for permits and regulations)*. A driveable part of the **Tahoe National Forest** *(map p. 303 A7, tel 530/265-4531)* can be found in the old **Foresthill Road District.** This stretch of road was once trod by Native Americans, then later by covered wagons and gold seekers. ■

Truckee & Donner Memorial State Park

The quaint little town of **Truckee** *(map p. 303 A7, Calif. 267, off I-80)* has emerged in recent years as a thriving place to visit, complete with a tolerably cute historic shopping district and several decent eateries. The town was founded in the mid-19th century, first as a stagecoach stop, then as a home to railroad workers maintaining the transcontinental railroad. Later decades saw the town become a center for the flourishing lumber and ice-harvesting industries.

In the early 20th century, the historic **Truckee Hotel** *(10007 Bridge St., tel 800/659-6921, www.truckeehotel.com)* briefly hosted actor Charlie Chaplin, who made his movie *The Gold Rush* (1925) here. A number of structures survive, including a **Chinese herb shop,** a reminder of the international workforce that built the railroads, and the **Old Truckee Jail** *(10142 Jibboom St., tel 530/582-0893)*, now a museum of the town's history.

Two miles (3.2 km) to the west is **Donner Memorial State Park** *(map p. 303 A7, off I-80, tel 530/582-7892)* on beautiful Donner Lake. Here you will find the **Emigrant Trail Museum** and **Donner Party Memorial.** The museum displays a rifle used by one member of the doomed 1846 band—forced by fierce weather to resort to cannibalism—to shoot a grizzly bear.

The world's single richest growing region, worth the heat to visit a rural culture intertwined with farming

Central Valley

Merced County Courthouse, built in 1875, is one of the region's oldest historical buildings.

BAY AREA p.231

Central Valley

Many visitors experience the great Central Valley of California in much the same way as the Spaniards, who were fearful of its "great heat and desolation"—they simply don't stop there. There is, to be frank, something to be said for such an attitude. The region is often "so hot that August comes on not like a month but like an affliction," to quote valley native Joan Didion. September, the beginning of fall in much of the civilized world, is often even hotter.

CENTRAL COAST p.171

Workers handpick cherries at family-run Simonian Farm in Clovis, north of Fresno.

NOT TO BE MISSED:

But in winter and spring, the valley can be an intoxicating, uniquely Californian place to visit. Then, as the heat slackens and the tule fogs rise up, earth and sky, as the native poet William Everson says, become "one mingle of color." The harvest in, another on its way (the land never rests here), the valley thrums with enterprise and optimism.

You will find here in the countryside a wild admixture of cultures, of Mexican Americans, Hmong tribesmen, fourth-generation Portuguese, and fifth-generation Japanese. One gets a feeling for the culture, in the words of writer Gerald Haslem, the dean of valley authors, who writes of "biscuits and gravy for breakfast, or *chorizo con huevos para desayuno* . . . this domain remains in many ways closer to Lubbock or Stillwater than to Hollywood."

Regardless of culture, California's Central Valley comprises a huge chunk of the state—15 million acres (6,070,284 ha) in all, stretching 430 miles (692 km) in length and, at its midriff, 75 miles (120 km) in width. Enormous economic power rests in the Central Valley. In fact, the valley is the centerpiece of California's $37 billion agriculture industry. Today, more money is made here from raisins, strawberries, almonds, and the like in one year than has been made since 1848 in all of the state's gold mines put together. ■

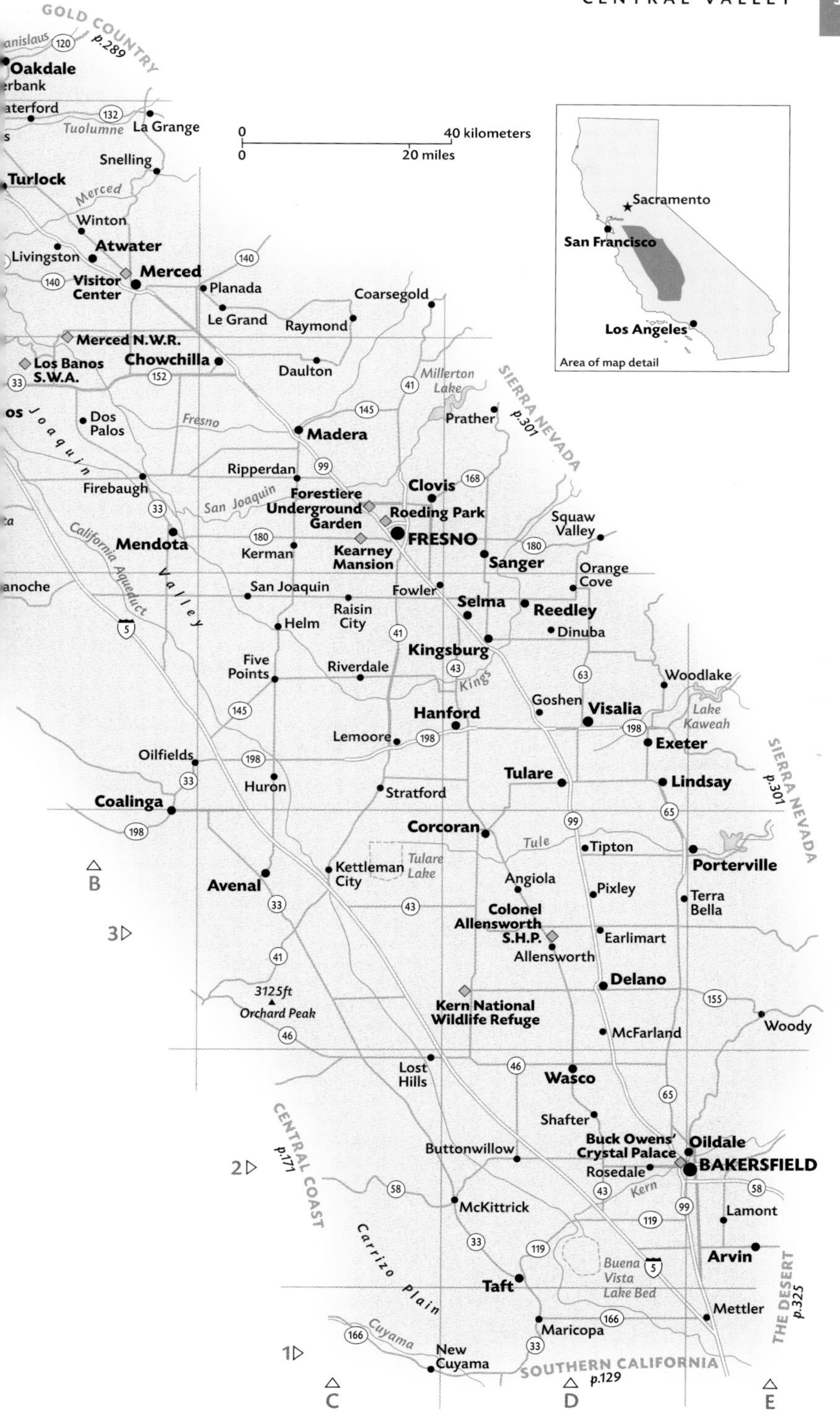

GOLD COUNTRY p.289
Oakdale
Turlock
Winton
Atwater
Livingston
Merced
Visitor Center
Planada
Le Grand
Raymond
Coarsegold
Merced N.W.R.
Los Banos S.W.A.
Chowchilla
Daulton
Millerton Lake
Prather
SIERRA NEVADA p.301
Dos Palos
Madera
Ripperdan
Firebaugh
Clovis
Forestiere Underground Garden
Roeding Park
FRESNO
Kearney Mansion
Mendota
Kerman
Squaw Valley
Sanger
Orange Cove
San Joaquin
Fowler
Raisin City
Selma
Reedley
Dinuba
Helm
Kingsburg
Five Points
Riverdale
Woodlake
Goshen
Visalia
Hanford
Lemoore
Lake Kaweah
Exeter
Oilfields
Huron
Tulare
Lindsay
Coalinga
Stratford
Corcoran
Tipton
Porterville
Avenal
Kettleman City
Tulare Lake
Angiola
Pixley
Terra Bella
Colonel Allensworth S.H.P.
Allensworth
Earlimart
Delano
3125ft Orchard Peak
Kern National Wildlife Refuge
McFarland
Woody
Lost Hills
Wasco
Shafter
Buck Owens' Crystal Palace
Oildale
BAKERSFIELD
Buttonwillow
Rosedale
CENTRAL COAST p.171
McKittrick
Lamont
Carrizo Plain
Arvin
Taft
Buena Vista Lake Bed
Mettler
Maricopa
THE DESERT p.325
New Cuyama
SOUTHERN CALIFORNIA p.129
0 40 kilometers
0 20 miles
Sacramento
San Francisco
Los Angeles
Area of map detail

Fresno

The story of Fresno, the raisin capital and the Central Valley's biggest city, goes a long way toward explaining the serendipitous *and* intentional nature of the valley's agricultural success. Founded as a station along the Southern Pacific line in 1872, the town held little allure for its original settlers. They named it Fresno—Spanish for "dry ash." Today, however, Fresno reigns as the nation's most prolific producer of high-value farm products, the Tuscany of the western United States.

Designed by Arthur Erickson, Fresno's angular City Hall echoes the Sierra Nevada to the east.

Fresno
319 C5
Visitor Information
Fresno Convention & Visitors Bureau, 1550 E. Shaw Ave., Fresno
559/981-5500, 800/788-0836
www.fresnocvb.org

Reedley
319 D4
Visitor Information
City Administration, 1717 9th St., Reedley
559/637-4200
www.reedley.com

At the turn of the 20th century, fruit growing was successful, but the marketing of Fresno's biggest cash crop, raisins, was so pitiable that many growers sold them under dubious Spanish labels. Then, in 1915, a head of the California Raisin Exchange "happened upon a young woman drying her curly jet-black hair under a red bonnet in the front yard of her Fresno home," writes Kevin Starr in *Inventing the Dream*. "[The executive] glimpsed what would eventually be one of the most famous trademarks in history . . . the Sun Maid, a marketing image so successful in its suggestions of health, abundance, and rural charm that in 1920 the Cooperative took Sun Maid as its formal name." The rest, as a glance along the shelf at any grocery store will tell you, is history.

As a travel destination, Fresno has improved over the past decade. One attraction is the **Blossom Trail,** a 62-mile (100 km) self-guided tour *(maps at 2220 Tulare St., www.gofresnocounty.com)* through orchards, vineyards, and wildflower meadows. March is the best time to view the blossoms. Along the way are growers such as **Simonian Farms** *(S. Clovis St., off Calif. 99, tel 559/237-2294, www.simonianfarms.com)*, growing more than a hundred kinds of fruit and vegetables.

Also along the drive is the quaint town of **Reedley,** named for wheat baron Thomas Law Reed, and it's worth a stop at the **Mennonite Quilt Center** *(1012 G St., Reedley, tel 559/638-3560, www.mennonitequiltcenter.com, closed Sun.)*, where you can see patient craftsfolk at work on their beautiful—and rare—quilts (buy one, it would make a wonderful family heirloom).

Fresno itself has some (sometimes eccentric) historical sites. The best is the **Forestiere Underground Gardens,** part of the

INSIDER TIP:

Spring is a great time to visit the Forestiere Underground Gardens, as orange blossom fragrance fills the subterranean courtyards.

—KENNY LING
National Geographic contributor

underground retreat of Baldasare Forestiere. Between 1906 and 1950, Forestiere sculpted a subterranean home with bedrooms, kitchen, library, and even a walk-under aquarium. More extraordinary still are the huge, productive skylit gardens and orchards from which he not only fed himself but also sold surplus crops.

More conventional is the **Kearney Mansion** *(Kearney Blvd., 7 miles/11 km W of downtown Fresno, tel 559/441-0862, www.valleyhistory.org, closed a.m. & Mon.–Thurs., $$)*. Built by the raisin king, Theodore Kearney, between 1900 and 1903, the house, constructed in French Renaissance style and furnished in keeping, is on the National Register of Historic Places. It is now a museum of local history.

For a different impression of early Fresno life, see the restored **Meux Home Museum** *(1007 R St., Fresno, tel 559/233-8007, www.meux.mus.ca.us, closed Mon.–Thurs. & Jan., $)*. Its 19th-century owner, T. R. Meux, was a Confederate surgeon.

Born in Fresno, author William Saroyan (1908–1981) spent many of his most productive years at 2729 W. Griffith Way. He lived to see many of his plays and novels produced on Broadway and rendered in films. But his enduring legacy is his collection of short stories about growing up in rustic Fresno, where immigrant tongues and oddball characters conjured a unique small-town drama.

The **Fresno Art Museum** is worth a visit for its Mexican and Impressionist collections, as well as American sculpture, native California art, and works on paper.

The **Fresno Chaffee Zoo** *(894 W. Belmont Ave., Fresno, tel 559/498-5910, www.fresnochaffeezoo.org, $$)*, located in **Roeding Park,** is home to more than 700 birds, mammals, and reptiles. Visit the Tropical Rain Forest and catch a "Winged Wonders" show, a free-flight performance of eagles, hawks, vultures, and parrots. ■

Forestiere Underground Gardens

- 5021 W. Shaw Ave., 2 blocks E of Calif. 99, Fresno
- 559/271-0734
- Closed Mon.–Tues. & Dec.–Feb.
- $$

www.undergroundgardens.com

Fresno Art Museum

- 2233 N. 1st St., Fresno
- 559/441-4221
- Closed Mon.–Wed.
- $

www.fresnoartmuseum.org

EXPERIENCE: Basque Celebrations

Basques began immigrating to California during Spanish colonial times, and in the late 1800s they began to form distinct enclaves in the Central Valley. In Fresno, you can tuck in at half a dozen Basque restaurants scattered around town, but to really immerse yourself, visit during the annual Fresno Basque Club Festival *(www.nabasque.org/members/fresno.htm)*. Held the first Saturday in May, the festival features a huge outdoor picnic, complete with hearty lamb stew, pork loin, and spicy sausages. Eventgoers eat at a long communal table and then celebrate with traditional dancing. For other Basque festivals in the area, consult the Kern County Basque Club *(www.kcbasqueclub.com)*.

North of Fresno

Classic Californian small towns and some excellent wildlife refuges, offering many superb opportunities for bird-watchers, characterize the Central Valley country north of Fresno.

Modesto
318 A6
Visitor Information
Modesto Convention & Visitors Bureau, 1150 9th St., Suite C, Modesto
209/526-5586, 888/640-8467
www.visitmodesto.com

Merced
319 B6
Visitor Information
California Welcome Center, 710 W. 16th St., Merced
209/724-8104, 800/446-5353
www.yosemite-gateway.org

Modesto

Modesto, established in 1870 by the Central Pacific Railroad, was the inspiration for the classic film *American Graffiti* (1973)—filmmaker George Lucas, who grew up here, modeled the memorable cruising scenes in his film after Modesto's own teen scene. Another mark of true Californiana is the **Modesto Arch,** one of the few early 20th-century icons of civic pride still extant.

Modesto is also a foodie paradise—not so much for its restaurants as for its orchards, vineyards, and food producers. **Nick Sciabica & Sons** *(2150 Yosemite St., Modesto, tel 800/551-9612, www.sciabica.com)* has been growing olives and pressing fine oil for four generations. At the **Hilmar Cheese Company** *(9001 N. Lander St., Hilmar, tel 209/667-6076, www.hilmarcheese.com)* you can take a free factory tour and munch a wide selection of cheeses produced on the premises. Shop for locally grown almonds at the **Blue Diamond Growers Store** *(4800 Sisk Rd., Modesto, tel 209/545-6230, www.bluediamond.com).*

Merced & Around

South of Modesto is the town of Merced, known to many visitors as the gateway to Yosemite. Just west of town you'll find the **San Luis National Wildlife Refuge Complex** *(7376 S. Wolfsen Rd., Los Banos, S of Calif. 140 between Merced and Gustine, tel 209/826-3508, www.fws.gov/sanluis),* which consists of three separate refuges totaling some 27,000 acres (10,926 ha) around the San Joaquin River. **Merced National Wildlife Refuge** is a haven for flocks of snow geese and sandhill cranes. Similar birdlife, as well as tule elk, flourish farther west at the **San Luis National Wildlife Refuge** and the **San Joaquin River National Wildlife Refuge.** The latter has a spectacular spring wildflowers. For herons and migrating geese, visit the **Los Banos State Wildlife Area** *(18110 W. Henry Miller Ave., Los Banos, tel 209/826-0463).* ■

EXPERIENCE: The Madera Wine Trail

Visit the boutique wineries of Madera County, between Fresno and Yosemite, to enjoy some of the Central Valley's best wines. Your visit should include the old-timers like Ficklin Vineyards *(30246 Ave. 7½, Madera, tel 559/661-0075, www.ficklin.com)* and the newcomers Chateau Lasgoity *(11219 Rd. 26, Madera, tel 559/674-8291, www.chateaulasgoity.com)* and Idle Hour Winery *(41139 Calif. 41, Oakhurst, tel 559/760-9090, www.idlehourwinery.com),* near Yosemite's south entrance. Download a map of the wineries at *www.maderawinetrail.com* and create your own itinerary.

South of Fresno

More wildlife refuges feature south of Fresno, but it is history that draws visitors to this hot, hot area. Agriculture rules in this region, and the towns have grown up around packing stations and food-processing companies.

Hanford

With its pleasant atmosphere, quiet ways, and railroad-era buildings, you would never guess that little **Hanford** *(W from Calif. 99 on Calif. 198)* was the scene of a bloody and historically important feud. In May 1880, a number of settlers in nearby Mussel Slough, understandably believing that the land that they alone had developed belonged to them, were outraged when the Southern Pacific Railroad decided to sell off several parcels from under their feet. When the settlers refused to move out, the railroad arranged for them to be forcibly removed. Guns were drawn on both sides, and seven men died, including two railroad employees. Five surviving settlers were later convicted and sentenced to eight months in the San Jose jail. They emerged as heroes. Later romanticized by Frank Norris in his antibusiness novel *The Octopus*, the Mussel Slough feud marked an important turning point in the campaign to rein in the powerful California railroad barons.

Today Hanford bakes lazily in the California sun. It is best known for the remains of its once thriving Chinatown. You can still tour **China Alley** and the historic 1893 **Taoist Temple** by contacting the visitor center. The worthwhile **Hanford Carnegie Museum** *(109 E. 8th St., tel 559/584-1367, www.hanfordcarnegiemuseum.org, closed Sun.–Mon., $)* focuses on local history and customs.

The "Bakersfield Sound"

To music buffs, Bakersfield (see p. 324) is the Nashville of the West. Local hero Buck Owens (1929–2006) had 21 number one hits on the *Billboard* country charts, including "Tiger by the Tail" and "Act Naturally." Hard-edged Merle Haggard (1937–) was born and raised in Oildale, on the outskirts of Bakersfield. His classic "Okie From Muskogee" is one of the great country music anthems of the last 50 years. Together, Owens and Haggard helped craft the "Bakersfield Sound," a rough-hewn West Coast version of the Nashville sound. Today you can catch live country music up and down the valley, including at Buck Owens' Crystal Palace *(map p.319 D2, 2800 Buck Owens Blvd., Bakersfield, tel 661/328-7560, www.buckowens.com).*

Visalia

A few miles to the east of Hanford on Calif. 198, Visalia was founded in 1852 by a bear hunter named Nathaniel Vise. It has since grown in classic Central Valley fashion, dominated by packinghouses, food-processing companies, and growers.

Two places in Visalia are worth a stop. Pay a visit to the **Tulare County Museum**

Hanford

319 D4

Visitor Information

Hanford Visitor Agency, 113 Court St. #306, Hanford

559/582-5024

www.visithanford.com

Visalia

319 D4

Visitor Information

Visalia Convention & Visitors Bureau, 303 E. Acequia Ave., Visalia

559/334-0141

www.visitvisalia.com

Lake Kaweah
319 E4

Allensworth
319 D3

(27000 S. Mooney Blvd., tel 559/733-6616, http://co.tulare.ca.us, closed Tues.–Wed.) to see a copy of the famed "End of the Trail Monument" and many artifacts detailing ancient Yokut Indian culture. Distinguished by its two 12-ton marble Shih Tzu lions, the **Central California Chinese Cultural Center** *(500 S. Akers St., tel 559/625-4545, by appt. only)* contains several fine holdings of ancient Chinese art and culture.

Tricolored blackbirds may be hardest to spot in summer.

Bakersfield
319 E2

Visitor Information

Bakersfield Convention & Visitors Bureau, 515 Truxtun Ave., Bakersfield

661/852-7282, 866/425-7353

www.visitbakersfield.com

Lake Kaweah

A popular outing (and a good way to beat the heat) is to head east on Calif. 198 to Lake Kaweah, in the foothills west of Sequoia National Park. Here, during the 1880s, a socialistic experiment called the Kaweah Colony briefly flourished.

Allensworth

A utopia of a different kind can be found farther south, west of Calif. 99 near Delano. Founded in 1908 by Col. Allen Allensworth, the highest ranking African-American military officer of his day, Allensworth was a "self-governing" town where liberated blacks could live free of discrimination. From 1909 to 1919, Allensworth thrived, but in the 1920s, the town's water supplies ran low, and a slow exodus began. By the late 1950s, it was a ghost town. In the 1970s, preservationists began restoring the town, which is now **Colonel Allensworth State Historic Park** *(Cty. Rd. J22, off Calif. 43 N of Wasco, tel 661/849-3433, www.parks.ca.gov, closed to vehicles Mon.–Thurs.)*.

Bird-watchers should visit the **Kern National Wildlife Refuge** *(19 miles/30.5 km W of Delano, off Calif. 155, tel 661/725-2767, www.fws.gov/kern)*, southwest of Allensworth. This managed wetland in the San Joaquin Valley supports a breeding colony of the endangered tricolored blackbird. If it is too hot to hike, there is a 6-mile (9.6 km) self-guided driving tour.

Bakersfield

The fine **Kern County Museum/Lori Brock Children's Discovery Center** *(3801 Chester Ave., tel 661/868-8400, www.kcmuseum.org, closed Mon.–Tues., $$)* in Bakersfield showcases Native American artifacts and local history. But the real reason to visit this town is for its music (see sidebar p. 323).

East from Bakersfield, Calif. 58 climbs through the wildly scenic Tehachapi Mountains to **Tehachapi,** a gateway to the Mojave (see p. 328) ■

One of the trendiest places to visit, attracting spiritual and ecological adventurers alike

The Desert

Cactus at the Living Desert wildlife and botanical park

The Desert

The vast area known to most Californians as "the desert" is actually two deserts. The northern one, Death Valley and the Mojave, is kept dry by the rain shadow cast by the Sierra to the west. The southern desert of Joshua Tree and Anza-Borrego is a small part of the Colorado Desert, itself part of the Sonoran Desert. The rain shadow here is provided by the Peninsular Range.

Death Valley dunes rise near Stovepipe Wells.

NOT TO BE MISSED:

- Death Valley's one-of-a-kind desert moonscapes **330–331**
- Rock climbing and trekking in Joshua Tree National Park **334–335**
- Riding the Palm Springs Aerial Tramway into the mountains **336–337**
- Cycling the San Andreas Fault **337**
- Glamorous Rat Pack hangouts in Palm Springs **338–339**
- Hiking the fantastic oasis canyons near Palm Springs **340**
- Communing with desert animals and plants from around the world at the Living Desert **341**
- Wildflower and star gazing in Anza-Borrego Desert State Park **343**
- Fishing and boating on the vast accidental lake known as the Salton Sea **344**

This is a land of extremes. In summer, temperatures soar by day to 110 or 120°F (43 or 48°C), plunging by 50° (10°C) at night. Winds shape entire dune canyons in a single season. Water is a rumor for most of the year, except in spring, when flash floods can carve new landscapes overnight. These extremes, paradoxically, have made the desert even more enticing to Californians. Since the 1920s, the Hollywood elite have been transfixed by the oasis of Palm Springs. In recent years, it has again become fashionable, attracting not only the rich and famous but also New Age crystal-gazers and a growing contingent who come to see its modernist architecture.

Desert extremes have wrought a highly diverse ecology. In the far north is the Owens Valley, its beautiful pale dust the consequence of lands being drained by Los Angeles's thirst for cheap water. More superlatives are to be found in Death Valley National Park, while Joshua Tree National Park is the showstopper of the desert experience.

The basics of desert travel bear repeating. If you will be camping in the desert overnight, register at one of the sign-up boards, usually found at visitor centers and trailheads. Take at least one gallon (4 L) of water per person per day just for drinking; for a strenuous trip, take two gallons (8 L) each. If you are going *anywhere* except along well-known trails, take a map and

CENTRAL VALLEY p.317

compass. In spring and winter, check at ranger stations for flood alerts.

To appreciate the desert's natural wonders, pack a few extras. A small telescope will enrich the powerful experience of the desert night sky. Constellation maps and guides to local flora are available at major visitor centers. ■

Toward Death Valley

The sites and towns that dot the Mojave Desert are a study in stubbornness, hinting at the tenacious if somewhat wistful pioneering mind-set of those who struggled to arrive here, and settled the area, in the 1800s. Here, as Ambrose Bierce once said, the "horrible is allied with the beautiful." The inhospitable terrain permits few roads, but the intrepid with time to explore will find opportunities for many memorable hikes. Even from your car, there is beauty—wrapped in dust and wind, but beauty nonetheless—to see as you go to Death Valley.

The exhausting climb up Mount Whitney involves an incredible 97 switchbacks.

Edwards Air Force Base

✉ 1 S. Rosamond Blvd., Edwards AFB

☎ 661/277-3517

🕒 Tours by appt. twice monthly on Fridays 9 a.m.–1 p.m.; book 2 weeks in advance

www.edwards.af.mi

The town of **Mojave** *(map p. 327 B4)*, gateway to the eponymous desert, is surrounded by intriguing sites, including **Edwards Air Force Base,** birthplace of supersonic flight and many other aviation firsts. The base's Air Force Flight Test Center Museum provides a fascinating review. The NASA Dryden Flight Research Center maintains the **Aerospace Exploration Gallery** *(38256 Sierra Hwy., Palmdale, tel 661/276-2662, www.nasa.gov/centers, tours by appt.)*, which features exhibits tracing NASA's exciting past, present, and future in outer space. In springtime, the 1,745-acre **Antelope Valley California Poppy Reserve** *(1501 Lancaster Rd., tel 661/946-6092, www.parks.ca.gov)*, 25 miles (40 km) west of Palmdale, bursts into audacious color with its bloom of native wildflowers.

Calif. 14 leads north to Death Valley National Park (see pp. 330–331) via **Red Rock Canyon State Park** *(Ridgecrest, 25 miles N of Mojave on Calif. 14, tel 661/946-6092, www.parks .ca.gov)*, geological wonder and

INSIDER TIP:

If you are driving to Mammoth Lakes (see p. 314) via U.S. 395, stop at Manzanar National Historic Site, where Japanese Americans were incarcerated during World War II.

—ERIN STONE
National Geographic contributor

setting for the opening scenes in *Jurassic Park* (1993).

The town of **Independence** stands not far from the ruins of old Fort Independence, where, in the 1860s, there occurred a number of often violent uprisings by the Paiute. The fort closed in 1872, after the Paiute were violently suppressed. Today the main attraction is the **Eastern California Museum,** which houses a detailed collection of pioneer and Native American history and a re-created village made from old buildings.

South of Independence is the site of the Manzanar Relocation Camp, where 10,000 Japanese Americans were interned during 1942–45, after the bombing of Pearl Harbor. This relic of a dark period in the nation's history has been marked as the **Manzanar National Historic Site.**

To reach Death Valley National Park, you turn east off U.S. 395 onto Calif. 136 just south of **Lone Pine** (see sidebar). Near the junction is dry **Owens Lake,** named after Richard Owen, a member of Frémont's 1845 expedition. The lake was a viable waterway for steamers into the early 1900s, but since the arrival of the Los Angeles Aqueduct in 1913, which sapped most of the feeder streams, it has shrunk away to nothing. It contains some of the world's largest sodium silicate deposits.

Along Calif. 136 are several ghost towns, including **Keeler** *(map p. 327 B5)*, a former mining town with a museum and ghost mines to explore. **Cerro Gordo** *(map p. 327 B5, tel 760/876-5030, www.cerrogordo.us)* was once known as California's Comstock, producing more than 4.5 million ounces (127,570 kg) of silver, lead, and zinc during the 19th century. ■

Lone Pine

The little town of Lone Pine, established in the 1850s, is a base for climbers and skiers on Mount Whitney, whose peak soars to 14,495 feet (4,418 m) 25 miles (40 km) to the west. Whitney Portal, several miles west of Lone Pine, is the start of several hiking trails, including the one that leads to the summit. Movie enthusiasts know Lone Pine for its October film festival *(tel 760/876-9103, www.lonepinefilmfestival.org)* featuring old cowboy movies. The visitor information center has a map to movie sites. Among the classics filmed around here were *Gunga Din* (1939) and *The Lone Ranger* (1956).

Independence
Map: 327 B6
Visitor Information
Tel: 760/878-0084
www.independence-ca.com

Eastern California Museum
Address: 155 N. Grant St., Independence
Tel: 760/878-0258
$: Donation
www.inyocountry.us/exmuseum

Manzanar National Historic Site
Map: 327 B6
Address: US 395, 9 miles N of Lone Pine
Tel: 760/878-2194
www.nps.gov/manz

Lone Pine
Map: 327 B6
Visitor Information
Address: Chamber of Commerce, 120 S. Main St., Lone Pine
Tel: 760/876-4444
www.lonepinechamber.org

Death Valley National Park

Perhaps more than any one of its singular geological wonders, it is the ride down into Death Valley on Calif. 190, through the dusty Panamint Mountains, that lingers in the memory. It is a descent of grandeur. There is no better way to appreciate the entire sweep of Death Valley National Park. Take it slowly.

Visitors get close to a shallow pool of salty water at Badwater Basin, the lowest point in the U.S.

Death Valley National Park

327 B6–C5

Visitor Information

Visitor Center, Calif. 190, Furnace Creek

760/786-3200

www.nps.gov/deva

Scotty's Castle

327 B6

760/786-2392, 877/444-6777

$$$

www.recreation.gov

The best time to visit is February through mid-April, when the desert wildflowers bloom and temperatures remain tolerable. Winter is the most crowded season. Visitors coming in summer will need an air-conditioned car, a supply of water, and a carefully timed plan: Walking is bearable very early or very late in the day. You will find accommodations, restaurants, and a store in **Furnace Creek** *(map p. 327 C5)*.

In the far north of Death Valley, at **Mesquite Spring** *(map p. 327 B6)*, on a sharp turn in Calif. 267, is one of the stranger manifestations of émigré architectural fever in the state. It is **Scotty's Castle,** a Moorish-style mansion built in the 1920s. Guides in period costumes give a lively account of the castle's builders. A few miles to the west is the **Ubehebe Crater** *(map p. 327 B6)*, thought to have been caused by volcanic activity.

Several popular natural wonders within a few miles of Furnace Creek (all well marked) include the **Devil's Golf Course,** a huge salt pan where winds push boulders across the slick surface during rare rains. Farther east is the **Artist's Palette** *(map p. 327 C5)*, a series of hills colored with a rainbow of various mineral hues. The colors are especially stunning around dawn and dusk. The same is true of nearby **Golden Canyon.**

If you have time and the heat is not too intense, explore the 4-mile (6.4 km) **Gower Gulch Loop,** a trail that winds through colorful badlands, multi-hued canyons, and old borax mines.

Though it lacks the romance of silver and gold, borax—a chemical deposited when alkaline lakes evaporate—was one of few valuable resources found in Death Valley. It was mined here from the 1880s. The **Borax Museum** at Furnace Creek tells the story of the mines through its collection of wagons and machinery. The **Harmony Borax Works Interpretive Trail**—at a quarter mile (.4 km) long, manageable in all but the worst heat—starts at the Borax Works parking area north of Furnace Creek.

Don't leave Death Valley without visiting one of its spectacular viewpoints—ideally at sunrise or sunset. **Zabriskie Point** *(map p. 327 C5)* is the site of the 1970 Antonioni movie of the same name. One of the valley's most memorable sights, it has inspired dozens of well-known plein air painters from around the world.

About 20 miles (32 km) south of Furnace Creek is **Dante's View** *(map p. 327 C5)*, which overlooks the valley from the Black Mountains. From here, you can see the 14,495-foot (4,418 m) peak of Mount Whitney and **Badwater Basin** *(map p. 327 C5)*, site of the lowest point in the U.S. (282 feet/86 m below sea level). West of Badwater, the land rises impressively, reaching 11,049 feet (3,367 m) at the top of **Telescope Peak,** only a few miles away. ■

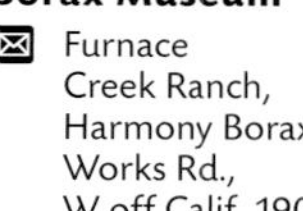

Borax Museum
Furnace Creek Ranch, Harmony Borax Works Rd., W off Calif. 190
760/786-3215

Singing Sands

With such place-names as Cowhole Mountain and Blind Hills, **Mojave National Preserve** *(map p. 327 D4, tel 760/252-6100, www.nps.gov/moja)*, more than three million desolate acres, lies south of I-15, southeast of Death Valley.

If you travel here, be sure to see the unique sand formation of **Kelso Dunes,** near Kelso. This sea of delicate, wind-created sand sculpture spreads out at the base of Providence Mountain. Golden-rose quartz grains, blown down from Afton Canyon over the course of 25,000 years, create a richly colored palette. Even more engaging is the unmistakable loud thrumming noise caused by loose sand sliding down the steep 600-foot (183 m) dunes. Study of such dunes has led some anthropologists to link their subaural wavelengths to religious experiences by native peoples.

This part of the Mojave contains a number of other unusual geological sites. North from Kelso on Kelso-Cima Road are extensive ancient lava flows traced by fossilized tube worms. This road takes you to **Cima Dome** *(map p. 327 D4)*, a high rounded hunk of rock thrust some 1,500 feet (457 m) above the desert floor. Turning back south from Kelso on Kelbecker Road, visit the **Amboy Crater** *(map p. 327 D3)*, a 250-foot (76 m) cinder cone.

Water, Water

There is, indisputably, a lot of it: Every year, some 200 million acre-feet (each enough to flood an acre of land under a foot of water) fall on California, two-thirds of it in the northern half of the state. And therein lies the rub. The water falls in the wrong place. It tends to evaporate or go where no one wants it to go. And most population growth has occurred in the south, a land of few rivers and even fewer lakes and streams.

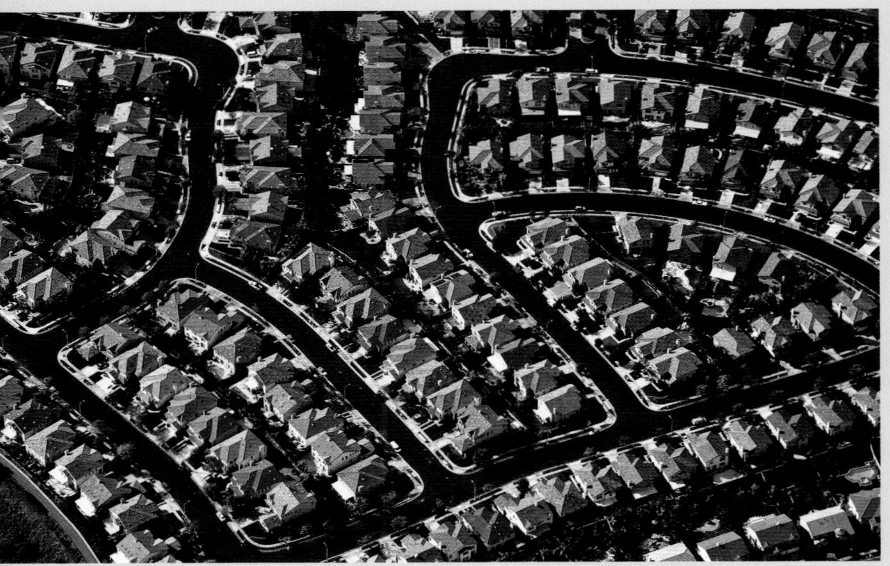

It takes a lot of water to support California's suburbs, like this one in San Bernadino.

The story of the first aqueduct is a familiar one to most Californians. A turn-of-the-20th-century Los Angeles business cabal, worried about the impact of drought on land prices, convinced a panicked citizenry to underwrite a 230-mile (370 km) water canal from Owens Lake. Visionary engineer William Mulholland built the aqueduct, the water from which was promptly used to "green up" San Fernando Valley real estate. The fat cats profited, but the public still needed water. A new study was commissioned, and a new aqueduct was built, this one from Sacramento. More water. More suburban growth. The story was repeated again and again.

The pattern persists to this day. Yet as suburban growth continues, many in California have come to question the belief that water needs can be filled by importing more and more water from far reaches of the state. Take the case of metropolitan Los Angeles. Today the region has 45 percent of the population on 6 percent of the state's habitable land—but only .06 percent of the state's total stream flow. With the population predicted to grow from 16 to 24 million over the next few decades, the region would seem ripe for yet another large-scale public works project.

Recent experience, however, suggests otherwise, says UCLA's Martha Davis, who

What Water Does in California

Left undirected and unrestrained, water has had a profound impact on the topography of California. Four interesting manifestations of this impact are:

Underground rivers (Mojave Desert): Created 15,000 years ago when sedimentation on above-ground rivers hardened to form a sandy "lid."

Alluvial fans (Death Valley): Formed when periodic downpours loosen hillside rubble and carry it to the bottom, creating fan-shaped mounds. *Bajadas,* also in deserts, are essentially spread-out, large-scale alluvial fans.

Badlands (statewide): Thin spires, thick columns, and undulating folds carved into soft sandstone hills by surface runoff.

Underground caves (throughout Sierra parks): Made by groundwater percolating through soluble rock.

studies water-use issues and the environment. In 1990, a drought that had begun in 1987 unexpectedly intensified. For the first time, the Metropolitan Water District mandated water rationing. "The response was dramatic," says Davis. "In 1990, water sales peaked at an all-time high of 2.6 million acre-feet; by 1993, these sales had plummeted to 1.5 million acre-feet . . . We have fundamentally changed the water demand curve for the southland. We are supporting more people with less (not more) water."

But can such policies really meet the water needs of L.A.'s future population? Ultimately such questions are resolved not by public policy planners but by politicians, who must balance the short-term needs of their constituents with the longer-term needs of the state as a whole. The former usually prevail.

Yet an enlightened public is beginning to alter water politics as well. A good example is the emergence of the Los Angeles River as an important political touchstone. For decades treated as little more than a giant drainage ditch, the river in recent years has become the focus of an intense debate over urban water use. A group named Friends of the Los Angeles River (FOLAR) has successfully fought to restore parts of the stream to a more natural state. The result is striking. Yet whether that kind of sustained civic activism can alter the larger patterns of water use is still unclear. The hand of *Homo sapiens,* after all, has made southern California what it is today.

Sand dune formations are no match for the hot sun in Death Valley National Park.

Joshua Tree National Park

Although there is much to see within this 800,000-acre park, no one element has attracted as much comment, speculation, and even poetry as the Joshua tree, a plant so biomorphically abstract that it might have been designed by a demented artist—its branches set at right angles to its trunk and then bent upward, as in prayerful supplication.

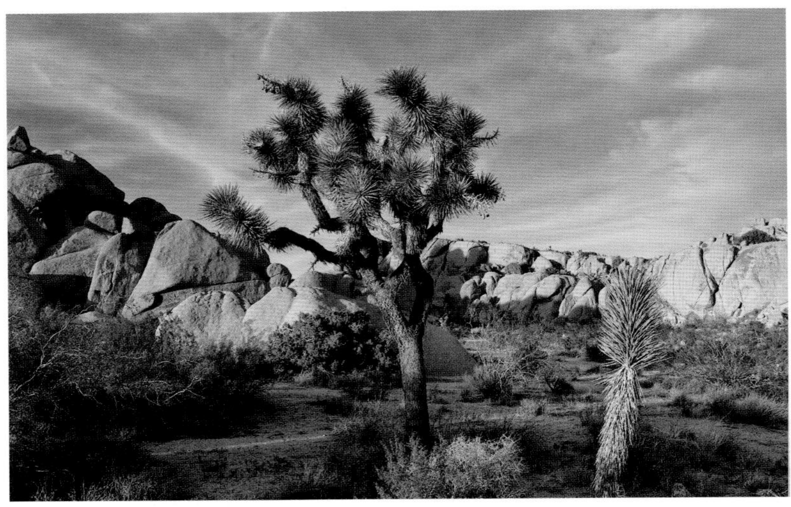

A characteristic sight: The afternoon sun warms a Joshua tree and rock formation near Split Rock.

Joshua Tree National Park

327 C3–D3

Visitor Information

Oasis Visitor Center, Calif. 62 & Adobe Rd., Twentynine Palms

760/367-5500

$ per person, $$ per vehicle

www.nps.gov/jotr

Not all have fallen in love with the Joshua tree. Capt. John C. Frémont, the first English-speaking traveler to record the trees, spoke of "their stiff and ungraceful forms . . . the most repulsive tree in the vegetable kingdom." To California Mormons, migrating back to Utah in the 1850s, the tree's branches seemed like prophetic guideposts. They promptly named the tree for the prophet Joshua. To naturalists such as Donald Peattie, the dean of California nature writing, they "look more like the blasted skeleton of a tree which has gone all awry." To many contemporary hikers, however, the Joshua tree's spareness, silhouetted against the evening sky, embodies the natural solitude they seek in the park.

Perhaps the most important natural aspect of the park is its merging of two distinct deserts: the hot, dry Colorado at its eastern end with the slightly wetter, cooler Mojave in the west. In the former grow the ground-hugging creosote bush and the spread-eagled ocotillo. In the latter, Joshua trees proliferate, as well as several distinctive groves of fan palms. The park represents a wide diversity of geological activity, its stones and alluvial fans and varnished rock producing a kind of desert mosaic.

Most visitors spend their time in the (slightly) cooler west. The focal point near the northern entrance is the **Oasis of Mara,** long the home of the Chemehuevi before becoming a popular stop for miners in the late 1800s. Later, cattle ranchers arrived. In the 1920s came homesteaders and the onslaught of cactus poaching—poaching that became so severe as to cause one prominent Pasadena matron, M. H. Hoyt, to lead a drive to win government protection, achieved in 1936 when the Roosevelt administration created Joshua Tree National Monument; in 1994 it was declared a national park.

Camping and Activities

If you plan on camping—and during the spring many do—the campground at nearby **Indian Cove** *(tel 877/444-6777)* is hard to beat. This is also the center of activity for the growing number of rock-climbing enthusiasts *(Joshua Tree Rock Climbing School, tel 760/366-4745, www.joshuatreerock climbing.com)*. Not far away, off Canyon Road, is the **Fortynine Palms Oasis.** Here a 1.5-mile (2.4 km) trail takes you to a desert oasis, replete with fan palms and animals slaking their thirst amid rare desert shade.

Another favorite drive and hike begins at the west entrance on Park Boulevard. Go south from the entrance station to **Hidden Valley,** a onetime redoubt of cattle rustlers and colorful ne'er-do-wells. Farther south is the trailhead for **Lost Horse Mine,** about 2 miles (3.2 km) away. (Do not enter this, or any other, mine.) Farther south still is **Keys View,** an overlook at 5,815 feet (1,772 m). A number of the more ambitious trails also originate around here *(maps from the visitor center)*. Though walking is the best way to experience the park, there is also the well-marked **Geology Motor Tour,** an 18-mile (29 km) self-guided trek through dramatic rockscapes. With more time, explore the central and eastern parts of the park. The former affords a rare glimpse at a desert-to-desert transition zone. Stop at the **Cholla Cactus Garden**. Here grows the teddybear cholla, a.k.a. the jumping cholla, named for the tendency of its spiny needles to "jump" onto the clothes of passing hikers. Elite Land Tours *(tel 760/318-1200, www.elitelandtours.com)* offers in-depth naturalist-guided tours by Humvee. ■

Hidden Oasis

South from the Cholla Cactus Garden is **Cottonwood Spring** *(map p. 327 D3, also accessible from I-10)*, one of the best kept secrets in Joshua Tree National Park and a welcome oasis. The spring, formed eons ago by an earthquake, was long used by Native Americans; their mortars, clay pots, and various other reminders of habitation can be seen throughout the spring area. Bighorn sheep can often be spotted in the Cottonwood Wash. For the hardy, the **Lost Palms Oasis Trail** rewards the 8-mile (12.8 km) effort with great views and the largest grove of fan palms in the park.

Palm Springs

The ultimate American oasis had its beginnings in 1885, when a San Francisco lawyer established a health resort in the place that had always been the home of the Cahuilla. Revivified as a celebrity hideaway in the 1920s by the likes of Rudolph Valentino and Marlene Dietrich, remade again as a permanent home to the ultra-rich by Bob Hope and Frank Sinatra, Palm Springs owes its irresistible charms to one simple fact: It has water.

Palm Springs's pleasant desert climate facilitates al fresco dining in downtown restaurants.

Palm Springs

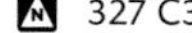
327 C3

Visitor Information

Visitor Center, 2901 N. Palm Canyon Dr., Palm Springs

760/778-8418, 800/347-7746

www.visitpalmsprings.com

Today, after an interregnum of benign neglect, Palm Springs has been revitalized with youthful vigor. The draw for the traveler can be summed up in five attractions: sun, pool, spa, golf, and more golf—more than 110 courses carpet Palm Springs and the seven adjoining communities that make up the Coachella Valley, rimmed by dramatically sculpted mauve mountains. A sixth might be shopping: **Palm Canyon Drive** and **El Paseo,** in nearby **Palm Desert** *(map p. 327 C3, visitor information, Visitor Center, 73-470 El Paseo, Ste. F-7, tel 760/568-1441 or 800/873-2428, www.palm-desert.org)*, are both upscale shopping areas where people-watching during the high season *(Oct.–May)* is a draw in itself.

One of the few unashamed tourist traps in California truly worth seeing is the **Palm Springs Aerial Tramway** *(1 Tramway Rd., tel 760/325-1449 or*

800/515-TRAM, www.pstramway.com, $$$$). Spanning the 2.5 miles (4 km) between the desert floor and the top of Mount San Jacinto, the tramway, which has the longest single span of cable in the world, was completed in 1963. The air-conditioned tram, which revolves through 360 degrees, offers fantastic views of desert and mountains. At the top, 8,516 feet (2,595 m) up, an upscale restaurant offers amazing views, while **Mount San Jacinto State Park** *(tel 951/659-2607, www.parks.ca.gov)* offers more than 54 miles (87 km) of trails.

Palm Springs Culture

Another magnificent aspect of the Palm Springs scene is the popular **Palm Springs Air Museum,** which has one of the largest collections of flying World War II planes, along with rare and original combat photography and an extensive collection of World War II artifacts, uniforms, and memorabilia.

The **Palm Springs Art Museum** has an outstanding collection (see p. 339) and a well-curated series of changing exhibitions. It also holds a number of Native American artifacts and offers concerts and lectures.

A small but engaging historical stop is **Village Green Heritage Center** *(221 S. Palm Canyon Rd.),* featuring the **Agua Caliente Cultural Museum** and the **McCallum Adobe** *(tel 760/323-8297, closed Mon.–Tues., a.m. Wed.–Sun., and June–Sept., $),* displaying artifacts of Palm Springs's original settler, John Guthrie McCallum. Also named for McCallum is the **McCallum Theatre for the Performing Arts** *(7300 Fred Waring Dr., Palm Desert, tel 760/340-2787, www.mccallumtheatre.com),* on the campus of College of the Desert. The McCallum presents a full program including theater and music.

Palm Desert's streets are enlivened by more than 150 public sculptures, notably along the ritzy El Paseo boulevard and in the 72-acre (29 ha) Civic Center Park *(San Pablo Ave.);* not to be missed in the park are David Phelps's "The Dreamer" and Dee Clements's 88-foot (27 m) "Holocaust Memorial." Pick up a map and booklet at the visitor center.

Scenic Calif. 111 links Palm Springs with Palm Desert and the other neighboring desert communities, including **La Quinta,** known for its premier golf courses and **La Quinta Resort & Club,** the region's most illustrious spa. ■

Palm Springs Air Museum

✉ 745 N. Gene Autry Trail, Palm Springs

☎ 760/778-6262

$ $$$

www.air-museum.org

Palm Springs Art Museum

✉ 72-567 Hwy. 111 Palm Springs

☎ 760/346-5600

🕒 Closed Mon.

$ $$ (free 1st Thurs. of month)

www.psmuseum.org

Agua Caliente Cultural Museum

✉ 219 S. Palm Canyon Dr. Palm Springs

☎ 760/778-1079

🕒 Closed Mon.–Tues. & a.m. Sun.

www.accmuseum.org

EXPERIENCE: Tracing the San Andreas Fault

To trace the San Andreas, California's notorious earthquake fault, take a sharp turn into the desert north of Los Angeles. As it reaches Palm Springs and the Coachella Valley, the San Andreas splinters into smaller but no less violent faults. For those who know what to look for (like sudden changes in desert vegetation), several of these faults can be spotted from the top of the **Palm Springs Aerial Tramway**. One of the smaller faults is also responsible for the string of hot springs along the valley's northern flank. Visitors can cycle the fault with **PS Bike Tours** *(tel 760/777-0120, www.psbiketours.com, $$)* or drive it on an **Elite Land Tours** *(tel 760/318-1200, www.elitelandtours.com, $$)* Hummer adventure.

Glamour in the Desert

There was a time in the not-too-distant past when Palm Springs conjured not wealth and glamour but, rather, the old, the outdated, and the déclassé. But since the late 1980s, when celebrity singer Sonny Bono was elected mayor (he later became its congressman before dying in a skiing accident in 1998), Palm Springs has staged an impressive comeback.

Modernist homes like the 1946 Kaufmann House have helped renew interest in Palm Springs.

One reason is that a new generation of urbanites has discovered the blessings of the desert. The blessings come in the form of quietude, raw natural surroundings, and a relaxed style perhaps best characterized as "desert Zen." Add to this the upsurge of interest in postwar modernist architecture, which the Springs has in abundance, and you have, as the trendy *Vanity Fair* recently put it, "a major revival."

Much of the renewed interest has been generated by younger bicoastal types who in recent years have snapped up and restored such architectural gems as the seven 1960s experimental steel houses *(Sunnyview Dr.)* by renowned architect Donald Wexler. This urban revival was epitomized by the purchase in 1993 of the famed Kaufman House *(470 W. Vista Chino),* built in 1946 by the great Richard Neutra in the swanky old Las Palmas area. Following a long restoration by two Newport Beach professionals, in 2008 it was to be auctioned by Christie's as a work of art with a staggering presale estimate of $15–25 million. The work of the late Albert Frey is also attracting attention. Near the Kaufman House stands one of his most engaging pieces of work, the Loewy House, which was commissioned in 1946 for Raymond Loewy, designer of the Coca-Cola bottle.

Celebrity, of course, fuels much of the scene (Palm Springs still hosts a number of celebrities, such as Barry Manilow and Jack Jones). Bob and Dolores Hope were the king and queen of the desert; their 1979 mansion was designed by architect John Lautner, a largely unsung genius of California modernism. The Hopes' first home *(1014 Buena Vista Dr.)* was just two blocks north of that of his inseparable sidekick Bing Crosby *(1011 E. El Alameda)*. Frank Sinatra's first Palm Springs house, on Alejo Road, is signaled by two palms the singer had planted so visiting friends would know the house.

Old-time celebrity homes abound. Local experts (see below) will guide the truly curious to several of them. De rigeur stops on the celebrity circuit include Liberace's Spanish Revival–style home *(501 N. Belardo Rd.)* and Elvis Presley's honeymoon house, known as "House of Tomorrow" *(1350 Ladera Circle)*, a dramatic structure originally built for Donald Alexander, the midcentury developer responsible for building many of Palm Springs's modernist homes.

INSIDER TIP:

Frank Sinatra's first Palm Springs house, on Alejo Road, can be rented for a cool $2,600 a night *(tel 877/318-2090, www.sinatrahouse.com)*.

—ANN MARIE HOUPPERT
Librarian, National Geographic Socitey

The younger crowd flocks to such places as the Korakia Pensione, a 1920s Hollywood getaway. Another place for the younger set is Miracle Manor in Desert Hot Springs *(tel 877/329-6641, www.miraclemanor.com)*. This low-slung 1940s motel was purchased and retooled by trendy L.A. architect Michael Rotondi and designer April Greiman. It is perhaps the sparest version of desert Zen, with putty tones, floors of varnished plywood and concrete, and linens of gauzy cotton. There are few of the traditional motel appliances—no TVs, phones, or clocks—but there is a natural-spring-fed hot tub, an on-call masseuse, and plenty of delicious desert scenery and silence.

Opening night of the Palm Springs International Film Festival

In Palm Springs itself, culture abounds, although much of it is the preserve of the locals, who have elevated fundraising parties to an art form and their own homes into architectural shrines. Fortunately, the Palm Springs Art Museum (see p. 337) offers a look into the collecting habits of this megaclass. Much of the museum's Western and Native American art was donated by film star Kirk Douglas and his wife, Anne, and author Sidney Sheldon. It includes some fine examples of work by British sculptors Henry Moore and Barbara Hepworth, American Old West master Frederic Remington, and California pop art maestro Edward Ruscha. Works by Maynard Dixon and Charles M. Russell are also represented in the museum's impressive collection. A treat awaits in the work of actor George Montgomery, who created a notable collection of sculpture and furniture.

Before setting out to see Palm Springs's celebrity homes, pick up a map of celebrity home locations at the Palm Springs Visitors Center (see p. 336). Palm Springs Celebrity Tours *(tel 760/770-2700, www.thecelebritytour.com)* offers standard "talk and gawk" trips. Modernist expert Robert Imber offers guided architecture tours *(PS Modern Tours, tel 760/318-6118)*, including tours conducted on Segways.

Indian Canyons

Four spectacular desert canyons lie outside Palm Springs (see pp. 336–337). Although today traversed by outdoor types, from hikers to SUVers to mountain bikers, the area was once the domain of a single hardy people, the Agua Caliente band of the Cahuilla. Their imprint on the area remains in the form of pictographs, used to mark holy places, and bedrock mortars, which the Cahuilla used to grind the nuts, seeds, and berries that sustained them for centuries. Their descendants administer the canyons—which are considered sacred—and are major sponsors of a new, 50-acre Agua Caliente Cultural Museum complex to be built next to the Indian Canyons.

Indian Canyons
- Map: 327 C3
- South Palm Canyon Dr., Palm Springs
- 760/323-6018
- Closed Mon.–Thurs. July–Sept.
- $$

www.theindiancanyons.com

Tahquitz Canyon
- 500 W. Mesquite, Palm Springs
- 760/416-7044
- $$$

www.tahquitzcanyon.com

Circled by barren hills, the four canyons each have a stream surrounded by steep rocky sides. The 15-mile-long (24 km) **Palm Canyon,** accessed via South Palm Canyon Drive, is the biggest of the four. The vast grove of *Washingtonia* palms that stretches for several miles along Palm Canyon is one of the biggest in the world.

After visiting the **Trading Post,** where you can buy hiking maps and Native American crafts, take the moderately graded trail into the canyon, which follows a beautiful palm-shaded stream before climbing up into the cactus-studded mountains. Nearby **Murray Canyon** has herds of wild horses running through it. Bighorn sheep and deer are also numerous in the vicinity. An easy hike leads to **Andreas Canyon,** the site of another enormous grove of *Washingtonia* palms.

Closer to the city center, **Tahquitz Canyon** is the setting for a huge natural amphitheater beneath Tahquitz Peak. Snowmelt from the peak feeds a spectacular waterfall. Ranger-led tours that depart the visitor center show ancient pictographs and irrigation systems. ■

EXPERIENCE: Floating the Colorado

A hundred miles (160 km) east of the Coachella Valley, the Colorado River is still largely wild and unfettered, a watery divide between California and Arizona protected within the confines of several national wildlife refuges and state parks. Float trips start from the tiny hamlet of Walter's Camp, 38 miles (61 km) south of Blythe *(map p. 327 E2)*. Whether in canoe, kayak, or home-made raft, the float trip is normally done over two days with an overnight at **Picacho State Recreation Area** *(tel 760/996-2963, www.parks.ca.gov)*, on the California side. The Colorado is strong and wide in these lower reaches, but lack of rapids makes for an easy passage. Wildlife along the banks includes coyotes and desert bighorn sheep, rattlesnakes, and myriad migratory waterbirds. Abandoned 19th-century mines and homesteads add a touch of human history. The 35-mile (56-km) downriver journey ends at Lake Martinez on the Arizona side. For those who don't have their own boats, **Lake Martinez Resort** *(tel 800/876-7004)* will deliver rented canoes to Walter's Camp and for a small fee drive your vehicle to the take-out point downriver.

The Living Desert

Deserts have long captured the minds of curious travelers and mystics, but seldom seem to have inspired those charged with putting together parks and zoos. Established in 1970, the Living Desert wildlife and botanical park is a rare exception.

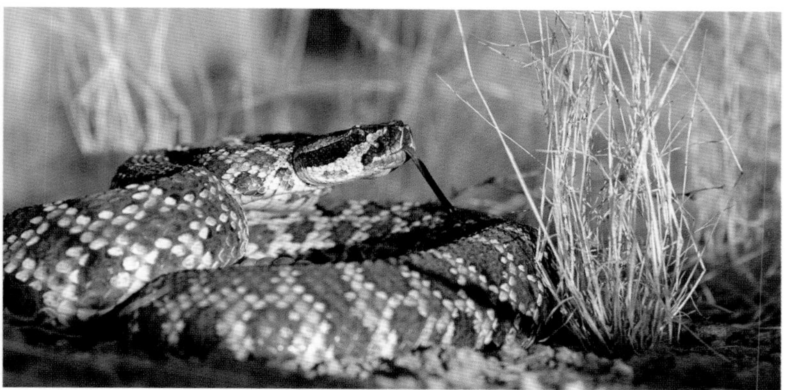

Rattlesnakes are among the deadliest inhabitants of the Living Desert.

The Living Desert offers a complete introduction to desert ecologies. Spread over 1,200 acres (485 ha) of the Colorado Desert, part of the vast Sonoran Desert, the park contains nearly 400 species of animals and a wide array of desert flora.

Although the new **Discovery Room** near the entrance is ostensibly set up for children, it provides all ages with a tutorial on desert basics. Animal exhibits are interspersed throughout specialized ecosystems, among them the shady Palm Oasis (with its walk-through aviary), the Mojave Garden, and the Sonoran Pond with its desert fishes. To the east is a section dedicated to African deserts and savannas, with animals ranging from gazelles and warthogs to giraffes and cheetah.

The big attraction is **Eagle Canyon,** with hiking trails, streams, and native fauna like mountain lions, bobcats, Mexican wolves, and golden eagles. Another exhibit explains the San Andreas Fault (see sidebar p. 337). Among the newest exhibits are the **Ant Lab, Native Bee Garden,** and large pronghorn antelope habitat. ■

INSIDER TIP:

The Living Desert allows your family to adopt a desert animal, or species, for one year *(www.livingdesert.org).*

—JENNIFER ALLARD
National Geographic contributor

Living Desert

- 327 C2
- 47900 Portola Ave., Palm Desert
- 760/346-5694
- Closed p.m. June–Sept.
- $$

www.livingdesert.org

Fragrant Trees of the Desert

Although the spring bloom of the desert wildflowers gets all the press, much of the glorious fragrance that accompanies it is provided by the spring and early summer flourish of the desert trees. The most numerous species are all represented at the Living Desert zoo and gardens (see p. 341).

This crowning bloom of paloverde illustrates the Living Desert's surprising flora.

Blue paloverde *(Cercidium floridum)* has a pale green trunk, spiny olive-green twigs, and sparse (if not entirely absent) foliage. Short and willowy, it is often found along stream and wash banks, performing a vital service in preventing erosion. Once a year, it bursts into bright yellow bloom. Desert burros can be seen champing on its soft wood in stupid delight.

Desert smoketree *(Dalea spinosa)* is one of the great landscape treasures of the Palm Springs area. It owes its mystical image—a fog-shrouded tangle of wooden antlers—to its evanescent foliage. Until its third year, its twigs are thickly coated with gray hairs, which explains the tree's ghostly appearance under the summer moon. It flowers precisely in the dead heat of summer, when tourists have departed.

Desert catalpa *(Chilopsis linearis)* was once used to make hunting bows. Fittingly known as the bow willow, it has long, thin, light green leaves and is willowlike in appearance. It often stands—hunches, rather—over washed-out culverts and ditches throughout the Colorado Desert. Its remarkable flowers are showy pink spikes with white and yellow spots in the throat. Later in the summer, the heat draws out their subtle fragrance, which resembles that of sweet violets.

Desert ironwood *(Olneya tesota)* more than lives up to its name. With a specific gravity of 1.14, a piece of it will sink in water. Its notable red-brown bark peels in long downward strips, and it has gray leaves. If you are in the desert in early summer, you will witness its remarkable flowering, a flourish of thousands of indigo and rose-purple blooms with a subtle perfume.

True mesquite *(Prosopis juliflora)* is among the Colorado Desert's dominant flora. It has dark, reddish-brown bark and slim, smooth twigs like tendrils waving at the bottom of the sea. Its usefulness to a range of inhabitants is legendary. Native American peoples of the Southwest used its strong wood to erect their homes; their children used it to make a wooden kickball; the elders made of its sugary fruit a nasty liquor. Spaniards fed their cattle on it; confectioners used it to make gum; the U.S. Cavalry fed it to their horses. Nevertheless, mesquite has rarely received its due praise, probably because it is one of the desert's most invasive plants. Its scent—piney and smoky—is the desert's own.

Anza-Borrego Desert State Park

The fact that this 600,000-acre (242,811 ha) park is tucked into one of the most remote no-man's-lands in the state doesn't stop thousands of wildflower lovers from making their spring pilgrimage. And little wonder: Anza-Borrego is a capital of desert botanica. These blooms begin in February, with the blue sand verbena. Then come the agave, the mallow, the ocotillo, and the brittlebush. By April, the desert has become a vast—albeit temporary—wonderland of color.

Memorable places to go include the **Borrego-Palm Canyon Trail** *(trailhead on Borrego-Palm Canyon, W of Borrego Springs)*. The path first winds through a bamboo-filled grove before ending at a waterfall and a grove of 800 fan palms. The **Tamarisk Grove** *(Calif. 78 and Yaqui Pass Rd.)* has a number of palm canyons and spectacular gorges. **Agua Caliente County Park** *(Cty. Rd. S2, S of Calif. 78)* is a site of the ancient Kumeyaay culture and a habitat for bighorn sheep and other desert wildlife. Ask for guides to archaeological sites at the visitor center.

For those staying in Borrego Springs, the one-hour round-trip east to see the views from **Fonts Point,** in the Borrego Badlands, is a must at sunset, when the sun boils dramatically down into the red-black horizon. If you really want to get to know the desert, naturalist Paul Johnson (reachable through the visitor center) conducts brilliant walking tours. ■

INSIDER TIP:

The night sky above Anza-Borrego offers stargazers a glorious view of the universe unavailable from most of southern California.

—DENNIS MAMMANA
Professional astronomer & sky guide

Anza-Borrego Desert State Park

327 C2–D2

Visitor Information

Visitor Center, 200 Palm Canyon, Borrego Springs

760/767-5311 (Park HQ), 760/767-4205 (Visitor Center)

www.parks.ca.gov

NOTE:

For up-to-date information on the spring bloom, contact the Anza-Borrego Desert State Park visitor center (see above) or the Payne Foundation *(tel 818/768-3533, www.theodorepayne.org, closed June–Feb.)*.

EXPERIENCE: Borrego Desert Stargazing

Clear arid skies and far distances from California's big coastal cities gives Anza-Borrego Desert State Park the distinction of being one of the best places in the U.S. to watch the heavens at night. The small desert town of Borrego Springs is the state's first and only designated International Dark Sky Community. In addition to the more common stars and constellations, dim objects like the Andromeda Galaxy and even rarities like the aurora borealis can sometimes be seen from Borrego.

The nonprofit **Anza Borrego Foundation** *(tel 760/767-0446, www.theabf.org, $$)* offers two-day stargazing and photography workshops under the guidance of a veteran astronomer. The **Springs at Borrego** *(tel 760/767-0004, www.springsatborrego.com)* RV resort has created its own small observatory with an 11-inch (38 cm) telescope, focus of the stargazing events that it organizes every year.

Salton Sea

About 30 miles (48 km) south of Palm Springs, the bizarre Salton Sea was formed in 1905, when the Colorado River burst out of irrigation canals in nearby Yuma, Arizona, and ran, unchecked for almost two years, into a 35-by-15-mile (56 by 24 km) desert basin with no natural outlet. The river water picked up salt, which was left behind when the desert heat evaporated the water. More river water ran in and evaporated, leaving behind increasingly high concentrations of salt. This process resulted in the Salton Sea's high salinity of 41 parts per million.

Seabirds flock to the shores of the Salton Sea.

Salton Sea
327 D2
Visitor Information
100-225 State Park Rd., North Shore
760/393-3052
www.parks.ca.gov

Sonny Bono Salton Sea National Wildlife Refuge
Sinclair Rd. & Gentry Rd., Niland
760/348-5278
Visitor center closed Sat. & Sun.
www.fws.gov/saltonsea

The Salton Sea's unique biology has had remarkable consequences. On the one hand, it has become one of the West Coast's great bird-watching areas, with a huge population of pelicans and egrets, among others. The birds come to feed on the equally huge fish population, particularly the tilapia, which are so numerous that fishermen have been known to pull hundreds of the fish from the sea in just one sitting. (There is no limit on how many tilapia you can catch.)

On the other hand, the sea is also a quagmire of ecological problems. Salt concentrations are increasing. For several summers, both birds and fish have been found dying in large numbers. One theory is that fertilizers from farm runoff have fueled enormous blooms of algae. When these colorful (and very smelly) blooms die, they pull enormous amounts of oxygen from the water, killing the fish in large numbers. The dead fish rot, encouraging botulism, which is then passed on to the birds, with fatal results.

Nevertheless, the sea remains a popular destination for fisherfolk, water-skiers, and campers. Winter is the favorite season for campers and hikers. The **Mecca Beach** campground, about 1 mile (1.6 km) south of park headquarters, is a perfect base camp for fishing fanatics. For bird-watchers, the months from October through May are a delight. At that time, up to four million migrating birds flock about the sea. The **Sonny Bono Salton Sea National Wildlife Refuge** is the preferred destination for ornithologists.

Authorities are shaping a plan to rehabilitate the sea, which is surrounded by the intensely irrigated farmland of the Imperial Valley—a lush Eden where avocados, dates, grapes, tomatoes, and other vegetables are grown in astounding abundance. ■

Travelwise

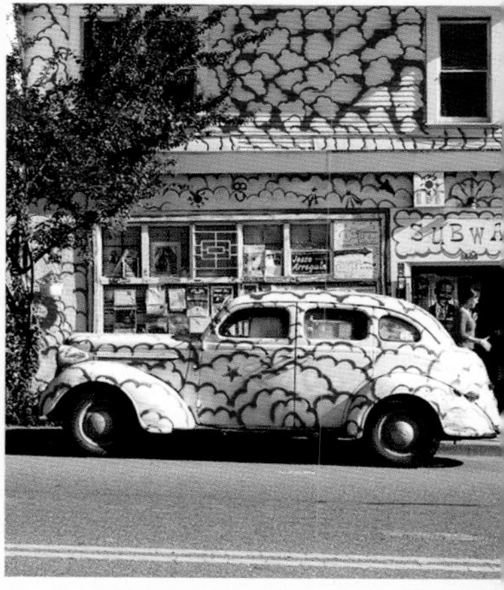

Traffic coordination, California style

TRAVELWISE

PLANNING YOUR TRIP

When to Go

Is there really a bad time to visit California? It depends upon which California you mean. If northern California, then the late winter and early spring months are a chilly proposition. If southern California, late August and September can be too hot for some. The basic climatic signposts are: In summer, go north; in winter, go south. Of course, this means you will encounter heavy tourist traffic. One alternative worth the effort is to explore the various tourist "cusp seasons" (very early spring in Wine Country, for example, or very early summer in L.A.).

Events & Festivals

California is full of cultural events: colorful agricultural festivals, seasonal music fests, sporting and ethnic venues. Check out each city's website and/or visitor information bureau for an up-to-date listing. Some favorites are:

January On Jan. 1, the Tournament of Roses Parade and Football Game *(www.tournamentofroses.com)* makes Pasadena one big party.

February San Francisco's Chinese New Year Parade *(www.chineseparade.com)* still outclasses L.A.'s *(www.lagoldendragonparade.com)* by far.

March The Mendocino Whale Watch Festival *(www.mendowhale.com)* commences with great gusto, and a lot of beer.

April The Antelope Valley's blooming of native poppies is a good excuse for music, art, food, and fun at the California Poppy Festival, in Lancaster *(www.poppyfestival.com)*.

May Mark Twain buffs will love the Jumping Frog Jubilee in Angels Camp, Gold Country *(www.frogtown.org)*.

June For pure Wine Country atmosphere, you must experience the Napa Valley Wine Auction *(www.napavintners.com)*.

July Right on the Central Coast are two great entertainment choices, the esteemed Carmel Bach Festival *(www.bachfestival.org)* and the Gilroy Garlic Festival *(www.gilroygarlicfestival.com)*.

August At the Old Spanish Days Fiesta in old Santa Barbara *(www.oldspanishdays-fiesta.org)*, you can get all dressed up and play hidalgo for a day.

September The Russian River Jazz Festival *(www.russianriverfestivals.com)* competes with the San Francisco Blues Festival *(www.sfblues.com)*–and everybody wins!

October The Tor House Poetry Festival in Carmel *(tel 831/624-1813)* really brings out the old-time California characters.

November This is a good time to see the desert. What better excuse than the Art of Food & Wine Festival, in Palm Desert *(www.artoffoodandwine.com)*. Many of southern California's best chefs prepare treats.

December Multimillion-dollar yachts, small boats, and even kayaks bedecked in Christmas lights emblazon Newport Beach harbor during the Christmas Boat Parade *(www.christmasboatparade.com)*.

GETTING AROUND

Airports

Californians pioneered the use of multi-passenger vans for to-and-from airport trips, and a number of companies ply their services (for example Shuttle Vans, Freeway Flyers, etc.) at all airports. Most are reliable, reasonable, and friendly. If you are staying at a major airport hotel, it will probably provide a free van ride to and from the airport; additionally, all the major car rental outfits provide a shuttle service to their outlets. Super Shuttle *(tel 800/258-3826, www.supershuttle.com)* offers door-to-door service in many cities.

John Wayne Orange County *(tel 949/252-5200, www.ocair.com)* This growing regional airport is a reasonable alternative to flying into L.A.

Los Angeles International *(www.airport-la.com)* A taxi ride to downtown or Beverly Hills will cost approximately $50.

Oakland International *(tel 510/563-3300, www.flyoakland.com)* A taxi ride to Oakland city center will cost about $40. A shuttle connects to the BART system.

Palm Springs *(tel 760/318-3800, www.palmsprings.ca.gov)* Taxi to center about $15.

Sacramento *(tel 916/929-5411, www.sacairports.org)* Taxi to center about $50.

San Francisco International *(tel 650/821-8211, www.flysfo.com)* For a taxi ride downtown, expect to pay $50. There is a BART station at the airport

San Jose *(tel 408/392-3600, www.flysanjose.com)* Taxi to center approximately $20.

By Car

Unless you plan on landing in San Francisco and staying within the metropolitan area, get a car. The most helpful motorists' organization is the California State Automobile Association *(tel 800/922-8228, www.csaa.com).*

California has a huge array of car rental agencies. If you respond to a "bargain" ad, only to find there are no longer any cars of the "bargain" line left to rent, ask for a free upgrade.

Avis: tel 800/230-4898, www.avis.com
Budget: tel 800/527-0700, www.budget.com
Dollar: tel 800/800-3665, www.dollar.com
Hertz: tel 800/654-3131, www.hertz.com

Public Transportation

Amtrak *(tel 800/872-7245, www.amtrak.com),* the nationwide rail network, has been enjoying good press and a revival among travelers who want to see the state more slowly. **Greyhound Lines** *(tel 800/231-2222, www.greyhound.com)* is the bus system, with services to most cities.

In San Francisco, the **Muni bus system** *(tel 415/701-2311, www.sfmta.com)* is quite well regarded. **BART** *(www.bart.gov),* the famous rapid transit train system, will whisk you fairly comfortably from downtown to the East, North, and South Bays. Call the visitor bureau for details on passes.

In Los Angeles, the **Dash bus system** covers much of the city *(tel 213/808-2273, www.ladottransit.com).* The Metro system, currently fairly limited, is being extended *(tel 323/466-3876, www.metro.net).*

PRACTICAL ADVICE

- California is still paradise, but even paradise has a few rotten apples. Behave appropriately; do not walk alone in unknown districts; do not display expensive equipment or jewelry.
- Do not call it "Frisco."
- Do not call it "The Big Orange," "La La Land," "Tinseltown," or "El-Lay."
- Use common sense. Do not use an ATM machine if you are alone late at night.
- Do not expect everyone to speak English, particularly in some of the more interesting parts of L.A. and San Francisco.
- Do not "flip the bird" to any other drivers, regardless of how badly they may be driving.
- Do not pick up hitchhikers and, save for extreme emergencies, do not stop to help anyone along the freeway unless there is another person in the car with you and you can telephone for help *(911)* immediately.
- Buy some good maps.
- Carry bottled water with you in the car.

Emergencies

In any part of the state, the 911 number is set aside for reporting all emergencies. If you are a victim of a crime, you may want to avail yourself of the counseling services at the Crime Victims' Hotline *(tel 800/394-2255).*

Visitors With Disabilities

The California legislature has enacted a number of laws requiring restaurants, universities, municipal facilities, and all transport systems to provide wheelchair access. To find out about your rights, call 510/644-2555. The hearing impaired can get information by calling 800/622-3277.

Visitor Information

The first resource is the **California Division of Tourism** *(1102 Q St., Ste. 6000, Sacramento, CA 95814, tel 916/444-4429, www.visitcalifornia.com),* which publishes a variety of helpful guides. Its website contains a list of regional convention and visitor bureaus and is linked to hundreds of region-specific sites, leading in turn to hotel, food, and attractions listings. The division has visitor information centers in 20 locations throughout the state.

An outstanding resource for outdoor folks is the **National Park Service** *(www.nps.gov).*

The principal city visitor information bureaus are in Los Angeles *(6801 Hollywood Blvd., Hollywood, tel 323/467-6412, www.discoverlosangeles.com),* San Diego *(1140 N. Harbor Dr., tel 619/236-1212, www.sandiego.org),* and San Francisco *(900 Market St., tel 415/391-2000, www.sanfrancisco.travel).*

BACKGROUND READING

To really get up on California culture and history, there is no better single volume in print than Carey McWilliams's classic *California: The Great Exception.* Unfortunately, McWilliams's narrative ends in 1949, leaving the rest of the tale to countless imitators and others, many of whom cannot be trusted. One generally reliable commentator is the omni-intellectual state librarian, Kevin Starr. See any title under his name, particularly *Inventing the Dream* and *Material Dreams.* The essays of Richard Rodriguez, though sometimes a bit elliptical, are worthwhile and entertaining; his *Days of Obligation* is a good, meditative, and thought-provoking read. John Muir's *The Mountains of California* is a must for all outdoor folk.

Hotels & Restaurants

California has an abundance of outstanding restaurants, with its principal cities at the top of the national culinary tree. Wealthy areas, such as Hollywood in the south and Silicon Valley in the north, have helped to attract some of the world's great chefs to the region. But the real deals—and some of the best food—are to be found in the ethnic restaurants run by first-generation immigrants from Asia and the Middle East. There the ingredients are fresh, the food is prepared with familial vigor, and the prices are modest.

The state's hotels, inns, and bed-and-breakfast establishments span a wide range of styles and amenities, from the super-chic Peninsula in Beverly Hills and the traditional Mark Hopkins in San Francisco to the indulgently quiet and restful Manka's Inn in tiny Inverness. Save yourself some money—sometimes up to 50 percent—by looking in the Sunday edition of the *L.A. Times (www.latimes.com)*, where many weekday and weekend bargains are advertised.

What to Expect

Most California hotels operate what has become known as the "American plan," which simply means breakfast is not included in the price. What *should* be included is attentive, pleasant service, knowledgeable and proactive staff, and a database of local and regional information about everything from local eateries to cultural and arts venues or sports teams. All of the hotels and inns listed below should be able to provide these, although the degree to which their staff will do so varies enormously. Service, even in the priciest of hotels, is a spotty commodity these days.

The listings that follow attempt to strike a balance between chain hotels and regionally unique hotels. The major chains listed all do a good job of the basics. The better bed-and-breakfasts are a worthwhile alternative; you may have to do a bit more homework before traveling, but, in general, you will get cheerier staff—and also breakfast.

Bed-and-Breakfast Association

California Association of Bed & Breakfast Inns: tel 800/373-9251, www.cabbi.com

Credit Cards

AE American Express, DC Diners Club, MC Mastercard, V Visa

Hotel Chains & Groups

Doubletree: tel 800/222-8733, www.doubletreehilton.com
Hilton: tel 800/445-8667, www.hilton.com
Holiday Inn: tel 877/834-3613, www.holidayinn.com
Hyatt: tel 888/591-1234, www.hyatt.com
Marriott: tel 888/236-2427, www.marriott.com
Ramada: tel 800/854-9517, www.ramada.com
Sheraton: tel 800/325-3535, www.sheraton.com
Westin: tel 800/937-8461, www.westin.com
Wyndham: tel 877/999-3223, www.wyndham.com

Hotel Restaurants

Outstanding restaurants in hotels are listed separately and a cross-reference is made in the hotel entry. Where a hotel restaurant is above the standard one would expect for a hotel of that quality, the restaurant symbol is given as well as the hotel one, and the restaurant is described in the entry. No indication is given where the hotel has a restaurant of no particular merit.

Parking

Where a hotel or restaurant has its own parking, the symbol P is included in the entry. Some hotels and restaurants offer valet parking, shown as P Valet.

Restaurants

Holiday closings may vary from year to year. It is advisable to check and to reserve a table.
L = lunch
D = dinner

Smoking

Smoking is not allowed in restaurants in California. By law, hotels must have nonsmoking rooms and nonsmoking areas in the lobby. A few hotels do not allow smoking at all, and this is indicated in the entry.

Tipping

Except in rare situations (or when large groups are involved), tipping in California restaurants is, in theory, entirely voluntary. In reality, you are expected to leave around 15 percent of the subtotal (before tax). Still, if you have a bad experience, do not hesitate to leave less, or even nothing.

Organization

In the following section, hotels are listed under each location by price, then in alphabetical order, followed by restaurants also by price and alphabetical order.

PRICES

HOTELS

An indication of the cost of a double room in the high season is given by **$** signs.

$$$$$	Over $280
$$$$	$200–$280
$$$	$120–$200
$$	$80–$120
$	Under $80

RESTAURANTS

An indication of the cost of a three-course meal without drinks is given by **$** signs.

$$$$$	Over $80
$$$$	$50–$80
$$$	$35–$50
$$	$20–$35
$	Under $20

LOS ANGELES

AIRPORT

RADISSON

$$$

6225 W. CENTURY BLVD.
TEL 310/670-9000, 800/967-9033
www.hilton.com

The closest hotel to LAX, L.A.'s airport, has features that will endear it to anyone who must stay near the airport; these include deluxe soundproofing, spacious public areas, and recently redecorated rooms.

580 P All major cards

BEVERLY HILLS

BEVERLY HILLS HOTEL & BUNGALOWS

$$$$$

9641 SUNSET BLVD.
TEL 310/276-2251
www.beverlyhillshotel.com

More than a hundred years old, this hotel has never seen better days than now. The gardens are lush, the service is very good, and the rooms are elegantly appointed with just about every amenity known to Hollywood-kind. The **Polo Lounge** is still a fine place to eat, particularly at the ideal hour (1–2 p.m.), when you can observe the local wildlife devouring fresh shrimp salad and cool tomato soup.

208 rooms, 23 bungalows P Valet All major cards

SLS LOS ANGELES

$$$$$

465 S. LA CIENEGA BLVD.
TEL 310/247-0400
www.slslosangeles.com

Emerging in spring 2008, the former Meridien has been given a complete transformation by Philippe Starck. If you like avant garde, this is the place. The hotel combines Japanese practicality and coolness with Western luxury and Starck's signature colorful textures. There's even a meditation garden in the lobby, and the hotel's chic bar and restaurants are considered places to see and be seen.

297 P All major cards

PENINSULA BEVERLY HILLS

$$$$–$$$$$

9882 S. SANTA MONICA BLVD.
TEL 310/551-2888
www.beverlyhills.peninsula.com

Without a doubt, the most elegant hotel in L.A. Rooms are the height of luxe—amazingly soft linens, deep soaking tub, tasteful period furniture. Outside are I. M. Pei's famous CAA headquarters and a whole lot of shopping. Here a splurge is a splurge—in the splurge capital of the Western world. The Belvedere restaurant (see this page) is the gilding on the lily.

196 P Valet All major cards

CAPITAL GRILLE

$$$$–$$$$$

THE BEVERLY CENTER,
8614 BEVERLY BLVD.
TEL 310/358-0650
www.thecapitalgrille.com

The Capital Grill serves old-school Americana, a combo of thick steaks (aged in-house for two to three weeks) and fresh-catch seafood (think crusted dry-aged sirloin with shallot butter and seared citrus-glazed king salmon). The wine cellar boasts 5,000 bottles of some of the world's best vintages. Or opt for a classic martini in the more lively mahogany bar.

250 P Closed L Sun. All major cards

BELVEDERE

$$$$

PENINSULA BEVERLY HILLS,
9882 S. SANTA MONICA BLVD.
TEL 310/551-2888

The Belvedere does not only fine modern American cuisine (sesame roasted prawns, New York steak with truffled hollandaise and fries) but also an outstanding brunch. A scene, but a quiet scene.

85 P Valet All major cards

MATSUHISA

$$$$

129 N. LA CIENEGA BLVD.
TEL 310/659-9639
www.nobumatsuhisa.com

The place to eat sushi in haute Los Angeles, Matsuhisa is not a sushi bar, it's a sushi monument. Chef Nobu specializes in the most delicate of tastes, from sea urchin and shiso leaf to truffled sea scallops with caviar.

76 P Valet Closed L Sat.–Sun. All major cards

SPAGO BEVERLY HILLS

$$$$

176 N. CANON DR.
TEL 310/385-0880
www.wolfgangpuck.com

This is still one of the top five restaurants in the city (in the country, some would argue). Wolfgang Puck is at the top of his form here, with chef Lee Hefter dishing out amazing works such as ragout of shrimp with chicken oysters (the morsels close to the backbone) and black truffles; osso buco and Knödel stuffed with pork crackling.
300 Valet Closed Sun. L DC, MC, V

CULINA
$$$–$$$$$
FOUR SEASONS HOTEL, 300 S. DOHENY DR.
TEL 310/860-4000
www.culinarestaurant.com
It may be located in the Four Seasons, but Culina feels and acts more like a modern Italian, neighborhood restaurant. The menu ranges from gourmet pizzas and panini sandwiches to *pesce spada* (Californian swordfish) served with eggplant caponata and a grape-tomato vinaigrette and *lombatina capricciosa* (veal chop) with aciabatta crust and arugula. For dessert try the delicious panna cotta (basil seed tapioca with strawberry sorbet).
231 Valet All major cards

CUT
$$$–$$$$$
BEVERLY WILSHIRE, 9500 WILSHIRE BLVD.
TEL 310/276-8500
www.wolfgangpuck.com
Another chicly contemporary offering from Wolfgang Puck, CUT—a contemporary twist on the classic steakhouse—has proved itself a cut above since opening in 2006, garnering awards everywhere and drawing Hollywood's finest. Try the lobster and crab Louis cocktail with spicy tomato horseradish, followed by the signature Kobe beef short ribs with Indian spices.
140 Valet Closed L All major cards

DOWNTOWN/LITTLE TOKYO

RITZ-CARLTON
$$$$$
900 W. OLYMPIC BLVD.
TEL 213/743-8800
www.ritzcarlton.com
From the California-chic rooms to the 3,400-square-foot Ritz-Carlton Club Lounge and the exclusive, rooftop pool and bar, this new high-rise hotel has become the hallmark for luxury in downtown L.A. Rounding out the offerings are a full-service spa and the nouvelle Chinese cuisine of Wolfgang Puck's **WP24** restaurant. Perched between the 22nd and 26th floors of a sleek 54-story tower, the Ritz-Carlton overlooks Staples Center, the Nokia Theatre, and the rest of the new L.A. Live complex.
123 Valet All major cards

KYOTO GRAND HOTEL & GARDENS
$$$–$$$$
120 S. LOS ANGELES ST.
TEL 213/629-1200
www.kyotograndhotel.com
Located in the heart of historic Little Tokyo, this hotel exudes simple Asian elegance and features a lovely oriental garden. Stylish rooms offer a choice of Japanese style, with futons, tatami mats, and deep bath tubs, or Western, spare, impeccable, and very comfortable.
434 All major cards

R-23
$$
923 E. 2ND ST.
TEL 213/687-7178
www.r23.com
Call ahead for exact instructions (you must drive here, even if in Little Tokyo). Fine sushi in tastefully decorated surroundings. This is a scene as well, with the trendy neo-industrial setting providing an interesting backdrop. Try the Dungeness crab salad.
48 Closed Sun. & L Sat. All major cards

SOMETHING SPECIAL

FUGETSU-DO CONFECTIONERY
$
315 E. 1ST ST.
TEL 213/625-8595
www.fugetsu-do.com
Step back in time, to an era when immigrant mom-and-pop candy shops made traditional Japanese sweet *manju* in hand-carved wooden forms, then wrapped them in maple leaves and ferns. The Fugetsu-do make their pastel-colored rice goodies exactly the way they did 100 years ago. A unique souvenir, a tasty treat.
Closed D No credit cards

CENTURY CITY

HYATT REGENCY CENTURY PLAZA
$$$$–$$$$$
2025 AVE. OF THE STARS
TEL 310/228-1234
www.centuryplaza.hyatt.com
A city within a city, the swank, chicly contemporary Plaza, President Reagan's favorite campaign stopover, is perfectly situated between Beverly Hills and nearby shopping, live theaters across the street and in Westwood, and cultural happenings at UCLA and the Getty.
726 All major cards

CHINATOWN

EMPRESS PAVILION
$–$$
988 N. HILL ST., 2ND FLOOR
TEL 213/617-9898
www.empresspavilion.com
The epitome of a giant Hong Kong restaurant, Empress

Pavilion does the best breakfast and lunch dim sum in Chinatown. Dim sum, in fact, is the only reason to come here, the dinners being mostly lackluster.
700 P All major cards

MON KEE
$–$$
679 N. SPRING ST.
TEL 213/628-6717
An old standby, Mon Kee does seafood better than anywhere in old Chinatown. Stir-fried rock cod, crab in ginger sauce, and shrimp in rock salt are the consistently outstanding mainstays. No reservations.
140 P Valet AE, MC, V

FAIRFAX DISTRICT

CANTER'S DELI
$
419 N. FAIRFAX AVE.
TEL 323/651-2030
www.cantersdeli.com
The original L.A. deli comes complete with wisecracking waitstaff, garish lighting, and characters out of a Bernard Malamud novel. The food is acceptable, predictable deli food. You won't leave any on your plate. Open 24 hours a day.
450 P MC, V

KOKOMO CAFE
$
7385 BEVERLY BLVD.
TEL 323/933-0773
Kokomo Cafe serves up Southern cookin' with an L.A. twist, as in turkey hash and apple-smoked bacon, a great Cobb salad (if you haven't had one in L.A. yet, this is the one to get), and a festive, pleasant atmosphere.
120 P AE, MC, V

HANCOCK PARK & KOREATOWN

HOUSE OF CHAN DARA
$$–$$$
310 N. LARCHMONT BLVD.
TEL 323/467-1052
www.chandararestaurant.com
A Thai hangout, where the waitstaff is at least as nice as the food, Chan Dara nevertheless is the best place to eat in Hancock Park. The mee krob is an old standard—and very good. Ditto the appetizers, particularly the shrimp in lemongrass.
115 P All major cards

HOLLYWOOD/ WEST HOLLYWOOD

CHATEAU MARMONT
$$$$$
8221 SUNSET BLVD.
TEL 323/656-1010
www.chateaumarmont.com
If you want to experience a slice of true Hollywood, you can do no better than the Chateau. Over the years, this 1929 castlelike mansion-hotel, with only 63 rooms, has hosted some of the great Hollywood eccentrics, from Christopher Walken (who once lived here) to John Belushi (who died here). The place has loads of charm and elegance, and the rooms are comfortable and well appointed, if a bit old. The Bar Marmont is a stylish hangout.
63 P All major cards

MONDRIAN
$$$$$
8440 SUNSET BLVD.
TEL 323/650-8999
www.mondrianhotel.com
Quintessential California chic draws the glamour set and hip executives to this sexy, showy, slightly surreal Ian Schrager hotel. The stunning lobby, with its diaphonous curtains and objets d'art, sets the urbane tone, as do full entertainment centers and well-chosen literature in suave guest rooms. The acclaimed Asia de Cuba restaurant (see p. 352) is quite the scene.
237 P Valet All major cards

THE REDBURY
$$$$–$$$$$
1717 VINE ST.
TEL 323/962-1717, 877/962-1717
www.theredbury.com
The hip new Redbury lures an arts and entertainment crowd to a celebrated corner of Tinseltown that is quickly becoming trendy again. In keeping with the area's funky repute, the design exudes a counterculture vibe highlighted by furnishings and decorative arts from around the globe. All rooms boast a seating area, kitchen, and washer/dryer, as well as a turntable and collection of classic vinyl albums, many of which were recorded within a mile radius. The **Cleo Restaurant** tenders tasty California -Mediterranean fare.
57 P Valet All major cards

HOLLYWOOD ROOSEVELT
$$$$
7000 HOLLYWOOD BLVD.
TEL 323/466-7000
www.thompsonhotels.com
Another onetime stronghold of the famous and rich, the Roosevelt is a more modestly priced alternative to the Chateau Marmont. It has recently been restored to its original 1920s grandeur, with painted ceilings, ornate tilework, and a balconied mezzanine. Rooms are a little on the small side, but quite comfortable. Gable and Lombard once romped here.
333 P Valet All major cards

STK

$$$$$

755 N. LA CIENEGA BLVD.

TEL 310/659-3535

www.stkhouse.com

Swanky and hip, this delicious steakhouse serves quality meat, cooked to perfection with sides like truffle fries, asparagus, and creamed corned pudding. As an added bonus, just about anything on the menu can be topped with truffles and/or lobster. As if to confirm its trendy vibe, STK flaunts a live DJ in the atrium bar Tuesday through Saturday.

200 Valet Closed L All major cards

ASIA DE CUBA

$$$$

MONDRIAN HOTEL, 8440 SUNSET BLVD.

TEL 323/848-6000

Jeffrey Chedorow's outstanding nouveau Asian-Latino cuisine is reason enough to dine here, but the Strip's hippest eatery also serves up a soupçon of catwalk divas, rock stars, and Hollywood idols. Choose roomy banquettes or an exquisite terrace with an arbor framed by terra-cotta pots on a Brobdingnagian scale. Try the chili-dusted pork with tasty tamal, or crispy yucca-coated mahi mahi in red wine miso, then end with the Bay of Pigs banana split sundae.

425 Valet Closed L Mon.–Fri. AE, MC, V

RED/SEVEN

$$$–$$$$

700 N. SAN VICENTE BLVD.

TEL 310/289-1587

www.wolfgangpuck.com

The Pacific Design Center is a perfect venue for Wolfgang Puck's red-themed lunch spot, with its fittingly minimalist decor and contemporary open design. Chef Yoshinori Kojima delivers superb Asian-influenced dishes combining local ingredients with the freshest seafood available.

60 Valet Closed D & Sat.–Sun. All major cards

AGO

$$$

8478 MELROSE AVE.

TEL 323/655-6333

Backer Robert De Niro and other Hollywood names help draw the hip industry crowd here for innovative Italian fare.

170 Valet Closed L Sat.–Sun. All major cards

THE EVELEIGH

$$$

8752 W. SUNSET BLVD.

TEL 424/239-1630

www.theeveleigh.com

Featuring a seasonal, largely local menu, the Eveleigh offers up a splendid gourmet take on country cooking. From rib-eye and braised beef cheeks to pork belly, there's plenty for carnivores to sink their teeth into. Equally delicious seafood includes roasted barramundi and crispy seasoned squid. The shady back patio is especially popular for weekend brunch.

150 Valet Closed L Mon.–Fri. All major cards

MAROUCH

$$

4905 SANTA MONICA BLVD.

TEL 323/662-9325

www.marouchrestaurant.com

This highly popular Middle Eastern restaurant does a little bit of Armenian, a little bit of Lebanese, a little bit of Arabic—very well. The portions are huge, the pita bread freshly baked, and the attitude totally upbeat. Enjoy—this is a part of L.A. cuisine that is not much publicized, but well worth twice the modest price, not least for the belly dancing.

70–80 Closed Mon. All major cards

PRICES

HOTELS

An indication of the cost of a double room in the high season is given by **$** signs.

$$$$$	Over $280
$$$$	$200–$280
$$$	$120–$200
$$	$80–$120
$	Under $80

RESTAURANTS

An indication of the cost of a three-course meal without drinks is given by **$** signs.

$$$$$	Over $80
$$$$	$50–$80
$$$	$35–$50
$$	$20–$35
$	Under $20

MUSSO & FRANK GRILL

See Hollywood, p. 80.

LOS FELIZ/GRIFFITH PARK

IZAKA-YA BY KATSU-YA

$$–$$$

8240 W. 3RD ST.

TEL 323/782-9536

www.katsu-yagroup.com

Here you'll find the freshest sushi together with Okinawa specialities like yakisoba and pork rib stew, with many different types of sake.

48 Valet Closed L Sun. All major cards

TRATTORIA FARFALLA

$$–$$$

1978 HILLHURST AVE.

TEL 323/661-7365

www.farfallatrattoria.com

Small and cozy, Farfalla cooks up consistently good southern Italian fare. The roasted chicken, the pasta in tomato-onion sauce, and the tiramisu are all delicious. No reservations—you may have to wait for a seat.

50 Valet Closed L Sat.–Sun. All major cards

CHA CHA CHA
$
656 N. VIRGIL AVE.
(NEAR MELROSE AVE.)
TEL 323/664-7723
In trendy Silver Lake–Los Feliz, a short drive from Griffith Park's elegant southern side, Cha Cha Cha has been serving outstanding Caribbean food for a decade. The jerk chicken, the St. Bart's curried shrimp, and the "rasta wrap" are favorites.
90 P All major cards

MALIBU/SANTA MONICA MOUNTAINS

GEOFFREY'S
$$$$$
27400 PACIFIC COAST HWY.
(4 MILES N OF MALIBU CANYON RD.)
TEL 310/457-1519
www.geoffreysmalibu.com
International cuisine dished up in the ultimate beachside location; some believe this is the only place where the food truly matches the quality of the view.
150 P All major cards

INN OF THE SEVENTH RAY
$$$$
128 OLD TOPANGA CANYON RD.
TEL 310/455-1311
www.innoftheseventhray.com
The ultimate New Age dining experience, this venerable inn, its open-air seating perched on the side of a babbling brook, offers fine vegetarian and other specialties. The baked salmon and pecan pie are outstanding.
200 P All major cards

SADDLE PEAK LODGE
$$$$
419 COLD CANYON RD.
(E OF MALIBU CANYON)
TEL 818/222-3888
www.saddlepeaklodge.com
The ne plus ultra of rustic California cuisine, this very woodsy and elegant canyon cottage offers adventurous game dishes, such as wild game trio with the chef's choice of three meats. For the tamer at heart, brunch on Sunday morning features delicious applewood-smoked bacon and waffles.
180 P Valet Closed L & Mon.–Tues. AE, MC, V

MARINA DEL REY

RITZ-CARLTON MARINA DEL REY
$$$$$
4375 ADMIRALTY WAY
TEL 310/823-1700
www.ritzcarlton.com
A luxury hotel with outstanding concierge service, tastefully decorated rooms, and quiet, impeccable service. The Ritz has the additional advantage of **JER-NE,** a fine restaurant that claims three Michelin fork-and-spoons for its California cuisine.
304 P
All major cards

MELROSE AVENUE & AROUND

CAMPANILE
$$$$
624 LA BREA AVE.
TEL 323/938-1447
www.campanilerestaurant.com
A foodie's dream, Campanile combines pure bold flavor with the freshest ingredients to produce some of the most satisfying cuisine in town. This is where the food critics go to get their fix of roasted black mussels in Meyer lemon aioli. The bitter almond panna cotta comes in a giant pool of coffee gelée.
160 P Valet Closed Sun. D All major cards

LUCQUES
$$$
8474 MELROSE AVE.
TEL 323/655-6277
www.lucques.com
The earthy, sensual fare comes straight out of the kitchen of Suzanne Goin, onetime chef at Campanile and an aficionada of ingredients from local farmers' markets. Even the *L.A. Times* has raved about her "fat asparagus topped with fried egg and parmesan," her Tuscan bean soup and greens, and her saddle of rabbit with pappardelle and black cabbage.
110 P Valet Closed L Sun.–Mon. AE, MC, V

BLU JAM CAFÉ
$–$$
7371 MELROSE AVE.
TEL 323/951-9191
www.blujamcafe.com
For those getting a late start, breakfast (their specialty) is served until 5 p.m., while Sunday brunch is the way to refuel between bouts of shopping. The eclectic dinner menu, designed by chef/co-owner Kamil Majer, is built around medium-size California cuisine dishes that are meant to share.
49 P Valet Closed D Sun.–Tues. All major cards

MOCA & AROUND

HILTON CHECKERS
$$$$
535 S. GRAND AVE.
TEL 213/624-0000
www.hiltoncheckers.com
A small, luxurious antidote to downtown's megahotels, Checkers has panache and quietude. Guest rooms are smallish but nicely appointed, with service—something rare these days at any price—among the best in town. The **Checkers Restaurant** is well known for its artful and satisfying California cuisine; the crab cakes are a favorite.
188 P Valet
All major cards

MILLENNIUM BILTMORE
$$$
506 S. GRAND AVE.
TEL 213/624-1011
www.millenniumhotels.com
If it's history and elegance you want, this is the place. Built in 1923, the Biltmore was one of the grandest hotels of its day. Now completely restored, it offers fine dining at **Sai Sai,** a top-rated Japanese eatery, well appointed guest rooms, and a sense of luxury, from old tiled fountains to a rococo-revival exterior.
473 Valet All major cards

KAWADA HOTEL

$$
200 S. HILL ST.
TEL 213/621-4455
www.kawadahotel.com
A budget alternative for downtown, close to Chinatown, MOCA, and various cultural venues, the Kawada provides serviceable rooms with TV, VCR, and two phones. The restaurant, **Epicenter,** makes for a good preconcert outing. The hotel shuttle is helpful for those who don't like driving.
116 Valet All major cards

PATINA
$$$$$
WALT DISNEY CONCERT HALL, 141 S. GRAND AVE.
TEL 213/972-3331
www.patinarestaurant.com
Executive chef Tony Esnault and his culinary team serve exceptional French cuisine, including game, seasonal tasting, market, and special-event menus, for which they have received a prestigious Michelin star. Impeccable service by seasoned professional staff only enhances this luxury dining experience.
160 Closed D Mon. & L All major cards

FIRST & HOPE
$$$–$$$$$
710 W. 1ST ST.
TEL 213/617-8555
www.firstandhope.com
Mere steps from the Walt Disney Concert Hall, this place takes you back in time with classic cocktails and a menu that offers modern takes on American comfort foods like grilled Caesar salad, lobster pot pie, bacon mac-n-cheese, a beef carpaccio "cheeseburger," and popcorn ice cream.
225 Valet All major cards

WATER GRILL
$$$
544 S. GRAND AVE. (E SIDE OF LIBRARY)
TEL 213/891-0900
www.watergrill.com
This is the place to eat fish—bluefin tuna tartare, grilled rock bass, black sea bass with eel pot stickers. The sea bass in braised fennel is popular with the bankers and attorneys who keep coming back again and again.
140 Closed L Sat.–Sun. All major cards

ORIGINAL PANTRY CAFÉ
$
877 S. FIGUEROA ST.
TEL 213/972-9279
www.pantrycafe.com
An original downtown eatery, in continuous operation since 1924, the Pantry is now owned by Richard Riordan, the former L.A. mayor, who often eats here with constituents and staff. The menu is pure diner fare: huge pancakes, omelettes, steaks, and a daily blue plate special. Bring a hefty appetite.
64 No credit cards

MONTEREY PARK/ ALHAMBRA

See also the feature on Monterey Park, pp. 124–125

EMPRESS HARBOR
$$
111 N. ATLANTIC BLVD.
TEL 626/300-8833
The dim sum, the steamed daily catch, and the *juk* (rice porridge) are so good that even Westsiders make the trip to this Hong Kong–style eatery.
336 All major cards

OCEAN STAR SEAFOOD
$$
145 N. ATLANTIC BLVD., #201
TEL 626/308-2128
www.oceanstarrestaurant.com
This always crowded place serves some of the finest seafood in town. On a weekend, go for the dim sum feast, selecting shu mai (shrimp dumplings) and smoky steamed veggies from steam tables that roll by your table.
800 AE, MC, V

PASADENA

LANGHAM HUNTINGTON HOTEL & SPA
$$$$$
1401 S. OAK KNOLL
TEL 626/568-3900
www.pasadena.langhamhotels.com
Pasadena has a long tradition as a winter haven for East Coast millionaires, so the luxury standards of this venerable hotel (the former Ritz-Carlton) are, in keeping with the tradition, quite high: The rooms are ample, with marble bathrooms and cozy robes; the services are impeccable; and the ancillaries make the stay as engaging as it is restful. The brunch is the best offering.
392 Valet All major cards

WESTIN PASADENA
$$$
191 N. LOS ROBLES AVE.
TEL 626/792-2727
www.westin.com/pasadena
This solid business hotel is perfectly located right in the

middle of the Plaza Los Flores. Stylish rooms are airy, the food at the **Ventanas Restaurant** is quite good, and the overall feeling is one of glowing ease.
350 All major cards

PASADENA HILTON
$$–$$$
168 S. LOS ROBLES AVE.
TEL 626/577-1000
www.hilton.com
This is Rose Bowl central come New Year's Day; during the rest of the year, the Hilton is the old standby, relied upon by businessfolk, visiting Caltech types, and many smaller conventions.
296 All major cards

DEVON
$$$
109 E. LEMON ST.
TEL 626/305-0013
Suburbia meets the frontier of urban cuisine at this 1890s carriage house. Some favorites: turtle-stuffed ravioli, or monkfish in tomatillo-Grand Marnier sauce. Smallish portions and a pricey wine list, but flavors you won't find anywhere else.
70 Closed Mon. & L Sat.–Sun. All major cards

SHIRO
$$$
1505 MISSION ST.
TEL 626/799-4774
www.restaurantshiro.com
Shiro pulls off a tricky blend of French-Japanese cuisine and is rated one of L.A.'s best restaurants. The sizzling catfish in ponzu and the shrimp-salmon mousse in smoked salmon sauce are the reason so many go here for the most special of occasions. A decent (and reasonably priced) wine list, too.
75 Closed L & Mon.–Tue. AE, MC, V

SOMETHING SPECIAL

EURO PANE BAKERY
$–$$$
950 E. COLORADO BLVD.
TEL 626/577-1828
Former Spago pastry chef Sumi Chang brings a penchant for fine ingredients, fresh fruits, and traditional baking methods to this unassuming but wildly popular bakery. Try some brioche bread or a slice of the famous pear spice cake.
20 Closed D MC, V

SALADANG
$–$$
363 S. FAIR OAKS AVE. (BETW. CALIFORNIA BLVD. & DEL MAR AVE.)
TEL 626/793-8123
Artsy and moderne, this thriving Thai eatery serves up all the basics with style. Try the green curry, the apple and chicken salad, the salad rolls, and the sweet rice dessert.
94 All major cards

ALL INDIA CAFÉ
$
39 S. FAIR OAKS AVE. (JUST S OF COLORADO BLVD.)
TEL 626/440-0309
www.allindiacafe.com
Intensely flavored Indian street fare done with a light use of traditional oils. The bargains, and some of the best cooking, are found in the lunch specials. These consist of a half dozen filling meals—curries, tandooris, thalis—made of smaller dishes.
45 All major cards

SAN FERNANDO VALLEY

SHERATON UNIVERSAL
$$$$
333 UNIVERSAL HOLLYWOOD DR. PKWY.
TEL 818/980-1212
FAX 818/985-4980
The best place to stay in the valley, this hotel is located on the Universal lot. A good business hotel, it has spacious rooms and a giant lobby in which to meet friends before setting off for sightseeing.
436 Valet All major cards

BEVERLY GARLAND'S HOLIDAY INN
$$–$$$
4222 VINELAND AVE.
TEL 800/238-3759
www.beverlygarland.com
This Holiday Inn is considered a homey place to stay. It sits on seven landscaped acres and has the usual Holiday Inn amenities, plus tennis courts. Free shuttle to Universal.
255 All major cards

SPORTSMEN'S LODGE
$$–$$$
12825 VENTURA BLVD.
TEL 818/769-4700, 800/821-8511
www.sportsmenslodge.com
Steeped in film history and within easy driving distance of Universal Studios, the lodge offers a "home on the range" theme in otherwise mod Studio City. The hotel's tiny but tasty restaurant pays homage to Hollywood Westerns and the celluloid heroes—like John Wayne, Roy Rogers, and Gene Autry—who used to hang out here.
190 All major cards

BISTRO GARDEN AT COLDWATER
$$$
12950 VENTURA BLVD.
TEL 818/501-0202
www.bistrogarden.com
Perhaps the prettiest location in the valley, the Garden offers Italian bistro food done to near perfection. Ravioli and the osso buco are favorites.
300 Closed L Sat–Sun. All major cards

SUSHI NOZAWA
$$$
11288 VENTURA BLVD.
(NEAR VINELAND ST.)
TEL 818/508-7017
Cool slices of flavorful seafood, from salmon to mussels to shrimp, done with a skillful hand. The chef is known for his delicate flavor combinations, such as seaweed noodle on salmon or mussels in rice vinegar broth.
30 Closed Sat.–Sun. MC, V

MISTRAL
$$–$$$
13422 VENTURA BLVD.
TEL 818/981-6650
www.mistralrestaurant.com
Outstanding Provençal cuisine with all the standards, from grilled entrecôte to the oniony French version of pizza, pissaladière. A good deal in an elegant place.
55 Valet Closed L Sat.–Sun. All major cards

PALATE+FOOD+WINE
$$–$$$
933 S. BRAND BLVD.
TEL 818/662-9463
www.palatefoodwine.com
Chef Octavio Becerra's bustling open kitchen serves up an eclectic array—crispy salt cod cakes and roasted bone marrow, steamed mussels with garlic and shelling beans, and lamb shank with grits. The cozy wine bar and cheese room is stocked with handmade, regional wines.
150 Valet Closed L except Fri. All major cards

LE PETIT RESTAURANT
$$
13360 VENTURA BLVD.
TEL 818/501-7999
www.lepetitrestaurant.net
Simple, authentic French food with the added benefit of charming surroundings. Try the eggplant and tomato tart.
80 Valet Closed L Fri.–Sun. AE, MC, V

PINOT BISTRO
$$
12969 VENTURA BLVD.
TEL 818/990-0500
www.patinagroup.com
Even well-seasoned fans of Joachim Splichal's more famous Patina (see p. 354) come here when they want just the essential City of Light fare. All the plats du jour are worth contemplating, if only to get a good dose of his irresistible brandade potatoes. Try the bacon-wrapped monkfish.
150 Valet Closed Mon. & L Sat.–Sun. All major cards

SANTA MONICA

LOEWS
$$$$$
1700 OCEAN AVE.
TEL 866/563-9792
www.santamonicaloews hotel.com
Another fine beachside hotel, the Loews features sun-filled atria, tasteful guest rooms, and up-to-date business services for those who must tear themselves away from the beach to send something back to the office. The Loews restaurant, **Ocean and Vine,** serves notable California cuisine.
359 All major cards

OCEANA
$$$$$
849 OCEAN AVE.
TEL 310/393-0486, 888/614-1750
www.hoteloceanasanta monica.com
In a great location just steps from the beach and Santa Monica Pier, and one block from upscale Montana Avenue, the designer-savvy Oceana is a boutique hotel reincarnation of a classic southern California oceanfront apartment building. Many of the large rooms have expansive ocean views, while the place to hang out is the center courtyard with the heart-shaped swimming pool.
70 Valet All major cards

SHUTTERS ON THE BEACH
$$$$$
1 PICO BLVD.
TEL 310/458-0030, 800/334-9000
www.shuttersonthebeach.com
Intimate and sun-filled, this luxury hotel on the coast featured spacious, bright rooms evocative of 1930s beachside cottages. The **One Pico** restaurant is a regular for local celebrities like Mel Brooks.
198 Valet All major cards

CHINOIS ON MAIN
$$$$
2709 MAIN ST.
TEL 310/392-9025
www.wolfgangpuck.com
Slick, breezy, and always crowded,

PRICES

HOTELS
An indication of the cost of a double room in the high season is given by **$** signs.

$$$$$	Over $280
$$$$	$200–$280
$$$	$120–$200
$$	$80–$120
$	Under $80

RESTAURANTS
An indication of the cost of a three-course meal without drinks is given by **$** signs.

$$$$$	Over $80
$$$$	$50–$80
$$$	$35–$50
$$	$20–$35
$	Under $20

Wolfgang Puck's family-style fusion cuisine (like Cantonese duck with plum sauce) is hard to beat. The charred tuna exemplifies Puck's puckishness with sauces.
100 P Valet Closed L Sat.–Tues. All major cards

VALENTINO
$$$$
3115 PICO BLVD.
TEL 310/829-4313
www.valentinorestaurants.com
For 25 years a revered L.A. institution, Piero Selvaggio's flagship is routinely rated among the best of the best. The wine collection warrants note for its depth and breadth of small specialty producers. Risotto, pasta and osso buco all feature on this earthy menu.
240 P Valet Closed Sun. All major cards

3-SQUARE CAFÉ & BAKERY
$$$–$$$$
1121 ABBOT KINNEY
TEL 310/399-6504
www.rockenwagner.com
Consistently rated as one of L.A.'s best places to eat, executive chef Wolfgang Gussmack's fine-dining yet casual, contemporary place is known for its sandwiches, salads, pastries, and such delights as truffle parmesan fries and octopus salad.
100 P Closed D Sun.–Mon. All major cards

BORDER GRILL
$$$
1445 4TH ST.
TEL 310/451-1655
www.bordergrill.com
Upscale Mexican cuisine from the kitchen of Mary Sue Milliken and Susan Feniger, hosts of the national TV cooking show *Top Chef Masters*. Among the menu favorites are tortilla soup, tamales, chile relleno, and more unusual items like pork slow roasted in banana leaves.
50 P All major cards

JIRAFFE
$$$
502 SANTA MONICA BLVD.
TEL 310/917-6671
www.jirafferestaurant.com
Another consistent performer, this one dishes up a version of California-French. Among the *plats* most desired are the roasted Jidori chicken and the vegetable ragout with sweet white corn. Signature cocktails are a highlight.
85 P Valet Closed L & Sun. D All major cards

PENTHOUSE
$$–$$$$
HUNTLEY HOTEL, 1111 2ND ST.
TEL 310/394-5454
www.thehuntleyhotel.com
Wrapped in glass, the Penthouse perches 18 stories above the California coast. Executive chef Seth Greenburg offers novel takes on traditional American dishes like an open-faced grilled cheese starter and a crispy-skin salmon main. In the lounge bar, resident mixologist Ryan Magarian conjures up creative cocktails (coconut espresso martini, spicy-hot margarita).
319 P Valet All major cards

VENICE

JOE'S RESTAURANT
$$$
1023 ABBOT KINNEY BLVD.
TEL 310/399-5811
www.joesrestaurant.com
Executive chef and owner Joseph Miller has crafted a sophisticated menu based on farmers-market-fresh produce. Signature dishes include New Zealand red snapper filet with potato scales and wild rice, grilled Vermont quail with almond bread and roasted beets, and prime pork tenderloin crepinette with wild mushrooms and roasted garlic jus. An affordable daily three-course prix fixe menu and chef's tasting menu are offered every day except Sunday.
90 P All major cards

ROSE CAFÉ
$$
220 ROSE AVE. (AT MAIN ST.)
TEL 310/399-0711
www.rosecafe.com
A big, airy cafeteria where the cappuccino is good, the breakfasts are satisfying, and the various cold salads are a favorite of the very trendy locals who hang out here.
150 P Closed L AE, MC, V

WESTWOOD/WEST L.A.

HOTEL BEL AIR
$$$$$
701 STONE CANYON RD.
TEL 310/472-1211
www.hotelbelair.com
For more than half a century, the Hotel Bel Air has charmed guests with its blend of mission architecture, lush gardens, and fine food (Wolfgang Puck at Hotel Bel Air is among the top California-Mediterranean eateries in the city). A good idea is simply to drop in for a drink at the Lobby Lounge, perhaps in the early evening when the gardens turn to pure magic.
58 rooms & 45 suites P All major cards

W LOS ANGELES
$$$–$$$$$
930 HILGARD AVE.
TEL 310/208-8765
www.starwoodhotels.com
This moderne California hotel is perfect for those who want to play on L.A.'s Westside at night while exploring inland during the day. Situated across the street from UCLA, the W offers a luxurious spa, spacious

suites, and a fine lobby bar where the people-watching just goes on and on.
258 rooms & suites All major cards

VINCENTI
$$$$$
11930 SAN VICENTE BLVD.
TEL 310/207-0127
www.vincentiristorante.com
Chef Nicola Mastronarti is noted as one of the best Italian chefs in L.A. The fresh whole fish cooked over glowing embers is the main attraction, with such innovations as penne with rapini and pressed tuna roe done in a surprisingly light, fresh manner. For fans of the trendy guanciale (pig's jowl), this is the place.
90 Valet Closed Sun. & L Sat.–Thurs. All major cards

ASAKUMA
$$
11769 SANTA MONICA BLVD.
TEL 310/473-8990
www.asakuma.com
Delivery of fresh, made-to-order sushi popular with local Japanese businessmen and UCLA types. The sushi is very fresh and skillfully prepared, particularly the toro—like butter when in season.
All major cards

SOMETHING SPECIAL

BOMBAY CAFÉ
$$
12021 W. PICO BLVD.
TEL 310/473-3388
www.bombaycafe-la.com
This well-known café brilliantly blends various Indian street foods with modern preparation techniques, yielding a relatively low-fat but very flavorful cuisine. For lunch, try the frankies, a kind of chutney-fried burrito. The crispy shrimp, tandoori-chicken sausages, and smoked *bharta* (eggplant) are favorites.
112 All major cards

FATHER'S OFFICE
$$
3229 HELMS AVE.
TEL 310/736-2224
www.fathersoffice.com
Close to the historic Sony MGM Studio, this edgy gastropub has 40 microbrews on tap, plus organic salads, steak, ribs, sweet potato fries, and what many consider the best burger in L.A. There is also a variety of tasty tapas.
150 Closed L Mon.–Thurs. All major cards

LA BRUSCHETTA
$$
1621 WESTWOOD BLVD.
TEL 310/477-1052
www.labruschetta westwood.com
Northern Italian fare—osso buco, risotto Milanese, and veal scaloppini—combines with an impressive wine list to make this local favorite a reliable, festive affair.
78 Valet Closed L Sat.–Sun. AE, MC, V

PASTINA
$$
2260 WESTWOOD BLVD.
TEL 310/441-4655
www.pastina.net
Tasty neighborhood Italian food that won't wreak havoc on a diet, despite the large portions of pasta, pizza, and gnocchi.
86 Valet Closed L Sat.–Sun. & D Sun. AE, MC, V

APPLE PAN
$
10801 PICO BLVD.
TEL 310/475-3585
The old-fashioned U-shaped counter is always packed with locals waiting for their hit of hamburgers, fries, and apple pie. Great if you've been shopping and need sustenance.
23 Closed Mon.
No credit cards

JOHN O'GROATS
$
10516 PICO BLVD.
(NEAR BEVERLY GLEN)
TEL 310/204-0692
Just the greatest little down-home breakfast spot on the Westside, O'Groats is legendary among UCLA grad students, who succor themselves on the café's homemade biscuits and fries, only to return with their families years later—just to order the same thing!
65 Closed D
All major cards

SOUTHERN CALIFORNIA

ANAHEIM

DISNEYLAND HOTELS
$$–$$$$
www.disneylandhotels.com
To extend the Disney experience try one of the Walt Disney Company hotels. The newly renovated **Disneyland Hotel** *(1150 Magic Way, tel 714/778-6600)* is located just off the Monorail. **Disney's Paradise Pier** *(1717 S. Disneyland Dr., tel 714/999-0990)* has a spa, shopping, and a grill where Disney characters appear regularly. The **Grand Californian Hotel** *(1600 S. Disneyland Dr., tel 714/635-2300)* is done in an Arts and Crafts style. The park/hotel packages offer good deals.
All major cards

CATALINA

VILLA PORTOFINO
$$–$$$$
111 CRESCENT AVE.
TEL 310/510-0555, 888/510-0555
www.hotelvillaportofino.com
Reliable and relaxed, the Portofino offers all modern amenities in a comfortable setting. Behind its classic Mediterranean exterior, rooms boast understated European elegance. It has a fine-

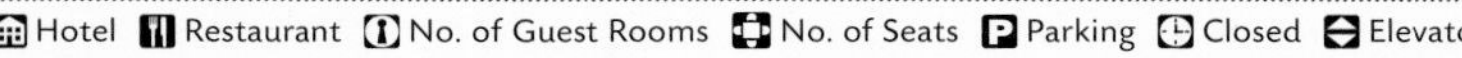
Hotel Restaurant No. of Guest Rooms No. of Seats Parking Closed Elevator

dining **restaurant** and splendid waterfront views.

34 All major cards

COSTA MESA

LEATHERBY'S CAFÉ ROUGE

$$$$$

SEGERSTROM CENTER FOR THE ARTS, 615 TOWN CENTER DR.

TEL 714/429-7640

www.patinagroup.com

Sophisticates with deep pockets and an eye for aesthetics appreciate the sexy contemporary surrounds, including a curvaceous glass wall and orange mohair booths. This stylish restaurant also delivers in the culinary arena, with an Asian-inspired fusion menu that offers such innovative items as sea urchin *brulé* over tilefish. The limited wine list is pricey.

120 Valet Closed L Mon.–Fri. & nonperformance weekends, D Mon., & D nonperformance Sun. All major cards

DANA POINT

RITZ-CARLTON LAGUNA NIGUEL

$$$$$

1 RITZ-CARLTON DR.

TEL 949/240-2000

www.ritzcarlton.com

Watch the wealthy old-timers take on body-crunching waves below, then retire to the wood-paneled elegance of the Ritz, where tea awaits. The Ritz's pan-Latin restaurant, **Raya,** has a knockout ahi tuna.

393 Valet All major cards

LAGUNA BEACH

INN AT LAGUNA BEACH

$$$$

211 N. COAST HWY.

TEL 949/497-9722, 800/544-4479

www.innatlagunabeach.com

The true beach romantic's favorite, the inn, low slung and unassuming, offers some of the best views in southern California. From a roomy guest suite, one can watch morning sea mists, blue afternoon skies, and spectacular boiling sunsets.

70 All major cards

DIZZ'S AS IS

$$$

2794 S. COAST HWY. (AT NYES PLACE)

TEL 949/494-5250

The aptly named Dizz serves up solid, honest fare. A great atmosphere in which to eat perfectly grilled fish, pink lamb chops, and steak au poivre. No reservations.

50 Closed L Mon. in winter All major cards

LONG BEACH

QUEEN MARY

$$$

1126 QUEEN'S HWY.

TEL 877/342-0742

www.queenmary.com

Launched in 1936, the *Queen Mary* set the standard for art deco luxury, and it remains much the same today. Guest rooms have ship-style bathrooms, wood paneling, and period furniture. Ask for an outside room with a view—and one of those swell round porthole windows!

365 All major cards

ALEGRIA COCINA LATINA

$$

115 PINE ST.

TEL 562/436-3388

www.alegriacocinalatina.com

A festive atmosphere (live flamenco music and dancing on stage) and good tapas add charm here. If you have a big appetite, choose the paella.

175 Valet Closed L Sat.–Sun. All major cards

NEWPORT BEACH

RESORT AT PELICAN HILL

$$$$$

22701 PELICAN HILL RD. S.

TEL 949/467-6800, 800/315-8214

www.pelicanhill.com

Opened in late 2008, this deluxe resort boasts a spectacular and serene seaside setting. Spacious and sumptuous rooms in bungalows and villas offer ocean views and lavish amenities. Other draws include a circular "Coliseum" pool, state-of-the-art spa, five restaurants, and a 37-hole Tom Fazio–designed golf course.

204 All major cards

THE ISLAND HOTEL

$$$$

690 NEWPORT CENTER DR.

TEL 949/759-0808, 866/554-4620

www.theislandhotel.com

Jumbo rooms with rich appointments combine with top-of-the-line service at this former Four Seasons. The indoor/outdoor **Palm Terrace** offers one of the better dining experiences on this coast.

295 All major cards

PASCAL

$$$

1000 BRISTOL ST. N.

TEL 949/263-9400

www.pascalnpb.com

Considered, at least by regulars, perhaps the best French cooking in Orange County. Sea bass is done with a deft hand.

100 Closed D Sun. All major cards

OJAI

OJAI VALLEY INN

$$$$

905 COUNTRY CLUB RD.

TEL 805/646-1111, 888/697-8780

www.ojairesort.com

This 1930s establishment in mission revival architecture was restored in the 1980s and again in 2005. Guest rooms are cozy and well appointed, many with antiques. The rolling grounds, spa, and fine dining at **Maravilla** enhance the charm.

308 All major cards

THE RANCH HOUSE

$$$

S. LOMITA AVE.

TEL 805/646-2360

www.theranchhouse.com

Many credit the founders of this rustic eatery with the creation of modern California cuisine. The influence persists, with brasserie staples like lamb chops and artichoke salad. Stunning gardens.

140 Closed L except Sun. & all Mon. All major cards

SAN DIEGO/LA JOLLA

THE GRAND DEL MAR

$$$$$

5300 GRAND DEL MAR CT.

TEL 858/314-2000, 855/274-5586

www.thegranddelmar.com

Tucked into a lush coastal valley behind Torrey Pines and the Del Mar coast, this eclectic resort is truly grand, starting with the super-wide hallways, capacious lounges, and full-scale, mission-style wedding chapel. Golf, tennis, fitness classes, spa treatments, horseback trail rides, mountain biking, hiking, and trips to the beach are among the many recreation options.

249 Valet All major cards

SOMETHING SPECIAL

LA VALENCIA

$$$$–$$$$$

1132 PROSPECT ST.

TEL 858/454-0771

www.lavalencia.com

Perched above the waters of La Jolla Cove, the historic Spanish-style La Valencia, one-time summer home to Charlie Chaplin and others, is still a great place to stay. Rooms and villas are old fashioned but comfortable, the lounge and bar have loads of hidalgo charm, and the views are unsurpassed.

112 rooms, suites, & villas All major cards

LOEWS CORONADO BAY RESORT

$$$$

4000 CORONADO BAY RD.

TEL 619/424-4000, 800/235-6397

www.loewshotels.com

Blessed with a spectacular location on the southern end of San Diego Bay, Loews, unlike the brassier Hotel Del across the way, specializes in elegant informality. Its in-house restaurant, French-inspired **Mistral,** ranks among the city's finest dining spots.

439 Valet All major cards

ANDAZ

$$$–$$$$

600 F ST.

TEL 619/849-1234

www.sandiego.andaz .hyatt.com

Andaz is a serene oasis in the midst of San Diego's hectic Gaslamp Quarter. The cool rooftop pool area is a place to relax during the day, but turns into a popular open-air nightclub on weekends. Sexy guest rooms have glass-enclosed bathtubs that come complete with mood lighting. All hotel guests receive VIP access to the über-hip Ivy Nightclub.

PRICES

HOTELS

An indication of the cost of a double room in the high season is given by **$** signs.

$$$$$	Over $280
$$$$	$200–$280
$$$	$120–$200
$$	$80–$120
$	Under $80

RESTAURANTS

An indication of the cost of a three-course meal without drinks is given by **$** signs.

$$$$$	Over $80
$$$$	$50–$80
$$$	$35–$50
$$	$20–$35
$	Under $20

159 Valet All major cards

ISLAND PRIME & LEVEL C

$$$$

880 HARBOR ISLAND DR.

TEL 619/298-6802

www.islandprime.com

Another creation by executive chef Deborah Scott, Island Prime & Level C combines incredible food with amazing waterfront views across the bay. The surf-and-turf menu features pan-roasted day-boat scallops and an array of artisan steaks finished off with a trio of rotating flavors of crème brulée.

180 dining room, 230 outdoor deck (Level C) Closed L All major cards

MILLE FLEURS

$$$$

6009 PASEO DELICIAS

TEL 858/756-3085

www.millefleurs.com

Mille Fleurs is a delight for those who appreciate a chef's dedication to fresh ingredients and impeccable preparation. Fish—grilled, poached, or baked—is outstanding; so are game meats and (seasonal) suckling pig. Extensive wine list.

120 P Closed L Sat.–Mon. All major cards

CUCINA URBANA

$$

505 LAUREL AVE.

TEL 619/239-2222

www.cucinaurbana.com

The cuisine of Italy is the star here, with California inspirations. Try the delicious braised black cod or ricotta gnudi. Great wine list; simple but decadent desserts.

130 P Valet Closed L Sat.–Mon. All major cards

BO-BEAU

$$

4996 W. POINT LOMA BLVD.

TEL 619/224-2884

www.bobeaukitchen.com

This neighborhood bistro aims to transport diners to another place and time with a French farm chic atmosphere. Main courses range from the burger royale (pork belly with Gruyère cheese, green peppercorn aioli) to boeuf bourguignon.

78 P Closed L All major cards

BERTA'S

$

3928 TWIGGS ST., OLD TOWN

TEL 619/295-2343

www.bertasinoldtown.com

It wouldn't be San Diego without *la cucina latina,* and if you're not heading south of the border, Berta's is the place. Big portions and remarkable breadth of menu are Berta's mainstays. Get the lamb.

45 P Closed Mon. AE, MC, V

MOTHER'S KITCHEN

$

33120 CANFIELD RD.

TEL 760/742-4233

www.motherskitchenpalomar.com

The only restaurant on Mount Palomar serves excellent vegetarian dishes in a rustic setting. Sit inside around a stone hearth or outdoors on the front balcony or beneath the towering pines out back. Among its specials are pancakes and French toast, breakfast burritos, club sandwiches, homemade mac & cheese and lasagna, and veggie chili.

48 P Closed L Sat.–Sun. All major cards

TEMECULA CREEK INN

$$$$$

44501 RAINBOW CANYON RD.

TEL 877/517-1823

www.temeculacreekinn.com

Enjoying a lush golf-course setting in the heart of southern California wine country, this lodge offers spacious guest rooms with rich Southwestern decor combining cozy comforts and modern amenities. In a town better known for fast food than gourmet fare, **Temet Grill** stands out as an oasis of fine dining.

130 P AE, MC, V

SANTA BARBARA & AROUND

ALISAL GUEST RANCH RESORT

$$$$$

1054 ALISAL RD.

TEL 805/688-6411, 800/425-4725

www.alisal.com

This 10,000-acre working cattle ranch welcomes guests with a range of resort-like activities, including golf, tennis, fishing, and spa services. But horseback riding is its claim to fame. Every Wednesday during the summer season, the ranch also puts on a full-scale rodeo. At the end of a day on the range, soothe your weary muscles with a deep-tissue massage and a glass of superb Santa Ynez Valley wine.

73 P AE, MC, V

FOUR SEASONS BILTMORE

$$$$$

1260 CHANNEL DR.

TEL 805/969-2261

www.fourseasons.com

Spanish-Mediterranean ele-gance, California amiability, and historic grandeur make this 21-acre resort a prime destination for Angelenos seeking respite from the city. The gardens, the mariachis in the sunset lounge, and the ever-pounding Pacific will lure you out of your impeccably appointed room. If you can't stay here, at least have lunch on the patio of the restaurant, **Bella Vista.**

207 rooms, 12 cottages P All major cards

SAN YSIDRO RANCH

$$$$–$$$$$

900 SAN YSIDRO LN.

TEL 805/565-1700

www.sanysidroranch.com

Nestled among the foothills of Montecito, this ranch is a perfect place for living out the fantasy of the good Santa Barbara life. The cottages are beautifully appointed, with soft gauzy linens, fireplaces, and little gardens outside. Call for an in-room massage, then eat at the **Stonehouse Restaurant,** where lobster and a saffron-potato soufflé await your discerning taste buds.

41 P All major cards

EL ENCANTO HOTEL

$$$–$$$$

1900 LASUEN RD.

TEL 805/687-5000

www.elencantohotel.com

Overlooking the city from verdant hills, El Encanto is all charm, from its nine Craftsmen and 11 Spanish Revival cottages to its breezy, sun-filled **dining room,** where you can sample classic California cuisine. The salads and soups in summer are simple, zesty, and beautifully presented. This exquisite hotel and restaurant are slated to reopen in 2013 after being closed for a lengthy restoration.

92 All major cards

SANTA BARBARA INN

$$–$$$

901 E. CABRILLO BLVD.

TEL 800/231-0431

www.santabarbarainn.com

This hotel offers solid value, consistently good service, big rooms—and it's just across the street from the beach!

71 Valet All major cards

HITCHING POST

$$$$

406 E. CALIF. 246 (OFF US 101)

TEL 805/688-0676

www.hitchingpost2.com

Eat here when visiting the Santa Ynez backcountry, where wineries spring from land that once belonged to old California dons. Think cowboy steak house, then add a moderne penchant for fresh ingredients. The steaks are huge, the french fries award winning.

125 Closed L AE, MC, V

ARIGATO SUSHI

$$–$$$

1225 STATE ST.

TEL 805/965-6074

This small, unpretentious eatery has the feel of a sushi bar in the older sections of the Ginza in Tokyo. The fish, particularly the various sushi rolls, keep the locals and out-of-town weekenders coming back.

40 Closed L AE, MC, V

DOWNEY'S

$$–$$$

1305 STATE ST.

TEL 805/966-5006

www.downeyssb.com

Elegant Downey's serves up a changing mix of outstanding California cuisine with a touch of traditional French cooking. Look for cassoulets, entrecôtes, and local fish offerings.

48 Closed Mon. & L AE, MC, V

LA SUPER-RICA TAQUERIA

$

622 N. MILPAS ST.

TEL 805/963-4940

An endorsement by the late Julia Child has made this modest taco stand a foodie icon. It also ensures long lines as locals line up for green chile and cheese corn tortilla soft tacos, *adobado* (marinated pork), *gorditas* (thick corn masa pockets filled with spicy beans), and the "Super-Rica Especial" (a combo of roasted pasilla peppers, cheese, and pork).

50 Closed Wed. No credit cards

CENTRAL COAST

APTOS

BITTERSWEET BISTRO

$$$

787 RIO DEL MAR BLVD.

TEL 831/662-9799

www.bittersweetbistro.com

Coastal bistro meets Mediterranean ristorante in a relaxed atmosphere. The rack of lamb is a feast for all senses.

100 AE, MC, V

MA MAISON

$$$

9051 SOQUEL DR.

TEL 831/688-5566

www.mamaisonrestaurant.com

One of the best eateries in the Santa Cruz area. Chef Lionel Le Morvan does outstanding California-French cuisine at a reasonable price, served in an intimate atmosphere.

90 Closed Mon. & L Sat.–Sun. MC, V

AVILA BEACH

AVILA LA FONDA

$$$–$$$$

101 SAN MIGUEL ST.

TEL 805/595-1700

www.avilafonda.com

Located just a block from Avila's pleasure pier and the long white-sand strand, Avila La Fonda is an artsy boutique hotel with an early 19th-century California-Mexico design theme, as well as Wi-Fi, wide-screen TVs, and Jacuzzi tubs

28 All major card

BIG SUR

POST RANCH INN

$$$$$

HWY. 1, ACROSS FROM VENTANA

TEL 831/667-2200, 888/524-4787

www.postranchinn.com

The inn is the exact opposite of Deetjen's (see below), from its Zen-ranch architecture to the spare California cuisine in the acclaimed **Sierra Mar** restaurant. Every known comfort is here: deep soaking tubs, thick terry robes, bedside massages, Indian slate bathrooms, stunning views of the ocean.

41 AE, MC, V

VENTANA INN & SPA

$$$$–$$$$$

48123 CALIF. 1

TEL 831/667-2331

www.ventanainn.com

Many people still consider the Ventana the ultimate in Big Sur luxury, with giant guest suites, fully equipped kitchens, open-air decks and hot tubs, and a decent

restaurant. Don't count on much in the way of room service, but do make your way to the breakfast and the afternoon wine and cheese spread.
60 All major cards

GLEN OAKS BIG SUR
$$$–$$$$$
CALIF. 1
TEL 831/667-2105
www.glenoaksbigsur.com
This classic 1950s adobe motor lodge has been updated with modern amenities and décor, but retains its rustic hipster ambience and the rates that make it a reasonable alternative to the super-high-priced lodges that spangle this coast. Rooms in the main lodge feature fireplaces, recycled peroba wood furnishings, modern bathrooms with walk-in showers and heated stone floors, and Wi-Fi. Many of them have private patios or outdoor seating areas.
20 MC, V

BIG SUR LODGE
$$–$$$
CALIF. 1, PFEIFFER BIG SUR STATE PARK
TEL 831/667-3100, 800/424-4787
www.bigsurlodge.com
Old-fashioned, basic family accommodations set in a scenic meadow surrounded by redwoods and pines make this an affordable and joyful destination. No TVs!
61 AE, MC, V

SOMETHING SPECIAL

DEETJEN'S BIG SUR INN
$$–$$$
48865 CALIF. 1, S OF BIG SUR
TEL 831/667-2377
www.deetjens.com
The ultimate in coastal rusticity, Deetjen's is a collection of woodstove-heated cabins planted deep in the redwoods. For romantics, old Deetjen's is a must, if only for a night of listening to the wind rustle the trees and reading old books left for nature lovers. Breakfasts are particularly good.
20 All major cards

NEPENTHE
$$$$
48510 CALIF. 1
TEL 831/667-2345
www.nepenthebigsur.com
A local institution since 1949, Nepenthe was one of the first eateries along the Big Sur stretch of Calif. 1 and continues to offer a quintessential California coastal experience. Perched 800 feet above the Pacific, the restaurant serves up Lolly's roast chicken, Ambrosia burgers, and filet mignon with a cabernet demi-glace, as well as local artisanal cheeses and celebrated triple berry pie, all served indoors or on long, outdoor tables with spectacular views.
36 Closed Sun.
All major cards

CAPITOLA

INN AT DEPOT HILL
$$$–$$$$
250 MONTEREY AVE.
TEL 831/462-3376, 800/572-2632
www.innatdepothill.com
Depot Hill has 12 tastefully decorated rooms, each inspired by a different region, from the Mediterranean to England.
12 All major cards

CARMEL

See more hotel listings p. 181.

PARK HYATT CARMEL HIGHLANDS INN
$$$$–$$$$$
120 HIGHLANDS DR.
TEL 831/620-1234
www.highlandsinn.hyatt.com
More coastal luxury, this time perched above the rocks of Point Lobos, where seals frolic on jagged rock islands and mists float to and fro. Big guest suites all have great views; in-room jacuzzis are perfect for after-hiking aches. Room service could be better, but the restaurant, **Pacific's Edge,** has few coastal peers. Steer for the caramelized sea scallops and potato and basil salad.
142 All major cards

LA PLAYA HOTEL
$$$$
8TH AVE. & CAMINO REAL
TEL 831/624-6476
www.laplayahotel.com
Cool and serene, with beautifully tended central gardens and views of the Carmel coastline, this 60-year-old favorite has plenty of charm. It was originally built by Christopher Jorgensen for his new bride, who was one of the famed Ghirardelli chocolate clan. A sweet retreat still.
75 rooms, 5 cottages All major cards

QUAIL LODGE RESORT & GOLF CLUB
$$$$
8205 VALLEY GREENS DR.
TEL 831/624-2888
www.quaillodge.com
A luxury deal on the coast, the Quail has great service, outstanding dining at its **Covey Restaurant,** and everything the golf fanatic could ever want, set in a serene and dreamy spot with rugged peaks and green valleys.
100 All major cards

ANTON & MICHEL
$$$
MISSION & 7TH STS.
TEL 831/624-2406
www.carmelsbest.com
Classic, elegant Continental cuisine with an emphasis on fresh ingredients makes Anton

& Michel's one of the first dining stops for many coastal regulars. The wine list, featuring several area vineyards, has grown substantially in recent years.
90 P All major cards

FRENCH POODLE
$$$
5TH & JUNIPERO STS.
TEL 831/624-8643
www.thefrenchpoodlecarmel.com
For more than 20 years now, some of the best French cuisine in town (try the duck and any of the sauced fish dishes) has been served here in a quiet, restful interior. The chilled desserts are a must.
36 P Closed Sun. AE

LITTLE NAPOLI
$$$
DOLORES & 7TH STS.
TEL 831/626-6335
Serving southern Italian country cooking from Pèpe family recipes since 1990. Here you can get all the favorites: antipasti, pizza, pasta, risotto, and traditional Italian desserts served in a friendly, inviting atmosphere. Being so close to the sea, there's also plenty of seafood on offer, and the garlic bread is outstanding.
60 P All major cards

MONTEREY

CASA PALERMO
$$$$$
1518 CYPRESS DR.
TEL 831/622-6666, 800/654-9300
www.pebblebeach.com
Evocative of a lush Mediterranean village, this elegant enclave features sun-drenched patios and lush landscaped grounds overlooking the Pebble Beach Golf Links. Lavish guest rooms feature wood-burning fireplaces, oversize soaking tubs, and plush robes. Tennis and billiards are among the refined activities to enjoy.
24 P All major cards

HYATT REGENCY MONTEREY HOTEL & SPA
$$$$–$$$$$
1 OLD GOLF COURSE RD.
TEL 831/372-1234
www.monterey.hyatt.com
The Hyatt Monterey perches on the edge of Del Monte Golf Course. Guest rooms feature private patios, wide-screen TVs, and bathrooms with walk-in rain showers. The resort offers direct access to the golf links, several swimming pools, 24-hour gym, and racquet club, as well as hiking, biking, and jogging trails. **TusCa Ristorante** serves up gourmet Italian cuisine with a California touch.
550 P Valet
All major cards

LODGE AT PEBBLE BEACH
$$$$–$$$$$
17 MILE DR.
TEL 831/647-7500, 800/654-9300
www.pebblebeach.com
This luxurious lodge has been setting the standard for the haute golf world since 1919. The rooms are impeccably appointed with crisp linens and richly burnished decor. The **Stillwater Bar & Grill** is the place for contemporary seafood, while the low-key **Gallery Café** offers homestyle meals.
161 P
All major cards

SEVEN GABLES INN
$$$–$$$$
555 OCEAN VIEW BLVD.
TEL 831/372-4341
www.thesevengablesinn.com
The ocean view, the European antiques and the gilded-age decor combine to make this clutch of yellow-gabled wood buildings a fine period hideaway.
14 P MC, V

PRICES

HOTELS
An indication of the cost of a double room in the high season is given by **$** signs.

$$$$$	Over $280
$$$$	$200–$280
$$$	$120–$200
$$	$80–$120
$	Under $80

RESTAURANTS
An indication of the cost of a three-course meal without drinks is given by **$** signs.

$$$$$	Over $80
$$$$	$50–$80
$$$	$35–$50
$$	$20–$35
$	Under $20

VISION QUEST RANCH
$$$–$$$$
400 RIVER RD.
TEL 831/455-1901, 800/228-7382
www.visionquestranch.com
The closest you can get to a safari in California, this unusual bed-and-breakfast is located inside the Vision Quest animal sanctuary, where more than a hundred exotic beasts get a second chance to enjoy a peaceful life. Elevated on wooden platforms, the canvas-walled bungalows contain all the comforts of a traditional hotel (including a full bathroom).
8 bungalows P All major cards

PÈPPOLI
$$$$
THE INN AT SPANISH BAY, 2700 17 MILE DR.
TEL 831/647-7433
www.pebblebeach.com
Exuding cozy Tuscan ambience, Pèppoli also offers flavorful, rustic Italian dishes paired to classic Italian wines. Consider these favorites: mussels and clams steamed

in a spicy shallot saffron broth, and slow-braised veal shank with Pèppoli wine and gremolata. The sweeping views over the Links at Spanish Bay and the Pacific Ocean are dessert enough.
120 P Closed L All major cards

MONTRIO
$$–$$$
414 CALLE PRINCIPAL
TEL 831/648-8880
www.montrio.com
For anyone who has grown impatient with the New American fad of recent years, this is where the form finds redemption in tasty, ingredient-savvy cooking by chef Tony Baker. Try the crab cakes or the rotisserie-cooked rib-eye steak.
200 P Closed L Sun. All major cards

TARPY'S ROADHOUSE
$
2999 MONTEREY-SALINAS HWY.
TEL 831/647-1444
www.tarpys.com
More American fare, but that would be to sell Tarpy's short. Inside the lovely ivy-shrouded stone house is some fine cooking, with the "American" menu including roast rabbit and a pecan-barbecued duck that will drive you quackers for more.
300 P All major cards

MORRO BAY

INN AT MORRO BAY
$$–$$$
60 STATE PARK RD.
TEL 805/772-5651, 800/321-9566
www.innatmorrobay.com
Simple and quiet, the inn sits above Morro Bay's rocky shore, where the famous Morro Rock juts from the ocean floor. Guest rooms are equipped with state-of-the-art amenities. The restaurant, **Orchid,** offers fine seafood at decent prices.
98 P All major cards

PACIFIC GROVE

GREEN GABLES INN
$$$–$$$$
301 OCEAN VIEWS BLVD.
TEL 800/722-1774
www.greengablesinnpg.com
A cross between an inn and a bed-and-breakfast, the Gables offers spacious rooms in its carriage house out back and more intimate, historic *chambres* in the main house, which was built, legend holds, by an enterprising sea captain for his mistress.
11 P AE, MC, V

FANDANGO
$$–$$$
223 17TH ST.
TEL 831/372-3456
www.fandangorestaurant.com
A fine midrange alternative to the French fever that possesses the peninsula these days, Fandango's zesty Mediterranean fare (from Spanish paellas to Moroccan couscous) has locals lining up. The osso buco is heady with wine and veal stock, simmered just right.
140 P All major cards

PASO ROBLES

BISTRO LAURENT
$$$
1202 PINE ST.
TEL 805/226-8191
www.bistrolaurent.com
If you're deep into cowboy wine country, you can't do better than this purveyor of rustic French cuisine, made with the freshest of local ingredients. The roasted squab is great, as is the roast chicken with garlic and rosemary.
50 P Closed Sun.–Mon. MC, V

SAN LUIS OBISPO

APPLE FARM
$$–$$$
2015 MONTEREY ST.
TEL 805/544-2040
www.applefarm.com
Down-home coziness, in the form of fireplaces, canopy beds, and flowers, greets visitors to this happy abode. Located along sycamore- and live oak–dotted San Luis Obispo Creek, this Victorian also offers affordable, satisfying dining at its **Apple Farm Restaurant.** Don't miss the homemade ice cream.
104 P AE, MC, V

SYCAMORE MINERAL SPRINGS RESORT
$$–$$$
1215 AVILA BEACH DR.
TEL 805/595-7302, 800/234-5831
www.sycamoresprings.com
A classic inland spa, complete with Mediterranean architecture, outdoor mineral spas (for soaking under crystal-clear summer skies), and luxury suites with fireplaces. The **Gardens of Avila Restaurant** is cozy and romantic.
55 P AE, MC, V

SANTA CRUZ

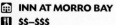

INN AT PASATIEMPO
$$–$$$
555 CALIF. 17
TEL 800/230-2892
www.innatpasatiempo.com
Set alongside Pasatiempo Golf Course, this fine country inn offers serene gardens, solid service, and rooms with fireplaces and jacuzzis. **Hollins House Restaurant** (at the golf course), with panoramic views of Monterey Bay, features no-nonsense (and very tasty) regional American cuisine.
54 P All major cards

SHELL BEACH

CLIFFS RESORT
$$$
2757 SHELL BEACH RD.
TEL 805/773-5000, 800/826-7827
www.cliffsresort.com
Pacific elegance in a tranquil clifftop setting characterizes this favorite weekend haunt. Many rooms come with wonderful ocean views.
160
All major cards

TEMPLETON

MCPHEE'S GRILL
$$
416 S. MAIN ST.
TEL 805/434-3204
www.mcpheesgrill.com
If all the walking at Mr. Hearst's little getaway has left you hankering for a bit of pampering, try McPhee's, a modernish grill room with inspired contemporary California cuisine. Locally raised meats make the steak offerings a good bet.
100 MC, V

SAN FRANCISCO

San Francisco is a grand city—and hard to beat for its wide range of hotels, inns, bed-and-breakfasts, and, of course, restaurants. Travelers also can consult the San Francisco Convention & Visitors Bureau *(900 Market St., tel 415/391-2000, www.sanfrancisco.travel)*. One of the best-run such organizations in the country, it offers a variety of free lodging and food guides that are constantly updated by an ambitious, discerning staff.

CHINATOWN & TELEGRAPH HILL

EMPRESS OF CHINA
$$$$
838 GRANT AVE.
TEL 415/434-1345
www.empressofchinasf.com
One of Chinatown's iconic eateries, the ornately decorated Empress serves a mixture of favorites, including shredded Cantonese duck lo mein, *hsiao lung pao* (Shanghai dumplings), and Szechuan beef. The menu is extensive, as are the views of San Francisco and the bay from the rooftop windows.
145
All major cards

HOUSE OF NANKING
$$
919 KEARNY ST.
TEL 415/421-1429
Not much to look at, and the service can be surly and abrupt, but aficionados of true Szechuan cuisine—fiery soups, even hotter sizzled eggplant—still come. Locals bring their out-of-town friends to show them that San Francisco Chinatown still has a few great eateries.
45 MC, V

PEARL CITY
$$
641 JACKSON ST.
TEL 415/398-8383
When you're finished antiquing in Jackson Square, check out one of the city's better dim sum hangouts—and consequently one that is always crowded. Try the shrimp-stuffed pot stickers and the crabmeat dumplings.
200 MC, V

HENRY'S HUNAN
$
924 SANSOME ST.
(AT BROADWAY)
TEL 415/956-7727
www.henryshunan restaurant.com
Hot and smoky—that's what great Hunan food is all about, and that's what you get at this very popular eatery, where connoisseurs go when they simply must have that steamed chili-tofu platter with deboned braised tilapia.
350 AE, MC, V

LUCKY CREATION
$
854 WASHINGTON ST.
TEL 415/989-0818
Lucky is the vegetarian who dines at Chef Kwok Lom's eatery. Try the various meatless meats—goose, pork, chicken—they're all good. Purists might stick with the mushroom-and-greens-stuffed dumplings or smoky oyster-sauce broccoli.
40 Closed Wed.
MC, V

CIVIC CENTER

SOMETHING SPECIAL

JARDINIÈRE
$$$$
300 GROVE ST.
TEL 415/861-5555
www.jardiniere.com
This lively, elegant place is presided over by the young Tracy des Jardins. Every detail of the cuisine here is perfect, from the pan-roasted chicken with chanterelles (which will change your mind about chicken altogether) and the essence of verdure that permeates her pastas to the amazingly refreshing sorbets and tortes that are on offer.
200 Valet Closed L
All major cards

FINANCIAL DISTRICT/ UNION SQUARE

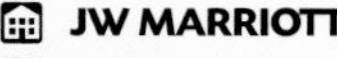

JW MARRIOTT
$$$$$
500 POST ST.
TEL 415/771-8600
www.marriott.com
A wonderful place to stay in the city's theater district, the JW Marriott fuses the comfort and amenities demanded by today's

luxe travelers with the services required by business travelers (complimentary limousines, etc.). The rooms are soothing (pastels dominate), and the lunch menu at the **Level Three Restaurant** is tasty and diverse. Check for weekday deals.
329 P All major cards

PALACE
$$$$$
2 NEW MONTGOMERY ST.
TEL 415/512-1111
www.sfpalace.com
Another classic San Francisco hotel, with grand mahogany furniture, old-style ambience, and large, well-lit rooms, combined with many modern comforts. The Palace even has an indoor lap pool for chilly summer days. Diners in the **Garden Court** restaurant eat under a high domed glass roof hung with chandeliers.
552 P All major cards

TAJ CAMPTON PLACE
$$$$$
340 STOCKTON ST.
TEL 415/781-5555
www.tajhotels.com
Set between Union Square and Chinatown, this chic boutique hotel lures guests with uncluttered, sophisticated rooms and discreet but friendly service. The rooms are cozy but cleverly designed, with large beds, soak tubs, writing desks, and handcrafted hardwood furniture. The outdoor fitness center offers great city views. The menu in the hotel's namesake **restaurant** revolves around California organic and free-range produce. The multi course tasting menus—paired with splendid California wines—are especially decadent.
100 All major cards

MONACO
$$$$–$$$$$
501 GEARY ST.
TEL 415/292-0100, 866/622-5284
www.monaco-sf.com
Audacious decor is the name of the game at this fun-loving hotel near Union Square. The suites are especially playful, blending old world glamour with modern amenities. The spa includes sauna, steam room, and jacuzzi. The Monaco goes out of its way to welcome pets. For guests who are traveling solo, companion goldfish are available on request.
100 All major cards

CLIFT HOTEL
$$$$
495 GEARY ST.
TEL 415/775-4700
www.clifthotel.com
Longtime tradition meets trendy style in this classic hotel given a makeover by Ian Schrager and his designer, Philippe Starck. Enjoy a cocktail in the Redwood Room (made from a single redwood tree, before such acts were considered abominations).
363 P Valet All major cards

HOTEL NIKKO
$$$$
222 MASON ST.
TEL 415/394-1111, 800/248-3308
www.hotelnikkosf.com
Solid, upscale service, roomy guest suites, a great location, and the award-winning **Anzu** restaurant make this a favorite. The spa services are worth checking out.
533 P All major cards

WESTIN ST. FRANCIS
$$$$ (TOWER $$$$$)
335 POWELL ST.
TEL 415/397-7000, 800/937-8464
www.westinstfrancis.com
A fine old downtown standby, the St. Francis is a hotel for people who love to stroll the city, like the grand boulevardiers of old. Its lobby is sumptuous, its rooms warm and charming (some with original Victorian details), and its restaurant-bar is the fifth location of the award-winning Michael Mina steak house **Bourbon Steak.**
1,219 P All major cards

HOTEL TRITON
$$$
342 GRANT AVE.
TEL 415/394-0500, 800/800-1299
www.hoteltriton.com
Another boutique hotel—one with outstanding decor (a kind of neo art deco), impeccable (but smallish) rooms, good service, and a great location: just steps from the old Chinatown Gate.
140 P Valet All major cards

PETITE AUBERGE
$$–$$$
863 BUSH ST.
TEL 415/928-6000, 800/365-3004
www.jdvhospitality.com
Another "personal suite" setup, this one with a tasteful French accent. Although the rooms are small, they are very comfortable. No concierge service to speak of, but the breakfast (included) and afternoon wine and cheese (free) are outstanding.
26 P Valet All major cards

POSTRIO
$$$$$
PRESCOTT HOTEL,
545 POST ST.
TEL 415/776-7825
www.postrio.com
Wolfgang Puck's stylish San Francisco restaurant is just as exciting as his Los Angeles ones. In the impressive downstairs room, feast on dishes such as stir-fried garlic lamb with chili and mint, Chinese-style duck with spicy mango sauce, and,

of course, pasta.
180 P Valet All major cards

MASA'S
$$$$–$$$$$
HOTEL VINTAGE COURT, 648 BUSH ST., UNION SQUARE
TEL 415/989-7154
www.masasrestaurant.com
It is a rarity for a leading-edge restaurant to be this good for this long. At Masa's, California-French cuisine reaches its apex. The primacy of ingredients shows in such items as venison in caramelized apples and zinfandel sauce, or spot prawns with fresh cranberry peas. Wines, cheeses, and desserts are equally good.
120 P Valet Closed L, Sun.–Mon., 1st 2 wks. Jan., & 1 wk in July All major cards

FARALLON
$$$$
450 POST ST.
TEL 415/956-6969
www.farallonrestaurant.com
Designer Pat Kuleto pulled out all the stops with Farallon, a marine-themed restaurant with so many oceanic references that you have to go—if only for a drink at the jellyfish bar. It's somewhat noisy, but the food is first rate, particularly the oyster dishes. The pastry chefs have been voted best dessertmakers in the city.
225 P Valet Closed L All major cards

FLEUR DE LYS
$$$$
777 SUTTER ST., UNION SQUARE
TEL 415/673-7779
www.fleurdelyssf.com
This is the place to get a surefire, and very memorable, dose of *la grande cuisine.* The room is stunning, royal in its use of fleur-de-lys fabrics and elegant mirrors. The food rivals the best of Paris, ranging from delicate fishes to hearty Alsatian versions of quail, venison, and foie gras. An unforgettable experience.
80 P Valet Closed L & Sun.–Mon. All major cards

MILLENNIUM
$$$$
580 GEARY ST.
TEL 415/345-3900
www.millenniumrestaurant.com
Healthy food for the gourmet—organic, vegan dishes such as Moroccan spice-roasted portobello mushroom, and almond-baked tofu with corn-garlic pudding.
150 P Valet Closed L All major cards

GRAND CAFÉ
$$$
HOTEL MONACO, 501 GEARY ST.
TEL 415/292-0101
www.monaco-sf.com
Even if the food were only so-so, the decor would warrant the name; very theatrical, it manages to take beaux arts style to new and elegant heights. Fortunately, the food is outstanding. Try the sweet-breads if they are on the menu, and don't skip dessert.
244 P Valet All major cards

LE COLONIAL
$$$
20 COSMO PL.
TEL 415/931-3600
www.lecolonialsf.com
With an atmosphere out of 1920s Vietnam, this stylish spot serves French-Vietnamese cuisine that might include scallop-ginger pot stickers or pomegranate-glazed Peking duck. For a lively scene and good appetizers, head for the upstairs cocktail lounge.
320 P Valet Closed L All major cards

PRICES

HOTELS
An indication of the cost of a double room in the high season is given by **$** signs.

$$$$$	Over $280
$$$$	$200–$280
$$$	$120–$200
$$	$80–$120
$	Under $80

RESTAURANTS
An indication of the cost of a three-course meal without drinks is given by **$** signs.

$$$$$	Over $80
$$$$	$50–$80
$$$	$35–$50
$$	$20–$35
$	Under $20

GOLDEN GATE & AROUND

HAMA-KO
$$$$
108B CARL ST.
TEL 415/753-6808
This impeccable restaurant turns out some of the freshest sushi (especially the yellowtail and giant clam) in town. Traditional Japanese meals, too.
22 P Closed L & Mon. MC, V

KABUTO SUSHI
$$$
5121 GEARY BLVD.
TEL 415/752-5652
www.kabutosushi.com
Though his restaurant is plain plain plain, Kabuto's chef is considered one of the city's best sushi masters, carving up some of the finest fatty toro and briny uni found anywhere.
31 Closed Mon. & L Sun. AE, MC, V

TON KIANG
$$$
5821 GEARY BLVD.
TEL 415/387-8273
www.tonkiang.net
One of the best Chinese restaurants in town, Ton Kiang is best known for its flavorful dim sum: veggie pot stickers with chili sauce, steamed pork dumplings with lemongrass broth, buns—all steamy white and pure—touched with sweet pork on the inside and gingery glaze outside.
90 All major cards

HAIGHT-ASHBURY

CHA CHA CHA
$$
1801 HAIGHT ST.
TEL 415/386-7670
www.cha3.com
This longtime Haight hangout is renowned for its Cajun shrimp and steamed black mussels dishes, but the eclectic menu also features a *plato vegetariano* (seasonal vegetables with black beans, fried sweet plantains, *yuca con mojo*) and Jamaican jerk chicken. It's often jam-packed, so make reservations.
60 All major cards

MISSION DISTRICT

LA TRAVIATA
$$
2854 MISSION ST.
(BETW. 24TH & 25TH STS.)
TEL 415/282-0500
A closely held secret of the younger, groovier folk now gentrifying the district, La Traviata offers affordable, classic Italian cuisine (tortellini, prosciutto, zuppa di pesce) in a delightful atmosphere.
60 Closed L
AE, DC

LA TAQUERIA
$
2889 MISSION ST. (AT 25TH ST.)
TEL 415/285-7117
Truly an amazing deal: downright seductive Mexican food with zesty fresh salsas, tacos so yummy you'll want to take some back to your hotel room, and fast service. Stop here after touring the Mission.
70 No credit cards

PANCHO VILLA TAQUERIA
$
3071 16TH ST. (BETW. VALENCIA & MISSION STS.)
TEL 415/864-8840
www.sfpanchovilla.com
A friendly purveyor of such specialties as barbecued pork burritos, prawn tacos, and an array of Tex-Mex as well.
90 AE, MC, V

NOB HILL

SOMETHING SPECIAL

THE HUNTINGTON
$$$$$
1075 CALIFORNIA ST.
TEL 415/474-5400
www.huntingtonhotel.com
For the money, the best San Francisco experience around. The staff is excellent, rooms large, opulent, and quiet, and the extras don't stop, from limo service to personal modems to unbelievable room service; the spa has an indoor infinity pool and elegant treatment rooms. The **Big Four** restaurant is soothing and rich.
136
All major cards

RITZ-CARLTON SAN FRANCISCO
$$$$$
600 STOCKTON ST.
TEL 415/296-7465
www.ritzcarlton.com
Pricey but, by most standards, one of the best hotels in the world. There is so much splendor: chandeliers, museum-quality oil paintings, flowers, chocolates, and personal maids. Staff is helpful and stylish. The brilliant, top-ranked **restaurant** celebrates the city's many cultural influences, from sashimi to fettucine. The variety makes it one of the best places on the West Coast, if not the country, in which to dine.
336 Valet
All major cards

STANFORD COURT
$$$$$
905 CALIFORNIA ST.
TEL 415/989-3500
www.marriott.com
Situated on the site of Leland Stanford's Nob Hill mansion, the Court takes its historical roots seriously, hence the amazingly elegant and grand lobby, with its high ceiling and stained-glass dome. Rooms are well appointed, and its restaurant, **Aurea,** is a classic coffee bar/café.
393 Valet
All major cards

FAIRMONT
$$$$–$$$$$
950 MASON ST.
TEL 415/772-5000, 800/441-1414
www.fairmont.com
The Fairmont, with its gilded-era lobby and soaring staircases, perhaps best evokes the city's golden age. Rooms are bigger in the new addition. The downright weird Tonga Room is worth investigation.
591 Valet
All major cards

INTERCONTINENTAL MARK HOPKINS
$$$$–$$$$$
1 NOB HILL
TEL 415/392-3434, 888/424-6835
www.intercontinentalmarkhopkins.com

Built by another of the Big Four railroad barons, the Mark, with an infusion of investment from the InterContinental Group, maintains much of the elegance, service, and atmosphere of old San Francisco. The lobby is grand and lively, the service polished. The views from the Top of the Mark cocktail bar are hard to beat.
380 Valet All major cards

ACQUERELLO
$$$$
1722 SACRAMENTO ST.
TEL 415/567-5432
www.acquerello.com
Acquerello serves up grand and very modern Italian cuisine, in the style of the edgiest Roman ristorante, with such zesty chemistry as salmon with lemon oregano oil and black olive and parsley salad Siciliana. If the house gelato is on the menu, don't miss it.
55 Closed L & Sun.–Mon. All major cards

NORTH BEACH

HOTEL BOHEME
$$$–$$$$
444 COLUMBUS AVE.
TEL 415/433-9111
www.hotelboheme.com
Some fine Beat-generation atmospherics in a well-run old hotel right in the center of historic North Beach. What you save on the room, you can spend on food—perhaps at the Rose Pistola (see below).
15 All major cards

SOMETHING SPECIAL

ROSE PISTOLA
$$$
532 COLUMBUS AVE.
TEL 415/399-0499
www.rosepistolasf.com
The author's favorite Italian restaurant in San Francisco, the Rose serves up light but flavorful Ligurian fare. The Rose does roasted fish better than any restaurant in town. The appetizers, from garbanzo-flour breads to pungent olive and mini-sarsone plates, are astounding; the potato leek soup with basil oil is worth returning for at lunch. Live jazz Thursday to Sunday.
135 Valet All major cards

MARIO'S BOHEMIAN CIGAR STORE
$
566 COLUMBUS AVE.
TEL 415/362-0536
Just across from Washington Square, Mario's is the classic Italian coffeehouse. The focaccia sandwiches are as good as the wonderful cappuccino.
65 MC, V

MO'S GOURMET BURGERS
$
1322 GRANT AVE.
TEL 415/788-3779
The namesake burgers rank among San Francisco's best; also good chicken and steaks.
40 MC, V

PACIFIC HEIGHTS/ JAPANTOWN

HOTEL DRISCO
$$$$
2901 PACIFIC AVE.
TEL 415/346-2880, 800/634-7277
www.hoteldrisco.com
A 1903 hotel located in the heart of Pacific Heights; views of the city, bay, and Golden Gate Bridge. Plush rooms and suites. No parking available.
48 All major cards

HOTEL KABUKI
$$$
1625 POST ST.
TEL 415/413-4709, 888/717-0743
www.jdvhotels.com/kabuki
A perfect compromise between bed-and-breakfast and the megahotel scene, this midsize hotel was renovated in 2007 and features an exquisite decor blending Japanese and Western themes. Some rooms have their own Japanese-style soaking tubs.
218 Valet All major cards

LAUREL INN
$$$
444 PRESIDIO AVE.
TEL 415/567-8467, 800/552-8735
www.jdvhotels.com
Units with kitchenettes, free covered parking, and stylish spare decor create a place well suited to an extended stay, located on the margin of Pacific Heights. A chic cocktail lounge and coffee club, Swank, is on the property.
49 All major cards

MAKI
$$–$$$
1825 POST ST. (AT WEBSTER ST.)
TEL 415/921-5215
The place where aficionados go when they want Japanese cuisine cooked the old-country way. Try the wappa meshi, a steamed-in-wood delight, or any of the grilled plates.
17 Closed Mon. & L Tues.–Fri. MC, V

BETELNUT PEJIU WU
$$
2030 UNION ST.
TEL 415/929-8855
www.betelnutrestaurant.com
Many foodies believe this is the only place to eat great Asian food in the city. Set in a noisy room, Betelnut specializes in the street food of Asia: anchovies with chilis and peanuts, savory lemongrass broths and giant noodles, satay- or tea-smoked duck.
138 DC, MC, V

ISOBUNE SUSHI
$$
JAPAN CENTER, 1737 POST ST.
TEL 415/563-1030
A fun "concept" restaurant, where little wooden boats float by in a tiny artificial brook, each bearing a different raw fish delicacy for your consideration. Decent, instant gratification. When it's quieter, in the late afternoon, the chef will custom-make special house rolls for you.
33 P MC, V

JUBAN
$$
1581 WEBSTER ST.
TEL 415/776-5822
www.jubanrestaurant.com
This lively Japanese barbecue, where you cook your own Kobe beef, comes with rare praise from none other than the curmudgeonly author John Krich (author of *Around the World in a Bad Mood!*). The barbecue is great, he says, and be sure to try the cold noodles, which are "superb."
128 P AE, MC, V

BARNEY'S GOURMET HAMBURGERS
$
3344 STEINER ST.
TEL 415/563-0307
www.barneyshamburgers.com
Located in the trendy Marina District, this local branch of the upscale California chain serves tasty beef, chicken, turkey, and 20 different types of vegetarian burgers, as well as sandwiches, hot dogs, and salads, plus amazing shakes and daily soup specials. Their signature Big Barney's Burger features a one-pound patty on a French baguette. Alfresco dining is available.
40 P MC, V

RUSSIAN HILL

LA FOLIE
$$$$$
2316 POLK ST.
TEL 415/776-5577
www.lafolie.com
Another top choice, La Folie has garnered acclaim in several surveys as the city's preferred purveyor of New French cuisine; that the room is simply breathtaking and the service perfect makes it a "can't miss" for a night out. Chef Roland Passot never misses with such dishes as roasted Scottish salmon with braised escarole, gnocchi, smoked ham hock, and sweet onion sauce.
62 P Valet Closed L & Sun. All major cards

WATERFRONT

ARGONAUT HOTEL
$$$$
495 JEFFERSON ST.
TEL 415/563-0800, 800/790-1415
www.argonauthotel.com
Occupying the old brick Del Monte warehouse, the hotel has a seagoing theme, right down to porthole-shaped windows and star-emblazoned blue carpeting in the guest rooms. A quiet retreat on Fisherman's Wharf.
252 P Valet

FAIRMONT HERITAGE PLACE
$$$$
900 N. POINT ST.
TEL 415/268-9900, 888/991-4300
www.fairmont.com
A large portion of Ghirardelli's renowned chocolate factory has been reinvented as a residential-style hotel near Fisherman's Wharf. The one-, two-, and three-bedroom units include gourmet kitchens and fireplaces. Prearrival grocery shopping, in-residence spa treatments, view terraces with fire pits, and chauffeured house cars are all available. For those who don't want to cook, the Fairmont can arrange a personal chef or help with reservations at the many nearby restaurants. Minimum three-night stay.
131 P All major cards

HARBOR COURT
$$$$
165 STEUART ST.
TEL 415/882-1300
www.harborcourthotel.com
A moderately priced business-tourist hotel with several outstanding amenities, including free area limousine service, a health club, and a pool with sauna. Rooms are comfortable.
131 P All major cards

LE MERIDIEN
$$$$
333 BATTERY ST.
TEL 415/296-2900
www.starwoodhotels.com
Freshly invigorated, this heart-hotel combines the Starwood chain's competence with class, plus plenty of business services. The **Park Grill** offers splendid fine dining.
360 P Valet All major cards

MANDARIN ORIENTAL
$$$$
222 SANSOME ST.
TEL 415/276-9888, 800/622-0404
www.mandarinoriental.com
Perched on top of the First Interstate Bank, one of the city's tallest buildings, the Mandarin has views of the entire cityscape. Much acclaimed for comfort and attention to detail by some of the pickiest travelers.
158 P All major cards

HOTEL GRIFFON
$$$–$$$$
155 STEUART ST.
TEL 415/495-2100, 800/321-2201

www.hotelgriffon.com
One of the better small hotels in the city, the Griffon is perfect if you don't need concierge services or the doting of a bed-and-breakfast. Rooms here are elegant yet conservative.
62 All major cards

RESTAURANT GARY DANKO
$$$$$
800 NORTH POINT ST.
TEL 415/749-2060
www.garydanko.com
Flawless California-French cooking and beautiful fresh ingredients add up to the city's hottest dinner ticket, where the menu may include horseradish-crusted salmon with dilled cucumbers, or lemon-herb duck breast with duck hash and rhubarb compote.
65 Valet Closed L All major cards

BOULEVARD
$$$$
1 MISSION ST., EMBARCADERO
TEL 415/543-6084
www.boulevardrestaurant.com
Boulevard, with its beautiful lush interior and memorable bay views, delivers some of the best brasserie cooking in town. At lunch, try the fish du jour, particularly if it happens to be roasted sea bass. The appetizers alone are worth coming for: the potato cake napoleon is not only satisfying but also artfully pretty.
180 Closed L Sat.–Sun. All major cards

SOMETHING SPECIAL

GREENS
$$$
BLDG. A, FORT MASON, OFF MARINA BLVD.
TEL 415/771-6222
www.greensrestaurant.com
The mecca for the modern vegetarian, Greens shines as one of the best restaurants in the Bay Area. Its chef, Annie Somerville, has shepherded along the new vegetarian cooking with such dishes as griddle cakes with corn served with tomatoes, crème fraîche, and tomatillo sauce; melon and figs paired with goat cheese and peppery vinaigrette; and desserts like cherry pie with honey ice cream. Marvelous waterfront views. Find a selection of bread and Italian sandwiches at Greens to Go up front.
200 Closed D Sun. & L Mon. D, MC, V

IL FORNAIO
$$$
1265 BATTERY ST.
TEL 415/986-0100
www.ilfornaio.com
Italian food from "The Oven" consists of excellent pizzas, well-prepared pastas, and grilled meats. Leave room for one of their luscious desserts.
148 Valet All major cards

PIPERADE
$$$
1015 BATTERY ST.
TEL 415/391-2555
www.piperade.com
Gerald Hirigoyen's Basque food is served among wine barrels and bright fabrics. Try the seafood and shellfish stew in red pepper sauce, or braised veal sweetbreads with madeira.
60 Closed L Sat. & Sun. All major cards

SLANTED DOOR
$$$
1 FERRY BLDG. #3, MARKET ST. AT EMBARCADERO
TEL 415/861-8032
www.slanteddoor.com
Chef Charles Phan does a spicy, bold Vietnamese cuisine featuring items like "shaking beef" (stir-fried filet mignon with garlic), peppery Chinese squid with mustard greens, and chicken simmered in a clay pot with caramel sauce.
150 Valet AE, MC, V

PRICES

HOTELS
An indication of the cost of a double room in the high season is given by **$** signs.

$$$$$	Over $280
$$$$	$200–$280
$$$	$120–$200
$$	$80–$120
$	Under $80

RESTAURANTS
An indication of the cost of a three-course meal without drinks is given by **$** signs.

$$$$$	Over $80
$$$$	$50–$80
$$$	$35–$50
$$	$20–$35
$	Under $20

BEACH CHALET
$$
1000 GREAT HWY.
TEL 415/386-8439
www.beachchalet.com
If you've been hiking on scenic Ocean Beach, this renovated historic bungalow is the place for a great designer beer and your basic minibrewery food. It's noisy but pretty—and the view is unforgettable; behind, the adjacent park chalet has indoor/outdoor dining by a fire.
140 MC, V

BAY AREA

BENICIA

JEFFERSON STREET MANSION
$$$$$
1063 JEFFERSON ST.
TEL 707/746-0684

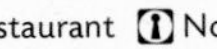
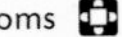
Hotel Restaurant No. of Guest Rooms No. of Seats Parking Closed Elevator

www.jeffersonstreet mansion.net
You will need to have made reservations to stay here. The reason? It has been rated one of the top three bed-and-breakfasts in the U.S. This Civil War–era mansion exudes period elegance throughout.
6 All major cards

BERKELEY

CLAREMONT HOTEL & SPA
$$$$
41 TUNNEL RD.
TEL 510/843-3000, 800/551-7266
www.claremontresort.com
This elegant and luxurious hotel in a giant white castle offers remarkable views of the bay. Built in the early 1900s, restoration has made it one of the Bay Area's top hotels. Its restaurant, **Meritage**, adds the finishing flourish.
279 All major cards

BANCROFT HOTEL
$$
2680 BANCROFT WAY
TEL 510/549-1000
www.bancrofthotel.com
There are only 22 rooms in this historic arts and crafts hotel, originally built in the 1920s as a women's club, a fact that gives the Bancroft its unique sense of elegant intimacy—for a great price, too.
22 All major cards

SOMETHING SPECIAL

CHEZ PANISSE
$$$$
1517 SHATTUCK AVE.
TEL 510/548-5525
www.chezpanisse.com
The temple, mecca, cathedral, and, just for fun, the Taj Mahal of modern California cooking, Chez Panisse has been turning out amazing food for more than 30 years. Legendary for its perfectionism and insistence on only the freshest ingredients—from Sonoma-raised duck to Meyer lemons from Ventura or San Joaquin Valley lamb and olive oils. Reserve as far in advance as possible.
50 Closed Sun.
All major cards

CAFÉ ROUGE
$$$
1782 4TH ST.
TEL 510/525-1440
www.caferouge.net
With a lively ambience and a packed bar in the burgeoning 4th Street scene, Café Rouge can be counted on for a great steak, fresh oysters, and other bistro standards. The friendly service is refreshing.
85 Closed Mon. D
AE, MC, V

MERITAGE AT THE CLAREMONT
$$$
41 TUNNEL RD.
TEL 510/549-8510
Superb views and great service make a visit to the restaurant here worth an evening—and you can also check out the Claremont Hotel without actually staying there! The wine-driven concept creatively pairs American wines with regional farm-fresh food.
175 Closed L Mon.–Sat. All major cards

BETTE'S OCEANVIEW DINER
$
1807 4TH ST.
TEL 510/644-3230
www.bettesdiner.com
The classic 1950s atmosphere complete with jukebox add to this diner's popularity. For breakfast, wait in line for a down-home feast of beef hash and poached eggs, soufflé pancakes, or even a cheesy herb omelet. If you can't wait, go next door to the bakery and dig into superb muffins.
50 Closed D
MC, V

HALF MOON BAY

ZABALLA HOUSE
$$
324 MAIN ST.
TEL 650/726-9123
www.zaballahouse.net
A converted farmhouse, almost engulfed in lush greenery and flowers, in a serene oceanside burg. If you want to get away from the crowds, this is a deal.
23 AE, MC, V

PRINCETON-BY-THE-SEA

PILLAR POINT INN
$$$
280 CAPISTRANO RD.
TEL 650/726-5400, 800/623-2661
www.pillarpointinn.com
Extension of Oceans Hotel & Spa. Try the supreme Pacific quietude and climate here, one of the best bed-and-breakfasts on the coast, and certainly one of the most luxurious. All rooms have fireplaces, feather mattresses, and lots of extras.
11 AE, MC, V

BARBARA'S FISH TRAP
$
281 CAPISTRANO RD.
TEL 650/728-7049
On the pier, this is the perfect place for a quick—but expertly executed—meal of fish and chips (or its local variant, calamari and chips).
38 No credit cards

INVERNESS

MANKA'S INVERNESS LODGE
$$$$

30 CALLENDAR WAY
TEL 415/669-1034
www.mankas.com
A rustic Marin bed-and-breakfast hideaway with a romantic atmosphere and views of Tomales Bay.
14 P AE, MC, V

POINT REYES

FERRANDO'S HIDE-AWAY
$$$$
31 CYPRESS RD., POINT REYES STATION
TEL 415/663-1966
www.ferrando.com
Set amid towering pines along the coast, Ferrando's, with cozy cottages and flowering gardens, is a home away from home for many vacationing San Franciscans, who love the interesting and friendly owners' dedication to detail and comfort.
6 P MC, V

LARKSPUR

SOMETHING SPECIAL

TAVERN AT LARK CREEK
$$$$
234 MAGNOLIA AVE.
TEL 415/924-7766
www.larkcreek.com
The little yellow-and-white eatery that changed the Marin restaurant scene forever is still one of the best dining experiences in the Bay Area. Perhaps it's the setting (amid redwoods) or the staff (helpful and unpretentious). Certainly it is the food: Yankee pot roast with ravioli stuffed with chard and ham hock, oven-roasted Dungeness crab with lime butter, or grilled flank steak and endive.
185 P Closed Sat. L
All major cards

MILL VALLEY

BUCKEYE ROADHOUSE
$$$
15 SHORELINE HWY.
TEL 415/331-2600
www.buckeyeroadhouse.com
Where foodies from the city come to PARTY! The Roadhouse's hearty, zesty, and impeccably prepared New American cuisine is the reason; the bar, where you can eat a dish called Oysters Bingo, is packed most nights.
40 P MC, V

FRANTOIO
$$$
152 SHORELINE HWY.
TEL 415/289-5777
www.frantoio.com
Someone once called chef Giovanni Perticone's cuisine "Italian soul food"–a good description of such satisfying dishes as roasted mussels with thyme-scented tomato broth, or risotto with chanterelles.
196 P Closed L & Mon.
All major cards

OAKLAND

WATERFRONT PLAZA
$$$
10 WASHINGTON ST.
TEL 510/836-3800
www.waterfrontplaza.com
Well-equipped modern hotel with spacious, light-filled guest suites, some with fireplaces, many with wonderful views across the bay.
154 P Valet
All major cards

JACK LONDON INN
$–$$
444 EMBARCADERO W., JACK LONDON SQUARE
TEL 800/549-8780
www.jacklondoninn.com
A tidy inn situated on the lively waterfront, close to Yoshi's (see p. 375), with friendly staff and comfortable rooms. A bargain.
110 P All major cards

BAY WOLF
$$$
3853 PIEDMONT AVE.
TEL 510/655-6004
www.baywolf.com
For more than 20 years, Bay Wolf has been serving up outstanding Mediterranean fare from its lovely converted old house. Check out its special "Dishes of" (Italy, France, Spain, Greece) series for some flavorful memories.
80–90 P Closed L AE, MC, V

CAMINO
$$$
3917 GRAND AVE.
TEL 510/547-5035
www.caminorestaurant.com
After apprenticing in the kitchen at the famed Chez Panisse for more than a dozen years, Russell Moore decided to create his own brilliant East Bay eatery. Camino's simple brick facade and rustic wooden tables belie the complex flavors coming from the kitchen. The selection changes daily, and the menu relies on the freshest California fish, meat, and produce: Dungeness crab grilled in the fireplace with farro; black trumpet mushrooms and chicory salad; artichoke gratin with Belgian endive, rutabaga, and egg; or chicken with garlic-and-herb sausage.
80 P Closed Tues. & L Mon.–Fri. All major cards

MILANO
$$–$$$
3425 GRAND AVE.
TEL 510/763-0300
Where the locals come to enjoy Italian cuisine with a creative edge. Redbrick walls and rich contemporary decor lend a glowing ambiance, and a

removable storefront provides open-air dining on warm summer nights. Specialties include cioppinos, risottos, wood-oven pizzas, and such delights as grilled prawns stuffed with provelone wrapped in spinach and pancetta.
120 P Closed L Sat.–Sun. All major cards

LE CHEVAL
$$
1019 CLAY ST.
TEL 510/763-8495
www.lecheval.com
What a deal: beautifully prepared Vietnamese-French food in a lively, unpretentious setting. Try the outrageously good Singapore noodles or the prawns in Vietnamese curry. Wash it down with decadent iced Vietnamese coffee.
385 P Valet Closed L Sun. All major cards

NAN YANG
$$
6048 COLLEGE AVE.
TEL 510/655-3298
www.nanyangrockridge.com
Savor Chinese cuisine created using excellent ingredients. A must is the garlic tomato spinach noodles with turmeric. The salads are also unforgettable.
20 P Closed Mon. MC, V

YOSHI'S
$$
510 EMBARCADERO W.
TEL 510/238-9200
www.yoshis.com
The Bay Area's top jazz venue also boasts a top-notch restaurant with classy contemporary decor. Take off your shoes in the traditional tatami seating and enjoy fresh sushi and classic Japanese dishes before taking in a show.
330 P Closed L Mon.–Sat. All major cards

PALO ALTO

EMPIRE GRILL & TAP ROOM
$$$
651 EMERSON ST.
TEL 650/321-3030
Unassuming and practical, the Empire, popular with everyone from Stanford professors to dating coeds, serves up basic American comfort food at a reasonable price. The burgers are made from some of the best beef in the U.S.
150 P All major cards

TAMARINE
$$$
546 UNIVERSITY AVE.
TEL 650/325-8500
www.tamarinerestaurant.com
Vietnamese food, including many vegan and vegetarian dishes, is the forte at this Silicon Valley favorite. The extensive menu includes dishes such as sugarcane prawns, wok pho noodles (rice noodles tossed with Chinese broccoli beef and eggs), tofu with basil leaves, clay pot cod (black cod caramelized in garlic, fish sauce and black pepper), and *bun cha* (grilled pork served in fish sauce with rice vermicelli noodles). Tamarine also boasts a good wine selection and a happening bar with happy hour specials.
150 P All major cards

SAN JOSE

FAIRMONT
$$$$
170 S. MARKET ST.
TEL 408/998-1900, 800/540-4493
www.fairmont.com
If you like the luxe treatment, you'll love this comfortable—and modern—San Jose variant of the San Francisco hotel.
551 P Valet All major cards

EMILE'S
$$$
545 S. 2ND ST.
TEL 408/289-1960
www.emilesrestaurant.com
New owners have reinvented this romantic culinary shrine, instilling new elegance and black-vested service. Beloved of loyal patrons, the French-inspired fusion cuisine includes such temptations as crêpes stuffed with basil-seasoned chicken, and ricotta baked in tomato and Mornay sauce.
60 P Closed L & D Sun.–Mon. AE, MC, V

HENRY'S HI-LIFE
$$
301 W. ST. JOHN ST.
TEL 408/295-5414
The house specialty here is barbecued ribs, chicken, or steak liberally slathered in exquisite barbecue sauce. But there are also hot dogs and burgers, as well as prime rib on Friday and Saturday nights. Henry's has been serving up the good food for more than 50 years.
74 P Closed L Sat.–Mon. All major cards

SAN RAFAEL

GERSTLE PARK INN
$$$$
34 GROVE ST.
TEL 415/721-7611, 800/726-7611
www.gerstleparkinn.com
Set among lovely gardens and a redwood grove, this inn was one of the first settlements in the area. The suites are full of fine linens and period antiques.
12 P AE, MC, V

SAUSALITO

CAVALLO POINT LODGE
$$$$$
601 MURRAY CIRCLE
TEL 415/339-4700, 877/322-0731
www.cavallopoint.com
When old Fort Baker was

transferred from the U.S. Army to the National Park Service in 2002, somebody got the bright idea that the bayside military outpost would make an incredible luxury hotel. The prize guest rooms are located in former officers' quarters overlooking a parade ground that tumbles down to the bay. Rooms feature gas fireplaces, elegant modern furnishings, and breathtaking views of San Francisco, Alcatraz, and the bridges. In **Murray Circle** the resort also boasts one of the best hotel restaurants in the Bay Area.
142 All major cards

INN ABOVE THE TIDE
$$$–$$$$
30 EL PORTAL
TEL 415/332-9535, 800/893-8433
www.innabovetide.com
Sausalito is relaxing and quiet—especially at this waterfront hotel, which blends the charm of a bed-and-breakfast (the breakfast is elaborate and tasty) and the professional services of a hotel (massage, concierge, turn-down, and morning paper).
29 All major cards

POGGIO
$$$$
777 BRIDGEWAY BLVD.
TEL 415/332-7771
www.poggiotrattoria.com
One of the broadest panoramic views of the bay can be caught from the portals of this classic Italian trattoria, where chef Chris Fernandez's soulful dishes include wood-roasted mussels with saffron tomato broth, and local Petrale sole with buttered spinach and poached potatoes with lemon caper sauce.
120 Valet All major cards

WALNUT CREEK

HAVANA
$$$
1516 BONANZA ST.
TEL 925/939-4555
www.havanarestaurant.net
A lively Cuban restaurant serving hearty, delectable dishes, including mango gazpacho, Havana crab cakes with pineapple aioli, and garlic-studded pork with mojo sauce, mashed yuccas, and black beans. The Latin rhythms create just the right mood for enjoying killer mojitos and Cuban cocktails.
100 Closed L Sat.–Sun. All major cards

LARK CREEK WALNUT CREEK
$$$
1360 LOCUST ST.
TEL 925/256-1234
www.larkcreek.com
If you are visiting the East Bay, you can do no better than this café. American cuisine prevails; grilled salmon and spoon bread is popular.
125 AE, MC, V

WOODSIDE

BELLA VISTA
$$$
13451 SKYLINE BLVD.
TEL 650/851-1229
www.bvrestaurant.com
Just out on Calif. 84 is this little rustic place offering French-Italian cuisine that will make you swoon. It is one of the few places to serve a decent Caesar salad made right at your table.
180 Closed L & Sun.–Mon. All major cards

WINE COUNTRY

Wine country has so many inns, hotels, and bed-and-breakfasts that many visitors rely on booking services to make reservations for them. This is particularly helpful during the high season (late spring through fall), when local wisdom (and a fee) will help you navigate the maze of available choices. Among the top services are: **Bed & Breakfast Inns of Napa** *(tel 707/944-4444, www.bbinv.com)*, **Napa Valley Reservations Unlimited** *(tel 800/251-6272, www.napavalleyreservations.com)*, and **Wine Country Concierge** *(tel 707/252-4472, www.winetrip.com)*.

PRICES

HOTELS
An indication of the cost of a double room in the high season is given by **$** signs.

$$$$$	Over $280
$$$$	$200–$280
$$$	$120–$200
$$	$80–$120
$	Under $80

RESTAURANTS
An indication of the cost of a three-course meal without drinks is given by **$** signs.

$$$$$	Over $80
$$$$	$50–$80
$$$	$35–$50
$$	$20–$35
$	Under $20

BOYES HOT SPRINGS

FAIRMONT SONOMA MISSION INN & SPA
$$$$-$$$$$
100 BOYES BLVD.
TEL 707/938-9000, 866/540-4499
www.fairmont.com/sonoma
A sprawling, modern, mission-style inn with outstanding spa facilities and wonderfully cozy and well-appointed rooms. A fine base for a visit to Sonoma Valley.
198 All major cards

CALISTOGA

MOUNT VIEW HOTEL

$$$

1457 LINCOLN AVE.
TEL 707/942-6877, 800/816-6877
www.mountviewhotel.com
The Mount View is one of the area's most pampering getaways. Located in a historic setting, its guest rooms are big, cozy, stylish–just like the "Southern Calistoga American" cuisine served at the popular **Catahoula Restaurant,** where Cajun meets California.
32 AE, MC, V

DR. WILKINSON'S HOT SPRINGS RESORT
$$–$$$
1507 LINCOLN AVE.
TEL 707/942-4102
www.drwilkinson.com
A wonderful, bare-bones, 1950s-style motel that somehow seems almost elegant, particularly when taken with the on-site hot springs, volcanic ash mud baths, and extensive spa services. Midweek specials offer "the works" (mud, aromatic whirlpool, mineral steam, and massage).
42 rooms, 17 cottages AE, MC, V

BRANNAN'S GRILL
$$$
1374 LINCOLN AVE.
TEL 707/942-2233
Delicious, unpretentious, bountiful cooking. Try the ginger-honey braised short ribs with pumpkin risotto.
190 All major cards

GLEN ELLEN

BELTANE RANCH
$$$–$$$$
11775 SONOMA HWY.
TEL 707/996-6501
www.beltaneranch.com
For anyone who really wants to get back to the land, as they said in the 1960s, this is the place. Beltane is a working ranch, full of cattle and grapevines, set amid miles of oak-bordered trails. The charming ranch is family run, which brings a warm feeling, particularly evident during long siestas on the old wraparound porch.
5 rooms, 1 cottage No credit cards

GAIGE HOUSE INN
$$$
13540 ARNOLD DR.
TEL 707/935-0237, 800/935-0237
www.gaige.com
A high-end country inn that prides itself on service and attention to detail. A great place from which to visit some wineries or to see Jack London State Historic Park.
14 rooms, 4 cottages AE, MC, V

HEALDSBURG

MADRONA MANOR
$$$$$
1001 WESTSIDE RD. (NEAR MILL ST.)
TEL 707/433-4231, 800/258-4003
www.madronamanor.com
This late 19th-century house is more than the usual redone Victorian–it's a three-story mansion, set on eight acres of wooded splendor (and some gardened splendor as well). Most guests prefer the rooms in the main house, where the food action is.
23 Closed Sun. AE, MC, V

BISTRO RALPH
$$$
109 PLAZA ST. (OFF HEALDSBURG AVE.)
TEL 707/433-1380
www.bistroralph.com
Another up-and-coming California-home-style bistro, with zesty Asian overtones. Try the peppery shrimp starter.
50 Closed Sun. MC, V

KENWOOD

KENWOOD RESTAURANT
$$–$$$
9900 CALIF. 12
TEL 707/833-6326
www.kenwoodrestaurant.com
The setting, right in the middle of Kenwood, draws locals from all around the valley to this bistro, where ingredients are just out of the ground and views are out of this world.
150 Closed Mon.–Tues. MC, V

MENDOCINO COAST

ALEXANDER'S
$$$$
21780 CALIF. 1, TIMBER COVE
TEL 707/847-3231
www.timbercoveinn.com
This romantic restaurant offers great food in a magical setting. With tables set inside glass walls or on the outdoor patio near a fire pit, the ocean views are expansive and magnificent. Frequently changing fare relies largely on local, sustainable, and organic ingredients.
40 All major cards

SPUD POINT CRAB COMPANY
$
1860 WESTSHORE RD., BODEGA BAY
TEL 707/875-9472
www.spudpointcrab.com
Picnic tables provide a simple but scenic spot to enjoy steamed crab and other seafood selections like clam chowder, shrimp cocktail, and shrimp sandwiches. Crab cakes are reserved for weekends.
Closed Wed. & 2 wks. Oct. All major cards

NAPA

SILVERADO RESORT
$$$

1600 ATLAS PEAK RD.
TEL 707/257-0200
www.silveradoresort.com
An upscale 1,200-acre retreat centered on a white-pillared mansion exuding yesteryear elegance and sophistication. Modestly furnished cottage clusters encircle swimming pools and line the fairways of this acclaimed golf resort. The **Royal Oak** restaurant serves grilled prime steaks and fresh seafood over mesquite.
280 All major cards

MUSTARDS GRILL
$$$–$$$$
7399 ST. HELENA HWY.
TEL 707/944-2424
www.mustardsgrill.com
The cradle of Napa California cuisine, Mustards has for more than 18 years served up a hearty menu including its famous smoked Peking duck, baby back ribs with corn pudding, and tempting hamburgers.
60 DC, MC, V

RUTHERFORD

AUBERGE DU SOLEIL
$$–$$$$
180 RUTHERFORD HILL RD.
TEL 707/963-1211, 800/348-5406
www.aubergedusoleil.com
Hotel meets country estate in this elegant getaway, where you can take in stunning views of olive groves while feasting on the Provençal cuisine.
52 All major cards

ST. HELENA

SOMETHING SPECIAL

MEADOWOOD
$$$$$
900 MEADOWOOD LN.
TEL 707/963-3646, 800/458-8080
www.meadowood.com
Perhaps California's best luxury destination, set amid groves of redwoods and firs, Meadowood is the kind of place you will tell your grandchildren about. Besides its huge guest cottages, it offers a spa, tennis courts, a golf course, and even a professional croquet court. The restaurant, rated among the state's top ten, has a menu with such delights as roasted rabbit with bay leaf gnocchi, crab and papaya confit appetizers, and seafood—steamed, fried, grilled—that will make you want to take up fishing. The cultural program aims high, too, with such visiting performers as the Vienna Boys' Choir.
85 All major cards

WINE COUNTRY INN
$$$
1152 LODI LN.
TEL 707/963-7077, 888/465-4608
www.winecountryinn.com
This inn sits on a delightful hilltop, its old stone tower conjuring the feeling of being in one of Robert Louis Stevenson's idylls about the place.
20 rooms, 5 cottages
Closed 3 wks. in Jan.
MC, V

EL BONITA MOTEL
$–$$$
195 MAIN ST.
TEL 707/963-3216, 800/541-3284
www.elbonita.com
The budget alternative for those who want to spend their money on wine rather than luxurious suites, El Bonita is a pleasant, well-tended old motel within walking distance of a number of wineries.
41 All major cards

TRA VIGNE
$$$
1050 CHARTER OAK AVE.
TEL 707/963-4444
www.travignerestaurant.com
This is the kind of Italian food—and surroundings—one would get in the very best Tuscan eateries: lots of fresh beans, fish, broths, and cracker-thin breads. The wine list is world class.
65 DC, MC, V

WINE SPECTATOR GREYSTONE
$$$
2555 MAIN ST.
TEL 707/967-1010
www.ciarestaurants.com
The restaurant of the Culinary Institute of America is in the old Christian Brothers Winery, a cavernous stone mansion. Dining here is akin to eating in a castle. The pastry chef is a genius; if the poached pears in zinfandel are on the menu, don't pass them by. A fine collection of cigars and aperitifs, many of the latter made in the valley, complete a wonderful experience.
125 Valet
All major cards

SONOMA

EL DORADO
$$$
405 1ST ST. W.
TEL 707/996-3220
www.eldoradosonoma.com
This impeccable hotel overlooks the Sonoma Plaza. With sumptuous rooms and equally sumptuous breakfasts, it is a true find. The **El Dorado Kitchen** *(tel 707/996-3030)* serves decent Italian cooking.
26 AE, MC, V

LA CASA
$$
121 E. SPAIN ST.
TEL 707/996-3406
An old-fashioned Mexican food hangout not far from Sonoma Plaza. Where better to celebrate General Vallejo's wise decision, 150 years ago, to "help out" the American insurrectionists?
180
All major cards

YOUNTVILLE

BARDESSONO

$$$$$

6526 YOUNT ST.

TEL 707/204-6000

www.bardessono.com

Bardessono is LEED Platinum certified, one of only three hotels in the U.S. that can currently make that claim. On the sumptuous side, it flaunts stylish, comfortable rooms, cozy fireplaces, and intimate private nooks.

51 P All major cards

YOUNTVILLE INN

$$$–$$$$

6462 WASHINGTON ST.

TEL 707/967-7900, 888/944-2885

www.hotelyountville.com

A rustic community just minutes away from some of the valley's finest dining, the inn offers luxurious amenities and your own patio.

51 P All major cards

SOMETHING SPECIAL

FRENCH LAUNDRY

$$$$

6640 WASHINGTON ST.

TEL 707/944-2380

www.frenchlaundry.com

A few years ago, a picky *New York Times* critic dubbed the French Laundry the best restaurant in America. So many people now agree that the only way you can get in is to call, between 10 a.m. and 7 p.m., exactly two months before the day you want to dine here. If you are a foodie, it's worth it. The nine-course lunch and dinner menus are prix fixe. The cuisine, dubbed California-French, offers entrées such as roasted rabbit saddles in pumpkin risotto and white truffle custard for an appetizer. Jackets are required for both lunch and dinner. If you can't make a two-month commitment but want to try chef Thomas Keller's fine food, go down the street to his equally raved-about **Bouchon** *(tel 707/944-8037, www.bouchon-bistro.com)* for a scaled-down version.

62 P Valet Closed L Mon.–Thurs. AE, MC, V

BISTRO JEANTY

$$$

6510 WASHINGTON ST.

TEL 707/944-0103

www.bistrojeanty.com

Phillipe Jeanty, the chef who put Domaine Chandon on the culinary map, has garnered outstanding reviews for his fine bistro fare here; the rabbit and cassoulet are huge favorites with the foodie class.

50 P MC, V

THE NORTH

ALBION

ALBION RIVER INN

$$$–$$$$$

3790 HWY. 1

TEL 707/937-1919, 800/479-7944

www.albionriverinn.com

A Mendocino Coast wonder, this one with fantastic coastal views, deluxe amenities, and a **restaurant** that has won raves from locals and out-of-towners.

22 P All major cards

ALTURAS

BRASS RAIL

$

395 LAKEVIEW HWY.

TEL 530/233-2906

It may not be much to look at, but the Basque food just keeps on coming. And it's good: big rib-eye steaks, lamb chops, fried chicken, red beans, Spanish rice, garbanzo beans, ravioli. For an amazingly low all-in price, you also get wine, homemade bread, soup, salad, coffee or tea, and ice cream.

200 P Closed Mon. MC, V

BOONVILLE

BOONVILLE HOTEL

$$–$$$$

14050 CALIF. 128

(AT LAMBERT LN.)

TEL 707/895-2210

www.boonvillehotel.com

If you're out cruising the backwoods area, this is a good place to stay or to stop for a meal at **Table 128,** which serves constantly changing prix fixe fare.

10 P Closed Jan. & part of Feb. MC, V

CHESTER

SOMETHING SPECIAL

DRAKESBAD GUEST RANCH

$$$

WARNER VALLEY RD.

TEL 530/529-1512, 866/999-0914

www.drakesbad.com

Set on natural hot mineral springs in the midst of Lassen Volcanic National Park (see p. 288), Drakesbad is the last of the 19th-century country lodges. The owner-hosts make a stay here absolutely delightful, with an informal atmosphere and satisfying, unfancy cooking (three meals a day are included in the price). Horseback riding, volleyball, and trail hiking are among the offered activities.

20 P Closed Oct.–Jan. MC,V

EUREKA

CARTER HOUSE

$$$$

301 L ST.

TEL 707/444-8062, 800/404-1390

www.carterhouse.com

Actually three properties—a hotel, a bed-and-breakfast, and a separate cottage, itself with three rooms—the award-winning

Carter is the place on the north coast. The decor is tasteful, with either period-perfect heirloom furniture or pleasing Southwesternalia. Big suites have all the right amenities, from whirlpool baths to jumbo beds.

33 All major cards

RESTAURANT 301
$$$
301 L ST.
TEL 707/444-8062, 800/404-1390
www.carterhouse.com

It would be an understatement to say the 301, at Carter House (see p. 381), is Eureka's best—it's every bit as good as Café Beaujolais in Mendocino (see this page). The elegant candlelit dining room serves up impeccably prepared dishes—fish, usually local, sautéed just right with chanterelle mushrooms brought in by a ranger from the nearby national forest.

45 Closed L All major cards

GARBERVILLE

BENBOW INN
$$$$–$$$$$
445 LAKE BENBOW DR.
TEL 707/923-2124, 800/355-3301
www.benbowinn.com

Host to Hollywood stars from Charles Laughton to Joan Fontaine, the Benbow, with its grand Tudor architecture and up-country setting, has been completely restored. Guest rooms are cozy and full of period decor, the **restaurant** serves fine regional cuisine, and there's boating, tennis, golf, swimming, and hiking.

55 All major cards

GUALALA

WHALE WATCH INN
$$$–$$$$
35100 CALIF. 1
TEL 800/942-5342
www.whalewatchinn.com

Large, airy modern rooms in a contemporary architectural complex perched high on a cliff overlooking the Pacific. A footpath takes you to a deserted beach. In the winter, watch whales through the telescope in the cozy lodge.

18 AE, MC, V

MCCLOUD

MCCLOUD HOTEL
$$–$$$$
408 MAIN ST.
TEL 530/964-2822, 800/964-2823
www.mccloudhotel.com

Big, light-filled rooms with Victorian-era decor, heirloom furniture, in-room Jacuzzis, and an atmospheric lobby make the McCloud a unique place from which to explore Shasta country and beyond.

17 All major cards

MENDOCINO

SOMETHING SPECIAL

STANFORD INN
$$$–$$$$$
CALIF. 1 & COMPTCHE-UKIAH RD.
TEL 707/937-5615, 800/331-8884
www.stanfordinn.com

This is the kind of place we would all build if we were as single-minded, as energetic, and as creative as the Stanford family. The Stanford Inn is wonderful, from its modern but woodsy guest rooms to its vegetarian **restaurant**. The Stanford sits at the mouth of the Big River, an unspoiled estuary, home to great blue herons, ospreys, and harbor seals.

41 All major cards

CAFÉ BEAUJOLAIS
$$$$
961 UKIAH ST. (BETW. EVERGREEN & SCHOOL STS.)
TEL 707/937-5614
www.cafebeaujolais.com

For many years, this rustic cottage set amid the wood and clapboard jumble of quaint Mendocino has attracted pickier diners from all over the country. The California country cuisine—with local wines, herbs, vegetables, and game—is a delight; the surroundings are intimate and memorable.

60 Closed L Mon.-Tues. All major cards

PRICES

HOTELS

An indication of the cost of a double room in the high season is given by **$** signs.

$$$$$	Over $280
$$$$	$200–$280
$$$	$120–$200
$$	$80–$120
$	Under $80

RESTAURANTS

An indication of the cost of a three-course meal without drinks is given by **$** signs.

$$$$$	Over $80
$$$$	$50–$80
$$$	$35–$50
$$	$20–$35
$	Under $20

GOLD COUNTRY

Although not as organized as San Francisco or Wine Country, Gold Country has its own unique brand of help for travelers. Friendly, informal "tourists bureaus" are found in almost every small city and town. As well as the larger places like Sacramento, even tiny Angels Camp, Sutter Creek, and Sonora have their own helpful offices, staffed through the week. Just follow the "Gold Country" signs.

COLOMA

COLOMA COUNTRY INN
$$$–$$$$
345 HIGH ST.
TEL 530/622-6919
www.colomacountryinn.com
Set on 5 acres, the inn is a beautifully restored 1852 Victorian, with period decor and antiques. The full breakfast is grand, the ballooning and rafting packages a deal.
5 None

GRASS VALLEY

HOLBROOKE
$$–$$$
212 W. MAIN ST.
TEL 530/273-1353, 800/933-7077
www.holbrooke.com
The rooms are spare, but prim and clean; the atmosphere is artsy Gold Country fun; and the food at the **Holbrooke Restaurant** is earthy, flavorful, and bountiful—New American with a sprinkling of local wild game and fruits (huckleberries, miners' lettuce, elderberries).
28
All major cards

MURPHYS

DUNBAR HOUSE 1880
$$$$
271 JONES ST.
TEL 209/728-2897
www.dunbarhouse.com
This historic house is overflowing with Victoriana, the service is impeccable, and the nascent (but tasty) local wine country is worth exploring.
5 AE, MC, V

NEVADA CITY

THE PARSONAGE
$$–$$$
427 BROAD ST.
TEL 530/265-9478
FAX 530/265-8147
www.theparsonage.net
A Victorian house built in the 1860s, the Parsonage has been restored to its gold rush grandeur. Breakfasts are hearty affairs. There is a cottage especially for families.
6 Closed Jan.
MC, V

PLACERVILLE

ZACHARY JACQUES
$$$
1821 PLEASANT VALLEY RD.
TEL 530/626-8045
www.zacharyjacques.com
Jacques serves a memorable earthy, country-French menu. The roast rack of lamb is the pièce de résistance.
55 Closed L & Mon.–Tues. AE, MC, V

PLYMOUTH

AMADOR HARVEST INN
$$
12455 STEINER RD.
TEL 209/245-5512, 800/217-2304
www.amadorharvestinn.com
Situated in one of the most lovely spots in Gold Country (or for that matter, the state), the inn is just next door to Deaver Vineyards and a deep blue lake. A full breakfast comes with the room price.
4 AE, MC, V

SACRAMENTO

DELTA KING
$$$–$$$$$
1000 FRONT ST.
TEL 916/444-5464, 800/825-5464
www.deltaking.com
Of the staterooms on this old riverboat, those toward the stern are the best, with views and elegant furniture. Breakfast is included.
44 Valet All major cards

AMBER HOUSE BED & BREAKFAST
$$$–$$$$
1315 22ND ST.
TEL 916/444-8085, 800/755-6526
www.amberhouse.com
Three architectural motifs—mission, Mediterranean, and colonial—and three separate houses make up this lovely historic complex. Some rooms have hot tubs and fireplaces.
14 All major cards

BIBA
$$–$$$
2801 CAPITOL AVE.
TEL 916/455-2422
www.biba-restaurant.com
Biba Caggiano, cookbook author and TV host, is responsible for the delicate and flavorful pasta dishes here. Her roasted meats and game are also amazing.
100 Closed Sun., L Sat. & L Mon. All major cards

SUTTER CREEK

FOXES INN OF SUTTER CREEK
$$$$
77 MAIN ST.
TEL 209/267-5882, 800/987-3344
www.foxesinn.com
With its elegant breakfast service, ornate period beds, and high ceilings, Foxes is a place where one can imagine what it was like to be a big-spending city slicker in gold-rush times.
7 MC, V

SIERRA NEVADA

LAKE TAHOE

RITZ-CARLTON HIGHLANDS
$$$$$
13031 RITZ-CARLTON HIGHLANDS CT., TRUCKEE
www.ritzcarlton.com
This top-of-the-line, ski-in, ski-out

property brings a whole new level of panache to Lake Tahoe with its deluxe suites themed with logs and granite.
170 All major cards

INN BY THE LAKE
$$$–$$$$
3300 LAKE TAHOE BLVD., SOUTH LAKE TAHOE
TEL 530/542-0330, 800/877-1466
www.innbythelake.com
This upscale motel is conveniently located just across the way from the swimming beach, close to Heavenly ski resort, accessed by free shuttle. Stay here and you can get a free ride to the casinos just east on the lake.
100 All major cards

SIX PEAKS GRILL
$$$$
RESORT AT SQUAW CREEK, 400 SQUAW CREEK RD., OLYMPIC VALLEY
TEL 530/581-6621, 800/327-3353
www.squawcreek.com
Though the view of the Sierra Nevada is what may attract people here, it is the food at Six Peaks Grill that brings them back again and again. The Grill has also received accolades from serious foodies for its California fusion cuisine and comfort foods, such as roasted corn chowder and grilled rib-eye steak. Leave room for the beehive-baked Alaska with meringue and raspberry sauce. The wine list is award winning.
75 All major cards

GRAHAM'S
$$$
1650 SQUAW VALLEY RD., OLYMPIC VALLEY
TEL 530/581-0454
www.dinewine.com
Glowing with cozy intimacy, Graham's intimate pine-paneled dining room is warmed by log fires in river-rock hearths. The California-Mediterranean menu is typified by the seared ahi with noodles appetizer, and three-peppercorn-crusted elk loin with lingonberry demi-glace. A vast wine list spans the globe.
125 Closed L & Mon.
AE, MC, V

MAMMOTH LAKES

WESTIN MONACHE
$$$$$
50 HILLSIDE DR.
TEL 760/934-0400
Catering to outdoorsy folks with deep pockets, the all-suite, full-service Westin Monache brings a new level of luxe to Mammoth.. Open-plan rooms here have gas fireplaces and flat-panel TVs.
230 All major cards

MAMMOTH MOUNTAIN INN
$$$–$$$$$
10001 MINARET RD.
TEL 760/934-2581
www.themammothmountaininn.com
At 9,000 feet, this modern alpine lodge offers cozy contemporary decor, blending comfort, convenience, and heaps of amenities, just steps away from the ski lifts. The Dry Creek Bar is the perfect spot for après ski.
216 AE, MC, V

OAKHURST

SOMETHING SPECIAL

CHATEAU DU SUREAU & ERNA'S ELDERBERRY HOUSE
$$$$$
48688 VICTORIA LN.
TEL 559/683-6860
www.chateaudusureau.com
After the French Laundry, perhaps the closest thing there is to "destination dining." **Erna's** *(tel 559/683-6800)* serves California-French with hints of the owner Erna Kubin. Impeccable food. Chateau de Sureau, run by the same owners, is fabulously luxurious: goosedown pillows, stone fireplaces, and staff who just won't let you do a thing!
12 Restaurant closed L Mon.–Tues. AE, MC, V

SEQUOIA NATIONAL PARK

WUKSACHI LODGE
$$–$$$
P.O. BOX 89, SEQUOIA NP
TEL 801/559-4948, 866/807-3598
www.visitsequoia.com
Beautifully blending into the big trees of Sequoia National Park, the lodge features roaring fireplaces, the park's best restaurant, and the likelihood of wildlife outside your window in the early morning light. Rooms have mission-style furnishings, ensuite baths, ski racks, and everything else you would expect from an upscale mountain resort.
18 Closed mid-Nov.–Apr. MC, V

CEDAR GROVE LODGE
$–$$$
P.O. BOX 909, CEDAR GROVE
TEL 559/335-5500
www.sequoia-kingscanyon.com
Modest, functional, and right in the middle of some of the park's most spectacular scenery, this little lodge is perfect if you just want a burger and a bed. You can also picnic here, right on the river's edge.
18 Closed mid-Nov.–Apr. MC, V

YOSEMITE NATIONAL PARK

AHWAHNEE
$$$$
1 AHWAHNEE DR.
TEL 801/559-4884, 866/875-8456

www.yosemitepark.com
Make reservations several months ahead if you want to stay in this delightful 1920s mountain lodge, replete with Native American decor, stone-and-sugar-pine construction, and cozy rooms with magnificent views of the valley's meadows and Half Dome. Also book ahead if you plan to luxuriate in the prettiest dining room in the state—the Ahwahnee's breathtaking light-filled **restaurant**, where the superb American cuisine comes with great service and memories to last a lifetime. (Dinner for hotel guests only.)
123 P All major cards

TENAYA LODGE
$$$
1122 CALIF. 41 (S OF YOSEMITE S ENTRANCE), FISH CAMP
TEL 559/683-6555, 888/514-2167
www.tenayalodge.com
Big, very professionally run, and with cozy rooms, the Tenaya offers what people who stay here want: a comfortable, amenities-filled getaway offering rest, relaxation, and food for those long evenings after a day's hiking. Past patrons will appreciate a recent multimillion dollar renovation. Its **Sierra Restaurant** is well regarded for its straightforward American cuisine.
244 P All major cards

WAWONA
$$–$$$
8308 WAWONA RD.
TEL 801/559-4884
www.yosemitepark.com
More modest than the Ahwahnee, the Wawona nevertheless holds its own on the Yosemite charm scale. The hotel consists of a sprawl of low-slung, whitewashed wooden cottages, with wraparound porches and views into a central meadow. Spend the day hiking, then come back to the **restaurant**'s grilled trout and steaks—satisfying and tasty. Rooms are austere but comfortable. Includes breakfast.
104 P Can be closed Feb.–Mar. All major cards

YOSEMITE LODGE AT THE FALLS
$$–$$$
YOSEMITE VALLEY
TEL 801/559-4884
www.yosemitepark.com
Right in the heart of the valley, close to Yosemite Falls, the lodge offers motel rooms with Southwestern decor, as well as more rustic cabins.
249 All major cards

EVERGREEN LODGE
$–$$$$$
33160 EVERGREEN RD., GROVELAND
TEL 209/379-2606, 800/93-LODGE
www.evergreenlodge.com
Evergreen offers a homey, hands-on alternative to the corporate hotels of Yosemite Valley. Guests can choose from a variety of different cabins, from furnished tents and vintage cabins to the roomy John Muir House, which can sleep as many as ten people. While the "unplugged" cabins have no televisions or phones, they do have comfy beds, satellite radios, minifridges, and an assortment of board games to entertain after dark. Internet and Wi-Fi are available in the lodge recreation building.
66 cabins P All major cards

CENTRAL VALLEY

BAKERSFIELD

NORIEGA'S ESKUALDUNEN ETCHEA
$–$$
525 SUMNER ST.
TEL 661/322-8419
www.noriegahotel.com
Hearty lunches and dinners are served family style. Entree choices might include lamb stew, prime rib, oxtail, fried chicken, red snapper, or liver and onions.
60 P Closed Mon. All major cards

CHALET BASQUE
$
200 OAK ST.
TEL 661/327-2915
People make a special trip just for the Chalet's wonderful roast lamb and pink beans special. Memorable Basque fare in a family atmosphere.
100 P Closed Sun. L AE, MC, V

FRESNO

PICCADILLY INN SHAW
$$–$$$
2305 W. SHAW AVE.
TEL 559/348-5520, 888/286-2645
www.piccadillyinn.com
The jumbo swimming pool will come in handy during the sweltering valley days; the amply sized guest rooms are neat, if austere, and even have their own refrigerators.
194 P All major cards

HANFORD

IRWIN STREET INN
$–$$
522 N. IRWIN ST.
TEL 559/583-8000
A nicely restored, tree-shaded Victorian, the inn is a pleasant place to stop on the way north or south. Rooms feature antiques and period reproductions.
30 P Closed Sun., D Mon.–Wed. & L Sat. All major cards

VISALIA

SPALDING HOUSE
$$
631 N. ENCINA ST.
TEL 559/739-7877
www.spaldinghouse.com

Another restored Victorian in farm country–this one complete with library, grand piano, and cozy sitting parlors for those long evenings, lemonade, ice cream, and seats on the quaint wooden porch. Full breakfast is included.
3 AE, MC, V

THE DESERT

Accommodations and eateries of note are thin in the deserts, except for the Palm Springs region, known for its bounty of spa resorts, trendy boutique hotels, and private rentals–from golf course condos to deluxe villas. Visitors seeking rental lodgings should consult specialist online booking services, such as **McLean Company Rentals** *(tel 760/322-2500 or 800/777-4606, www.ps4rent.com)* and **Vacationhomes** *(tel 888/689-9709, www.vacation-homes.com)*. The **Palm Springs Desert Resorts Convention & Visitors Authority** *(tel 760/770-9000, www.giveintothedesert.com)* is a helpful resource.

DEATH VALLEY

INN AT FURNACE CREEK
$$$$$
CALIF. 190
TEL 760/786-2345, 800/236-7916
www.furnacecreekinn.com
Cool off at this historic inn, where the pool is supplemented by a natural mineral spring, the food is climate adjusted, and the golf course is equipped with plenty of refreshing sprinklers, beer, and umbrella drinks.
66 All major card

DESERT HOT SPRINGS

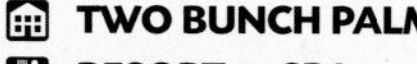

TWO BUNCH PALMS RESORT & SPA
$$$–$$$$
67425 TWO BUNCH PALMS TRAIL
TEL 760/329-8791, 877/839-3609
www.twobunchpalms.com
It was here that director Robert Altman located the spa scene in his film *The Player,* about the Hollywood elite. Trendy and luxurious, Two Bunch is a wonderful, serene place, where the massages and mud baths are first-rate, the guest rooms stylish and calming, and the California cuisine in the intimate **Casino Restaurant** is exquisite.
52 AE, MC, V

LA QUINTA

LA QUINTA RESORT & CLUB
$$$$$
49499 EISENHOWER DR.
TEL 760/564-4111, 800/598-3828
www.laquintaresort.com
The quintessential desert escape, this legendary hacienda resort features 41 swimming pools, 53 hot spas, and 23 tennis courts, and guests can dine in a different restaurant each night of the week.
796 All major cards

PALM DESERT

CUISTOT
$$$$
72595 EL PASEO DR.
TEL 760/340-1000
www.cuistotrestaurant.com
The menu has been officially dubbed California-French, but that's really a bit tame and buttoned-up for the savvy, freestyle cooking here. Try the quail stuffed with sweetbreads in white wine sauce to get a notion of the chef's deftness with essential flavors. The desserts are equally complex and, ultimately, satisfying.
290 Closed Aug. & L Sun.–Mon. All major cards

PALM SPRINGS

SOMETHING SPECIAL

VICEROY PALM SPRINGS
$$$$$
415 S. BELARDO
TEL 760/320-4117
www.viceroypalmsprings.com
This luxurious boutique hotel is a perfect refuge, and Hollywood's finest are often seen lounging beside the three pools, sipping mojitos at the stylish bar, or relaxing in the spa. Chef Stephen Belie conjures divine California fusion cuisine in the **Citron** restaurant. Try the pumpkin-seed-crusted Chilean sea bass with lobster asparagus ravioli and uni butter.
68 All major cards

MOVIE COLONY HOTEL
$$$$–$$$$$
726 N. INDIAN CANYON DR.
TEL 760/320-6340, 888/953-5700
www.moviecolonyhotel.com
With its minimalist furnishings and fabrics from the modernist heyday, this chic compact hotel draws Hollywood mavens. Contemporary rooms and two-story townhouses set a 21st-century tone, and the open-air bar is a popular spot for martinis by the fire pit.
17 All major cards

SMOKE TREE RANCH
$$$$–$$$$$
1850 SMOKE TREE LN.
TEL 877/730-4409
www.smoketreeranch.com
The last of Palm Springs's venerable dude-ranch lodges, this one still revolves around its stables while retaining the rusticity that drew erstwhile regulars Cary Grant and Walt Disney. Timber-beamed cottages are simply appointed and have fireplaces.
85 cottages DC, MC, V

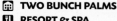

THE PARKER PALM SPRINGS

$$$–$$$$$

4200 E. PALM CANYON DR.

TEL 760/770-5000

www.theparkerpalmsprings.com

Among the current crop of deluxe, retro-themed desert spa hotels, the Parker has won accolades for its cutting-edge chic and fine dining. The fun yet glamorous atmosphere is enhanced by the swank Palm Springs Yacht Club spa.

144 All major cards

PURPLE PALM

$$$–$$$$

572 N. INDIAN CANYON DR.

TEL 760/969-1801

www.colonypalmshotel.com

Overlooking and open to the garden and pool of the Colony Palms Hotel, Purple Palm serves largely Mediterranean dishes with some notable fusion inclusions like fried squid with Szechuan sauce and tandoori Jidori chicken served with basmati rice, spinach, poppadom, and preserved kumquat.

100 Valet All major cards

PEAKS

$$$

ONE TRAMWAY RD.

TEL 760/325-4537

www.pstramway.com

At this elegant mountaintop aerie (accessed by the Palm Springs Aerial Tramway), chef David Le Pow delivers delicious California fusion dishes such as rack of lamb with fresh peach compote and truffled mashed potatoes. Go not least for the peerless vistas from 8,560 feet.

125 All major cards

JOHANNES

$$–$$$

196 S. INDIAN CANYON DR.

TEL 760/778-0017

www.johannesrestaurant.com

At chef Johannes Bacher's hip, high-end shrine to cosmopolitan dining, the minimalist decor is matched by precise service and attention to detail in the imaginative California-Asian-Austrian fusion cuisine.

Closed Mon. All major cards

FISHERMAN'S MARKET & GRILL

$–$$$

235 S. INDIAN CANYON DR.

TEL 760/327-1766

www.fishermans.com

You're guaranteed only the freshest seafood at this homey local favorite. The oyster shooters are a hit at adjoining Shanghai Red's, where live R&B music can be heard on Friday and Saturday nights.

140 All major cards

RICK'S

$–$$$

1973 N. PALM CANYON DR.

TEL 760/416-0090

A friendly Cuban-American 1950s-style diner that packs in the locals for hearty American favorites, Cuban *ropa vieja,* and eclectic treats such as seared ahi tuna salad.

104 Closed D AE, MC, V

RANCHO MIRAGE

RITZ-CARLTON RANCHO MIRAGE

$$$$$

68900 FRANK SINATRA DR.

TEL 760/321-8282

www.ritzcarlton.com

Set on a plateau in the mountains, this sumptuous modern resort hotel emerged in 2008 from a $500 million remake and is now perhaps the desert's most luxurious hotel.

260 All major cards

DESERT SPRINGS JW MARRIOTT RESORT & SPA

$$$–$$$$$

74855 COUNTRY CLUB DR.

TEL 760/341-2211, 800/331-3112

www.desertspringsresort.com

This large hotel combines style with all the amenities you could wish for, not least a massive state-of-the-art spa, the hottest nightclub in the valley, and excellent dining options.

884 All major cards

WALLY'S DESERT TURTLE

$$$$$

71775 CALIF. 111

TEL 760/568-9321

www.wallys-desert-turtle.com

To some minds, this lavish restaurant serves the best cuisine in the desert. Try the pan-broiled Lake Superior whitefish, with mussels, leek fondue, and lemon beurre blanc apricot soufflé.

180 All major cards

LAS CASUELAS NUEVAS

$$

70050 CALIF. 111

TEL 760/328-8844

www.lascasuelasnuevas.com

An upbeat California-Mexican restaurant with free-flowing Mexican beer, hearty Mexican-American classics (burritos, tacos, quesadillas), and some actual Mexican food as well (soups, *carne asadas*). Go a little early.

450 All major cards

TWENTYNINE PALMS

29 PALMS INN

$–$$$$

73950 INN AVE.

TEL 760/367-3505

www.29palmsinn.com

Each room has a patio, hot tub, and fireplace, and the **restaurant** means you don't have to leave the place for a good meal. Located on the famed Oasis of Mara.

19 All major card

Shopping

Even the locals regard shopping as recreation in California. This section suggests some places where you can find the unusual, the special, or the bargain.

LOS ANGELES

Antiques

Rose Bowl Flea Market
Rose Bowl, Pasadena, www.rgcshows.com, 2nd Sun. of month
Second Time Around Watch Co.
8763 Rosewood Ave., West Hollywood, tel 310/271-6615, www.secondtimearoundwatchco.com

Art

Gagosian Gallery 456 N. Camden Dr., Beverly Hills, tel 310/271-9400, www.gagosian.com
L.A. Louver Galleries 45 N. Venice Blvd., Venice Beach, tel 310/822-4955, www.lalouver.com
Latin American Masters
2525 Michigan Ave., Santa Monica, tel 310/829-4455, www.latinamericanmasters.com
Margo Leavin Gallery 812 N. Robertson Blvd., tel 310/273-0603, www.margoleavingallery.com

Arts & Crafts/ Mission-Period Pieces

Gamble House Bookstore
4 Westmoreland Pl., Pasadena, tel 626/793-3334, www.gamblehouse.org
Jack Moore Craftsman Furniture 1419 N. Lake St., Pasadena, tel 626/577-7746

Books & Music

Amoeba Music 6400 Sunset Blvd., West Hollywood, tel 323/245-6400, www.amoeba.com
Book Soup 8818 Sunset Blvd., West Hollywood, tel 310/659-3110, www.booksoup.com

Fashion & Boutiques

American Rag Company 150 S. La Brea Ave., Melrose District, tel 323/935-3154, www.amrag.com
Fred Segal 8118 Melrose Ave., Hollywood, www.fredsegal.com
Grove 189 The Grove Dr., Los Angeles, tel 323/900-8080, www.thegrovela.com
Maxfield 8825 Melrose Ave., tel 310/274-8800, www.maxfieldla.com. Designer clothes.
Y-Que 1770 N. Vermont Ave., tel 323/664-0021, www.yque.com. T-shirts and kitsch.

Food

Grand Central Market 317 S. Broadway, tel 213/624-2378, www.grandcentralsquare.com
Pasadena Farmers Market Various locations, tel 626/449-0179, www.pasadenafarmersmarket.org
Santa Monica Farmers Market
Various locations, tel 310/391-9996, www.smgov.net

Furniture & Design

Arte International Furnishings
5356 Riverton Ave., Hollywood, tel 818/753-4510, www.arteshowrooms.com
Pacific Design Center 8687 Melrose Ave., tel 310/657-0800, www.pacificdesigncenter.com
Rehab Vintage
7609 Beverly Blvd., tel 800/668-1020, www.rehabvintage.net

Hollywoodalia

Frederick's of Hollywood
6751 Hollywood Blvd., Hollywood, tel 323/957-5953, www.fredericks.com. Madonna's alleged choice.
Hollywood Book & Poster Company 6562 Hollywood Blvd., Hollywood, tel 323/465-8764, www.hollywoodbookandposter.com
Western Costume 11041 Vanowen Blvd., North Hollywood, tel 818/760-0900, www.lawardrobesupplies.com. Studios' choice.

Pampering

Beverly Hot Springs
308 N. Oxford Ave., tel 323/734-7000, www.beverlyhotsprings.com
Burke Williams Spas
tel 866/239-6635, www.burkewilliamsspa.com. Check website for locations.
Frederic Fekkai Beauté de Provence 8457 Melrose Pl., tel 323/655-7800, www.fredericfekkai.com

SOUTHERN CALIFORNIA

Antiques

Michael Haskell Antiques
539 San Ysidro Rd., Santa Barbara, tel 805/565-1121, www.michaelhaskell.com

Art

California Art Gallery
305 N. Coast Hwy., Laguna Beach, tel 949/606-6830, www.californiaartgallery.com. Plein air revivals.
Laguna North Gallery
376 N. Coast Hwy., Laguna Beach, tel 949/494-4324, www.lagunanorthgallery.com
Santa Barbara Contemporary Arts Forum 653 Paseo Nuevo, tel 805/966-5373, www.sbcaf.org
Scott White Gallery 7655 Girard Ave., San Diego, tel 858/255-8574, www.scottwhiteart.com

Books

The Book Den 15 E. Anapamu St., Santa Barbara, tel 805/962-3321, www.bookden.com

Fashion

Las Americas Premium Outlets
4211 Camino de la Plaza, San Ysidro, tel 619/934-8400, www.simon.com

Food

Julian Pie Company
2225 Main St., Julian, tel 760/765-2449, www.julianpie.com. In fall, the apple of everyone's eye.

Olympics

Olympic Training Center
2800 Olympic Pkwy., Chula Vista, tel 619/656-1500, www.teamusa.org. Free tours.

CENTRAL COAST

Food

Casa de Fruta 10021 Pacheco Pass Hwy., Hollister, tel 408/842-7282 or 800/543-1702, www.casadefruta.com. Fresh produce.
Pezzini Farms 460 Nashua Rd., Castroville, tel 831/757-7434 or 800/347-6118, www.pezzinifarms.com. Artichokes.

Funk

San Juan Bautista Peddlers Fair
Mission San Juan, 1 Polk St., tel 831/623-2454, www.sjbca.com

Outlet Stores

American Tin Cannery Factory Outlets 125 Ocean View Blvd., Monterey, tel 831/372-1442, www.americantincannery.com

Wine Guides & Maps

Chateau Julien Winery
8940 Carmel Valley Rd., Carmel, tel 831/624-2600, www.chateaujulien.com

SAN FRANCISCO

Art & Antiques

Gump's 135 Post St., Union Square, tel 800/766-7628, www.gumps.com
Hang Gallery 567 Sutter Square., tel 415/434-4264, www.hangart.com
Isak Lindenauer Antiques
4143 19th St., tel 415/552-6436, www.isaklindenauer.com
Kuromatsu 722 Bay St., tel 415/474-4027. Japanese art & antiques.
Montgomery Gallery
460 Jackson St., tel 415/788-8300, www.montgomerygallery.com. Art of California.
W. Graham Arader III
435 Jackson St., tel 415/788-5115, www.aradersf.com. Maps, prints, & books.

Beauty

Elizabeth Arden Spa
126 Post St., tel 415/989-4888, www.reddoorspas.com

Books

City Lights 261 Columbus Ave., North Beach, tel 415/362-8193, www.citylights.com. Landmark literary bookstore.
Green Apple Books
506 Clement St., tel 415/387-2272, www.greenapplebooks.com. New and used books.
Museum Books SFMOMA, 151 3rd St., tel 415/357-0037, www.sfmoma.org

Fashion

Diesel 800 Market St., tel 415/398-4055, www.diesel.com
Jeremy's 2 South Park, SoMa, tel 415/882-4929, www.jeremys.com. Labels like Prada, Barney's, and Armani at discounted prices.
Union Square www.unionsquareshop.com. Serious shopping, with Hermès, Gucci, Cartier, Celine, etc.
Wasteland 1660 Haight St., Haight-Ashbury, tel 415/863-3150, www.shopwasteland.com. Vintage and trendy secondhand clothes.

Food

Ferry Street Farmers Market
1 Ferry Bldg., Embarcadero, tel 415/983-8030, www.ferryplazafarmersmarket.com. Tues., Thurs. & Sat.
Ghirardelli Chocolate 900 N. Point St., Ghirardelli Square, tel 415/474-3938, www.ghirardelli.com
Scharffen Berger Chocolates
1 Ferry Bldg. #14, Embarcadero, tel 415/981-9150, www.scharffenberger.com. Gourmet chocolate.
Super Mira Market
1790 Sutter St., tel 415/921-6529. Japanese favorites.
Swan Oyster Depot 1517 Polk St., Polk Gulch, tel 415/673-1101

Funk

Aria 1522 Grant Ave., tel 415/433-0219

BAY AREA

Art & Antiques

Alameda Point Antiques Faire
Alameda Point, Alameda, tel 510/522-7500, www.alamedapointantiquesfaire.com, 1st Sun. of month. Antiques/collectibles.
Dove Place Antiques & Consignments 160 Sir Francis Drake Blvd., San Anselmo, tel 415/453-1490, www.doveplaceantiques.com
Imari Gallery 40 Filbert Ave., Sausalito, tel 415/332-0245, www.imarigallery.com. Japanese antiques.
Oriental Corner 280 Main St., Los Altos, tel 650/941-3207
Telegraph Avenue, Berkeley. This street is lined with off-beat stores and street vendors selling antiques, artwork, jewelry, and clothing.
Traywick Gallery 1316 10th St., Berkeley, tel 510/527-1214, www.traywick.com. By appt. only.

Books

Book Passage Marin 51 Tamal Vista Blvd., Corte Madera, tel 415/927-0960 & 1 Ferry Building, San Francisco, tel 415/835-1020 www.bookpassage.com

Food

Civic Center Farmers Market
Marin Civic Center, San Rafael, tel 415/472-6100, www.marincountyfarmersmarkets.org. Thurs. & Sun.

Downtown Farmers Market Festival 4th St., San Rafael, tel 415/492-8007, www.sanrafaelmarket.org. Thurs. & Sun.
Johnson's Oysters Near Point Reyes Lighthouse (look for signs), tel 415/669-1149
Oakland Farmers Market 9th St. betw. Broadway & Clay, tel 510/745-7100, www.urbanvillageonline.com. Fri. 8 a.m.–2 p.m.
Paul Marcus Wines Rockridge Market Hall, 5655 College Ave., Oakland, tel 510/420-1005, www.paulmarcuswines.com
Tomales Bay Foods & Cowgirl Creamery 80 4th St., Point Reyes Station, tel 415/663-9335, www.cowgirlcreamery.com. Fresh cheeses, organic everything.

Funk
Berkeley Flea Market 1837 Ashby Ave., tel 510/644-0744, www.berkeleyfleamarket.com
San Jose Flea Market 1590 Berryessa Rd., San Jose, tel 408/453-1110, www.sjfm.com

Music
Amoeba Music 2455 Telegraph Ave., Berkeley, tel 510/549-1125, www.amoeba.com. Thousands of titles from classical to hip-hop.

WINE COUNTRY

Food
Jimtown Store 6706 Calif. 128, Healdsburg, tel 707/433-1212, www.jimtown.com. From Brie to baguettes.
Oakville Grocery 124 Matheson St., Healdsburg, tel 707/433-3200, www.oakvillegrocery.com. Local cheeses, oils, etc.
Sonoma Cheese Factory 2 Spain St., Sonoma, tel 707/996-1931 or 800/535-2855, www.sonomacheesefactory.com
Sonoma Country Farm Trails 930 Shiloh Rd. #7, Santa Rosa, tel 707/571-8288, www.farmtrails.org. Chart course for local farms.
Vella Cheese Company 315 2nd St. E., Sonoma, tel 707/938-3232, www.vellacheese.com

Outlet Stores
Napa Premium Outlets 629 Factory Stores Dr., Napa, tel 707/226-9876, www.premiumoutlets.com
St. Helena Premium Outlets 3111 N. St. Helena Hwy., St. Helena, tel 707/963-7282

Wines
Napa Cellars 7481 St. Helena Hwy., Yountville, tel 800/535-6400, www.napacellars.com
Napa Valley Vintners 900 Meadowood Ln., St. Helena, tel 707/963-3388, www.napavintners.com
Sonoma Valley Vintners' Association 783 Broadway, Sonoma, tel 707/935-0803, www.sonomavalleywine.com
V Wine Cellar 6525 Washington St., Yountville, tel 707/531-7053, www.vwinecellar.com

THE NORTH

Food
Apple Farm 18501 Greenwood Rd., Philo, tel 707/895-2333, www.philoapplefarm.com

Wines
Mendocino Winegrowers Alliance 525 S. Main St., Ukiah, tel 707-468-9886, www.mendowine.com
Navarro Vineyards 5601 Calif. 128, Philo, tel 707/895-3686 or 800/537-9463, www.navarrowine.com

GOLD COUNTRY

Art
Gold Country Artist's Gallery 379 Main St., Placerville, tel 530/642-2944, www.goldcountryartistsgallery.com. Paintings, photography, pottery, sculpture, glass, and jewelry.

Flowers
Amador Flower Farm 22001 Shenandoah School Rd., Plymouth, tel 209/245-6660, www.amadorflowerfarm.com. Specializes in daylilies.

Fruit
Boa Vista Orchards 2952 Carson Rd., Placerville, tel 530/622-5522, www.boavista.com. Fruit, wine, pies, and pastries.

Wines
Sierra Ridge Winery 14110 Ridge Rd., Sutter Creek, tel 209/267-1316, www.sutterridgewine.com

CENTRAL VALLEY

Food
Sciabica and Sons 2150 Yosemite Blvd., Modesto, tel 800/551-9612, www.sciabica.com. Olives/olive oils.
Simonian Farms 2629 S. Clovis Ave., Fresno, tel 559/237-2294, www.simonianfarms.com. More than 100 kinds of fruits and vegetables.

THE DESERT

Fashion
Trina Turk's 891 N. Palm Canyon Dr., Palm Springs, tel 760/416-2856, www.tinaturk.com. Bold designs for fashionistas.

Food
Hadley's Fruit Orchards 48980 Seminole Rd., Cabazon, tel 951/849-5255, www.hadleyfruitorchards.com. Dried fruit.

Outlet Stores
Desert Hills Premium Outlets 48400 Seminole Rd., Cabazon, tel 909/849-6641, www.premiumoutlets.com. With 130 stores.

Activities

With a hospitable climate year-round, California has become the nation's unofficial sports capital. The tourism bureaus, accessible through the California Division of Tourism (see p. 347), publishes guides and lists on all outdoor activities. Also useful are the Sierra Club *(85 2nd St., San Francisco, tel 415/977-5500, www.sierraclub.org)*, the National Park Service *(333 Bush St. #500, San Francisco, tel 415/623-2100, www.nps.gov)*, and the California Department of Parks and Recreation *(1416 9th St., Sacramento, tel 800/777-0369, www.parks.ca.gov)*.

Bicycling

Backroads 801 Cedar St., Berkeley, tel 510/527-1555, www.backroads.com

Getaway Adventures 2228 Northpoint Pkwy., Santa Rosa, tel 707/568-3040 or 800/499-2453, BIKE, www.getawayadventures.com

Bird-watching

Point Reyes Bird Observatory 4990 Shoreline Hwy., Stinson Beach, tel 415/868-0371, www.prbo.org

San Francisco Bay Bird Observatory 524 Valley Way, Milpitas, tel 408/946-6548, www.sfbbo.org

Deep Sea Fishing

H & M Landing 2803 Emerson St., Point Loma, San Diego, tel 619/222-1144, www.hmlanding.com

Helgren's Oceanside Sportfishing 315 Harbor Dr. S., Oceanside, tel 760/722-2133, www.helgrensportfishing.com

Golf

LOS ANGELES AREA

Brookside Men's Golf Course 1133 N. Rosemount Ave., Pasadena, tel 626/585-3594, www.brookside.lagolfclubs.com

Rancho Park Golf Course 10460 W. Pico Blvd., Beverly Hills, tel 310/838-7373, www.lagolfclubs.com

SOUTHERN CALIFORNIA

Alisal Golf Course 1054 Alisal Rd., Solvang, tel 805/688-6411, www.alisal.com

Balboa Park Municipal Golf Course 2600 Golf Course Dr., San Diego, tel 619/235-1184, www.sandiego.gov

Sandpiper Golf Course 7925 Hollister Ave., Santa Barbara, tel 805/968-1541, www.sandpipergolf.com

Torrey Pines Golf Club 11480 N. Torrey Pines Rd., La Jolla, tel 858/452-3226, www.torreypinesgolfcourse.com

CENTRAL COAST

Del Monte Golf Course 1300 Sylvan Rd., Pebble Beach, tel 831/373-2700, www.pebblebeach.com

Links at Spanish Bay 2700 17-Mile Dr., at Pebble Beach Resort, Spanish Bay, tel 831/647-7495, www.pebblebeach.com

Pasatiempo Golf Course 18 Clubhouse Rd., Santa Cruz, tel 831/459-9155, www.pasatiempo.com.

Pebble Beach Golf Links At the Lodge at Pebble Beach, 17-Mile Dr., Pebble Beach, tel 831/624-3811 or 800/654-9300, www.pebblebeach.com

Rancho Cañada Golf Course 4860 Carmel Valley Rd., Carmel, tel 831/624-0111 or 800/536-9459, www.ranchocanada.com

SAN FRANCISCO & BAY AREA

Half Moon Bay Golf Links 2 Miramontes Point Rd., Half Moon Bay, tel 650/726-1800, www.halfmoonbaygolf.com

Presidio Golf Course 300 Finley Rd., Presidio National Park, San Francisco, tel 415/561-4661, www.presidiogolf.com

THE DESERT

La Quinta Resort & Spa 49499 Eisenhower Dr., La Quinta, tel 760/564-4111, www.laquintaresort.com

PGA West 56150 PGA Blvd., La Quinta, tel 800/742-9378, www.pgawest.com.

Tahquitz Creek 1885 Golf Club Dr., Palm Springs, tel 760/328-1005, www.tahquitzcreek.com

Hang Gliding

High Adventure 4231 Sepulveda Ave., San Bernardino, tel 909/379-9095, www.flytandem.com

Torrey Pines Glider Port 2800 Torrey Pines Scenic Dr., La Jolla, tel 858/452-9858, www.flytorrey.com.

Hiking

Sierra Club tel 415/977-5500, www.sierraclub.org

Yosemite Mountaineering School & Guide Service Curry Village, Yosemite Valley, tel 209/372-8344, www.yosemitepark.com

Horseback Riding

Drakesbad Guest Ranch End of Warner Valley Rd., Lassen Volcanic National Park, tel 866/999-0914, www.drakesbad.com

Los Angeles Equestrian Center 480 Riverside Dr., Burbank, tel 818/333-1408, www.la-equestriancenter.com.

Smoke Tree Ranch Stables 1850 Smoke Tree Ln., Palm Springs, tel 877/730-4409, www.smoketreeranch.com

Hot Air Ballooning

California Dreamin' 33133 Vista Del Monte Rd., Temecula, tel 951/699-0601 or 800/373-3359, www.californiadreamin.com

Fantasy Balloon Flights 74181 Parosella St., Palm Desert, tel 760/568-0997, www.fantasy balloonflight.com

Lake Tahoe Balloons South Lake Tahoe, tel 530/544-1221 or 800/872-9294, www.laketahoe balloons.com

Napa Valley Balloons 301 Post St., Napa, tel 707/944-0228 or 800/253-2224, www.napavalleyballoons.com

Hot Springs

Golden Haven Hot Springs 1713 Lake St., Calistoga, tel 707/942-8000, www.goldenhaven.com

Keough's Hot Springs 7 miles S of Bishop, tel 760/ 872-4670, www.keoughshotsprings.com

Two Bunch Palms 67425 Two Bunch Palms Trail, Desert Hot Springs, tel 760/329-8791, www.twobunchpalms.com

Houseboat Rentals

New Melones Lake Marina 6503 Glory Hole Rd., Angels Camp, tel 877/468-7326, www.houseboats.com

Shasta Marina Resort 18390 O'Brien Inlet Rd., Lakehead, tel 530/238-2284 or 800/959-3359, www.shastalake.net

Kayaking

Mission Bay Sports Center 1010 Santa Clara Pl., San Diego, tel 858/488-1004, www.mission baysportcenter.com

Monterey Bay Kayaks 693 Del Monte Ave., Monterey, tel 831/373-5357 or 800/649-5357, www.montereybaykayaks.com

Santa Barbara Adventure Company Santa Barbara, tel 888/773-3239, www.sbadventu reco.com

Mountain Biking

Another Side of San Diego Tours 300 G St., San Diego, tel 619/566-2077, www.another sideofsandiegotours.com

Bicycle Trails Council tel 510/761-6825, www.btceb.org

Mountaineering & Rock Climbing

Joshua Tree Rock Climbing School tel 760/366-4745, www.joshuatreerockclimbing.com

Yosemite Mountaineering School & Guide Service Curry Village, Yosemite Valley, tel 209/372-8344, www.yosemite park.com

Sailing

Marina Sailing 4633 Admiralty Way, Marina del Rey, tel 310/822-6617; 1551 Shelter Island Dr., San Diego, tel 619/221-8286; www.marinasailing.com

Santa Barbara Sailing Center 133 Harbor Way, Santa Barbara, tel 800/350-9090, www.sbsail.com

Skiing

Alpine Meadows 2600 Alpine Meadows Rd., tel 800/403-0206, www.skialpine.com

Badger Pass Glacier Point Rd., Yosemite National Park, tel 209/372-8430, www.yosemitepark.com

Bear Mountain Ski Resort 43101 Goldmine Drive, E of Big Bear Lake City, tel 909/866-5766, www.bearmountain.com

Kirkwood 1501 Kirkwood Meadows Dr., tel 209/258-6000, www .kirkwood.com.

Mammoth Mountain Ski Area tel 800/626-6684, www.mam mothmountain.com.

Mount Shasta Ski Park 104 Siskiyou Ave., Mount Shasta, tel 530/926-8610, www.skipark.com

Squaw Valley 1960 Squaw Valley Rd., 5 miles N of Tahoe City, tel 800/545 4350, www.squaw.com

Skydiving

Perris Valley Skydiving Center 2091 Goetz Rd., Perris, tel 800/832-8818, www.skydiveperris.com

Skydive Elsinore 20701 Cereal St., Lake Elsinore, tel 951/245-9939, www.skydiveelsinore.com

Surfing

Club Ed Surf School & Surf Camp 5 Isabel Dr., Santa Cruz, tel 831/464-0177, www.club-ed.com

San Diego Surfing Academy tel 800/447-7873, www.surfsdsa.com

Undersea Diving

Aquarius Dive Shop 2040 Del Monte Ave., Monterey, tel 831/657-1020, www.aquarius divers.com

Oceanside Scuba & Swim Center 225 Brooks St., Oceanside, 760/722-7826, www.oceanside scubaswim.com

Whale-watching

Dolphin Charters 1007 Leneve Pl., El Cerrito, tel 510/527-9622 or 800/472-9942, www.dolphin charters.com

Monterey Whale Watching 96 Fisherman's Wharf #1, Monterey, tel 212/209-3370 or 800/979 3370, www.monterey whalewatching.com

Oceanic Society Expeditions 30 Sir Francis Drake Blvd., Ross, tel 415/256-9604 or 800/326-7491, www.oceanic-society.org

Whitewater Rafting

American River Touring Assoc. 2400 Casa Loma Rd., Groveland, tel 800/323-2782, www.arta.org

Whitewater Voyages 5225 San Pablo Dam Rd., El Sobrante, tel 510/222-5994, www.whitewater voyages.com

Entertainment

San Francisco has some of the most way-out bars and clubs in the country and a theater scene that is in constant turmoil. L.A. is not far behind, and San Diego seriously enjoys its theater, too. Taking in a game is part of California life whatever your passion. And music happens everywhere.

LOS ANGELES

Comedy Clubs

Comedy Store 8433 Sunset Blvd., tel 323/650-6268, www.thecomedystore.com

Groundlings Theater 7307 Melrose Ave., tel 323/934-4747, www.groundlings.com

Music

Gibson Ampitheatre 100 Universal City Plaza, tel 818/622-4440

Hollywood Bowl 2301 N. Highland Ave., tel 323/850-2000, www.hollywoodbowl.com.

House of Blues 8430 W. Sunset Blvd., tel 323/848-5100, www.hob.com

L.A. Opera Dorothy Chandler Pavilion, 135 N. Grand Ave., tel 213/972-8001, www.losangelesopera.com

L.A. Philharmonic Walt Disney Concert Hall, 111 S. Grand Ave., tel 323/850-2000, www.laphil.com

Nokia Theater 777 Chick Hearn Ct., tel 213/763-6000, www.nokiatheatrelalive.com

Roxy 9009 W. Sunset Blvd., tel 310/278-9457, www.theroxyonsunset.com

UCLA Live B100 Royce Hall, tel 310/825-2101, www.uclalive.org

Whiskey a Go Go 8901 W. Sunset Blvd., tel 310/652-4202, www.whiskyagogo.com

World Stage 4344 Degnan Ave., tel 323/293-2451, www.theworldstage.org

Nightclubs

Bar Marmont 8171 W. Sunset Blvd., tel 323/650-0575

Viper Room 8852 W. Sunset Blvd., tel 310/538-1880, www.viperroom.com.

Public Arts Events

John Anson Ford Ampitheatre 2580 Cahuenga Blvd., tel 323/461-3673, www.fordamphitheater.org

Spectator Sports

Angel Stadium 2000 Gene Autry Way, Anaheim, tel 714/940-2000. L.A. Angels *(www.losangeles.angels.mlb.com)* baseball.

Dodger Stadium 1000 Elysian Park Ave., tel 323/224-1507. L.A. Dodgers *(www.losangeles.dodgers.mlb.com)* baseball.

Hollywood Park 1050 S. Prairie Ave., Inglewood, tel 310/419-1549, www.hollywoodpark.com. Horse racing.

Home Depot Center 18400 Avalon Blvd., Carson, tel 310/630-2000. L.A. Galaxy *(www.lagalaxy.com)* soccer.

Santa Anita Racetrack 285 W. Huntington Dr., Arcadia, tel 626/574-7223, www.santaanita.com. Horse racing.

Staples Center 1111 S. Figueroa St., tel 888/895-8662. L.A. Clippers & L.A. Lakers *(www.nba.com)* basketball. L.A. Kings *(www.kings.nhl.com)* hockey.

Television

Audiences Unlimited Tel 818/260-0041, www.tvtickets.com

Theater

Ahmanson Theatre 135 N. Grand Ave., tel 213/628-2772, www.centertheatregroup.org

Geffen Playhouse 10886 Le Conte Ave., Westwood, tel 310/208-5454, www.geffenplayhouse.com

Pasadena Playhouse 39 S. El Molino Ave., Pasadena, tel 626/356-7529, www.pasadenaplayhouse.org

SAN DIEGO

Music

Anthology 1337 India St., tel 619/595-0300, www.anthologysd.com

Belly Up Tavern 143 S. Cedros Ave., Solana Beach, tel 858/481-8140, www.bellyup.com. Rock.

Brick by Brick 1130 Buenos Ave., tel 619/275-5483, www.brickbybrick.com. Alternative.

Croce's 802 5th Ave., tel 619/233-4355, www.croces.com.

Humphrey's 2241 Shelter Island Dr., Shelter Island, tel 619/244-3577, www.humphreysconcerts.com. Outdoor venue. Popular.

La Jolla Music Society 7946 Ivanhoe Ave., Ste. 103, La Jolla, tel 858/459-3728, www.ljms.com. Classical.

Nightclubs

Pacific Beach Bar & Grill 860 Garnet, Pacific Beach, tel 858/272-4745, www.pbbarandgrill.com

Stingaree 454 6th Ave., Gaslamp Quarter, tel 619/544-9500, www.stingsandiego.com

Spectator Sports

Del Mar Thoroughbred Club 2260 Jimmy Durante Blvd., Del Mar, tel 858/755-1141, www.dmtc.com. Horse racing.

Qualcomm Stadium 9449 Friars Rd., tel 619/280-2121. San Diego Chargers *(www.chargers.com)* football.

Petco Park 100 Park Blvd., tel 619/795-5000. San Diego Padres *(www.sandiego.padres.mlb.com)* baseball.

Theater

La Jolla Playhouse 2910 La Jolla Village Dr., UC San Diego, tel 858/550-1010, www.lajolla playhouse.org.

Old Globe Theater 1363 Old Globe Way, Balboa Park, tel 619/234 5623, www.oldglobe.org. Contemporary and classic.

San Diego Opera
Civic Center Plaza, 1200 3rd Ave., tel 619/533-7000, www.sdopera| .com. Classical.

San Diego Repertory Lyceum Theatre, 79 Horton Plaza, tel 619/544-1000, www.sdrep.org. Classic dramas to musicals.

Viejas Arena San Diego State University, tel 619/594-6947, www.cox-arena.com. Popular.

SAN FRANCISCO

In San Francisco unless indicated.

Comedy

Cobb's Comedy Club 915 Columbus Ave., tel 415/928-4320, www.cobbscomedy.com

Punch Line 444 Battery St., tel 415/397-7573, www.punchline comedyclub.com.

Dance

San Francisco Ballet War Memorial Opera House, 301 Van Ness Ave., tel 415/865-2000, www .sfballet.org.

Music

Boom Boom Room
1601 Fillmore St., tel 415/673-8000, www.boomboomblues.com. Venerable jazz and blues joint.

Bottom of the Hill 1233 17th St., tel 415/621-4455, www.bottom ofthehill.com. Alternative.

Cal Performances 101 Zellerbach Hall #4800, UC Berkeley, Bancroft Way & Telegraph Ave., tel 510/642-9988, www.calperfs. berkeley.edu. Eclectic.

Fillmore 1805 Geary St., tel 415/346-6000 or 800/745-3000. Rock.

Freight & Salvage Coffeehouse
2020 Addison St., Berkeley, tel 510/644-2020, www.thefreight .org. Folk.

San Francisco Opera War Memorial Opera House, 301 Van Ness Ave., tel 415/864-3330, www .sfopera.com

San Francisco Symphony
Davies Symphony Hall, 210 Van Ness Ave., tel 415/864-6000, www.sfsymphony.org

SF Jazz 3 Embarcadero Center, Lobby Level, tel 866/920-5299, www.sfjazz.org

Slim's 333 11th St., tel 415/255-0333, www.slimspresents.com

Yoshi's 510 Embarcadero, Oakland, tel 510/238-9200, www.yoshis.com. Jazz.

Nightclubs

Café du Nord 2170 Market St., tel 415/861-5016, www.cafedu nord.com. Everything from swing to salsa.

El Rio 3158 Mission St., tel 415/282-3325, www.elriosf.com. Salsa.

Starlight Room Sir Francis Drake Hotel, 21st Floor, 450 Powell St., tel 415/395-8595, www.harryden ton.com. Stylish live-music lounge.

Tonga Room Fairmont Hotel, 950 Mason St., tel 415/772-5278, www.tongaroom.com. Kitsch.

Public Arts Events

Shakespeare in the Park
Tel 415/558-0888, www.sfshakes .org. Various Bay Area venues. Summer weekends only. Free.

Stern Grove Summer Music Festival Sloat Blvd. & 19th Ave., tel 415/252-6252, www.stern grove.org.

Spectator Sports

AT&T Park
24 Willie Mays Plaza, tel 415/972-2000. San Francisco Giants *(www .sfgiants.com)* baseball.

Buck Shaw Stadium
451 El Camino Real, Santa Clara, tel 408/556-7700. San Jose Earthquakes *(www.sjearthquakes .com)* soccer.

Candlestick Park 490 Jamestown Ave., tel 415/464-9377. San Francisco 49ers *(www.sf49ers .com)* football.

Golden Gate Fields 1100 Eastshore Hwy., Albany, tel 510/559-7300, www.goldengate fields.com. Horse racing.

O.co Coliseum Oakland 7000 Coliseum Way, Oakland, tel 510/762-2255 (tickets). Oakland A's *(www.oaklandas.com)* baseball, Oakland Raiders *(www.raiders.com)* football.

Theater

American Conservatory Theater
Geary Theater, 405 Geary St., tel 415/749-2228, www.act sf.org. Repertory.

Berkeley Repertory Theater
2025 Addison St., Berkeley, tel 510/647-2949, www.berkeleyrep .org. Eclectic productions.

Club Fugazi *(Beach Blanket Babylon)* 678 Green St., tel 415/421-4222, www.beachblanketbabylon .com. Cabaret.

Curran Theater 445 Geary St., tel 415/551-2000 or 888/746-1799. Large productions and musicals.

Exit Theater 156 Eddy St., tel 415/931-1094, www.sffringe.org. Experimental to classical offerings. Produces San Francisco Fringe in September.

Golden Gate Theater 1 Taylor St. at Market & 6th Sts., tel 415/551-2000 or 888/746-1799. Host to nationally renowned productions.

Magic Theater Fort Mason Bldg. D, Fort Mason Center, Marina Blvd. at Buchanan St., tel 415/345-7575, www.fortmason.org.
New plays.

Theater Rhinoceros 1360 Mission St., tel 415/552-4100 or 800/838-3006, www.therhino.org. Gay and lesbian productions.

INDEX

Bold page numbers indicate illustrations.
CAPS indicates thematic categories.

N

O

P

ILLUSTRATIONS CREDITS

All photographs by Gilles Mingasson unless otherwise noted:

2-3, S. Borisov/Shutterstock; 4, Jerry Lee Hayes, San Francisco Convention & Visitors Bureau; 8, Steve Beer/Shutterstock.com; 14-5, Doreen Keith/National Geographic My Shot; 16, Frederic J. Brown/AFP/Getty Images; 24, bonchan/Shutterstock; 26-7, Tom Bean/Corbis UK Ltd.; 28, Brendan Howard/Shutterstock.com; 32-3, The Route to California. Truckee River, Sierra Nevada. Central Pacific railway, 1871 (litho), Currier, N. (1813-88) and Ives, J.M. (1824-95)/Private Collection/The Bridgeman Art Library; 35, DB Apple/dpa/Corbis; 37, David Paul Morris/GYI NSEA/iStockphoto.com; 38-9, Half Dome, Yosemite (oil on canvas), Bierstadt, Albert (1830-1902)/Private Collection/Photo © Christie's Images/The Bridgeman Art Library; 44, Hulton Archive/Stringer/Getty Images; 49, Fox Photos/Hulton Archive/Getty Images; 55, nito500/123RF.com; 59, Gerry Boughan/Shutterstock.com; 73, egd/Shutterstock.com; 112, Photo Works/Shutterstock.com; 121, Jose Gil/Shutterstock.com; 123, Richard Thornton/Shutterstock.com; 124, Corbis UK Ltd/Phil Schermeister; 127, Jim Richardson/National Geographic Stock; 128, JustASC/Shutterstock; 134, Barry King/WireImage/Getty Images; 137, Bureau L.A. Collection/Sygma/Corbis; 139, hoangkhainhan/Bigstock.com; 144, Chad McDermott/Shutterstock; 147, MindStorm/Shutterstock; 150, sburel/Veer; 152, S. Greg Panosian/iStockphoto; 157, Sprokop/Dreamstime.com; 159, Mariusz S. Jurgielewicz/Shutterstock; 160, Scott Prokop/123RF.com; 162, Livia Corona/The Image Bank/Getty Images; 167, Daniel Ochoa/FOTOCHOA/Shutterstock; 172, Mariusz S. Jurgielewicz/Shutterstock; 179, Corbis UK Ltd/Ansel Adams Publishing Rights Trust; 223, Giorgio Fochesato/iStockphoto; 234, Lynn Watson/Shutterstock; 240, Visit Berkeley; 243, Jerry Moorman/iStockphoto; 246, Jonathan Lenz/Shutterstock; 248, David Madison/Stone/Getty Images; 252, Arvind Balaraman/Shutterstock; 261, Andy Z./Shutterstock; 268, Bromberger Hoover Photography/Getty Images; 274, Corey Rich/Getty Images; 278, Peter Kunasz/Shutterstock; 280, David Stubbs/Aurora/Getty Images; 283, Phil Schermeister/National Geographic Stock; 286, Caitlin Mirra/Shutterstock; 301, Nick Stubbs/Shutterstock; 302, Danny Warren/iStockphoto; 304, Andrey Tarantin/123RF; 307, Steve Heap/Shutterstock; 309, JustASC/Shutterstock; 310, Jim Lopes/Shutterstock; 315, topseller/Shutterstock; 324, pix2go/Shutterstock; 328, amygdala_imagery/iStockphoto; 333, Katrina Brown/Shutterstock; 338, Arcaid Images/Alamy; 339, Michael Buckner/Getty Images For Palm Springs International Film Festival; 341, Rusty Dodson/Shutterstock; 342, EuToch/iStockphoto.

National Geographic
TRAVELER
California

Published by the National Geographic Society
John M. Fahey, *Chairman of the Board and Chief Executive Officer*
Timothy T. Kelly, *President*
Declan Moore, *Executive Vice President; President, Publishing and Digital Media*
Melina Gerosa Bellows, *Executive Vice President; Chief Creative Officer, Books, Kids, and Family*
Lynn Cutter, *Executive Vice President, Travel*
Keith Bellows, *Senior Vice President and Editor in Chief, National Geographic Travel Media*

Prepared by the Book Division
Hector Sierra, *Senior Vice President and General Manager*
Jonathan Halling, *Design Director, Books and Children's Publishing*
Marianne R. Koszorus, *Design Director, Books*
Barbara A. Noe, *Senior Editor, National Geographic Travel Books*
R. Gary Colbert, *Production Director*
Jennifer A. Thornton, *Director of Managing Editorial*
Susan S. Blair, *Director of Photography*
Meredith C. Wilcox, *Director, Administration and Rights Clearance*

Staff for This Book
Matt Propert, *Illustrations Editor*
Carl Mehler, *Director of Maps*
Michael McNey and Mapping Specialists, *Map Production*
Marshall Kiker, *Associate Managing Editor*
Galen Young, *Rights Clearance Specialist*
Katie Olsen, *Production Design Assistant*
Sarah Alban, *Contributor*

Manufacturing and Quality Management
Phillip L. Schlosser, *Senior Vice President*
Chris Brown, *Vice President, NG Book Manufacturing*
George Bounelis, *Vice President, Production Services*
Nicole Elliott, *Manager*
Rachel Faulise, *Manager*
Robert L. Barr, *Manager*

KKComm, LLC
Kay Kobor Hankins, *Project Manager/Art Director*
Mary Stephanos/Justin Kavanagh, *Project Editors*
Jack Brostrom, *Contributor*

First edition: Edited and designed by AA Publishing (a trading name of Automobile Association Developments Limited, whose registered office is Norfolk House, Priestley Road, Basingstoke, Hampshire, England RG24 9NY. Registered number: 1878835).

Cutaway illustrations drawn by Maltings Partnership, Derby, England

Tide pool illustration drawn by Ann Winterbotham

The National Geographic Society is one of the world's largest nonprofit scientific and educational organizations. Founded in 1888 to "increase and diffuse geographic knowledge," the Society works to inspire people to care about the planet. National Geographic reflects the world through its magazines, television programs, films, music and radio, books, DVDs, maps, exhibitions, live events, school publishing programs, interactive media and merchandise. *National Geographic* magazine, the Society's official journal, published in English and 33 local-language editions, is read by more than 60 million people each month. The National Geographic Channel reaches 435 million households in 37 languages in 173 countries. National Geographic Digital Media receives more than 19 million visitors a month. National Geographic has funded more than 10,000 scientific research, conservation and exploration projects and supports an education program promoting geography literacy. For more information, visit www.nationalgeographic.com.

For more information, please call 1-800-NGS LINE (647-5463) or write to the following address:

National Geographic Society
1145 17th Street N.W.
Washington, D.C. 20036-4688 U.S.A.

For information about special discounts for bulk purchases, please contact National Geographic Books Special Sales: ngspecsales@ngs.org

For rights or permissions inquiries, please contact National Geographic Books Subsidiary Rights: ngbookrights@ngs.org

National Geographic Traveler: California
(Fourth Edition)
ISBN: 978-1-4262-1021-1

Printed in China
12/TS/1

The information in this book has been carefully checked and to the best of our knowledge is accurate. However, details are subject to change, and the National Geographic Society cannot be responsible for such changes, or for errors or omissions. Assessments of sites, hotels, and restaurants are based on the author's subjective opinions, which do not necessarily reflect the publisher's opinion.